The Anthropology of Childhood

How are children raised in different cultures? What is the role of children in society? How are families and communities structured around them? Now available in a revised edition, *The Anthropology of Childhood* sets out to answer these questions, and argues that our common understandings about children are narrowly culture-bound.

Marshaling evidence from several lines of research, David Lancy shows that, while the dominant society views children as precious, innocent, and preternaturally cute "cherubs," there are other societies where they are regarded as unwanted, inconvenient "changelings," or as desired but pragmatically commoditized "chattel." Enriched with anecdotes from ethnography and the daily media, the book examines family structure and reproduction, profiles of children's caretakers within family or community, children's treatment at different ages, their play, work, schooling, and transition to adulthood. The result is a nuanced and credible picture of childhood in different cultures, past and present.

Organized developmentally, moving from infancy through to adolescence and early adulthood, this new edition reviews and catalogs the findings of over 100 years of anthropological scholarship dealing with childhood and adolescence, drawing on over 750 newly added sources, and engaging with newly emerging issues relevant to the world of childhood today.

DAVID F. LANCY is Emeritus Professor of Anthropology at Utah State University. He is author/editor of several books on childhood and culture, including *Cross-Cultural Studies in Cognition and Mathematics* (1983), *Studying Children and Schools* (2001), *Playing on the Mother Ground: Cultural Routines for Children's Learning* (1996), and *The Anthropology of Learning in Childhood* (2010).

"If I were to assign just one book as required reading for students of child psychology, this would be it. It opens our all-too-parochial eyes to childhood's possibilities."

Peter Gray, Boston College

"The scholarship in this book is incredibly sound and thorough in breadth and scope."

Rebecca Zarger, University of South Florida

"the most comprehensive, and perhaps only, review of the human child in terms of evolutionary biology and sociocultural anthropology. Based on the best of theory and field ethnography, it is essential for any study of human development and human nature."

Barry Bogin, Loughborough University

"David Lancy's *The Anthropology of Childhood* was essential the moment it appeared; the second edition is even better! He has digested the survey material even more, used updated materials, and held back less on his criticism of contemporary Euro-American childrearing."

Susan D. Blum, University of Notre Dame

"a valuable forum to better understand childhood as a rapidly growing subfield of anthropology."

Akira Takada, Kyoto University

"this revised version of the volume is very welcome, providing students, teachers and generalists who are interested in the subject with a broad overview of the anthropology of childhood, supported by a comprehensive and helpfully interdisciplinary bibliography."

Sally Crawford, The University of Oxford

The Anthropology of Childhood

Cherubs, Chattel, Changelings

Second edition

David F. Lancy
Utah State University

CAMBRIDGE UNIVERSITY PRESS

CAMBRIDGE
UNIVERSITY PRESS

University Printing House, Cambridge CB2 8BS, United Kingdom

Cambridge University Press is part of the University of Cambridge.

It furthers the University's mission by disseminating knowledge in the pursuit of education, learning and research at the highest international levels of excellence.

www.cambridge.org
Information on this title: www.cambridge.org/9781107420984

© David F. Lancy 2015

First published 2015
6th printing 2015

Printed in the United States of America by Sheridan Books, Inc.

A catalogue record for this publication is available from the British Library

Library of Congress Cataloging-in-Publication Data
Lancy, David F.
The anthropology of childhood : cherubs, chattel, changelings / David F. Lancy, Utah State University. – Second edition.
    pages   cm
ISBN 978-1-107-07266-4 (Hardback) – ISBN 978-1-107-42098-4 (Paperback)
1. Children–Cross-cultural studies.   I. Title.
GN482.L36 2014   305.23–dc23
2014014319

ISBN 978-1-107-07266-4 Hardback
ISBN 978-1-107-42098-4 Paperback

Contents

Plates

Preface

Second edition preface

The Anthropology of Childhood was first published in November, 2008; however, I had delivered the manuscript to the publisher much earlier. At that time, I did not feel that the book was "complete." The flow of "new" sources was unabated. So, I proceeded as if the book was incomplete and continued to collect and annotate relevant work. Then too, there has been a virtual explosion in the size of our formerly rather miniscule community of anthropologists (and archaeologists!) studying childhood. This has produced a spate of journals and books. New scholarly organizations have sprung up, including the Anthropology of Children and Youth Interest Group (ACYIG, of the American Anthropological Association) and the Society for the Study of Childhood in the Past. Several institutions in North America and Europe host regular, open seminars highlighting recent research, and international conferences have been convened in the US, Canada, UK, Belgium, Greece, Norway, and India.

This edition incorporates over 750 sources that were not referenced in the first edition, which drew on roughly 1,400 sources. Certain topics have been blessed with lots of new material, in particular: infancy and "delayed personhood"; child labor; adoption and fosterage; infants and children as autonomous learners; the limited role of teaching in children's acquisition of their culture; gamesmanship; the benefits of free play; the chore curriculum; apprenticeship; the impact of economic transformation and civil conflict on childhood; children as a reserve labor force; the historical antecedents of schooling; resistance to education; the impact of schooling on thought; the culture of street kids; and children's *agency*. Readers familiar with the first edition will also find a great deal of new visual material to complement the text.

The second edition also afforded me an opportunity to refocus the book to make it even more useful to the intended audiences. First, I can unashamedly claim that this is a reference volume, given the comprehensive nature of my literature survey and the thoroughness with which I document each source, including specific page numbers. I couldn't have done it without Google

Books and Google Scholar! Second, I know very well that readers find this work to be extremely accessible, all-encompassing, and engaging. Feedback suggests that students feel a justifiable sense of mastery of the field, once they've read it. Third, I want to provide a valuable resource to childhood scholars, whether in anthropology or elsewhere. Child psychologists, in particular, may be blinded by the dominance of Western culture in their theories, methods, and population samples. There are many ideas here that correct or even overturn conventional wisdom regarding child development and, particularly, the role of parents.

I likened the production of the original book to the careful handling of an awkward and obtrusive gorilla. For the second edition I would invoke the metaphor of a barn-raising. I have always been fascinated by the idea of a barn-raising, and one of my favorite cinematic moments is the Amish barn-raising in the 1985 film *Witness*. I have gained a wonderful community of friends and scholars in the last six years who've created forums for the discussion and promotion of the anthropology of childhood, and these discussions gave birth to many of the "big" ideas introduced in this edition. I would like to acknowledge my enormous debt to these very wonderful organizers/hosts. These include Susan Blum, James and Tanya Broesch, Alyssa Crittenden, Sandra Evers, Peggy Froerer, Rob Gordon, Peter Gray, Diane Hoffman, Marida Holos, Heidi Keller, Stephen Laurence, Alice Lesnick, Courtney Mehan, Leslie Moore, Élodie Razie and Charles-Edouarde de Suremain, Andria Sherrow, and Gerd Spittler. Funding from the Society for Psychological Anthropology allowed me (and colleagues John Bock and Suzanne Gaskins) to host a marvelous interdisciplinary seminar to thrash out the role of stage in theorizing about childhood. As I extended my reach, endeavoring to make this edition more comprehensive, I was aided by numerous patient scholars who expertly fielded my queries. A special thanks to David Bjorkland, John Bock, Barry Bogin, Adam Boyette, Suzanne Gaskins, Heather Montgomery, David Olson, Sanae Okamoto-Barth, and Alice Schlegel. Last, a shout-out to ACYIG board members Kristen Cheney, Jill Korbin, David Rosen, Susan Shepler, Aviva Sinervo, E. J. Sobo, Rachael Stryker, and Tom Weisner, who have been so critical in the process of building an organization to shelter our enterprise.

October 10, 2013

First edition preface

In 2002, an article entitled "Why don't anthropologists like children?" appeared in *American Anthropologist*. The author argued that anthropologists, in their comprehensive study of every society on the planet, had ignored or mishandled childhood (Hirschfeld 2002). Since I'd devoted my career to the study of children in culture, I was personally affronted. Moreover, I had had no difficulty finding dozens of accounts of children in the ethnographic record to corroborate a thesis I advanced in a book published just a few years earlier (Lancy 1996). Consequently, I wrote a careful and thorough rebuttal and submitted it as a commentary. The journal editors rejected it as too long. I whittled and whittled but it was still over the 500-word limit. I gave up trying to shrink my rebuttal and, instead, decided to expand it. You are reading the result.

I realized that while I might be aware of a treasure trove of material in the ethnographic record, others might not. The field, in fact, seems balkanized. For example, I've noted that anthropologists who study children in schools – there are more than 700 members of the Council on Anthropology and Education – may not pay much attention to the work of ethnographers studying children learning to farm or to hunt. Anthropologists looking at language socialization; archaeologists studying mortuary practices; biobehavioral anthropologists studying fertility – these and numerous other lines of inquiry run in parallel, rarely crossing. Theoretical perspectives that are treated as antithetical when they might better be seen as complementary divide us as well.

This volume aims to include, therefore, the work of anthropologists interested in childhood who, heretofore, may have been unaware or at least unappreciative of each other's work. I achieve this synthesis partly through a comprehensive literature review but also by eschewing lengthy treatment of theoretical formulations that might act as a bar to the uninitiated. Ideally, this work should serve as a catalyst that promotes much greater interaction among those who study children.

The book quite consciously sets out to capture and offer at least a passing reference to most studies in anthropology where children are in the foreground. All of the major themes – for example, infancy, children's play, and adolescent initiation – are covered at length. Furthermore, where these themes abut the disciplines of history and primatology, I draw liberally from those bodies of scholarship to strengthen and enrich the presentation.

A seminal work that provided a model for my research was Sarah Blaffer Hrdy's *Mother Nature*. In that book, Hrdy draws on the literature on motherhood outside the dominant culture, and, in constructing a more representative portrait, she also dismantles many taken-for-granted notions about the phenomenon – the maternal "instinct," to choose just one example. It has been my intent to do for childhood what Hrdy did for motherhood. Here, too, we see that many assumptions that are made about what is "normal" or natural in children's development are, in fact, quite narrowly culture-bound. Indeed, throughout this work, the formula employed in child development texts will be turned on its head. In these texts, research on middle-class Euroamerican children defines the standard and "anecdotes" from anthropological studies illustrate "deviation from the mean." In the pages that follow, common aspects of Western childhood are examined through the lens of anthropology. This lens reveals that what we take for granted as customary appears to be rather strange when compared with prevailing practices found elsewhere. The goal is not to offer a competing volume to standard child development texts but, rather, to offer a supplement or corrective.

The alliterative terms in my subtitle suggest three compass points in this landscape. Our own society views children as precious, innocent, and preternaturally cute *cherubs*. However, for much of human history, children have been seen as anything but cherubic. I will introduce readers to societies, indeed entire periods in history, where children are viewed as unwanted, inconvenient *changelings* or as desired but pragmatically commoditized *chattel*. These perspectives will be employed in the study of family structure and reproduction; profiles of children's caretakers – parental, sib, and community; their treatment at different ages; their play; their work; their schooling; and their transition to adulthood. Again and again, our views and treatment of our cherubs will stand in sharp contrast to views of children constructed by anthropologists and historians from their work in other societies.

Another audience I hope to reach is the legion of teachers, fieldworkers, and policymakers who are laboring to improve the lives of children not fortunate enough to have been born into a privileged society. All are aware of the importance of taking culture into account in their work, and "multiculturalism" has become an oft-heard mantra. But the concept is often used to provide some exotic spices to season the otherwise standard prescriptions for children's schooling and welfare. Throughout this work we'll probe deeply into the literature to discover the ways in which child development is truly shaped by culture. But *The Anthropology of Childhood* goes beyond this analysis in consistently building bridges between the rich cultural traditions documented by ethnographers in the past and the contemporary scenarios confronted by interventionists.

Gradually, the 500-plus-word commentary has grown into a 500-lb gorilla dominating my life and rendering me an insufferable companion. I couldn't see a play or a movie or read a novel without finding something that might fit. Joyce has not only tolerated the beast but has groomed it on regular occasions. Other family and friends fed it snacks. Thank you Nadia, Sonia, Leslie, Bob, Judy, Quinn, Rick, and Melissa. Many others often asked after the gorilla's growth and wellbeing. At Utah State, these included (among many others) my colleagues Michael Chipman, Richley Crapo, Christie Fox, Kermit Hall, Norm Jones, Rick Krannich, Pat Lambert, Lynn Meeks, and Mike Sweeney. Colleagues elsewhere who joined the vigil included Katie Anderson-Levitt, Nigel Barber, Jay Black, Gary Chick, Gary Cross, Aaron Denham, Bob

Edgerton, Heather Rae Espinoza, Hilary Fouts, Rob Gordon, Judy Harris, Shep Krech, Jon Marks, Jim Marten, David Olson, Aaron Podolefsky, Paul Raffaele, Deborah Reed-Danahay, Jaipaul Roopnarine, Peter Smith, Brian Sutton-Smith, Glenn Weisfeld, and Becky Zarger. Thank you all for your support, guidance, and tolerance of my persistent queries.

As this project took on visible proportions I began to bring the gorilla into my Anthropology of Childhood class. Students in the class also did much to nurture it from toddlerhood on, notably Helen Brower, JeriAnn Lukens, Amy Montuoro, Tonya Stallings, Mary Sundblom, and James Young. However, no one was more critical to this enterprise than Annette Grove, who evolved from stellar student into untiring and incredibly effective research assistant and editor. My debt to Annette is simply incalculable. Cecylia Maslowska assisted with the translation of Gerd Spittler's *Hirtenarbeit* and the late Professor Renate Posthofen with Barbara Polak's work. Professor Sarah Gordon assisted with material in French.

Many colleagues assisted in the creation of what eventually coalesced into this oversize creature, beginning before I had any idea of what was coming. Utah State's Honors Students in 1995 selected me to give the annual "Last Lecture," and I used the opportunity to develop the child-as-commodity ideas presented at the end of the book. A general outline of Chapters 6 and 7 emerged at a presentation I made at UCLA in February 1999. Hosted by Alan Fiske, the talk was followed by extremely stimulating discussions with Alan, Patricia Greenfield, Tom Weisner, Candy Goodwin, and others. In April 2004, Pierre Dasen and Jean Retschitzki invited me to a symposium in Switzerland to present early versions of Chapters 5 and 6 on learning and play. Sid Strauss had me speak in December 2004 to an incredibly diverse and stimulating group – sponsored by the McDonnell Foundation – on culture and children's social learning. Chapter 6 was drafted, initially, in response to an invitation from Gerd Spittler to give a presentation in Bayreuth in July 2005. Bryan Spykerman's inspired photographs of children added personality to the text. These gratefully acknowledged efforts to assist me in gestation are complemented by the work of many midwives who critically reviewed chapters and provided often extensive and invaluable feedback. Chief among these I would thank Rob Borofsky, John Gay, Barry Hewlett, Howard Kress, Mark Moritz, Barbara Polak, Ali Pomponio, Alice Schlegel, and, particularly, John Bock and Suzanne Gaskins. Two anonymous reviewers for Cambridge University Press provided extensive, on-target feedback.

This work is dedicated to the late Nancy Hylin. Our next-door neighbor, she became, in effect, a close older sibling. Nancy, in adulthood, met and married a Norwegian, Hans Jacob Hylin, settled in Norway and proceeded to raise four sons and assist in the rearing of nine grandchildren. She also enjoyed a distinguished career as a secondary school teacher. Nancy was a natural participant observer and, for nearly fifty years, she shared her observations of childhood and adolescence with me and my family through the media of long, intimate letters and photographs. So, while my research and fieldwork has been episodic, I could count on a steady stream of "field reports" emanating from Norway, year after year. In spite of her passing in 2000, Nancy served as muse throughout this project, a silent but insistent reviewer and critic. Lastly, I need to acknowledge a muse of another sort. Katherine Iris Tomlinson will turn three in a few days and, since birth, her weekly play-dates with "Uncle David" have been both therapeutic and inspirational. As you read this text, please remember that I much prefer cherubs.

April 23, 2007

1   Where do children come from?

The anthropologist's veto

Americans are the most individualistic people in the world. (Henrich *et al.* 2010: 76)

The field of developmental psychology is an ethnocentric one dominated by a Euro-American perspective. (Greenfield and Cocking 1994: ix)

A robust tradition in anthropology, dating at least to Mead's (1928/1961) *Coming of Age in Samoa*, calls attention to the culture-bound flaw in psychology. Mead's work undermined the claim by psychologist G. Stanley Hall that stress was inevitably part of adolescence. Less well known was Malinowski's earlier critique of Freud's Oedipal theory based on fieldwork in the Trobriand Islands (Malinowski 1927/2012). Universal stage theories of cognitive development, such as that of Jean Piaget, met a similar fate when cross-cultural comparative studies demonstrated profound and unpredicted influences of culture and the experience of being schooled (Greenfield 1966; Lancy and Strathern 1981; Lancy 1983). Ochs and Schieffelin's (1984) analysis of adult–child language interaction also showed that ethnographic studies in non-Western societies could be used to "de-universalize" claims made in the mainstream developmental psychology literature. Bob LeVine has taken on one of psychology's most sacred cows – mother–infant attachment (see also Scheper-Hughes 1987a). LeVine's observations of agrarian, East African Gusii parents suggest the possibility of weak attachment and consequent blighted development. He finds that, while mothers respond promptly to their infant's distress signals, they ignore other vocalizations such as babbling. They rarely look at their infants or speak to them – even while breastfeeding. Later, when they do address their children, they use commands and threats rather than praise or interrogatives (LeVine 2004: 154, 156; in press). In spite of these obvious signs of "pathology" on the part of Gusii mothers, LeVine and his colleagues – who have been studying Gusii villagers for decades – find no evidence of widespread emotional crippling. He argues that the problem of excessive claims of universality arises from the "child development field's dual identity as an ideological advocacy movement for the humane treatment

1

of children and a scientific research endeavor seeking knowledge and under-standing" (LeVine 2004: 151).

Another sacred cow slain by anthropologists has been "parenting style" theory (Baumrind 1971). Central African Bofi farmers fit the so-called "authoritarian" parenting style in valuing respect and obedience and exercising coercive control over their children. According to the theory, Bofi children should be withdrawn, non-empathetic, and aggressive, and should lack initia-tive. On the contrary, they display precisely the opposite set of traits, and Fouts concludes that the theory may work when applied to Americans, but "it has very little explanatory power among the Bofi" (2005: 361). Throughout this book the reader will find similar examples of anthropologists "exercis[ing] their veto" (LeVine 2007: 250).

The view that many well-established theoretical positions in psychology cannot be as widely generalized as their authors assume was given a boost by a carefully argued paper published in 2010. Joe Henrich and colleagues challenged the very foundations of the discipline in arguing that psychologists fail to account for the influence of culture or nurture on human behavior. From a large-scale survey they determined that the vast majority of research in psychology is carried out with citizens – especially college students – of Western, Educated, Industrialized, Rich, Democracies (WEIRD). They note that, where comparative data are available "people in [WEIRD] societies consistently occupy the extreme end of the ... distribution [making them] one of the worst subpopulations one could study for generalizing about *Homo sapiens*" (Henrich *et al.* 2010: 63, 65, 79).

Primatologists as well have taken Western psychologists – who rely on lab experiments – to task for claims re uniquely human characteristics that are belied by evidence for these characteristics among free-living non-human primates. "The disdain of observational data in experimental psychology leads some to ignore the reality of animal cognitive achievements" (Boesch 2005: 692).

Some years earlier I had been struck by this same paradox – that both our popular and our scientific understanding of childhood were based on experience with and data from a single and unique culture. In studying Kpelle children in a remote interior village in Liberia, I took note of how radically different their experience of childhood was than that depicted in the textbooks I'd studied from. To capture this difference I created a polemical contrast between the society from which most of the generalizations about childhood had been made with the rest of the world. The contrast was best captured by the terms "neontocracy" and "gerontocracy" – as illustrated in Figure 1.

This contrast, along with continued reference to the atypicality of WEIRD society and field studies of apes, will channel much of the discussion throughout the book. My goal is to offer a correction to the ethnocentric lens that sees children only as precious, innocent, and preternaturally cute

US mainstream neontocracy

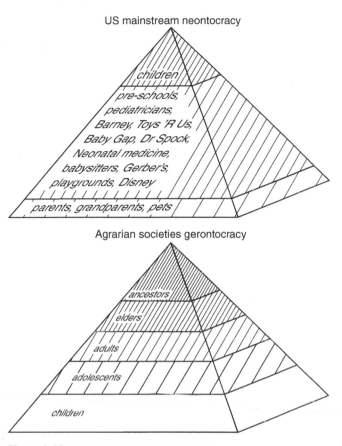

Figure 1 Neontocracy versus gerontocracy

cherubs.[1] Building on a firm foundation of research in history, anthropology, and primatology, I hope to uncover something close to the norm for children's lives and those of their caretakers. I will also make the case for alternative lenses whereby children may be viewed as unwanted, inconvenient changelings[2] or as desired but pragmatically commodified chattel.[3]

---

[1] "Cherub" has a diversity of meanings, depending on the particular historical epoch or text one consults. In modern usage, a cherub is a plump, angelic, child-like creature that personifies innocence.

[2] "Changeling" is a pagan concept borrowed by medieval Christians. Like the cuckoo, trolls or elves might substitute their peculiar offspring for a human infant. The mother of the infant had recourse to a number of punitive measures designed to rid herself of the nest usurper in hopes its parent would bring back the human child and re-exchange the two.

[3] "Chattel" has its origin in the Latin *capitale* or wealth, property. The closely related term "cattle" has a similar origin. A typical Roman patrician household might employ more than a

But I intend to move well beyond vetoing the theoretical assertions of non-anthropologists. I believe that the vast ethnographic archives[4] contain an almost undiscovered vein of data that can be mined for insights into the nature of childhood – outside the neontocracy. Ethnography has some unique virtues that make ethnographic "data" particularly valuable.[5] One such virtue is that by gathering information as a *participant observer*, the ethnographer weaves together three strands of information. First, ethnographers *describe* what they're seeing – compiling an impressive observational log (complemented with photos and audio/video recordings) from which patterns can be detected. Second, by interviewing or engaging their informants in a discussion of what they've witnessed, they may gain an insider's (*emic*) perspective, which often makes intelligible the foreign or exotic practices. These perspectives typically coalesce into what has been termed a cultural model (Quinn 2005: 479; Strauss 1992: 3) or ethnotheory (Harkness and Super 2006). These models are useful in trying to place particular childcare practices into a broader, more comprehensive cultural context. Third, ethnographers record their own (*etic*) perspective. As a reader of ethnography, I pay particular attention to the anthropologist's "aha" moments when they are surprised or shocked by something that violates their own cultural model of childhood.[6]

My approach is comparative (the method is termed *ethnology*; Voget 1975) and inductive. That is, to take an example from Chapter 2, as I annotated the many ethnographic accounts of the handling and treatment of newborns and infants, a pattern emerged. Although the specific details vary a great deal, a majority of the world's societies delay the conferral of personhood. This pattern, in turn, has enormous implications for the practice of infanticide, attachment theory, the diagnosis of child illness, and interment practices

---

100 slaves, so their monetary value represented a significant portion of a man's estate. Even in societies that didn't practice slavery, children were treated as the property of the head of the household.

[4] Prominently, but by no means exclusively, contained within the Human Relations Area Files. Available at www.yale.edu/hraf/collections.htm. Accessed February 1, 2014.

[5] For a broader discussion of the value of ethnography in studying childhood, see Lancy (2001a).

[6] It is only fair to note a major failing of most ethnographers. Because each culture is treated as unique and there is the expectation that the ethnographer be clear-eyed in collecting the data, unbiased by ethnocentrism, little attention may be paid to other ethnographic work on the topic(s) of interest. In short, the review of literature as well as analyses designed to gauge the generalizability of results may be quite cursory. Consequently, there has been little accumulation and refinement of findings from ethnography – as typically occurs in science (Tooby and Cosmides 1992: 44). Thus ethnographies rarely get connected to the web of scholarship and they are forgotten with time. Which goes some distance in explaining why there's untapped material in the ethnographic record and why this book fills a void. This might be an appropriate time to tip my hat to the resources and staff of the Merrill-Cazier Library, without whose assistance I would not have been able to resurrect these obscure or forgotten treasures.

for the very young – among others. These patterns serve as the major organizing axes and themes of the book.

But first, a little history.

Is there such a thing as childhood?

"Child" is itself not an uncomplicated term. (Boswell 1988: 26)

Like the icy month of January to a farmer waiting to plant seed, children were considered a worthless season "without wit, strength, or cunning." (Schorsch 1979: 23)

In the Middle Ages, children were generally ignored until they were no longer children. (Schorsch 1979: 14)

In order to begin our work, we'll start with a clean slate. Consider the notion that childhood didn't exist at all until recently. This is the thesis of an extremely influential book by French philosopher/historian Philippe Ariès published in 1962. In it, he argued that the concept of childhood as a distinct state is largely absent until the past few hundred years. His case is based primarily on an analysis of figurative art.

Medieval art until about the twelfth century did not know childhood or did not attempt to portray it. It is hard to believe that this neglect was due to incompetence or incapacity; it seems more probable that there was no place for childhood in the medieval world. (Ariès 1962: 33)

And, if we limit our database to images of children in portraits, we would have to acknowledge that they are rare or don't look very child-like. The infrequency with which children are depicted in art should be taken as a measure of their insignificance (Wicks and Avril 2002: 30) – also reflected in burial practices. That is, studies of infant and child burials show a characteristic pattern of their being interred informally in house floors, walls, at the edge of garden plots, and lacking any special treatment or burial goods (Lancy 2014). What Ariès said, in effect, was that there are two pre-adult life-stages: the baby–toddler stage when, lacking speech, manners, and proper locomotion, the individual isn't yet fully human; and the proto-adult stage when the individual is treated as a smaller, less competent adult. This characterization is probably not far off the mark for peasant society throughout much of civilization (Shon 2002: 141) and it may fit quite a few tribal societies studied by anthropologists. Osteological analysis, while scarce, shows skeletal evidence of adult activity (heavy, dangerous work, warfare) on juvenile remains (Thompson and Nelson 2011: 269).

Scholars, however, quickly picked up the gauntlet Ariès had thrown down. Sommerville (1982) documents virtually continuous evidence of childhood as a distinct stage from the Egyptians onward. In fact, when Flinders

Petrie excavated the Middle Kingdom (*c*.1900 BCE) village of Lahun, he found many children's toys, including balls and pull toys that wouldn't look out of place in a contemporary toy store.

Barbara Hanawalt, exploring various textual sources, finds ample evidence of children in the medieval period, and, in fact, is able to document consistent variation in children's lives as a function of their parents' social standing: "By 1400 professional toy-makers had shops in Nuremburg and Augsburg and began to export their wares to Italy and France. Manor children also played chess and backgammon and learned falconry and fencing" (Hanawalt 1986: 208).

To be sure, as Shahar's meticulous study shows, illness, high infant mortality, and the need to become self-sufficient, or, at least, to unburden one's parents, at an early age, meant that childhood with its carefree and pampered associations must have been rather short; for example, "boys and girls, designated for the monastic life, were placed in monasteries and convents at the age of five, and, in exceptional cases, even younger" (Shahar 1990: 106). Evidence of childhood in the past is irrefutable but the length of childhood and the child's role in the family and in society were very different than in our neontocracy.

What's so special about human childhood?

The majority of mammals progress from infancy to adulthood seamlessly, without any intervening stages. (Bogin 1998: 17)

For those immersed in the neontocracy, the question "What's so special about human childhood?" might never arise. But, for anthropologists impressed with unique aspects of human life history as well as the enormous cross-cultural variability in childhood, it is one of the most vital issues in human evolution. Why does the chimpanzee, our closest relative, hover on the brink of extinction while we threaten to overpopulate the planet? Barry Bogin found an explanation for this gross disparity in early childhood as a "unique stage of the human life cycle, a stage not to be found in the life cycle of any other living mammal" (Bogin 1998: 17). As compared with the other apes, humans have much higher fertility, which Bogin attributes to the crèche-like character of childhood. Its purpose is to provide a kind of holding pattern in which the child can be weaned – freeing the mother to bear another child – while it is still somewhat dependent on others.

Relative to chimps, humans are weaned early, when they've reached about 2.1 times their birth weight, at twenty-four months or even earlier. Chimps wean at five to six years and are independent and sexually mature soon after. So while female chimps must wait at least six to seven years between births, humans can, under favorable circumstances, have another one every two years. But while they may be weaned at two or earlier, human children still need adult support and provisioning. Their brains, growing rapidly and gobbling up calories like mad, are still developing. Indeed, nutrients that fuel body growth in other species are diverted to the brain in humans (Bogin and Smith 1996: 705). Babies lack vital skills like speech. They are small, slow, and easy prey. They can't chew or digest adult foods. So, unlike most chimpanzee mothers, who are often their child's sole caretaker, human mothers rely upon child-care assistance from the child's closest kin – the father, older siblings, and grandparents. Because their genes are proliferating in each of their wife/ mother/daughter's children, their genetic interest is almost as great as hers (Hrdy 2005a).

But childhood is lengthened in the human species not only in the period from six months to four years when others can care for the child. Middle childhood is also an "extra" stage not found in the life histories of the other apes, and human adolescence is relatively longer than the comparable stage in apes. The model that best seems to explain this extended period of juvenility is referred to as "embodied capital" (Bock 2002a, 2010; Kaplan and Bock 2001). The long period of dependency on others and heightened risk of perishing before passing on one's genes is offset by a longer, healthier, and more fertile adulthood. Children, while experiencing relatively slow growth of their brains, and then their bodies, are, also, acquiring vital immunities and resistance to pathogens as well as developing skills and knowledge of the means their culture has accrued to insure survival and reproduction. As they mature, youth are getting physically stronger, fatter, more competent and socially connected.[7] Individuals who begin adulthood having accumulated a store of embodied capital are likely to live longer and produce more offspring who will be healthier and more likely to survive. This life history course should be favored by natural selection.

However, as this volume will amply demonstrate, the length of childhood overall, and the sub-stages, vary a great deal. In Chapter 7 (pp. 278–282) I discuss the possibility of childhood being curtailed so that children can "step up" and fill in for the loss of older members to the domestic labor force (e.g. death of the mother leads the eldest daughter to take over the role). During the prolonged period of childhood, the child acquires considerable "reserve capacity" (RC) biologically and socially that they can activate under adverse circumstances (Bogin 2013: 34). For example, the loss of one or both parents may trigger the acceleration of mating and

---

[7] The early period of slow growth in childhood means the cost of provisioning the dependent child is lower (small bodies don't require as many calories) while the adolescent growth spurt signals that the child can now take care of most of his or her own needs (Gurven and Walker 2006).

family formation (Belsky *et al.* 1991; 507; Draper and Harpending 1982). The child "grows up early" and shifts from the "slow" life history track to the "fast" track (Schlegel 2013: 303–304). This alternate trajectory would facilitate the replication of one's genes in spite of a shorter, less robust adulthood (Kaplan and Bock 2001: 5566, Figure 2). There is growing evidence that middle childhood represents a decision point where a stress-filled, precarious existence[8] will lead to earlier puberty, shortened adolescence, and opportunistic mating (del Giudice and Belsky 2011; Geronimus 1992, 1996; Low 2000: 333). Although prospects for the offspring are not very good (Bogin 1994: 32), the juvenile may already have mastered a significant fraction of his or her culture's adaptive system and can, therefore, keep themselves and at least some offspring alive. The life history of "street kids" (Lancy 2010b, and this volume, Chapter 10, pp. 387–393) certainly fits this trajectory as well. This twin trajectory model may help us to understand how the human population may have been sustained under adverse conditions.

As I have indicated, my goal has been to thoroughly search the ethnographic record[9] seeking emergent patterns – especially those relevant to "big" questions such as the consequences of varied periods of juvenility. Historically, human life history scholars would have employed a narrower search process. That's because it was assumed that, to understand childhood from an evolutionary perspective, we should privilege hunting-and-gathering or foraging societies that, presumably, came closer to matching the "Environment of Evolutionary Adaptedness" (Bowlby 1980: 40). That is, if the fossil record of human evolution revealed a predominantly foraging mode of subsistence, then we should focus on contemporary societies that followed that aboriginal way of life. The ground-breaking work done on childhood among the !Kung – perhaps the most thoroughly studied foraging society in the world – set the "norm." This view is losing its currency, however. Even though there are undoubted commonalities among contemporary foraging peoples (Konner in press; this volume, Chapter 2, pp. 66–70), the differences are also quite evident (Hewlett 1996: 216). Then too, the !Kung are now seen as somewhat atypical in that the period when !Kung children are free from responsibility for providing food for themselves and family is quite long relative to that in other foraging groups. Many scholars now view the Late Pleistocene as the

---

[8] However, if the stress is largely caused by food shortage, which may be temporary in a famine, for example, the response may be only a temporary slowing of growth and maturation (Lasker 1969: 1485).

[9] Less thoroughly, I have canvassed a considerable library of secondary sources in history. Where historians are looking at change over time and the impact of specific events or individuals, I treat historical cases as analogous to ethnographic cases. I found, for example, near perfect homology between the nature of apprenticeship in the historic and ethnographic records (Lancy 2012a).

Ursprung of modern man, as that was the period of the spectacular population growth and global dispersal of *Homo sapiens*. The modal subsistence strategy of these mobile populations was to travel and live near water, taking advantage of readily exploitable marine resources such as shellfish. This is a very different lifestyle than that of the !Kung, whose diet was chronically short on protein (meat), and much more like that of the Meriam (island dwellers in the Torres Straits). Unlike !Kung children, on Mer, children just older than toddlers easily obtain edible marine resources (Bird and Bird 2002: 262). There is growing evidence for evolutionary adaptation also occurring as the human population expanded rapidly during the Holocene, where we see an enormous diversification in human culture (Hawks *et al.* 2007; Volk and Atkinson 2013: 182). So I take the position that we may learn as much about the "nature" of childhood from studying the culture of street kids as from studying African arid-land foragers.

While there is a wealth of material on childhood in anthropology, the reader should appreciate that such information may be hard won.

The challenges of studying children in culture

Adolescent [Aboriginal] girls were quite happy to spend time with me, often for hours on end, as long as I did not ask them questions and as long as they did not have to talk to me. (Young 2010: 87)

Archaeologists write of how elusive the search is for evidence of children in most habitation sites. Their primary focus is on artifacts and physical remains. It may be difficult to differentiate "toys" from utensils or votive objects (Horn and Martens 2009: 188; Crawford 2009). Archaeologists excavating an early Thule culture site determined, for example, that the smaller-sized "tools" they recovered were likely toys because they were made of wood whereas the adult-sized versions were made of other materials (Kenyon and Arnold 1985: 352). Another clue to children's use of an artifact as a toy is that it may be crudely made (Politis 2007: 224). A child's involvement in ceramics manufacture may be detected by the size of fingerprints on recovered shards (Kamp 2002: 87). Earlier I noted that, since children are often not yet considered fully human, there is little perceived need to bury their remains in a formal context. So while we can learn a great deal years and centuries later from adult burials, child burials – if located at all – will be much less well preserved (Lewis 2007: 31).

Ethnography can be equally challenging. Considering the hierarchy inherent in the gerontocracy, anthropologists interested in children are treated in a bemused fashion; after all, why bother to observe or talk to individuals who "don't know anything" (Lancy 1996: 118; also Barley

1983/2000: 61)? Often the first challenge is to obtain basic demographic and census data. Parents rarely keep track of children's ages (Bril *et al.* 1989: 310) and the process of recall can be laborious. Among the Kpelle, a frequent aide-memoire to calculating a child's age was to recollect where the garden had been – in swidden cultures the cultivated fields are moved each year to allow the land to fallow – when the child in question was born. And then the respondent painstakingly works forward, year by year, recalling details of the particular location or other noteworthy attribute such as a locust attack while the ethnographer patiently keeps a tally of the elapsing years (Lancy 1996). Estimating age on the basis of the child's size is unreliable because our notions of age-size relationships come from living in a culture where children likely consume too many calories rather than too few. I learned to gradually recalibrate my estimator. Confusion can arise from naming conventions that vary over the lifespan, and it is extremely rare for an individual to bear the same name from birth to death. A child may be called, simply, "third-born" or "born late." Nominal terms for son, daughter, cousin, father, and so on may take on different meanings than in standard Euroamerican kin terminology. This is especially true in the context of extended or polygynous (one husband, multiple wives) families. Above all, people may be reluctant to talk about children for fear of calling them to the attention of jealous neighbors or malevolent spirits. Or, contrariwise, the ethnographer may be specifically warned off from associating with particular children. One of my best child informants was cheeky, bright, very talkative, and unguarded – all attributes identifying him as a "bad child" and "un-Kpelle."

It is extremely rare for anyone to interrogate anyone else. Considering how little privacy there might be in a small, close-knit community, it would seem unnecessary. Referencing again the gerontocracy, it is particularly inappropriate for adults to interrogate children (unless they've misbehaved) to discover their views or reasons for doing things. Children make challenging informants, as these examples illustrate:

Initiating oneself as an adult into [Asabano] children's groups can prove difficult, particularly if the researcher is ... foreign to the children. It took me more than a week before many children felt comfortable enough to talk with me or have me sit around with them. Some children, particularly the youngest girls, never overcame their fear of me and there was one child that broke out into hysterics every time I walked near her, up until my very last day. (Little 2008: 29)

Befragte Mädchen oder Junger reagierten auf meine Frage entweder einsilbig oder reproduzierten Phrasen von Erwachsenen.
   (When questioned, Bamana girls and boys reacted either with mono-syllables or would parrot back something they'd heard an adult say.) (Polak 2011: 112)

The question as to the meaning of Wagenia circumcision is easier asked than answered. This is ... because the informants were of so little help on this point. (Droogers 1980: 159)

Given these problems, I tend to discount descriptions of cultural practices derived largely from interviews with adults that aren't buttressed by observational data. As Chris Little (2011: 152–153) has found in his work with the Asabano, parents' *accounts* of how they raise their children have been heavily influenced by their exposure to Christianity and bear little resemblance to how children are actually raised.

Outline of the volume

Societies take what are essentially straightforward, biologically grounded dispositions, for example puberty, or pregnancy, or menstruation, and weave around them the most intricate webs of custom, attitude, and belief. (Broude 1975)

In the remainder of this chapter, I highlight the contents of the subsequent chapters. Each chapter offers numerous examples from the rich archives on childhood from cultural anthropology, primatology, archaeology, and history. Whenever possible, these sources are "triangulated," in order to gauge how old or widespread the phenomenon under examination might be. Themes are drawn, inductively, from the literature. For example, while all societies acknowledge stages or milestones in the child's development, there is considerable variation in how these are identified and marked. We will need to tease out the broad commonalities among many individual cases.

As patterns are noted, an attempt is made to identify the underlying forces that shape them. In some cases, biological fitness is a proximal force; in others, subsistence systems can be linked to aspects of childhood. Childhood in foraging bands looks different from childhood in farming communities. In yet other cases – object play by very young children, for example – we find true biological universals at work. And, obviously, there are many aspects of childhood that are not easily linked to either child biology or adaptation to the local ecology. Importantly, as we'll see, children have a great deal of autonomy and freedom to construct a novel "children's culture."

Each chapter also features contrasts drawn between dominant, modern (e.g. WEIRD, neontocracy) views on a particular aspect of childhood and views derived from ethnographic cases. Often, we will see the contemporary view as being at odds with wider, older patterns and seek to explain how changes in the nature of parenthood and the exigencies of the modern, information economy have changed the nature of childhood. Contrast will also be drawn between the children observed in intact, self-sufficient villages and their contemporary counterparts living in societies racked by poverty, disease, and civil strife.

Valuing children

As we will explore in Chapter 2, a child's worth varies widely across cultures, across social classes, even within a single family (e.g. the family may favor boys). While the norm for much of human history has been a society dominated by attention to the oldest members – a gerontocracy – our society is uniquely a neontocracy. Figure 1 graphically depicts this distinction (Lancy 1996: 13; this volume, p. 26).[10] In a gerontocracy, children may be devalued, seen largely as a liability until they reach an age when they become useful. Korowai "adults express an expectation of pleasurably consuming the bounty of a grown child's work" (Stasch 2009: 143). The child that survives also promises to carry forward the parents' genes and patrimony. In a neontocracy, by contrast, children are accorded a great deal of social capital – from conception in some quarters – and are under little or no obligation to pay back the investment made in them. Their account is always in the black.

Louise Brown, who, in 1978, became the world's first "test-tube baby," can be contrasted with the unnamed infants born to impoverished mothers in northeast Brazil studied and befriended by Nancy Scheper-Hughes. Louise might carry the title "most wanted child," considering her parents' ardent pursuit of a child and society's willingness to support their quest. In contrast, the Brazilian babies are so unwelcome that their mothers, in effect, starve them to death and no one – save the gringo anthropologist – is at all concerned (Scheper-Hughes 1987b). In rural Bangladesh, children are expected to help out with farming and household work, and by age fifteen the break-even point is reached: parents can now turn a "profit" on them. Girls, however, often marry before fifteen, and their marriage requires the payment of a dowry, while young men, obviously, bring in dowry when they marry. Not surprisingly then, infant/child mortality is three times as high for girls as for boys (Caine 1977).

I use admittedly extreme examples to make the point that for much of human history, children were, and still are in most of the world, treated as a commodity. Children enhance their parents' inclusive fitness (e.g. reproductive success), they assist with the care of younger siblings, and they do farm-work. They may be sold into slavery, be sent to urban areas to fend for themselves in the streets, or have their wages incorporated into the family's budget. In the Middle Ages, children were donated to the church as oblates to intercede with the divine on behalf of their parents. And, most extraordinary to our sensibilities, children in many societies were sacrificed to insure the favorable attention of the gods.

---

[10] A vivid illustration of the phenomenon is "child-proof" packaging which is, unfortunately, senior-proof as well.

In earlier times, the "difficult" or unwanted child might be dubbed a "changeling" or devil-inspired spirit, thereby providing a blanket of social acceptability to cloak its elimination (Haffter 1986). In cases where mothers are forced to rear unwanted children, the young may suffer abuse severe enough to end their life. While our society may treat such behavior by the parent as a heinous crime, "This capacity for selective removal in response to qualities both of offspring and of ecological and social environments may well be a significant part of the biobehavioral definition of *Homo sapiens*" (Dickeman 1975: 108).

The child's value is continually recalibrated. Infants occupy a liminal position. Not yet fully human, they are treated as living in an external womb where their gestation continues. They are kept hidden and, often, tightly swaddled. Stimulation such as making eye contact or addressing speech to the infant is to be avoided in the interests of keeping the baby as calm and quiet as possible. An alternative view sees children as occupying two worlds, that of humans and the spirit world. As such, they are seen as worthy candidates to carry messages of supplication between the two. Once the neonate is past the gauntlet of birth trauma, illness, and deliberate termination, it will be welcomed joyfully by its kin. A naming ceremony or other means may be used to recognize the child's emergent personhood, acknowledging its more fully human nature. The child is welcomed as a contributor to the household economy. Evidence that the child is now acknowledged as fully human or a full member of society is revealed in burial practices, which change from about five years of age. Additionally, at this age children may be "circulated" or fostered into other families where their contributions may be more critical.

Aside from the neontocracy, there is a small sample of the world's least complex, most egalitarian societies that are very "indulgent" toward children. Living close to the land as foragers, in these societies, everyone in the band interacts with and cares for the child. It is never scolded or punished and no one expects the child to rapidly "grow up" so that it can take care of itself and others. The !Kung were the earliest such society to be documented by anthropologists (Draper 1978: 37).

Children are typically viewed as chattel, so, when times are hard, families have no recourse but to force children to "earn their keep." The work they do – for low wages – on plantations, in mines, and in factories is physically demanding and dangerous. With industrialization, a child's potential worth grows, as it can now augment the family account with wages it earns through regular employment. Growing wealth in the society at large also expands opportunities for the employment of the young in "domestic service." But then, 150 years ago, the idea of the useful child began to give way to our modern notion of the useless but also priceless child (Zelizer 1985). Children become innocent and fragile cherubs, needing protection from adult society, including the world of work. Their value to us is measured no longer in terms of an economic payoff or even genetic fitness but in terms of complementing our own values – as book lovers, ardent travelers, athletes, or devotees of a particular sect.

To make a child

This chapter highlights the interplay of biology and culture. It is my fond hope that readers will discover aspects of childhood influenced profoundly by biology that they assumed were all about "nurture," and vice versa. Biology can explain the physiological processes underlying reproduction but can't account for the following: while the average age of first pregnancy in the US edges above twenty-five, in some areas of the country pregnancy at fourteen is common and socially acceptable (Heath 1990: 502). The decision to make a child will be examined in all its variation and complexity. Using contrasting cases, like the pair just cited, we will identify key stakeholders in this agreement and try and understand their agendas.

In a previous section, I touched on the relative reproductive success of chimps and humans, but cross-culturally as well there will be great variability in fertility. Societies that have reached the carrying capacity of their territory – increasingly the case – must either find ways to limit growth voluntarily or face famine, civil war, and genocide. Similarly, individuals must make difficult decisions regarding reproduction depending on their personal and material wellbeing. Furthermore, thanks to the brilliance of Robert Trivers (1972, 1974), we now realize that mothers, fathers, and children have differing agendas. The nursing child wants to be the last child his mother will ever have so that he can enjoy her care and provisioning exclusively. The father will be opportunistic in seeking mating opportunities and display a similar fickleness toward the provisioning of his offspring. He will, in other words, spread his investment around to maximize the number of surviving offspring. The mother has the most difficult decisions of all. She must weigh her health and longevity and future breeding opportunities against the cost of her present offspring, including any on the way. She must also factor in any resources that might be available from her children's fathers and her own kin network.

These differing agendas form the nucleus for the soap-opera-like quality of family life in many societies. Many common customs and institutions studied by anthropologists, including marriage, polygamy, the extended family, adoption, and witchcraft, represent the cross-currents generated by these biologically based conflicts. I refer to polygyny, for example, as a great compromise whereby men can increase their progeny without preying on other men's wives and daughters. Another very common source of discord is the sex and paternity of the newborn. Girls may be unwelcome, in general, and fathers, especially stepfathers, disavow any child they aren't sure is their own.

In a majority of the world's diverse societies, women continue as workers throughout pregnancy and resume working shortly after the child is born. This work is physically demanding, so, for many, there is a peak period in their lives when they have the stamina and fat reserves to do their work and have babies. How many babies they successfully rear will depend heavily on their access to a supportive community of relatives who can help with household work, assist with childcare, and provide supplementary resources. Hence a woman's "fitness" or the number of her offspring who survive and reproduce themselves is at least partly a function of her social skills, her ability to recruit allies.

Another factor to take into account is infant mortality. Until recently, as many as one infant in three didn't survive until its first birthday. Typically women operate from an estimate of the ideal number of offspring and increase their fertility by a factor that reflects the incipient rate of infant mortality. If the world is perceived today as overcrowded, the blame might be placed on the disconnect between public health measures, like child vaccination and sterile obstetrics procedures, which sharply reduced infant mortality, and the reproductive calculus of millions of individual mothers. These mothers continued to use the old "ideal" as the benchmark for gauging how many children to have – Olusanya (1989) refers to them as "fertility martyrs." The agencies that intervened to reduce infant mortality were not as ready with contraception and family-planning interventions, and the result has been masses of humanity living on the ragged edge of poverty.

While high infant mortality may be met by stoicism or the manufacture of a special, not-fully-human character for the newborn, pregnancy and childbirth are heavily buttressed by well-established and widely embraced customs. Folk theories encompass the process of conception (not all societies associate it with sexual intercourse), taboos to be practiced by parents during pregnancy, and specified procedures for childbirth. Because childbirth is seen as inherently dangerous – to the community as well – mother and infant may be secluded for a period of time. There are well-known prescriptions for the proper care and feeding of infants, and a young mother violates them at the risk of ostracism. Similarly, there is a folk pharmacopeia for common child illnesses, most of which is, unfortunately, harmful to the child. However, a common diagnosis traces the problem to jealous discord or infidelity in the family.

Adults are rewarded for having lots of offspring when certain conditions are met. First, mothers must be surrounded by supportive kin who relieve them of much of the burden of childrearing so they can concentrate their energy on bearing more children. Second, those additional offspring must be seen as "future workers," on farm or in factory. They must be seen as having the potential to pay back the investment made in them as infants and toddlers, and pretty quickly, before they begin reproducing themselves. Failing either or both these conditions, humans will reduce their fertility (Turke 1989). Foragers, for whom children are more of a burden than a help, will have far fewer children than neighboring societies that depend on agriculture for subsistence (LeVine 1988).

As a society modernizes, economic opportunity may require the loosening of ties to one's extended family. Working parents who have moved away from supportive kin must shift to a strategy of bearing fewer children on whom they lavish much attention. Unable to recruit other family as caretakers, parents must invest more in childrearing, including forging stronger emotional bonds with their child. The net result is that parents take advantage of modern contraception options and only give birth to children they can "afford." This pattern has become a worldwide phenomenon and is referred to by demographers as the "Great" transition (Caldwell 1982) leading to dramatically lower birth rates.

It takes a village

In middle-class Euroamerican society, we take conception, pregnancy, childbirth, nursing, and infant care largely for granted. The real challenge for parents, their job, if you will, begins when the child starts to become vocal, mobile, and capable of learning. In most of the rest of the world and in the historical record, this distribution of responsibility is skewed in exactly the opposite direction. That is, conception is critical because the assurance of paternity determines whether the husband or partner and his kin will provide resources and care for the infant or abandon the mother and/or the child (Wilson and Daly 2002). Pregnancy is a critical period because of the threat of miscarriage, stillbirth, and birth defects. Pregnant mothers and spouses are ringed around with taboos, and among the most common is the proscription against intercourse either during pregnancy or (up to three years) afterward. Childbirth is critical because of the enormous risks faced by both mother and newborn (Hern 1992: 36). Again, most societies mark this critical rite of passage with ritual, folk medicine, and taboos. For the subsistence-farming Semai people, living in the forests of Malaysia, death in childbirth accounts for 50 percent of adult female mortality, and "Puerperal blood and afterbirth are so dangerous that people use euphemisms to talk about them" (Dentan 1978: 110–111). However, as the post-partum threats to the infant diminish, the parents' role typically *declines*, as others now provide care.

Nearly all societies hold very strict views on the necessity for almost constant contact between a mother or other nurturing adult and the infant. Infants are fed on demand, carried constantly, and sleep with their mother.

Young mothers are severely chastised for any lapse in infant care. However, once the infant begins to walk, it immediately joins a social network in which its mother plays a sharply diminished role – especially if she's pregnant – and its father may play no role at all. Again, this is precisely the reverse of our views of what is normal. The child is cosseted in a blanket of humanity, an idea captured by the African proverb "It takes a village" – the title of Chapter 4.

Once the infant has been judged worthy of rearing, it will be displayed to a community eager to interact with it. In particular, its older sisters will be in the forefront of those wanting to share in the nurturing process. The circle of caretakers may gradually widen to include aunts, grandmothers, and, occasionally, the father. Even more distant kin can be expected to cast a watchful eye on the child when it is playing on the "mother-ground" (Lancy 1996: 84). Indeed, the toddler must seek comfort from relatives as it may be abruptly weaned and forcibly rejected by its mother as she readies herself for the next child.

Moving from the village to the more complex societies of the ancient world, we see various "professionals," such as wet-nurses and tutors, helping at the nest. By the seventeenth and eighteenth centuries, responsibility for child-rearing becomes more firmly placed on parents' shoulders. This occurs in response to increasingly modern notions that target the early years as being critical for imparting moral values and literacy. These views become accentuated by the demographic transition whereby smaller, more mobile families preclude sibling and grandparent caretakers. The rapid growth in knowledge pushes "education" earlier and earlier, ultimately into the nursery.

Making sense

The lens I use in Chapter 5 is developmental. How does the child become an adult? How does it acquire the culture of its ancestors? We talk to our babies as if they were sentient. When the internal mechanisms of their metabolism (e.g. bowel movements) provoke a panoply of facial expressions, we rush to interpret meaningful responses. Elsewhere, societies – including Western society until 150 years ago – treated the infant as semi-human. Young children lack speech and control of bodily functions. They crawl on the ground and mouth whatever they find, all suggesting an animal of the lowest sort. Christians saw them as inherently sinful. These views tend to provoke one of two extreme responses. One response is "benign neglect" – everyone waits until the child can talk sensibly before acknowledging its existence. A second typical response is to aggressively humanize the child, including ruthless suppression of all "sub-human" tendencies (e.g. bawling, crawling, thumb-sucking).

In spite of the widely shared view that infants cannot participate in society, it is evident from research on infant cognition that babies are definitely learning a great deal about the world around them. This rapid growth in understanding – correlated with a rapidly growing brain – emerges in early childhood as two powerful motives. These are, first, to "fit in," to be liked, appreciated, and accepted. The second motive force is a drive to become competent, to replicate the routine behaviors enacted by those who're older and more capable. The presence of these drives accounts for the child's ability to learn through observation, imitation, and, by extension, playing with objects and ideas in make-believe.

In most societies, the child's autonomous and socially conforming learning process will arrive, without much intervention, at the desired end. However, in Oceania, particularly, family members intervene directly to shape children's demeanor ("manners") toward those whose rank and/or kinship require appropriate recognition. Etiquette may also include notions about reciprocity and altruism toward kin. While such social savvy can be expected to develop spontaneously in nearly all children,[11] where inter-community relations are particularly formal, the child may be "pushed" to acquire correct behavior and speech early.

Children learn in particular contexts that are conveniently structured to facilitate such learning. The very family members assigned to care for toddlers – older siblings – are also playmates *and* role models. The "play group" has at least some of the character of a classroom. A "bossy" older sister ordering one around is, effectively, teaching. When a toddler accompanies an older brother on an errand, they are "apprenticing." Domestic activity such as processing game and gathered tubers, cooking, and craft-work, as well as farm-work and construction, are all carried on openly with children as spectators and, when appropriate, helpers.

The *laissez faire* stance on children's autonomous learning extends broadly to their development as a whole. Intervention to redirect the child's activity or to force it to learn something it can't or won't learn on its own is rare but noticeable. The infant's motor development may be accelerated to ease the burden of its care. In a warrior society, the child's aggression may be cultivated, while in the opposite – egalitarian and pacific – society it may be suppressed. The same polemic accounts for the use of fright tactics and corporal punishment and their prohibition. Gender roles, while not taught explicitly, may be emphasized by controlling the child's activity (girls work more and play less), their dress, and with whom they associate.

---

[11] The neontocracy may be the singular exception where adults tolerate "ill-mannered" youth; Chapter 2, pp. 71–72.

The shift in attitude toward children who've "gotten sense" is quite apparent. While schooling for us may begin with the fetus (if you can believe the hype about expectant mothers listening to Mozart), most societies don't see children as sophisticated learners until their cognitive and linguistic skills have matured. This change usually occurs during the fifth to seventh years and may correspond to the eruption of the first molars. Children become capable of following directions and attending to and copying the correct behavior of others. Imperfect at first, they will keep practicing until, with perhaps the merest acknowledgment of their mastery, they are treated as full participants in the household economy.

The concluding section dissects the role of active, intentional teaching or instruction in children's acquisition of their culture. Once again, prevailing wisdom in WEIRD society fails to hold up very well outside this exclusive segment of the population.

Of marbles and morals

The great Swiss psychologist Jean Piaget was noted for crafting ingenious experiments to tease out the child's underlying level of mental acuity. But when he wanted to describe the child's nascent ideas about morality and social convention, he focused on boys playing marbles (Piaget 1932/1965) – hence the title of Chapter 6, on children's play. Piaget, however, was not alone in seeing play as a kind of "natural curriculum" for children.

Play is a truly universal trait of childhood. The one thing that children can appropriate for themselves, without the sanction of culture or explicit blessing of parents, is play. It is ubiquitous. A baby will play with its mother's breast. The first glimmer of understanding about the natural world and how it works comes through play with objects. After its nurturing mother, the child's first close relationships are with its playmates – usually siblings. The child's first active engagements with the tasks that will occupy most of its adult life – hunting, cooking, house-building, baby-tending – all occur during make-believe. The games of youth are among the most mobile of cultural artifacts; "hopscotch" had diffused to every continent before the age of mass media. Children given a full menu of chores still manage to weave play into their work.

Many of the child's most basic needs seem to be fed by play – their need to socialize with peers and their need for physical, sensory, and, to a lesser extent, cognitive stimulation (Lancy 1980a). The demands of earning a living and reproduction gradually extinguish the desire to play. This happens earlier in girls than in boys – almost universally. However, where these demands are light, as, for example, with males in some segments of our society, play will continue unabated. While we take our children's play seriously, in traditional societies play's greatest value is that it keeps children distracted and out of adults' way. It is not often looked upon as of special value in children's socialization.

As in so many aspects of childhood, our society is not content to let nature take its course. The child's play is managed by adults. From a mother teaching an infant how to interact with "educationally oriented" objects to the highly charged atmosphere of professionally coached youth hockey, we capitalize on children's passion for play to pursue more serious ends. These ends may range from inculcating in children the competitive ethos of the culture to fostering early literacy to affording parents cultural capital – bragging rights – with peers. However, I argue that there may be a downside to the contemporary attenuation of children's "free" play in that they lose opportunities to develop the kind of social savvy (which I refer to as gamesmanship) that involves cooperation, negotiation, and compromise.

The chore curriculum

The theme of Chapter 7 is children's work and, more particularly, the processes through which children acquire the skills implicated in various "chores." The term "curriculum" conveys the idea that there is a discernible regularity to the processes whereby children attempt to learn, then master, and finally carry out their chores. Work is central both to the nature of childhood (excepting in the neontocracy) and to the child's progress toward adult standing and competence. Our society reacts with disapproval at the "exploitation" by parents of child models and actors. And yet, if one visits the area around Kisoro, a prosperous area in western Uganda, one will see far more young (four to eight years old) children working than playing. A four-year-old might be tending his first goat – a proudly achieved milestone in his development. A slightly older brother drives a small flock of goats, a ten-year-old cousin tends a cow and calf, and so on up to the fifteen-year-old who's driving a herd of forty cattle to another pasture. Not only would the children see these "opportunities" in a positive light, their parents would wax eloquent on the many benefits to their children's character and maturation that animal husbandry provides. I've found several references in the literature to parents, semi-jokingly, referring to their "little slaves." Today, and even more so in the past, children may be treated as chattel.

Chapter 7 will offer snapshots of children at work in a wide variety of societies, leading to several critical generalizations. For example, the Hadza are more fertile than neighboring groups because children as young as four can meet a substantial part of their own nutrition by gathering and processing large quantities of baobab fruits. Since they take care of some of their own provisioning, their mothers can have another child more quickly (Blurton-Jones 1993: 405). We also note that, outside modern industrialized society, children are rarely taught these critical work skills. They learn them by observing older, more proficient individuals and trying out their fledgling skills in make-believe play with miniature tools.

Societies vary in their need for child helpers, but most girls will be welcomed as "helpers at the nest," and a boy as young as four may be trusted with the care of a chicken. By eight or nine, a child might be working for more hours a day than it is playing, and it may be earning real money for its family through street sales and other odd jobs or a regular shift in factory, mine, or plantation. Most children are, in fact, quite eager for these opportunities to assume more adult responsibilities.

The chapter details the intricacies of various "chore" curricula from running errands/marketing to camel-tending to bean cultivation. In each case we see realms of work conveniently staged into tasks of varying levels of difficulty so that even the youngest may assay to "help out." Older siblings act primarily as role models who only occasionally need to intervene in correcting a youngster's miscues. The acquisition of vital subsistence skills is a leisurely process, but, nevertheless, competency is achieved at a young age. And this yields a paradox as children seem to become competent at food acquisition or production well before they are expected to fully provision themselves and others. I attempt a resolution in a theory of "children as a reserve labor force."

Somewhat later, the child may elect to move beyond the core skills expected of everyone to tackle more challenging endeavors such as learning pottery or weaving. She or he must demonstrate adequate strength, physical skill, and motivation before anyone will deign to spend time on his or her instruction. An apprenticeship escalates these demands and its coercive quality reinforces the high status of the master. Still, in both informal crafts and the formal apprenticeship, adults are reluctant to spend time in teaching and learners must make headway largely on their own.

Living in limbo

The enduring paradox of adolescence is that when children are biologically ready to claim the rights of adulthood – such as family formation – society is not prepared to grant them. But there's nevertheless the expectation that they'll give up their youthful pastimes. So they're living in limbo, and they drive people crazy. Societies have devised various means for dealing with this problem. The pastoralist Masaai of East Africa send young men away from the compound to act as roving patrols; the Kpelle require youths to endure a challenging, four-year-long indoctrination in "bush" school before they're given the stamp of approval; Trobriand Islanders grant adolescents limited rights: they can have sexual relations but cannot begin to form their own households.

Like childhood, adolescence is of variable length. Several factors, notably diet quality, influence the onset of puberty. Worldwide, the average age of menarche can be as low as twelve and as high as seventeen. Puberty for boys is delayed by a year or two relative to girls. Attention to and aroused feelings toward the opposite sex may begin even earlier. Indeed, by flirting with prepubescent girls, men may accelerate the onset of menarche and, consequently, the onset of breeding. Girls typically transition directly from their mother's "hearth" to their own; hence, adolescence as a social stage may be quite short. On the other hand, older men may resist younger men's access to post-pubescent females, and/or marriage may carry steep financial requirements. In either case, delayed marriage and family formation will extend adolescence for males.

In most societies, adolescents are involuntarily assigned to their futures – as apprentices, as soldiers, as clerks in an office – and their marriages are arranged. Meanwhile, and until these new roles are assumed, their marginality can sometimes be of benefit to society. Living on the fringe of the community (literally in many cases), the risks they take may lead to the detection of useful resources or, alas, lurking dangers – a pattern found widely in the order *Primata*. During periods of rapid social change, adolescents may adopt new customs and survival strategies more quickly than adults and thus serve as a conduit for social change.

In our society, we are almost obsessed with marking off milestones in the child's development: birthdays, physiological events (sleeping through the night, first tooth, control of elimination), and, above all, the passage through academic grade levels. In the societies we'll be studying, such milestones are rarely noted. Nevertheless, even in the simplest societies, the child's transition to adolescence and/or adulthood may be marked by, sometimes elaborate, rites of passage. I will argue throughout the book that the norm for humans is to adopt a *laissez faire* attitude toward the young – in sharp contrast to the anxious ministrations characteristic of the neontocracy. However, rites of passage signal broad and undeniable course corrections in the child's trajectory. The milestone is acknowledged by the entire community. The child is treated differently; expectations have changed.

Circumcision rites that occur just before or after the onset of puberty apply a stamp of approval to the individual's "coming of age." Such rites signal a shift from permissive attitudes regarding the commingling of the sexes to the imposition of strict controls over – especially the girl's – sexuality. Societies where warfare is central use these rites of passage to forcibly wrench the boy from his mother's company and brutally indoctrinate him in the rigors and secrets of the male side of the culture. The process of conditioning and indoctrination may take years, and in a few cases includes the reinforcement of a status quo where men are oppressively dominant over women.

Marriage is the succeeding rite of passage, but it may occur early in adolescence or quite late. Where virginity is highly valued, girls will be married at the onset of puberty or earlier. In warrior cultures marriage is delayed for young men. In any case, marriage is usually tightly controlled as it involves the transfer of wealth between families.

As these customs give way in the face of missionary and government intervention and the spread of modern communication, the transition to adulthood changes. Frequently this has meant a lessening of the influence of adults over the next generation, and the oral transmission of traditional culture is imperiled. In its place, adolescents appear to adopt a universal culture that is heavy on Coca-Cola, pop music, and, above all, school attendance.

Taming the autonomous learner

I mentioned earlier in this chapter that my approach is inductive. This is very evident in Chapter 9, which is devoted to the role of schooling. I was struck by how strange schooling looks once one adopts an anthropological perspective on childhood. There is so much about formal education that is antithetical to the "usual" way that children learn. The enormous variety of children's pathways must all converge, in the modern era, on the school or at least the exams that measure one's progress up the academic beanstalk.

A second inductive insight is that there seem to be two broad patterns to schooling. The earliest schools in the eastern Mediterranean to train scribes look identical to the various apprenticeships discussed in Chapter 7. The characteristics of the apprenticeship – such as a distant, aloof master whose primary tasks seem to be to model (rather than actually teach) and to punish; repetitive menial chores for the student; a harsh and unforgiving learning environment; and a paucity of teaching material – are all characteristic of schooling. And this is true well into the modern era in the West and continuing in most of the rural schools in economically undeveloped areas today. More recently, schools – especially in WEIRD society – have become "progressive," and much more benign. And yet not every student succeeds in this more student-centered institution; indeed, in many schools, the majority fail. Even "passing" students display "resistance" to academic learning.

As schools are introduced into the kinds of villages featured throughout this book, they may provoke a mixed reaction. In spite of harsh conditions, children may embrace the opportunity to "become modern," to abandon the hard work of herding or hoeing for a comfortable white-collar job in the city. Of course, most discover that the school has poorly prepared them for the very few salaried positions in an economy that's not expanding and/or is being consumed by graft. Parents are considerably less eager, although they too may harbor dreams of a share of the hoped-for pay-check. As we've seen, children are a vital part of the rural labor force, so parents may resist the added expense of school fees, books, and uniforms. This is particularly true for girls, whose contributions to family support are critical and whose marriageability may be compromised by going to school. On the other hand, when girls do have an opportunity to acquire at least rudimentary literacy their life prospects, and especially their children's, are enhanced. A few years of schooling does seem to alter the individual's worldview and reasoning – changing the holistic outlook of the village into a more analytical perspective. The schooled villager can now place themselves, at least hypothetically, in a different world than that of their parents (Lerner 1958).

The chapter title reflects the fact that to turn children into eager, bright, and successful students may require them to be "tamed" and turned into "nerds." They must learn obedience, self-control, discipline, and, above all, rapt attention to a teacher – initially a parent. Two broad cultural patterns are associated with families that succeed in transforming their autonomous learners into diligent students. These patterns are associated with "intensive parenting" in Euroamerican or WEIRD communities and the "Tiger Mom" syndrome in many Asian communities, as well as among Asian immigrants to the US and Europe. Contrariwise, we can see that this sort of active parenting is absent in the (unsuccessful) schooling experience of children in rural villages and urban slums.

Too little childhood? Too much?

Popular misconception would assign anthropology the exclusive role of studying the past. On the contrary, as we pursue the study of childhood in the present and project toward the future, we see anthropologists in the forefront of such efforts. The concluding chapter will focus on emerging issues in the lives of children that are likely to preoccupy policymakers in the coming years. With apologies to Charles Dickens, we might say that, for children, these are the best of times and the worst of times. For a fairly small sample of the world's children, life is good. Considering the obesity epidemic, perhaps too good. Children in the neontocracy are cosseted and enriched to a degree unprecedented in human culture. A much larger portion of the world's children live in very straitened circumstances, facing hard labor, poverty, exploitation, and the perils of urban or civil strife. And the overpopulated rural area may no longer be a secure haven. To obtain food, "surplus" children may elect or be forced to leave rural homes to find work or join the ranks of street kids or "rebel" militias.

Still, many poor children cling to families even as they may be exploited and abused. The mores of the gerontocracy exercise a powerful hold on children's sense of obligation and duty – precisely the opposite to the mores of the "me" generation. Children are the breadwinners in families devastated by AIDS or the broken spirits of the chronically unemployed. Once children make a break from their families to make a living in the streets, they may find that their living standard actually improves. The study of street kids' culture is in its infancy but already we can see an outline emerging. Very young kids may be taken under the wing of those who're older and more experienced. They are permitted to shadow the more experienced in learning a trade (e.g. begging, street selling) and the learning environment bears some resemblance to the chore curriculum. Resources may be shared among children and these relationships evolve into "family," with fictive kin terms employed to characterize specific relationships ("brother," "wife"). Street kids occupy particular home territories that provide protection and anonymity. They develop unique slang and modes of dress. In short, children participate in the construction of a new culture. However, this very independence erects barriers to aid agencies that would help street kids by herding them into institutions where they can be protected and cared for.

The problems facing children in the neontocracy revolve around the blanket of overprotection that anxious parents throw over them. Above all, anxiety about their unhappiness leads to a degree of overreaction, with negative consequences (e.g. sugar-rich diet, mood-altering drugs, academic ennui). Raising children to protect them from overrated perils, pitfalls, and disappointments means that their ability to learn from the environment will be impaired. Instead, they are taught in appropriate and "safe" environments, using an "expert-approved" curriculum by intrusive parents, and the "best" coaches and teachers. The result may be a child who is often bored, disrespectful, and overweight, if not "depressed."

The chapter concludes by enumerating the many contrasts between our popular assumptions about the nature of childhood and the picture constructed by using the lens of anthropology.

2   Valuing children

Introduction

In Salic [sixth-century Europe] law ... one who killed a free young woman of childbearing age had to pay 600 sous [but] one who killed a male baby only had to pay 60 sous (30 sous if it was a girl). (Alexandre-Bidon and Lett 1999: 10).

For Korowai ... terms such as "famine," "hungry," and "wanting sago" are popular children's names ... A child is a person in a state of pronounced want, dependent on others for well-being. (Stasch 2009: 168)

The Old Testament witnesses a view of children as essentially a benefit to adults. Like all benefits, such as livestock or crops, children were understood as proof of divine favor. (Horn and Martens 2009: 43)

Much of the contemporary literature on children identifies the parent–child relationship as central to the functioning of society. Furthermore, this relationship is seen as largely unidirectional. That is, the parent has manifold obligations to her child, while the child has few, if any, to her parent. However, as we review literature on children in other societies, a very different picture emerges. For example, West African "Ijo perceive of inheritance as flowing from sons to fathers as readily as the reverse" (Hollos and Leis 1989: 29). This contrast is captured in the two "value pyramids" labeled gerontocracy and neontocracy in Figure 1 in the first chapter. Viviana Zelizer details the gradual change over the past century, in Europe, North America, and East Asia, that transformed children from future farmers or factory workers – adding their critical bit to the household economy – to economically costly but emotionally priceless cherubs: "While in the nineteenth century a child's capacity for labor had determined its exchange value, the market price of a twentieth-century baby was set by smiles, dimples, and curls" (Zelizer 1985: 171). Viewing our culture from a more universal perspective, I see a *neontocracy*, in contrast to the *gerontocracy* I found in my study of a West African village – Gbarngasuakwelle – populated primarily by members of the Kpelle tribe (Lancy 1996: 13). In a neontocracy, kids rule. For example, our entire round of holidays, passed down over millennia, have nearly all become occasions to celebrate – and spend money on – children (Cross 2004: 6). Any cruise through the supermarket will bring one face to face with a weary, overweight, and unkempt mother, accompanied by her Barbie-doll-perfect daughter. In our child-centered society, moralists hurl invectives at mothers who work in lieu of paying constant attention to their offspring (Eberstadt 2004).

The idea of neontocracy also encompasses the trend to steadily lengthen that part of the life-cycle we call childhood. Nowadays, twenty-somethings – who would have married, established their own domicile, and borne or sired several children in an earlier era – are still "in the nest" (Armstrong 2004). At the other end of the continuum, medical practice and the religious right have steadily advanced the point in the life-cycle when the conglomeration of embryonic cells is defined as a child.

This chapter opens with some arresting cases from the US and Japan that illustrate the extreme devotion expected of parents to their adored offspring. A dramatic contrast is drawn as we then examine widespread practices in which children are sacrificed to the more important interests of their parents, families, and the community at large. These actions toward infants are not only tolerated; they may be enshrined in respected and ancient customs. A utilitarian attitude to children is also associated with the widely shared view that children should contribute to the welfare of their families through their labor – as farmhands, child-minders, traders, and craft workers. This perspective also colors traditional attitudes toward adopted children, in marked contrast to the contemporary perspective. But there is one group of societies – foraging bands – that cannot make good use of children's labor. Foraging requires physical attributes they lack. Further, reproduction and childcare practices in these highly mobile societies emphasize the survival of the few offspring produced. And, as a consequence, adult–child interaction among foragers partially resembles a neontocracy. The chapter concludes with a brief history of how our children became cherubs and some concerns about the future of the neontocracy.

Expensive little cherubs

Parents talked about spending $450 on a five-year-old's birthday party . . . and hundreds of dollars on Halloween costumes. (Pugh 2009: 84–85)

In the US, children have become the ultimate "big-ticket" consumer purchase. The meter starts running long before the child is born. A well-known Los Angeles obstetrician quit his practice in 1999 to offer expectant parents 3D sonograms of the fetus for $250. By 2014, 3D and 4D video fetal imaging services are available nationwide for as little as $300.[1] Another booming business devoted to children is the birthday party. One helpful website asks re the "princess party": "Are you ready to turn your home into a family fun castle and your porch into the palace bridge?" Parents are expected to expend hours of effort and a small fortune to host this memorable and unique event. Those pressed for time can contract with "Natalie" to organize a two-hour "princess" party for only $180 plus mileage.[2] Sheila Chapman willingly spent $3,000 on her son's birthday party because "I want him to know how important and special I think he is" (Mitchell 2008: B1). There seems to be no limit on what we will do for our cherubs. A 2007 report from the US Department of Agriculture estimates a family will expend over $200k on raising a child from birth to age eighteen (an eighteen-fold increase in fifty years),[3] but this is a minimum figure and doesn't take into account sono-grams, birthday parties, nannies, or private school tuition (Paul 2008). In Kusserow's ethnography of childrearing in three communities in New York City, "Parkside" is the most exclusive:

> by age three Parkside children were already considered little competitors – small but complete "little people" with their own tastes, desires, needs, and wants ... children enrolled in private preschools ... [where] competition to get in was fierce ... [A father saw similarities] ... between the venture capital business and the upbringing of a child ... [and a mother] ... said "there was nothing that would stop her children from being the best" ... though developing the child through various lessons and classes cost quite a lot, it ... must be done ... "My daughter is extraordinary at chess and ice skating, for which I pay through the nose." (Kusserow 2004: 81, 82)

Slavish devotion to one's progeny can also be found in Japan, where "mothers cater to [the] baby's every whim" (Shwalb et al. 1996: 170). T'ae-kyo, for example, is a complex set of practices and overarching philosophy to guide the expectant mother, who must get in synch with her unborn child. She should expose herself to uplifting thoughts and pleasing sights, sounds, and aromas while avoiding their antitheses (Kim and Choi 1994: 239–240). A Korean proverb says, "It is more effective to be educated during the ten months of pregnancy rather than the years of education after birth" (Shon 2002: 141). T'aekyo now includes the use of new technologies to facilitate the

---

[1] Inner View Ultrasound. Available at www.innerviewultrasound.com/pricing/pricing.html. Accessed February 1, 2014.

[2] The Princess Party. Available at www.birthdaypartyideas.com/html/the_princess_party.html. Accessed December 20, 2012. Princess Parties. Available at www.princesspartiesbynatalie. com/Services.html. Accessed February 1, 2014.

[3] Expenditures on Children by Families, 2007. Available at www.cnpp.usda.gov/Publications/ CRC/crc2007.pdf. Accessed February 1, 2014.

child's academic success, including, for example, "English-language texts to be read aloud by the mother-to-be into a sort of resonating device strapped to her belly" (White 2002: 134–135).

While these parents might be seen as a trifle "overindulgent," no one would seriously question the duty of a modern American or Japanese parent to devote a significant amount of their resources in time and money to their offspring, with no expectation of any material or tangible return aside from the child's love and affection. Indeed, parents' near-obsession with their children, their paranoia about their health and safety, drives them to a state of "hyper-vigilance." Aside from "nannycams," which are enjoying record sales, children are now monitored by an array of sophisticated, Pentagon-inspired, eavesdropping equipment (Katz 2005: 109). Hyper-vigilant US parents who, despite taking all necessary precautions, end up giving birth to a "flawed" child feel themselves the victims of a great injustice (Landsman 2009: 30). As we will see throughout this chapter, the modern neontocracy is at odds with virtually every pre-modern society where childcare has been studied.

Our views on the treatment of fetal and infant mortality and pre-term and medically challenged infants can be contrasted with a far more common pattern: among the ancient Greeks and Romans sickly, unattractive, or unwanted infants were "exposed" or otherwise eliminated; the Chinese and Hindus of India have, since time immemorial, destroyed daughters at birth, to open the way for a new pregnancy and a more desirable male offspring; the Japanese likened infanticide to thinning the rice plants in their paddies; among foragers such as the Inuit or the Jivaro, unwanted babies were left to nature to claim; and in nineteenth-century London, infant corpses littered parks and roadsides (Scrimshaw 1984: 439). Even today,[4] the decision to bring the infant to term and to raise it is by no means automatic. Let's examine some of the factors that come into play.

Calculating the costs

When offspring have low chances of survival or become too energetically expensive, a switch in the ... brain turns off mother's love. (Maestripieri 2007: 113)

[On Chuuk abortion] may also be practiced if divination indicates that the child is a soope (ghost or spirit). If a child is born malformed ... it is sometimes killed for similar superstitious reasons. (Fisher 1963: 530)

---

[4] Demographic studies indicate that infanticide is still very much with us. In China, "abandonment contributes notably to the annual million-plus 'missing' female births" (Johnson 2004: 73).

Just how do parents decide how much to invest in a given child? Consider that a "sick infant simultaneously increases the cost of parental investment and reduces the likelihood of the investment paying off" (Volk and Quinsey 2002: 439). Hrdy (in press) suggests that the infant's gaze-following and close attention to facial expressions and moods – along with a plump body and other neotenous features – are designed to send a clear signal to its mother and other caretakers: "Keep me!" Autistic behavior, by contrast, may send the signal "Don't keep me!" (Shaner et al. 2008). A society's willingness to accept a new arrival is usually contingent on the presence of a set of parents. For example, the death of the mother or father is grounds for infanticide among the Ache, a Paraguayan foraging society.

The baby was small and had very little hair on its head. The Ache felt little affection for children born without hair. No woman volunteered to cradle the baby while the mother recovered from the birth. No man stepped forward to cut the umbilical cord. The signs were clear, and it took only Kuchingi's verbal suggestion to settle the point. "Bury the child," he said. "It is defective, it has no hair." "Besides, it has no father [killed by a jaguar]. Betapangi [the mother's current husband] does not want it. He will leave you if you keep it." Pirajugi [the mother] said nothing, and the old woman Kanegi began to dig silently with a broken bow stave. The child and placenta were placed in the hole and covered with red sandy soil. A few minutes later the Ache packed up their belongings and Grandpa Bepurangi began to break a trail through the undergrowth with his unstrung bow. Pirajugi was tired, but she had nothing to carry, so she was able to keep up without difficulty. (Hill and Hurtado 1996: 3; see also Mull and Mull 1987)

The Ache are particularly direct in disposing of surplus children (approximately one-fifth) because their peripatetic, foraging lifestyle places an enormous burden on the parents. The father provides significant food resources, and the mother provides both food and the vigilant monitoring required by their dangerous jungle environment. Both men and women face significant health and safety hazards throughout their relatively short lives, and they place their own welfare over that of their offspring. A survey of several foraging societies shows a close association between the willingness to commit infanticide and the daunting challenge "to carry more than a single young child on the nomadic round" (Riches 1974: 356).

Among other South American foragers, similar attitudes prevail.[5] The Tapirapé from central Brazil allow only three children per family; all others must be left behind in the jungle. Seasonally scarce resources affecting the entire community dictate these measures (Wagley 1977). In fact, the

[5] Infanticide and/or abortion were once ubiquitous throughout the world. The peoples of the South American rainforests have been singled out in this discussion only because their practices were studied in advance of missionary and government efforts to suppress infanticide.

availability of adequate resources is most commonly the criterion for determining whether an apparently healthy infant will be kept alive (Dickeman
1975). Among the Ayoreo foragers of Bolivia, it is customary for women to
have several brief affairs, often resulting in childbirth, before settling into a
stable relationship equaling marriage. "Illegitimate" offspring are often buried
immediately after birth. During Bugos and McCarthy's (1984) fieldwork, 54 of
141 births ended in infanticide.

In farming communities, additional farmhands are usually welcomed.
Still, in rural Japan, a family would be subjected to considerable censure for
having "too many" children and might find themselves ostracized if they failed
"to get rid of the 'surplus'" (Jolivet 1997: 118; see also Neel 1970). Bear in
mind that breastfeeding is more costly – metabolically – than pregnancy
(Hagen 1999: 331). In the impoverished northeast of Brazil, women can count
on very little support from their child's father, and their own resources are
meager. Hence, "child death *a mingua* (accompanied by maternal indifference
and neglect) is understood as an appropriate maternal response to a deficiency
in the child. Part of learning how to mother ... include[s] learning when to
'let go'" (Scheper-Hughes 1987b: 190). Early cessation of nursing – one
manifestation of the mother's minimizing her investment – is supported
by an elaborate folk wisdom that breast milk can be harmful, characterized
as "dirty," "bitter," "salty," or "infected." Another folk illness category,
doença de crianca, is used flexibly by mothers in justifying a decision to
surrender the child into the hands of God or, alternatively, raise it as a real
"fighter." Of 686 pregnancies in a sample of 72 women, 251 infants failed to
reach one year of age (Scheper-Hughes 1987a). We see a similar fatalism
among mothers living in a slum adjacent to the Kimberly (South Africa)
diamond-mining concession. Their infants frequently die of *skelmsiekte*
(rogue-sickness) due to:

Vuil melk (dirty milk) – the effects of promiscuity on breast milk ... mothers engag[e]
in prostitution ... to obtain money to buy food for their children ... If one asked who
was the "rogue" in *skelmsiekte*, one would invariably be told that the rogue is the
circumstances. (Lerer 1998: 239, 243)

Child malnutrition is not limited to the "poor." Tamang mothers in Nepal
leave weaned infants behind as they work in distant fields. Alone all day,
children eat contaminated leftovers and scraps (Panter-Brick 1989). In the
Himalayan kingdom of Ladakh, high-altitude living imposes an extra cost
on the expectant mother who does farm-work throughout her pregnancy.
Her infant's life chances, owing to inevitably low birth-weight and other
complications, are sharply reduced (Wiley 2004: 6). The worth of a new child
in Ladakh will always be calculated as a tiny fraction of that of his fully
mature, productive mother. While the mother's health is closely monitored

and she is treated with great solicitude, her infant's fate is of less concern. Its death will be "met with sadness, but also with a sense of resignation ... they are buried, not cremated like adults" (Wiley 2004: 131–132).

Are Third World mothers who neglect their infants or, more actively, expose or kill them, acting this way because they are, somehow, "uncivilized" or lack any sense of aspiration, purpose, or pleasure in having children? Not at all. The Ache – whom we saw burying an inconvenient infant – constantly gossip with each other about the growth of their children, and their passage through important developmental landmarks. "'Chejugi knows how to sit'; 'My child can walk now'; 'She really knows how to talk'; 'He is quite a grown up young man'; 'She has almost reached menarche, she is sexually active now.' These types of comments are important filler information in any casual conversation" (Hill and Hurtado 1996: 341).

Two anthropologists who've devoted their careers to the study of mothering, Sarah Hrdy and Nancy Scheper-Hughes, argue, respectively, "Nurturing has to be teased out, reinforced, and maintained. Nurturing itself needs to be nurtured" (Hrdy 1999: 174), and "the usefulness of such ill-defined and culturally de-contextualized terms ... as 'bonding,' 'attachment,' 'critical period,' and so forth ... [must be questioned] ... The terms seem inadequate to describe and to contain the experiences of mothering and nurturing under conditions of extreme scarcity and high risk of child death" (Scheper-Hughes 1987a: 149).

While new mothers may be evaluating the actuarial odds,[6] we know that many are also suffering from post-partum depression or, less severely, detachment from and indifference toward their offspring. An argument can be made that this failure to bond immediately with the infant is adaptive in that it permits the mother to keep her options open, and also shields her emotionally from the impact of the infant's death – often, a likely outcome (de Vries 1987a; Eible-Eibesfeldt 1983: 184; Hagen 1999; Konner 2010: 130, 208; Laes 2011: 100). In a study undertaken in Jaipur, India, the entire sample of mothers interviewed – Hindu and Muslim – had experienced multiple miscarriages and child deaths (Unnithan-Kumar 2001). Among the Bajau, boat-dwellers and fishers in the Sulu Sea, "infant mortality is so high that some parents cannot even recall the number of their deceased children" (Nimmo 1970: 261).

Before we've finished this chapter, we'll have cataloged an extensive list of utilities that justify the costs of bearing and raising children but, bottom line, the unstated, possibly unconscious, goal for every adult is to pass on his or her

---

[6] A 2007 report from UNICEF states that "In 2006, for the first time since records have been kept, the number of children dying before their fifth birthday fell below ten million." However, in sub-Saharan Africa, 174 of every 1,000 children die before celebrating their fifth birthday, and these statistics have shown only modest decline (UNICEF 2007: 20).

genetic inheritance. This means not only making babies, but rearing them in a way that insures they will survive and themselves successfully reproduce. One's success at this fundamental enterprise is referred to as "inclusive fitness." The extended family, some of whose genes are passed on each time a new member is added, also has an interest in viability decisions. Investing in a high-risk child is often, or usually, seen as a waste of resources that might be better invested in existing, healthy offspring, the mother herself, or future offspring. Furthermore, as anyone who has observed a parent struggling to maintain a handicapped child will be aware, the effort and expense involved may be two or three times higher than that required by a "normal" child. However, as Hrdy notes: "the same mother who regretfully eliminates a poorly timed neonate will lovingly care for later ones if circumstances improve" (Hrdy 1999: 314).

Being a "calculating" mother is not synonymous with wickedness; on the contrary, it is adaptive behavior.[7] While the well-to-do mothers in the first section seem to "live for their children," in the next section, we discover just how recently these attitudes have become incorporated in Western society. We will trace the fluctuating value of infants in history and see that what we now consider horrible crimes were, in earlier periods, the principal means of birth control.

The value attached to infants in antiquity

The history of childhood is a history of death. (Volk and Atkinson 2013: 182)

Infanticide in . . . Japan was rationalized by maintaining that the death of a newborn was not the extinction of a life but a return to the other world, allowing for the possibility of rebirth at a more favorable future time. (Kojima 2003: 116)

Huang Liuhong [ranked] infanticide with the failure to cultivate fruit trees and repair roads, view[ing it] as a violation of public order. (Waltner 1995: 209)

Classical Greece is justly famed for its self-reflective examination of all aspects of society. For the first time, philosophers questioned traditional ways of doing things and offered theoretical alternatives. Infanticide was one such practice that came in for a great deal of consideration; however, no one seems to have doubted the fundamental necessity for it. Infants, being speechless and spastic, were considered little better than animals (Kleijueqgt 2009: 55). Indeed, the Greeks were puzzled by the fact that in Egypt infanticide was officially discouraged (Sommerville 1982: 23). There is

---

[7] In this sense, all stepmothers should be "wicked," in that it is adaptive for them to deny resources to their stepchildren, preferentially investing in their own offspring.

evidence in Egypt of careful, ritually correct infant interment (Halioua and Ziskind 2005: 75), and Egyptian medicine was particularly advanced when it came to women's health issues, including birth control. Plato believed that, in an ideal society, parents should keep only those children that they could personally afford; the poorest should remain childless (Boswell 1988: 82). Undoubtedly these views were colored by the fact that Greece, unlike Egypt – where the bounteous Nile almost invariably yielded a surplus of food – was chronically short of food.

Illegitimacy was usually a death sentence. "Identity was given by the family, and without a recognized father and family, the child had no proper guardian (*kurios*) since its mother could not legally fulfill such a function. Without a father, the child had no true place in the patrilineal kin structure, no right to the family name" (Patterson 1985: 115). Until at least the end of the eighteenth century, any Venetian infant of questionable parentage would have been abandoned or destroyed (Ferraro 2008).

The infant's vital signs were closely monitored for ten days, and if a decision to expose had been forestalled, the *amphidromia* or naming ceremony was held, welcoming the infant as a member of the family. Excavations at ancient Greek sites of myriad artifacts related to children – toys, child-size furniture, including "potty" chairs, and scenes of loving childcare inscribed on vases – reveal that the calculating attitude toward potentially surplus youth coexisted with a deeply caring and positive attitude toward those who were wanted (Golden 1990).

Roman society fully accepted the idea that each infant was subject to a valuation. The *lacteria* or "nursing column," where nursing babies were abandoned, could be found in nearly every public market (Boswell 1988: 110). Many abandoned children were claimed by those needing a child. "The child's father ... (or, if still alive, his grandfather) ... had the power to decide whether or not the child should be reared."[8] By "raising up the child (*tollere*) [he showed his] willingness to rear it" (Rawson 1991: 12). The next rite of passage occurred nine days after birth (eight for girls): the *lustratio*. The child was given a name and an official, formal identity (Rawson 1991: 13). An accepted child was, nevertheless, not bound closely to parents as the high infant mortality rates precluded the formation of strong emotional ties (Rawson 2003: 220).

Long before the "one-child policy," abortion was common in China. The oldest Chinese medical text found so far, some 5,000 years in age, includes reference to mercury as an abortifacient. In spite of high infant mortality, families were expected to limit growth to maintain the economic viability of

[8] Current "evidence suggests that men may use cues of paternity to influence the likelihood of caring for, or abusing, or abandoning, infants and children" (Volk and Quinsey 2002: 439).

the household. The pictogram for "abandonment" from the Shang period shows a basket being held by two hands, ejecting a baby. Another iconic image is of the "drowning bucket" kept nearby during delivery (Colón with Colón 2001: 57, 262).

Attitudes toward infants changed very slowly. The Jewish writer Philo of Alexandria wrote condemning infanticide in the first century CE because it implied that intercourse had been for pleasure rather than reproduction (Noonan 1970: 6). Meanwhile, as Christian influence spread throughout the Roman Empire, more and more church leaders wrote condemning abandonment and infanticide, following St. Paul's injunction that, in effect, parents may not avoid paying the "wages of sin." One of the more bizarre arguments advanced (by Clement, the patriarch of Alexandria) was the threat that a father might, inadvertently, commit incest because so many abandoned children ended up in brothels. The first Christian emperor, Constantine, outlawed infanticide in 318 CE,[9] and the death penalty was prescribed for it in 374 CE (Sommerville 1982: 43), but abandonment was not effectively prohibited until 600 CE (Colón with Colón 2001: 108). Making infanticide a sin or crime without providing the means for parents to limit conception fails to address the underlying problem. Consequently, the number of infants who were accidentally suffocated under their parents' bodies grew (Nicolas 1991: 38). The creation of hundreds of monasteries and nunneries during the late Roman Empire and the early medieval period also provided an outlet for surplus children. Mothers had been encouraged to drop off their unwanted infants at churches, and this practice grew into the officially sanctioned act known as oblation.

The monastic establishments could not handle the influx, and many soon discovered that hosting a gaggle of youngsters quickly undermined the very principles upon which they were founded. So the church began to establish homes for unwanted children called *brephotrophia*, the earliest opened in Milan by the end of the eighth century CE (Sommerville 1982: 50). Supply could never keep up with demand. The Ospedale degli Innocenti in Florence (one of sixteen *brephotrophia* in Tuscany alone) admitted 100 infants in its first year and as many as 1,000 in succeeding years; ultimately, it accepted 5,000 unwanted babies, *two-thirds of whom perished before their first birthday* (Kertzer 1993, emphasis added; see also Guy 2002: 144, 147, on colonial-era South America). A major challenge arose from the fact that an adequate, safe substitute for mother's milk was still not widely available and wouldn't be until the perfection of Liebig's formula in 1860 (Sunley 1955: 154). Wet-nurses were preoccupied with babies whose parents wanted to keep them,

---

[9] Ironically, he was to kill his own son. Putting members of one's immediate family to death was by no means out of the ordinary during Rome's imperial era.

and they were no longer paid after their milk stopped, but they were not penalized if the infant in their care died. Not surprisingly, therefore, they usually failed to notify the authorities of their changed condition, and the infant perished (Gavitt 1990: 197).

Contemporary echoes of this tragedy can be heard in Russia, where 800,000 orphans – the majority abandoned by living parents – are ware-housed in unfit facilities. Russians show an aversion to adoption because, rather than seeing orphans as innocent cherubs, they see them as contamin-ated by the "bad blood" of the shiftless, alcoholic parents who abandoned them (Fujimura 2005: 17). Eyewitness descriptions of Russian orphanages include these:

Healthy babies are lying in hospital beds all day ... completely ignored. No one plays with them or provides any kind of stimulation ... in a central Russian hospital another patient noticed a room of abandoned babies with their mouths taped shut to stop them from crying ... Reports of babies tied down in their cots are common ... it's often immediately clear to visitors that abandoned babies are left to "rot alive."[10] (Feifer 2007)

Russian orphans have been snapped up by foreign adoptive parents (60,000 to the US alone), but Russia has capitalized on this demand as a political weapon, turning the adoption pipeline off and on at will (Carey 2012).

The situation in China has been comparable: orphanage mortality rates of one-third to one-half of the resident children. Parents might adopt an orphaned baby girl to raise with their infant son. As the daughter grew she could look after the son and eventually the two would be married, insuring the subservi-ence of the daughter-in-law and saving the cost of the bride-price. "An orphanage was [also the logical] place to go to obtain a *tongyangxi* or a servant" (Johnson 2004: 7, 29).

Parents will make decisions regarding their offspring that reflect their own personal criteria. And if they choose not to raise them, it should be clear from the foregoing that even the most sympathetic public and religious institutions are not prepared to incur anywhere near the full costs of acting *in loco parentis*. Even amid relative affluence, many children may not be afforded adequate familial care and the state or church rarely, if ever, has provided adequate substitute or supplemental care. Leaping into the twenty-first cen-tury, we see a parallel situation today in the USA where meager public pre-school services cannot adequately perform parental functions and children suffer accordingly.

Ironically, church and government prohibition of infanticide was not accompanied by a parallel concern for infant mortality, which wasn't even

---

[10] Other accounts paint a more favorable picture (Garrels 2008).

recognized as a problem until the early twentieth century.[11] Fertility rates had dropped as a corollary of changing economic opportunities but infant mortality had not. One concerned politician in Britain went so far as to distribute promissory notes to newly delivered women offering them a £1 bonus if they kept their infants alive for a year. "The reverse side of these promissory notes was printed with . . . advice on infant hygiene and feeding" (Dyhouse 1978: 249). As we've seen, the church's prohibitions weren't very effective, and poor communities continued to limit population through the only means available, although these actions were often enveloped in a fog of folk beliefs.

And in the present, social critics argue that "however heinous and unnatural, [infanticide] is an extreme consequence of recognized ills: poverty, child and spousal abuse, mental instability" (van Biema and Kamlani 1994: 50). Studies also show that the same cluster of variables that trigger infanticide is also implicated in post-partum depression (Hagen 1999). While the termination of the fetus or of the infant's life is most often the parents' decision and we've seen numerous possible reasons for this behavior, societies often legitimize that decision. Overpopulation, the burden on the community of a hard-to-raise child, the social disharmony created by illegitimacy: all give the society a stake in this critical decision. Ultimately, also, the community must value the life and emotional wellbeing of its experienced, productive adult females over any potential value a tiny infant might have. So that, even today, when the penalties and censure for infanticide are higher than at any time, the young women who deposit their new infants in trash bins "are excused because society failed them" (Lee 1994: 74).

Anthropologist Jill Korbin argues that "neglect . . . appears to be more frequent in the cross-cultural literature than deliberate killing, even if the end result is frequently the same" (Korbin 1987a: 36). For example, a study in Hungary finds that mothers of high-risk infants breastfed them for shorter periods than their normal infants; as well, they smiled less often at them, and stimulated or played with them less frequently. They also became pregnant more quickly following the birth of a high-risk infant (Bereczkei 2001). In short, they scaled back their investment in the high-risk infant and acted as if they didn't expect it to survive.[12] But, as the child grows older, especially as it survives the pre-five period of greatest mortality, its value climbs.

One way to characterize the foregoing discussion is that the newborn is, effectively, on probation. The costs are evident, but its asset value is

---

[11] Punishing sin was more important than saving lives. Indeed, death and illness were always ascribed to "God's will."

[12] Middle-class Europeans often display the same adaptive reactions to high-risk offspring as their counterparts in developing nations (Mann 2002: 373).

undetermined. As we've seen, its existence is precarious from birth until some time, even years, later. This liminal state is shaped by cultural beliefs in a variety of patterns, but one common feature is that the conferral of personhood is delayed.

Delayed personhood

During this period no one is very certain whether the [Ashanti] infant is going to turn out a human child or prove, by dying before this period has elapsed, that it was never anything more than some wandering ghost. (Rattray 1927: 187)

In a recently published work, I was able to identify numerous issues affecting the lives of babies that lead to a "wait-and-see" posture and a postponement of an acknowledgment of humanity (Lancy 2014). Several have been discussed previously, including high infant mortality. Data from a range of societies past and present suggest that from one-fifth to one-half of children don't survive to five years (Dentan 1978: 111; Dunn 1974: 385; Kramer and Greaves 2007: 720; Le Mort 2008: 25). The first-century CE philosopher Epictetus cautioned, "When you kiss your child, say to yourself, it may be dead in the morning" (Stearns 2010: 168). Extrapolating from these figures I'd guess that miscarriages and stillbirths were also common by comparison with modern, post-industrial society. And I'd expect that if half the children died, then the majority were seriously ill in childhood. Indeed, in many villages studied by anthropologists the level of clinical malnutrition is 100 percent, as is the level of chronic parasite infestation and diarrhea. There are, then, ample reasons for withholding investment in the infant and maintaining a degree of emotional distance.

Throughout much of human history, pregnancy was treated as a serious illness. Childbirth can be extremely risky (Dentan 1978: 111) and even if the mother survives she may become the target of evil forces, including jealousy and witchcraft. She and the babe are both contaminated by the process of birth and the spilling of puerperal blood. Women may need to obey food taboos at critical junctures such as menstruation and pregnancy, and these taboos often involve restricting their intake of high-quality, fat- and protein-rich (nutritious) foods (de Vries 1987b: 170; Spielmann 1989: 323). At the peak of her childbearing years the young mother is also a critical contributor to the household economy through gathering, farming, or craft-work. She is likely to be responsible as well for maintaining a household and caring for a husband, older children, and parents or parents-in-law. The health and recovery of the mother are seen as far more urgent than the health of the infant (Wiley 2004: 132).

In the next chapter I discuss at length the prevalence of discord within families – especially those that practice polygyny. This atmosphere can be poisonous for children – literally. The Dogon are a particularly egregious example with consequent effects on child mortality.

It was widely assumed that cowives often fatally poisoned each other's children. I witnessed special masked dance rituals intended by husbands to deter this behavior. Cowife aggression is documented in ... court cases with confessions and convictions for poisoning ... sorcery might have a measurable demographic impact – [given] the extraordinarily high mortality of males compared with females. Males are said to be the preferred targets because daughters marry out of the patrilineage whereas sons remain to compete for land. Even if women do not poison each other's children, widespread hostility of the mother's cowife must be a source of stress. (Strassmann 1997: 693)

The response to these threats on the part of the anxious mother is to keep her children well out of the public eye. If she talks about them it is not to brag on their good looks or accomplishments but to complain about their faults and blemishes. The Fulani, for example, roll a child in dung or give it a name such as *Birigi* (cow turd) to make it less attractive and immune from malicious jealousy (Riesman 1992: 110).

The list of factors that contribute to the phenomenon of delayed personhood could be extended almost indefinitely. But it is more interesting to review the cultural models (Strauss 1992: 3) that have been created to frame or explain what is going on. These models are derived primarily from interviewing informants about their beliefs and observing their practices. Film footage is also available showing two vivid examples of cultural models of infancy. In one, de Suremain (2007) shows an Aymara mother swaddling her infant in such an efficient and mechanical fashion that it is clear she does not think of him or her as a "person" yet. A second, equally striking example (Bonnet 2007; see also Edel 1957/1996: 173; Worthman 2010: 67) shows a Mossi mother very roughly scrubbing her baby in a pan of water and then holding it by one arm to shake it dry. In both these cases, the child is treated as an inanimate object and its howls of protest are largely ignored until the operations are complete and the mother can calm the child by rocking it or giving it the breast.

One characteristic shared by these cultural models is that most societies place the infant in a dynamic between two poles, expressed by concepts like hard versus soft or colored (pigmented skin) versus pale. The infant's movement between these poles is closely monitored and carefully orchestrated. There is, however, relatively little consensus regarding the age at which personhood is achieved. In fact, of 200 cases in my data corpus in which there is an evident delay in granting personhood, only in forty-three has the investigator indicated a likely stage or transition point after which personhood is acknowledged. The most common marker is to accord the child its own (as opposed to "baby," "born at night") name, as the Barue do at six months (Wieschoff 1937: 498). In roughly fifteen cases, in my sample, the point falls within the first year, with a second cluster (sixteen) at ages five to nine – the age of "sense."

In my survey (Lancy 2014) a few at least partially distinct models emerged. I will briefly elucidate several in turn, beginning with the idea that the newborn remains in a kind of external or second womb.

The external womb model

Evolutionary anthropologists have noted that, in many respects, the human infant (kangaroo-like) remains in a near-fetal state (Trevathan and McKenna 1994: 91) for at least three months after birth. Many societies seem to construct a cultural model of infancy reflecting this fact (Gorer 1967; Grove and Lancy in press). Kept in seclusion indoors or largely hidden in the voluminous layers of its mother's clothing (Aymara – Tronick *et al.* 1994) the infant is still in a womb-like state. Swaddling – an extremely common practice at one time – also creates an external womb.

The new-born [Vlach] child sleeps tightly swaddled in a wooden rocking cradle which is enveloped from end to end in a blanket, so that he lies in a kind of dark airless tent. (Campbell 1964: 154)

The post-partum [Japanese] child remains, inseparably a part of its mother. The infant continues to develop within the protective, womb-like environment of its mother's presence, excluding others. (Lebra 1994: 261)

A [Bakkarwal] baby is kept swaddled "for its comfort" till it begins to crawl. Too much kicking about (*kisiti marnan*) is not considered healthy for the little arms and legs. (Rao 1998: 93)

Many ... post-natal practices [involve the] gradual shedding of the symbols for maternal ties ... [of] a [Hubeer] child that has not yet passed through the first ceremonies (e.g. the *banaan bixin*) that declare his agnatic links, it can be said that "his bones are not yet hard." (Helander 1988: 150)

After a [Telefol] woman has given birth, the baby remains in close contact ... nestled within the airy but secure space [of the] *men am* [net bag] ... providing the external equivalent of the *man am* [womb, literally child house] ... Often the "cradle" is worn hanging above the chest, somewhat in the manner of a marsupial pouch ... and the baby can if necessary be suckled in route while the mother's hands remain free for foraging. (MacKenzie 1991: 130)

Personhood is denied to infants on the basis of their patent deficiencies as social beings. Among the Punan Bah "the baby is ... hardly considered human ... [it] is like unripe fruit, it must ripen, only then will you know the taste of it" (Nicolaisen 1988: 209, 202). Similarly, the Wari liken the newborn to unripe fruit or say it is "still being made" (Conklin and Morgan 1996: 672–73). Aside from the lack of speech, various attributes are singled out, including, for example, the infant's softness and lack of motor control. Significantly, these models are used both to explain the basis of non-personhood but also include prescriptions for turning the baby into a person (Bonnet 2007). They have "directive force" (Strauss 1992: 3). Here are a few examples illustrating the ripening process:

Asked why infants are swaddled, [Nurzay] women explained that the newborn baby's flesh is *oma* (lit. unripe) like uncooked meat, and that only by swaddling will it become strong and solid like cooked (*pokh*) meat. (Casimir 2010: 16)

Food taboos [affecting Huaorani parents] are aimed at "hardening" the [baby's] body ... The goal is to make the baby vigorous and strong, so it can grow fast and develop into an independent member of the longhouse. (Rival 1998: 623)

New-born [Amele] infants are cold and soft ... and must be strengthened by the application of warm hands heated over a fire ... As strength develops and the infant can hold up its head, it is known as *momo memen*, literally "infant becomes stone." (Jenkins *et al.* 1985: 39)

Other areas singled out as needing ripening to transform the infant into a human being are: speech (Bird-David 2005: 97; Kleijueqgt 2009: 55); self-locomotion (Ayoreo – Bugos and McCarthy 1984: 510; Mbya – Remorini 2011); teeth and the ability to masticate (Bariba – Sargent 1988: 82); acquisition of social knowledge and skill (Montague 1985: 89; Warlpiri – Musharbash 2011; 66); and "sense" or intelligence (Javanese – Geertz 1961: 105; Fulani – Riesman 1992: 130; Woolf 1997: 71). To become fully human, the infant must exit from this metaphorical womb and enjoy a second birth whereby it is joined to its father, his clan, and the extended family (Blanchy 2007; Fricke 1994: 133). To achieve this requires survival and maturation on the part of the newborn, but, as well, various rites of separation and attachment are mandated. Soninké rites of separation involve proper treatment of umbilical cord and placenta, while attachment rites include a ceremony with singing by a griot and the exchange of gifts and acknowledgment of the child by ritual leaders (Razy 2007).

The most *common* rationale for withholding personhood is that the infant itself has not yet committed to being human. It exists in two worlds, the human world, and the "other" world of spirits, ghosts, ancestors, and gods (Montgomery 2008: 93). The Javanese explain that a child who died young "didn't want to be cared for" (Keeler 1983: 154).

The "two worlds" model

The part-spirit/part-human model, includes characterizations of the child that emphasize its purity and innocence (Little Angels below), or that emphasize the child's potential as a conduit of evil forces (Little Demons below). Among many culture-specific "two worlds" models, here are six examples:

The perceived relationship of [Mende] infants with the world of spirits generates loyalties in conflict with the world of the living ... infants are presumed to develop unusual powers of vision and the powers to move across different sensory domains. (Fermé 2001: 198)

[The Qiqiktamiut Inuit explain] general or prolonged fussiness, a refusal to eat or outright sickness ... as symptomatic of the spirit's withdrawal from the body. (Guemple 1979: 41–42)

The small [Ijaw] child who cries out with fright because he thinks he has seen something while in the forest [may have] seen the *bouyo* ("forest people"), potentially dangerous creatures whom adults cannot always see. (Leis 1982: 155)

A newborn [Yukui] has been contaminated by [puerperal] blood and is also more likely to succumb to disease or birth defects during these first few weeks of life. The baby was therefore regarded as not yet belonging fully to the world but lay somewhere between the spirit domain and that of the living. (Stearman 1989: 89)

As a marginal being, the [Roman] child is only partially a member of the citizen society; but that implies that he is nearer to the world of the gods than the [human]. (Wiedemann 1989: 25)

In the Tibetan tradition, it is believed that babies may have special attributes or abilities that adults no longer possess, or that infants may have relations with supernatural elements. (Maiden and Farwell 1997: 127)

The "two worlds" cultural model not only explains observed phenomena but also prescribes actions to be taken by the infant's caretakers. In the Bolivian Andes, a precise and elaborate swaddling procedure guards the infant against *susto*, an illness that results in the separation of body and soul (Aymara – de Suremain 2007). A caretaking style that emphasizes keeping the infant in a womb-like state – always quiet and sheltered – is also often justified on the basis of insuring that the spirit doesn't flee (Kogi – Reichel-Dolmatoff 1976: 277; Bonerate – Broch 1990: 31).

A [Mandok] newborn's inner self (*anunu*) was not yet firmly anchored inside its body ... and for this reason both new parents observed many food and behavioral taboos after the birth ... As the child grew, the Mandok believed that the *anunu* gradually moved from the surface of the skin to the inside of the body, a common belief in other areas of Melanesia as well. (Pomponio 1992: 77)

[In rural Japan] a baby was considered to be transferred into the human world by a god. A midwife ... played a role in guiding the baby from the gods' world to the human world and giving social recognition to the baby as a member of the community. (Yanagisawa 2009: 88)

When the [Azande] child is born the soul has not become completely and permanently attached to its abode. Hence it is feared that the soul may flit away and this is one of the reasons for confining infant and mother to a hut. (Evans-Pritchard 1932: 404)

The "two worlds" cultural model calls attention to the child's vulnerability; its slender hold on life. But this impermanence may be construed in a more positive light. Quite a few societies, especially in ancient times, saw opportunity in the child's indeterminate – part-spirit, part-human – state.

Little angels

Children are, in some societies, seen as pure and without the stain of sin or corrupting knowledge of the world.[13] Their innocence makes them both worthy sacrificial offerings to the gods and potential intermediaries. Child "spirits" could be utilized to appease or otherwise communicate with the other world of ancestors and gods (Muchik – Klaus et al. 2010). In an example from the ethnographic record, the Bolobo believe that exchanging a bewitched adult's soul with the uncontaminated soul of an infant can save the adult. As the adult gradually recovers health, the infant sickens and dies (Viccars 1949: 223). Following are other examples from antiquity.

The Olmec were the precursors of later and better-known Mesoamerican civilizations. They appeared to have sacrificed children at points during their development (starting with the fetus) to correspond to that of the growing corn (Orrelle 2008: 73). In much of Mesoamerica,[14] there was a direct association between the child's tears and rain. The Aztecs sacrificed children on the first day of the month of Atlachualo to appease Tlaloc, the rain god. According to de Sahagun, the more the sacrificial victims cried and carried on, the better the prospects for rain (de Sahagun 1829/1978). Aztec

---

[13] Of course, it doesn't take a huge leap of imagination to see mothers who are members of the neontocracy as treating their "cherubs" rather worshipfully. Indeed, Viviana Zelizer, whose 1985 book first called attention to the uniqueness of modern conceptions of childhood, refers to the "rise of the sacred child" (Zelizer 1985: 52).

[14] Studies of children's remains in Latin America present an extremely varied picture, ranging from the Chinchorro (Peru), who mummified even fetuses – suggesting therefore that children were considered persons from birth (Arriaza et al. 1998: 195); to forty-eight children packed into a sacrificial container at the great Aztec temple at Tenochtitlan (Berrelleza and Balderas 2006: 240); to coastal Oaxaca (Mexico) where children were excluded from house burials, suggesting low or less-than-fully-human status (S. M. King 2006: 185); to post-classical Cholula (Mexico), where children were formally buried but without the grave goods that accompanied adult interments (McCafferty and McCafferty 2006: 42).

children – "human paper streamers" – were dressed in bright colors and were sacrificed in seven different locations. The streaming tears of the children insured rain (Carrasco 1999: 84–85). This model continues into the present with Aymara (Andean) children carrying appeals for rain on their post-mortem journey "home" (Arnold 2006: 95, 97). Aztec children were also sacrificed to the god of death. This was the fate of forty-eight children – mostly boys aged around six – whose remains were analyzed by Berrelleza and Balderas (2006).

In cases of drought or famine, Maya from all over the lowlands would gather at one of the sacred cenotes, natural wells, where priests officiated at sacrificial ceremonies to honor and appeal to the gods. At daybreak, children were thrown into the cenote and those who were – miraculously – still alive by midday were rescued and questioned by the priests regarding any mes-sages they might have received from the gods (Sharer 1994: 10–11). Child sacrifice was highly institutionalized among the Inca. Represented as *capa-cochas*, or "royal sins," children were destined to appease the gods who might have been inadvertently angered by the rulers. Celebrated for days of feasting and ritual, these semi-divine children were likely drugged and taken to the high (up to 6,000 meters) Andean peaks by priests to be buried alive, in effect freezing to death (Besom 2009: 117). They were carefully wrapped in costly textiles and interred with toy-like miniatures of animals, crops, people, and tools. Both historical and archaeological evidence sug-gests that the children were highly valued and, in all likelihood, were the offspring of the elite (Sillar 1994). These mummified children, some in their teens, have come to light recently as disappearing snow cover opens areas to climbers.

In the Pacific, children were sacrificed to attract the attention of the gods:

Two practices intended to appease angry gods … mentioned by many of the early European visitors to Tonga, were child strangulation (*no'osia*) and finger-joint amputation … carried out [as examples] when a high chief was ill, [or as] a form of atonement for the desecration of the tapu place … those chosen were the children of chiefs by "inferior" female attendant[s]. (Morton 1996: 175, 176)

In Greco-Roman society, children's indeterminate state indicated the possession of a divine gift for prophecy and the ability to function "as intermediaries between the divine and human worlds" (Horn and Martens 2009: 179). A natural extension of this idea justified Carthaginian child sacrifice. Infants or young children up to the age of four were sacrificed – burned on an altar, then interred in a ceramic urn (Stager and Greene 2000: 31). Evidence from numerous sources suggests that these were valued children, but that parents were required to suppress the urge to mourn. Childless couples bought children to donate (Brown 1991: 35, 24). In times of emergency, such as the invasion by Agathocles, the tyrant of Syracuse, many children may have been sacrificed at one time to Ba'al Hammon. A special area or Tophet was set aside for these sacrifices and the stored remains. It was most extensively used between 750 and 146 BCE when Carthage was destroyed by Rome (Lee 1994: 66). Stillborn or miscarried remains are rare, suggesting that, like the Inca, the Phoenicians were sacrificing truly valued children and not just limiting their population (Stager and Wolff 1984; for a contrastive view see Schwartz *et al.* 2010).

The construction of buildings, especially those with a religious character, usually called for the ceremonial burial of "foundation deposits" at the base of important buildings. And these often included sacrificed children (Tlingit Indian – Colón with Colón 2001: 64; Iron Age Europe – Green 1999: 65; Roman Britain – Scott 1999: 86; Late Neolithic Turkey – Moses (2008: 49). Excavation of the Hanoi citadel (eleventh century CE) revealed the skeletons of eight-year-old children who had been interred in the foundation – probably alive – to drive off evil spirits (Sachs and Le 2005). Also fairly common was the practice of sacrificing children (and adults) to accompany the deceased in the afterlife. Women and children were sacrificed as companions for Mayan rulers, as a recent royal tomb excavated in northern Honduras attests (McGirk 2012). Hill and Hurtado describe this practice among the Ache in considerable detail, especially with respect to the process of selecting the accompanying child (Hill and Hurtado 1996: 68–69).

Children can be treated as sacred without sacrificing them! In ancient Egypt, the deceased expected to be provisioned in the afterlife by his dutiful children. Quite early in its history, Egypt transitioned from putting servants and family members to death to accompany and care for the deceased to using substitutes engraved on tomb walls or freestanding sculptures. In the tomb of necropolis inspector Nikau-Anpu from the sixth dynasty, his five children appear in wall paintings "doing all sorts of menial work ... [they engage in these] exaggeratedly humble activities in order to demonstrate their humility and dependence on their father and ... usefulness to him in the afterlife" (Roth 2002: 110). Young boys, for centuries, have been donated by their parents to Buddhist monasteries. In Mustang, the second-born son joins a monastery at six or seven (Peissel 1992). In the Hindu *devadasi* rite, lower-caste girls may be donated to the village temple to serve the sexual needs of the priests (Verma and Saraswathi 2002: 127). A letter describes the "joyless" childhood of a Christian girl (*hostia* = offering) in the fourth century CE being "relentlessly" groomed for a life in the nunnery (Katz 2007: 118). Biographies of medieval Anglo-Saxon saints describe the privations and beatings they endured as child oblates consigned to monastic life (Crawford 1999: 151).

Figure 2 Novice monk in Rangoon (Yangon)

For the Beng people of the Ivory Coast, babies are ancestors who've been reincarnated and returned from *wrugbe*, the land of the dead.[15] Consequently, Beng adults not only treat infants with great respect and devotion, they talk to them as well because the child/ancestor can serve as an intermediary with powerful spirit forces. This conception of children also works to cushion the shock of infant death (Gottlieb 2000: 80–81). In Indonesia, the rice-growing Balinese hold similar beliefs.[16] Spirits of ancestors return to inhabit the infant in the womb. Following birth, the baby is believed to be divine for a period of 210 days (Hobart *et al.* 1996), "the nearest thing to a god which man may know" (Belo 1949: 15). A Balinese woman who marries a man from a higher-ranking family may have children who outrank her. Proper respect for the child must be shown or the child may die, choosing to return to the gods rather than remain with a disrespectful mother (Mead 1955). The same general orientation in Japan rationalizes the often-observed public misbehavior of young children. As semi-divine, a child cannot be held to the same standards of conduct as an adult, and any attempt to control his or her behavior might disrupt the transition from the world of the gods to our world (Naito and Gielen 2005: 69).

These examples underscore that the child is in a liminal state – not yet fully human and not yet completely attached to the family. These incomplete emotional bonds may enable the child's family to more easily relinquish the child to serve ritual ends. Regardless of whether a given infant ends up in an urn in the Tophet or, eventually, gracing the recital stage, its destiny is influenced greatly by the iconized image of the child that exists in the culture. Our society is only apparently child-centered when compared with, say, Phoenicia, because our children, too, must fulfill our needs.

Little demons

The same "two worlds" notion undergirds many cultural models in which the infant may be viewed as threatening either in its own right or as a vessel or avatar for ghosts and evil spirits (Soninké – Stoller 1989: 45; Bhils – Nath 1960: 187). A wide range of societies including Greek, Roman, and

[15] Similarly among the Yoruba, children "are watched for the unfolding of resemblances to the ancestors they reincarnate" (Zeitlin 1996: 412; also characteristic of the Wolof of Senegal-Rabain 1979), and in "traditional [Iñupiaq-Inuit] culture, a newborn was considered a recycled soul of a recently departed relative" (Sprott 2002: 48). An interesting belief found in ancient Greece held that, since infants were as yet empty vessels, when they died their bodies could be used to transport the souls of the dead to the underworld (Liapis 2004).

[16] In Mormon theology, children are "little angels," waiting in heaven for a married couple to, in effect, adopt them. They must spend at least some time among the living in order to earn a permanent place in heaven with "their Heavenly Father." Retrieving these "little angels" is offered as part of the rationale for very high Mormon birth rates.

Figure 3 Child participant: Kuningan Festival, Munduk, Bali

Anglo-Saxon took steps to contain the potential malevolence of the potent and dangerous newborn (Wileman 2005: 82, 86). The "two worlds" model is often invoked if there is a problem. Bumbita (from the Sepik region of New Guinea) infants who are colicky suffer from *ambohis* spirits eating them from the inside out. Bumbita sorcerers are accused of using the potent fluids from a deceased infant to render themselves invisible (Leavitt 1989). The Navajo believe epileptic children result from a violation of the incest taboo.[17] Bariba infants with physical anomalies or developmental delays are feared as witches who threaten the family and must be put to death, given to a neighboring tribe as slaves or, more recently, given to missionaries (Sargent 1988). "Defective" newborns are readily perceived as threatening or corrupting.

Among the Songye (same as Soninké), those defined as "bad" or "faulty" children, including albino, dwarf, and hydrocephalic children, are considered supernaturals who have been in contact with sorcerers in the anti-world; they are not believed to be human beings, and they are expected to die. (Devleiger 1995: 96)

The first cries of the nursling were ... often interpreted by the [Christian] clergy as a sign of a person's sinful condition or as a manifestation of the devil. That is why recipes existed for quieting these cries [such as] administering poppy [opium]. (Alexandre-Bidon and Lett 1999: 12)

In Han China, infanticide was justified in the case of "ill-omened" children born during an inauspicious period. The "wolflike cries" of newborn[s] were used as evidence of their inborn wickedness ... foreshadowing ... future unfilial behavior. (Kinney 1995: 24–25)

What is a spirit child? It is a child that has a large head, is born with teeth or a beard, spies on its parents, and vanishes when the parents are not looking ... A woman who gives birth, continuously falls sick, and doesn't get well has given birth to a spirit child [Elder Nankani woman]. (Denham *et al.* 2010: 608)

Because the very young are seen as a potential conduit allowing the transmission of dangerous forces into the family or community, steps have to be taken to guard against this possibility while the infant is not yet acknowledged as human. These steps include practices like baptism, swaddling, avoiding eye contact with the infant, or bloodletting.

The belief that infants were felt to be on the verge of turning into totally evil beings is one of the reasons why they were tied up, or swaddled, so long and so tightly. (Haffter 1986: 11)

When a [Pamiri] child is born and fidgets and cries [a lot] and he has a black circle around his mouth and eyes, it means that he may have jinn [genie or spirit]. To solve the

---

[17] Alice Schlegel, personal communication, April 6, 2006.

Figure 4 Korowai child accused of being a *khahkua* or witch

problem, one has to open the child's mouth and look at the roof of his mouth. If you observe black veins, you need to make a hole in the veins with a needle and mop up the blood with a swab. The child gets better and does not cry again. (Keshavjee 2006: 75)

[On Truk Island in Micronesia, women might give] birth to ghosts ... deformed children [who were consequently] thrown into the sea, burned or buried – [as were] normal children who exhibited peculiarities of behavior such as a lack of desire to eat. (Fisher 1963: 533)

Cannibalism was once widespread in New Guinea, but it survives now only in isolated communities, such as the Korowai, where inter-group warfare and raiding are so common, houses are erected on 20-meter-high platforms – for safety. There is a pervasive atmosphere of threat from witchcraft that extends to the newborn. "They [do] not consider infanticide itself an immoral act [because] birth processes are repulsive and dangerous [and] a newborn is demonic (*laleo*) rather than human (*yanop*)" (Stasch 2009: 151). The Korowai are also quick to accuse, convict, and then consume individuals practicing witchcraft. Journalist Paul Raffaele found the boy shown in Figure 4 hiding among distant kin who feared for his life after he'd been accused of culpability in the death of his parents (Raffaele 2006).[18]

---

[18] Of course, as we saw in the earlier discussion of the Ache, orphans – even those well beyond infancy – are often put to death because no one will be able to feed them. So accusing the orphan boy Waw'a of witchcraft might have the effect of either justifying his elimination or

Changelings represent a special sub-group of "demon" children who provoke a negative response from caretakers. The changeling was an *enfant changé* in France, a *Wechselbag* in Germany, and, in England, a "fairy child." Strategies to reverse the switch included tormenting the infant or abandoning it in a lonely spot (Haffter 1986). A Beng mother-to-be who breaks a taboo may have her uterus invaded by a snake. The snake takes the fetus's place and, after birth, is gradually revealed by the infant's strange behavior. "The child may be harassed and hit by stones; however, being boneless like a snake, the snake-person is thought to feel no pain" (Gottlieb 1992: 145). A Papel infant deemed abnormal may be a spirit that's entered the mother's uterus. Two procedures are available to determine whether the child is human, but surviving either procedure seems improbable (Einarsdóttir 2008: 251). Dogon children thought to be evil spirits are taken:

Out into the bush and you leave them ... they turn into snakes and slither away ... You go back the next day, and they aren't there. Then you know for sure that they weren't really [Dogon] children at all, but evil spirits. (Dettwyler 1994: 85–86)

Among the Nuer, it is claimed, a disabled infant was interpreted as a hippopotamus that had mistakenly been born to human parents; the child would be returned to its proper home by being thrown into the river. (Scheer and Groce 1988: 28)

In ... northern Europe, changelings were left overnight in the forest. If the fairies refused to take it back, the changeling would die during the night – but since it was not human, no infanticide could have occurred. (Hrdy 1999: 465)

[For Lurs] Djenn are said to be ... jealous of the baby, especially during the first ten to forty days; they might steal the baby or exchange it for their own, sickly one. A baby indicates that it might be a changeling by fussiness, weakness, or lack of growth. (Friedl 1997: 69)

Our data are not limited to the accounts of ethnographers or historians. Archaeological excavations and analyses of post-mortem treatment of the young offer very strong support for the claim that personhood is delayed.

Post-mortem treatment and delayed personhood

Children's remains located outside the confines of communal burial grounds are a common finding throughout the world, and during all time periods. (Lewis 2007: 31)

provoking a humanitarian rescue from his kin. Paul Raffaele was able to move the boy to a more acculturated Korowai village where he attends school and, in the photo he sent me, looks quite happy (personal communication, February 4, 2009).

Ethnographic studies reveal a fairly consistent pattern of post-mortem treatment of infants and children. And these patterns strongly reinforce the delayed personhood argument (Senior 1994). Burial rites and mourning may be minimal or actively discouraged in the case of a child younger than five (Fricke 1994: 133; Ndege 2007: 103) or even as late as ten (Rawson 2003: 104). The variability is consistent with the variability in marking the age at which the child is considered a person (Conklin and Morgan 1996: 679; Lancy 2014). The attention of the family and community should be on the next child, not on the one that's died. For example, "the average duration of a birth interval is substantially shorter following an infant death than when an infant survives" (Kramer and Greaves 2007: 720). Some illustrations follow:

It is not unusual for the [Ayoreo] newborn to remain unnamed for several weeks or months, particularly if the infant is sickly. The reason given is that should the child die, the loss will not be so deeply felt. (Bugos and McCarthy 1984: 508)

[East Africa Bagesu] children often died at birth or in infancy, and the bodies were thrown out into the bush. (Roscoe 1924: 25)

[When a Chippewa infant died] weeping was frowned upon for the fear that the sorrow would be passed on to the next child. (Hilger 1951: 79)

When a [South Africa Tonga] child died before it was named, there was no mourning for no shades were involved . . . the old women will tell the mother to hush her wailing, saying this is only a ghost (*cello*). (Reynolds 1991: 97)

When we turn to the archaeological record, excavators find that, save for a few societies such as ancient Egypt (Meskell 1994), during the city-state period in Athens (Houby-Nielsen 2000), or in the case of royal or elite burials (Greece – Lebegyiv 2009: 27; Berón *et al.* 2012: 59), infants and children were buried apart from older children and adults (Mesoamerica – King 2006: 185).

In Mesoamerica Xaltocan . . . burials of infants and young children less than four years-of-age were recovered . . . under room floors and . . . also incorporated into house walls. (de Lucia 2010: 612–613)

[Mapuche] infants are not buried in the cemetery, but are buried in the old family plot or somewhere near the house, it is believed that it would be harder for the child to be turned into a demon if it is closer to the house. (Faron 1964: 91)

In Early Mycenaean Greece, infants of less than one year-of-age were differentiated by their total exclusion from organized extramural cemetery areas and by the absence of complete vases in their graves . . . Children of between one–two and five–six years-of-age were still only included in formal extramural cemeteries in exceptional cases. (Lebegyiv 2009: 27)

An analysis of Etruscan child burials in Tarquinia enables one to conclude that the absence of children below the age of five and a half years from the principal cemeteries was suggestive of a major shift at that age. (Becker 2007: 292)

Children in medieval England . . . were normally buried in churchyards beneath shallow mounds. The mounds had no permanence or lasting memorials, because the ground was constantly re-used for burials, especially in towns . . . Burial inside churches was restricted to adults and children of rank. (Orme 2003: 120)

A consideration of post-mortem treatment, including funerary rites and interment practices, reveals their complementarity to the ethnographic record of infancy. The archaeological reports also underscore the child's liminality and lack of integration into the social world of the community (Alexandre-Bidon and Lett 1999: 29; Wileman 2005: 77). At death, the child is mourned privately or not at all and it is interred discreetly, without ceremony.

If parents and the larger society can countenance the abandonment, killing, or fatal neglect of children, as discussed earlier, then selling them won't seem beyond the realm of possibility. And, indeed, the prospect of providing the parent with some economic return, however small, has probably kept many children alive.

Children as chattel

[Kpelle] children are a form of property that fathers must pay for and maintain if they are to be considered legal owners. (Bledsoe 1980a: 91)

[In] the sixth century the peasants of southern Italy got rid of their children at the marketplace during a large fair. (Alexandre-Bidon and Lett 1999: 38)

[Landowners in Pakistan think] children are cheaper to run than tractors and smarter than oxen. (Silvers 1996: 82)[19]

The sale of children must be viewed from a utilitarian perspective. Among the Nigerian Ibo, children represent social capital: sons are initiated into the various secret societies, with credit redounding to the father, and daughters are married to cement relationships with other families. Simon Ottenberg notes that, in sub-Saharan Africa, "babies are thought of as material goods" (Ottenberg 1989: 3). The same is the case in Micronesia: Trukese "children may easily be viewed as capital goods" (Fisher 1963: 527). The term "chattel" can mean any kind of real property, including human beings. And children throughout much of history have been indistinguishable from slaves

---

[19] Comment of a landowner who employs children as young as four as farm laborers in Rawalpindi, Pakistan.

(Woolf 1997: 71).[20] Their masters/parents hold the power of life or death; they can and often do use corporal punishment to discipline them; they provision them with food and clothing and a roof over their heads (or not); they program their lives of work and leisure and determine whom or whether they'll marry. And this fate has been shared as well by children of the wealthy. Indeed, their lives are often more tightly circumscribed than those of their lower-class age-mates.

Slaves outnumbered every other class of society by a wide margin in ancient Rome and so, not surprisingly, there were statutes regulating the sale of children. The rights of biological parents to reclaim abandoned children from their adoptive parents when they were old enough to earn a wage were, perpetually, in a state of flux (Sommerville 1982: 44). Abandoned children were "rescued," reared, and then sold into slavery or prostitution, or castrated to serve as eunuchs. "Employing *expositi* as beggars, possibly even crippling them to make them more pitiful, as Seneca describes, may have been common" (Boswell 1988: 113).

The sale of human beings, including children, was a dominant feature of Western European society and around the globe for better than two thousand years. "Throughout the Middle Ages ... landowners possessed hundreds of subjects, often children ... [treated as] human livestock subject to the whims of the master" (Alexandre-Bidon and Lett 1999: 36). After slavery had been abolished in Europe it continued to flourish in the Americas, and in the Rio de Janeiro slave markets the majority of sales were of children from eight to fourteen (Kuznesof 2007: 191). Child slavery was well entrenched in Asia, and anthropologists have studied the conditions that promote it. For example, in north India, the demand for lower-caste brides creates a scarcity exploited by child thieves. "Sales of women to become concubines, courtesans, prostitutes, bondservants, or slaves [are found] in those provinces where both female infanticide and oppressive landlordism were intense" (Dickeman 1979: 345). In Pre-Columbian society children might be donated to the state to meet a tax obligation (Dean 2002: 44). In Europe, from the late Middle Ages until quite recently, impecunious gentry routinely restored their fortunes by marrying off sons and daughters to social-climbing merchant families.

Anthropologist Woody Watson documents the common practice of selling male children in China's Canton Delta region that persisted into the twentieth century. Referred to as *hsi min* or "little people," these children were identified by itinerant rice merchants who knew which families were destitute. "At the death of a slave owner his *hsi min* were divided among the surviving heirs like any other form of property" (Watson 1976: 364–365). In rural Japan:

---

[20] "The same word, 'pais', was used [by the Greeks] to denote both a child and a slave" (Beaumont 1994: 88).

The most destitute families would sell their nubile daughters into prostitution. So as not to alert the whole neighborhood to the fact that they had a daughter for sale, the parents would discreetly light a fire at night which could be seen from a long way off ... 3,222 young girls from the Shimabara region had been transported in this way between 1889 and 1894 ... These young women ... accepted their fate through a sense of filial duty and sent their parents money. (Jolivet 1997: 124)

War often presents opportunities to gain a return from one's offspring. During the American Revolutionary War, parents turned idle boys into soldiers, earning money from their pay, from their enlistment bonuses, and from payments received when they entered the service as a "substitute." Obadiah Benge, aged fifteen, "was bartered into the service by his step-father ... as a substitute for one James Green, [who provided] ... horse, bridle and saddle" (Cox 2007: 20).

And just as infanticide continues in spite of laws to prevent it, so, too, does the sale of children (Raffaele 2005). Many argue that slavery never ended in Africa, and reports continue to surface, especially with respect to children. At the end of 2012, the UN reported 175 Malian children bought from their parents for US$1,000-plus to serve the Islamic insurgency (Callimachi 2013). In the prosperous modern city of Abidjan, Côte d'Ivoire, girls are bought and sold at the "maid market" (Bass 2004: 149). In Senegal, thousands of boys who've been "donated" by parents or stolen by traffickers live at a Qur'anic school. These *almajirai* spend their days begging on the streets of Dakar and can expect to be beaten by the "teacher" if they don't bring back a daily minimum amount (Callimachi 2008). Boys are likely to be donated to these "schools" (the only training is in memorizing portions of the Qur'an) by divorced parents who need to shed children in order to appease a new mate (Hoechner 2012: 161). Throughout Africa, children work on plantations for little or no pay (Bourdillon 2000: 168; Chirwa and Bourdillon 2000: 134). Surveys in Nigeria and Benin find child slaves, as young as four, working under appalling conditions in rock quarries. The slavers obtained the children with payments to their parents of as little as US$15 (Ahissou and McKenzie 2003; Polaski 2011). Until fairly recently, the Yoruba might pawn (*iwofa*) their children, whose work would serve as interest on a debt. They would be bound to work for the lender until the debt was paid off (Renne 2005). In Mesopotamia it was common to put up a child as collateral for a loan, which, if unpaid, led to the child's enslavement (MacGinnis 2011). "Trokosi girls, some as young as ten, are forced to become physical and sexual slaves of shrine priests to please the gods [and] to atone for their families' sins" (Bass 2004: 151–152).

Children of working age in Nepal and Bangladesh are sold for US$50–$75 to coal-mine owners to serve as bonded laborers to pay off their purchase price. Collapsing mine shafts represent one (usually fatal) among numerous hazards (Anonymous 2009). In contemporary China, the domestic demand for sons, coupled with demand from overseas to adopt Chinese children, has turned child trafficking into a lucrative industry. Many of the children are sold to orphanages and they, in turn, resell them to eager adoptive (including foreign – one-third of foreign adoptions into the US are from China) parents.[21] In 2012, crackdowns netted 355 traffickers and led to the rescue of 54,000 children (McDonald 2012). The demand for healthy adoptable babies by well-off parents has led to baby farming, whereby adoption agencies provide clandestine funds to rural mothers who "give up" their baby to the agency (Liefsen 2004: 185).

I want to stress that child slavery is far more often associated with complex, socially stratified societies and only rarely found in the ethnographic record. Yet the underlying model of children's worth as determined by their usefulness is almost universal. As the child matures from infancy to early childhood, nothing confers the imprimatur of personhood quite like the ability to work. Recall that, in a gerontocracy, children are at the bottom of the pecking order. What that means is that those who're older expect to be taken care of by youth. Investing in the young – feeding, dressing, and caring for them – is seen as insuring a secure old age. The labor of children also lightens the work of their parents. Grove and I described the transition from invisible non-personhood to participating member as "Getting Noticed" (Lancy and Grove 2011a).

Milk debt

In accord with the belief that lactation uses up maternally irreplaceable body substances, it is seen [in rural Mexico] as incurring debts on the part of children, who thus are obligated to attend their mother's wants in old age. (Millard and Graham 1985: 72)

[Bumbita] children, in eating food that parents have grown and given them, literally sap the parents of their strength. (Leavitt 1998: 193)

[Baining] women are thought to lose increments of their flesh and blood to each successive child they bear. Men also experience this gradual debilitation. (Fajans 1997: 62)

With the exception of the children of the very rich in the past, a few foraging societies (see "Children in paradise," pp. 66–70), and modern families where children are to dedicate themselves to schooling, every society has the

---

[21] Orphanages have a robust history of supplying child laborers, from seventeenth-century Portugal and Brazil (dos Guimarães Sá 2007: 29) to eighteenth-century Russia (Gorshkov 2009: 30) to nineteenth-century "orphan trains" in the US (Kay 2003: iii).

expectation that a child will contribute to the household economy. In Europe until well into the nineteenth century, "seven was an informal turning point when the offspring of peasants and craftsmen were expected to start helping their parents with the little tasks around the home, the farm or workshop" (Heywood 2001: 37). "The word *moço*, which originally meant 'child,' came to be used in Spanish and Portuguese for a young servant ... in Italian, the term *fante* ... derived from *infante* (child) ... applied to the domestic servant" (Stella 2000: 33). Rairoans (Polynesia) believe:

> that children, like all the other members of the family, ought to make themselves useful, and they give even quite small children astonishingly heavy and difficult tasks. Children of four or five are sent regularly to fetch water from the large communal tank; many of them do as many as ten trips a day with their gallon bottles. (Danielsson 1952: 121)

Among the Iñupiaq, children provide critical support to the family through their labor. Young people embrace this opportunity to contribute: "They respect[ed] me, because I could do ... my chores ... without them telling me. That's my reward [but sometimes] I got reward[ed] with good meals" (Sprott 2002: 229).

When I asked Kpelle parents what constitutes a "good" child, one mother answered, without hesitation, "What makes a child good? If you ask her to bring water, she brings water. If you ask her to cook, she cooks, if you tell her to mind the baby, she does it. When you ask her to plant rice, she doesn't complain" (Lancy 1996: 76; see also Dybdahl and Hundeide 1998: 140; Cronk *et al.* 2009: 331). Women traders in urban markets in Ghana proudly delegate virtually all domestic work – particularly infant care – to their children (Asante – Clark 1994: 332). A Giriama mother who demands obedience and hard work from her children earns the community's respect (Wenger 1989: 93; see also the Sebei – Goldschmidt 1976: 259). Tom Weisner has done a masterful job of contrasting the ever-solicitous parent depicted in Western child development textbooks with what he observed in an Abaluyia farming village in East Africa. Parents and adults rarely assist children with tasks. More often help is provided by other children, and even this token aid is "often indirect and delayed" (Weisner 1989: 72). The only direct communication is to assign the child its chores; indirect communication also includes teasing and aggression. "Food is used consistently to reward and acknowledge the child's contribution and vice-versa, recalcitrance is rewarded by food denial" (Weisner 1989: 78; see also Barlow 2001: 86). Similarly, the "Kwoma child ... learns by experience that no work means no food" (Whiting 1941: 47).

Moni Nag and her colleagues took a very close look at the contribution of children to the household economy in Java and Nepal. They found that girls as young as six spend upward of two hours per day in childcare. Teenagers (fifteen–nineteen-year-olds) spend as much as eight to eleven hours per day working (Nag *et al.* 1978: 294–296). Unlike in East Asia, girls are welcomed into the family as eagerly as boys, and infanticide seems rare. Indeed, the attitude seems to be to have "as many children as they can afford and find useful" (Nag *et al.* 1978: 301). This folk wisdom is borne out by "econometric analyses of fertility ... [that] have demonstrated significant positive correlations between measures of child labor-force participation and birth rates" (Nag *et al.* 1978: 293; also Ember 1983).

As societies "modernize" and wage-earning opportunities arise, we can expect that parents will seek employment for their children, even if it means that childhood will be curtailed (for example, "higher child wages lead to decreased leisure hours of both boys and girls"; Skoufias 1994: 346). In trying to understand how Thai parents can earn money from their children's prostitution, Montgomery explains that:

According to the Thai Buddhist moral scale, parents are entitled to be "moral creditors" (*phu mii phra khun*) because of their presumably self-sacrificing labour of bearing and rearing children ... while children are moral debtors ... one raises a child in expectation of explicit returns. A daughter repays the debt to her mother by remaining in the parental household to care for her parents in old age, while a son ordains as a Buddhist monk to pay his mother back for her breast milk. (Montgomery 2001a: 73)

Anthropologists have also called our attention to an extremely widespread aspect of childhood related to "being useful." Adoption and fosterage provide legitimate avenues to "circulate" children in ways that enhance their contributions and/or their opportunities.

Adoption

In places where land is scarce and surplus children cannot be absorbed in agricultural labor, they are sent to live with wealthier households that can use them. (Ravololomanga and Schlemmer 2000: 301)

Fofao was taken out of school by his step-father and "given" to an aunt who set the 6-year-old up selling ice pops on the streets of Recife. (Kenny 2007: 78)

There is no stigma associated with sterility. If [Baining] partners do not have children, they simply adopt them. (Fajans 1997: 68)

Adoption is quite common in the ethnographic record, and we earlier touched on practices in antiquity that facilitated the transfer of unwanted infants to others who'd be willing to rear them. Similar practices can be found in the ethnographic record (Balicki 1967). For example, on Vanatinai Island,

"The verb 'to adopt' literally means 'to feed.'" An unwanted infant would be placed in the crotch of a tree and anyone was then "free to retrieve the infant, wash it, and raise it as their own" (Lepowsky 1985: 63). What is less appreciated is that there are a number of societies or even whole regions where a significant portion of *all* children are given in adoption, such as the pan-Arctic region (Bodenhorn 1988: 12), Oceania (Shore 1996: 290), and West Africa (Martin 2012: 203). There appear to be several motives for moving children among families. An obvious motive is to keep the child alive in the event of the death of one or both parents – an all-too-common likelihood among both tribal peoples (Aka – Hewlett 1991a: 19) and those living in the past when life expectancy was around thirty-three to thirty-five (Anglo-Saxon – Crawford 1999: 129–130). As Silk (1980, 1987) has demonstrated, children are likely to be adopted by close kin who are, in the process, enhancing their own inclusive fitness. But as noted earlier for the Ache, family members may not be able to pick up the slack and the child is not kept. More recently, the AIDS epidemic has nullified the "traditional kin obligations to orphans" (Cheney 2012: 101).

A second motivation appears to be to redistribute children from families that have children to those that don't (Fajans 1997: 67) or to redistribute children from families that cannot make full use of them to families or individuals (like Fofao's aunt) who can. On Truk (now Chuuk) island, fertility is low and fertile women donate one or more of their children to the infertile in return for food and gifts (Fisher 1963: 530). A similar situation exists among East African pastoralists such as the Masaai (Talle 2004: 64). Another common transfer is across generations. As we will see in Chapter 4, grandmothers are extremely likely to serve as allomothers or substitute mothers for a newly weaned child. One step beyond would be to transfer the child more or less permanently to a grandparent's domicile. They are useful in running errands and doing menial work that would compromise the elder's prestige (Clark 1994: 367). The Javanese child is "put into service" with a relative who might also expect emotional comfort from their young kinsman "in exchange for tangible and intangible goods" to the parent (Jay 1969: 73).

Most commonly the child is transferred "to fulfill another household's need for labor" (Fée – Martin 2012: 220) as a "helper" (Inuit – Honigmann and Honigmann 1953: 46). The request may be for a girl in families with a shortage of female labor (Kosrae – Ritter 1981: 46; Bellona – Monberg 1970: 132). On Raroia boys are requested as they can work in copra processing (Danielsson 1952: 120). On the other hand, the impetus may begin with a family that has a surplus of children (Bodenhorn 1988: 14), or children too close in age, or discord within the family; or as the means to defray a debt. Stepchildren are often moved out of the natal home to make way for the new parent's biological offspring. On Suau "adopted children were sent along the same 'roads' of exchange as bride wealth pigs and the services of sorcerers" (Demian 2004: 98).

A number of societies value adoption for improving child outcomes. Many societies believe parents cannot enforce sufficient discipline to socialize children in proper behavior. Adoptive parents are less restrained by emotional ties and can be more effective parents (Java – Geertz 1961: 116). Indeed, the Baatombu share "the idea that children are better off raised by foster parents than biological parents" (Alber 2012: 182) because the latter are "too lenient with them" (Alber 2004: 41).[22] They take steps to minimize the emotional ties between the child and birth parent. "Even in the first hours after birth I observed mothers expressing distance towards their newborn child in the presence of a watching crowd of friends and relatives" (Alber 2004: 40).

In exchange for payment, a Palauan happily arranges for his child "to become the protégé of more influential and wealthy men" (Barnett 1979: 54). In Sierra Leone, girls who will be trained as *garrah*-cloth-makers are readily fostered into cloth-making households (Isaac and Conrad 1982: 244). Increasingly, girls are sent from rural villages to live with urban kin as "maids," where they may hope to earn their dowry (Jacquemin 2004: 384). In fact the practice of well-off families "taking in" the children of their poorer relations has been one of history's most enduring means of transferring wealth downward. However, the reality today may be less benign. "Under the pretext of 'helping' poor rural relatives, some women [in Abidjan] have created networks to place little maids, which under the cover of fosterage, are close to child trafficking" (Jacquemin 2006: 394; for Ghana see Derby 2012). Leinaweaver discusses this moral dilemma in the Peruvian context and the difficulties it poses for child welfare agencies.

"Improving oneself" is a reason for relocating children into the homes of better-off urban relatives ... In this migration of the young, children provide assistance in the home of the receiving family, who in turn provide for their care and upbringing ... [but] child circulation can involve unpaid labor (sometimes to exploitative degrees), sexual abuse, and other serious risks. (Leinaweaver 2008a: 60, 65)

Leinaweaver's (2008b) study documents a change in the nature of adoption as rural communities adapt to social change.[23] The term "child circulation"[24]

---

[22] On the flip side, children may escape from onerous work and domestic conflict by moving in with less demanding kin such as a grandmother (Hewlett 2013: 75).

[23] Child circulation seems likely to occur whenever a community is subject to the instability and change characterized by economic shifts (up and down), warfare, or persistent strife and plague (Alexandre-Bidon and Lett 1999: 54; dos Guimarães Sá 2007: 30).

[24] Child circulation in the European Middle Ages looked much the same and was undertaken for the same reasons (Alexandre-Bidon and Lett 1999: 54). An emerging area of child circulation is associated with failed adoptions; cf. Twohey (2013).

better captures the dynamics than "adoption" or "fosterage." One can "improve oneself" and the family economy by joining a wealthier household. Typically, schooling engages the younger family members while their niche in the household economy is filled by the circulated children. Civil war in the Andean region prompted many parents to transfer their children to other, safer villages. Parents' economic opportunities often involve relocation to job sites where a family would be inconvenient, so children are placed, temporarily, with extended family or at the local orphanage.

[One mother] has strategically dispersed her children around the region: the eldest daughter lives in her mother's house to make sure no one robs it, the second daughter resides permanently with her aunt and uncle, and the only boy works with another uncle in the jungle region. (Leinaweaver 2008b: 86–87)

Not surprisingly then, we see parents socializing their children to behave respectfully toward their elders or betters, "and this attitude is admonished, swatted, and even beaten into them." They are also "taught how to address their relatives properly, and ... how they should behave [toward them]" (Leinaweaver 2008b: 124, 141).

We are likely to view adoption from the perspective of the neontocracy. The motivating force is not genetic continuity, as we are likely to adopt non-kin. It is not physical resemblance, as cross-national and cross-race adoption is common. We aren't looking to augment our harvests with child labor inputs. We aren't acquiring children as an insurance policy providing social security as we age. We adopt because we "want" and "love" children in spite of the unfavorable cost–benefit ratio. As Hrdy explains: "Unlike other animals, humans are able to consciously make choices counter to their self-interest. Indeed, much of what we consider 'ethical behavior' falls in this category" (1999: 460).

Since children are already expected to participate in domestic labor and family enterprises such as herding, the threshold to laboring for a stipend is shallow. They readily transfer any earnings to their families – doing their duty as a regular member of the domestic economic unit (Baas 2011: 197). While child trafficking receives a great deal of attention from the press, child labor is a more pervasive phenomenon. Children can be viewed as chattel – their labor available without cost to families – even in the absence of outright slavery.

Child labor

In Brazil, over six million children between the ages of 10–17 and 296,000 between 5 and 9 are working [producing] much of what Brazilians eat, wear, and sleep in ... The cacao, gems, minerals, soybean, and grape industries have all required the use of cheap (children's) labor. (Kenny 2007: 2)

In many of the impoverished areas of the world, decreases in the carrying capacity of the land have not corresponded to a decline in fertility (Chirwa and Bourdillon 2000: 128). In worst-case scenarios, like Guinea-Bissau, mothers who can barely feed themselves continue to obey the dictum: "you never have too many children" (Einarsdóttir 2004: 63). And children suffer the consequences of this Malthusian dilemma. Parents go to desperate lengths to unburden themselves of child maintenance and/or to earn even a pittance from the child's labor (Baas 2011: 106). Overpopulation in Zimbabwe leads impoverished parents whose farms can no longer provide food for the family to force their children to work long hours in chrome and gold mining. Mining areas are characterized by "extreme environmental degradation ... where younger children collect chrome from the surface and pan for gold. Older children work in the mine shafts where 'they age early'" (McIvor 2000: 176, 179).

In Guatemala, Miguel is one of nine siblings who spend their days turning rocks into gravel – by hand – to help their parents (Ruiz 2011a: 87). Each child has a proportionally sized hammer to crush the larger rocks, which they hold between their feet (van de Berge 2011a: 71). Parallel to overpopulation and the scarcity of arable land is the monetization of the rural economy. Villagers need cash – to pay taxes and school fees, to obtain medicines and other essentials – but find few opportunities to obtain it. Earnings from their children's labor may be their best bet.

The main reason for [Quechua] children – from four years – to be active in the stone quarries is that they have to contribute to the family income ... All families have a little piece of land (0.5 or 1 ha) on which they grown corn or potatoes. Most also have [some livestock]. Some of the products, such as milk and butter, are sold for cash. However, this is not sufficient to cover the costs of daily expenditures. (van de Berge 2011a: 75)

In Colombia (in fact throughout the Andes) parents benefit from the earnings of their child (coal) miners:

Children are preferred for ore extraction in the deepest, narrowest parts of the gallery because they are so small and agile. They work in hot, humid, contaminated spaces with no ventilation and constant exposure to lung-damaging toxic gases and dust. [They] start ... from as young as six years old [, able] to work as soon as they can pick up objects and drag them along. The smallest children work at the pithead: sorting coal, carrying wood, tools, water, and food. Older ones do jobs that demand a greater degree of resistance. Working hours usually extend from one or two a.m. through eight or nine a.m. when the children are released for school before later going to work in the fields. (Sastre and Meyer 2000: 87–88)

In Bolivia, typical rural families have many children and all are sent to the mines. The very youngest cannot be legally employed but are able to work alongside their parents and augment their production (Baas 2011: 112). The child miners' health, not surprisingly, is very poor. They show signs of evident malnutrition with accompanying parasites, anemia, and decaying teeth. Diseases associated specifically with mining include pharyngitis, tonsillitis, sinusitis, influenza, pulmonary ailments, and silicosis. Skin and limb infections as well as deformity are evident in long-term employees (Sastre and Meyer 2000: 89).[25]

Urbanization further expands the economic potential of children. In rural Thai villages, children, especially daughters, are seen as assets to be carefully managed. As their chores are assumed by younger siblings, they may go to school for a couple of years until they can be sent to the towns to make their living in street work, including prostitution. In the village, families whose daughter(s) send home a part of their earnings are distinctly better off (Taylor 2002).

Throughout this book, we look at children through different lenses, avoiding the tendency to evaluate childhood in one society by the ideals espoused in another. But it goes without saying that the lives of impoverished children in the Third World are miserable compared with those of contemporary children in the developed world – including those living in relative poverty in urban ghettos or rural hideaways. But I don't think I fall prey to the "noble savage" myth when I assert that children in traditional villages not yet blighted by overpopulation and outside influence also enjoy lives that are idyllic compared with those of the children we've just been reading about. Yet another lens we might use is historical, and here we see many children whose experiences were akin to those of contemporary child miners and prostitutes.

Childhood in the past

Daughters working with their mothers [in Naples] are unlikely to get any wages at all, and their contribution to the household is made directly through their labour. (Goddard 1985: 19)

It is sobering to realize that the horror stories I've just been recounting would have been commonplace in the West until quite recently. Children earning wages or augmenting their parents' production is attested throughout history. Linear B tablets from Mycenae (1400 BCE) indicate that children were employed in a variety of menial tasks (Aamodt 2012: 37). Sippar

---

[25] Similar cases can be found in other countries and industries. Huichol youth who work on tobacco farms face severe threats of poisoning from pesticides and nicotine, for example (Gamlin 2011).

(Mesopotamia) temple archives from 535 BCE indicate that 20 percent of the construction crew were five or younger (MacGinnis 2011). The Code of Justinian (534 CE) suggests that children were working by the age of ten, and exceptionally by the age of five (Bradley 1991: 115). Epitaphs from ancient Rome convey eloquently the child's economic importance to their parents:

In memory of Viccentia, a very sweet girl, a worker in gold. She lived nine years.

In memory of Pieris a hairdresser. She lived nine years. Her mother Hilara put up this tombstone. Shelton. (1998: 112)

Many of the nastiest jobs such as cleaning chimneys and wells and tunneling into the earth as miners (Alexandre-Bidon and Lett 1999: 77–78), were favored for children because of their diminutive size. The industrial revolution had a major impact on childrearing cost–benefit calculations as factories offered parents the opportunities to earn wages through their children. While the size of one's landholding limited the scope for child employment, the industrial revolution loosened restraints on fertility (Sommerville 1982: 152). As early as the fourteenth century, "children worked in the mines of the Montagne Noir in France, leaving their small footprints in the clay [floor]" (Wileman 2005: 64). By the 1720s, four-year-olds were employed in French textile mills, and a hundred years later in Lancashire, one-quarter of all the ten-to fifteen-year-old girls were making cotton (Sommerville 1982: 250).

One-quarter of the labor force in eighteenth-century Russian textile factories was eight or younger. A typical child-assignment was to climb under and around whirring spinning machines to clean away lint. Their hours were the same as those of adults (typically two six-hour shifts in twenty-four hours) and the tasks demanding, but child wages were a fraction of the adult wage (Gorshkov 2009). Mechanization represented a very direct threat of children "falling into brewery vats, under the wheels of flour or water mills, under the hoofs of pack animals or the donkey turning the millstone" (Alexandre-Bidon and Lett 1999: 76).

In the West, restrictions were gradually imposed so that, by 1830, factory workers had to be at least eight years old; still, a fourteen-hour or longer working day was the norm, and they could be beaten for tardiness (Sommerville 1982: 103). An initial wave of reform aimed at children in the nineteenth century was actually less concerned with child labor (considered a good thing) than with children who were "vagrants" (Zelizer 1985: 61), who'd somehow broken free of their families and the constrictions of the factory, like the boys in Dickens' *Oliver Twist*. The termination of child labor was strongly resisted, mostly by parents as an infringement on their economic interests in their children and, in many cases, as a loss of critical family income. In a US study of child labor conducted in 1895, it turned out that, while the children came from homes with a father present, he was often unable to support the family (Hine 1999: 125).

A 1909 investigation of cotton textile mills reported that fathers and mothers vehemently declare that the State has no right to interfere if they wish to "put their children to work," and that it was only fair for the child to "begin to pay back for its keep." In New York canneries, Italian immigrants reportedly took a more aggressive stand ... against a canner who attempted to exclude young children from the sheds: [He was] besieged by angry Italian women, one of whom bit his finger "right through." Parents routinely sabotaged regulatory legislation simply by lying about their child's age. (Zelizer 1985: 69)

Figure 5 Spinners and doffers in Mollahan Mills (1908)

Immigrant parents resisted compulsory schooling on the same grounds (Lassonde 2005). However, as Zelizer (1985) shows, the movement to sanctify children, to remove them from adult spheres of influence, was inexorable (Clement 1997: 132). In 1900, one-fifth of children between ten and fifteen were employed. "By 1930, the economic participation of children had dwindled dramatically" (Zelizer 1985: 56). Demand for child laborers was curtailed primarily by improvements in technology that eliminated some of the more perfunctory, menial chores children were so good at. And, as documented in the Value of Children (VOC) surveys, in the modern world there has been an ongoing transition from valuing children for their economic contributions to valuing them for the psychological rewards they bestow (Kagitiçbasi and Ataca 2005: 318).

In the next section, I want to turn to another group of societies – both similar to and very different from our own – where children are treated like cherubs. They have affection and attention lavished on them – especially as infants.

Children in paradise

Kaingáng (South American forest foragers) children are valued for their potentialities as emotionally satisfying living things, like most other pets. There is no idea expressed that when they grow up they will feed and protect their parents. (Henry 1941/1964: 31)[26]

[!Kung] children are valued ... for their ability to make life more enjoyable. (Shostak 1981: 179)

There is a world in which children almost always feel "wanted" and where "there is no cultural preference for babies of either sex" (Howell 1988: 159). Infants are suckled on demand by their mothers and by other women in her absence. They are indulged and cosseted by their fathers, grandparents, and siblings. Children wean themselves over a long period and are given nutritious foods (Robson and Kaplan 2003: 156). They are subject to little or no restraint or coercion. Infants and toddlers are carried on long journeys and comforted when distressed. If they die in infancy, they may be mourned (Henry 1941/ 1964: 66). They are rarely or never physically punished or even scolded (Hernandez 1941: 129–130). They are not expected to make a significant contribution to the household economy and are free to play until the mid to late teens (Howell 2010: 30). Their experience of adolescence is relatively stress free (Hewlett and Hewlett 2013: 88). This paradise exists among a globally dispersed group of isolated societies – all of which depend heavily

---

[26] The Pirahã – another Amazonian people – also treat pet animals similarly to infants and children, including nursing them (Everett 2014).

on foraging for their subsistence. They are also characterized by relatively egalitarian and close social relations, including relative parity between men and women (Hewlett *et al.* 1998).[27]

In the Paraguayan rainforest, Ache infants are almost never separated from their mothers and may suckle whenever they choose; "they are never set down on the ground or left alone for more than a few seconds" (Hill and Hurtado 1996: 219). In other foraging societies, infants are frequently played with. Noted ethologist Eibl-Eibesfeldt traveled the globe to study patterns of infant care among less complex foraging and/or horticultural societies. He notes mothers and other caretakers kissing infants, rubbing noses, playing peek-a-boo, and fondling and stimulating their genitals (Eibl-Eibesfeldt 1983: 194). Others who've studied foraging bands also find ample evidence of affectionate mother–infant play (Gusinde 1937; Burling 1963), which, however, may end at about one year (Morelli and Tronick 1991: 104). "The [Agta] infant is eagerly passed from person to person until all ... have had an opportunity to snuggle, nuzzle, sniff, and [provide] affectionate genital stimulation" (Peterson 1978: 16). Eibl-Eibesfeldt (1983) reports that fathers engage in infant play less frequently than others, and, despite high levels of father involvement in infant care among Aka foragers, there's very little father–infant/child play (Hewlett 1991b: 95).

In central Malaysia, small bands of Batek people survive off the forest's bounty. Batek fathers as well as mothers spend a lot of time cuddling, holding, and talking with infants of either sex. Parents are quite relaxed about discipline: one two-year-old child used a bamboo flute his father had just finished making as a hammer. The father didn't care since he could easily make another. Parents rarely strike a child or use physical force on them, since their word *sakel* means both to hit and to kill, an abhorrent concept to them (Endicott 1992). Among the Airo-Pai foragers of Amazonian Peru:

> Men and women have explicit ideas about family size and spacing. They say that the ideal number of children is three and that a woman should not become pregnant until her last child is capable of eating and moving around independently ... Closely spaced children are said to suffer, cry, and develop angry characters. (Belaunde 2001: 136; see also Huaorani – Rival 1998: 630)

In the Sarawak region of Borneo, the Punan Bah explain the devoted care of infants as mediated by their belief that the child is a reincarnated ancestor. Further, its body and soul are only tenuously linked, hence it is fragile, easily

[27] Thinking of Malinowski's ethnography of the Trobriand Islanders, I'm tempted to argue that any society with conspicuous gender parity is likely to be a paradise for children (Malinowski 1929: 18).

harmed by the distress arising from separation from its mother. Treated with great care, at least until four years of age, children are "never punished physically so as not to scare off their souls" (Nicolaisen 1988: 198–199). The Garo, who live in the forests of Bengal, all share in infant and childcare, and parents "seldom roughhouse with their children, but play with them quietly, intimately, and fondly" (Burling 1963: 106). In the Northwest Territory of Canada, the Inuit (aka Eskimo) would never leave a child alone or let it cry for any length of time. Infants receive a great deal of solicitous care and lots of tactile comfort, anticipatory of "the interdependence and close interpersonal relations that are an integral part of Inuit life" (Condon 1987: 59; Sprott 2002: 54).

It is noteworthy that extremely attentive childcare is accompanied by respect for the child as a unique individual. For the Sioux living on the Great Plains of western North America, the child was invested with a great deal of character from birth. Care was taken not to suppress or divert the natural course of the child's personality: "there was within the ... Sioux community a profound respect for individual autonomy" (Wax 2002: 126). Draper observed a similar mindset operating among !Kung foragers in the Kalahari:

Adults are completely tolerant of a child's temper tantrums and of aggression directed by a child at an adult. I have seen a seven-year-old crying and furious, hurling sticks, nutshells, and eventually burning embers at her mother ... Bau (the mother) put up her arm occasionally to ward off the thrown objects but carried on her conversation nonchalantly. (Draper 1978: 37)

As the examples have already suggested, the entire band may participate in nurturing the child. Typical are the forest-dwelling Canela (Brazilian foragers) who live in small-scale consanguine communities of related women and their children.

While each mother is basically oriented to taking care of her own children, she can get help from her sister, her female cousins, and her mother should she need to absent herself for whatever purpose, including an extramarital tryst. Because female kin like to help one another have a good time in this way, the domestic unit has a number of willing baby-sitters built into its social structure. The ... domestic unit includes from ten to twenty children of all ages. They call each other brother and sister, though some may be first or even second cousins. (Crocker and Crocker 1994: 177)

A similar egalitarian, collective ethos[28] animates pygmy (Aka, Mbuti, Bofi – Central African rainforest foragers) childcare (Fouts 2005: 355). For example,

---

[28] The Okiek – mountain foragers in East Africa – do not share this ethos. Their "honey economy" creates rank among men, and men, in turn, dominate (and beat) women (Blackburn 1996: 208–209).

there are no sanctions against a Bofi child who fails to heed a request, and he is not "pestered" by a repeat of the request (Fouts 2005: 358).

There is a cluster of factors that undergird this pattern of infant and childcare. First, unlike agrarian and industrialized societies, among most foragers, children's lack of strength and stamina renders them incapable of contributing very much to family subsistence or income (Kaplan 1994). Second, foraging is, by definition, the active pursuit of food resources and mothers will, of necessity, carry their newborn constantly unless they can pass it off to another caretaker. Third, as discussed in the next chapter, foragers adopt a "survivorship" reproductive strategy. Around-the-clock nursing and a post-partum sex taboo combine to insure long intervals between births, leading to lower fertility. Low fertility is offset by the attention bestowed on the few offspring, enhancing their chances of survival (Fouts *et al.* 2001). An older Aka woman tells Bonnie Hewlett:

It is not good to become a parent when you are older, or too quickly again, because you fear your birth will have lots of blood. You risk death. With the loss of blood you will be sick and die. For the infant, the little baby you already have, this baby will have a sickness and this will take the baby. You risk this baby, and also the other may die. Some women, if they are pregnant again quickly, they take a traditional medicine to abort the baby, the bark of a tree. You do this so that the baby you have may live. (Hewlett 2013: 135)

Fourth, there are absolutely zero alternative life courses available within a foraging community. Children will either learn what they need to – including important social skills – to feed themselves and find a mate, or starve. So there is no need to rein them in, guide them, or teach them.

Huaorani people consider learning an integral part of growing. Children . . . become full members of the longhouse through their increased participation in ongoing social activities [and] by getting food and sharing it, by helping out in the making of blowguns, pots, or hammocks . . . adults never order children around; they do not command, coerce, or exercise any kind of physical or moral pressure, but simply suggest and ask. (Rival 2000: 115–116)

To be sure, the paradise that forager children enjoy is not quite the same as that enjoyed by our cherubs. Bodenhorn describes Inuit society, for example, as "'child-inclusive' rather than child-centered" (1988: 9). Aka babies are held by someone almost constantly, fed on demand, and not allowed to cry or fuss, whereas our infants are more often held by inanimate containers – cribs, playpens, and strollers – and tended on a schedule (Hewlett *et al.* 1998: 654; Lozoff and Brittenham 1979: 478).[29] Euroamerican babies are much more

---

[29] Containers are not completely absent from forager childcare. A Drysdale River aboriginal baby is placed in a trough-like vessel called "*puluyur* . . . lined with a thick layer of paper bark . . .

likely to be tickled, played with, and talked to than forager babies (Hewlett *et al.* 2000: 164). Further, in even the most indulgent forager bands, children are often malnourished (Howell 2010: 64)[30] and suffer from untreated injuries and infections. Children and adolescents maintain a cheerful, optimistic outlook in spite of infant/child mortality rates as high as 45 percent (Hewlett and Hewlett 2013: 95). Forager youth are exposed to violence, particularly as more powerful outsiders grab the group's territory, and they must cope with the early death of close relatives. This paradise for children may have been common for much of human prehistory but the foraging way of life has become ephemeral. Only in the modern era have we seen the emergence of, parallel, paradise-like conditions in childhood.

The priceless child

It is incumbent on good parents to cultivate happiness by meeting on the ground of the child's interest, not the concerns of adults. (Stearns 2010: 167)

Zelizer, in her landmark work *Pricing the Priceless Child*, describes a dramatic shift in attitudes toward the young in the nineteenth century.[31] Until then, "there was ... little appreciation of the need to cherish an infant, to give it the security of a warm nest and, as it grew up, to help it to develop" (Mitterauer and Sieder 1997: 100). The death of a child was no great cause for sorrow, and newborns were often referred to as "it" or "little stranger." The next child replaced the deceased; indeed, "it was a common practice to name newborns after a sibling who had recently died" (Zelizer 1985: 24–25). Others noted an earlier shift during the Protestant Reformation, with a new emphasis on the sacred duty of parents to rear all children and prepare them for a blameless life. However, in heeding admonitions from some reformers to invest more in their children (childrearing tracts were published from the fifteenth century), Protestants ran the risk of, according to a fifteenth-century archbishop, "'serv[ing] their children like idols [and thereby] earn[ing] damnation!'" (Cunningham 1995: 38).

---

providing the baby with a mattress and the mother an easy means of cleaning the baby's defecations, a task most repugnant to aborigines" (Hernandez 1941: 125).

[30] Unpublished data on the Aka from Courtney Mehan (personal communication, November 5, 2012).

[31] Cherubs appear fairly early in Chinese history but they are not entirely analogous to the cherubs that arose in Victorian times. There is evidence from the eleventh century CE of Chinese indulgence of children through the gift of toys, and vase paintings frequently depict (well-to-do) children at play. However, children's playtime was limited by the heavy burden of academic work necessary to succeed in the frequent "civil service" exams (Barnhart and Barnhart 2002: 55).

By the Victorian era, the child (of privilege) looks more and more cherubic as parents used dress and hairstyle to render children sexless. The goal was to create an ideal "of androgynous (that is, angelic) innocence" (Calvert 1992: 109). Linda Pollock's analysis of diaries dating from early modern England gives us glimpses of this attitude, at least among the "gentry." Already in the eighteenth century, children were seen as expensive to maintain and rear; however, they began to be seen as a source of:

Emotional satisfaction and as providing interest and variety in life ... they were valued for the amusement they offered and their company. They ... offer[ed] a second chance for an individual to achieve for his children the things he did not manage to have and as providing ... pleasure ... in old age. (Pollock 1983: 208)

Similarly, during the immediate post-World War II period in Japan, children were romanticized "as cute, dependent, and needing much tender care ... in contrast to the earlier utilitarian conception" (Uno 1991: 398). Recent research shows these attitudes developing further as parents go to great lengths to socialize children to embody the "outgoing, warm, loving ... cheerful ... qualities one might like in a friend" (Hoffman 1988: 118).[32] Children are increasingly valued for their contribution to parents' emotional wellbeing rather than to their material comfort. By the early twentieth century, the death of children also becomes more and more a cause for public concern, with newspaper editorials chiding parents for failing to prevent their children from often fatal accidents in the burgeoning vehicular traffic. The fight to limit child labor and child insurance, indeed any practice that permitted parents to earn a return from their children, became one of the twentieth century's great civil rights crusades, with strong moral overtones. Culpable "neglect" began to replace the fatalistic "god's will" as the most common post-mortem verdict after child death (Zelizer 1985: 37).

And, incrementally, the gerontocracy becomes a neontocracy. But I would argue that the neontocracy has, lately, gotten out of control. For example, it has been "argued that the rights of the fetus have now come to supersede the rights of pregnant women themselves" (Landsman 2009: 53; Paltrow and Flavin 2013). An ethnographic study in Madrid charted the gradual "take over" by the child (accoutrements like toys, furniture, and special foods, and the removal of "dangerous" or breakable items) of the domicile, leaving less and less "adult" territory (Poveda et al. 2012). "Power struggles" have now become an integral part of parent–child relations in the neontocracy (Hoffman 2012; Paugh 2012: 153). A survey in the US found that for the 60 percent of

---

[32] Some parents may be going well beyond this point. There is increasing use of pre-implantation genetic diagnosis, or PGD, to deliberately *increase* the odds of producing an offspring that shares the parent's disability, such as dwarfism (Sanghavi 2006) or deafness (Templeton 2007).

women who are employed, taking care of one's children ranked near the bottom of a preference scale, just ahead of housework and commuting (Kahneman *et al.* 2004: 1777). Middle-class parents feel "burdened" by their children's needs (Kremer-Sadlik *et al.* 2010: 47). One reason for this ennui may be that, from being a reliable helper in the household in nearly all (discussed more fully in Chapter 7) traditional societies, the child has turned into a parasite. There has been a flurry of studies recently on middle-class children's contributions to the household – or lack thereof. In one of the earliest, Anglo-Australian parents expressed the view that they can't ask their children to do more than self-care. Chores that involved caring for other family members and their property were "extra" and deserving of pay (Goodnow 1996). Other examples:

In West Berlin] parents alone are responsible for . . . the reproduction of daily life . . . the child is the recipient of care and services. (Zeiher 2001: 43; see also Wihstutz 2007: 80)

In a case study from Los Angeles, a parent spends a lot of time cajoling/guiding a 5-year-old into making her bed. It becomes a big dramatic production after she initially refuses, claiming incompetence. In a comparative case from Rome, the father doesn't even bother trying to get his 8-year-old daughter to make her bed, he does it himself, while complaining that her large collection of stuffed animals and her decision to move to the top bunk make his task much harder. (Fasulo *et al.* 2007: 16–18)

[Genevan children] use the vociferous defeat strategy. They comply with what is asked of them but . . . cry, scream, bang doors, lock themselves up in their rooms to sulk and so on . . . Some . . . agree to submit if their parents can prove their demands are well-founded. (Montandon 2001: 62)

A lengthy description of "shepherding" a four-year-old Swedish child to bed at night shows this as a major undertaking, consuming the mother's time and energy (Cekaite 2010: 17–19).

[In a second study of thirty families in Los Angeles] no child routinely assumed responsibility for household tasks without being asked . . . the overall picture was one of effortful appeals by parents for help [, who often] backtracked and did the task themselves . . . [becoming, in effect,] a valet for the child. (Ochs and Izquierdo 2009: 399–400)

In the neontocracy, children have authority – lording it over their valet parents – but little freedom and no responsibility (Lancy 2012b). By contrast, in the Tallensi gerontocracy children "are remarkably free from over-solicitous supervision . . . they can go where they like and do what they like [but] are held fully responsible for tasks entrusted to them" (Fortes 1938/1970: 41).

Nothing speaks the "times have changed" refrain more poignantly than the statistics on youth employment in the US: "[while] most high school seniors . . . work part-time during the school year . . . this work is not required by their school program, nor is it undertaken primarily to save for college or help with family finances" (Bachman *et al.* 2003: 301). They spend nearly 100 percent of their earnings on their own, conspicuous consumption (Mortimer and Krüguer 2000: 482). Further, the more hours adolescents devote to employment, the more likely they are to smoke, drink, and use marijuana and the weaker are their plans and aspirations for college and career (Bachman *et al.* 2003: 307; Mortimer and Krüguer 2000: 482). Middle- and upper-class US parents gain no return from their children's employment; in fact, they may incur a loss. In contrast to these cases, Orellana's research on Central American migrant families in Los Angeles shows children – particularly girls – making a large contribution to the care and wellbeing of the household (and attending school). Not only do they do household chores, they do odd jobs and bring in needed cash, and assist their parents and older relatives around the barriers of culture and language (Orellana 2001, 2009; Eksner and Orellana 2012).

When children become cherubs, rather than chattel, parents and society at large no longer view them as helpers, contributing significantly to the domestic economy. In a Nahua village, children's work has diminished and the elders regret that "children nowadays are not what they used to be, they get sick easily, they are more delicate" (Sánchez 2007: 94). And children absorb these values – trading a willingness to emulate and assist for an eagerness to express needs and preferences.[33] But in spite of the burden they impose, cherubic children are so attractive, so desirable, so much a reflection of our longing for innocence and naiveté – while still allowing us the pursuit of sensual indulgence and materialism – that they've become essential components of "the good life." Modern Americans and Europeans often want children even when they don't want to go through the pain and/or hassle of pregnancy or marriage. Never mind gourmet cooking, orchid cultivation, or photography, "parenting" has become the ultimate hobby, allowing us to indulge our values and tastes in shaping a real live human being (Matchar 2013). And, as our talented cherubs gather public acclaim for their good looks, cleverness, and many accomplishments, we contentedly bask in their reflected glory.

Another stage in the evolution of the neontocracy is playing out now. Pope Benedict called for "world leaders to show more respect for human life

[33] The neontocracy model has gradually taken over public policy as guiding the "correct" approach to childrearing and thereby defining the parenting strategies of immigrant, poverty-class and minority communities as deficient (Bernstein and Triger 2011). Some US states insist that day care providers be trained to adopt this view in their practice. Uttal (2010) documents a small-scale revolt on the part of would-be providers who happen to be Latina immigrants. "The Latina providers are especially . . . critical of the concept of 'self-esteem.' They wonder why it is so important . . . especially if it produces a self-centered, individualistic child" (Uttal 2010: 734; see also Ochs and Izquierdo 2009: 296).

at its earliest stages by saying embryos are dynamic, autonomous individuals"
(Associated Press 2010). US society has become increasingly

"fetally fascinated" [as the] American understanding and classification of premature
infants has changed dramatically from the late nineteenth century to the present. What
were categorized previously as miscarriages ... are now called "premature infants,"
subject to a variety of medical and social interventions designed to finish what nature
has failed to complete. (Isaacson 2002: 89)

This relentless push to extend and sanctify childhood comes at a cost in the
USA, annually, of US$26 billion just for the birth, intensive care, and further
postnatal complications (Muraskas and Parsi 2008: 655) associated with
"preemies." This cautionary note about the downside of the neontocracy
should make us wary of recoiling from newspaper accounts of an unmarried
mother on welfare giving birth to her sixth child; or a woman drowning her
sons to make herself a more attractive match for a husband; or a boyfriend
shaking to death his girlfriend's infant; or a husband leaving his wife and four
children to marry a younger woman. All reflect a view of childhood that
existed for far longer and affected far more children than our taken-for-granted
neontocracy.

3   To make a child

Introduction

The [Sisala] father of many children commands respect since the potential labor of his offspring will eventually contribute to his wealth and position in society. (Grindal 1972: 11)

In the previous chapter, I surveyed the relative rank of children over time and across cultures. Children may occupy the apex of society (neontocracy) or the basement (gerontocracy) or points in between. In this chapter my intent is to view the beginnings of life in the more common gerontocracy. Figure 6 depicts a specific case from Pamela Reynolds' study of the Tonga of Zambia. Note that the lowest level is the earth and a stillborn is returned directly to the wild, without ceremony. As the individual survives, she or he ascends a ladder of value reflected in the place of burial – which progresses from fully wild to domestic or man-made – and the manner of burial. It is not until the age of ten that a child is accorded an adult burial, but, unlike the adult's, this will not be recalled on the first anniversary of the funeral. "Only those who reproduce (both as parents and householders) are granted full adult status after death, only their spirits are secured a position of influence over the living" (Reynolds 1991: 96–98).

This chapter is founded on a paradox or a series of paradoxes. In our own society we expect to have few offspring and to treat them almost worshipfully – yet our children suffer from a near epidemic of psychological disorders (Lancy 2010c). We deny the dictates of our hormones to delay reproduction until we've created a well-furnished and stocked nest to nurture our "cherubs." And, if nature then thwarts us and we are unable to bear our own children, we go to extraordinary lengths – traveling half-way around the world and spending our life savings – to adopt (or create in a lab) a baby that may not be remotely representative of our own genetic and cultural heritage.[1] Other societies welcome children – lots of

---

[1] In India, baby factories are springing up where young women earn good money "renting their wombs" to infertile couples (Dolnick 2008).

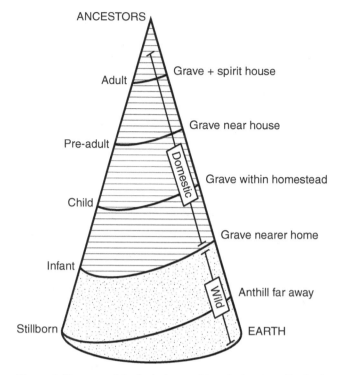

Figure 6 Tonga model of relative position during the Life-Cycle

them – yet, in those societies, children may suffer from evident hunger, illness, and neglect. In the wealthiest communities that can "afford" lots of children, the birth rate is low, and vice versa.

The gerontocracy model is probably more representative of "humankind" at least statistically. The model can be detected in the attitude expressed by the agrarian Sebei people of Uganda as recorded by American anthropologist Walter Goldschmidt. He says, reflecting the bias of his own culture, "It would appear that progeny are desired, but children are not particularly wanted" (Goldschmidt 1976: 244). Among Ashanti farmers, childless adults are taunted and "after death had great thorns ... driven into the soles of the feet ... with these words ... 'do not return again'" (Rattray 1927: 66–67). "Israelite society regarded it as a curse for a man to die childless, a status equivalent to the end of his name [, and] barrenness brought shame ... upon a woman for ending a lineage" (Horn and Martens 2009: 73). For Hokkien-speaking villagers in East Asia: "The dominant theme of the marriage ritual is fertility and ... yet ... birth is considered unclean and actually dangerous to others" (Wolf 1972: 56). "One of the duties [Roman] citizens had to the state ... was to produce heirs, but ... this ... was to increase ... the privileged classes, not to encourage a love of children" (Boswell 1988: 58).

Bearing children is bound up with a more general preoccupation with fertility. Ceremonies and symbols link childbearing to the fecundity of domestic stock, crops, and wild game (Gray 1994: 92). So powerful is this imperative to "be fruitful and multiply" that it may lead to the Malthusian nightmare found in deeply impoverished areas where famine is common and yet the birth rate remains high.[2]

While men and women must cooperate in creating a child, they may bring diametrically opposed perspectives to the corollary task of raising the child. This lack of congruence gives rise to the variation we see in family structure and function. We will be particularly interested in polygyny, the very common pattern where a single male controls a household consisting of multiple wives and their children.

Although high fertility is almost universally applauded, boys are sometimes desired over girls and vice versa. These calculations are influenced by the economic roles men and women fulfill. Female babies are devalued where women are prevented from contributing to the domestic economy. Factors like birth order – first-born girls are welcome as future helpers in raising the preferred sons – also come into play. In foraging societies, where children are dependent and unproductive well into their teens, fewer children are preferred. In farming societies, such as the Beng, children may be welcomed as "little slaves" (Gottlieb 2000: 87). In pastoral and industrial societies, where young children can undertake shepherding a flock, or do repetitive machine-work, women are much more fertile. And, while the traditional culture of the village affords a plethora of customs and taboos for the protection of the pregnant mother and newborn, these coexist with customs that either dictate or at least quietly sanction abortion and infanticide.

In recent history, changes in the economic basis of society, in particular the need for future workers to spend long years in schooling, have led to a demographic transition. "Modern" families make use of effective and inexpensive methods of contraception to reduce their fertility significantly. Children have been transformed from economic assets to liabilities to personally rewarding "projects." But not all segments of the world's population have made this transition, and high fertility may still be the ideal even in the absence of opportunities to earn economic benefits from one's offspring.

In the decision to create a child, the child's wellbeing and happiness are rarely the issue. In fact, reproduction decisions draw in many parties who bring strikingly different interests to the table.

---

[2] As Davis notes, in Darfur (Sudan), "famine is part and parcel of ordinary social life, and is not a breakdown of normal social experience" (Davis 1992: 151).

One big unhappy family

Mating systems are not the same as marriage systems. (Low 2005: 16)

The behaviours that make individuals successful in mating are often mutually exclusive of the behaviours that result in successful parenting. (Bereczkei and Csanaky 2001: 501)

Popular media are replete with rhetoric on the "dysfunctional" family and this has broadened to include any form of chronic conflict – even at a low level. In the section that follows, I want to make the argument that, as much as we might wish to see families as cooperating harmoniously for the common good, especially for the sake of children, in reality, members sometimes follow different agendas that may clash.

Two important ideas need to be introduced. The first is that the "selfish gene" reveals the compelling drive for each organism to reproduce itself as often as possible (Dawkins 1989). The second idea is that the reproductive interests of men, women, and children are different (Trivers 1972). The first idea leads to a big family; the second means it could be unhappy. Men and women have evolved fundamentally different reproductive preferences. Men, under ideal circumstances, will impregnate as many women as possible and invest only enough in their offspring to keep them alive (Borgerhoff Mulder 1992: 362). Women, ideally, want fewer children, for the children's sake and to protect their own bodies.[3] And they'd like the father or fathers of their children to be good providers. Many societies – even the most conservative – endorse men's promiscuity (*machismo*) and women's resistance (defending their honor). Other common-sense notions that have been confirmed by science include the tendency for men to use deception ("Of course I love you"), whereas "feminine wiles" include a range of tactics designed to unmask the male's intentions (Grammer *et al.* 2000).

Men, knowing what women are looking for, are likely to "show off." In a society where whale hunters rule the roost, "young women on [Nantucket] island ... pledged to marry only men who had already killed a whale. To help ... young women identify them as hunters, boatsteerers wore chock-pins ... on their lapels. Boatsteerers, superb athletes with the prospect of lucrative captaincies, were considered the most eligible of Nantucket bachelors" (Philbrick 2000: 13). More subtly, in several societies where men hunt, researchers have discovered some interesting facts. First, hunters

---

[3] As we'll see in the next chapter, grandmothers often assist with childcare and can have a positive effect on grandchildren's survival and wellbeing. But the effect is much more pronounced for maternal grandmothers. Evidently, paternal grandmothers invest less in daughters-in-law and their offspring because of the uncertainty of genetic ties (Leonetti *et al.* 2005).

sometimes pass up easily captured small game to pursue larger, more spectacular prey. Second, upon returning to the community, the hunter will conspicuously share his catch with other households (Blurton-Jones *et al.* 2005: 235). Third, successful, generous hunters enjoy more mating opportunities than unsuccessful hunters (Hawkes 1991). Even when they can earn more calories for their families through gardening, men in several South American forest-resident tribes prefer to hunt, because game provides a much more visible indicator of one's ability to provision a woman and her children (Kaplan and Hill 1992: 189). In southern Africa, the !Kung San[4] explain that poor hunters will remain bachelors because "women like meat" (Biesele 1993).

In another method of showing off – "baby-parading" – fathers, who otherwise spend little time with their offspring, in effect "borrow" them from their mothers to take on a stroll around the village. Here are three examples:

Among the Eipo [of Papua New Guinea], fathers pick up their baby at the women's area and carry it ... for half an hour or so, getting friendly attention. (Eibl-Eibesfeldt 1983: 208)

[Chipewyan] men are often seen walking around the village carrying their small children. (van Stone 1965: 53)

His [Fijian] father does not play with him often, but occasionally he takes the child on his back to attend a meeting or to visit a neighbour. (Thompson 1940: 39)[5]

A man who parades his healthy infant and demonstrates his own nurturing personality may, like a show-off hunter, improve future mating prospects (Konner 1975: 101). However, promiscuity on the part of either parent may be viewed as threatening to the child. *Phiringaniso* is a childhood "illness attributed to violation of the [Tsonga] norms of sexual behavior by a parent" (Green *et al.* 1994: 11).

Even in otherwise simple, egalitarian societies, such as the !Kung, violent conflict may arise – usually over access to women (Edgerton 1992: 71). The unending tribal warfare that anthropologists describe in unacculturated

---

[4] A note on African terminology: the !Kung Bushmen are among the most heavily studied group of people in the world and will be cited often throughout this book. However, there are other related groups that have been studied and, collectively, these foraging peoples are called San. The !Kung are referred to (more accurately) as Ju/'hoansi in more recent literature. Moreover, they are no longer referred to as Bushmen, partly because the term has pejorative connotations, partly because they no longer live "in the bush." I use the name chosen by the author of the particular article or book I'm drawing on.

[5] Other examples of baby-parading: Bali – Covarrubias (1937: 132); Dogon – Paulme (1940: 439); Amhara – Messing (1985: 205); Maya – Elmendorf (1976: 94); Ngandu – Hewlett (1991b: 148); Java – Geertz (1961: 106); Lurs – Friedl (1997: 115). Typically, the father returns the child to its regular caretakers at the first sign of fussiness or impending evacuation.

(and "unpacified") South American (Chagnon 1968/1992) and Papua New Guinean (Gardner and Heider 1969) groups is often sparked by the drive to add women to the community. By the same token, diplomacy, marriage, and filiation customs are rooted in the necessity to exchange women who have reached breeding age and thus avoid inbreeding (Fox 1972: 309). Open conflict between competing males is also avoided by the operation of mechanisms that create and reinforce relative rank. Among the Yanomamo of South America, those who have risen to the rank of chief have access to more women and significantly higher inclusive fitness (Chagnon 1979).

Very often young men are blocked from access to females[6] until they have been initiated into the society of older men (Fox 1972: 308). And this happens when they've "proven their manhood" through success as hunters (Spencer 1970) or pursuit of an arduous spiritual quest (Benedict 1922), or when they and their family have amassed sufficient "bride-price" (Rappaport 1967). Meanwhile, at the top of the pecking order, wealthy and/or powerful men – via the mechanism of polygyny or multiple marriages – can monopolize access to young women (Low 2005: 17).

However, the dominance hierarchy, while present in our species (Weisfeld and Linkey 1985: 110), plays much less of a role in the mating process than it does among our primate relatives (Strier 2003: 168–169). Neither the harem, where the ruler sequesters (guarded by eunuchs) a large number of females, nor a Don Juan, riding about the countryside deflowering damsels, is common – hence their legendary status. Rather, every society exercises some control over mating via institutions such as marriage, rules governing property, and prescriptions for the living arrangements of men, women, and their children. Not that these institutions are ever 100 percent successful in suppressing the mating game.[7]

The alternative offered by marriage and the explicit or implied fidelity contract may reduce but certainly does not eliminate the conflict provoked by competition between males and the differing tactics of men and women. Charges of adultery filled the "docket" in the (Kpelle) town chief's court in Gbarngasuakwelle. A very typical case pitted an older husband, whose relative wealth enabled him to acquire a young wife, against a young lover – her ace in the hole, in the likely event her aged husband died and left her without resources (Lancy 1980a).

---

[6] The Ache may attack excessively randy young men in periodic group stick fights (Hill and Hurtado 1996: 227). An interesting exception to the tendency to keep young men from mating occurs in several tropical South American foraging groups, such as the Wari, where they are paired with a prepubescent girl. The young man's semen is seen as essential to bringing the girl to sexual maturity, just as his semen will, later, build his offspring in the womb (Conklin 2001).

[7] Draper and Harpending (1982) offer two alternative strategies – dad vs. cad – that capture much of the observed variation. That is, men can achieve high fitness either by devoting themselves to their wife (wives) and children, insuring high certainty of paternity and higher survival of offspring, or by playing the field.

At the other extreme from societies where the bonds of marriage are "loose" are those where premarital relations and adultery, with the implications of illegitimacy, are treated as capital crimes. Clitorodectomy, the surgical removal of a girl's genitalia, has become a rallying point for international human rights (Wilson and Daly 2002: 302). Cliterodectomy's ostensible purpose is to protect the virtue of women and reduce the likelihood of illegitimacy by destroying any sexual desire they might have (Ciaccio and el Shakry 1993: 47–48).

Other oppressive restrictions imposed on breeding-age women include the medieval (European) chastity belt (Potts and Short 1999: 92); full-length clothing and head covering such as the Iranian *chador* (Ansar and Martin 2003: 177); and virtual house imprisonment (*purdah*) for higher-caste Indian wives (Deka 1993: 126). In lower-caste marriages, the wife may be terrorized into fidelity through frequent beatings (Rao 1997). Among the Dogon of Mali, monitoring a woman's sexual activity is a community affair; specifically, their menses are verified to insure that, prior to marriage, they aren't already pregnant by another man (Strassmann 1993). In China, higher-class women had their feet permanently deformed (foot-binding), in part symbolizing their virtual imprisonment (Wilson and Daly 2002: 301).

Anthropologists find that there is an inverse relationship between restrictions imposed on women and their economic contribution to the household. That is, where women's labor is critical, attitudes regarding fidelity are, necessarily, more relaxed. Women suffer these restrictions to preserve their virtue, even as a society valorizes the promiscuous male. Nevertheless, given the risks and wear and tear of promiscuity, men's long-term genetic interests may be served by faithful attachment to a mate (Hrdy 1999: 231) (or multiple wives in polygyny), and anthropologists have studied the calculus that comes into play in these decisions (Hill and Reeve 2004; Kanazawa and Still 2000): "males confront a problem of how to budget their reproductive efforts between seeking, courting, and contesting new mates, on the one hand, and doing whatever it takes to monopolize the ones already acquired, on the other" (Wilson and Daly 2002: 291). A Hadza man can be expected to remain in a relationship if his mate is fecund, bears healthy young that thrive, is a hard worker who provides a significant amount of the household's needed resources (Marlowe 2004: 365), and shows little interest in other males (Apicella and Marlowe 2004: 372). A woman's commitment is leavened by similar concerns, particularly that her mate should be a "good provider" and not harm her or the children. Research affirms that women show a clear preference for potential mates who appear to enjoy children (Brase 2006: 151).

Residence is also a contributing factor. Where couples reside "patrilocally" – with the husband's family – the husband can rely on his kin to keep a close watch on his spouse(s) and aid him in insuring the legitimacy of any offspring. Studies show that the father's kin are more likely to invest in children whose paternity is certain (Huber and Breedlove 2007). The "family," obviously, extends well beyond the husband, wife, and nurseling. There may be multiple wives (or, rarely, husbands), which we'll discuss shortly, and extended family members such as the husband's mother in residence. Grandparents may play a vital role in childcare. Indeed, among the Ache of South America, orphans are likely to be put to death unless rescued by grandparents (Hill and Hurtado 1996: 438). On the other hand, it is the rare mother-in-law who does not attempt to usurp the wife's authority, and mothers-in-law are often identified as the primary culprits in the frequent bride-burnings in India. Grandfathers may not be available to assist with childcare because, at least among the Hadza of East Africa, where divorce and multiple marriages are common, a grandfather is busy siring new children on his young wife (Blurton-Jones *et al.* 2005: 224).

In our hypothetical large, unhappy family, the unhappiest member may be the child who is being weaned. Robert Trivers (1974) formulated the theoretical version of what every harried parent knows, namely, that, at a certain point in the life-cycle, the interests of the child and its mother clash. The mother may be ready to begin investing in her next baby well before this baby is willing to give up the nutrition and comfort only the breast can provide. The mother is also eager to shed what has become a heavy appendage while the toddler is reluctant to give up a free ride and locomote on her own. The result of these conflicts can set the entire family on edge: "Mothers in all societies recognize aggressive behavior by the young child towards its follower as rivalry or jealousy . . . in the [East African] Kikuyu language, the word for the adjacent younger child has a stem meaning 'rival'" (Whiting and Edwards 1988a: 173). Nisa, a !Kung woman interviewed in old age, still held vivid memories of her life's great trauma: "Some mornings I just stayed around and my tears fell and I cried and refused food. That was because I saw him (brother) nursing. I saw with my eyes the milk spilling out. I thought it was mine" (Shostak 1976: 251).

Among all the ape species, temper tantrums thrown by displaced juveniles are both likely and effective in garnering additional attention and food (Fouts *et al.* 2001: 31). An Inuit weanling, confronted with her nursing sister, screams and carries on until her mother makes her second breast available (Briggs 1970: 157). Briggs recorded fascinating interchanges between toddlers and adults in which the latter encouraged consideration of siblicide, designed, apparently, to assist the child in vocalizing its jealousy (Briggs 1990: 35).

Even the new infant may be seen as threatening to its family. Throughout West Africa, infants are seen as arriving from a "beforelife" that they are reluctant to leave. Further, they may harbour "witch spirits who complicate pregnancy, labour and delivery" (Fermé 2001: 199).

As troublesome as they are, children just may be the glue that holds the family together. Sarah Hrdy argues persuasively that humans, like a number of other species (e.g. wolves), are cooperative breeders (Hrdy 2005b). Bogin's theory, touched on in Chapter 1, holds that human fertility is enhanced, relative to that of other apes, because our young, while yet immature and not entirely self-sufficient, can manage just fine without the attentions of their mother, who is free to have another child (Bogin 1998). They survive through the care of other family members, a phenomenon that we will examine in Chapter 4. Another critical human trait, missing in other primate species, is the sharing of food. Older individuals – of both genders – routinely share food with younger individuals (Lancaster and Lancaster 1983). And men share food with women they'd like to mate with, who, in turn, share with their offspring. The care and feeding of children, then, may have been the *raison d'être* for the creation of families as we know them.

Love the one you're with

Kpelle social fatherhood is a complex matter often involving intrigues far beyond the simple fact of biological relationships. (Bledsoe 1980a: 33)

It would be a mistake to view women as without resources in the mating game. Beauty may be in the eye of the beholder, but physical attractiveness or sex appeal has long been a woman's weapon of choice. In studies conducted in the USA, physically attractive women are more likely to delay the onset of sex and "hold out" for a higher-ranking male (Elder 1969). Mende women of West Africa "are especially proud of their full, rounded buttocks, displayed to advantage in the way they tie their clothes, and in dance ... [they] display [their] full rounded contours in a message of fecundity" (MacCormack 1994: 112).

Women may have an interest in concealing their ovulation cycle to maintain discretionary control over the onset of pregnancy. Unlike other primates, female humans are never conspicuously oestrous. They are almost continuously available as sex partners and reproductive targets. And this phenomenon has been used to explain the origin of male–female pair-bonding that is absent in chimpanzees, for example. That is, if men want frequent sexual access and want to prevent others from access, they had better "stick around" to ward off suitors (Alexander and Noonan 1979). Another common tactic used by new mothers is to exaggerate the resemblance between the newborn and their husband (Apicella and Marlowe 2004: 372). In spite of the confidence with which humans claim "he looks just like his father," experimental studies show that babies cannot be reliably paired to their parents on the basis of appearance (Pagel 2012: 315). Studies in our monogamous, adultery-condemning society have shown that 10 percent of men designated as the biological father of a particular child are not (Buss 1994: 66–67), so the baby's anonymous appearance confers a survival advantage.

One of the more interesting and extreme manifestations of this, often deliberate, obfuscation is called "partible paternity" (Conklin and Morgan 1996: 657). The Kpelle child is said to resemble "individual men in proportion to the number of times the mother has had intercourse with them" (Bledsoe 1980a: 33). For the Bumbita, the man who had had intercourse most often during the first trimester becomes the "father" (Leavitt 1989: 117). In foraging societies found over a large area of South America, cutting across geographical and language barriers, babies are said to be "made" by everyone who has intercourse with the mother. While the "real" father is the individual who was most closely linked to the mother on the eve of delivery, a strategic female, once she's conceived, will seduce (Hrdy 1999: 35)[8] several good hunters who will then be designated "secondary" fathers (Crocker and Crocker 1994: 83–84). These men constitute an insurance policy in the event the primary father dies or reneges on his obligations, and they are referred to by the same term as the primary father (Hill and Hurtado 1996: 249–250). This strategy apparently is effective: studies of the Bari – South American forest dwellers – demonstrate that children with multiple fathers have a higher survival rate than those with one (Beckerman *et al.* 1998; Beckerman and Valentine 2002). On the other hand, among the Ache, "too many" fathers can nullify the insurance policy in terms of men's willingness to support an orphan (Hill and Hurtado 1996: 444).

While it is always in the woman's interest to maintain a relationship with a reliable provider,[9] it isn't necessarily in her interest to bear as many children as he would like to sire. Each pregnancy, birth, and infant nursed and carried to toddlerhood takes a huge physical toll on a woman's body. If "sex appeal" was a factor in securing her first mate, bearing multiple children will rapidly erase that asset. Concerns for her own health and the wellbeing of present and future children may all render conception at a particular time unpropitious. If fortunate, she may have access to herbal contraception with some degree of effectiveness (Lindenbaum 1973: 251).[10] In the Sepik area

---

[8] Hrdy (1999), from her research with Hanuman langurs (primates), noted that females were promiscuous, mating with males other than the alpha male, as opportunity permitted. Coupled with the fact that newly dominant males routinely kill the infants sired by their deposed rivals, it seemed obvious that the mothers were protecting their offspring by obscuring paternity. Males rarely kill their own offspring. See also Sugiyama (1967).

[9] Clark notes that, in many societies, a mother is much more dependent on long-term relationships with her own kin than with an ephemeral or irresponsible husband. Her West African informants insisted that "giving precedence to husbands over kin was actually considered morally wrong or selfish" (1994: 103).

[10] Lindenbaum also discusses *clusters* of cultural practices that either promote or reduce overall fertility, and indicates that these are mediated by resource availability. In Papua New Guinea, the Dobu and others embrace beliefs and practices that increase fertility while the Enga, among others, embrace customs that militate against high fertility.

(Papua New Guinea), *kip*, "magic" bark from a tree, is eaten by women to successfully prevent conception (Kulick 1992: 92). The Hottentots from southern Africa had several abortifacients in their pharmacopoeia (Schapera 1930). In the high Andes of Peru, modern forms of contraception are not available; hence villagers "rely on traditional knowledge to prevent conception" (Bolin 2006: 16–17).

Abortion and infanticide, prior to the influence of Western moral standards, would have been widespread (Ritchie and Ritchie 1979: 39). However, the mother may need to conceal her actions from her husband and his kin because contraception or abortion is often seen as a tacit admission of promiscuity (Einarsdóttir 2004: 69). One strategy for family formation that may work to reduce these conflicts is polygyny.

Polygyny as the great compromise

Polygyny was quite common across past human societies ... the practice had adaptive value under a range of conditions, and ... this remains true for individuals in populations where it persists. (Sellen 1998a: 331)

Each wife of the [Ottoman] sultan was known as *kadin*, which means simply "woman" [; however,] the two who were the first to bear sons ... took precedence as first (*birinici*) and second (*ikinci*) *kadin*. (Freely 1996: 195)

Contemporary Euroamerican society, being heavily influenced by Christian traditions, values monogamy highly. To support this "unnatural" condition, we've evolved elaborate wedding ceremonies, neolocal residence (husband and wife establish their own residence away from his and her parents), and the pervasive culture of romantic love. Polygyny, as the special form of polygamy in which a man may be legally married to more than one woman, is much more "natural," or at least far more common. Estimates range from 85 percent (Murdock 1967: 47) to 93 percent (Low 1989: 312) of all societies ever recorded (about 1,200) having practiced polygyny. The proportion might be even higher if we were to include foraging societies where egalitarian relations between and within the sexes all but preclude polygyny, but where divorce and remarriage are so common they are said to practice "serial monogamy" (Marlowe 2007: 179).[11]

The compromise arises because men are able to translate wealth and power into breeding opportunities while reducing the perils associated with the Don Juan model. Women in a polygynous relationship gain access to a

[11] Among South American foragers, sexual relations are even more fluid, and fidelity is not routinely expected of either partner (Howard Kress, personal communication, February 7, 2007).

higher-ranking, reliable provider at the cost of emotional strain in sharing resources (including the husband's affection) with others. In one study, children of senior wives were better nourished than children in monogamous unions, who were, in turn, better nourished than children of later wives (Isaac and Feinberg 1982: 632). A woman must weigh the trade-offs between marrying a young man in a monogamous union or marrying an older man and joining a well-established household as a junior wife. Studies show that, if they choose monogamy, they enjoy slightly higher fertility (Josephson 2002: 378) and their children may be somewhat better nourished (Sellen 1998a: 341). However, they are, perhaps, more likely to be abandoned or divorced by their husbands.

Anthropologists have documented the, potentially negative, impact on children of the decline in polygyny. In Uganda, monogamy has led to less stable marriages. A man, rather than bringing a second wife into the household, now abandons the first wife and her children to set up a second separate household with his new mate (Ainsworth 1967: 10–11). A typical case among the Nyansongo in Kenya describes a mother, whose childhood was spent in a large polygynous compound where multiple caretakers were always available, who must cope alone in a monogamous household. She leaves her three-year-old to mind her six-month- and two-year-old infants as she performs errands like bringing the cow in from pasture. Unfortunately, the three-year-old is simply not mature enough for this task and is, in fact, "rough and dangerously negligent" (Whiting and Edwards 1988a: 173).

Older wives in polygynous unions may find they are ignored and their share of the family larder may diminish, but they're rarely evicted. Indeed, living quarters in polygynous unions are often constructed to facilitate the rearrangement of the female pecking order (Altman and Ginat 1996: 214), as brilliantly depicted, for example, in the Chinese film *Raise the Red Lantern* (Yimou 1991). On the other hand, separate and distinct living quarters may also signal the autonomy and upward mobility available to women. West African women, in particular, often parlay their high status in polygynous households into important positions in the community. They become the managers of the, sometimes substantial, household economy and can direct the labor of their co-wives, their children, and any extended kin (Clark 1994).

In monogamous marriages, divorce is always a threat. It is most often precipitated by infertility or loss of fertility – Henry VIII's (of England) divorce of Catherine of Aragon a well-known case in point. Adultery is almost universally considered legitimate grounds for divorce (or worse: Henry VIII had wives 2 and 5 beheaded). But far more prosaic reasons can be found. As societies become more mobile and men migrate seeking employment, the likelihood that the male will abandon (or neglect) his family in the village in order to establish a new family in the city is increasingly high (Bucher and d'Amorim 1993: 16; Timaeus and Graham 1989). And, perhaps most common of all, women whose fertility is on the decline are replaced by younger wives in peak breeding condition (Low 2000: 325), popularly referred to today as "May to December" unions.

The abandoned spouse and her children may face severe difficulties. One might think that an obviously fertile woman would be a "catch," but "Having a child towards whom a new husband will have to assume step-parental duties diminishes rather than enhances a women's marriageability" (Wilson and Daly 2002: 307).[12] In the case of a young, pregnant widow, ancient Roman law permitted both annulment and the exposure of the infant in order to enhance her chances of remarriage (French 1991: 21). Raffaele describes an unfortunate case in a Bayaka[13] foraging band in Central Africa: "Mimba had been in a trial marriage . . . her partner's father had refused to pay the bride price and she had just been forced to return to her own family. She is two months' pregnant, and it is a disgrace for an unmarried Bayaka woman to give birth" (Raffaele 2003: 129). Fortunately for Mimba, the tribe's pharmacopoeia includes *sambolo*, a very reliable and safe herbal abortifacient,[14] which she will use. Mimba will return to the pool of eligible mates and, hopefully, will find a family willing to pay the bride-price so their son can join her in raising a family – something she could not accomplish by herself.

Systems that confer/deny legitimacy to the child are complemented by elaborate customs to protect the child through pregnancy and birth.

Pregnancy and childbirth

[Kako] Women draw an analogy between the cooking of food and the cooking of children in the womb. (Notermans 2004: 19)

---

[12] As marriage becomes more fragile, women face a classic Catch-22. If they have "too few" children, they're in danger of being divorced for low fertility. If, on the other hand, they have "many" children and are later abandoned by their spouse, they face the prospect of being unable to support their "large" brood.

[13] The Bayaka (also Biyaka) are just one of several foraging peoples of the Central African rainforest to be cited in this book. Others are the Efe, Aka, Baka, M'buti, and Bofi. Aside from sharing the rainforest habitat and a minimal material culture, all these people also evince an unusually short stature, and were referred to as *pygmies* – a term now considered pejorative. All of these groups also live in a symbiotic relationship with sedentary farming peoples. Collectively, they represent several unique adaptations that are of special interest to students of culture and childhood.

[14] From an evolutionary perspective, abortion seems quite straightforward and predictable. Women will seek the means to abort the fetus if they are unwell, if they lack a support system, if they're living with a man who is not the father of their fetus, and, especially, if their *future* prospects of bringing a child into a supportive environment are more favorable (Low 2000: 325).

"A pregnant woman has one foot in the grave" according to a proverb from Gascony. (Heywood 2001: 58)

[Tibetan] women rarely prepare a layette until after the birth, because, "Where there is too much preparation, the baby may die at birth." (Craig 2009: 150)

Throughout much of human history, pregnancy was treated as a serious illness and childbirth was, until recently, extremely risky. "Childbirth is by far the greatest peril faced by [Semai] women in their reproductive years, accounting for thirteen of twenty-nine deaths (forty-five per cent), and half of all deaths from known causes" (Dentan 1978: 111). This reality is accommodated via culturally constructed theories of the gestation and birth process and by remedies or prophylactic strategies to protect the mother and fetus. On the fertile, volcanic island of New Britain, the Kaliai believe – in common with peoples around the globe – that "a successful pregnancy requires numerous acts of sexual intercourse [which] should continue until the foetus … quickens" (Counts 1985: 161). While that particular prescription for a healthy baby may be welcomed by parents, other Kaliai prescriptions may be less popular:

If either parent ate the flesh of the flying fox, the child might be mentally defective or it might shake and tremble as the animal does, or it might be unable to sit at the normal time because the animal does not sit erect. A pregnant woman [should] not eat wallaby because the child might develop epilepsy and have seizures during the full moon. (Counts 1985: 162)

For the Maisin in the Sepik Region of Papua New Guinea, various species of fish are prohibited, as are crabs, which inhibit the production of milk. Mangoes and pumpkin are to be avoided during lactation, as they'll turn the baby's skin yellow (Tietjen 1985: 129). For the Bambara and Bakong there are pregnancy taboos against eating most types of game (Bril *et al.* 1989: 309). The Drysdale River Aboriginals forbid many "bush delicacies," including wild turkey and emu (Hernandez 1941: 125). On the other hand, we do find cases where a mother's food cravings are indulged, as among the Hmong (Liamputtong 2009: 162).

Food taboos are often woven into a broad theory of illness and health: in Guatemala, pregnancy provokes a "hot" state so, to protect mother and fetus, cool foods are recommended (Cosminsky 1994: 201). There is little evidence that these food taboos are efficacious;[15] just the reverse may be true, especially where women are prohibited from eating fat and protein-rich meat (Einarsdóttir 2004: 70). Several studies have shown lower birth-weights

---

[15] A modern parallel can be found in the explosion in sales of higher-priced "organic" baby-foods to "protect" infants from pesticides and additives in regular baby-food.

for babies born to malnourished women (Spielmann 1989: 323). One careful study in four African societies determined that, in at least one, overall fertility was reduced by 5 percent as a result of malnourished women obeying food taboos (Aunger 1994). The Masaai (East African pastoralists) pregnancy diet is positively guaranteed to harm the fetus, as "the woman abandons her normal diet and exists on a near starvation diet" (de Vries 1987b: 170).

Of course, foods are not the only things to be avoided. "In Fiji nothing tight must be worn around the mother's neck lest the umbilical cord strangle the foetus" (Ritchie and Ritchie 1979: 43). For the same reason, Maisin mothers-to-be must not wear necklaces, make string bags, or encounter spider-webs. "When going along a path towards the garden, they must either be preceded by another person or hold a large leaf in front of them to break any webs that might block the path" (Tietjen 1985: 125).

Anthropologists refer to beliefs of this sort as "sympathetic magic." A connection is made between a symptom of the child's and a similar attribute in something that may have been ingested or encountered by the mother during pregnancy. In the Kaliai epilepsy example, note that the wallaby is a small kangaroo that locomotes in sudden, rather jerky movements.

Women may be so concerned about potential miscarriage, deformity, or the neonate's failure to thrive that an elaborate fiction is played out. The Baganda – small-scale subsistence farmers in East Africa – do not have a term for fetus and discuss pregnancy through euphemisms like "'some disorder has caught me' or even 'syphilis has caught me'" (Kilbride and Kilbride 1990: 104). In the Himalayan kingdom of Ladakh, women "hide or conceal their pregnancy to avoid the evil eye" (Wiley 2004: 103). An expectant Ashanti mother is in a liminal or intermediate state and is both vulnerable and a danger to others (Rattray 1927: 187).

Another chapter in our hypothetical folk medical handbook covers labor and delivery. In Bisayan villages in the Philippines, a woman in labor may be given a concoction including dried manure with the idea that, as her stomach violently expels this vile stuff, her uterus will expel the fetus (Hart 1965). Folklorists have collected many such customs, which, sympathetically, emulate unlocking, opening, untangling, and expelling (Bates and Turner 2003). Generally speaking, women during delivery are expected to be stoic, "enduring pain in silence" (Bengali – Afsana and Rashid 2009: 128), although, in many societies, they are also comforted by the presence of a midwife and/or other women (Truk – Fisher 1963: 535).

Also common is the provision of a separate structure or a specially designated area in the forest for the actual birth. In Qiqiktamiut (Inuit) society, a tent or igloo is constructed and provisioned for use as a birth hut – where the expectant mother will be lodged at the commencement of labor (Guemple 1969: 468). Ju/'hoansi women who survive in the rugged Kalahari espouse a "cultural ideal of giving birth outdoors in the bush alone. This ideal is usually achieved after the first birth, which *is* attended by older female relatives" (Biesele 1997: 474). A Yanomamo woman will give birth in the forest near by, with only women in attendance. Men are said to become ill if they are present. The pregnant woman squats on a log, and another woman, usually the mother or a sister, holds her from behind. At birth the infant drops onto banana leaves. The baby is quickly picked up and washed with water before being given to its mother (Peters 1998: 123). Another group from the South American rainforest – the Pirahã – prefer that women give birth in the river (in spite of the presence of caimans, piranhas, and anacondas), alone, without assistance (Everett 2014).

Seclusion of the mother and new infant is an extremely common practice (Holmes 1994: 222).[16] "For the first forty days after the birth, the [Vlach] hut or house after dusk is like a city under siege, with windows boarded, the door barred, the salt and incense at strategic points such as the threshold and window cracks to repel any invasion of the Devil" (Campbell 1964: 154). While one function of seclusion may be to protect them from communicable disease, another function may be to provide, in effect, a privacy curtain to allow the discreet termination of an unwanted infant's life (Caldwell and Caldwell 2005: 210). This function is specifically acknowledged when an Onitsha (Nigerian farming community) woman gives birth to twins, an abomination that could be discreetly erased in seclusion (Bastian 2001: 18).

The new mother may not be released from these strictures at delivery; on the contrary, she and her newborn remain vulnerable and need to rest and recover. "In the *Ubugoya*, [the Japanese mother was] exempted from daily work and could concentrate on taking care of the baby" (Yanagisawa 2009: 88). The birthing house may be their home for quite a while. In Gapun-speaking villages in the Sepik area of Papua New Guinea, pregnant mothers may be threatened by sorcerers who attack with magical substances that prevent her from expelling the infant or placenta. Continued danger, post-partum, leads the mothers to remain in the "maternity house ... for weeks or months" (Kulick 1992: 93). Not only are mother and child vulnerable, they may be viewed as a danger to others (Stasch 2009: 151). In China *zuoyuezi* or seclusion is designed to "counter the ill effects of the birth pollutants and to prevent infant soul loss" (Harvey and Buckley 2009: 64). "During confinement, a [Hmong] woman's body is seen as particularly unclean, dirty, and polluted," leading to seclusion until the danger is passed (Liamputtong 2009: 168). At delivery, a Tamil mother enters a birthing house, which is:

---

[16] The Mehinacu of Brazil are a rare case in which, with the first child, *both* parents go into seclusion – for up to a year (Gregor 1970: 242).

Completely shuttered and closed during the actual delivery and ... much of the postnatal pollution period ... in order to protect the mother and baby from marauding spirits, ghosts, and demons which are attracted to all the blood and contamination ... The end of the 31 days of childbirth pollution is marked ... by a purification of the house, a ritual bath for the mother, and the shaving of the child's head. (McGilvray 1994: 48–50)

Throughout most of Christian history, the childbed was regarded with dread, even horror ... Childbirth was exclusively women's business ... that men were thankful to be relieved of and careful to distance themselves ... the pain mothers endured was ... perceived as the curse of Eve, and birth itself as a re-enactment of the Fall, requiring that both mother and child be cleansed of its polluting effects [in the] rite of "churching" ... The newborn was also regarded as a sinful polluting presence until the protective act of baptism had taken place. Even then, the "little stranger," as babies were often called, would be scrutinized for signs of original sin. (Gillis 2003: 88)

Another common element of the folk wisdom surrounding pregnancy and childbirth is the tension that may be omnipresent in the "unhappy" family. For the Mende, a difficult delivery may provoke a witch hunt – literally. When a witch is not found, the woman in labor is pressed to confess any recent adulterous mating that introduced competing sperm into her womb (MacCormack 1994: 118–119). Witchcraft – undertaken by jealous co-wives, barren women, or rivals for the husband's affection – is a common diagnosis. In any case, it behooves the expectant or new mother to throw her enemies off the scent. For the people living in the Kerkennah Islands off Tunisia,

boys are ... more desirable than girls, so preparing for the birth of a girl is sometimes used as a ruse to disinterest the envious spirits ... a mother ... will go out begging from the single women in the village to buy earrings for the baby ... [suggesting] the birth of a girl and hopefully throw[ing] the envy of the jinns (and the single women of the village) off the scent of a healthy baby boy ... after the birth ... a very fearful mother might publicly give [her son] a girl's name and dress him in female clothing for a period to ward off misfortune caused by envious influences. (Platt 1988: 273–274)

In some societies, such as the southern African Azande, it is the father and his family that are a danger to the infant, especially if there's a hint of illegitimacy. "The birth usually takes place at the home of the husband, unless the oracles have decided that it is a dangerous place; then the wife goes to her parents' or brother's home" (Baxter and Butt 1953: 72). Women may feel threatened particularly by their co-wives and mother-in-law and elect to give birth in their natal home or a clinic offering Western medical services (Einarsdóttir 2004: 73). Among the Macha Galla of Ethiopia, the mother returns to her natal home to give birth in order to avoid named (*budda* and *tolca*) harmful forces unleashed by other women in her husband's community (Batels 1969: 408). Other precautions against malevolent jealousy – common throughout the ethnographic record – include the Galla use of "bad names … usually those of the Mao or Nuak, the indigenous ethnic groups from whom the Galla took slaves [, because using] a good name may provoke the aggression of hostile people or spirits" (Batels 1969: 417). The Dongria believe the newborn gets its soul from an ancestor who looks after it, but "when enraged may also invoke fever and other illness in the child … [so parents must take steps to] please the … ancestor" (Hardenberg 2006: 66).

In a matriarchal society, such as the Ashanti (Ghana), the birth will take place in the home of the mother's parents under the care of close maternal kin. Aside from the wellbeing of mother and infant, this tradition "fixes, in a very tangible way, the lineage affiliation … of the child" (Fortes 1950: 262). Even in patrilocal societies, such as the Aka (Meehan 2005: 71) and Rotuman (Howard 1970: 27), women may elect to reside in their parents' village during the birth and infancy of their children. And research confirms that "infants residing matrilocally have significantly more alloparents and receive higher frequencies of care-giving behaviors from maternal kin" (Meehan 2005: 76). The operative force here is that the mother's kin have more certain genetic ties to the infant than do the father's kin.

Once the period of seclusion is over, the mother returns to her work, and a celebratory rite of passage may follow. The Azande hold a feast in which the child is taken from the hut and passed through the smoke from a greenwood fire. The whole community is involved, prominently the kin of both parents. However, the celebration is restrained to the extent that the midwife goes unpaid and the infant unnamed until "it is certain that the child is hale" (Baxter and Butt 1953: 72). Among the Lepcha of Sikkim, the first three days of the newborn's life pass with no acknowledgment of its birth. In effect, it is still in the womb, and it is referred to as "rat-child." Only after the house and its members have been thoroughly cleansed will the infant be welcomed into the world of humans with a special feast (Gorer 1967: 289). The fourth-night welcoming party on Gau Island (Fiji Islands) is called "falling of the umbilical cord" (Toren 1990: 169). In Ladakh, the newborn's welcoming party (*rdun*) – celebrated by the assembled with barley beer, music, and dance – is delayed a month; even then, the child won't necessarily be named and "there appears to be no hurry to do so" (Wiley 2004: 125).

But the child may not *always* be welcomed by its kinfolk, nor even by its mother. What then? In the next section we examine the widespread practice of infanticide.

Gene roulette

Lower probability of parentage for males does tend to make them less likely than females to provide care. (Queller 1997: 1555)

When one child must be sacrificed so others can be saved, it is apparently a cross-cultural universal that the youngest is the likeliest victim. (Salmon 2005: 509)

There is every indication that, absent accessible and reliable contraception, abortion, abandonment, and infanticide always have been and will continue to be "common," at least according to modern sensibilities. Successive surveys of the ethnographic literature are consistent with this view (Devereux 1955: 134; Ford 1964: 51). John Whiting (1977) found that in a sample of ninety-nine societies, infanticide was specifically noted in eighty-four. A much larger and more complex study of nearly four hundred societies, similarly, found infanticide practiced in 80 percent (Mays 2000: 181). Given the ease of concealing the act, and the possible stigma attached, the practice is undoubtedly more widespread than these data suggest. And then there's physical abuse and neglect (Das Gupta 1987), which take a toll that's almost impossible to estimate. For example, anthropologists have documented many cases of culturally sanctioned dietary taboos and feeding patterns aimed at very young children that may have the unstated effect of culling the less vigorous (Lepowsky 1987; Scrimshaw 1978; Langness 1981; Miller 1987; Cassidy 1980). In the most recent survey of infanticide, of sixty societies, thirty-nine show definite evidence of the practice (Daly and Wilson 1984: 490).

For the Yuqui (South American forest nomads) there are a variety of circumstances that might lead to abortion or infanticide.

The first pregnancy was almost always aborted since this child was considered weak.[17] Abortion was accomplished by having the woman's husband or mother kneel on her abdomen until she expelled the fetus. This was termed "breaking the child" (*taco siquio*) ... A woman still nursing a child or who for some other reason did not want to give birth would use the same method to terminate her pregnancy. When women were angry at their husbands, they might kill their children, particularly boys, in retaliation ... In the case of a nursing child who lost its mother, sacrificing the infant to appease the mother's spirit as well as to resolve the problem of finding someone to care for the baby was common. (Stearman 1989: 88–90)[18]

Many grounds for infanticide were positively sanctioned by the community including adultery (six out of fifteen cases observed among the Eipo – Schiefenhovel

---

[17] This is mentioned as Yanomamo practice as well, suggesting that it may be more widespread in South America. Young mothers may be so poorly nourished that their first-born is at risk (Peters 1998: 123).

[18] But Stearman's ethnography also makes clear the great care with which the Yuqui protect the viability of the fetus and newborn under favorable circumstances. The historical record also indicates that the unfettered practice of infanticide is associated with improved treatment of children, who "are more likely to be mourned deeply when they do die" (Golden 1990: 87).

1989). Among the Masaai, every male newborn was subject to a paternity trial. The infant was placed in the pathway of the clan's cattle returning to the homestead in the evening. "If, in this process, the baby was killed, or so badly injured that he died, he is thought to have been a bastard child" (de Vries 1987b: 171).

The Inuit, among others, were known to cull females in anticipation of high mortality among males through hunting accidents, homicide, and suicide (Dickemann 1979: 341). Multiple births were often seen as unlucky (de Vries 1987b: 171). In medieval Europe, it was believed a woman could not conceive twice (simultaneously), so twins could not be from the same father. A woman might abandon twins to protect her reputation (Shahar 1990: 122). Mothers are unable to sustain two infants, especially where both are likely to be underweight. As Gray (1994: 73) notes, "even today, with the availability of western medical services it is difficult to maintain twins." On Bali, which is otherwise extraordinary in its elevation of babies to very high esteem, giving birth to more than one child at a time is seen as evidence of incest. Priests consider the birth of twins as sub-human or animal-like (Lansing 1994; Barth 1993; Belo 1980). Similarly, the Papel (Guinea-Bissau) believe that

it is *mufunesa* to give birth to many children at the same time like animals. Pigs have many offspring. Human beings give birth to only one each time. Therefore twins have to be thrown away. If not, the father, the mother, or somebody in the village may die. (Einarsdóttir 2004: 147).

Among the !Kung, Nancy Howell found that mothers whose toddlers had not been weaned might terminate the life of their newborn. In a society with high infant mortality (IM), an unweaned but otherwise thriving child is a better bet than a newcomer of unknown viability. The mother is *expected* by the band to kill one of a pair of twins or an infant with obvious defects. She would not be committing murder because, until the baby is named and formally presented in camp, it is not a person (Howell 1979: 120). We can juxtapose this picture – paralleled in pre-modern communities the world over – with the almost legendary affection and love the !Kung show their young (Konner 2005). Similarly, Trobriand Island (Papua New Guinea) women, who also shower affection on their children, "were surprised that Western women do not have the right to kill an unwanted child . . . the child is not a social being yet, only a product manufactured by a woman inside her own body" (Montague 1985: 89).

The decision to raise, abandon, or destroy a newborn is not only governed by immediate concerns. Fertility may be driven by a broad array of beliefs that establish an "ideal" family size as well as assigning relative value to male versus female offspring.

Pink ribbons or blue, many or few?

The dowry system makes every [Sicilian] daughter represent a debt that sooner or later must be paid. (Chapman 1971: 30)

When you have lots of children, there is lots of help for the family ... if you are sick, your children can help. (Ngandu – Hewlett 2013: 128)

In the Andes, Quechua farmers/herders have created a society in which there is relative parity of men and women. Both play critical roles in subsistence and both participate in the modern economy to some degree. This might explain why Bolin finds that South American Chillihuani parents treat their children largely the same, regardless of sex. This includes dress during infancy (Bolin 2006: 36). A display of equanimity toward the sex of one's new baby is more common among foraging peoples, again, where status differentials of any kind, but particularly between the sexes, are minimized. For example,

the Chewong are a small group of aboriginal people of the tropical rain-forest of the Malay Peninsula. Traditionally they are hunters, gatherers, and shifting cultivators ... Value judgments are not attached to gender ... nor are these made the basis for further social or symbolic distinctions ... There is no cultural preference for babies of either sex. (Howell 1988: 148, 158–159)

More commonly, we find that the infant's sex is highly salient in determining its fate. Some years ago, I came across a United Nations report, on the cover of which was a picture of a mother holding on her lap a boy and girl of about the same age, possibly twins. The girl was skeletal, obviously in an advanced state of malnutrition, the boy robust and healthy. He sat erect, eyes intent on the camera; she sprawled, like a rag doll, her eyes staring into space. That picture and what it represented has haunted me ever since. In high-caste India, where daughters can neither contribute to the household economy nor find a marriage partner,[19] girls are a burden, which families easily shed. One estimate put the number of "missing" women at 41 million (Deka 1993: 123), and "there are grim reports that a few villages in the north-western plains [of India] have never raised one daughter" (Miller 1987: 99). Some hospitals in India now ban amniocentesis (and presumably ultrasound as well) because

---

[19] India presents a classic Catch-22. Families use daughters to enhance their status by marrying them into higher-status families, an arrangement facilitated by the payment of dowry. Hence in families at the top of the caste structure, there is no one of higher rank to match their daughter to. On the other hand, girls aren't trained for a trade or profession because to do men's work, to venture out into the world, spoils their value as future wives/mothers. However, as the Indian economy modernizes, opportunities for girls and women will be enhanced.

a female fetus is inevitably aborted (Miller 1987: 103), and China has prohibited such procedures altogether for the same reason.[20]

Esther Boserup first noted that, in the transition to plough agriculture, women's contribution to farming along with their relative worth and autonomy plummeted (Boserup 1970). Other forms of agricultural intensification, including the adoption of irrigation, also diminish women's contribution to subsistence (Martin and Voorhies 1975). In the Highlands of Papua New Guinea, where women are the primary food producers, clans must pay an enormous bride-price in pigs and other valuables to acquire a woman in marriage. By contrast, in high-caste India, where women play almost no role in subsistence,[21] a family must provide a dowry to induce a higher-status family to take their daughter in marriage (Rao 1993; Naraindas 2009: 99).

Customary arrangements for caring for the elderly also come into play. Except in the rare matriarchy, sons are expected to inherit the family farm or business and, with these resources, care for elderly parents. Daughters marry out. They leave their parents to join their husband's family. In Bangladesh, children's farm and household labor set against the "cost" to raise them has been measured by economists. The break-even age is around fifteen and sons remain in their natal home for several more years, yielding their parents a "profit." Girls are married and gone before fifteen, carrying precious family resources with them as dowry (Caine 1977). This equation creates an atmosphere like that found in Hokkien (Taiwan) villages where a girl's fate was decided shortly after her birth. "If the family had a surfeit of girls, she was simply allowed to slip into a bucket of water" (Wolf 1972: 54). More recently on the Chinese mainland, new mothers of a girl baby might expect to be "blamed, abused, or sometimes abandoned" (Johnson 2004: 5). Or, worse, they might be forced to give her up in order to more quickly "gain another chance to produce a boy" (Johnson 2004: 30). Similarly, among the Yomut of Turkmenistan,

---

[20] Technology became available in the mid-1980s permitting parents to identify the sex of the fetus, which facilitated the selective termination of females. The result has been a sharply skewed sex ratio in China, Pakistan, and India. So, today, tens of thousands of young Asian men are "bare branches" of the family tree that won't bear fruit. They are unable to mate because they lack the means to acquire now-scarce females. Social analysts believe this will have a profound destabilizing effect, as bare branches are prime candidates for crime and violence (Hudson and den Boer 2005). Further, Goodkind argues that selective abortion is preferable to selective infanticide (or abuse and neglect), which would be the likely alternative (Goodkind 1996). Interestingly, because the USA has not banned medically assisted sex selection (Canada and the EU have), it has become a Mecca for foreign parents-to-be, especially from China. A couple may spend their life savings to visit the US to have sex-specific embryos harvested from the mother's store and implanted in her uterus (Hudson and den Boer 2005).

[21] An implication that hasn't been discussed is that the care of children is not seen as a vital woman's role, since childcare is usually delegated to older siblings and grandmothers.

when a child dies, neighbors come to offer condolences, and it is customary to say to the bereaved, "May God give you another son!" This is said whether the deceased child was a boy or a girl. When a girl is born, especially if a series of births has produced girls, it is common practice to give the girl a name expressing a wish for a son. Names such as "Boy Needed" (*Oghul Gerek*) or "Last Daughter" (*Songi Qiz*) are common for girls. (Irons 2000: 230)

Nursing is another arena where sex preferences play out (Wolf 1972: 60). In rural Lebanon, girls are weaned a year earlier than their brothers, because:

long nursing will pamper her. If the girl does not early learn to control herself she will later bring shame upon her family ... Among the bottle-fed babies, boys were more likely to be fed from a standard store bought bottle and girls from an improvised bottle. (Williams 1968: 30, 33)

While male preference and selective female infanticide is the norm (Dickeman 1975: 129), anthropologists are finding examples of *female* preference. Because girls may so effectively serve as "helpers at the nest," in Japan, where boys are preferred, parents hope the first child will be female so she can assist with the care of her future male siblings (Skinner 1987 cited in Harris 1990: 218). Several studies confirm that, if the first-born is a daughter, a woman's completed fertility is increased (Turke 1988; Crognier and Hilali 2001). In Polynesia, Tongans acknowledge that girls are easier to manage than boys; they're more compliant.[22] They also mature faster socially and physically (Morton 1996: 105). Girls are preferred in the relatively rare matriarchal societies (Lepowsky 1985: 77; Clark *et al.* 1995). North American Hopi Indian mothers say "you raise up a daughter for yourself," whereas "you raise up a son for somebody else" (Schlegel 1973: 453).

One thorough study compared Hungarian Gypsies (matriarchal) with mainstream Hungarian (patriarchal) society. Gender preferences were as expected and behaviors tracked preferences. Gypsy girls were extremely helpful to their mothers and tended to remain at home longer than their brothers, helping even after marriage. They were nursed longer than their brothers, while Hungarian boys were nursed longer than their sisters. "Gypsy mothers were more likely to abort after having had one or more daughters, while Hungarians are more likely to abort pregnancies when they have had sons" (Bereczkei and Dunbar 1997: 18).

Similarly in Jamaica, women are employed at much higher rates than men, who are seen as troublesome pests. This attitude carries over into a preference for daughters, which translates into a much lower survival rate for sons (Sargent and Harris 1998: 204). Parallel results obtain in the USA: "women

---

[22] Even without such evident bias, studies find that boys are more costly, physiologically, for mothers (Blanchard and Bogaert 1997).

with annual household incomes of less than $10,000 or without an adult male present were more likely to breast-feed their daughters an average of 5.5 months longer than their sons" (Cronk 2000: 214).

A change in subsistence patterns can affect preference for daughters or sons. The Mukogodo are an East African group studied by Lee Cronk who have made the transition from hunting and gathering to the pastoralism of their Masaai neighbors. But, as the Mukogodo are new to it, their herds are small and males have difficulty acquiring the necessary cattle for the bride-price. Female Mukogodo, on the other hand, are in demand from cattle-rich Masaai communities and thus serve as a conduit of wealth to their families. As a result, the gender ratio has become heavily skewed because daughters are nursed longer than sons and parents are much more likely to take their daughters for medical care than their sons (Cronk 2000: 206). However, the ancestral culture still holds sway, as "Despite their behavior, most Mukogodo mothers claim to prefer sons" (Cronk 1993: 279). For the Netsilik (Arctic hunter-gatherers) the birth of a child may trigger a clash between the parents. Ideally, the gender ratio should be equal but fathers prefer boys – their future helpers – and vice versa for mothers (Freeman 1971: 1015).

Subsistence patterns also have an impact on the preferred *number* of children. For the !Kung San moving opportunistically through the Kalahari desert, children were a burden. Unable to support themselves in the harsh environment until adolescence, they were carried constantly and nursed on demand – several times an hour and throughout the night. Infants were indulged, never disciplined, and permitted to wean themselves. As a result, inter-birth intervals (IBIs) were relatively long – four years (Draper 1976). Likewise for the Ache, who travel frequently through difficult terrain where placing a child on the ground exposes them to immediate hazards, children aren't "weaned from the back" before five (Konner 2005: 53). Their IBI is calculated to be slightly more than three years.[23] By contrast, the Hadza – another East African foraging society – inhabit territory where children *can* provision themselves from an early age and are much less burdensome. They are weaned at two-and-a-half; left behind in camp from the age of three; and are often treated rather harshly by their mothers (Blurton-Jones 1993: 405).

In Central Africa, systematic comparisons have been drawn between foragers and farmers in the same region. Bofi-speaking foragers follow the !Kung model. Babies are carried or held constantly, by mothers *and* fathers, are soothed or nursed as soon as they cry, and may wean themselves after three to four years.

---

[23] Howard Kress reports for the Ache and the Houarani that, as these foragers settle into permanent villages with public areas cleared of creatures such as snakes and bullet ants (their bite is likened to the pain of a bullet wound), "birth rates explode" (Kress, personal communication February 7, 2007).

Children are treated with the affection and respect consistent with preparing them to live in an egalitarian society where the principal subsistence strategy is *cooperative* net-hunting. Bofi-speaking farmers, on the other hand, tend not to respond as quickly to fussing and crying, are likely to pass the infant off to a slightly older sibling, and are verbally and physically abusive to children, who are treated like the farmhands they are soon to be. Bofi (farmer) mothers cover "their nipples with red fingernail polish, and/or a bandage to resemble a wound" (Fouts 2004a: 138) to initiate the weaning process, which may be completed by eighteen months (Fouts 2005: 356). Not surprisingly, "Bofi forager parents criticized them for weaning children at too young an age, describing how farmer children cried so frequently when weaned" (Fouts 2004b: 71). This comparative study replicated closely an earlier comparison between East African Aka foragers and their farmer-neighbors, the Ngandu (Hewlett *et al.* 2000). Farmers' having a Darwinian attitude toward their offspring seems consistent with a competitive culture in which status differentials are marked.

These competing strategies (or trade-offs; cf. Kaplan and Bock 2001: 5562) have been referred to as "survivorship," where (typically forager) parents[24] invest heavily in relatively few children, and "production," where less effort is expended on many infants – some of whom will survive (Blurton-Jones 1993: 406).[25] The latter strategy is more likely observed where mothers work in distant fields while their young can be more easily "minded" by siblings or grandmothers in the village (Nerlove 1974) *and* where children can, from an early age, help out with household chores, fieldwork, and herding (Sellen and Mace 1997: 888; Zeller 1987: 536). It also helps that domesticated foods and food-preparation options facilitate the creation of suitable "weaning" foods (Fouts 2004a: 135). Dogon (Mali) farmers can serve as an archetypal example of the "production" strategy. Their children are so poorly nourished that many starve. Women are almost constantly pregnant, but when a woman secretly took contraceptives after her ninth child, her husband, thinking she'd entered menopause, took another, younger wife (Dettwyler 1994: 158). Interestingly, as the !Kung relinquished their peripatetic lifestyle to settle down as gardeners and ranch-hands during the 1970s, their reproduction strategy switched over as well (Lee 1979).

---

[24] The Agta are an exception to this pattern. Agta foragers inhabit remote mountain territory in the Philippines and, uniquely, women hunt using the tools and methods "normally" employed by men. Despite this evidence of egalitarianism, "women have many children, have short birth intervals, and lose many infants ... approximately forty-nine per cent of prepubescent children die" (Griffin and Griffin 1992: 300).

[25] Another way to characterize this distinction is to contrast "slow" and "fast" life history strategies (LHSs). Species, communities, and individuals pursuing the former strategy spend more time growing; begin reproducing later; and have fewer offspring; to which they devote greater attention. A fast LHS means early onset of reproduction, multiple offspring, and minimal care (Schlegel 2013: 303).

Kramer draws a comparison between a trio of South American foraging bands, where eighteen-year-olds are still dependent on relatives to supply about 20 percent of their calories (Kaplan 1994), and Mayan farming villages where:

> juvenile economic dependence ends and positive net production is achieved well before males and females leave home and begin families of their own. Females achieve positive net production at age twelve, the mean age at marriage is nineteen ... Males become net producers at age seventeen, also prior to the average age of marriage, which is twenty-two. (Kramer 2002: 314)

In South/Central America there are two contrasting reproduction models (LeVine 1988). The Maya value having lots of children – of either gender – whereas the Machiguenga, Piro, and Ache clearly value reproductive restraint. But, regardless of which strategy seems paramount, abortion and infanticide will be employed to eliminate unwanted children, and there will be an array of customs designed to preserve those children who are wanted.

Promoting survival

A fat baby is considered to be a healthy one. (Lepowsky 1985: 64)

More than 60 percent of all [Bonerate] children born in Miang Tuu die before the age of three ... This grim fact may be reflected in the attitude toward infants. The major goal of their parents during the first three years is to keep them alive; the demands of enculturation are low. (Broch 1990: 19)

In this section, we sample from among a rich array of customs that buttress infant care. One set of customs supports continuous, prolonged nursing, which provides nutrition for the current baby and may also forestall pregnancy. Daniel Sellen has created a model of the ideal infant-feeding program that includes the immediate onset of nursing so the infant benefits from immunogens found in colostrum, and at least eighteen months of breastfeeding,[26] supplemented, from six months, by appropriate foods. Unfortunately, few infants, even in developed countries, enjoy this ideal (Sellen 2001). The Datoga (East African pastoralists) believe "that the colostrum would give the infant digestive problems, because early milk was thought to be 'too heavy' for the infant's stomach" (Sellen 1998b: 485–486). Nor is this omission unusual. In a survey of fifty-seven societies, in only nine did nursing begin shortly after birth (Raphael 1966).

The length of the inter-birth interval (IBI) is a key factor in an infant's survival. A minimum IBI of three to four years is ideal. In a study conducted in the USA – where we enjoy sophisticated obstetrics and calorie-rich

---

[26] The range in Sellen's survey is six to thirty-six months (2001: 236).

diets – women who gave birth eighteen months or sooner after the birth of a previous child were 50 percent more likely to deliver a premature baby and/or a baby with "adverse perinatal outcomes" (Conde-Agudelo *et al.* 2006: 1809). In the village, early weaning replaces a sanitary, easily digestible and nutritious food with an alternative that may be none of these. A common outcome is frequent diarrhea and the attendant weakening and susceptibility to disease and parasites (Gray 1994: 72).

It turns out that frequent, prolonged nursing and permitting the infant to handle the breast freely increase production of the prolactin hormone, which, in turn, makes conception less likely (Konner and Worthman 1980). Another way in which nature contributes to increasing IBI is through post-partum depression following a miscarriage, stillbirth, or infant death. Binser notes that depression elevates cortisol and leaves the mother lethargic and sleepy, which may just serve to put off the next pregnancy until she has had a chance to recoup her vigor (Binser 2004).

Nature is aided by culture in promoting longer IBIs through injunctions that militate against long intervals between nursing bouts. Frequent, round-the-clock nursing maintains high prolactin levels. The post-partum taboo on intercourse between husbands and wives also plays a critical role in spacing births. In Fiji, a nursing mother must cease fishing because the cold water will sour her milk. Aside from fishing, she should avoid traveling any distance from the village as well because she may not be available when her infant is hungry. Were she to become pregnant, her nursling might develop *save* – wobbly legs. If she succumbs to the temptation to resume sexual relations, she runs the risk of falling ill herself (West 1988: 19).

Whittemore's Mandinka (Senegal) informant explained that:

first I gave the breast to Fatu, who held it and gave it to Séku, and so on, naming her way through the ordinal sequence of her offspring. This suggests not only that her breasts define her role as mother, but also that they temporarily belong to the nursling whose milk they contain. (Whittemore 1989: 97)

The notion of a succession of infants "owning" the breast is complemented, in the Gambia, by the notion that a woman's age is measured not in a linear fashion but as a reservoir of life that is "used up" by successive births (Bledsoe 2001).

Frequent nursing is complemented by a concern for the *quality* of the breast milk. Kaliai parents, for example, are cautioned to avoid sex because semen poisons the milk[27] – especially the semen from a male who's not the infant's father. Nursing and the post-partum taboo on sex should continue until the child is able to recount "its dreams or when it is old enough to gather

---

[27] This notion was common in Europe at least until the nineteenth century (Pollock 1983: 50).

shell-fish ... about three years of age" (Counts 1985: 161). Elsewhere in Papua New Guinea, the Enga see the man's semen as a component of his war magic. Were this potent substance to mix with breast milk the result for the infant could be fatal (Gray 1994: 67). The couple may be aided in avoiding temptation by separating. The wife may be lodged in a birthing or "lying-in" house (Lepowsky 1985: 64), or secluded in her own home, until, in the Trobriands, "mothers lost their tans and their skin color matched that of their infants" (Montague 1985: 89). The expectant mother may move back to her natal home just prior to giving birth and remain there for a prescribed period. A new father may move into the men's house or, in a larger communal dwelling, move his sleeping mat some distance away from his wife's.

A nursing mother who becomes pregnant may be treated with repugnance (Basden 1966: 188). The young Gogo woman can expect to be publicly ridiculed by the community, by senior women, in particular (Mabilia 2005: 83). There must be considerable tension involved, nonetheless, as she must also be concerned about alienating the affections of the child's father. On the Micronesian island of Truk, when "the post-partum sexual taboo prove[s] especially frustrating, sexual relations may be arranged with the wife's sisters and the brothers' wives" (Fisher 1963: 532). Among M'buti foragers in Central Africa, where polygyny is not an option, "There is no ... prohibition against sleeping with other women, least of all unmarried girls" (Turnbull 1978: 212).

Of course nursing is not the only aspect of mother-infant relations that comes in for attention. The ethnographic record includes numerous examples of cultural traditions aimed at restoring the mother's health following childbirth. For example, the traditional Malay view – but common throughout Southeast Asia – is that pregnancy is a hot state and that with parturition the mother plunges into a dangerously cold state. Aside from diet, elaborate steps will be taken – accurately referred to as "mother roasting" – to restore her equilibrium.[28]

Other traditions highlight the fragility of infants, and urge special efforts on their caretakers to keep them alive (Guemple 1979: 42). In Sarawak villages children are "never punished physically so as not to scare off their souls ... [they] must be handled with the greatest care at least till they are about four years old when they become more secure" (Nicolaisen 1988: 199).

The Javanese feel that a baby is extremely vulnerable ... if the baby were suddenly or severely disturbed by a loud noise, rough handling, strong taste ... his weak psychic defences would fail and evil spirits (*barang alus*), which hover constantly around the mother and child, could ... cause him to be ill ... infant care can be seen as an attempt to ward off this danger. The baby is handled in a ... gentle, unemotional way. (Geertz 1961: 92)

---

[28] Cases of third-degree burns from this treatment are not unknown (Manderson 2003: 142–143).

A "fussy" baby is often thought of as possessed. On Luzon the cure involves fumigating the mother and child over a smoky fire. The smoke "shields the doors, the windows ... with preventive powers" (Jocano 1969: 30). Later in life, a sick child is fumigated by burning the preserved hair from his first haircut (Jocano 1969: 32).

In more complex societies, the precautionary measures undertaken after the birth may become quite elaborate. In Japan, the mother and baby emerge from her mother's house only after the viability of the newborn seems assured. Prior to a visit to the *hatsu-miyamairi* tutelary shrine for blessings, a series of ceremonies in the home solidifies the child's hold on life, because "the baby's soul is believed not to be firmly implanted in its body during this period, and is therefore surrounded by many dangers" (Sofue 1965: 152). Various rites promote the infant's continued health and development, such as the *yuzome* ceremony (first hot bath), *kizome* (new clothes provided by the maternal grandmother), and *kamisori* (first head shaving) (Sofue 1965: 150). In Java a similar series of rites, such as the first time the child is allowed to touch the ground or the first haircut, occur at regular intervals marking each transition to a "more secure stage in life" (Jay 1969: 99).

The whole village carefully scrutinizes the new mother and feels free to chastise and correct her.[29] Indeed this policing mechanism may extend to visitors. Achsah Carrier and I both did fieldwork on Ponam Island (ocean foragers and traders) in the North Bismark Sea accompanied by our children. My experience was quite similar to hers:

when I went back for my first visit with my son ... The women began right away to correct my behavior and insist that I ... feed my son, wash him, dress him and carry him properly at all times. They were angry if I did not and would tolerate no excuses ... women came running out of their houses to yell at me for carrying him improperly or not holding my umbrella at the right angle to provide him with shade. (Carrier 1985: 189–190)

Pragmatic advice is mixed with appeals to the supernatural. A Mandinka mother needs to purchase from a shaman antelope horns filled with "medicine" to wear around her waist to guard her fetus against malevolent spirits during pregnancy. After the birth, it is customary to provide the child with amulets of various kinds: "the mother gathers grains of sand or earth from the birth place, a bit of charcoal from her hearth, all of which are later packed and sealed in leather sewn charms (*boro*) soon to be tied to the child's wrist"

---

[29] Field and colleagues, working with Haitian immigrant mothers in Miami, find these mothers often have difficulty feeding their offspring, who are therefore hospitalized for dehydration and malnutrition at a high rate (Field *et al.* 1992: 183). I think it's possible these young women immigrants lost the opportunity to learn how to care for infants from older women.

(Whittemore 1989: 86). "Among the Bofi ... infants and children are adorned with magical waist cords, necklaces, bracelets, and charms to protect them from ... taboos, sorcery, dangerous animals ... and cold temperature" (Fouts 2005: 353). It is worth noting that these practices are applied prophylactically on the assumption that all children are in jeopardy. "This notion, that through special treatment children can be saved from the death which has overtaken their predecessors, finds widespread expression in Eastern Africa" (James 1979: 204). The Uduk ratchet up their efforts for a *Gurunya* – a newborn whose mother has had difficulty keeping alive previous offspring:

> The normal rite for taking a baby out consists of carrying him through the front door of the hut ... But [for] the Gurunya baby a ... special hole is made in the hut wall. The Gurunya is carried round ... the village and laid at the door of each hut, where he is given some little presents such as a cob of maize ... Two important themes dominate this rite ... One is the idea of his being "led" carefully into it ... The other ... is that of the child being a charge upon the whole community. Everyone should contribute to his "rescue" or "adoption." (James 1979: 213–215)

There are reports of culturally prescribed methods for strengthening the infant. Infants may be massaged for reasons ranging from stimulating their physical development (Einarsdóttir 2004: 93) to "soothing them to sleep" (Morton 1996: 62). Mandinka grandmothers massage the infant to get its "body ready for the multiple caregivers upon whom [it] will depend" (Whittemore 1989: 89). Regardless of the folk rationale, if we extrapolate from research in neonatal medicine, it's likely that this sort of stimulation does increase the infant's chances of survival.

Unfortunately, an objective appraisal reveals that many customs are not efficacious; if anything, they may be harmful. In the next section we will review culturally sanctioned infant and childcare practices aimed at diagnosis and cure.

Illness and folk medicine

The high rate of infant mortality may explain the fact that all of the Attic [Greece] reliefs depicting babies are dedicated to healers such as Asklepios and Pankrates. (Lawton 2007: 45)

Childhood, according to the seventeenth-century French cleric Pierre de Bérulle, "is the most vile and abject state of human nature, after that of death." (cited in Guillaumin 1983: 3)

Infancy [in the Victorian era] represented such a precarious existence that parents regarded it essentially as a state of illness. (Calvert 2003: 67)

It may seem a macabre subject to dwell on, but the pervasiveness of infant treatments that undermine rather than enhance their health deserves at least some attention. Infants might be tightly swaddled for lengthy periods, resulting in suppurating sores (de Mause 1974: 11; Friedl 1997: 83). A Pilgrim-era prescription for rickets ran: "Dip the child in cold water, naked in the morning, head foremost" (Frost 2010: 34). In ancient Egypt, children in pain were treated with widely recorded nostrums the ingredients of which included an opiate and fly excrement (Halioua and Ziskind 2005: 83–84). In Southwest Iran, Deh Koh villagers "protect" infants when the grandmother dips a finger in cow dung and sticks it into the newborn's mouth. This guards against the "child-stone," a favored tool of jealous sorcerers. "In order to purge the child's body from the impurities of the mother's blood in the womb . . . incisions are made . . . on various parts of the body. A baby was said to need such purging again whenever it cried a lot" (Friedl 1997: 59). Bloodletting sickly (or cranky) babies is practiced by the Pamirs in Tadjikistan. Different sites (roof of the mouth, for example) are bled depending on the child's symptoms" (Keshavjee 2006: 76).

Malaria is a very common childhood malady and the Zaramo people attribute the symptoms to "a coastal spirit (*mdudu shetani*) that takes the form of a bird and casts its shadow on vulnerable children on moonlit nights." The stricken child is immediately bathed in its mother's urine: "the smell of urine is believed to repel the spirit in possession of the child's body" (Kamat 2008: 72–74). This repulsion strategy is fairly common. When a typhoid or cholera epidemic strikes, the Dusun believe that supernaturals will refuse to "eat" a really filthy child, and they take appropriate steps (Williams 1969: 92). When asked why the Zaramo child was brought to a *mganga* rather than to a government clinic, parents explained that the injection "needle will puncture the skin and allow malevolent spirits to enter the body, causing rapid death" (Kamat 2008: 75).

Childhood diarrhea is attributed to the "snake in the stomach" in southern Africa. If the child is contaminated – by the touch of his unfaithful father, for instance, or the parents' failure to perform funerary rites for a deceased relative – the snake expels the contaminants via diarrhea. Treatments are patently harmful and include denying the child food and liquids (Green *et al.* 1994: 11–15). From her work with West African subsistence farmers, Alma Gottlieb describes the Beng practice of giving babies frequent enemas because "Mothers bear great shame if clothes are soiled due to inadequate toilet training" (Gottlieb 2000: 86; see also Riesman 1992: 4). Given that diarrhea, and the consequent dehydration, are a leading cause of infant mortality (IM) worldwide (2.2 million infant and child deaths; cf. Mabilia 2000: 191), this widely reported (at least in West Africa) practice seems perverse.

A frequent folk diagnosis for child illness is family conflict, such as the machinations of a jealous co-wife (Strassmann 1997) or other relative. The Amele often attribute a child's chronic illness to a curse imposed by the mother's brother "because he has not received the full promised bride price, particularly the pork component" (Jenkins *et al.* 1985: 43). In the Ecuadorian village of San Gabriel, children often died of *colerin*, caused by drinking poisoned breast milk when the mother is distraught over her husband's affair. Hence he will be blamed for the death (Morgan 1998: 70). When an Ashanti child is sick, the shrine priest will focus on possible discord between the parents. Not surprisingly, such discord often emerges, and appropriate remorse and reform are supposed to effect a cure (Field 1970: 119). In my fieldwork in Gbarngasuakwelle, I lived (as a guest) in a large, polygynous household and the tensions were palpable. This was seen as harmful to children. The shaman (village blacksmith in this case) came often to divine the cause and, using appropriate rituals (inevitably involving the sacrifice of a chicken), would attempt to ameliorate it (Lancy 1996: 167). The pairing of child illness with familial discord in the annals of ethnography reflects a very real phenomenon, as established by Mark Flinn and colleagues. Flinn has conducted long-term studies of the pronounced impact on children's endocrine function (cortisol levels, for example) of familial instability and stress in rural villages on Dominica (Flinn and England 2002). This suggests that conflict reduction has an impact on child wellbeing even though it often appears to be a case of the tail wagging the dog: the child's illness providing a convenient pretext for addressing the "real" problem – disharmony (Howell 1988: 155).

Divorce may reduce the immediate threat but does not bode well for the child in the long run. One of the best-established findings from the field of evolutionary anthropology is for altruism, or caring for others, to be channeled by genetics. People tend to care for related individuals. Studies from the least (Hadza – Marlowe 1999) to most complex societies (urban-dwelling Xhosa – Anderson *et al.* 1999; residents of Albuquerque, NM – Anderson *et al.* 2007) consistently show that fathers are much more likely to invest in their biological children than in their stepchildren. Abuse of one's non-biological children is also more likely than abuse of biological children – referred to as the "Cinderella Effect" (Burgess and Drias-Parillo 2005: 315). Resources that flow to the mother of one's offspring are categorized as "parental effort." Investing in stepchildren is referred to as "mating effort," as it seems to be motivated by the desire to gain or maintain sexual access to the stepchild's mother (Borgerhoff Mulder 1992).[30]

---

[30] On the other hand, men are more likely to divorce their wives following the birth of a child about whose paternity they are not confident (Anderson *et al.* 2007).

Stepparents often live up to their fictional reputation (in medieval England a "meager portion ... was called a 'stepmother's slice'"; Orme 2003: 56). Indeed, studies in the USA indicate that living with a stepfather and stepsiblings leads to elevated cortisol levels, immunosuppression, and general illness (Flinn and England 1995)[31] as well as poorer educational outcomes (Lancaster and Kaplan 2000: 196). Daly and Wilson find that a child is a hundred times more likely to be killed by a stepparent than by a biological parent (1984: 499). In some respects, contemporary children may be more vulnerable to the threat of mom's boyfriend/new husband than are their village counterparts. Highly mobile urbanites are separated from kin who could be expected to care for the child while the mother was working and to protect it from harm.

But the greatest threat to the child is, probably, his next younger sibling. For example, an Ijaw woman unable to conceive or bring a child to term will be told by the diviner that her "living child ... wants no younger rivals, and that it is killing her unborn babies" (Leis 1982: 163). Among the Luo, an African pastoralist tribe, if a pregnant woman continues to nurse her infant, it will contract *ledho*. This illness "is characterized by a wasting away, becoming very thin, diarrhea, skin changes, and swelling of the stomach" (Cosminsky 1985: 38). We would recognize in *ledho* all the symptoms of malnutrition brought on, not by the "poisonous" milk, but by inadequate weaning foods. As Brenda Gray notes, the most common label for child malnutrition is *Kwashiorkor* – a term native to Ghana, translated as "the disease of the deposed baby when the next one is born" (Gray 1994: 75–76). In Morocco, there is a term linking fetus and infant, which is based on the verb "to snatch away" (Davis and Davis 1989: 80).

While many societies acknowledge the need for a "special diet" for the child[32] who is being weaned or still nursing (Lepowsky 1985: 80), the efficacy of such diets is open to question. Tibetan babies are given adult foods from four months, leading to "health problems, particularly diarrheal diseases" (Craig 2009: 156). On the other hand, Hadza babies are fed "rendered soft fat ... from the zebra, and bone marrow ... followed by a thin gruel-like mixture made of the ... ground seeds, of the baobab fruit," and this diet produces clinically well-nourished babies (Jelliffe *et al.* 1962: 910). Aside from a demonstrable shortage of food (Hill and Hurtado 1996: 319), undernutrition may be attributable to customs that support a shortening of the

---

[31] A caveat is perhaps in order. We all know wonderful stepdads – I can think of several. However, our great wealth and the absence of any apparent need to be cared for by our children in old age permits us to defy the genetic imperative.

[32] By no means all, however; the Aymara have no special weaning foods: "Give them everything, they will grow accustomed to it" (de Suremain *et al.* 2001: 52).

nursing period, such as the belief by some East African pastoralists that certain babies nurse "too much" and should, therefore, be weaned early (Sellen 1995). On Fiji, nursing beyond one year is condemned as keeping "the child in babyhood [, leading to] a weak, simpering person" (Turner 1987: 107). The Alorese use threats to discourage nursing: "If you continue nursing, the snakes will come . . . the toad will eat you" (Du Bois 1941: 114).

Worldwide, the trend to bottle-feed babies infant formula, sometimes of dubious quality, so the mother can cease nursing earlier, is deplored as very harmful to infant survival (Howrigan 1988; Trevarthen 1988).[33]

Meat is usually among the foods kept from children. This is probably harmful, as a protein shortage, in particular, is often found in recently weaned children. However, malnutrition is rarely identified by parents as the root of a child's illness. Katherine Dettwyler pointedly titled her study of the Dogon *Dancing Skeletons*, describing, in graphic detail, the horrific sight of severely malnourished children. She finds that, while the mothers are aware of something amiss, they attribute the problem to locally constructed folk illnesses and seek medicine from the anthropologist to effect a cure. When she tells them to provide the child with more food, they are skeptical. Children can't benefit from good food because they haven't worked hard to get it, and they don't appreciate its good taste or the feeling of satisfaction it gives. Anyway, "old people deserve the best food, because they're going to die soon" (Dettwyler 1994: 94–95). Yoruba mothers feed children barely visible scraps compared to the portions they give themselves. Good food might spoil the child's moral character (Zeitlin 1996: 418; also true for the Tlingit – cf. de Laguna 1965: 17). The prescription for a sick child among the Gurage tribe in southwest Ethiopia is often the sacrifice of a sheep: "The flesh of the sacrificial animal is eaten exclusively by the parents of the sick child and others who are present at the curing rite; no portion of the meat is consumed by the patient, whose illness may well stem from an inadequate diet" (Shack 1969: 296).

Overall, one has the impression that parents in resource-poor societies (recall the gerontocracy pyramid in Figure 1, Chapter 1) are investing only enough in the infant to keep it alive. But because malnutrition renders the child vulnerable to a host of other problems, death is likely. A 2010 estimate suggests that 40–60 percent of IM is "potentiated" by malnutrition (Worthman 2010: 41).

---

[33] UNICEF estimates that a formula-fed child living in unhygienic conditions is between six and twenty-five times more likely to die of diarrhea and four times more likely to die of pneumonia than a breastfed child, and these statistics have led many developing nations to ban the sale of formula and baby bottles (www.unicef.org/nutrition/index_breastfeeding.html, accessed January 9, 2013).

Accounting for death

The most common reason given for death was thus that the [Fulani] child's "time had come." Maternal displays of overt grief, or even concern, for a child's death are considered to be ... un-motherly, because a mother who cries at her child's death is seen as impeding its chances in the afterlife. (Castle 1994: 322)

A hard exterior shell was a necessity amongst the village poor to protect them from the grief of repeated infant deaths. (Heywood 1988: 39).

In the modern, industrialized world, IM is almost unknown: five deaths per 10,000 live-born children. By contrast, the figure for Africa is 150 per 10,000, and it is significantly higher in very poor or strife-torn areas. Child mortality is linked to the quality of the neonatal environment, and the prevalence of infectious and parasitic diseases. "Acute respiratory infections and diarrhea together are at the root of approximately one third of child deaths" (UNICEF 2004: 4). In the rural Iranian village of Deh Koh, 100 percent of the children in 1994 were suffering from some combination of "avitaminoses, protein deficiencies, sub-nutrition, chronic internal parasitic infections including giardiasis and ameobiasis ... respiratory infections, eczema, cuts and bruises, bone fractures, eye diseases, toothaches" (Friedl 1997: 131).

Even among relatively affluent pastoralists such as the Datoga (Sellen 1998b: 482) and the Kashmiri Ladakh (Wiley 2004: 6), IM is at least 20 percent, with double that figure classified as malnourished. The rise of urbanization did nothing to alleviate this problem. If anything, IM was higher in the first urban environments. IM is estimated at 25–35 percent in ancient Athens (Golden 1990: 83)[34]; estimates for Europe in the Middle Ages were 30–50 percent (Hanawalt 2003); in late eighteenth- and early nineteenth-century Russia, the estimate was 50 percent (Dunn 1974: 385); and somewhat below 50 percent in eighteenth- and nineteenth-century Japan (Caldwell and Caldwell 2005: 213).

Humans have always had to cope with the loss of infants, and societies have developed an elaborate array of "cover stories" to lessen grief and recrimination (Martin 2001: 162; Scrimshaw 1984: 443). As discussed in the previous chapter, the primary strategy is to treat the infant as not yet fully human. Most importantly, if the baby is secluded initially and treated as being in a liminal state, its loss may not be widely noted. The precarious status of the newborn is reflected in naming rituals common in both the historical record and the

---

[34] In a large-scale demographic survey of hundreds of well-preserved remains covering almost a 3,500-year span (2000 BCE to 1500 CE) from coastal Chile and Peru, infant and child mortality was consistently high (50 percent by age fifteen) and did not drop appreciably with the transition to sedentism and agriculture (Allison 1984).

cross-cultural record of contemporary tribal societies (de Vries 1987b; Sharp 2002). Among the Bena-Bena, a tribal society in the New Guinea Highlands, "children were often not regarded as truly human until they had survived for several years" (Langness 1981: 14). On Vanatinai Island:

it is not customary to name a child until a few weeks after birth, and the ritual presentation by the mother's family of shell currency necklaces or greenstone axe-blades to the father's kin to "thank him" for siring a new member of the mother's matrilineage does not take place for about six months. Presumably these delays assure that naming and "child-wealth" exchanges are only performed for children who are expected to survive. (Lepowsky 1987: 78–79)

In ancient Greece, children under the age of two are never (or hardly ever) said to have died *ahoros*, "untimely" (Golden 1990: 83), and in Renaissance Italy, parents waited until their child had survived a year to register its birth – forgoing tax incentives to register it straightaway – because so many didn't survive (Klapisch-Zuber 1985: 98–99).

Treating the child as semi-human affords other opportunities to account for unfavorable outcomes. For example, when a woman experiences multiple miscarriages or early infant deaths, the Yoruba believe that, by going abroad at night, the woman has exposed her uterus to invasion by *abiku*. An "*abiku* child will come back time and again to torment the parents with its temporary presence, only to die in due course" (Maclean 1994: 160). Other societies use what I've referred to as the "trickster theory" (Lancy 2014). Among the Toradja of Sulawesi:

[such] children were ... put away in a hole that was made in a large, living tree ... The body was placed ... on end, with the head downward ... after which the hole was nailed shut with a small board. This was done so that the child's *tanoana* would not return to earth and call the *tanoana* of other children, so that the latter would also be stillborn or die soon after birth. (Adriani and Kruijt 1950: 708–709)

The Bhils take even more extreme measures to destroy the malevolence reflected in stillbirths or abnormal births and infant deaths. They dismember the corpse, stake the pieces to the ground, and burn them to drive out the *Jam* (Nath 1960: 188). It should be understood that these folk theories and treatments not only serve to dampen the sense of grief or loss but, more importantly, they deflect blame from the living. The Nankani have constructed an elaborate myth of the "spirit child not meant for this world" to explain away the tragedy of mother or infant death in childbirth and/or chronic infant sickness and, eventual, death (Denham 2012: 180). The alternative to, in effect, blaming the deceased child or "evil forces" is to blame the parents or other family/community member. And we've seen how readily this line of reasoning is adopted in the "unhappy" family. One illustration of this shielding effect is the post-mortem diagnosis – by the Fulani – of *foondu* ("the bird") or *heendu* ("the wind") as the cause of death. "These diagnoses tend to exonerate the child's caretakers, and because they are conferred by senior women in a patrilineage, they ... also encourage social support from affines for the woman whose child has died" (Castle 1994: 314).

Unfortunately, the ubiquity of infant death along with well-established coping mechanisms inures people to a phenomenon that, given the state of medical knowledge and a pharmacopeia adequate to the task,[35] shouldn't be happening. The wastage of young human life and the debilitating impact this has on mothers are staggering and cannot possibly be justified. And, in the West, we remain largely oblivious of the problem of child malnutrition and death in the Third World until it reaches such proportions that the story becomes newsworthy. And the response – the provision of massive, but too little, too late, food aid – does nothing to address the underlying problems (UNICEF 2004: 2).

The extremes of high and low fertility

[In rural SW Iran women – despite poor health due to high fertility] don't use birth control because they are afraid that their husbands will take another wife if they do not have a child every year. (Friedl 1997: 38)

Change in demand for children is the prime mover behind the large and enduring decline in fertility ... that has occurred in society after society during the course of modernization. (Turke 1989: 61)

The transition from foraging to agriculture was and is certainly important in influencing fertility. Demand for farm laborers creates demand for children, leading to shorter IBI, earlier weaning, higher fertility, *and* higher IM. Archaeologists studying human remains in the US southwest find that meat and wild plant foods in the diet declined as maize became the mainstay. Less protein in women's diets led to a nutritional deficit, which led, in turn, to a decline in the health of their unborn and newly born children (Whittlesey 2002: 160). Consequently, "children's health in the Southwestern US after the introduction of agriculture illustrates a pervasive pattern of high infant mortality, malnutrition, and disease infestation" (Sobolik 2002: 150). A similar pattern of severe child malnutrition in the wake of the transition to agriculture was found recently at a Neolithic site in Vietnam (Oxenham *et al.* 2008).

---

[35] For example, the role of clean water in reducing parasites and infection, or the availability of low-cost vaccines that are, nevertheless, not universally distributed. Information from Lifewater International website, www.lifewater.org, accessed January 5, 2013.

Numerous studies have shown the deleterious effects on children's health in the agriculturalist's pursuit of the "production" strategy. However, as the land is brought fully into cultivation, population-limiting mechanisms (such as the post-partum sex taboo) should develop to curtail further growth (Sear *et al.* 2003: 34). And this seems to have happened in many, many cases. However, Western influence in the past hundred years seems to have dismantled these mechanisms, including, especially, abortion and infanticide.[36] Improved nutrition and healthcare for mothers and infants has no doubt brought benefits (Kramer and Greaves 2007: 722). But missionary efforts to stamp out "pagan" practices like polygyny also undermined the post-partum taboo on intercourse, even while they simultaneously blocked the introduction of modern contraceptives (Morton 1996: 53; Hern 1992: 33). Additionally, "fashion" and commercial interests pushing infant "formula" have drastically reduced the number of infants being breastfed (Small 1998: 201). The result has been, in many parts of the world, population growth outstripping opportunities for either employment or improved food production (Hern 1992: 36; Condon 1987: 35–36). For example, from Malaita Island in the South Pacific, traditional Kwara'ae practice was to keep men separated from their nursing wives for at least a year. However, the "abolition of the *tabu* system and the ascendance of Christianity has meant that . . . ritual separation [is] no longer practiced" (Gegeo and Watson-Gegeo 1985: 240–241). As a result, fertility has jumped and families with ten to thirteen children are not uncommon.

The quality of life . . . has begun to deteriorate . . . [forest-grown] building materials . . . are now scarce . . . The carrying capacity of the land has been reached . . . resulting in continuously planted gardens, soil exhaustion, lower productivity, and less diversity in garden crops . . . Streams and rivers have been nearly fished out . . . Traditionally, food exchanges among households ensured sharing in times of . . . famine or flood [but] in the past 20 years there has been a reduction in food exchanges, influenced by lower garden productivity and the growth of the cash economy. (Gegeo and Watson-Gegeo 1985: 239–240)[37]

Living conditions following the cessation of population limiting mechanisms can deteriorate rapidly. Xavante women in central Brazil are so preoccupied

[36] The impact of Western influence on reproduction patterns and children's wellbeing is not well documented. Carrier's informants on Ponam spoke about a decline in IBI and increase in birth rates following the invasive presence of foreign troops during World War II (Carrier 1985: 202). And there are similar oral history accounts that identify a sharp increase in fertility associated with the establishment of permanent Western facilities – military, mission, governmental, and commercial (plantations) – in tribal areas.

[37] By contrast, the island peoples of Manus Province in Papua New Guinea apparently have obtained access to contraceptives and are using them in the face of the overpopulation confronting them (Ataka and Ohtsuka 2006).

with caring for their larger broods, they are "gradually withdrawing from participation in dances and rituals, simply because they are too tired from work" and the cultural heritage is thereby lost (Nunes 2005: 219).

Jónína Einarsdóttir and Nancy Scheper-Hughes provide thorough case studies of the next stage in this descent into extreme poverty and environmental degradation. The former studied a very poor area of Guinea-Bissau (West Africa); the latter studied Ladeiras, an even more impoverished area of northeast Brazil. Severe overpopulation has been a problem for quite some time. Land and job scarcity conspire to render men unable to support their families, leading to a breakdown, if not the dissolution of marriage. Einarsdóttir (2004: 27) reflects: "I experienced the hopelessness and desperation of the mothers. Despite heavy and incessant work they could hardly feed themselves and their children. Their husbands, and men in general, were frequently commented on as *ka bali nada* (totally worthless)." Nevertheless, when she asked mothers how many children they would prefer, many responded: "You never have too many children" (Einarsdóttir 2004: 63). Birth control is resisted[38] in part because the motive ascribed to the use of contraceptives is an adulterous liaison (Einarsdóttir 2004: 69). And in Ladeiras, a woman is said to be "used up" (*acabado*) from multiple pregnancies. Her weakness will be transferred to her fetus, who will, therefore, be born weak and thin, lacking the will or strength to battle for its own survival. Locating the problem of IM in the mother's depleted body and the infant's lack of vigor justifies the mother's neglect of the child and her emotional detachment (Scheper-Hughes 1987b, 2014).

While the plight of mothers and children in severely impoverished areas seems invisible to us, ample precedent can be found in the past. Throughout Euroamerican history, infant malnutrition and mortality rates were as high as they are today in Ladeiras or Biombo. However, the starvation, abuse, and neglect of children were largely invisible because they took place among the "lower orders" (Scheper-Hughes 1987a: 135). At the other end of the social scale, in eighteenth-century Paris (France), IBI, fertility, and IM were all affected by the mother's social status. The richest women had the shortest IBIs, highest fertility, and lowest infant mortality. Rich women[39] were able to hire the best wet-nurses to sustain their infants as they quickly became pregnant. However, on the downside, the women's bodies suffered various

---

[38] Strassman reports on the Dogon of Mali – where the per capita income in 2006 was US$470 – "USAID made condoms and . . . contraceptives available in 2010; however . . . the demand for these products in rural areas is nonexistent. The modal fertility per woman per lifetime is ten live births," fewer than half of whom survive childhood (Strassman 2011: 10895).

[39] In the upper echelons of society, fertility was probably always valued as an end in itself, unmotivated by any utility that children might have as workers. While studies still find a positive correlation between the number of offspring and wealth, the relationship is much

symptoms related to high fertility, including anemia and prolapsed uteruses (Hrdy 1992: 422).

But something was afoot in a small corner of Europe. In the Netherlands in the seventeenth century, society was shifting to the forager's "survivorship" reproduction model. At this time, the Netherlands were "modern," that is, society was highly urbanized and commercial interests took precedence over courtly customs. Protestantism had been embraced along with Weber's "work ethic." The arts and literature flourished. This liberalization of society was applied to children.[40]

In the seventeenth century, foreigners were already recording their astonishment at the laxity of Dutch parents ... they preferred to close their eyes to the faults of their children, and they refused to use corporal punishment ... foreigners remarked on something else: since the sixteenth century, most Dutch children – girls as well as boys – had been going to school. (Kloek 2003: 53)

Among the growing middle class, children were no longer viewed merely as chattel but as having inherent value. Consequently, people had fewer of them so they could afford to "pamper" and educate them (Heywood 2001: 87). A wonderful scene painted by Jan Steen between 1663 and 1665, called *The Feast of St. Nicholas*, shows a family just after St. Nick's visit. He has left toys, candy, and cake for the children.[41] There are also paintings from this era depicting a well-dressed mother reading to her one or two children. These are women with the leisure to enjoy and educate their (relatively) small broods (Durantini 1983). John Locke – exiled to Holland in 1685–1688 – was profoundly influenced by what he saw. His treatise on childrearing, published in 1693, brought Dutch ideas on childcare to England (Locke 1693/1994). At the end of the eighteenth century, the Quakers also embraced population control and used various means to reduce their fertility. "The drop in the birth rate also reflected ... a rejection of the view that women were chattels who should devote their adult lives to an endless cycle of pregnancy and childbirth" (Mintz 2004: 78).

---

weaker than in eighteenth-century bourgeois French society. Indeed, the same study finds that "better educated people have fewer biological children" (Hopcroft 2006: 106).

[40] The Dutch are still leading the way in terms of promoting liberal policies toward children. They have legalized euthanasia for terminally ill children in severe pain and are withholding heroic medical intervention for fetal and perinatal children expected to suffer severe handicaps (Vermeulen 2004) as well as severely pre-term fetuses (Lorenz *et al.* 2001). In a 2007 survey of child wellbeing in rich countries, the top two countries across the various measures were the Netherlands and Sweden. The bottom two (of twenty-one) were the USA and Britain (Adamson:2007).

[41] Rijksmuseum Amsterdam permanent collection. Can be viewed online: www.rijksmuseum.nl/en/collection/SK-A-385, accessed January 9, 2013.

It took the rest of Europe a few centuries to catch up with the Netherlands – for example, "From 1730–1750, seventy-five per cent of the [children] of greater London died by the age of five" (Sommerville 1982: 156–157) – but the change has been dramatic. Italy, which had one of the world's highest birth rates, now has one of the world's lowest,[42] in spite of the majority of the population being at least nominal members of the Catholic church, which vociferously condemns contraception. In Sweden, where women postpone childbearing to their mid-to-late twenties, the fertility rate is 1.67, in spite of extremely liberal, government-subsidized parent-support services (Welles-Nyström 1988). Worldwide, fertility rates fell from an average of 4.95 children per woman in the 1960–1965 period to 2.59 children in 2010.[43]

Many factors have contributed to what is called the "Great" or demographic transition (Caldwell 1982). First, we have repeatedly noted that individuals – backed by consensually supported social customs – *have* found ways to limit family size in the face of resource scarcity. Second, "As societies modernize, social and economic success is increasingly achieved outside the sphere of kinship" (Turke 1989: 67).[44] That is, one is no longer dependent on family for employment, and indeed, a characteristic of the modern economy is that it forces those who would be successful to relocate frequently. Hence families are surrounded by neighbors who are non-kin. Third, if parents no longer have easy access to extended family as part-time caretakers of their dependent children,[45] they will need to purchase childcare. The cost and quality of such services should have a depressive effect on fertility.[46] Fourth, successful employment requires years of formal education, an activity that is incompatible with childrearing; thus marriage and the age of first pregnancy are now delayed at least a decade beyond the onset of puberty.

---

[42] Information obtained from www.cia.gov/library/publications/the-world-factbook/rankorder/ 2054rank.html, accessed January 9, 2013.

[43] Information obtained from the CIA, available at www.cia.gov/library/publications/the-world-factbook/rankorder/2054rank.html, accessed: January 9, 2013.

[44] Among the Pare of Tanzania, Hollos finds pre- and post-transition families in a single village: some families want cherubs, others want chattel (Hollos 2002: 187).

[45] Research suggests that there is considerable cross-national variation in the persistence of extended family ties and grandmother involvement with grandchildren – high in Poland, Spain, and Italy, low in the USA, the Netherlands, and Sweden (Harkness *et al.* 2006). During a month-long visit to some of Italy's most popular vacation spots in 2011, an often-repeated scene struck me. There would be a multi-generation family enjoying the sites while a single child occupied center stage. Family members seemed to be taking turns – even competing – for the child's attention. Basically, the extended family, alloparenting cluster of caretakers was still functioning even though the necessity for this service had been sharply diminished.

[46] This assertion is supported by research showing that the middle-class birth rate is higher in northern European countries such as Norway and the Netherlands where there is strong government support for childcare leave and daycare (Shorto 2008).

Fifth, contemporary urban environments, unlike the village, are not conducive to the free-wheeling, minimally monitored playgroup.[47] Children now
have to be supervised, which carries new costs and burdens for parents. Sixth,
as we'll discuss in Chapter 5, children in the village learn much of their culture
through observation and imitation with minimal instruction from adults.
In contemporary society, training someone to become a competent member
now requires the costly services of full-time teachers, tutors, and coaches. And
parents cannot just hand over their child as an unformed lump of protoplasm to
these professionals (Jolivet 1997). They must invest a great deal of their
precious time in prepping kids for school and other demanding but necessary
institutions. Seymour documents this aspect of the transition among upwardly
mobile families in Bhubaneswar (India), providing "evidence that the child
care strategies of middle- and upper-status households were adapting to a
society increasingly characterized by an emphasis on formal education and
competition for new kinds of jobs" (Seymour 2001: 16).

Lastly, parents may still "need" children: "a child makes a couple into a
family. Childlessness is, for many, a tragedy" (Cross 2004: 5; Braff 2009: 5).
But the need can no longer be reckoned in terms of additional workers or
augmented security in old age. In short, quality meets the current need,
quantity doesn't (Lawson and Mace 2010: 57).[48] These and other changes
all reward parents who limit reproduction and punish those who do not
(Kaplan and Lancaster 2000: 283). During the economic depressions of the
1890s and 1930s, educated middle-class individuals reduced fertility – primarily by postponing marriage (Caldwell 1982). This stands in sharp contrast to
cases cited in this chapter where fertility is not reduced in the face of famine.[49]

As widespread as this transition has been, it is by no means inevitable.
Mexico represents an interesting patchwork of the old and new. Among the
emerging middle class, women sought birth-control medication on the black
market during an era when both the church and state opposed its use. As
the government, belatedly,[50] has begun to offer family planning, it is eagerly

---

[47] As we'll see in Chapter 4, villagers readily "keep an eye on" their neighbors' children. In
modern (sub)urban society where neighbors are not even friendly let alone related to each other,
such casual supervision isn't available (Spilsbury and Korbin 2004: 197).

[48] However, one consequence of having just one or two "precious" children is that parents exhibit
what borders on paranoia in their child-directed anxiety. Many fear their child might be
kidnapped and killed, despite the infinitesimally small probability of that happening (Glassner
1999).

[49] Another case of rural privation coupled with high fertility can be observed in Nepal (Baker and
Panter-Brick 2000: 165–166). One important variable appears to be life expectancy, which is
negatively correlated with fertility. Evidently, when individuals expect a short lifespan they
begin bearing at puberty and continue bearing at short IBIs thereafter (Low et al. 2008).

[50] The Mexican economy (even when the US migrant economy is included) cannot keep pace with
the post-World War II exponential population growth, even though the birth rate is now falling.

welcomed by women with seven or more years of education but rejected by women with less education (Uribe *et al.* 1994). The women interviewed in a rural village that Browner calls San Francisco "expressed sharply negative attitudes about childbearing and childrearing" (Browner 2001: 461). They were frustrated because the mandatory school attendance policy robbed them of children's labor. They were also frank about the debilitating effects on their health that frequent childbearing exacted. However, their husbands and males generally are opposed to fertility reduction and birth control. The women then "revealed an extreme reluctance to engage in socially disapproved behavior" (Browner 2001: 466).

Similarly, Kress finds that fertility has plunged among indigenous people in northern Ecuador who are enjoying great success marketing handicrafts,

Figure 7 Otavalo market, Ecuador

while it has not declined in the neighboring communities that are not involved in craft production (Kress 2005, 2007). Indeed, I visited the Otavalo market and was struck by how lavishly dressed many of the children were – they were definitely being treated as cherubs.

Even though IM rates have been falling steadily throughout the world, they're falling much more slowly or not at all in the poorest communities.[51] In 1970, eight times as many children perished in the world's five poorest than in the five richest countries; by 2000 that ratio had risen to twenty times (Gielen and Chumachenko 2004: 94). These trends are part of a worldwide phenomenon best captured by the aphorism "The rich get richer and the poor get lots of sickly children." In Nigeria, for example, the fertility rate is 5.9, with gross national income (GNI) per capita at us $260. Western Europe, on the other hand, has a fertility rate of 1.5 with a GNI of us $25,300 (Gielen and Chumachenko 2004: 85).

Indeed, in the worst-off regions of the world, it's almost as if all vestiges of rationality have disappeared. Somalia has, for decades, been beset by the twin evils of rapid degradation of the subsistence system (owing to overuse of thin soils and periodic drought) and civil war. Nevertheless, Somali women vie for the title of world's most prolific breeders, and when asked how many children they'd like, the *average* number desired was twelve (Dybdahl and Hundeide 1998: 139). In Burkina Faso, overpopulation has placed whole villages in jeopardy of starvation – if HIV/AIDS doesn't wipe them out first. Yet villagers live in complete ignorance of contraception and see no connection between sexual relations and AIDS (Hampshire 2001: 117).

Madagascar is another country where the persistence of the "production" strategy has had dire consequences. Ancestor worship has always been very important and adults must depend upon their progeny to insure the "quality of their ancestral afterlife ... [A]t a wedding ... future husbands and wives [are wished] 'seven sons and seven daughters.'" However, for decades, the island has witnessed severe erosion and spreading desertification due to land overuse. Consequently, "a large number of families can no longer even feed their children, never mind clothe them ... parents with disabled children refuse to have them fitted with artificial limbs free of charge because handicapped beggars bring in higher earnings" (Ravololomanga and Schlemmer 2000: 300, 310).

For many parts of the world, modernization will come too late. Instead of the voluntary lowering of fertility associated with the "Great" transition, the effect will be accomplished via history's oldest forms of population

---

[51] These are critical times in much of the underdeveloped world. It's as if there's a race between overpopulation and environmental disaster versus investment in human capital, including birth control (Caldwell *et al.* 1998).

control – famine and epidemic (Boone and Kessler 1999: 261; Kovats-Bernat 2006: 1). And, surprisingly, some enclaves in post-industrial society, such as among lower class African-Americans and Utah Mormons (Lancy 2008: 63–69), continue to pursue a high fertility, production strategy in spite of the unfavorable outcomes for children.[52]

---

[52] A very thorough study found that "mothers and fathers can only achieve large family size at a significant cost to the quality of care provided to individual children," leading to unfavorable child outcomes (Lawson and Mace 2009: 180).

4   It takes a village

Introduction

Most of the time spent in childcare is spent not by [Javanese] mothers, but by other household members. (Nag *et al*. 1978: 296)

There is a [Nso] saying: "A child belongs to a single person while in the womb, and after birth he or she belongs to everybody." (Keller 2007: 105)

In the fall of 1973, I took up residence in the polygynous household of Chief Wolliekollie in the Liberian village of Gbarngasuakwelle (Lancy 1996). While the chief was very gracious in welcoming me, in facilitating my research on the children of the village, and in providing me with accommodation in his sprawling house, he failed to introduce me to other members of his household. Strangers rarely visited Gbarngasuakwelle and, when they did, the chief knew they usually meant trouble and expense, so he did his best to insure their stay was short and unobtrusive. There was no protocol for dealing with a resident ethnographer.

The household consisted of three of the chief's four wives, an unmarried sister of one of them, their children, and a steady stream of temporary residents related to the chief or his wives. I gradually sorted out all the adults, and it was relatively easy to match the nursing babies with their mothers, but then I struggled for weeks to match up the various children to their respective mothers. Bear in mind that, initially at least, given my lack of fluency, I had to rely largely on observation. I was stymied because the children, once they were no longer attached marsupial-like to their mother's body with a length of cloth, spent far more time in each other's company and in the company of other kin, particularly grandmothers and aunts in nearby houses, than with their mothers. And as far as the chief was concerned, I just had to assume that since these were his wives, the majority of the children in the vicinity must be his as well. Aside from dandling the occasional infant on his knee during the family's evening meal, I never saw him enjoy more than the most fleeting interaction with a child.[1]

My impression was that, far from being the dominant influence in their children's lives, the biological parents were just two of a large cast of potential child-minders. And, even while acknowledging the mother's near-constant proximity to her nursing infant, the relationship is best described as "casual nurturance [where] ... mothers carry their babies on their backs and nurse them frequently but do so without really paying much direct attention to them; they continue working or ... socializing" (Erchak 1992: 50). Mazahua nursing mothers often display a "distracted air and pay almost no attention to the baby" (Paradise 1996: 382). Pashtu mothers rarely make eye contact with their infants when nursing unless there's a problem (Casimir 2010: 22). This seeming indifference may be reinforced by custom whereby a mother is chastised by peers if she is overly fond of her child (Toren 1990: 172). Figure 8 illustrates this phenomenon quite well.

Since I was enamored of the exotic – and what anthropologist isn't – these strange family customs were exciting. And yet, twenty years after completing my work in Gbarngasuakwelle, I began to see their family arrangements and childcare customs as neither unusual nor exotic, rather as close to the norm for human societies, and, simultaneously, to see the customs of the middle-class Utah community I live in now as extraordinary. My neighbors are predominantly adherents of the LDS or Church of Jesus Christ of Latter-Day Saints (Mormons), which maintains a very pronounced position on the nature of the family, reflected in the following: "This divine service of motherhood can be rendered only by mothers. It may not be passed to others. Nurses cannot do it; public nurseries cannot do it; hired help cannot do it" (Packer 1993: 24). There is a steady stream of moral injunctions that issue forth from the church hierarchy to the effect that a Mormon wife's calling is the production and care of children. Further, this effort should be seen as a demanding, full-time occupation.[2] While the husband is the designated breadwinner and head of the family, the LDS church goes further than perhaps any contemporary moral authority in also obligating the father to participate in childcare.

---

[1] As much as anything else, the chief, like any polygynist, is loath to stir up the cauldron of jealousy that is usually simmering in his household. Paying particular attention to any of his children might be construed by the mothers of his other children as "favoritism."

[2] I don't want to imply any uniqueness in the LDS perspective. These views on the "proper" role of women as sole caretakers and guardians of children's virtue are broadly representative of the political/religious right throughout the world (Coleman 1999: 76). Furthermore, in the US, the intensive parenting movement demands extraordinary efforts on the part of mothers, leading them to reject any and all aid from individuals (family, daycare, hospital delivery) or modern technology (prepared baby food) (Matchar 2013).

Figure 8 White Karen mother playing mouth-harp as baby nurses, north Thailand

In contrast to this view,[3] I hope to show that in the large and growing archive on comparative childcare patterns, the mother's role may be quite

---

[3] Judith Harris makes a very cogent argument that evolution would not favor exclusive reliance on biological parents, especially on the mother. The mother may be incompetent or she may perish; others – who are already "wired" to the child, so to speak – readily take up the slack. Also, the more caretakers the child has, the more "role models" she or he may learn from (Harris 1998: 119).

attenuated[4] and the father's role is, in many societies, perhaps in the majority, virtually non-existent (Gray and Anderson 2010: 168). In a telling study of West African Hausa children's ability to identify kin and construct their own genealogies: "some children omitted their parents; more than a third of the girls failed to mention their fathers" (LeVine 1974: 41).

Alloparents as mother's helpers

Guayqueries children … are almost continuously in direct touch with the skin of some other person. (McCorkle 1965: 73)

Hadza mothers are quite willing to hand their children off to anyone willing to take them. (Marlowe 2005: 188)

The notion that "It takes a village" to raise a child has become part of our national folk wisdom, immortalized in a book with that title penned by Hillary Rodham Clinton (Clinton 1996). But few people seem to have any clear sense of how the original aphorism gains its force. For many, I suspect the vision conjured up is of the child cosseted by an adoring chorus of family and neighbors. As I will demonstrate, if one actually looks at real kids in real villages, either one sees infants and young children in a group of their peers, untended by an adult, or one sees a mother, or a father, or an older sister, or a grandmother tending the child. These helpful family members are referred to in anthropology as "alloparents." The rule governing their behavior would not necessarily be "Everyone's eager to have a hand in caring for the child," but, rather, "Whoever can most easily be spared from more important tasks will take care of the child." And the next rule we might derive from our observations might be, "The mother is often too busy to tend to the child." At the same time, babies are not simply passive recipients of care. They not only *look* cute, they beguile caretakers with their gaze, their smiling and their mimicry (Spelke and Kinzler 2007: 92). While alloparents may want to minimize their effort (Trivers 1974) in caring for the child, the very young have an arsenal of tactics they can deploy to secure additional resources (Povinelli *et al.* 2005).

We'll examine the role of swaddling and similar technologies that, at least partially, relieve the mother of her burden. A contrast will be drawn between patterns of infant care and the treatment – tantamount to rejection in many cases – of toddlers (Lancy and Grove 2010: 148–149). The village is a community of caretakers and, in this chapter, we will systematically examine the roles played

---

[4] When Freudian theory was in fashion, the mother was seen as potentially harmful to her children's psychological wellbeing, so, in at least one utopian community, children were placed in the care of professionals at the earliest opportunity (Siskind 1999). The kibbutz movement embraced a similar philosophy (Spiro 1958).

by the mother, father, older siblings, and grandparents as well as the community at large. For example, "on Fiji, an un-weaned infant is as likely to be in the arms of another as with its mother" (West 1988: 22). This phenomenon is so common cross-culturally that it has its own name: "child shifting" (Lange and Rodman 1992: 190). After examining the nature of childrearing in the village, we'll conclude with a functional analysis of the radically different childrearing program utilized by contemporary parents in mid- to upper-echelon western society. The following are reasonably typical cases that introduce the notion that the "whole village" may share responsibility for childrearing.

In West Africa, the expectant Mende mother moves "back home" to have her baby and returns to her husband's home only after the baby is walking. She does this in order to take advantage of the support of her own close kin (as opposed to less supportive in-laws) during the most precarious period of her child's life. (Isaac and Feinberg 1982: 632; the Fulani as well – cf. Dupire 1963)

Central African Efe mothers are not always the first to nurse their new infant, who, at four months, will spend 60 percent of the time being cared for by many other band members. The child will, in fact, be "passed around the band, an average of 8.3 times per hour" (Tronick *et al.* 1987). Life expectancy among the Efe is low, leaving many children orphaned. A child who has been nurtured from birth by others will be cared for should the parents die. (Morelli and Tronick 1991)

[A woman] called the *tapare* ... is responsible for ... the [Ache] child's care during its first few days of life ... she will sometimes adopt her godchild if the child's mother dies ... a single man ... called *mondoare*, cuts the umbilical cord of the child with a bamboo knife. He is expected to provide for his godchild in times of need, and ... other individuals who lift and hold the child, or wash it in the first few minutes after birth, are designated as *upaire*, "those who lifted it," and they too take on a godparent-like relationship. (Hill and Hurtado 1996: 66–67)

From weaning, [Kako] children get used to a hierarchical relationship with their mother ... There is no play, no talk, no cuddle; the relationship is one of authority and obedience. In this way children learn to be emotionally independent of the mother and to fit in a wider network of kin who care for them. (Notermans 2004: 15)

In Arab society, a special kin term, *rida'a*, denotes the relationship between a child and a woman, not its own mother, who nursed it. (Altorki 1980: 233)

In Hong Kong, rather than experiencing the birth of a baby as a beginning, the new mother considers it as "a project finished." The nine-month period of symbiosis for which she is solely responsible is over. The responsibility can now be shared with others. (Martin 2001: 164)

Needing attention and clinging to the mother in lieu of alloparents are treated as symptoms of illness among rural farmers in Argentina. (Remorini 2012: 152–153)

There were numerous constraints put on young [Orissa India] mothers to prevent them from focusing too much attention on a new infant. Close, intimate mother-child bonds were viewed as potentially disruptive to the collective well-being of the extended family ... In such families, much early child-care was organized so as to subtly push the infant away from an exclusive dependence on its mother toward membership in the larger group. (Seymour 2001: 15)

These are not isolated cases; in fact, as I explained in Chapter 1, our approach designating the mother as the primary if not sole caretaker of the very young is atypical. We might well ask how this sharing of childcare came about. Several scholars have contributed to this discussion. As noted in Chapter 1, Bogin (1998) lays out the unique human life history pattern and the corollary reproductive advantages. Even though human children take a relatively long time reaching a state of self-sufficiency, they can well survive "early" weaning at three years or less. That's because others step up to feed and nurture the infant, freeing up the mother to bear another child (Hrdy 2005a). Alloparenting also means that weaned babies are quite likely to survive the death of their mothers (Sear and Mace 2008: 5). A systematic study of the Aka found that children from age two received more food from others than from their mothers (Fouts and Brookshire 2009). Howell's reanalysis of !Kung data collected in the late 1960s, when they depended almost entirely on nomadic foraging, showed that a nuclear family with two or more children could not keep them alive without supplemental provisioning by fellow band members (Howell 2010). Hadza infants receive care from a wide variety of individuals but, statistically, the bulk of care is provided by more closely related individuals (Crittenden and Marlowe 2008: 249). Sarah Hrdy (2009) characterizes the process whereby family members – all of whom have a genetic investment in the infant – pitch in to assist in rearing as "cooperative breeding." The burden is likely to fall most heavily on women who don't have children of their own, namely the infant's young sisters, cousins, and grandmothers.

Infant-care

The added weight of carrying infants while lactating [is] much like carrying a heavy backpack. (Strier 2003: 173)

Conversational interaction is minimal with [Mayan] infants. (de León 2000: 143)

!Kung mothers respond quickly and consistently to a crying infant (Kruger and Konner 2010: 323). And with very few exceptions, mothers nurse the child, "on demand."[5] Of course, this still allows for wide variability; for example,

---

[5] In Euroamerican society, where babies are precious cherubs, new mothers often express amazement at how "demanding" their baby can be: "I mean really I was rooted to the sofa and she was wanting to feed all the time which I hadn't prepared for" (Murphy 2007: 111).

one study compared the agrarian Ngandu with their foraging neighbors the Aka and found the latter nursing four times an hour, on average, and the former, twice. In addition, Aka mothers hold their infants for more of the day than do the Ngandu. This occurs in spite of the fact that for the small-stature Aka, the energetic costs are higher (Hewlett *et al*. 1998, 2000). These differences may reflect differing reproduction strategies in the two societies, "production" for the Ngandu versus "survivorship" for the Aka and !Kung – as discussed in the previous chapter.

In many societies the baby is attached to the mother with a sling, woven bag, or length of cloth and rides on her chest, her back, or her hip. The infant is simultaneously kept warm and comforted by proximity to her body, is kept clean and out of harm's way, and travels with her as she moves from place to place. In short, the infant is at all times accessible to the mother should it need attention. Naturally, mothers vary their ministrations according to perceived need.[6] Gusii mothers "provided more protective attention in the early months of life for those infants who showed signs of being vulnerable. Those ... rated as not well organized ... were held more by their mothers ... Babies who weighed less during the first nine months were held more by mother and other caregivers" (LeVine and LeVine 1988: 31–32).

Breastfeeding and carrying a growing child impose additional (up to five times) energy costs (Lee 1996) on a woman. "Maternity leave" in traditional societies is short (Hadza mothers resume foraging three to four days after giving birth; cf. Marlowe 2010: 65) while the labor demands on women are typically high. Aka mothers rely upon others in the camp to care for their older infants so that they don't have to carry them on arduous foraging rounds in the forest (Meehan 2009: 389).[7] My female housemates and neighbors in Gbarngasuakwelle were hard at work hoeing in the rice fields shortly after the birth of their children. Not surprisingly, mothers appreciate offspring who are wiry, agile, and early walkers (Zeitlin 1996: 412). One convenient way to reduce this cost is to "swaddle" the child or use some device like a cradleboard that keeps the child safe and secure without being constantly tethered to its mother:

A swaddled baby, like a little turtle in its shell, could be looked after by another, only slightly older child without too much fear of injury, since the practice of swaddling made ... child care virtually idiot proof. (Calvert 1992: 23–24)

---

[6] Ironically, because infants are often nursed at the first sign of movement or fussiness (recall the external womb notion from Chapter 2), an infant can be overfed and the true cause of its discomfort may be ignored (Howard 1973: 118).

[7] I asked Courtney Mehan, an Aka anthropologist who studies infancy: "Who orchestrates the highly fluid pattern of Aka alloparental care? The mother?" Her immediate response: "No, it's the child" (personal communication, November 5, 2012).

A Navajo mother appreciates the utility of the cradleboard in protecting the child but also in protecting her work environment from a clumsy, curious, and grasping infant (Chisholm 1983/2009: 218). The Navajo (North American pastoralists) are, undoubtedly, the best-known exponents of the cradleboard but its use was widespread throughout North America (e.g. Pearsall 1950: 340). There were four graduated sizes designed to be lashed to a horse's saddle in such a way that a kind of awning could be stretched from the saddle-bow over the cradle to shield the child. The Navajo had an elaborate rationale for its use; for example:

Babies are kept . . . in the cradle to make them straight and strong. Some women let their children lie on sheep skins and roll about, but they are always weak, sick children. (Leighton and Kluckhohn 1948: 23)[8]

There are many variations on this theme. In Bukkitingi, Sumatra, I observed unattended infants in cradle-baskets, suspended on long cords, which swung, pendulum-like, in the slightest breeze. As recently as 2007, I found cradles that immobilized the infant on sale in the markets of Uzbekistan. They featured an amazing add-on that collected the child's urine – keeping it dry and diaper-free. In an article on transhumance in Mongolia, there's a photo of an infant in a cradle-like structure strapped to the back of an ox in the middle of a milling herd. The herd is being driven over a mountain pass to winter pasture. The caption reads: "An ox-back ride is sometimes dangerous and always rough but there's no other way to go: The adults are too busy herding to babysit" (Hodges 2003: 108). The same scenario occurs when Sámi (sub-Arctic nomads) reindeer herders move their camp (Kleppe 2012: 78).

One of the most interesting baby-tenders is the manta pouch used by Quechua farmers who live high in the Andes. It turns out this low-tech device is quite efficacious in promoting the infant's wellbeing.[9] In this micro-environment, heightened temperature and humidity make breathing easier and sleep more likely than wakefulness. During nursing, the infant remains in the pouch to reduce the chance it will be aroused, thus further conserving energy that would waste precious calories (Tronick et al. 1994: 1009–1010). Modern substitutes, including strollers, cribs, and playpens, have dispersed the

---

[8] The autobiography of noted Hopi Don Talayesva includes many interesting details on life in a cradleboard (Simmons 1942: 33).

[9] A study in the US found that swaddled infants "sleep longer, spend more time in NREM sleep, and awake less spontaneously than when not swaddled" (Franco et al. 2005: 1309). But then it is unlikely to be popular because, as Margaret Mead (1954: 405) noted, swaddling is "peculiarly horrifying to Americans" as it suppresses the child's free will.

Figure 9 Chinese child-minding device

cradleboard concept around the world.[10] Another popular childcare "tool" is the "child – minder" (Figure 9).

The infant invariably sleeps with its mother for the same reasons it's usually attached to her during the day – ease of nursing. This suggests that the mother may not be sleeping with the child's father[11] and, indeed, the post-partum taboo on intercourse is widespread. Each society will operate with tacit ideas about how long the inter-birth interval (IBI) should be, but a father's threat to withhold provisions until relations resume may hasten weaning.

A lengthier nursing period is usually associated with a more casual weaning process. An Efe mother, teased because she's still nursing her three-year-old, replies: "'I've tried to wean him, but he refuses, so I guess he's not ready.' Everyone laughs" (Wilkie and Morelli 1991: 55; see also Fouts *et al.* 2001).

[10] And these aren't the only widely used child-management aids. Ceramic baby bottles and potty chairs are clearly depicted in Greek vase paintings (Oakley 2003). One can view the genuine items on display in the small museum inside the Stoa of Attalus in Athens.

[11] I believe that one of the unacknowledged reasons for separating the child from its parents at bedtime and during bathing in the USA, in contrast, say, to contemporary European and Asian custom, is concern for sexually polluting the child.

By contrast, Kpelle mothers withhold the breast and force-feed infants rice water to accelerate weaning. The abruptness and severity of weaning were studied intensively in research initiated by the Whitings during the 1960s (Whiting and Whiting 1975). In many societies, children are threatened with all sorts of terrors to discourage them from nursing (Williams 1969). It can be a traumatic experience for the child – a key element in Freud's theory of personality development.

A casual and relaxed attitude toward weaning usually signals a relaxed attitude toward toilet training. The Fore, in the Eastern Highlands of Papua New Guinea, are representative:

> Although disposal of body wastes was a matter of great concern to adult Fore because of their use in sorcery, toilet training was not imposed ... A toddler could repeatedly defecate in the hamlet yard, even during a feast, without being chastised ... [someone] would ... clean up ... As the child grew older, he began to adopt ... practices governing excretion by modeling ... on those of older children ... who often treated ... "errors" in behavior as a cause for amusement. (Sorenson 1976: 177)

This view is widely shared. It certainly characterized my Kpelle informants. In the next section, we'll see that the infant's almost magnetic attractiveness to other members of the community is commonplace and is also typical of non-human primates as well.

Playing with dolls

All female primates find babies ... fascinating. (Hrdy 1999: 157)

I have seen a little [West African Afikpo] girl of about five or six carrying a newly born baby over her shoulder, or sitting down and giving it water to drink. (Ottenberg 1968: 80)

The mother of an infant benefits from the fact that other women, particularly her own daughters and other younger female relatives, will find her baby irresistible. In Uganda in 2003, I observed and filmed numerous primate species and, after resting, eating, and play, "baby-trading" is the most common occupation. Often I observed what amounted to a "tug-of-war" between the nursing mother and her older daughters for possession of the infant, which may lead to what Sarah Hrdy (1976) referred to as "aunting to death." By contrast, mothers tend to discourage interest shown by juvenile males in their offspring (Strier 2003).[12]

---

[12] Barbara King describes an episode in which a mother successfully thwarts an attempt by an older brother, who'd already demonstrated his incompetence as a caretaker, from spiriting off his infant brother (King 2005).

Several studies have documented the gender bias in "baby lust" (Hrdy 1999: 157). Females show far more interest in babies, images of babies, and even silhouettes of babies than do males. In fact, there's some evidence that young chimp females will cradle, groom, and carry around a "doll" (a stick or a dead animal) in the absence of a live infant (Kahlenberg and Wrangham 2010: 1067). Somewhat unexpectedly, this line of research also shows such interest peaking just before women enter their childbearing years (Maestripieri and Pelka 2001), suggesting that they are preparing for the emotional distance required of new mothers discussed in Chapter 2.

The advantages to the nursing mother of having "helpers at the nest" (Turke 1988) are numerous. She can move through the environment foraging more readily with less energetic expense and she has an additional ally or two in responding to threats of predation or attacks from, sometimes indiscriminately aggressive, males. Among cotton-topped tamarins, having a daughter to carry the infant is the critical variable in successfully rearing offspring (Bardo et al. 2001), and some daughters, influenced evidently by pheromones released by their mother, never ovulate. As they never have offspring of their own, they can continue to provide allomothering services to their mother until she is past childbearing (Ziegler et al. 1987; Savage et al. 1988). Jane Goodall (1973) has documented several cases of juvenile chimps who perished shortly after the death of their mother, except in one case where an older sister "adopted" the orphan.

While comparable research with human populations is sparse, Mark Flinn, working in rural Trinidad, has demonstrated delayed pregnancy in young women who are assisting in the care of younger siblings, but also that, after age thirty, mothers "pay back" by investing in their daughters' reproduction efforts (Flinn 1988, 1989). Another critical study, undertaken on Ifaluk atoll in the western Pacific by Paul Turke, found "that parents who produce daughters early in their reproductive careers ... out-reproduce parents who produce sons early" (Turke 1989: 73). Among Efe foragers in the Congo, "The number of child caregivers who assisted a mother was positively related to the time that mothers spent acquiring food away from camp" (Henry et al. 2005: 202). Among Indo-Fijian farmers, sib-care "was associated with a 1.3-fold increase in the number of surviving offspring" (Mattison and Neill 2013: 121).

In the previous chapter, I discussed "baby-parading," in which a father uses his healthy child as a tool in marketing his own genetic fitness. Across several societies, mothers may similarly display or market a child to potential allo-parents. The baby's cherub-like features aid the mother in her quest for helpers. Young mammals, generally, but especially humans, display a suite of physical features that seem to be universally attractive to others, and these features are retained longer in humans than in other mammalian species (Lancaster and Lancaster 1983: 35; Sternglanz et al. 1977). Also critical is the fact that human infants vocalize, make eye contact, and smile from very early on (Chevalier-Skolnikoff 1977) – unlike chimps, for example, whose mothers make more limited use of helpers.

Mothers may not always rely on the inherent cuteness of their babies; they may take pains to showcase the baby – at least among close kin. The Kpelle mothers I observed didn't stop at frequently washing and cleaning their babies. They oiled the babies' bodies until they gleamed – an ablution carried out in public view with an appreciative audience. The Kaluli mothers studied by Bambi Schieffelin in Papua New Guinea not only hold their infants facing toward others in the social group – a practice often noted in the ethnographic record – but treat the baby as a ventriloquist's dummy in having him or her speak to those assembled (Schieffelin 1990: 71). The Beng advise young mothers:

Make sure the baby looks beautiful! . . . put herbal makeup on her face as attractively as possible . . . we Beng have lots of designs for babies' faces . . . That way, the baby will be so irresistibly beautiful that someone will feel compelled to carry her around for a while that day. If you're lucky, maybe that person will even offer to be your *leng kuli*. (Gottleib 1995: 24)

When [Guara] neighbors visit . . . relatives – identified by kinship terms – are repeatedly indicated to the child. (Ruddle and Chesterfield 1977: 29)

[Marquesan mothers] . . . spent much time calling the baby's name, directing him to look and wave at others . . . directing three- to six-year-old siblings to play with him. (Martini and Kirkpatrick 1981: 199)

[Among the Kwara'ae, in the Solomon Islands] an infant of six months given a piece of fruit is immediately told to "Give some to your sister/brother" . . . In helping the infant to hand the piece to its sibling, the caregiver tells the infant to say, "Here's your fruit." Infants who cry or resist sharing are gently chided, teased, or laughed at. (Watson-Gegeo and Gegeo 1989: 61)

Most babies enjoy the contacts with many people, which occur at any casual gathering; some, however, tend to retreat into mother's arms. This, the Chiga deem as unfortunate sulkiness, a sign of an unpleasant, bad-tempered disposition. (Edel 1957/1996: 174)

Samoan . . . caregivers routinely prompted infants to notice . . . others. Infants were held face outward to witness . . . interactions nearby. Toddlers were fed facing others and prompted to notice and call out to people. (Ochs and Izquierdo 2009: 397)

From the moment a [Warlpiri] child is born . . . she will hear every day . . . for the next few years; "Look, your granny," 'That's your big sister, your cousin, your auntie." In fact, they make up the bulk of verbal communication with babies and little children. (Musharbash 2011: 72)

In the Sepik area of Papua New Guenia, recently weaned youngsters are encouraged to act solicitously toward the neonate, if they wish to "remain in the proximity of ... mother's breast" (Barlow 2001: 97). These examples are typical of many one finds in the anthropological literature of mothers actively teaching their children politeness or etiquette conventions and terminology (Lancy 1996: 23). As we'll see in Chapter 5, mothers otherwise rarely act as their children's teachers, so this may be directly related to their dependence on older children and kin to assist with childcare. For example, having been taught politeness and respect for kin, a recently weaned Qashqa'i child begs food from other households and is successful (Shahbazi 2001: 54–55). The mother must, however, accept the consequence that virtually anyone older than her child can scold or even discipline them (Whiting 1941). In societies like our own, where childcare is handled within the nuclear family and/or by professionals, the necessity for learning manners and kinship arcana is reduced. At the same time, we are often reluctant to concede to outsiders, even "professionals," the right to discipline our young.

That "good" mothers are those who are able to amass social capital is borne out in research with primates in the wild. Joan Silk and her colleagues conducted a study of fitness (number of surviving offspring) among savannah baboons and found that: "Females who had more social contact with other adult group members and were more fully socially integrated into their groups were more likely than other females to rear infants successfully" (Silk *et al.* 2003: 1234). Studies also show high-ranking mothers as more mellow, allowing their infants to wander more freely, trusting in their high status to insure that troop members will aid and not harm their offspring – in contrast to low-ranking mothers, who must be much more protective and vigilant (Altmann 1980). These socializing skills are passed on to daughters that are active in grooming higher-ranking females and, in effect, acquiring social capital within the troop (Walter 1987: 365).

Comparable research with humans is rare, but we should, for example, expect better conditions for children of higher-ranking wives in a polygynous household. A study of the Mende found that senior wives did have higher fitness while junior wives had fewer surviving children than their counterparts in monogamous unions (Isaac and Feinberg 1982). Similarly, in Botswana, children of more senior wives enjoyed nutrition and school attendance advantages (Bock and Johnson 2002: 329). Given the fact that our species in its most primitive state as foragers in a marginal environment still manages to raise roughly 50 percent of its offspring, compared with a range of 12–36 percent for other primates (Lancaster and Lancaster 1983: 37), the ability to recruit childcare assistants must be seen as central to the success of individual mothers and the species as a whole.

While the benefits to the mother are obvious, allomothering daughters also clearly benefit by learning how to care for infants (Fairbanks 1990). A study of captive chimpanzees showed that females prevented from interacting with their mothers and younger siblings were themselves utterly incompetent as mothers (Davenport and Rogers 1970). The Canela in Brazil hold an annual round of festivals – to proclaim and reinforce values – in the center of their circular village. One "hilarious" skit in the Fish Festival mocks young women who've failed to learn mothering (Crocker and Crocker 1994: 124).

Riesman, in describing the situation for the pastoral Fulani of West Africa, could be referring to almost any traditional, non-urban society in the world:

> All women caring for their first babies will have had years of experience taking care of babies ... under the watchful and sometimes severe eyes of their mothers, aunts, cousins or older sisters. The other women ... will immediately notice, comment on, and perhaps strongly criticize any departure from customary behavior on the part of mothers. (Riesman 1992: 111)

An interesting contrast can be made with WEIRD society, where girls are not usually assigned sibcare duties and where young mothers labor alone without the guidance of their older female relatives.[13] "The relative isolation of the nuclear family ... means that each woman rears her newborn infant from scratch" and young, urban mothers are unprepared for squalling, active, and very unhappy babies (Hubert 1974: 46–47). The foibles of clueless parents have proven to be quite entertaining, as evidenced by "reality" TV shows such as *Nanny 911*, which aired in the USA between 2004 and 2007, and *Supernanny* (2004–2011),[14] in which a competent nanny brings order and harmony to dysfunctional families.

Toddler rejection

The "dethronement" of the infant not only follows weaning, but is also quite commonly coincidental with the birth of the next child. (Prothro 1961: 66)

[On Malaita Island] children are pushed to be adult as soon as possible. (Watson-Gegeo and Gegeo 2001: 3)

If "peek-a-boo" or parent–infant play is uncommon (Lancy 2007), parent–toddler play is virtually non-existent. The toddler's mother not only faces potential conflict between childcare and work, she's likely pregnant as well.[15]

---

[13] Programs have sprung up in the US in which young expectant mothers with no access to competent role models are "mentored" from pregnancy through the end of their child's infancy by competent volunteers (Blinn-Pike *et al.* 1998).

[14] Still running in early 2013 was *America's Supernanny: Family Lockdown*. Available at www.mylifetime.com/shows/americas-supernanny. Accessed February 3, 2014.

[15] "The Kaingáng do not feel that a woman should be accompanied by a little child [as] its presence may prevent a swift and surreptitious sex encounter" (Henry 1941/1964: 15).

At one end of the continuum, Central African foragers display long IBIs and relaxed weaning – toddlers are indulged. Fouts documents the contrasting pattern found among their farming neighbors where IBIs are much shorter, and weaning is forced (Fouts 2004a: 138). Commonly, the mother applies hot pepper to her nipples and this is quite effective (Culwick 1935: 338). Even among the "indulgent" !Kung, tantrums erupt when the mother refuses to continue carrying her fully mobile youngster or attempts to leave him in camp when she goes foraging (Shostak 1981: 47). Pirahã infants and children are treated with great attention and affection but when weanlings throw enormous tantrums, screaming for hours and injuring themselves in their epileptic-like "fits," they will be studiously ignored by everyone (Everett 2014). Efe toddlers are "desolate" following the mother's departure from camp (Morelli and Tronick 1991: 48). Mothers are also eager to "wean the child from [their] back," which may be just as tearfully resisted as weaning from the breast (Maretzki and Maretzki 1963: 447).

Somewhat ironically, we find a number of societies – including the !Kung – that accelerate the transition to the toddler stage (Lancy and Grove 2010: 146). !Kung foragers accelerate sitting, standing, and walking because "in the traditional mobile subsistence pattern . . . children who cannot walk constitute major burdens" (Konner 1976: 290). The agrarian Nso claim that "A standing baby . . . makes less work for the mother" (Keller 2007: 124), hence they accelerate locomotor development as well. Other foraging societies where this acceleration has been documented include the Mbya Guarani (Remorini 2011), the Baka (Hirasawa 2005: 166), and the !Xun San. The !Xun – in common with many other societies – hold babies under the arms and dandle them on their laps. This stimulates a "stepping" reflex and if this "gymnastic" exercise is kept up, the babies will walk sooner – relieving their caretakers of the burden of transporting them (Takada 2005: 290).[16] Agricultural societies that are reported as accelerating development using this and other techniques include Kipsigis (Harkness and Super 1991: 226–227; Super 1976: 290), Bambara (Bril et al. 1989: 315), Bamana (Polak 1998: 106), Chiga (Edel 1957/1996: 174), Aymara (de Suremain et al. 2001: 50), Gujarati (Keller 2007: 122), Ganda (Ainsworth 1967: 321), Malaita (Watson-Gegeo and Gegeo 2001: 3), and Kogi (Reichel-Dolmatoff 1976: 277).

The Zulu of South Africa use a more direct approach; they place the child on an ant's nest to motivate it to stand and walk (Krige 1965/2005). Also in Melanesia, Gau Islanders expect children to grow up quickly, and they treat harshly any child who seems to be lagging behind in their developmental timetable. A two-year-old will be scolded and teased as acting baby-like if it

---

[16] Empirical tests have confirmed that activating this "stepping" reflex leads to the child walking at an earlier age (Zelazo et al. 1972).

whines to be picked up and held (Toren 1990: 174). Similarly, a fourteen-month-old that is still not walking will be given a chili-pepper enema (Toren 1990: 171). Baka foragers encourage toddlers to keep trudging along the forest trail by poking them with a prickly seedpod (Higgens 1985: 101). Parents will accelerate the child's motor development when an impending infant threatens to absorb all of the caretaker's attention and/or because the child needs to begin making a useful contribution to the household as soon as possible. Where this is not the case and/or where eager sib-caretakers are available, the baby will continue to be indulged.

Refusing to carry the child and denying access to the breast is only one among many signs of rejection (Du Bois 1944: 51). Long-term observers of the !Kung have noted the dramatic transformation in childhood as the foragers gave up their itinerant lifestyle and settled down to farming. The IBI shortened, fertility increased, and the formerly loving, indulgent mothers had to ruthlessly separate their toddlers from themselves (Draper and Cashdan 1988; Lee 1979: 330; true also for the !Xun Bushman – cf. Takada 2010: 165). The child's demanding character at this time may be characterized as an "assault on the privileges of rank, for only the senior-ranking individual in an interaction has a right to make demands" (Howard 1973: 119). Toddler rejection[17] is by no means limited to the mother; a common theme suggests that the rejection[18] is community-wide.

One of the most striking features in the [Akan] attitude to the child is the contrast between the lavish affection meted out to infants … and the harsh disregard which is the lot of most older children. The adored small child has to suffer the trauma of growing into an object of contempt. (Field 1970: 28)

[Lurs] adults and elder siblings likely will deny any request, interfere in any activity, foil any intention a toddler may initiate or express. (Friedl 1997: 124)

As they begin to become more and more children rather than babies, and begin to be a bit irritating and willful because they are "thinking for themselves," [Tahitians] begin to find children less amusing. Instead of being the center of the household stage, the child … becomes annoying. (Levy 1973: 454)

[Bonerate] mothers do not establish eye contact with their nursing [toddlers] as they … are nursed quickly, without overt emotional expression either from the mother or from the child. (Broch 1990: 31)

An unsteady [Bakkarwal] toddler who stumbles is not picked up when it cries: "it must learn on its own," is the argument. Two toddlers who shriek after a fight are not helped out: "In life the stronger wins," is the motto. (Rao 1998: 100)

---

[17] Term from Weisner and Gallimore (1977: 176). Other examples: van Stone (1965: 51); Levine (1965: 266).

[18] Toddler rejection is not universal. The Sinhalese give in to the child's every demand, "no matter how outrageous" (Chapin 2011: 356)."

Leavitt devotes a great deal of attention to toddler rejection among the Bumbita Arapesh. Infants are weaned relatively early and show obvious signs of malnutrition. Tantrums are to be expected and the infants are often successful in gaining brief access to the breast. On the other hand, the mother and entire extended family collaborate to deflect the toddler's attention using various scare tactics and promises (largely unmet) of future bounty. Another common tactic is to suggest that the complaining child will be treated preferentially vis-à-vis a sibling, such as a father promising to give one child lots of (edible) beetles and another only few (Leavitt 1989: 143–152).

Fortunately, as the mother and other adults lose interest, the toddler is taken up by older siblings who may be more patient and willing to "baby" him or her.

Her brother's keeper

Like many firstborn children, I learned to care for children by baby-sitting my two younger brothers. (Clinton 1996: 9)

[Mayan] siblings structure play activities for their younger charges to keep them out of the way of adults and to keep them entertained and happy. (Maynard 2004a: 245)

While we have certainly seen the truth of the African proverb, "It takes a village to raise a child," some members play a bigger role than others. In a landmark study, Weisner and Gallimore examined hundreds of ethnographies in the Human Relations Area Files (HRAF) archive and found that, in accounts of childcare, 40 percent of infants and 80 percent of toddlers are cared for primarily by someone other than their mother, most commonly older sisters (Weisner and Gallimore 1977). For the nomadic Pashtun, older siblings take over much of the care of infants after the first few weeks (Casimir 2010: 24). In the Ngoni (Bantu pastoralists) village, one sees "nurse girls" herding toddlers to a "playground" on the outskirts of the village where they meet peers to "practice dancing, thread beads and chatter" (Read 1960: 82). The investment in one's younger siblings may incur a distinct cost, as demonstrated in a study of Amazonia-dwelling Tsimané. Tsimané girls acting as sib-caretakers have less fat and muscle accumulation than girls without such duties (Magvanjav et al. 2012: 17).

Sib-caretakers must not let themselves get too engrossed in their own pursuits. "One of the worst things a [Hopi] girl can do is to neglect an infant charge. This can result in ostracism for days, shaming [her] deeply" (Schlegel 1973: 454). In Kipsigis villages: "Child nurses are expected not only to carry the baby around, but also to play with it, sing lullabies to it, feed it porridge … and help the baby in learning to talk and walk" (Harkness and

Super 1991: 227; see also Sigman *et al.* 1988: 1259). In Gbarngasuakwelle, one often observes a trio of the nursing mother accompanied by one of her daughters who's carrying the sleeping infant on her back. At the first cry from the infant, it will be transferred to the mother to nurse, then, once sated, transferred back again to the sister – who may be as young as five (Lancy 1996: 146). The involvement of siblings in infant care also facilitates the weaning process. Among the Mandinka:

With the arrival of the next sibling, infancy is over. Now, play begins and membership in a social group of peers is taken to be critical to *nyinandirangho*, the forgetting of the breast to which the toddler has had free access for nearly two years or more. As one mother put it, "Now she must turn to play." (Whittemore 1989: 92)

One reason why mothers do not play with their young may be that they don't want to diminish the seductive power of the play group (Konner 1975: 116; Shostak 1981: 48). Aside from expediting weaning, it has other functions. "Three-year-old children are able to join in a play group, and it is in such play groups that children are truly raised" (Eibl-Eibesfeldt 1989: 600).

Marquesan mothers have a fully articulated theory of the toddler's development in the company of older siblings. The toddler wants to be with and be like older peers from whom she learns to take care of herself, proper elimination, and various household chores assigned to children. (Martini and Kirkpatrick 1992)

Several authors have carefully documented the stratagems employed by sibling caretakers, who are, after all, just slightly older than their charges in many cases. Older Hadza children act more indulgently toward their younger kin than do mothers.[19] For the Fore, older children were expected to be tolerant toward toddlers and accept their aggression with mild amusement. Older children usually defer to younger ones when they both want the same thing. Not surprisingly, "sibling rivalry"[20] may be non-existent (Sorenson 1976: 162, 180, 187).[21] Suzanne Gaskins reports that older Maya siblings are well aware

[19] Alyssa Crittenden (personal communication, November 5, 2012).

[20] On a personal note, I didn't understand, until I wrote this chapter, why my mother, the youngest of twelve (ten who survived childhood) and nicknamed "Babe," cared least for her sister (my aunt) Becky, only a year older, and was much closer to sisters Marie and Verona, who were at least a decade older. I realize now that the latter would have been her primary caretakers while the former was her only rival for their attention. My mother was rather indifferent toward Aunt Theresa – who had married and formed her own household before my mother was born.

[21] Harris argues that sibling rivalry occurs in our society because parents suppress the natural dominance hierarchy among siblings based on age (Harris 1998: 93–94). This is vividly illustrated in Barbara Rogoff's (2003: 145–146) account of conflict over possession of a doll. My sense is that the key factor is the degree to which sib-caretakers have carte blanche. When they don't and parents actively manage and correct sib-caretaking behaviors, there will be evident signs of rivalry (Broch 1990: 81).

that their young brothers and sisters "must always be kept happy." Caretakers can expect no help from or oversight by adults except to abruptly terminate the play activity if work needs doing, or if play becomes too rambunctious, or a child begins to cry (Gaskins *et al.* 2007). Mandinka sib-caretakers employ an arsenal of tactics to keep their charges in line. The term *manené* covers everything from persuasion, verbal or physical threats and mock blows, to teasing and promises (usually unfulfilled) of treats (Whittemore and Beverly 1989).

However, while the Mayan play group is expected to remain within earshot of the family compound, in the Marquesas the play group is not welcome in the vicinity of adults. As a consequence, caretakers are not nearly as deferential to the young ones (Martini and Kirkpatrick 1992). In Quechua-speaking areas of Ecuador, child-minders are also given a great deal of latitude in trying to control the behavior of toddlers: teasing, shaming, and threatening are all legitimate tactics (Rindstedt and Aronsson 2003). On Gau Island a youngster "who disciplines one even younger with a slap or a sharpish knock with the knuckles on the side of the head is rarely rebuked" (Toren 1990: 183). Bolivian village children have considerable latitude with their charges, delegating chores to them and imposing punishment for misbehavior (Punch 2001: 29). Quechua boys are occasionally recruited for sib-care duties, which include "combing their hair ... for head lice ... helping to toilet train them ... [and acting as] an 'interpreter' explaining to others what his/her charge has just said" (Rindstedt and Aronsson 2003: 8).

Evidence of competent childcare by older siblings in the village setting contrasts with evidence of their incompetence in our own society (Farver 1993). Brian Sutton-Smith offered these comments on the Weisner and Gallimore sib-care study:

Maximal ... development of infants is produced by the mother ... who interacts with them in a variety of stimulating and playful ways ... the intelligence to do this with ever more exciting contingencies is simply not present in child caretakers. It is difficult enough to impart these ideas of infant stimulation even to mothers ... children as major caretakers maintain social life at a much lower level. (Sutton-Smith 1977: 184)

His point is no doubt true and has received considerable empirical support (Rogoff 1990: 165). But the comment is culturally biased. He is evaluating the socialization practices of non-Western people by the standards of WEIRD society. Other researchers have demonstrated how effective sibling caretakers can be in the context of village-based, agrarian society (Watson-Gegeo and Gegeo 1989). Indeed, they show that siblings are often more patient toward and tolerant of toddler mood swings than are adults (Zukow 1989) and more likely to use special speech forms to aid their understanding (Toren 1990: 175). With a few noteworthy exceptions, such as the Marquesas cited above, village play groups will be reliably found in areas of the community where watchful adults aren't far away.

Playing on the mother ground

[Gusii] children soon learn that any grownup can rebuke them and has authority over them. (LeVine 1973: 135)

[Palauan children are] usually found playing around the spot where their fathers are working or gossiping. (Barnett 1979: 6)

One of the great facilitators of reduced workload effort for childcare is something that the Kpelle refer to as *panang lè-ma* or mother ground. This is a flat, open area in village or garden[22] where children gather to play under the watchful eye of adults working or relaxing nearby.[23] These are not purpose-built playgrounds but areas that have been cleared to facilitate traffic and discourage snakes, and as occasional areas for work such as laying out house-building materials, or drying clothing or crops. These are mixed-age play groups with older children casually minding infants and toddlers while they engage in their own play (Takada 2010: 171). In the rare event of conflict or injury, or when a distressed child can't be comforted, an adult is close enough to detect a problem and intervene. Situating play areas in close proximity to adults serves two ends. It affords adults the opportunity to oversee the children, almost effortlessly, but it also gives watchful children a source of scenes of adult activity to incorporate into their play (Lancy 1996; also discussed more fully in Chapter 6). However, adults rarely intervene in children's play except when fighting threatens to get out of hand. Interestingly, primatologists note the same watchful behavior, benign neglect, and rapid intervention on the part of mothers of actively playful primate juveniles (Baldwin and Baldwin 1978).

For the Lebou of Senegal, the mother ground has a constantly changing cast but, in one observational study, an average of nine two- to six-year-olds were casually supervised by a couple of adults (Bloch 1989: 143). A similar configuration can be found among the Dusun rice farmers of Borneo (Williams 1969: 75). In Chaga villages one finds "a children's play area, often at the edge of or near the village commons" (Raum 1940: 95). It is clear from Hewlett's description that the entire Aka camp – and this would

---

[22] Like the Fore gardens described by Sorenson (1976: 50), Kpelle gardens are a place for adult singing, dancing, and socializing, and for children's games, as well as hard work (Lancy 1996).

[23] We can even find something approximating the mother ground in primate bands (Sussman 1977: 522).

certainly be true for other foraging bands (Turnbull 1978) – functions as the mother ground. He describes the campsite with its maximum of twenty-five to thirty-five inhabitants as "about the size of a large Euroamerican living room" (Hewlett 1992: 225). In camp, even one-year-olds are free to roam widely within the perimeter and interact with whomever they wish. The camp isn't "child-proof": no one panics if the baby handles knives or wanders into, say, a butchering site.

Indeed, small towns in remoter corners of the USA once offered the kind of shared responsibility noted among the Aka. The following is from rural Maine in the 1950s.

> Children's escapades through town were observed by many eyes … and parents seemed comfortable with the idea that someone would contact them if their child misbehaved. Such joint, unobtrusive supervision permitted children's free-ranging play and also drew multiple other adults into the role of … audience for the plays, circuses, animal shows, and other productions that interviewees remembered putting on. (Beach 2003: 192)

While rarely mentioned in the literature, the mother ground may have been overlooked by scholars because of its very ubiquity and because, perhaps, there may be no specific term for it in most languages. The most familiar yet unrecognized example is Peter Breughel's 1560 masterpiece *Children's Games* in the Kunsthistoriches Museum, Vienna. He depicts eighty-four distinct children's "pass-times" or games and, with few exceptions, children are playing within view or hearing of adults either in the workplace or in their homes. However, it is sadly the case that modern society is no longer likely to provide a mother ground.[24] In an ethnography of a suburban neighborhood, anthropologists found that adults were reluctant to intervene in settings where children were involved, deferring to public agencies. There was also the fear that intervention might be misconstrued "as an attempt to kidnap or otherwise harm the boy or girl" (Spilsbury and Korbin 2004: 197).

Among the mother ground custodians in the village, we are likely to find grandparents. Aside from any concern they might feel toward their grandchildren, nieces, and nephews, they are, simply, available. That is, the relatively sedentary (their work keeps them stationary and close to home) observers at the periphery of the mother ground are more likely to be the children's grandparents than their parents.

---

[24] Urban centers have probably always been less hospitable to children and, as we explore early European society later in the chapter, we'll see that child mortality was often the indirect result of the absence of adult supervision.

Going to grandma's place

[Hadza] grandmothers [as caretakers of grandchildren] increase their own genetic success because their daughters can have more babies sooner. (Hawkes *et al.* 2000: 253).

[Folk wisdom of northern India claims] none but a grandmother should oversee a child. Mothers are only fit for bearing. (Kipling 1901/2003: 120)

The ethnographic literature is replete with examples of grandmothers caring for their daughter's offspring. Grandmothers substitute as primary caretakers far more often than do fathers (Black *et al.* 1999: 974). But it was Kristen Hawkes and colleagues – who study the Hadza – who first put forward the notion that this particular solution to the problem of freeing mothers from childcare may have deep evolutionary roots. They point out that, compared with other great apes, our species is unique in that women routinely live well beyond their reproductive years after passing through menopause. Hawkes *et al.*'s explanation for this phenomenon is that older women, by forgoing reproduction, are preserving their bodies so they can invest their energy and skills in rearing their grandchildren, thereby increasing their own genetic fitness (Hawkes *et al.* 2000). And, in a study on Ifaluk, Paul Turke also found that adults whose parents were living had more offspring than those who did not have the help of grandparents (Turke 1988). In another relevant study, among the Oromo of Ethiopia, the authors found that grandmothers can enhance the survivorship of their grandchildren indirectly as well. In this case some grandmothers visit their daughters who have small children, in order to help them with their most arduous chores. This intervention evidently frees the mother to devote more time to childcare, increasing the child's viability (Gibson and Mace 2005).

Of course, the opportunity to have more children is not the mother's only concern. She must address her own personal needs and those of her mate, who may be providing critical resources for her and the children. And she will, inevitably, have a vital economic role to play. In all these endeavors, a child may literally "get in the way." For Sepik women, their principal protein source is fish and "young children are a hindrance to subsistence fishing" (Barlow 2001: 84). Aka mothers on the hunt have been observed to set a (crying) infant down on the ground to run in pursuit of their quarry (Hewlett 1991b: 79–80). In the Marquesas, adults shoo away children when they're processing raw coconuts into copra because the children might interrupt the activity. Parents disavow any desire to teach children these skills, arguing that, in effect, when they're old enough, they'll figure it out themselves (Martini and Kirkpatrick 1992: 205). In many cases, then, the child may be placed in the care of a grandmother – usually more tolerant of the child's curiosity and "interference." The Tlingit claim that a child enjoys greater love and constancy from its grandmother than from its parents (de Laguna 1965: 8).

Grandmothers intervene at critical times, particularly during weaning (de Laguna 1972: 507; Fouts 2004a; Hawkes *et al.* 1997; Hilger 1957: 30; Raphael and Davis 1985). One grandmother is described as suckling the fussy baby on "her wizened breasts" (Rohner and Chaki-Sircar 1988: 71). And in the event of the mother's death, "The Chiga insist that a grandmother ... who has borne a child in the past can produce milk again if a child is set to her breast earnestly enough" (Edel 1957/1996: 72). Figure 10 shows a grandmother minding two of her grandchildren in the Toradja area of Sulawesi.

When the child is sick or injured, grandmothers serve up a stock of comforting stories (Raum 1940: 160). They are there to spell the mother when she is sick, doing critical work or caring for a subsequent infant. It is not

Figure 10 Grandmother tending two grandchildren, Marante Village, Sulawesi

uncommon to find grandmothers moving from part- to full-time childcare (Bove *et al.* 2002: 459). For the Mende of Sierra Leone, "grannies" step in to care for babies suspected of being illegitimate whose mothers are in high school; babies whose unmarried mothers spy a marriage opportunity; or babies whose mothers are anxious to resume sexual relations with their husbands and/ or get pregnant. Compared with young mothers, grannies are perceived as more knowledgeable, patient, and attentive (Bledsoe and Isiugo-Abanihe 1989: 453). On the other hand, as noted by Sutton-Smith for sibling caretakers (Sutton-Smith 1977), they have their limits. Fijian children raised by their grandmothers acquire unattractive traits. They are "said to be either presumptuous and 'too inquisitive' or 'childish' and unable to take on the tasks proper to their age" (Toren 1990: 172).

[I]n the Mende view, grannies are notoriously lax with children. They are said to feed children upon demand and do not beat them or withhold meals from them for bad behavior or for failing to work ... Children raised like this are said to grow up lazy and dishonest ... children can even insult their grannies in play or in anger ... Mende teachers ... argue ... that children raised by grannies perform the most poorly in school. They attend only fitfully, because grannies are said to encourage them to stay home and avoid the rigors and discipline of the classroom. (Bledsoe and Isiugo-Abanihe 1989: 454–455)

A Mende granny may not actually be the child's biological grandmother; other relatives may also be called upon and "fosterage" is extremely common. A study of fosterage among the Gonja of Ghana found that at least half the sample had spent all or a significant part of their childhood in the care of an adult other than the biological parent. It commonly occurs where one household has a surplus of children while another suffers a dearth (Goody 1982b). Among the Kpelle, children are given to childless adults to raise and form ties with so the children will care for them as they age (Lancy 1996: 145). In fact, as discussed in Chapter 2, practices designed to provide reliable caretakers for children and insure their future usefulness may be much more fluid than our common notions of adoption. Among Tswana cattle herders, children are:

Moved between caregivers, going to live with a mother or an uncle in town for a few months, then back to a home village to stay with grandmother, then out to an arable agricultural site or a cattle-post for weeks or months. (Durham 2008: 168)

As we might expect, foster or adoptive parents tend to be closely related to the child. Among Herero herders from southwest Africa, where the proportion of fostered children is high, fewer than 4 percent were being cared for by non-kin (Pennington and Harpending 1993). Silk has pursued this question with vigor and shown the importance of kin-ties in adoption in Polynesia (Silk 1980) and the Arctic (Silk 1987). She has also shown that, in a range of primate species, animals can differentiate between close kin, non-kin, and distant kin and that this awareness mediates their altruistic behavior (Silk 2002). In fact, the expression "It takes a village" might be better phrased "It takes an extended family."

However, we conclude this section as we concluded the last, by acknowledging that, like the mother ground, grandparents as child-minders may fade into history. In the USA, communities like Sun City, Arizona, are infamous for no-child rules, barring residence for families with children. Sun City and its sisters are part of a much larger trend to segregate the older generations from the younger. Many contemporary Japanese grandmothers resent being asked to assist with childcare: "Having at last got rid of their own children, they want to enjoy their new-found freedom – some would like to knit, others to do calligraphy or aikido" (Jolivet 1997: 56). Will fathers be available to take up the slack? Let's see.

Life with(out) father

Fathers have surprisingly little effect on child survival. (Sear and Mace 2008: 1)

Strange as it may seem, it is a rare father who is accorded an important place in the [Chinese] son's autobiography. (Wu 1995: 131)

Of all the cast of characters in this melodrama, the role of father is the most subject to creative script variation. Hrdy notes that "human males may nurture young a little, a lot or not at all" (2009: 162). One reason for this variability arises because it is hard to find a father as the head of an isolated nuclear family, or what we'd consider the "normal" father's role. In my home in Gbarngasuakwelle, the "head" of the household was clearly the chief's senior wife; the chief himself was actually a rather shadowy figure around the house. In other parts of Africa, one might find people living in large, diverse groups in a "compound." There are multiple males – brothers, cousins, and grandsons – whose relationship to the corresponding group of women in the compound is not easy to discern. In large sections of Papua New Guinea, married women live in modest huts with their younger children while men, married and single, live in dorm-like bachelor quarters where homosexuality is completely accepted.

In Maningkabau villages in western Sumatra, the paterfamilias adds sections on to the communal home, like a vertical layer-cake, to accommodate his married daughters and their offspring. Similarly, among the Nyars of southern India, husbands and wives live apart except for conjugal visits, and fathers have little to do with their children (Menon 2001: 354). Among the Na, a Chinese minority group living near the border with Burma, women mate secretly with their lovers, whose paternity is never acknowledged (Hua 2001). By contrast, I might cite the Pashtu, nomadic pastoralists in Afghanistan, where women carry a higher workload than men – especially during milk-processing season – and, consequently, "men take care of the infants more often than women do" (Casimir 2010: 23). Similarly in China, women's education has kept pace with men's, as has employment, and there are many fathers caring for their offspring full-time – an unthinkable state of affairs until just recently (Jankowiak 2011). In short, the role of father varies in part because the role of husbands, and/or adult males, generally, varies so much cross-culturally.

In large parts of the world, males are absent from the household for lengthy periods herding livestock, fulfilling military service, or earning money as migrant workers. In a Caribbean Garifuna community, Munroe recorded a conversation in which the (rarely) visiting father asks the mother the name of their seven-year-old son (Munroe 2005). Under these circumstances, not only is there little opportunity for the *Ozzie and Harriet* style[25] of open display of affectionate cooperation in childcare, but the only episodes of affectionate relations between husband and wife may be conducted furtively in the bush.

Looking at our primate cousins, the situation is similarly unpromising. The general pattern for non-human primates is for adult males to keep their distance from infants – as they are seen as potentially threatening by the mothers. Among orangutans, the juvenile male not only doesn't interact with its biological father, it may not even see another male as it grows up (Horr 1977). Gorilla fathers frequently play with their infants in the wild, whereas play is uncommon in chimpanzee fathers. However, "chimpanzee paternity is usually not known either by observers or apparently the chimpanzees … whereas it is certain in gorilla harems" (Bard 1995: 36). Of course, humans are much more closely related to chimpanzees than to gorillas. It is a fairly safe generalization that the father's primary contribution to children occurs at conception.[26] For example, among a forest-dwelling tribe who refer to themselves as Chewong, the father "builds up" the fetus with his semen, which is, in turn, nourished by the mother during pregnancy. "The prenatal stage is the one in which parental responsibility is at its strongest since

---

[25] *The Adventures of Ozzie and Harriet* was only one among a dozen or more US TV programs popular from the early 1950s to mid-1960s that portrayed life in "typical" families that consisted of a man, a woman, and their two to three children living in suburbia. Both parents were quite engaged with the children from infancy through adolescence.

[26] In the Trobriand Islands off eastern New Guinea, intercourse and pregnancy are not linked and males aren't viewed as essential for procreation. Further, in this matrilineal society, it is the mother's brother, not her husband, who acts in a "paternal" capacity vis-à-vis the children (Malinowski 1929; Roscoe and Telban 2004: 104).

congenital malfunctions of any kind are attributed to the behavior of one or other of the parents during this period" (Howell 1988: 155).

On Ifaluk Island, no men, not even husbands, are permitted to witness the birth of a child (Burrows and Shapiro 1957), and this prohibition is typical (but see also Huber and Breedlove 2007: 214). Post-partum, fathers are discouraged from attending on their wives and new babies, as well: "the [Kipsigis] father is forbidden to see his wife or new baby ... for fear that he might be tempted to break the postpartum sex taboo, or that he might unwittingly harm the vulnerable newborn by his very presence, or even that his own masculinity might be compromised by close contact with a baby" (Harkness and Super 1991: 223). Societies construct elaborate rationalizations for the father's absence from the nursery (Makey 1983: 394; Munroe and Munroe 1992: 218; Hewlett 2001: 49). Kwara'ae "men's degree of interaction with infants was limited by beliefs that urine and feces were polluting.[27] The infant's skin was also considered potentially polluting until it reached full pigmentation" (Gegeo and Watson-Gegeo 1985: 248). For the South African Thonga (Junod 1927: 169–170) and East African Logoli (Munroe 2005), it is taboo for a father to pick up an infant. The Han Chinese thought that men were incapable of infant care and might, for example, "become confused and drop the child" (Jankowiak 2011: 114). The Fijian child learns early "not to touch or take anything ... of his father – his mat, pillow, comb, or lavalava ... if he ... disobey[s, he] ... will be scolded, perhaps whipped" (Thompson 1940: 39).

Japanese society historically ridiculed "the 'kind' or 'accommodating' man who helps his wife" (Jolivet 1997: 58), but attitudes are changing dramatically and fathers are increasingly seen as playing a role in childcare (Nakazawa and Shwalb 2012). Although the idea of a nurturing father dates to 1966 in the USA (Pleck 1987: 84) this telling anecdote suggest that old attitudes persist:

Sandy's and Ben's images of fatherhood were quite different. Ben thought about the new baby much as an athlete might think about a trophy: After it has been won, it sits on the shelf to be viewed from a distance. Sandy thought about fatherhood in much more personal terms and imagined an active participant in Kim's childhood. When the baby arrived and Ben walked away from his responsibilities, Sandy's illusions about Ben began to crumble. (Berrick 1995: 43)

Hillary Fouts' characterization of Bofi (Central African farmers) fathers would strike a familiar chord with fieldworkers all over the globe. Although they spend many days "at home" in the village, "they rarely perform care giving

---

[27] Malinowski's vivid description of Trobriand fatherhood shows that the father seems delighted to nurture the infant and suffer whatever indignities may occur as a consequence. But then, the matrilineal Trobrianders afford the father only a marginal role in family life. So childcare is the male's way of demonstrating his worth to the family (Malinowski 1929).

tasks for their children and instead spend the majority of their time politicking with other ... men" (Fouts 2005: 358). Even when fathers "tend" children, they don't exactly replicate "maternal" behavior. Yanomamo (South American foragers) men

> are not comfortable with infants – they are afraid, for one thing, of being urinated or defecated [on] ...When they carry young infants [their] arms are slightly extended away from their bodies ...Women carry infants placed firmly against their own bodies. If a child cries while a man is tending it, he will quickly pass it to a woman. (Peters 1998: 89)

On forest treks, the Yanomamo mother may be carrying material in a basket secured by a sling over her forehead and a child, perched on the basket or attached to her hip with a sling. "All the while the husband may walk empty-handed ahead of her along the forest trail" (Peters 1998: 135).

Barry Hewlett has been the most dedicated student of the father's role in childcare, his interest stemming from his discovery that Aka foragers are extraordinary in the critical direct role played by fathers. He attributes this to two general phenomena: the nature of one of their principal subsistence activities – net-hunting – and a community ethos of gender equity. Net-hunting obligates the mother to strenuous work in which a baby is especially burdensome, but other women are similarly burdened. Older siblings may lack sufficient strength to carry infants and toddlers for the extended distances (eight to twelve kilometers per day) required, may be unable to adequately protect children from the forest's dangers, and are actively engaged in foraging on their own. Hence, fathers spell mothers on the hunt, and in camp – where grandmothers also make a significant contribution (Hewlett 1986). However, Hewlett, in subsequent research, also found that male status is inversely correlated with time allocated to childcare (Hewlett 1988): "males gain greater fitness returns by engaging in status maintaining or resource accumulation than from childcare activities" (Hames 1992: 225). In addition, he also acknowledges that new Aka (and Bofi, another Central African foraging group) fathers are required to contribute bride-service to their new in-laws and, consequently, tend to absent themselves from the camp at long intervals to hunt. In these cases, grandmothers take up the slack (Hewlett 1991: 41–42). Fouts' work among the Bofi and Aka also delimits father involvement, which is reduced when there were other – especially post-menopausal – women in camp (Fouts 2008: 300). While ethnographers of the !Kung, Hadza, and Ache, among others, note the occasional direct involvement in childcare by men, there is greater evidence of indirect care or provisioning. However, because hunters tend to "spread the wealth" of their prowess widely to attract additional mates (Hawkes 1991), researchers find, not surprisingly, that when a Hadza father dies, there is no noticeable effect on his children's survival or wellbeing (Blurton-Jones et al. 2000).

Divorce is extremely common in foraging societies. Divorced men invariably select younger mates with consequently greater childbearing potential than the mates they're divorcing (Low 2000). In pastoralist and horticultural societies, polygyny substitutes for the "serial polygamy" of frequent divorce, but family relationships remain fluid and divorce is not uncommon. Thus, the relative lack of involvement of fathers in childcare in traditional societies may attenuate the negative impact of divorce on children.

The role of the father's close kin may also vary widely. As we've seen, many women look to their families for child support and view their husbands' families as essentially hostile. In traditional Chinese and Muslim societies and others that are profoundly patriarchal, the father literally "owns" his children. The child's mother is seen not so much as the caretaker but as an incubator. It is entirely acceptable, therefore, for the father to remove his children from their mother's care and place them in the care of his family (Fernea 1991: 450) – a phenomenon that some estranged US wives of Middle Eastern men have discovered to their horror and eternal sorrow.

Employment opportunities associated with modernization bring new costs and benefits for village children and their mothers. Bock and Johnson conducted a very sophisticated natural experiment in Botswana on the impact of Botswana fathers on their children. They compared children of migrant workers with children of fathers resident in the village. The researchers reasoned that since the former were unable to enjoy the benefits – if any – of direct father involvement, they should show a decrement in traditional skill acquisition compared with their peers. No such decrement was found, indicating that fathers have little impact on children's skill acquisition. Bock and Johnson also reasoned that the remittances sent home by migrant fathers might be used to enhance child nutrition, and this prediction was confirmed for both boys and girls, who showed greater weight for their age than their peers (Bock and Johnson 2002: 329).

But it's not clear how consistently mothers and their offspring benefit from these new economic opportunities. On Java, women complain about their parasitic and irresponsible husbands, who "lack the self-discipline needed to bring money home at the end of the day instead of squandering it" (Brenner 2001: 147).

One positive role that fathers do seem to play in their offspring's lives is that of stern disciplinarian (Munroe 2005). In Central Asia, Tajik "children fear their father for his strictness and ability to hurt them" (Harris 2006: 66). Turkish fathers "play the role of the relatively distant authority whose main duty is to establish and enforce strict rules of conduct for the children" (Kagitçibasi and Sunar 1992: 82). This role also extends to guarding the virtue of daughters (Davis and Davis 1989: 78), who, in the absence of a father figure, are more likely to be promiscuous (Howard 1970: 76; see also Draper and Harpending 1982; Coley *et al.* 2009). Absent fathers may, therefore, leave socially maladjusted adolescents in their wake. To conclude this section, let me quote from a description of Yoruba fatherhood, which strikes me as quite representative:

Fatherhood exists almost independently of any engagement with … a child. Simply by having impregnated a woman, a man becomes a father – and remains "the owner of the child," irrespective of whether he makes any contributions to the child's upkeep. Men retain entitlements to children they have fathered … and through children who are publicly acknowledged as a man's offspring, women are able to make claims on men as the fathers-of-their-children. A child without a recognized father is stigmatized and bullied, and can turn against its mother in anger and shame. Having a father, then, is important for children as having children is for men, whether or not the two have any contact. (Cornwall 2001: 147)

As we noted in the previous chapter, a father's primary interest in the newborn is in deciding whether to keep it alive. And that decision is mediated not only by the physical condition of the infant and its mother but also by concerns about its paternity. "If he believes that the child is his own, he will ordinarily accept the 'minding' responsibility for the child" (Lange and Rodman 1992: 188). "Minding," in this case from the Caribbean, refers to indirect care or provisioning, not direct care of the child. The former is far more common than the latter. Palauan fathers are "conscientious providers" but are "bystanders" when it comes to direct care (Barnett 1979: 7). In one of the most thorough examinations of this issue, a study of 220 foragers in six camps, Hadza fathers brought home twice as much meat (measured in calories) to their biological offspring as to stepchildren (Hawkes 1991). Indirect care, in Marlowe's (1999: 401) research, does seem to make an appreciable difference in both reproductive success and child survival. Yet investigators are not finding much effect of father absence or death on child wellbeing, survival, or fitness (Winking *et al.* 2010: 87).

Next let's look at what happens to childcare as society becomes more complex, with greater social distance between classes of people.

Professional child-minders

If we turn to vase painting to look for evidence of what activities Athenian fathers shared with their young sons, the picture is meager indeed. (Shapiro 2003: 98)

The [Roman state] continually expresses … a low estimation of the desirability of or need for direct parental involvement in childrearing. (Boswell 1988: 82)

The most notable effect of the transition to more complex, urban society on the lives of children is that, for the well-off, biological parents are even less involved in childcare than before. Where there is wealth, leisure, and servants or slaves, mothers quickly divest themselves of any residual childcare responsibilities (Janssen and Janssen 1990). Wet-nurses, nannies, and tutors are essential and often quite valued members of the household (Emery 2010: 751). Indeed, one of the most spectacular tombs uncovered in Egypt is that of Maya, King Tut's wet-nurse. "From the Han dynasty to the Ming, there were numerous cases of emperors lavishing noble titles and other favors on their wet nurses" (Wu 1995: 133). Sculpture and vase paintings give us many clues to domestic life in ancient Greek society. Graves have yielded thousands of small statuettes of women holding children; these are the *kourotrophoi* or "child rearers." There's also a revealing scene on a large calyx krater (*c*.400 BCE) that depicts the death of two children. The parents look on, seemingly unconcerned, while their nurse and tutor show obvious signs of mourning (Neils and Oakley 2003).

The Romans went further than their predecessors in that abandonment and infanticide were at least loosely regulated, laws regarding the legal status and property rights of children were promulgated, and, during the reign of Augustus and later emperors, childbearing was encouraged and subsidies provided to parents. But at no time did Rome consider it important to promote the notion that parents (or siblings or grandparents, for that matter) should play any direct role in childrearing. Rather:

It was the *nutrix* [nurse] who ... took responsibility for ... early infant care: breast-feeding, powdering and swaddling, bathing and massaging, rocking and singing the child to sleep, weaning the child from milk to solid food ... The *nutrix*, in fact, was only one of a sequence of child-minding functionaries who influenced the early lives of children. (Bradley 1991: 26–27)

Paedagogues ... male slaves ... looked after young children. They played with them, took them on outings, taught them table manners, and generally baby-sat ... the paedagogue escorted [the child] to and from school ... baths, the theater, and social functions. The paedagogue might ... be responsible for teaching the child some simple reading and writing ... close bonds between upper-class children and their slave or lower-class caretakers [were discouraged, however, because] social distance must be maintained. (Shelton 1998: 33)

Expert advice was offered on how to select a wet-nurse since the infant could acquire the nurse's personal traits through her milk (Dasen 2010: 669). The use of professionals for childcare gradually spread downward. By the Middle Ages, women married to skilled laborers could afford to hire a wet-nurse, a task consigned to peasants. "One biographer noted that Michelangelo's nurse was a stonecutter's wife, by way of explaining his interest in sculpture" (Sommerville 1982: 80). Infants were usually lodged with wet-nurses, rarely visited, and then reclaimed once weaned – if they survived. Since the wet-nurse offered her services for money and not out of a love of babies,[28] her charges were usually swaddled and tucked out of harm's way while she went about her work (Sommerville 1982: 80).

This raised little concern because infants were widely seen as insensible. Almost like plants, their care could be rudimentary and not much "was actually expected of a caretaker ... virtually anyone could safely tend or carry a swaddled baby" (Calvert 1992: 23). Of the 21,000 babies registered in Paris in 1780, only 5 percent were nursed by their own mothers (Sussman 1982). This statistic is brandished by Hrdy as clear evidence of maternal indifference and her "prime exhibit in the case against maternal instincts in the human species" (Hrdy 1999: 351). But wet-nursing is evidence of a heightened investment in children by those who could afford it. The well-off also hired child-minders to look after and protect their children from manifold dangers:

A baby in the cradle might be caught in straps or cords ... burnt in a fire, choked by smoke, or attacked by an animal ... pigs were a particular source of danger, wandering into houses through open doors. (Orme 2003: 99)

Most parents had neither the time to "mind" their children nor the wealth to hire a minder. Children were left indoors or otherwise out of sight of adults. Potential sib-caretakers had economically more important work to do on a farm or in the craft workshop. Six- and seven-year-old wage earners were not unusual. Hence, nearly 60 percent of medieval English children who perished before they were a year old died in fires. "Most ... accidents ... happened during the workday, when [family members] were busy and distracted by work" (Colòn with Colòn 2001: 207).

From medieval times, if they didn't serve as farmhands, children left their natal home at an early age. Among the nobility, children were routinely sent to live with relatives or higher-status patrons in hopes of "advancement" (Colòn with Colòn 2001: 209). Children as young as five were donated by parents to the monastic life (Shahar 1990: 191). Outside the nobility, parents sent their five- to seven-year-old children (who were, in their view, no longer actually children) to the homes of master-craftsmen or merchants as apprentices, where the first decade of service might well be "scut-work" rather than the acquisition of usable skills. Daughters were sent into domestic "service."

Parents in sixteenth-century England were considered particularly callous in shipping off their offspring at an early age (Anonymous Venetian Diplomat 1847). However, Linda Pollock (1983), in her analysis of personal diaries, finds a gradual shift taking place in the seventeenth century. Cavalier

---

[28] The pervasive use of wet-nurses persisted in the US into the twentieth century and was commonly referred to as "baby-farming" (Riis 1890/1996: 184).

attitudes give way to solicitation. Even though childrearing is still a minor occupation for mothers compared with bearing them and managing the household, they now regularly visit their wet-nursed infants (Calvert 1992: 23). As the century advances and over the following two hundred years, a profound change will occur in notions about childrearing, fostered, in part, by the Reformation.

New metaphors for childrearing

The patriarchal family was the basic building block of Puritan society ... Male household heads exercised unusual authority over family members ... Childrearing manuals were thus addressed to men, not their wives. (Mintz 2004: 13)

Very gradually, popular views of infants changed, so that there was a growing sense of the need to *socialize* the young.

Like wild men [or beasts], babies lacked the power to reason, speak, or stand and walk erect. [They were] nasty, brutish, and dirty, communicating in wordless cries, grunts, and screams, and were given to crawling on all fours before they could be made to walk like men ... Left to their own devices, they would remain selfish, animalistic, and savage. Parents[29] believed they had to coerce their babies into growing up, and they expected protests and resistance. (Calvert 1992: 26, 34)

Swaddling remained popular, not only for the convenience of the caretaker but because it prevented the baby from crawling – which reinforced the child's animal nature and was dangerous, as homes were not "child-proofed." Swaddling also served to stretch the child's legs, which might otherwise atrophy.[30] "Standing stools" (today called "walkers") served the same function. In the Enlightenment era (seventeenth and eighteenth centuries) well-to-do parents hired governesses even though many were considered by "experts" to be unsuited to the demanding task of educating children for bourgeois society. In France, "conduct books" offered a substitute means of socializing girls whose professional caretakers were from the "wrong" class of society (Bérenguier 2011: 67).

The Puritans were the first society to create a truly comprehensive theory of childrearing, reflected in a steady stream of advice manuals published from the seventeenth century. They believed in the child's essentially animalistic and ungodly nature, taming which was the great challenge of

---

[29] Upper-crust parents had always held this view of children and expected the various child-minders in the household to shape up the children efficiently and turn them into miniature adults as soon as possible. But the "common" folk had, heretofore, thought about their infants much as parents in tribal societies still do – as hardy plants that needed little close attention.

[30] Most probably attributable to rickets.

parents. Anticipating contemporary Mormon views as noted early in this chapter, the Puritans argued that neither professionals (e.g. wet-nurses) nor neighbors could be expected to fulfill the arduous task of raising truly righteous individuals. Gradually the focus shifted from the father as the architect of the child's character to the mother, as there was growing recognition of the malleability of the very young (Mintz 2004: 71). But parents were cautioned against "natural" parenting instincts. For example, parents should not "cocker" or indulge their children or laugh at their high jinx because they'd only have to beat the waywardness out of them later in life (Sommerville 1982: 110). In fact, any sort of play on the part of the child was seen as "a sinful waste of time" (Mintz 2004: 19). The Puritans were perhaps the first anxious parents, fearing they might fail and their children would turn out badly. Many migrated to found new communities in order to isolate their children from the harmful effects of non-believing peers (Sommerville 1982: 112–113), much like parents today moving to a neighborhood because it has "good" schools.

But then along came Darwin, whose theory of natural selection influenced every area of thinking, including child psychology. Swaddling was condemned as protecting and restraining the child excessively, prohibiting it from being toughened up by nature's slings and arrows. Meanwhile, rapid industrialization absorbed the labor of women who formerly earned a living as wet-nurses and/or domestic help. So the child's mother was faced with fewer childcare options, and "many mothers turned to alcohol, opium, or other drugs to soothe a restless baby"(Calvert 1992: 76).

Entering the modern era, Western parents were discovering that they couldn't start too soon to prepare their children for the rigors of formal education. This is an imperative that had driven the childcare philosophies of East Asian societies for far longer. Since sons provided social security for elderly parents, it was in the parents' self-interest to prepare them[31] for the civil service examinations. Success demanded self-discipline, concentration, and rote memorization. Concepts like "womb education" or *T'aekyo*, and sayings such as "like three [years old], like a hundred" reflect a philosophy of child-rearing emphasizing the child's malleability (Uno 1991: 396) and the parent's obligation to make the most of it.

Attitudes about the care of children have changed so dramatically! We now take for granted the "need" to stimulate the infant through physical contact, motherese, and playing games like peek-a-boo to accelerate physical and intellectual development. Contrast these assumptions with the pre-modern

---

[31] In Singapore, "with the greater education and paid employment of females, many parents now say that daughters are 'as good as sons'" (Wee 1992: 192).

objective of keeping babies quiescent so they'd make fewer demands on caretakers and not injure themselves (LeVine *et al.* 1994).[32] Among the Maya, the overarching goal of childcare is to keep the baby quiet. Babies are provided with soothing comforts and never stimulated. Opportunities to explore the environment or interact with others are limited (Howrigan 1988: 41). Similarly, Chiga babies are kept quiet and not spoken to (Edel 1957/1996: 175), and traditional Chinese provide the infant "a tranquil and protective environment" (Bai 2005: 11).

If parents are to become the sole caretakers of children and, further, if this is now seen as requiring a much more interactive and demanding relationship with the child, broods can be expected to shrink.

The "Great" transition

Children become more costly to parents as societies modernize and this increased cost leads to decreased demands for [them]. (Turke 1989: 76)

Since I was sticking my nose into the lives of my neighbors in Gbarngasuakwelle (Lancy 1996), it was only fair to open up my personal life to them. They were particularly interested in my family and were appalled that someone as old as I was (twenty-eight) and so obviously wealthy – my clothes didn't have holes, I owned a radio and shoes – had no children. Indeed they were surprised I had only one spouse and I had to politely deflect matchmakers throughout my fieldwork. There was nothing in my explanation of why we felt the need to limit reproduction that made any sense to them. And it wouldn't have made sense to 99 percent of the world's pre-modern peoples. That evidently well-fed, clothed, and generally prosperous adults should choose to have few children is the paradox that scholars refer to as the "Great" or "demographic" transition, discussed in Chapter 3.

There is an ongoing shift in the burden of childcare from a widely dispersed kin network to the biological parents. Substitutes for kin as caretakers are both costly and unreliable (Turke 1989: 67, 71). This chapter has been replete with documentation of the first part of that equation. All other things being equal, the more you can shift the burden of childcare on to those who don't have small children of their own to care for, the more offspring you can have, thereby increasing genetic fitness. But, to participate in the modern economy, one must absent oneself from the household to attend school, accept

---

[32] The Dutch maintain a model of infancy in which plenty of sleep and restful, quiet waking periods is ideal. By contrast, US mothers are committed to keeping infants stimulated via physical contact, speech, and toys (Harkness and Super 2006: 69).

employment at a considerable remove, and establish a separate household from one's parents,[33] so shared childcare is no longer an option.

The *demographic transition* has been monitored around the globe. In Ireland, rigorous enforcement of child labor and compulsory schooling laws denied parents the opportunity of earning a direct return on their children. But government gave as it took away, providing new guarantees of social security, which "made it unnecessary for the poor to think of children as their main defense against misfortune, unemployment, or disability" (Sommerville 1982: 159). Fertility plummeted.[34] Mexico has undertaken a national effort to check its population growth.

Like many old-style Mexican matriarchs, Emma Castro Amador bore so many children that she can't keep their birthdays straight. Sometimes she even loses track of whether Oscar, her 10th, came before David, her 11th, or vice versa. "But I never regret having so many," said Mrs. Castro, 59, who had 14 children in 25 years. Mrs. Castro's offspring, however, have a different view. In a generational divide repeated in millions of Mexican families, all 14 say they are determined to limit their families to two or three children.[35] (Dillon 1999)

The demographic transition is becoming a worldwide phenomenon. The Samburu villagers studied by Swadener and colleagues have invested in building and staffing a pre-school, purchased or made toys for the children, and, most significantly, claimed that these new expenses were leading to a decrease in the number of children *and* wives in polygynous families (Swadener *et al.* 2000: 94). Even as women's work moves out of the home and into the public sphere, and as their dollar contribution to the household economy increases, their responsibility in the domestic sphere has not lessened (Tingey *et al.* 1996: 184). A "baby adds about ten days' worth of tasks to the household per month" (Seiter 1998: 304). Although lip service has been paid to husbands as "partners" in the home, at best they "help out" with jobs that the wife owns (Mederer 1993). That's assuming there is a husband around. "The percentage of US children living with their fathers has declined steadily since the 1960s" (Black *et al.* 1999: 967).

---

[33] When I worked for the Ministry of Education in Papua New Guinea, I was initially puzzled to find that teachers requested *not* to be assigned to teach in schools in their home area. But it soon became clear that, whatever they might gain by proximity to kin, they'd lose far more as relatives would "eat" all their wages.

[34] I'm one of two children while my mother was the youngest of twelve (nine living when she was born). Her immigrant parents were from East European peasant stock and she loved telling the story of her father (who lived to ninety-seven) relieving his still-resident sons of their pay packets from the (steel) "mill" each fortnight.

[35] And what is especially striking about these three cases (Ireland, Eastern Europe, and Mexico) is that individuals, in limiting the number of offspring, are, quite obviously, defying the teachings of their (Catholic) church.

Meanwhile, the task of childrearing has become vastly more demanding. Preparing a child to succeed in the modern economy so she can leave the nest and start a family of her own takes both time and money. Much of what we think of as the routine duties (e.g. reading bedtime stories; cf. Lancy 1994) or expenses (e.g. orthodontics) of modern parents are completely unknown outside modern, mainstream societies. On the other hand, the economic benefits of children also decline dramatically, as we saw in Chapter 2.

While these social changes were taking place, seismic shifts were occurring in the culture of childhood, as documented by Zelizer (1985) and discussed in Chapter 2. Basically, non-economic value was added to the child to counterbalance the obviously increased costs. The child became adorable, precious, special, cute as a bug's ear, the parents' pride and joy, Mom's best friend.

Raising children in the twenty-first century

Child-rearing is not physics. (Harris 1998: 86)

Mealtimes form part of the symbolic foundation of [middle-class] family life. (Fiese *et al.* 2006: 85)

To the French ... it seems like American kids are in charge ... the parents never say, "no." (Druckerman 2012: 68)

If children can be brought to fully competent adulthood in the hands of a cross-section of villagers, including, prominently, other children, then, following Judith Harris, childrearing surely isn't physics. Or is it? What I want to argue in the concluding section of this chapter is that preparing children to succeed in our contemporary, fast-paced, technologically dynamic, and information-charged society is extremely challenging. In East Asia, for example, the road to success passes through what is widely known as "examination hell," which the child cannot successfully navigate without the devoted attention of his mother (Lebra 1994: 264).

Unfortunately, childrearing can no longer follow the village model because, today, being raised by your older siblings probably means you're on your way to becoming a gang member (Achpal *et al.* 2007). Indeed, one might reasonably argue that video games and TV have become the typical child's sibling caretakers. And, in France, in the fall of 2005, when young African immigrants on a rampage torched hundreds of vehicles, we had tragic evidence of the failure of the village-based enculturation model to transfer to a modern, urban setting. Asked why the African parents had been unable to prevent their sons from running amok, a mosque director responded: "France is a democratic country. It gives rights to women and children, now parents cannot do anything – if they hit their 12-year-old, police will come to their door. There's a hot line the kids can call to report parental abuse" (Faramarzi 2005). In the USA, people often signal their aversion to other people's children by saying to the mother, in effect, "You are solely responsible for your kid, make sure she doesn't intrude into our lives." They may fear reprisal if they intervene to constrain the dangerous or illegal behavior of other people's children (Spilsbury and Korbin 2004).

To gauge how demanding this task is, I scanned the parenting guides selection at Amazon.com. There are literally hundreds available, and most parents will "own a small library on the subject" (Harkness *et al.* 1992: 175), including Dr. Spock's guide, second only to the Bible in sales of thirty million plus (Sommerville 1982: 12). At Amazon, I found books for every stage and milestone of the child's life. There are books for Christian parents, Jewish parents, combos, and those who find inspiration in astrology. There are books for homosexual parents and homophobic parents; young parents and older parents; books for confident parents, anxious parents, and clueless parents. There are parenting books for every ethnic and religious group. There are books for divorced parents and for parents who want to avoid divorce. There are books to cope with underachieving kids and overachieving kids, sick kids and super-athletes. Books guide the parent in meal preparation, bedroom decoration, birthday-party organization, vacation planning, children's book choices, choosing a pre-school, a nanny, a music teacher, a team, and a teacher. The list is almost endless. So, rather than rely on the wisdom of grandparents, we turn to books, newspapers, and magazines for the "latest scientific information" (Welles-Nyström 1988: 79).

The "Mommy Wars" (Steiner 2007) notwithstanding, studies consistently show that "the impact of maternal employment on child wellbeing [is] negligible" (Bengston *et al.* 2002: 158). Two things do matter[36] a great deal: family income and mother's education (Black *et al.* 1999: 974). Income has an impact on the extent to which the mother can purchase aids like playpens, walkers, high-chairs, strollers, Tommee-Tippee cups, and disposable diapers that reduce the labor of infant-care. Infants in the United States are held much less than their counterparts from an African village and they "spend a considerable amount of time in various sorts of 'containers,' such as high chairs and playpens" (Richman *et al.* 1988: 70). Also, child-oriented "videos provide tired mothers time to cook dinner, feed the baby, or clean the house. Toys keep children entertained while they [ride] along . . . on errands" (Berk 1985: 306).

---

[36] Other variables that don't seem to have much impact on children's successful adaptation, by themselves, are: father absence, homosexual parents, and being conceived in a test-tube (Harris 1998: 51).

The well-off mother can purchase devices to reduce domestic labor; for example, "very small kitchen areas ... [and] lack of a dishwasher [mean that] Japanese mothers uniformly washed dishes at least three times a day; American mothers did so an average of about once a day" (Fogel *et al.* 1992: 38). Her up-scale home or apartment will have private recreation areas and/or be located near public playgrounds or parks where she can safely allow her children to play without supervising them while she does the chores. She can afford to pay someone to come in and do her household work. A higher income purchases quality daycare[37] – consistently shown not to diminish the child's life-chances as compared with those of children raised by "fulltime moms" (Scarr 1997). After school there is youth soccer, little league, girl scouts, as well as music, ballet, and *tai kwan do* lessons – all correlated with enhanced academic success or standing in one's peer group.

Education contributes to a mother's success in childrearing[38] in a number of, sometimes quite subtle, ways. "Getting an education" usually means delaying childbearing until one has acquired a comparably educated, supportive husband (Fogel *et al.* 1992: 38–39). Continuing one's education through college may delay childbearing until one has achieved a measure of emotional and financial stability. Better-educated women may have the learning skills and motivation to acquire the cultural capital associated with successful childrearing – even in the face of adverse circumstances, like the child's attention deficit disorder, unfavorable schools, or divorce. Better-educated women make smarter choices in terms of childcare aids and personnel; they know which parenting guides to buy from Amazon.com! Education level implicates particular childcare behaviors.

Among the middle class, it is customary to hold babies *en face* and to talk to them using a special form of language referred to as *motherese*. We respond contingently to the baby's reactions.[39] Signs of displeasure, excitement, engagement, and distraction provoke nuanced and varied speech, including

---

[37] In Europe, public, surrogate caretakers loom even larger in the overall picture; northeastern Italy and Sweden, in particular, are noted for their comprehensive and effective pre-school programs. Subsidized by progressive civil authorities, they are open to all children, not just those whose parents can afford them. Public attitudes in Europe reflect a view of the family that echoes the utopian ideals of the Israeli kibbutz from the mid-twentieth century. While the mother might be the primary caretaker during infancy, shortly afterward the child should be placed in a nursery with trained staff as she returns to her job. This policy is seen as beneficial to the mother's self-esteem, the economy, and the child itself (Corsaro 1996; Dahlberg 1992; Eibl-Eibesfeldt 1983: 181). Publicly supported pre-school or daycare in the US has been blocked by the politically powerful religious right, which insists on keeping wives tied full-time to the kitchen and nursery.

[38] Mother's education is an extremely powerful predictor of children's academic success and this is especially true in poorer communities in the industrialized world, as well as throughout the developing world, (LeVine *et al.* 2012).

[39] Talking to one's fetus is becoming popular, too (Han 2009: 13).

tone and non-verbal signals. In comparative studies, "American middle-class parents show the most extreme prosodic modifications ... in infant-directed speech" (Fernald 1992: 399–400). Additional research demonstrates convincingly that, when adults speak often to infants, the infants pick up certain linguistic skills, such as word segmentation, earlier (Thiessen *et al.* 2005: 68). The child's first words are marked as important milestones and vocabulary development is accelerated through naming games of various kinds. "What is ____?" questions gradually expand to the full panoply of Socratic interrogation routines.

US child psychologists have fostered the idea of teaching pre-linguistic babies to use American Sign Language (ASL). Enthusiastic devotees offer dazzling testimonials such as the following:

Our oldest (now three) has a vocabulary more than most five-year-olds. Even our pediatrician commented on his vocabulary skills .... My son is only twelve months old and he can communicate what he wants and needs and is very patient with me by nodding "yes" or "no" when I am learning to understand his talk. No language barriers, and he talks [signs] better than most two-year-olds. Hurray for Baby Signs! ... Considering how slowly babies learn even easy words like ball and doggy, let alone difficult words like scared or elephant, many months are lost that could be spent having rich and rewarding interactions, both for the child and the parent. (Acredolo and Goodwyn 2002: testimonials, 3)

This intense and varied early language curriculum is all the more remarkable in that it is totally unnecessary (MacNeilage and Davis 2005: 708). Children become fluent speakers of their mother tongue in societies where no language instruction occurs – which is the norm. Clearly Euroamerican and Asian parents are preparing children to be more than merely competent native speakers. They encourage the development of narrative ability through frequent queries about the child's activity, including their subjective assessments: "mothers pick up on children's ... topics, repeat and extend what their children say, and adjust their language ... to support the child's projects" (Martini 1995: 54). Toddlers are expected to hold and to voice their opinions! As parents seek "explanations" from their children, they also tolerate interruptions and contradiction (Portes *et al.* 1988). And this entire package of cultural routines is almost completely absent in the ethnographic record (Robinson 1988).

Savvy parents carefully manage their children's access to food, TV, video and computer games, and, above all, peers – all of which have the potential to help or harm the child. Regular times for family meals, waking, and bed allow the child to internalize orderly practices so that family regulation becomes self-regulation (Fiese *et al.* 2006: 85). The parents believe "that their investment in the 'right' education toy, software, summer camp, or home teaching program [will] help their offspring avoid the temptations of an indulgent society and gain the competitive edge to win the brass ring of success" (Cross 2004: 194).

While the parent-as-(patient-)teacher role has become enshrined as the gold standard (Goodnow 1990: 280), studies, in fact, show wide variability in contemporary parents' effectiveness as teachers. If we look outside the hypothetical mainstream of modern parenting, the teaching role shrinks drastically. Poorly schooled teen parents in the USA rarely talk with their children and in standard free-play sessions, they don't know how to play with them (Gross *et al.* 2003). Mothers who live in urban high-rise ghettos seldom converse with their small children; most verbalizations are short commands or reprimands (Heath 1990). Mothers from West Africa living in France "do not usually talk to their children during childcare or diapering, which, in contrast, are rich exchange periods for French ... mothers" (Jamin 1994: 156).

Village parents don't use the same strategies we've seen as prevalent in mainstream Euroamerican society because they aren't necessary. Far less demanding socialization routines and processes (see Chapter 5) will suffice. Parents don't need to look for teachable moments. "In a Mayan community ... children are taught to avoid challenging an adult with a display of greater knowledge by telling them something" (Rogoff 1990: 60). West African Wolof parents never quiz their kids by asking known-answer questions (Irvine 1978) – a favorite trick of Euroamerican parent-teachers. Fijian children are never encouraged to address adults or even to make eye contact. Rather their demeanor should express timidity and self-effacement (Toren 1990: 183).

It is only when confronted with the challenge of preparing for the demands of schooling and white-collar employment that these *laissez-faire* strategies can't get the job done.[40] The comfortable learning atmosphere of the village is severely altered when societies become so complex that only a well-educated and knowledgeable bureaucracy can keep things running smoothly: "schooling exploded in thirteenth-century Italy ... in 1333 it was decreed that public officials and judges must be able to read and write to hold their jobs" (Olson 2003: 16). Civil service usually implies a meritocracy, which in turn implies formal means of education and assessment. A new stratum of society is created, access to which may be open only to those with merit.

---

[40] Interestingly, when attempts have been made – by a museum in this particular case – to create settings in which children are to learn didactic or factual information through the informal means practiced in the village, the results are disastrous. Researchers report that: "informal learning environments, in and of themselves, have no greater claim on solid, conceptually accurate, deeply meaningful interpretations than any other form of learning. We should not expect too much" (Leinhardt and Knutson 2004: 17).

Families who aspire to place their offspring in contention must adopt an entirely new approach to childrearing. It is no longer practical to wait until the child is "ready." Training in self-discipline, the deferral of reward, and verbal fluency must begin very early.[41] An ethnographic study comparing childrearing in the modern sector of Bhubaneswar (India) versus "Old Town" revealed that little or no parental teaching occurred in Old Town, while "upper status households were adapting to a society increasingly characterized by an emphasis on formal education and competition for new kinds of jobs" by active teaching at home (Seymour 2001: 16; see also Tahiti – Levy 1996).

However, this brings up some consideration of contemporary debates on parenting philosophies across the spectrum of societies that have made the demographic transition. Striking differences emerge even between Euroamerican society and one as similar as modern Japan. The mid-upper-class American mother, in talking to and stimulating her baby, acts on the belief that it is autonomous and eager to become a distinct social being. The Japanese mother, by contrast, lulls and comforts her baby. She sees the baby as an appendage, "and psychologically the boundaries between the two of them are blurred" (Caudill 1988: 49, 67).

In the USA parents pursue an optimization strategy. Its core belief is that each child has the potential to be a standout – at something. They see their role as a diagnostician searching out the child's strengths and weaknesses, nurturing the former and remedying or downplaying the latter (Pugh 2009). A middle-class US mother explains that:

She first sent her daughter Hailey to swimming lessons at age six when another mother told her that the young girl had the body of a swimmer. The mother proudly recounts how Hailey immediately excelled in the sport and was accepted to the club swim team the first time she tried out. (Kremer-Sadlik *et al.* 2010: 40)

A secondary and related goal in the US is that the child should be popular with peers and "well liked by all," which accounts in part for the extraordinary investment parents are willing to make in the child's extracurricular activity and in his or her wardrobe and treasury of possessions. This creates a striking contrast with the East Asian model, where high academic achievement is the primary objective and the belief is that the child should willingly forego popularity for exceptionality (Li 2012: 43).

A best-selling book, *Battle Hymn of the Tiger Mom*, sought to create a clear distinction between models of "good" childrearing in China (and among Chinese-Americans) and the USA. The Tiger Mom insists on high

---

[41] On the downside, in the USA, a three-year-old – denied admission to the "best" private pre-school – may now carry the burden of failing to "make the grade" (Kusserow 2004: 81).

academic and musical achievement; US mothers feel that "stressing success was not good for children" (Chua 2011: 5). Tiger Moms expect their children to work hard, to suffer, and to suppress any feelings of aversion or resistance. US Moms want their kids to "have fun" and to like them, to be their "best friends." Chua records this telling conversation with her daughter: "'My friend Maya is so lucky,' she said wistfully, 'she has so many pets' ... I said 'Maybe that's why she's only in Book One of violin because she's too busy taking care of pets ... Your violin is your pet'" (Chua 2011: 65). A second best-seller in this vein, *Bringing up Bébé*, contrasts French and US parenting ideology. Like the Chinese, the French aren't afraid to assert parental authority and rule by fiat – for the child's good. The French believe that parental needs should, generally, take precedence over child wants, and, more specifically, French children are expected to follow an adult diet and "proper" table manners without complaint and to avoid disturbing parents who are otherwise engaged. And, compared to US and Chinese parents, "French parents ... don't push their kids to read, swim, or do math ahead of schedule. They aren't trying to prod them into becoming prodigies" (Druckerman 2012: 80).

At the outset of this chapter, I set up a juxtaposition. One view holds that, to succeed in life, children require the near-full-time attention of a mother who treats childrearing as a vocation and prepares herself assiduously. A contrary view is that this is a task best shared among a variety of individuals, a village. What can we conclude? I would argue that, to prepare a child for life in the village, it is neither necessary nor an efficient use of scarce resources to put the burden on any one individual. However, to prepare a child for the modern world, spreading the responsibility among a variety of individuals – none of whom is in charge – invites disaster. Hillary Clinton, in *It Takes a Village*, tries to apply the village model to the modern situation. She argues for improvements in schools and social service agencies, an increase in library and playground facilities, and after-school programs – among other things (Clinton 1996). All these proposals are helpful, but all these agents – teachers, librarians, playground supervisors, Boys & Girls Club volunteers – cannot, collectively, substitute for a dedicated, resourceful parent. They are not related to the child and, in our society, the village is not responsible. The parent is. At best, these agents can only assist the parent in fulfilling their plan for the child (Fosburg 1982).

Having said that much, I want immediately to disavow any claim that this task requires the full-time ministrations of the child's biological mother. There is overwhelming evidence – not reviewed here – that fathers, adoptive parents, lesbian partners of the biological mothers, and grandparents can all do a fine job. Any of them, or the child's mother, can and usually do avail themselves of an array of supplementary caretakers. A working mother, in particular, may well bring home cultural, intellectual, and, certainly, economic resources that a non-working mother cannot provide.

So parenting in contemporary society is at least somewhat like physics, as it is tough to insure the child's future success and a close, lasting filial relationship. But, ultimately, we come full circle in that, as long as a reasonably competent and caring individual is in charge, the more loving, intelligent, and dedicated helpers surrounding the nest, the better off the twenty-first-century child will be.

5   Making sense

Introduction

Learning to work was like play. We [Hopi] children tagged around with our elders and copied what they did. (Simmons 1942: 51)

Chiga children, like Topsy, just grow. They learn the ways of their culture by observation and participation, and only occasionally by precept. (Edel 1957/1996: 173)

In the previous chapter we looked at childhood through the lens of dependency. Infants and children can be distinguished from the young of mammals, generally, because, while their brains are large and growing rapidly, representing over half of their metabolism, yet they remain virtually helpless and in an immature state for a very long time. Others must care for them. In this chapter, we will examine the flip side of that coin and look at how "brainy" but incompetent children set about acquiring their culture and becoming competent members, ultimately supporting their erstwhile caretakers. This process we might characterize as "making sense," which incorporates two ideas. One is that the child must strive to understand or make sense of all that's going on around her, and this begins in infancy. And two, the child strives to be accepted, to fit in. This social milestone (see the "Delayed personhood" section in Chapter 2, pp. 38–40) may be marked by acknowledging that the child now has "sense."

One of the most compelling attributes of childhood is the children's tendency to be avid spectators. Babies are quite attentive and continue, through childhood, to relish the role of observer. Observation and imitation or, more specifically, make-believe (in play) seem to serve complementary ends. Being a spectator and incorporating what one has observed into one's play are simultaneously entertaining and educational. Further, there is a clear expectation held by adults that children's observation/imitation predilections insure that they are learning their culture largely without explicit instruction (Phillips 1983: 63).

Children also learn from their universal need to explore and handle objects – possibly as a precursor to tool-handling. This tendency may be accommodated by adults who donate items that can function as miniature tools, dolls, or other props to be woven into make-believe scenarios. Adult encouragement of play must be offset by concern for the child's safety and wellbeing, if the child is left to play without restraint (Lancy 2001b).

As children engage in play, they are typically under the supervision of siblings and other young neighbors, who, coincidentally, serve as excellent role models for more mature behavior. While active play is tolerated within limits, the child's need to "fit in" will be thwarted until he can join the family circle and be seen but not heard. The "good" child will be encouraged to observe and emulate those engaged in helpful acts such as errand-running, fetching water and firewood, cleaning the domestic space, and so on.

In contemporary society, the child is a pupil from birth, if not before. The domains where the village child is free from adult control, during play, for instance, are co-opted by Euroamerican and Asian parents to serve very specific ends in the child's preparation for schooling. Whereas we intervene to accelerate the child's intellectual development, elsewhere children under the age of seven or eight are seen as lacking sense, unable to benefit from instruction. Nevertheless, we do see parents, however infrequently, "pushing" children to learn proper etiquette and kin terminology. At least one reason appears to be to make the child a more attractive candidate for shared nurturing. A polite child will garner willing child-minders to relieve the mother of this burden (Kilbride 1975: 88, 93). A second reason is the strong desire to encourage more mature, socially acceptable behavior on the part of the child.

Parents welcome a child's display of "sense" at the onset of middle childhood (Nerlove *et al.* 1974: 271). Although various interpretations are placed on the term, they cluster around acting responsibly, showing respect, and carrying out chores effectively – rather than, say, intelligence, cleverness, or verbal fluency. Village children conform readily to family expectations – they may not be fed, otherwise! Of course, kids being kids, deviation will occur. And I discuss some of the most common means of encouraging compliance, including the use of scare tactics and corporal punishment.

Gender role socialization follows a similar path, in that children gravitate to appropriate behaviors well before puberty, bearing in mind that village life is highly gendered. Men's and women's roles are quite distinct. Nevertheless, the symbolic, political, and economic importance of gender raises the bar in terms of parental concern, and steps may be taken to accelerate or highlight the transition from "child" to "girl."

In the last section, I acknowledge the elephant in the living room: teaching. I discuss the prevailing view in WEIRD society – among most scholars as well as the public at large – that children's development into mature, competent members of society depends critically on the guidance and lessons, beginning in infancy, provided by an eager parent who's a "naturally gifted" teacher. Based on unequivocal evidence of the relative unimportance of teaching in the ethnographic record, I question that assumption as well as its evolutionary foundation.

The wisdom of babies

Primate infants seem to have been selected to be information extractors. (King 1999: 21)

Babies as young as 4 months already possess a "theory of physics." (Norenzayan and Atran 2004: 151)

Zinacanteco infants ... quiet and alert, attentively observed their surroundings, laying the foundation for later observational learning. (Greenfield *et al.* 1989)

A recent development in the West but of greater antiquity in the Far East is the conviction that the fetus and newborn require mental stimulation. Elsewhere, most would agree with the !Kung:

A child who is nursing has no awareness of things. Milk, that's all she knows. Otherwise, she has no sense. Even when she learns to sit, she still doesn't think about anything because her intelligence hasn't come to her yet. Where could she be taking her thoughts from? The only thought is nursing. (Shostak 1981: 113)

Defying such conventional wisdom, since the mid-1980s, there has been a revolution in research on infants with the invention of very interesting paradigms to study what would earlier have been called an oxymoron – infant cognition (Gopnik *et al.* 2000). Studies have established that babies automatically deploy a range of capacities that aid them in making sense of the world, including basic principles of physics, mathematics, biology, and psychology (Bloch *et al.* 2001; Norenzayan and Atran 2004: 151). This catalog of capacities can also be mined for evidence of *core knowledge* (Carey and Spelke 1996) systems that function as "learning devices" (Baillargeon and Carey 2012: 58). As an alternative to Locke's *tabula rasa* or the empty vessel waiting patiently to be filled, infant cognition scholars posit the untutored emergence of key concepts and modules that facilitate learning about the world (MacDonald and Hershberger 2005: 25).

Among the infant's suite of capacities for learning the culture, "parsing" is getting increased attention. The most obvious application is in language acquisition (Saffran *et al.* 1996: 1927). The infant's segmentation or parsing capacity has been extended to the realm of physical objects (Spelke 1990: 54). Infants may also be able to parse the behavior of their companions. The young seem to apply a parsing strategy to "'see below the surface' of behavior, and detect the logical organization that produced it" (Byrne 2006: 494). This, according to Byrne, may account for children's evident ability to acquire complex skills through observing others – referred to as *social learning* (Bandura 1977).

Aside from decoding their physical world, babies must also be busy decoding their social world, and learning their native language must be seen as the keystone of this effort (Flinn and Ward 2005: 27). Earlier models assumed infants were "taught" to speak by their parents but "there is growing evidence that ... children are able to create and negotiate complex communication systems from scratch and relatively quickly, without a prior model" (Steels 2006: 347).

Well before language develops, studies document the child's early understanding of social relations (Callaghan *et al.* 2011). Human infants are confronted with the need to secure care from potentially uncommitted mothers and a shifting cast of alloparents. "To prosper in such a system, infants have to be adept at monitoring caretakers, reading their moods and intentions and eliciting their solicitude" (Hrdy 2006: 25). In short, instead of a "scientist in the crib" (the title of the Gopnik *et al.* 2000 volume), we may have a "Machiavellian in the crib" (Lancy 2010a: 97; see also Maestripieri 2007: 122).

The "precocity" of infants as social actors is now well established. By three months they can distinguish faces and familiar vs. unfamiliar individuals; they can detect various facial expressions; by five months, they can decode these expressions; and at seven months, they discriminate between more and less emotional expressions and respond appropriately (LaFrenicre 2005: 192). At twelve months, they attend to and follow their mother's gaze (Okamoto-Barth *et al.* 2011), which launches the "education of [the child's] attention" (Ingold 2001: 139). At a year they can respond, appropriately, with pride or shame (Trevarthen 2005). By eighteen months, infants reliably use other's facial expressions as a guide to their own behavior, reacting appropriately to expressions showing fear, joy, or indifference (Klinnert *et al.* 1983).

By the time they reach the toddler stage, children can enact powerful strategies for learning the culture.

Young children also go beyond imitating observable outcomes and instrumental techniques; strikingly, they also abstract the adult's goals. Children will skip over a poorly performed accidental act and instead imitate acts that appear purposeful. If an adult is unsuccessful in an attempt to complete a task, toddlers will copy the intended goals instead of the observed outcome ... An important characteristic of human imitation is that it can be deferred; a child may watch his father behave in a certain way and store it in memory. This stored representation then is tapped at a later time when the child finds himself in a similar situation and is uncertain how to behave ... The fact that children can imitate over such lengthy delays suggests that imitation is a powerful learning mechanism before other processes, such as direct instruction through language, are possible. (Meltzoff and Williamson 2009: 481)

Not at all the "buzzing confusion" William James referred to as the infant's mind (1890/1981: 542), infancy and early childhood are now seen as periods of intense, almost non-stop learning. Infant cognition studies are generally supportive of the position that children take the initiative in the acquisition of culture. But, at the same time, universal aspects of culture seem designed to facilitate this process as well (Ingold 2001: 142). Importantly, children are allowed – even expected – to act as voyeurs or spectators.

Children as spectators

Male camels seem to have problems in copulating successfully, and [Pashtu] boys and girls of all ages stand next to the pair and look closely to see whether they succeed. (Casimir 2010: 64)

[Talensi] children learn who their ... ancestors (*banam ni yaanam*) are by listening at sacrifices. (Fortes 1938/1970: 22)

Speech and other sources of language – overheard speech, stories – provide such rich input that children should eventually learn enough of their language for all their needs. (E. V. Clark 2005: 429)

Children are great observers. In the Kpelle village of Gbarngasuakwelle, the average court case is just slightly more interesting than watching grass grow. Imagine a forty-minute debate about the failure to promptly return a borrowed lantern or an even longer debate over the amount of compensation appropriate in the case of an adulterous liaison (the juicy details are discreetly glossed over). And yet the court never failed to attract a good crowd of juvenile male spectators (Lancy 1980a). While the boys watching the chief's court were quiet and blended in with their surroundings, it was obvious that the chief saw them as "pupils" in an open-air classroom. Targeting his youthful audience, his rhetorical questions and judicial "opinions" often reflected basic principles of Kpelle morality. Observation soon turns into imitation.

Ngoni boys ... played ... at law courts ... in their high squeaky voices [they] imitated their fathers whom they had seen in the courts, and they gave judgments, imposing heavy penalties, and [kept] order in the court with ferocious severity. (Read 1960: 84)

Most societies are keenly aware of the child as voyeur and fully expect to use public events for their didactic value (Atran and Sperber 1991). Elizabeth Fernea illustrates this phenomenon for the Middle East. One of the

Figure 11 Child spectators at a funeral in Toradja, Sulawesi

time-honored public ceremonies is the post-nuptial display of a bloodstained sheet. Signaling the bride's virginity and the husband's potency, the gesture preserves the honor of bride and groom and their families. Children are present on these occasions, "so these tests of honor were made clear through observation and . . . through admonition and discussion of honor" (Fernea 1991: 454). Simon Ottenberg describes the Igbo feast of the tortoise in West Africa as a "rite of reversal" in which normally private behavior is publicly exposed. The feast includes dancing and singing, where bawdy songs openly describe sexual practices. Children are spectators of all these events, and "the content of the songs may help children to learn sexual rules and constraints" (Ottenberg 1989: 113). Further, children continue singing these songs as they work for months afterwards. Figure 11 shows child spectators at a funeral in Toradja, Sulawesi.

Children's "education" among the Talensi includes eavesdropping on adult conversation. "No one would inhibit his conversation or actions because children are present" and, no surprise, children demonstrate "comprehensive and accurate sexual knowledge" at six (Fortes 1938/ 1970: 37). Tlingit children learn "by listening to the stories of ... the old men gathered in the sweathouse to bathe and chat" (de Laguna 1965: 15). Bonerate children are "content to sit around ... for an hour or so" watching adults at work (Broch 1990: 72). On Fiji, "any lively gathering in the house or village hall attracts small groups of children, who range themselves outside the building and peer at the proceedings through the chinks and crevices in the bamboo slats" (Toren 1988: 241).[1]

[Biyaka] children are almost constantly in the presence of at least one adult and have therefore almost ubiquitous opportunity for observational learning of adult subsistence behaviors. Furthermore, "watching," a behavior that is necessarily the commencing act of any visual observational learning, was a very high-frequency activity across all age groups. (Neuwelt-Truntzer 1981: 109)

Could children's tendency to observe closely the actions of others convey an evolutionary advantage? One of the most exciting debates in biobehavioral research since the mid-1990s has been over whether "culture" is a uniquely human phenomenon. Studies of chimps in the wild have added the most fuel to this fire.[2] We now have a lengthy catalog of practices that are associated only with specific chimp populations, meaning they aren't hard-wired. These practices include: making sponges out of leaf bundles to soak water up from puddles; using stones to crack open nuts; group-hunting of prey; and using twigs stripped of their leaves to "fish" termites out of their nests (Marks 2003). Tool use among chimpanzees – as among early hominins – affords access to hard-to-get foods, permitting an expansion and diversification of the resource base (Yamakoshi 2001: 547). These practices are enduring, they are passed from one generation to the next, ergo, culture! Furthermore, the transmission of culture for apes and humans seems to occur largely through juveniles imitating an expert model (Matsuzawa *et al.* 2001: 571). Studies of the acquisition of the complex skill of termiting in Gombe show that female chimps learn it from their mothers roughly two years earlier than do juvenile males. The females stay nearer to their mothers, watch them closely, and emulate their behavior – while males are busy playing. The mothers never actually "teach" the skill, learning depends mostly on careful observation and, secondarily, on diligent practice (Lonsdorf 2005: 680–681).

---

[1] Unfortunately, the universal predilection for learning through observation leads, eventually, to TV addiction and couch potatoes.
[2] Orangutans also have unique cultural traditions within populations: "In Sumatra, orangutans use sticks to pry calorie-rich seeds from prickly, hard-to-eat Neesia fruits, a clever trick that youngsters pick up from adults" (Knott 2003: 78).

Of course human culture is several orders of magnitude more complex than chimp culture. A framework that I have found inspirational in this context I owe to Jack Roberts, who wrote:

> It is possible to regard all culture as information and to view any single culture as an "information economy" in which information is received or created, stored, retrieved, transmitted, utilized, and even lost ... information is stored in the minds of ... members and ... artifacts ... [In this view, children are seen as] ... storage units [which] must be added to the system ... as older members of the society disappear. (Roberts 1964: 438, 439)

If culture is information, then we can ask: how do children acquire it? There are a variety of possible mechanisms, but first and foremost, children observe and copy the behavior of more mature individuals.[3] Humans share with most primates – baboons, for example (King 1999: 21) – the ability to learn from others even when the models aren't intending to demonstrate or instruct. It is patently less costly for an individual to observe and attempt to replicate the proficient behavior of an expert, rather than operate in a social vacuum or "learn individually" (McElreath 2004). In fact, Richerson and Boyd (1992: 70) argue that this trait is the key facilitator for the establishment of cultural traditions. In species in which the young don't automatically observe and imitate others, such as Cebus monkeys, cultural traditions don't arise (Visalberghi and Fragasky 1990). Even when social learning is likely, learners may well introduce variation in technique, which may be retained and passed on (Byrne 1995: 57; see also Toshisada 2003) or not (Boyd and Richerson 1996).

Children's capacities to learn through observation serve them well as they explore and learn about the natural environment. Hilger claims that Araucanian children have "keen" eyesight, hearing and "powers of observation ... going along a path, they will trace the steps of tiny insects I can hardly see" (Hilger 1957: 50). I was similarly impressed by Kpelle children's ability to parse the environment:

> I was led into the bush on a mushroom-hunting expedition by a group of children barely out of toddler-hood. The atmosphere was entirely playful, yet the children were able to locate and gather [edible] mushrooms that were completely invisible to me. (Lancy 1996: 156)

---

[3] Think about the complex defensive mechanisms that we've developed to combat academic cheating. What we are doing, in essence, is recalibrating the cost–benefit equation to favor individual effort to counteract the more "natural" approach, namely, copying the answers from a classmate. For a scholarly discussion of the trade-offs between individual and social learning, see Rogers (1989) and Richerson and Boyd, who aver: "Plagiarism is usually easier than invention" (1992: 65).

The Ache are Paraguayan forest foragers, and children

learn to follow the signs indicating that Ache have walked through an area. These signs, which are almost invisible to the untutored, consist of bent leaves, twigs, and shrubs that the Ache call a *kuere* or "trail." Following these trails is one of the most important forest skills, and *most children are successful by about eight years of age*. This enables children to navigate between camps without always being in the sight of adults, and it allows boys to begin small hunting forays without getting lost. (Hill and Hurtado 1996: 223 – emphasis added).

Children's interest in and profound knowledge of the natural environment is not at all limited to foraging societies and does not depend on adult guidance or demonstration (Chipeniuk 1995: 492).[4] The Bakkarwal are pastoralists and yet children learn to navigate their surroundings and to exploit appropriate and relevant natural products (Rao 2006: 58). Zapotec (Mexican farmers) children's excellent command of ethnobotany is described as "everyday knowledge acquired without apparent effort at an early age by virtually everyone in town" (Hunn 2002; 610).

Children's ability to take in and process information from the environment suggests an unlearned capacity for what Gaskins and Paradise call "open attention," which can be deployed to good effect in social settings as well as in the natural environment (2010: 104).[5] They describe open attention as wide-angled and abiding. The first means that the individual is aware of and attends to a great deal of the environment at one time – rather than attending to only one information source (video game, teacher). The second means that attention is sustained rather than episodic or short-term (2010: 99–100). Further examples:

As observers, in both detail and precision, the Aivilik continually amazed me. Again and again, they saw what I did not. A seal on the ice was known to them long before I could see it, even when the direction was indicated. Yet my eyes are 20–20. Standing at the floe edge they could tell at a glance whether it was a bird or seal, a seal or square-flipper ... the children would continue to watch long after it had disappeared from my view. (Carpenter 1973: 26)

An Eveny [Siberian pastoralist] adolescent can remember each reindeer in a herd ... recognize a reindeer from a different herd – or a wild reindeer which [had] joined [the] herd – and other tiny details. (Ulturgasheva 2012: 114)

---

[4] There are exceptions to these two generalizations. First, urban youth in the US do not – without instruction – acquire a sophisticated knowledge of the natural world (Atran and Medin 2008: 128). Second, there are a few cases in the literature of grandmothers conducting educational tours through the bush to acquaint their younger kin with medicinal plants (Ngandu – Hewlett 2013: 76; Tonga – Reynolds 1996: 7).

[5] Open attention seems to be of singular importance to Mongolian pastoralists (Lattimore 1941: 209).

In comparative research, children and adults from the WEIRD society displayed short, fleeting attention (think of a teenager on the living room floor doing homework with the TV on and listening to music through earphones) whereas Mayan mothers and children displayed sustained attention (Chavajay and Rogoff 1999). In a second relevant study, the investigators found that Mexican village children learned a great deal from carefully observing an instructional episode in which they were *not* the target of instruction, compared to acculturated migrants in the US who ignored the instruction when they weren't targeted (Sliva *et al.* 2011). In an Australian study, Aboriginal children solved a visual pattern task by deploying a visuo-spatial approach, in contrast to white children who attempted to use a less successful verbal strategy (Kearins 1986). It may well be that open attention is subject to a critical period during which, if it is not exercised (because, for example, WEIRD parents spend so much time focusing the infant/child's attention on them as a teacher, on educational toys and the like), it will be extinguished. A case in point:

The [middle-class] mother . . . made suggestions for pretend play . . . she asked the child "What does Mommy do when I put mail in the mailbox that the postman needs to pick up? Remember?" By reminding her son to put the red flag up on the pretend mailbox, she used the play as a context to teach her child about the world. (Vandermaas-Peeler *et al.* 2009: 93–94)

In an early and enduring theory of child development, humans, from birth, are motivated to act on the environment in every way open to them in order to develop competence. Humans find such mastery rewarding and experience a "feeling of efficacy" (White 1959: 329). This drive transitions at age three or four into a more general motive to "strive for success," according to Weisfeld and Linkey (1985: 110). They argue that children are able to translate practical accomplishments, such as successful foraging or carrying home some firewood, into social capital. As we've seen, a great deal of what one needs to master the culture can be learned through observing and emulating conspecifics. Frans de Waal makes the case that the drive to observe and imitate is paired with a drive to "fit in" or the "desire to be like others" (de Waal 2001: 230). Other incentives for hanging around with older members of one's group include the facts that they are more likely to identify and deal with threats[6] and they are better at finding food (Johnson and Bock 2004).

Enumerating these various "drives" across a spectrum from psychology to primatology might seem like the proverbial five blind men describing an

---

[6] We also have evidence of what psychologists call "one-trial learning," where the organism experiences a non-fatal encounter with a threat source – predator, treacherous stream, pitfall – or observes someone else's encounter (McGrew 1977; see also Barrett and Broesch 2012: 499). The reoccurrence of these threats will, subsequently, provoke an immediate avoidance reaction.

elephant. Summing up, it seems to me that children learning their culture are demonstrating at least two powerful drives: one, to acquire the skills to survive, and two, to affiliate securely to a group. Happily for the child, the domestic world is usually organized in a way that facilitates these goals. In the next section we'll consider another universal human trait with practical benefits: the playful manipulation of objects. In many societies, curious children are afforded opportunities to learn from common artifacts.

Exploration and play with objects

[Wagenia boys] build miniature fish-traps close to the river bank or, after rain, in small channels. (Droogers 1980: 80)

Humans are nothing more than souped-up primates, chimpanzees with certain enhanced abilities. (Bloom 1999: 306)

The object play of toddlers seems to be a continuation of the infant's visual exploration of objects. Now the child can explore the properties of objects with its hands; its mouth; it can throw them; use them as hammers; toss them into puddles, and so on. But, more to the point, the child will inevitably lay hands on objects that are tools. These may be rough replicas made by an older sibling (Peters 1998: 90); they may be broken or cast-off tools (Ruddle and Chester-field 1977: 34); they may be miniatures or scaled-down versions of the real thing (Hewlett *et al.* 2011: 1174; Politis 2007: 224); or they may be adult tools, perhaps "borrowed" (Odden and Rochat 2004: 44). Figure 12 depicts young Bamana boys using "their" hoes.

Theorist Richard Byrne sees a clear connection between the predilection towards object play and later use of tools (Byrne 1995: 86–87). The only two species where play with objects is common are humans and chimpanzees, which also happen to be the only two primate species that routinely use tools. Gorillas are an interesting intermediary case. In the wild, they neither play with objects nor use tools. They don't need to – their foods can be harvested without tools. However, under circumstances where there are no age-mates to play with, they do play with objects, so the capacity is certainly there; captive gorillas, in fact, show considerable tool-using ability (Byrne 1995: 86). Byrne also postulates a more general impact of object play on cortical growth, and it's worth noting that, as we age, the "decline in the rate of object play coincides with decline in synaptic density in the cerebral cortex" (Fairbanks 1995: 144).

A "tool" may be an outrigger canoe. Ifaty village in Southwest Madagascar depends, primarily, on marine resources, and a modest-sized outrigger sailing canoe is the primary means of accessing such resources as well as marketing them. Virtually all adult males use such canoes almost daily. On the beach and

Figure 12 Young Bamana "farmers"

in the shallows, I observed (almost simultaneously): (a) a two-year-old splash-
ing alone in a tide-pool, learning about water; (b) three boys aged around five
clambering over a beached canoe, learning an agile dance from thwart to
gunwale;[7] (c) two boys aged about seven, independently, preparing and then
sailing model canoes, making appropriate adjustments to sail angle and rudder;
(d) two boys of eight playing with an abandoned outrigger in the shallows –
they climbed on, paddled it, capsized it, took turns as captain and mate;
(e) when two young men began to rig and prepare to launch a full-size
outrigger, the two boys paddled over to watch this unfold; and (f) shortly after
they sailed away, a boy of about ten came *paddling* in to shore in a half-size
canoe (Lancy 2012c: 26–27). Extrapolating from more thorough studies of
children learning to use canoes (Hatley 1976: 84; Pomponio 1992: 72), I am
confident that these experiences prepare Ifaty boys to become mariners with
little need for any formal instruction. The Warao, for example:

put in so much practice time on make-believe canoe rides that by the age of three all
children, boys and girls alike, know how to maneuver a canoe perfectly ... It is truly
breathtaking to observe a three-year-old child push off and paddle a canoe across an
enormous river in full control of the craft. (Wilbert 1976: 318)

---

[7] Even when the craft is a large whaling ship, Nantucket boys – who went to sea at fourteen –
already at ten were using "the waterfront as their playground. They rowed decrepit whaleboats
up and down the harbor and clambered up into the rigging of the ships" (Philbrick 2000: 2).

As noted by Donald (1991: 309) and others (Flinn 2005: 78), a significant amount of cultural "information" is encoded in human artifacts, including tools (Portisch 2010: 71), houses (Winzeler 2004: 70–71), and the arrangement of the village itself (Strathern 1988). All serve as a form of *external storage*. This point is obvious when we consider writing, books, computer programs, and the like (Goody 1977), but information is also embedded in the simplest artifact (Renfrew 1998).[8] When a Bamana child plays with the characteristic short-handled hoe (Polak 2011: 103), there are only so many ways it can be effectively grasped. If he uses it to pierce the soil – as he's observed his siblings doing – the number of possibilities is further reduced. Neither the grasping end of the handle nor the top side of the head makes much impression on the earth compared to the bottom edge. This proposition was supported in an experiment derived from Köhler's study of thought in apes. Children aged eighteen to thirty-six months were given a range of tools of varying utility to pull a desired object within reach. Nearly all quickly eliminated the unlikely candidates and succeeded in the task (Brown 1990: 121). And, of course, children at play have an almost inexhaustible reservoir of curiosity and energy to apply to the task of decoding the information embedded in objects.

The literature is replete with instances of children transitioning from scaled versions of tools to potent, usable versions as they matriculate, seamlessly, from playing to working (Lancy 2012a). Perhaps the most persuasive evidence regarding the attitude of adults toward children acquiring culture through play – without the need for adult guidance – comes from widespread reports of parents' indifference and even encouragement of toddlers playing with machetes and other sharp and dangerous tools (Howard 1970: 35). For example, from the Kwoma of Papua New Guinea: "I once saw Suw with the blade of a twelve-inch bush knife in his mouth and the adults present paid no attention to him" (Whiting 1941: 25). Aka mothers regret it when their infants cut themselves while playing with knives but they don't want to restrain their

---

[8] The typical village tool inventory is pretty basic. The Wanka are farmer-potters in Highland Peru. Their tools are homemade or scavenged from local materials. The two most complex tools are the plow and kiln – both pretty simple. Most tools have multiple uses (Hagstrum 1999). If we adopt a historical perspective, we come to a similar conclusion. The primary tool used by early man was the handaxe. "Handaxes are found in the archaeological record for more than 1 million years. During this time there is no significant change in their range of forms, their manufacturing techniques or the way they were used" (Mithen 1999: 494). When we survey hunting-and-gathering societies, we are unable to find evidence of technological "progress." "There is no directional trend among hunter-gatherer societies. Numerous examples reveal complexity coming and going frequently as a result of adaptive necessities" (Rowley–Conwy 2001: 64). In fact, there are cases of societies (Tasmanians – Jones 1977: 45; Mapuche-Politis 2007: 339) voluntarily giving up practices and the associated technology and thereby significantly lowering their resource base. The child learning to use his society's tool inventory isn't learning rocket science.

exploration and learning (Hewlett 2013: 65–66). The Aka provide scaled versions of items in their tool inventory to their very young children and enjoy observing (and, occasionally correcting) their practice strikes (Hewlett *et al.* 2011: 1175). Four-and-a-half-year-old Okinawan children readily peel the outer skin off a length of sugar cane with a sharp sickle. When a mother was asked how the child acquired this skill she was at a loss for a reply. "'I don't know! He must have watched us and learned himself by trying it out!' she said" (Maretzki and Maretzki 1963: 511). On Vanatinai Island in the South Pacific, "children … manipulate firebrands and sharp knives without remonstrance … one four year old girl had accidentally amputated parts of several fingers on her right hand by playing with a bush knife" (Lepowsky 1987: 79). An entirely parallel case is described for the Asabano (Little 2008: 50–51). Lepcha babies "will crawl to fire and burn or scald themselves … There is scarcely a grown-up who does not carry scars from childhood burns" (Gorer 1967: 297). !Kung children were filmed playing with scorpions – in full view of at least one parent (Marshall 1972). "Hadza parents allow, even command, children to take risks [, for example] to approach and throw rocks at snakes" (Blurton-Jones *et al.* 1996: 171). They say "children will learn on their own what is dangerous" (Marlowe 2010: 198). De León (2012) records an episode from her Zinacantecan site where a three-year-old boy nearly runs, barefoot, through a fire. Adults do not react sympathetically. Instead, they comment that the child is flawed in not developing awareness of its surroundings, not paying close attention, and not figuring things out. There is an uneasy trade-off here. On the one hand, by indulging their curiosity about the environment and the things in it, parents insure that children are learning useful information without the necessity of parental intervention. This efficiency comes at a cost of the occasional damage to or loss of one's offspring (Martini and Kirkpatrick 1992).

This rather extreme *laisssez-faire* attitude is not universal. Because of the dangers and the likelihood of getting quite dirty, infants and toddlers, in many societies, are kept off the ground and denied access to found objects (Kaplan and Dove 1987: 195). For example, to a Balinese, crawling is animal-like behavior; hence the baby "may not even touch the earth and is carried everywhere" (Covarrubias 1937: 129). On Gau Island, children have the freedom to crawl but their territory is limited, and should they stray they are roughly picked up and placed back in the safe zone with harsh admonitions. Similar treatment is meted out to the curious child who would examine or play with an adult's possessions (Toren 1990: 172). Once children are ambulatory, however, they are almost inevitably granted great freedom to play and explore – as long as they remain in the company of sibling or adult caretakers. Found and crudely made toys will, inevitably, be used as "props" in the elaborate make-believe scenarios frequently recorded by anthropologists.

It's only make-believe

When [Talensi] adults are asked about children's mimetic play they reply: "That is how they learn." (Fortes 1938/1970: 23)

As anthropologists have consistently shown, in the village, make-believe[9] play is critical (Schwartzman 1978). It is the "classroom" where children try on and practice their culture. The walls of the mastaba tomb of Mereruka, an Egyptian official who died c.2300 BCE, are a virtual "picture encyclopedia" of daily life in the Old Kingdom. The visitor will discover several reliefs depicting children playing, including boys playing at war. Some boys are dressed as soldiers, while another has his hands bound – a captive. In a lower panel, girls (their youth conveyed by the iconic side-lock) have formed a living merry-go-round and the inscription refers to their activity as "pressing the grapes" (Strouhal 1990: 26).

In "Becoming a blacksmith in Gbarngasuakwelle," I described Kpelle children's amazingly detailed and faithful replication of the blacksmith's forge in an episode of make-believe. The blacksmith's compound was a lively gathering point in the village, consistently attracting a crowd of onlookers and gossips, young and old. Children could watch the action of the smiths and eavesdrop as village affairs were discussed. They thus built up a stock of script material that could be woven into their make-believe play. The boy playing the smith, in particular, had obviously absorbed a great deal of the processes, both technical – he constructed reasonable replicas of bellows, anvil, tongs – and social – assigning the roles of novice, wives, and helpers to his playmates. The terminology for tools, actions, and relationships used in the "script" was also a faithful rendition (Lancy 1980b). It's impossible to say whether this boy will actually become a blacksmith, although, in studies of apprenticeship, this evidence of early interest is sometimes cited in accounting for the decision to place a child with a master craftsperson (Lancy 2012a).

Ethnographic descriptions of make-believe play are rich and varied. "Dhebar boys ... use camel and sheep droppings to practice herding sheep and lambs" (Dyer and Choksi 2006: 170). Goody (1992) describes a continuum from make-believe to "for real" food preparation in which older children model for younger ones, real but scaled-down pots may substitute for toy pots, and, if mother's willing, edible ingredients go into the pot rather than weeds. While the everyday work activities of adults provide a common theme, we also see replicated the processes involved in carrying out trance-induced shamanism (Katz 1981); simulated marriage, including copulation (Gorer 1967: 310); and religious rituals (Fortes 1938/1970: 68).

---

[9] Also referred to in the literature as role-playing, pretend, socio-dramatic, and fantasy play.

Figure 13 Hadza boys target shooting

As noted above, parents (and older siblings; cf. Shostak 1981: 83) are generally supportive of children's learning through make-believe, as evidenced by the widespread practice of supporting such play through the donation of appropriate objects and materials as props. Figure 13 shows Hadza boys target shooting using "tools" that may have been donated.

[Aka] parents place fabric slings on toddlers, sometimes placing a bottle or corncob in it to represent an infant. (Hewlett *et al.* 2011: 1175)

When a small [Sisala] boy first goes to the farm with his father, he is told to sit in the shade of a tree and observe what his elders are doing. When he asks to help, someone gives him a hoe with which to play. (Grindal 1972: 29)

[A Javanese] father may make a miniature carrying pole for a young son to use, or he may be given [an] adze-shaped spade. (Jay 1969: 32)

Little [Tlinglit] girls learned how to cook, not only from helping their mothers, but also because they were given toy pots, and dishes to use. (de Laguna 1965: 14)

In order for children to take the initiative and get a head start on learning their culture, it must be an open book. The public nature of most adult activity facilitates children's engagement (Puri 2013: 289) at a safe distance where they are not interfering. Anthropologists often note adult awareness and sympathy toward children's mimicry. And this presumption on the part of both anthropologists and parents was supported in a series of empirical tests carried out among several groups in Botswana (Bock 2005; Bock and Johnson 2004). In some villages, adult women pound grain in a mortar and pestle to remove the outer husk. Not surprisingly, girls (not boys) play at pounding, and, in communities that derived less of their food from grains, girls were much less often observed playing at grain processing. Similarly, the "aim game," which sharpens hunting skills, was seen less often in villages that derived most of their food from agriculture. Furthermore, the ethnographers noted that children were prohibited from practicing with actual grain for fear they'd spill it, so that play-pounding was the only means to practice this critical skill (Bock and Johnson 2004).

The idea that make-believe play may have an important role in the child's acquisition of culture (Barber calls it "vocational kindergarten"; 1994: 85) has also received theoretical support. The importance of children acquiring useful skills from those older and more expert via imitation is widely acknowledged. "We are such a thorough-going cultural species that it pays children, as a kind of default strategy, to copy willy-nilly much of the behavioral repertoire they see enacted before them" (Hopper *et al.* 2012: 105). Donald argues that mimesis "adds a representational dimension to imitation ... [and] mimetic skill results in the sharing of knowledge, without every member of a group having to reinvent that knowledge" (Donald 1991: 169, 173). And, of course, among humans, the quintessential display of mimesis occurs in make-believe play (Harris 1998).

Lastly we might consider that learning through play can be more efficient than learning from instruction, not least because the latter is rather boring to the young while play is arousing, and because the latter "requires an investment by a second party, the teacher" (Lancy 1980c: 482). In fact, when the very young receive tutelage, an older sibling, not a parent, likely delivers it.

Learning from peers

Mayan toddlers learn primarily by observing and interacting with their sibling caretakers. Much of this learning occurs in the context of make-believe play. (Maynard 2002: 978)

Fore children are expected to focus their attention as learners on older children, not adults. (Sorenson 1976: 198)

In the previous chapter I noted the case of a Mandinka mother shooing her toddler away to join the play group. This pattern of behavior is so common, it has a name: "toddler rejection" (Weisner and Gallimore 1977: 176). Obviously, it is a complement to weaning in that, where infants are weaned relatively early, their displeasure can lead to an escalating battle in which others – grandmothers and older siblings particularly – come to the mother's aid (Leavitt 1989: 147). Native Hawaiian mothers closely attend their infants but, following the birth of a new child, the toddler's "overtures are increasingly punished and he is forced to rely on older children" (Gallimore *et al.* 1969: 393).

Under ideal circumstances, the rejected toddler will be afforded opportunities to overcome her feeling of rejection. The play group serves as a distraction from one's personal tragedies. Second, the toddler may well receive more than adequate attention and comfort from mother substitutes (Barnett 1979: 6; Casimir 2010: 24), particularly older sisters. Across the primate order, juvenile females show great interest in infants (Hrdy 1999: 157), and it is not hard to sustain an argument that their supervised interaction with younger siblings prepares them for the role of motherhood (Fairbanks 1990; Riesman 1992: 111). The weanling's need for mothering corresponds to the allomother's need to mother.

In the process of becoming initiated into the peer group, the toddler must shape up or suffer the consequences. It must "fit in." Teasing, being made the brunt of pranks, and other forms of correction are to be expected (Broch 1990: 81) except where parents exercise close oversight and intervene to keep things amicable (Gaskins *et al.* 2007). This is a familiar scene to those studying childhood in village settings:

When [Hadza] children are one to three years of age, they often throw tantrums, during which they may pick up a branch and repeatedly whack people over the head. The parents and other adults merely fend off the blows by covering their heads, laughing all the time. They do not even take the stick away. When the child hits another child who is a little older, however, that child often grabs the stick and hits the little one back. This is the way young children learn they cannot get their way; older children train them. Thus, it is not necessary for adults to discipline them. (Marlowe 2010: 197)

Children consigned to the company of older siblings and their friends have joined a cadre of excellent role models (Sorenson 1976: 198).

[By imitating their sib-caretakers, Marquesan] toddlers learn to run, feed, and dress themselves, go outside to urinate and defecate, and help with household chores. (Martini and Kirkpatrick 1992: 124)

Little [Bengali] girls accompany older girls in gathering, and they gradually learn the needed skills. (Rohner and Chaki-Sircar 1988: 33)

Martu ... adults recall a childhood spent foraging with other children to keep themselves fed ... Women hunt on foot with digging stick, and they often remark that children are too slow to keep pace while they are searching and tracking. (Bird and Bird, 2005: 135)

Young Penan girls ... feel peer pressure to produce "beautiful" rattan baskets and other handicrafts that are the trademark of Penan and other hunter-gatherer groups. (Puri 2013: 295)

Because sib-caretaking is so pervasive, children are far more likely to be in the company of peers than parents. Weisner argues that "children care for other children [under a mother's or other adults' management] within *indirect chains of support*" (1996: 308, emphasis added; see also Rogoff 1981a: 31). That is, toddlers are managed by slightly older siblings, who are, in turn, guided by adolescents, while adults serve as rather distant "foremen" for the activity, concentrating, primarily, on their own more productive or profitable activity. This phenomenon is well illustrated in Polak's study of Bamana families engaged in farming (2003, 2011, 2012).

Kaluli mothers direct their daughters to cooperate with and emulate their older sisters (Schieffelin 1990: 218), perhaps because siblings can be more patient and sympathetic teachers than adults (Maynard and Tovote 2010).[10] A contrasting pair of anecdotes is illustrative. Raum observed a Chaga mother and her daughter cutting grass to take home to feed the cattle. Tying the stalks into a bundle is difficult and the daughter was struggling with the task. But the "mother refuses requests for [guidance] by saying: 'Haven't you got hands like me?'" (1940: 199). Now consider a vignette of Pushtun children gathering and bundling shrubs (*buti*) to bring home.

Khodaydad showed and explained to his younger brother Walidad ... how to put *buti* together: He made up a small pile while Walidad squatted next to him and watched. Tying them together, he explained how to do it. Then he untied the bundle and bound it up again to show how it was done. Walidad then wanted to carry it home. His elder brother helped him shoulder it and his sister guided him home, and it was obvious that little Walidad was very proud of being able to accomplish the work. (Casimir 2010: 54)

It is not hard to construct a scenario where the rejected toddler – in the course of group play and by emulating the more mature behavior of older peers – is socialized and made ready to rejoin the family circle. No longer throwing tantrums, demanding the breast, and making a mess, he is again made welcome. And a new phase of culture learning may begin.

---

[10] Maynard found that sib-caretakers tried to utilize the formal approach to teaching they'd experienced in school "until they realized that that model was not resulting in the younger child's compliance in doing the task" (Maynard 2004b: 530).

Fitting in to the family circle

[Matsigenka] Infants and young children are embedded in the middle of quotidian activities where they are positioned to quietly observe and learn what others are doing. (Ochs and Izquierdo 2009: 395)

There is amazingly little verbalization in the whole learning process. [Chiga] children seem never to ask "why" questions which are so much a feature of learning in our culture. (Edel 1957/1996: 178)

From the distant past, humans must have conducted much of their business in a public setting with multiple participants and onlookers including, especially, children. Studies of the stone scatter from sites where stone tool production occurred show incomplete tools and debris consistent with a mixture of skill levels, including that of beginners (Dugstad 2010: 70; Pigeot 1990: 131). At two Magdalenian sites in France, "highly skilled [flint] knappers occupied places closest to the hearth, the less skilled knappers and the novices sat further back from it" (Shennan and Steele 1999: 375). Iban children observe their parents working in the fields from an early age and "both boys and girls begin to join in tasks which lie within their powers, and soon come to make valuable contributions to the working of the family farm" (Freeman 1970: 231–232). For chimpanzees, the "family circle" most often consists of a mother and her one or two offspring.

In the case of nut-cracking ... we have often seen infants stealing kernels from their mothers just after she finished cracking ... Infants less than 3 years old have ... free access to kernels, nuts, and stone tools that are in use by their mother ... The mother's behavior toward her offspring is thus typified by high levels of tolerance ... It takes at least three-five years for young chimpanzees to combine the three objects (a nut, a hammer stone, and an anvil stone) in the appropriate spatial and temporal arrangement for successful nut-cracking. During this extended learning process, their manipulatory behavior is never once reinforced by an edible item [and hence, the] learning process is not supported by feeding motivation but by the motivation to copy the mothers' behavior. (Matsuzawa *et al.* 2001: 571–572)

Ingold defines the essence of this dynamic as the "education of attention" (2001: 139).

In the passage of human generations, each one contributes to the knowledgeability of the next not by handing down a corpus of disembodied, context-free information, but by setting up, through their activities, the environmental contexts within which successors develop their own ... skills. (Ingold 2001: 142)

Just as "artifacts" contain embedded information, we can also see that culture is conveniently packaged in conceptual artifacts such as songs, rituals, and customary procedures – what Bourdieu (1977) called "habitus" and what I called "cultural routines" (Lancy 1996: 2). Medaets, for example, describes a Breugelian tableau in an Amazonian village where a family of mixed ages is busy around the house with gardening, processing, and roasting cassava flour and tidying up. There are no fewer than eight children aged four to fifteen distributed across this scene – each one busy with a chore but also observing others (Medaets 2011: 3). Here follows a small sample of cases illustrating the atmosphere of the family circle.

At the age of three he chooses his own place at the [Wolof] family meal, and here he is encouraged to gradually acquire social norms. (Zempleni-Rabain 1973: 222)

[Vlach] children ... [of] all ages are tolerated on almost all family occasions and no topic of discussion is considered unfit for their ears. They hear their elders interminably discussing and criticizing the behavior of adults and children in other unrelated families. (Campbell 1964: 157)

Because Inuit children are present in many multi-age situations, they are exposed to a great deal of talk by older people. Yet, it became apparent in this study that they were neither expected to participate nor to ask questions of adults who were speaking together. If they did ask questions, the adults ignored them, leaving their questions unanswered. (Crago 1992: 494)

[Ganda] children over two years of age ... sit politely, with their feet tucked under them out of sight, listening to the talk of their elders and speaking only when spoken to. If any young child becomes rambunctious and draws attention to himself, he is told to sit properly [and] be silent. (Ainsworth 1967: 12)

[Mazahua] children participate in ... family ... activities [, and] conversation and questions ... usually occur for the sake of sharing necessary information ... Talk supports and is integral to the endeavor at hand rather than becoming the focus of a lesson. (Paradise and Rogoff 2009: 118)

Indeed, were the Mazahua children to ask questions it would be considered immature and rude (Paradise and Rogoff 2009: 121; see also Penn 2001: 91), an attitude widely characteristic of traditional societies (Lancy and Grove 2010: 153). Instead, learning takes place largely through children's initiative to observe the activity and to become engaged – even if discouraged. The parent need not change his or her behavior to accommodate the learner or evince any intent to instruct (Paradise and Rogoff 2009: 117), because the tasks themselves "can also function as 'knowledge transmission' events" (Puri 2013: 277). Contrast this with WEIRD society, where a mother may totally restructure a domestic task, inviting the son's participation, so that she can construct a lesson for him (Gauvain 2001: 3). Gauvain's cake-making lesson points to a deep divide between the WEIRD and village models of childhood. Typically, in the former, the child's striving for competency trumps the drive to fit in; whereas, in the latter model, fitting in or not disturbing others is of greater value.[11]

The WEIRD equivalent of the family circle might be the dinner table (the family vehicle another). WEIRD parents use "dinner-table conversations" as a forum for socializing children (Larson *et al.* 2006: 5). Family dinners indicate that there is structure built in to home life and this structuring (along with a regular bedtime hour, after-school events, and attending church) will help the child adapt to the highly structured school routine. An opportunity is provided for children to observe adult role models – not always available where parents and children may be separated for much of the day. Moral lessons may be transmitted (Pontecorvo *et al.* 2001; Sterponi 2003). Finally, the use of various speech genres (interrogation, joking, narrative) provides a fertile training ground for the child's linguistic, cognitive, and academic development. Children are immersed in academic language, which "is intrinsically more difficult than other language registers." Compared to colloquial speech, it is more concise, denser, with a high lexical diversity (Snow and Uccelli 2009: 114, 119). Examples of the family dinner as classroom abound (Israel – Ariel and Sever 1980: 173; Sweden – Dalhberg 1992: 113–134; USA – Ochs *et al.* 1992: 38; Brazil – Rojo 2001: 64).

From her ethnographic work, Mary Martini describes a typical dinner-table conversation in an average white, middle-class home:

Parents engage children in teaching routines. Typically, a child asks "Why?" and the parent answers at length. Common topics are aspects of the physical world: sea life, animals, dinosaurs, stars, astronauts, and how everyday things work ... parents and children invent stories, jokes, and riddles. They set up "what if" scenarios and experiment with new ways of doing things. Parents listen to, watch and comment ... Children learn to "show off" ... inventing songs, jokes, games or implausible situations ... parents also laugh when children break rules or violate expectations in imaginative ways. (Martini 1996: 30)[12]

Martini observed something quite different in her Marquesan study: "children defer to elders, initiate few topics of conversation, and take only brief speaking turns" (Martini and Kirkpatrick 1992: 203). Bamana children rarely talk with adults, who are to be treated with deference and respect. "They can always listen to adults' conversations, yet they are urged to not interfere by posing

---

[11] There has been a flood of studies from WEIRD societies in the US and Europe documenting how extraordinarily unhelpful children have become (Lancy 2012a: 44–45; this volume, Chapter 2, pp. 71–72). WEIRD parents in protecting and cherishing their toddlers extinguish their drive to "fit in." It disappears in the family context even while it is rekindled in the peer group.

[12] And we shouldn't be surprised to learn that French parents also use mealtimes as an opportunity for *education de gout* or the education of taste (Sjögren-de Beauchaine 1998).

questions or expressing opinions" (Polak 2012: 88). Nor are adults likely to ask a child for their opinion (Luo – Blount 1972: 127).

In the village, the child does not remain as a passive observer for long. As a "legitimate peripheral participant" (Lave and Wenger 1991) she will "pitch in" and help with ongoing activity such as food preparation, crafts, and housework as soon as she can do so without damaging resources or interfering with those who are more productive (Krause 1985: 95; Portisch 2010: 67). Children can expect some attention from family members[13] as long as they are focused on the task at hand (Weisner 1989: 78). Indeed, scholars have advanced the idea that merely by approving/disapproving children's early attempts, older family members can dramatically improve their efficiency as social learners – a facultative feature less evident in non-human primates (Castro and Toro 2004). For example, Little recorded the interaction as a six-year-old Asabano girl emulated her mother's construction of a string bag. If uncertain where to put the next knot, the girl asks: "Here?" and the mother "would respond with a grunt indicating 'yes' or 'no.' [If the child were] tying a knot at the wrong place, her mother would preempt her [by saying] nothing more than 'no'" (Little 2011: 154).

For the Chiga, the "assumption of work and responsibility comes about gradually, and largely on the child's own initiative" (Edel 1957/1996: 178). "[Mayan children] are eager to participate in the economic activities of the household" (Rogoff 1981a: 31).

[Hadza] five-year-olds fetch anything adults want. Sometimes they fetch things they see the adult will need before they are even asked. For example, when seeing a man getting out his pipe and tobacco, a child may grab an ember from the fire and take it to the man to light the pipe. They never complain. In fact, they seem to enjoy being helpful. (Marlowe 2010: 198)

As soon as a Cree child learned to walk, she was expected to help with and share in the work of the bush camp. The child was not usually given verbal instruction but encouraged to learn skills by playing and by imitating adults through participation in subsistence production[14] activities ... [she] was told, "Keep trying, never give up until you get it right." (Ohmagari and Berkes 1997: 206).

---

[13] Outright praise for children's work efforts is fairly rare; the "reward" is subtle signs that one fits in: being fed regularly and adequately, for example. By contrast, in WEIRD society, children are often praised excessively and indiscriminately, undermining their success striving (Boyd and Richerson 1985: 43; Mueller and Dweck 1998). I suspect as well that, in a gerontocracy, praise, if it occurs, is directed at the deed or accomplishment, not the child.

[14] The family circle (and its kin such as the market; cf. Paradise and Rogoff 2009) is the setting for the learning of the great majority of practical and subsistence skills, which children must acquire. This topic will be explored much more fully in Chapter 7.

Nothing is more cheering for a Huaorani parent than a three-year-old's decision to join a food gathering expedition . . . . carrying his/her own *oto* basket and bringing it back to the longhouse filled with forest food . . . to share with co-residents. (Rival 2000: 116)

[Japanese] children . . . show filial devotion to their parents and grandparents at the [public] bath . . . washing their backs and lightly massaging their shoulders. (Clark 1998: 243)

These claims of early altruism and prosociality are supported by a study that simulated a home environment where mothers and fathers were carrying out various tasks with young children in attendance (and since replicated: Warneken and Tomasello 2006: 1301). Children as young as eighteen months of age:

Spontaneously and promptly assisted the adults in a majority of the tasks they performed. Furthermore, the children accompanied their assistance by relevant verbalizations and by evidence that they knew the goals of the tasks, even adding appropriate behaviors not modeled by the adults. (Rheingold 1982: 114)

We might say that that the extraordinary capacity for social learning of the very young is exercised to its fullest extent in the family. Children can create a kind of mental spreadsheet of the behavior and needs of other family members. They can create a map of activities within the domestic sphere, fitting themselves into the flow of events, and attempting to help out or mimic the actions of those older "as if" they were helping out.

The importance of good manners

Instruction in Tikopia in matters of etiquette and decorum in the house begins . . . almost before the child can fully understand what is required of it. (Firth 1970: 79)

What happens when the child does not fit in, or at least does not do so soon enough? In the majority of cases this doesn't seem to be a problem: "The [Melpa] child grows into social maturity rather than being trained into it" (Strathern 1980: 197). But it is treated as demanding intervention in a significant minority of societies, particularly in the South Pacific. Keeping in mind that, outside the neontocracy, children may not be viewed as adorable cherubs, families may feel their reputation is tarnished by their children's immature behavior (Fajans 1997: 54). Children are "socialized" or trained to decode the social and kin hierarchy and demonstrate appropriate speech and demeanor in public.

The Rotuman child is subtly instructed in kin relations: "Why don't you go outside and play with Fatiaki, he is your *sasigi*" or "You must show respect to Samuela, he is your *o'fa*.' (Howard 1970: 37)

[Inuit children] are drilled daily on their terms for relatives. (Guemple 1979: 43)

[Kwara'ae caregivers use] ... repeating routines ... telling the child what to say, line by line ... Encoded in [these] routines is information on kin terms and relationships and on polite ways of conversing ... important goal[s] ... in a society where *enoenoanga* (delicacy) and *aroaroanga* (peacefulness) are key values ... for maintaining harmony in the extended family and descent group. (Watson-Gegeo and Gegeo 1989: 62)

As young as four, the Fijian child will be expected to bend double in exaggerated respect as he passes by adults. Failure to show sufficient respect will earn the child a scolding, "if not a blow." (Toren 2001: 166)

[Samoan] children are encouraged in a variety of ways to be sociocentric, to notice others and take their point of view. (Ochs 1988: 85)

Maung social structure is deeply organized according to ... hierarchical relationships ... I observed persistent prompting and guidance of children's practices of respect. (Howard 2012: 350, 358)

The Hopi – North American Puebloans – provide] deliberate instruction in kinship and community obligations. (Eggan 1956: 351)

[The Javanese mother repeats "polite" kin terms over and over and corrects her child's mistakes, urging it to observe proper etiquette. Hence] children little more than a year old ... go through a polite bow and say an approximation of the high word for good-by ... a *prijaji* (aristocrat) child of five or six already has an extensive repertoire of graceful phrases and actions. (Geertz 1961: 100)

Among the Basotho of South Africa, mothers and older siblings prompt children in politeness ... and proper terms of address. (Demuth 1986: 62–63)

A number of societies intervene early to promote sharing (Aka – Boyette 2013: 126;[15] Inuit – Guemple 1979: 43; Araucanian – Hilger 1957: 52; Kaoka – Hogbin 1969: 33; Ifaluk – Lutz 1983; Wolof – Zempleni-Rabain 1973: 227). For example, Papel infants are given something desirable, such as a snack, then, immediately told to pass it on to another, particularly a sibling (Einarsdóttir 2004: 94). Generosity is demanded of even small Ngoni children both directly – forcing them to donate prized resources to peers – and indirectly, through proverbs lauding generosity and condemning meanness (Read 1960: 155). The !Kung grandmother most often takes on the task of teaching *hxaro*, their quite formal system of exchange and mutual support. The very young child is given beads and told which kinsmen to pass them on to (Bakeman *et al.* 1990: 796).[16] The Whale River Eskimo also provide formal instruction in this area only (Honigmann and Honigmann 1953: 41). It is

---

[15] But such intervention is not always successful. Boyette reports on a seven-year-old "notably greedy" Aka boy who is repeatedly chastised by the "boys in his age group" (2013: 113).

[16] Like other hunter-gatherers, the !Kung are "fierce egalitarians." They "consider refusal to share as the 'ultimate sin'" (Howell 2010: 194).

certainly the case that sharing – especially of food – is a core value in most societies (Mauss 1967) and children are hastened into compliance. But a related goal for sharing lessons is to make the child as attractive as possible to alloparents or foster parents (Chapter 4).

Good manners constituted the most important attribute when describing a good child. For all Nso mothers, the concept of good manners includes learning to greet others and showing obedience and respect for elders ... mothers spoke of vigorous training sessions in order to habituate their children to others: "I will not like it [when he clings to me]. I will try to at least make him to know people around me and make them close to him by forcing him to them." (Otto and Keller in press).

There's considerable evidence that children will learn the appropriate prosocial behaviors with time (d'Andrade 1984: 97; Fehr *et al.* 2008),[17] including proper kin terms (Beverly and Whittemore 1993: 239; Fortes 1938/1970: 53–54; Read 2001). For example, on Samoa

children as young as six ... begin to pick up the distinctive features characterizing people of rank and authority without any explicit instruction. This was particularly the case for distinctive behavioral aspects of common ritual events associated with chiefs that children could readily witness. (Odden and Rochat 2004: 46).

There are many societies that value "proper" behavior highly without engaging in this kind of enforced compliance and training. After all, the very success of the human species has rested on *voluntary* compliance with social norms (Boyd and Richerson 2006: 469). Nevertheless, while Kpelle adults, for example, expect their children to learn manners through emulation, they are quick to censure – either directly or via the use of proverbs – a child for any of a range of behaviors and attitudes that show lack of respect or sloth. And they are keenly aware that a "bad" or disrespectful child reflects poorly on its parents (Lancy 1996: 96).

American anthropologist Laurence Wylie's wonderful ethnography of village life in France, recorded in the early 1950s, reveals how important it was to inculcate a fine sense of proper social behavior – *à la table* – in children:

Everyone considers it important for a child to know how "*se tenir comme il faut à la table*." He must sit up straight and keep both wrists on the edge of the table when his hands are not being used for eating. An elbow must never be on the table, and a hand must never be below the table. If a hand slips down in his lap, his parents will say, "What's that hand doing, hiding down there? Put it on the table where it belongs!" ... if

---

[17] Recent laboratory studies underscore that human children exhibit pro-social behavior spontaneously from the age of three or earlier and are more readily pro-social than juvenile chimps (House *et al.* 2012).

*"I thought we had the sort of relationship where
'please' and 'thank you' were implicit."*

Figure 14 No need for politeness

he wants to be served he must say, "Thank you, papa or maman" after he is served. If he forgets to repeat the formula, his parents will pretend to be deaf and refuse to serve him until he remembers. (Wylie 1957: 45)

Wylie ruefully acknowledges that "Even though we thought that at home our children seemed normal in social situations, we saw that in Peyrane they were *mal elevés* by the standards of any of the villagers, even the most humble" (Wylie 1957: 44). Sixty years later, the gap between French children's manners and American children's lack thereof had clearly grown – inspiring a best-selling book (*Bringing up Bébé*, Druckerman 2012) and parental angst. It is ironic that mid-upper-class US society, placed at the upper extreme on a continuum from high to low incidence of active teaching by parents, gives relatively short shrift to teaching children kin terminology, politeness, and etiquette, particularly in contrast to Japan (Hendry 1986: 73–74) and East Asia, generally. In fact, the press for conformity in Western society is very weak compared to that in non-Western societies (Henrich *et al.* 2010: 71).

In Figure 14, the cartoonist suggests that our emphasis as teachers of our children seems to be on creative and fluent language use and interdependence between parent and child to the exclusion of more distant kin. Another pointed example:

Molly, a seven-year-old, suddenly declared to her friend Lila, "I got tired of playing with you today." Later Lila's mother brought it up to Molly's mother, Eve, who told her that Molly was "just being honest." Eve saw nothing wrong with Molly's hurtful words; after all, she was raising her daughter to know that it was important to recognize and express her own feelings. (Gross-Loh 2013: 216)

While other societies spread the burden of childrearing among a variety of individuals, to whom the child must learn to relate in the "proper manner," in the USA, we assign near-exclusive responsibility to mothers. And the tactic these mothers are most likely to use to insure the child's cooperation is to establish bonds of friendship, a process that is probably not aided by didactic instruction on inviolable rules of etiquette and kin relations.

Socializing aggression

Small children sometimes threaten adults as an extension of the encouragement [Tongan] babies are given to behave violently. (Morton 1996: 211)

The Yang emphasis on socializing cooperation and politeness can be juxtaposed with those societies that take a more Yin approach. The Yanomamo – famous for their evident enjoyment of fighting and warfare – encourage boys to "be fierce." They are rarely punished by their parents for whacking each other or their unfortunate sisters (Chagnon 1968/1992: 126).[18] A child that is attacked will not be defended by a parent; rather, it will be given a stick and sent back into the fray. "This is socialization for the fisticuff duels that are so central to the Yanomamo justice system" (Peters 1998: 136–138).

Education in bravery and aggressiveness among Pashtun nomads starts quite early, and little boys, often toddlers, are called upon to fight with words "*jan work*" (make war, fight). They are held close to each other by their respective fathers or other male relatives so that they can hit each other. (Casimir 2010: 40)

Fulbe pastoralists in Northern Cameroons encourage boys to engage in aggressive attacks on peers, simultaneous with the start of their career as cattle herders. Boys are "encouraged from a very early age to fight with sticks and ... challenge each other with insults" (Moritz 2008: 112) In southern

---

[18] The warrior cult is often paired with extreme misogyny, even abuse of women by men, hence boys are encouraged to beat up on girls. The warrior Bena-Bena in Papua New Guinea are a case in point (Langness 1981).

Africa, Xhosa tribesmen terrorized their neighbors and defeated the Europeans trying to usurp their farmland. Preparing warriors started at an early age:

In what is called *thelelekisa*, women will catch hold of the hands of two little boys two or three years old, and make them hit each other in the face, until the children get excited and angry and start lunging out on their own account, scratching and biting for good measure. The women look on with loud laughter. Slightly older boys are given reeds or other soft "weapons" and encouraged to have a bout together; or an adult (man or woman) will pretend to fight the child with a prodding finger, and encourage him to show how hard he can hit back. (Mayer and Mayer 1970: 165)

Don Kulick describes Gapun villagers (Sepik Region, Papua New Guinea) as extremely argumentative and assertive, constantly picking fights and abusing each other. Without that understanding we might find his description of their socialization practices incredible. Like the Xhosa, mothers actively pit their three-year-olds (girls as well as boys) against each other, holding them in proximity and shouting orders to strike out at the opponent. Children are also encouraged and praised for hitting dogs and chickens, and "raising a knife at an older sibling will be rewarded with smiles and cries of 'Watch out, he's *kros* now'" (Kulick 1992: 119). Elsewhere in Papua New Guinea, the phenomenon is related to inter-village and inter-sexual conflict that is persistent and, often, vicious – including socially sanctioned rape, warfare, head-hunting, and cannibalism. In one such society, the Kwoma, children are verbally and physically abused by adults and each other, and their play is infused with violent themes. Adults continually remind children of the need to cling to kin while being vigilant toward enemies (Whiting 1941: 62). Athapascan adults in sub-Arctic Canada egg on child combatants, "pushing them together and forcing them to strike provocative blows ... challenging them to attempt certain tactics to prove their ... superiority," but they do this because as adults *they* must be reserved. "So they use the boys to express vicariously emotions they feel but may not display" (Savishinsky 1982: 118–119).

The deliberate socialization for aggression cited in these few examples was, a few centuries ago, much more common. Inter-tribal warfare would have been more widespread and polities like those in ancient Mesoamerica would have been dependent on a constantly renewed cadre of young, fearless fighters (Hassig 1945). Pacification efforts since European contact led, after a lag period, to the reduction and elimination of the socialization of children to be aggressive (Ember and Ember 2007).[19]

Severe corporal punishment may be an aid in the preparation of warriors. The Codex Mendoza is a sixteenth-century manuscript prepared by Aztec

---

[19] Even today, African pastoralist societies are noted for continuing the cattle rustling and aggression against neighboring tribes practiced for centuries (Leff 2009).

scribes. Much of the third part, about twenty pages, deals with youth. In colorful pictures and accompanying text in Spanish and Nahuatl, the scribes detailed Aztec (or Mexican) childrearing practices. The most noteworthy aspect of this is the frequent depiction and description of severe corporal punishment, which includes being forced to inhale chili smoke. Young soldiers are shown having their hair cut off and their scalp singed with a firebrand (Berdan and Anawalt 1997).

Corporal punishment is by no means limited to nascent warriors. Early childhood is a period when children have great latitude and may behave in ways that provoke gratitude or outrage. In the absence of explicit lessons to socialize the child, or in the event those lessons aren't completely successful, parents must have the means to curb their children.

Controlling children's behavior

Cultural evolution created cooperative groups [, in turn favoring] the evolution of a suite of new social instincts suited to life in such groups including . . . new emotions like shame and guilt, which increase the chance that norms are followed. (Boyd and Richerson 2006: 469)

Ridicule, a common recourse in training Ulithian children. (Lessa 1966: 95)

The beating constitutes a lesson in [Pukapukan] social relations. (Borofsky 1987: 97)

The first, lengthy epigraph reinforces a theme repeated throughout the chapter. Children are born with a package of capacities that aid them in acquiring their culture. The need to affiliate or fit in makes perfect sense when one considers that the child must rely upon others for food and other necessities until well into the teen years (Rochat 2009: 25). However, the various capacities don't always mesh perfectly. The child that's curious and eager to learn about the world may expose itself to danger. The child's need to play may lead to property damage or otherwise provoke displeasure, perhaps from a parent noting unfinished chores. The child's eagerness to engage in competition and contesting the dominance hierarchy (discussed more fully in the next chapter) may lead him across a politeness or respect boundary into dangerous waters. In short, "nobody's perfect," and most communities employ an arsenal of tactics to control wayward behavior ranging from subtle to severe.

A proverb might suddenly be dropped like a stone into a pond. The conversation rippled away into silence, and the [Ngoni] boy or girl who had refused to share some peanuts or had been boasting began to wonder to himself: "Can that be for me? No? Yes? It is me. I am ashamed." No one said anything but the shamed one took the first chance of slipping away to avoid further public notice. The use of proverbs [was] an effective way of making a child learn for himself and apply the lesson. (Read 1960: 44–45)

The main cultural tool [Bofi foragers] use to maintain their egalitarian sharing is rough joking. Someone who does not share appropriately ... will become the butt of jokes or be made fun of in community-wide stories. (Fouts *et al.* 2013: 345)

De León (2012; see also Campbell 1964: 157; Sliva *et al.* 2011) describes the "over-hearer" as one of the cornerstones of traditional Zinacantecan childrearing. Older family members critically discuss the child's behavior when it is present but is not otherwise interacting with them. The child, who is expected, at all times, to pay attention to those older, listens and reflects upon his or her actions – a nice example of what Kline *et al.* refer to as "subtle, low cost teaching" (2013: 353).

In much of Asia, crowded living conditions have been the norm for millennia, no more so than on densely populated Bali, and not surprisingly children are taught to control their emotions at a young age; positive emotions, fear, and jealousy should all be hidden. If a child throws a tantrum, even if his or her mother "borrows" another child to nurse, the child will be ignored (Bateson and Mead 1942; Jensen and Suryani 1992). Emotional restraint, modesty, and cooperation are also inculcated early on in young Chinese.

For ... the Chinese ... shame is an essential social and moral emotion, a virtue. Developing a sense of shame is ... important ... in becoming a full member of their culture. (Li *et al.* 2004: 794; see also Fung 1999)

Appeals to concern for maternal feelings, shaming, and ridicule are part of the socialization arsenal (Wu *et al.* 2002). Corporal punishment is very much a part of the arsenal as well (Jankowiak *et al.* 2011: 158).

Taiwanese mothers – with their errant child present – construct a narrative of current and past transgressions for an audience. They spotlight the child's misdeeds in front of others in order to provoke shame (Miller *et al.* 2001: 166). Javanese cultivate the emotion of "*isin* ... (shame, shyness, embarrassment, guilt) [so] that at any formal public occasion [children] are exceedingly quiet and well-behaved and will sit docilely ... through hours and hours of formal speeches" (Geertz 1961: 113). On Fiji, the same emotions "are inculcated in the child by ridicule, mockery, laughter, or plain disapproval" (Toren 1990: 183). Ifaluk Islanders see *metagu* or the ability to exercise restraint as "the primary inhibitor of misbehaviour" (Lutz 1983: 252). The Kaluli use teasing and shaming to socialize children and bring them into conformity with adult expectations. Mothers tease toddlers in order to discourage them from nursing, and children are teased when they are greedy or disrespectful (Schieffelin 1986: 169; see also Eisenberg 1986: 189; Loudon 1970). The Javanese – and others – tease and shame five-to-six-year-olds to encourage an end to sex play and greater modesty and decorum (Geertz 1961: 102). Marquesan toddlers are teased, criticized, and attacked without provocation by adults and peers. They are provoked to anger and then punished for becoming angry (Martini 1994: 79). Indigenous Taiwanese villagers tease and roughly handle children – playfully – to toughen them up (Stafford 1995: 52). A similar pattern of teasing – and observing the child's response – allows South Indian villagers to evaluate the child's character (Nichter and Nichter 1987: 75).

From Borneo to the American southwest, children are warned repeatedly that improper behavior can bring the wrath of some harmful being. Dusun parents regularly use fear of the supernatural as a means of insuring that children conform to expected behavior. Parents tell children folktales with themes of violence (inflicted on) a child because of some error in his behavior (Williams 1969: 114; see also Mathews 1992).

[Navajo children] are told that if they misbehave the big gray Yeibichai will carry them off and eat them … [And in children's autobiographies there is evidence that these threats are effective.] "The first time I saw the Yeibichai I was scared. I thought they eat the children, and I cried." (Leighton and Kluckhohn 1948: 51–52)

In Papua New Guinea, Bena-Bena (a warrior society) "boys and girls are threatened 'in fun' with axes and knives and they run crying in terror" (Langness 1981). Children in Punan Bah village on Sarawak are threatened by various evil beings, including *penjamun*, creatures that abduct and sacrifice children, and by Europeans bearing injections. Adults claim "that children should be afraid … or they will never take advice nor pay respect to their elders" (Nicolaisen 1988: 205). Samoan children are reined in by threats to call on horrific beasts to come and eat them. A fretful baby will be distracted by: "Pig! Elenoa is here, come and eat her!" (Ochs 1988: 183). My personal favorite in this large collection is from the Kaoka on Guadalcanal:

The elders tell tales of the giants called *umou* that … inhabit the remote mountains. These beings, they say, are ready to pounce on naughty boys and girls and carry them off to a cave, where the bodies are cooked and eaten. (Hogbin 1969: 34)

The historical record is replete with parallel cases, and the roster of demons that were invoked to frighten children from Labartu (Assyria) to Mormo (Greece) was long indeed (Colón with Colón 2001: 47). The most frightening Bible stories were used to control the less compliant (Horn and Martins 2009: 154).[20] As recently as nineteenth-century England, children "were taken

---

[20] Abelow advances the thesis that the prevailing model of childrearing (e.g. Peisner 1989: 122) was "mapped onto a religious cosmos." Christianity absorbed themes of (child) waywardness, punishment, reform, and filial obedience and then, in turn, legitimated folk beliefs about children by turning them into dogma. Rearing children to feel sinful and guilty creates willing adherents to a religion whose core "reward" for allegiance is salvation and remission of sin (Abelow 2011: 11).

on visits to the gibbet to inspect rotting corpses hanging there while being told moral stories" (de Mause 1974: 14). They were whipped by their parents "on returning home to make them remember what they had seen" (Bloom-Feshbach 1981: 88). Somewhat more benign, but still pretty hair-raising, are the folktales compiled – since the eighteenth century – into books to "instruct" children (Tatar 1992).

If proverbs, shaming, teasing, and threats of the bogeyman aren't effective, many societies prescribe corporal punishment. The Matsigenka (Peru) punish the lazy or uncooperative by scalding or the application of skin irritants (Ochs and Izquierdo 2009: 395). Freeman tallies the frequency and severity of child beating on Samoa, where they "believe in the unique efficacy of pain as a means of instruction … severe discipline … is visited on children from an early age" (Freeman 1983: 206, 209–210). Corporal punishment is, thus, often seen as a legitimate tool in shaping the child's behavior. The Rwala Bedu (Syria) utilize an arsenal of physical punishments ranging from spanking with a stick (small children) to slashing with a saber or dagger (older children). They hold that the rod of discipline leads to paradise (Musil 1928: 256). Ainsworth recorded several episodes of physical punishment – for a variety of misdemeanors, including selfishness – in her observation in several Ganda villages (1967: 113).[21] Quinn presents the Mfantse (Ghana) menu of methods for "getting the child's attention."

If a child is small and the infraction slight, he is likely to be hit with a cupped hand to deaden the blow (but adults were disapproving of those who spoiled their children by not beating them hard enough when called for). Even an infant might be lightly cuffed for crying for no good reason … an older child who misbehaves will be beaten repeatedly with [a cane, which] was left on prominent display, and sometimes called attention to or brandished by one of the women working or sitting in the courtyard. Women had special and unmistakable voices that they used to threaten caning or to otherwise warn [or] to head off anticipated misbehavior before it happened. They could also send these messages with a certain sidelong stare. (Quinn 2005: 492–493)

Rural Moroccans, similarly employ a variety of punishments – on a daily basis. Beating is considered necessary "for the survival and growth of the child." Parents using harsh disciplinary practices do not expect their children to be timid as a result; on the contrary. They expect obedience but also they want to prepare their children for life's vicissitudes. "Tahtanis also often used harsh teasing to teach children to contain their hurt feelings and instead be able to

---

[21] To us it may seem perverse to punish a child for failing to behave altruistically. We tend to juxtapose aggression and pro-social behavior. But an important line of research finds an association between the tendency to punish selfish behavior severely and a high value attached to altruism (Henrich *et al.* 2006).

wittily retort to such prodding, encouraging the 'strong management of emotions'" (Nutter-El Ouardani 2013: 112, 99).

The variability in the use of corporal punishment is extremely wide. At one extreme, the Piaroa – South American foragers – totally disallow the display of violence; children are never physically punished, and this is pretty typical for foraging societies (Overing 1988: 178; this volume, Chapter 2, p. 66). Pashtu nomads are reluctant users of corporal punishment. They use verbal directives to chastise a child for bed-wetting, but resort to beating if the child persists (Casimir 2010: 35). In Greece and Rome, "physical punishment was taken for granted" (Horn and Martins 2009: 30). An extreme case, the Bulusu' (Borneo) believe that *severe* corporal punishment is necessary for learning because children are inherently naughty (*jayil*). Beating a child to unconsciousness or even death is not unknown (Appell-Warren 1987: 160–161).

Physical punishment is particularly prevalent in societies where the violence of tribal warfare, inter-village conflict, and wife-beating are endemic (Ember and Ember 1994). It may also be more frequent in modernizing or urbanizing societies, such as the Caribbean (Lange and Rodman 1992; Munroe 2005) or Turkey (Kagitçibasi and Sunar 1992: 85), or among lower-class populations in the developed nations (Landy 1959: 134). The collective pressure of the "village" shaping the child's behavior is missing in contemporary society, and more forceful or explicit disciplinary tactics may be necessary. Furthermore, while the father is generally absent from the childrearing scene, he is expected to play a role as "disciplinarian" (Kagitçibasi and Sunar 1992: 82; Roopnarine *et al.* 1994: 16).

Summing up, there seem to be several strategies for shaping children's behavior. The most widespread and largely implicit strategy is to promote the idea that children should monitor and attempt to replicate mature, correct behavior. A poorly behaving or immature child is scorned or scolded (Erchak 1980). The Japanese give children a great deal of leeway, but when they "misbehave," shame is engendered by calling attention to their filial obligations (Lebra 1994: 263; Fogel *et al.* 1992), e.g. "When you do that it makes mommy sad." Less subtle shaming is widely used in other societies. We have seen that the use of mythical figures, like *Yeibichai*, to coerce correct behavior is common as well. This strategy is extremely efficient. In effect it's like casting a spell that works without further intervention. Verbal and/or physical abuse is common, occurring "as a frequent or typical technique of discipline in societies in all major regions of the world ... about forty per cent of the sample" (Ember and Ember 2005: 609). Experimental research suggests that memory is enhanced at higher states of arousal (McGaugh 2006: 345), so these coercive tactics are used because they probably work. However, if a parent is to any degree dependent on neighbors/kin for assistance with childcare, they may not want to broadcast the fact that their child is unmanageable.

The rarest strategy, favored in WEIRD society, is to "reason with" children (Kousholt 2011: 106). This may not be as effective at controlling behavior but, as a side-benefit, it does give some early preparation for being an effective negotiator. Reasoning with children accomplishes two goals. It is a way to manage children's behavior, especially when shaping more complex skills, and it also facilitates the development of the (parent-as-)teacher–pupil relationship, discussed in the last section of Chapter 4.

A very significant change in the child's pattern of social interaction occurs at the outset of middle childhood, a stage in biological development character- ized by changes in dentition and brain organization and the onset of *adrenarche*. Widespread cultural recognition of this transition includes heightened expectations for more mature, "sensible" behavior (Lancy and Grove 2011a: 282).

The age of reason

[Azande] children are set to perform useful tasks as soon as they are old enough. (Baxter and Butt 1953: 47)

[Theologian Chrysostom wrote in the fourth century CE] the summit of wisdom is refusal to be excited at childish things. (Horn and Martens 2009: 158)

On Ifaluk Island, before the age of two, children have no thoughts or feelings; they just eat and play. Since they lack sense or morals, it is useless to get angry or to try to control their behavior. It is believed that children do not gain *repiy* (intelligence) until they are five or six years old (Burrows and Shapiro 1957; Lutz and LeVine 1983: 339). Contrast with WEIRD society, where parents eager to optimize their children's academic success are invited to begin their education in the womb (Robbins 2006: 334).[22] The age at which village children are considered teachable is "delayed" vis-à-vis the WEIRD model.[23] There is also little concern about the achievement of developmental milestones – save perhaps walking. For the Chewong

---

[22] For example, there is the Brill(iant) Baby Prenatal Education program. Available at www.brillbaby.com/prenatal-before-birth/introduction-to-prenatal-education.php. Accessed January 26, 2013.

[23] Theorists also note that learners should be primed to seek more instruction than experts are willing to give (Aka – Hewlett *et al.* 2011: 1172; Wogeo – Hogbin 1946: 282), as the experts incur a lower cost "if the trait is transmitted when the learner is at a developmental stage where (s)he is most receptive to such learning" (Shennan and Steele 1999: 369). And this prediction fits actual observation precisely – children want to learn before they're "ready" and experts are extremely reluctant to invest in instruction (Lancy 1996: 149–153).

(Malaysia) no developmental timetable is acknowledged. Nor is the child's development a subject for discussion. The onus for learning is entirely on children and they are rarely "pushed." Examples of children treated as lacking any sense, as being essentially uneducable, are legion in the ethnographic record. In Gbarngasuakwelle, I was chastised for spending my time with children because "they don't know anything, they haven't yet 'gotten sense'" (Lancy 1996: 118). Olga Nieuwenhuys, conducting fieldwork in an Indian coastal village, found that adults treated her attempts to observe and analyze children's culture with derision (1994: 34). Puerto Rican village children are *sin capacidad* and, therefore, "seldom taught anything deliberately" (Landy 1959: 99).

In Yemen, children love to play around construction sites, but in spite of the obvious danger, workers only half-heartedly curtail the risky behavior. More importantly, "builders adopted the prevalent Yemeni position that 'explaining' [the dangers] to children was pointless ... as they ... have no '*aql* (reason)" (Marchand 2001: 91). One of the consequences of treating young children as senseless, incomplete, and amoral is that adults feel no qualms about their exposure to sexual activity. Yanomamo parents "blowkiss, lick or manually rub the vaginal orifice of baby girls and stroke the scrotum of boys or mouth his penis until the age of three" (Eibl-Eibesfeldt 1983: 208). A Javanese mother rubs her son's penis during his bath and reacts with pleasure to his erection (Geertz 1961: 102). Young Dusun (Borneo) "children rarely are censured for open sexual behavior ... Adults look upon sexual play between children under four years of age with tolerance, in much the same manner as they view sex play in young animals" (Williams 1969: 102). Among the Bajau boat-dwellers in the Sulu Sea, children "wear no clothes until the age of eight or ten ... commonly explore one another's genitals ... [and] parents do not become upset with such behavior" (Nimmo 1970: 253). Similar attitudes prevailed in European society until the end of the seventeenth century, when "the custom of teasing small children with sex play was suppressed" (Sommerville 1982: 94).

The foregoing suggests that the child has no sense at this early age, that, in fact, nothing that happens to him or her can make a lasting impression. Children, before the age of five, roughly, are too immature to really absorb important lessons.[24] However, a survey of fifty societies confirmed that there

---

[24] The late Renaissance (Europe) ushered in the novel idea that children were sensible or educable at a much earlier period. Perhaps this occurred as an indirect response to the explosive growth of knowledge and the spread of literacy during what historians call the "Age of Enlightenment." Children's intellectual development needed to be accelerated to hasten the onset and effectiveness of schooling.

are two common transitions in children's development, at five to seven and at puberty, when new duties are assigned (Rogoff *et al.* 1975). At five to seven the child arrives at the "age of reason" and will be "noticed" (Lancy and Grove 2011a). This transition is found in many, perhaps most, of the world's cultures.

"An Ayoreo [South American] forager child is not considered a complete human being [until attaining] . . . *aiuketaotiguei*, which means 'understanding' or 'personality'" (Bugos and McCarthy 1984: 510). For Fulani pastoralists: "It is when children begin to develop *haYYillo* (social sense) that adults in turn change their expectations and behavior" (Riesman 1992: 130). For Sisala farmers, children from six years should display *wijima* (Grindal 1972: 28). For the Kipsigis, children are said to have sense or *ng'om* when they can not only take care of themselves but undertake certain routine chores – watering the cows, sweeping the house – without supervision (Harkness and Super 1986). For the Bakkarwal – nomadic pastoralists in Jammu and Kashmir – "*Osh* comes to a human child increasingly from the age of seven or eight years [and] it is *osh* which enables a shepherd to tend his flocks well, day and night" (Rao 1998: 59). For the Bulusu' of East Kalimantan, the comparable idea is *kakada'*, which means to be responsible and able to control one's emotions (Appell-Warren 1987: 161). For the Sepik people, when the child is able to fulfill social obligations even when it would rather not, it has achieved *Save* – the essential trait separating adults from children (Kulick and Stroud 1993: 44). Sinhalese children achieve *tere-neva* (understanding) at seven (Chapin 2011: 360).

"Intelligence" in the village is associated with qualities like self-sufficiency, obedience, respect toward elders, attention to detail, willingness to work, and effective management of younger siblings and livestock (Wober 1972). "It is common in the lower Tapajós to hear about someone who's 'very smart' that 'she doesn't need to observe more than once, just by watching us do it here, she can do it herself'" (Medaets 2011: 6). Qualities we value, such as precocity, verbal fluency, independent and creative thought, personal expression, and ability to engage in repartee, would all be seen by villagers as defects to be curtailed as quickly as possible.[25] These are danger signs of future waywardness. "Inquisitiveness by word or deed is severely censured, especially in [Kogi] women and children" (Reichel-Dolmatoff 1976: 283). "A [Sisala] child who tries to know more than his father is a 'useless child' (*bichuola*),

---

[25] While we may see cognitive "development" from early childhood to adulthood as some inevitable march to greater sophistication and rationality, that's not the typical view. As Christina Toren points out, in the Fijian society she studied, children do not grow into a more rational, instrumental worldview. They learn to see the world as adults do: it is populated with spirit forces, superstitions, supernatural powers, and taboos (Toren 1993).

for he has no respect" (Grindal 1972: 28). In rural Turkey the trait most valued by parents (60 percent) was obedience; least valued (18 percent) was independence (Kagitçibasi and Sunar 1992: 81).

Of course, "getting sense" occurs across an age span of several years. The child will have taken responsibility for a few chores; she will be noted observing and attempting to replicate adult skills; and she may be sent on errands. Novel or inappropriate use of adult tools or wasting valuable materials will provoke a scolding, as will failure to take care of oneself or to perform simple tasks correctly (Martini and Kirkpatrick 1992: 211). Albeit casually, adults will be sizing up the child, evaluating her potential for further learning. In an important study, Guatemalan villagers were found to rate the "intelligence" of children from their spontaneous demonstration of initiative and competence, and then assign greater responsibility to "smarter" kids (Nerlove et al. 1974).

The intervention by adults to redirect the child from the path of play to the path of work is one of the clearest indicators of this important transition in the child's development. Indeed, parents who fail to curb their five-to-seven-year-olds and to demand compliance and cooperation are ostracized by the community (Einarsdóttir 2004: 95; Lancy 1996: 76). If this is seen as a critical period for learning to act responsibly, the child will only succeed if provided opportunities to be useful. The consequences of not assigning chores in a timely manner are discussed in Chapter 2 (p. 57). So parents must assign chores (discussed fully in Chapter 7) at the appropriate level and intervene forcibly if the child shows a failure to mature on schedule. This is a very clear statement of that philosophy:

Giriama [Kenyan farmers] attach importance to providing children with duties that teach responsibility and mutuality. In their view, a mother who does not expect her children to help is remiss, even neglectful. A child so treated would inevitably emerge as an adult with few prospects and without the respect of the community. (Wenger 1989: 93)

Middle childhood also carries the expectation of greater self-awareness of gender conventions. The child now must insure that its behavior conforms to gender stereotypes while properly concealing the physical signs of its sex. In appearance and behavior there is now a sharp divergence in the lives of girls and boys. The former are particularly constrained by rules of modesty, and these are associated with territorial constraints. That is, while boys enjoy increased freedom of movement and access to realms unsupervised by adults, girls are more tightly bound to the domestic sphere and are either working in tandem with their mother or serving as her junior surrogate (Lancy and Grove 2011a: 298–299). Once again we will see a mixture of *laissez-faire* "let nature take its course" and stricter, more interventionist tactics.

Socializing gender

[Russian] peasants considered infants and very young children, from birth to five or six, as neutral – without gender. (Gorshkov 2009: 18)

If a [Qashqa'i] girl approaches a group of males, she will be re-directed to a gathering of women ... a lesson in gender. (Shahbazi 2001: 54)

We are girls who cannot do what boys do, we stay in the house to work [San Blas song lyric]. (McCosker 1976: 44)

In a few societies gender differences are of relatively little importance. On Vanatinai Island (Papua New Guinea), egalitarian relations between the sexes mean that "Gender identity ... is formed primarily after puberty. Children of both sexes live substantially similar lives" (Lepowsky 1998: 129; see also the Walpiri – Musharbash 2011: 67). Among the Inuit "at thirteen-years-of-age ... sex distinctions took on greater significance, and young people were called either *inuuhuktuq* (boys) or *arnaruhiq* (girls). In the previous stage *nutaraq*, sex distinctions were not made" (Condon 1987: 55). At the other extreme are societies where gender is so important that it must be created through ritual action. In the New Guinea Highlands, "maleness, unlike femaleness, is not a biological given. It must be artificially induced through secret ritual" (Herdt 2001: 165).

Similarly, in the Dogon worldview "children are born as androgynous beings," and only through circumcision (boys) and excision of genitalia (girls) can they become adult males and females, capable of reproduction (D. Y. Arnold 2006: 50; Dettwyler 1994: 27). Ceremonies – many involving circumcision – to transform children into adults will be reviewed in Chapter 8. In this section we'll review some of the more subtle ways that gender is marked and shaped by the society.

Parents may act on perceived differences from birth. Commonly, babies are given gifts of miniature versions of tools they'll use in the gender-specific tasks they'll later fulfill (Greenfield *et al*. 1989: 203; Hewlett 1992: 234; Whittemore 1989: 88). Other rites include the Highland Maya custom of cutting a boy's umbilical cord over a corncob and a girl's over a grinding stone (Modiano 1973: 28). Among the Aztecs, a boy's umbilical cord would be buried in a battlefield, a girl's under the hearth (Shein 1992: 25).

Feeding is also reflective of gender roles and relative status. In the Kerkennah Islands (Tunisia), females are weaned and expected to become physically independent much sooner than boys. Even so, compared with girls, boys are seen to "be very difficult to wean" (Platt 1988: 276–277). In southwestern Ethiopia, Gurage boys are always fed before and more generously than their sisters. On ceremonial occasions, boys are invited to partake of food; girls serve but do not consume any food themselves (Shack 1969: 296). Differences in the quality and amount of food are paralleled by differences in the way illnesses are treated. For example, in Hokkien villages on Taiwan, "illnesses contracted by girls were approached with a wait-and-see attitude, whereas similar illnesses in their brothers received prompt treatment" (Wolf 1972: 61).

In societies that treat children as asexual, middle childhood provokes a change in attitude (Lancy and Grove 2011a: 287–288). Children should now be clothed and limit interaction with the opposite sex (Barnett 1979: 6; Lawton 2007: 46). At five or six Ulithian children must begin to wear clothing.

Boys wear a long grass like garment made of hibiscus bast that is shredded and made to hang down over the genitals and the buttocks. Girls abandon their nakedness by putting on a bulky "grass" skirt made of shredded coconut leaflets. Children fidget a lot when first they put on clothing and must be trained through scolding, warnings, and rewards to keep from discarding them. (Lessa 1966: 98)

Whereas small [Wagenia] boys were still allowed to go around naked as they pleased, initiated youths had to cover their genitals. Their maleness had acquired relevance. Circumcision put the finishing touches to the process whereby the boy became conscious of his sex role. (Droogers 1980: 161)

A distinct segregation of roles is the rule. In the case of male Berber children, the close physical contact with the mother begins to end. Accession to this age-status is marked by the child being given a pair of under-drawers (*serwal*) to wear under his *jellaba*, and a small skullcap for his head (Hatt 1974: 139). The names assigned to children may change; among Dusun farmers, boys are called "without loincloth," girls "without a skirt" until five years, and then "child man" or "virgin" (Williams 1969: 86). Segregation in play may be imposed and reinforced by hazing (Henderson 1970: 107). These strictures are often imposed earlier for girls than for boys (Barnett 1979: 6; Geertz 1961: 102; Marlowe 2010: 199; Rao 1998: 93–94).

Aside from clothing, food, and care, societies may accentuate gender divisions through ritual. In Tamang (Nepal) custom, the first rite of passage – for boys only – is the *chewar*, a ceremony marking the first haircut. It is performed by the mother's brother (Fricke 1994: 134). Wogeo (Papua New Guinea) males have the distinction of playing flutes, and each male must pass

through a series of initiation ceremonies that begin in babyhood and end in later youth ... to make certain that the boy will grow into a man ... in his pubescent period they scarify his tongue to enable him to play the flutes ... his first artificial menstruation ... [to eliminate] the injurious elements absorbed from females during his infancy and childhood ... cleansing the tongue renders it pliable and hence better fitted for coping with a woodwind instrument. (Hogbin 1970: 103, 114)

Girls and boys are often subject to varying "tether lengths," meaning that the limits imposed on them differ (Watson-Franke 1976: 194). "Around the age of six to seven years, [Matsigenka] boys start accompanying father to hunt, fish, and plant in the gardens, while the girls remain close to their mothers" (Ochs and Izquierdo 2009: 396). Giriama boys "spend more time than girls beyond the range of scrutiny . . . because the chores [they] do take them outside the homestead" (Wenger 1989: 110). Tongan boys "are eager to move into the boys' huts, to be associated with the older boys, and to experience their comparative freedom" (Morton 1996: 112). Girls' behavior may also be subject to other restrictions not imposed on boys. Pashtu girls are beaten more often than boys to insure their obedience to their husbands (Casimir 2010: 36). In medieval Europe a girl had to learn obedience early as she was subservient to nearly everyone – to her parents, tutor, and husband, or, if she took the veil, to the rule of her monastic order (Shahar 1990: 166).

In East Asian society, "Under the principles of Confucian ideology, women [must] observe the virtues of three submissions: to their fathers, their husbands, and their sons" (Kim 1993: 188). Consequently, girls found themselves suffering under severe restrictions – from an early age. In aboriginal Taiwan, a mother will berate or even beat

a four-year-old girl who does something that endangers her small brother . . . She has heard from the time she could understand . . . that she was a "worthless girl." Wan-iu (a four-year-old girl) was sitting on a small stool near the well. A neighbor came out and said, "Wan-iu, let Thiam-hok (a two-and-a-half-year-old boy) sit on your stool so he won't get dirty." Wan-iu pushed him away . . . Wan-iu's mother shouted at her angrily, "You are a girl! Give him that stool. I'll beat you to death!" . . . By age five most little girls have learned to step aside automatically for boys. (Wolf 1972: 65–67)

Katherine Platt observes that Kerkennek boys are encouraged in verbal dueling and their anger and impatience are readily tolerated, while aggression or any sign of strong emotion is discouraged in girls, who are rewarded for being reticent and unassuming (Platt 1988: 279). A parallel picture emerges from Tonga, where "boys' . . . cheeky and aggressive behavior is often given covert approval" (Morton 1996: 105).

Whatever contribution adults make to gender socialization is amplified, even exceeded, by that of the child's peers. This description of Amhara (Ethiopia) childhood is quite representative: peers, through hazing, mold wayward behavior. A little boy will be harassed and insulted for crying, for not defending himself, or for exhibiting soft or effeminate traits. And a "girl who shows signs of daring (k'obba) is mocked and hazed" (Messing 1985: 207).

The assignment of chores is another area where gender differences are highlighted, and we will discuss the various "chore curricula" in Chapter 7. Scholars who have reviewed the ethnographic literature find great consistency in role assignments across cultures (Edwards and Whiting 1980), which may be the reason parents, generally, are not expected to take special pains to insure their children adopt gender-appropriate behavior and tasks. Girls, in particular, assume the role of mother's helper at a very young age, well before boys start to contribute. Girls, in fact, are often credited with "sense" well before their male counterparts (Friedl 1997: 297).

However, there are plentiful examples of families with "too few" girls, and childcare is assigned to boys (Ember 1973: 425–426). But boys strenuously resist "women's work" while demanding of their sisters the same degree of deference and servitude their fathers expect of their mothers (Nicolaisen 1988: 216). On the other hand, there are a few cases of helpful boys being rebuffed. "Mahmud wanted to help his [Lurs] mother wash clothes. She ... scolded him: 'Do you want to turn into a girl?! Go away!'" (Friedl 1997: 142). Lourdes de León (cited in Paradise and Rogoff 2009: 117) describes a Tzotzil Maya boy who applied himself to learning a variety of women's tasks including tortilla making and embroidery in spite of vigorous discouragement.

Lastly, I want to stress that the gender role socialization practices I've been discussing may be more commonly talked about than observed, because children so readily attend to and adopt the clothing, manner, and tasks of same-gender adults (Ames 1982: 115) – prominently during several years of ardent make-believe play.

But what about teaching?

Culture is learned less because of the pedagogical efforts of the adults than because of the predispositions, agency and intentionality of the children. (Goody 2006: 11)

An individual does not learn from another but through another. (Schönpflug 2009: 466)

[In learning to become a Touareg camel herder] Es gibt keine systematische Ausbildung, keine institutionalisierte Lehre. (Spittler 1998: 238)[26]

In the first chapter I threw down the gauntlet and argued that many of contemporary psychology's notions about childhood and, especially, child development could be challenged if not fully discounted by a thorough analysis of the ethnographic record. One such opportunistic target has been cultural transmission. In this chapter I have tried to spread out for the reader's inspection segments of the ethnographic record that have a bearing. It's hard to conclude other than that active or direct teaching/instruction is rare in cultural transmission, and that when it occurs, it is not aimed at

[26] "There is no systematic training, no formal instruction."

critical subsistence and survival skills – the area most obviously affected by natural selection – but, rather, at controlling and managing the child's behavior. This shouldn't be news, because from the earliest to the most recent ethnographic accounts of childhood (Fortes 1938/1970; Raum 1940; Whiting 1941; Read 1960; Grindal 1972; Lancy 1996; Bolin 2006; Casimir 2010; Marlowe 2010; Hewlett and Hewlett 2013: 76), the authors describe children acquiring culture through social learning without the necessity for instruction. Furthermore, anthropologists often find that the absence of teaching is specifically endorsed in parental ethnotheories. Nevertheless, as Barbara King notes "anthropologists seem to take teaching in humans for granted" (1994: 111).

Psychologists make the same assumption but tend to treat the dominant WEIRD culture as normative vis-à-vis all theoretical considerations. This certainly includes theories of cultural transmission and child development (Pitman *et al.* 1989: 18). But consider that, on most attributes important to an understanding of childhood, WEIRD society is just that, a weird or anomalous outlier (Henrich *et al.* 2010; Lancy 2007, 2010a; Ross 2004: 24).

In contrast to American parents, who seem to feel that knowledge is something like medicine – it's good for the child and must be crammed down his throat even if he does not like it – Rotuman parents acted as if learning were inevitable because the child wants to learn. (Howard 1970: 37)

From the WEIRD perspective there is the strong presumption that the child is an empty vessel ("storage unit"; cf. Roberts 1964: 438) that is filled with culture by parents, kin, religious authorities, and educators. Cultural transmission is seen primarily as a top-down process with the parent playing a key role as organizer, mentor, and instructor for the recipient of cultural knowledge – usually a child. As examples: "The central concern has been with how infants and children are *taught* to 'think, act, and feel appropriately' [as they] are recruited to be members of a culture" (Pelissier 1991: 82, emphasis added). Socialization is "a process applied 'from above' by [those who are] older ... to originally asocial infants until they conform to some standard known as 'adulthood'" (Rowell 1975: 126). "Ethnographic work in traditional cultures has been hamstrung by the assumption that any knowledge deserving of notice is culturally transmitted" (Chipeniuk 1995: 494).

The bias inherent in theory derived exclusively from WEIRD society can distort our understanding of the infant cognition research discussed at the beginning of this chapter. From studies on infant gaze preferences, Gergely and associates have argued for the primacy of parental teaching in the transmission of culture.

Humans are adapted to spontaneously transfer ... fast and efficiently ... relevant cultural knowledge to conspecifics and to fast-learn the contents of such teaching through a human-specific social learning system called "pedagogy." Pedagogical knowledge transfer is triggered by specific communicative cues (such as eye-contact, contingent reactivity, the prosodic pattern of "motherese," and being addressed by one's own name). Infants show special sensitivity to such "ostensive" cues that signal the teacher's communicative intention to manifest new and relevant knowledge about a referent object. Pedagogy offers a novel functional perspective to interpret a variety of early emerging triadic communicative interactions between adults and infants about novel objects they are jointly attending to. (Gergely *et al.* 2007: 145, 139)

This argument is built on a mountain of weak assumptions. Outside WEIRD or post-industrial society, this suite of parent–infant interaction patterns is rare. Mothers don't often engage cognitively with infants, they may only respond contingently to their distress cues, and they probably do not gaze at them or engage in shared attention to novel objects (de León 2011: 100; Göncü *et al.* 2000; LeVine 2004: 161). In fact, when Nso babies gaze at their mothers during nursing, the mother blows in their eyes so that they avert their gaze (Otto 2014). Akira Takada makes the point – based on his extensive observation of mother-infant interactions among Kalahari San – that the mother is engaged in a whirlwind of activity while holding or nursing her infant. This may include a complex series of verbal interactions with others. In short, she's much too busy to gaze at the infant or attempt to engage it in a mutual activity (Takada 2012: 69; see also Meehan 2009: 389).[27]

In the many societies where infants are not held *en face* as a rule but attached to the mother's body or held facing away from the caretaker (e.g. Field and Widmayer 1981; Jay 1969: 99; Ochs and Izquierdo 2009: 397), the infants may be far "more attuned to their caregivers' postural positions than to their caregivers' gaze direction" (Akhtar and Gernsbacher 2008: 61)".[28] Motherese and baby-talk are not found universally (Ochs 1986: 8; Pye 1991; Solomon 2012: 129). The absence of mutual gaze and motherese can be accounted for in part because rest and quietude are usually considered essential for the infant's growth and survival (Lancy and Grove 2010: 147; this volume, Chapter 3, p. 54).

---

[27] For instance, in constructing an argument about the genesis of teaching in the (universal) parent-infant relationship, Tomasello and colleagues offer this exemplar: "suppose a child and adult are building a block tower together" (Tomasello *et al.* 2005: 682). Nowhere in the entire ethnographic record of childhood have I found any instance of a parent and child building a block tower together or anything else whose purpose is to entertain while also instructing the child. In order to sustain the idea that the top-down pedagogy model is biologically based, *all* parents in *all* cultures should be engaging in this kind of behavior with infants because, in the theory, it establishes the foundation on which later and, presumably more instrumental teaching is built. But they don't.

[28] The infant's sensitivity to the mother's movements is reciprocated. !Kung "mothers are aware of their children's movements and sounds and learn to anticipate defecation, and move the child off their body before it occurs" (Howell 2010: 27).

In many societies, probably the majority, children who're *speaking* don't usually have conversations with adults (Toren 1990: 171), so the likelihood of adults conversing with speechless infants[29] is very low.[30] Infant pointing is also part of this nascent "pedagogy" referred to by Gergely and colleagues, as it shows the infant is inviting instruction (Tomasello *et al.* 2005: 683) from the parent. But many infants are swaddled or otherwise confined, so how can they point? And if they do, does anyone take notice (de León 2011: 100)?

Spontaneous pointing by Tzeltal Maya and Rossel Island [Papua New Guinea] infants is rare, not evidenced in the data for all infants, and the infants are not yet very competent at pointing ... pointing ... does not have the canonical result observed in postindustrial societies, with the adult labeling the object pointed at ... On the basis of these observations, it is hard to believe that indexical pointing *per se* is playing a critical role in the infants' understanding that others have minds and communicative intentions of their own. (Brown 2011: 48)

In most societies, infants don't receive a name until their viability is assured and they are considered "ripe" or ready to "become persons" (Chapter 2). Also, there is little evidence in the ethnographic literature that adults feel any urgency to transfer knowledge to children "fast and efficiently." The primary examples of adults shaping the behavior of infants occur in the acceleration of motor development (Chapter 4) and self-management skills to render the children easier to take care of (this chapter). In other words, whatever "pedagogy" we might see applied to the very young is done for the benefit of caretakers, not children.

Brazelton published what amounts to a succinct rebuttal to Gergely's theory thirty-five years ago. On the basis of field research carried out in 1966–1969, he wrote:

Differences in the stimulation provided by mother–infant interaction in the U.S. and Zinacantecan cultures are dramatic. Zinacantecan infants are not reinforced contingently for vocalizing, smiling and motor development; yet, they continue to develop, as reflected in the results of the Bayley scales ... These findings suggest that the imitative mode for learning ... may serve well [and] may be activated by stimuli that seem non-contingent and are not directed through the usual visual and verbal channels. (Brazelton 1977: 177)

---

[29] In fact "infant" comes from the Latin *infans* = speechless.

[30] There are a few societies, such as the West African Beng, that consider infants to be reincarnated ancestors, in between the human and spirit worlds (this volume, Chapter 2, p. 47). The Beng do sometimes direct speech to infants, but they're speaking not to the baby but, rather, to the reincarnated kinsman, pleading for him to intercede with the ancestors (Gottlieb 2000: 80–81).

Contra Gergely *et al.* (2007), I think the infant cognition studies are far more congenial to a child-initiated acquisition of culture rather than an adult-directed "transfer of cultural knowledge." Setting aside these specific studies, *parental investment theory* (Trivers 1972) should make us wary of ascribing to parents any "non-essential" investment in their offspring – such as teaching them. The *cultural niche theory* argues that the human ability to learn through observation of others reflects an evolved psychology (Boyd and Richerson 1996: 82) and that learners are predisposed to learn selectively from more successful role models – rather than relying exclusively on parents (Boyd *et al.* 2011: 10921).

Teaching will be favored by selection only where the costs to teachers of facilitating learning are outweighed by the long-term fitness benefits they accrue once pupils have learned, and these benefits will be scaled by *the ease with which pupils could learn without teaching.* (Thornton and Raihani 2008: 1823, emphasis added; see also King 1994: 125)

One of the most unequivocal findings re childhood from the ethnographic record is children learning their culture *without teaching.* "Navahos abhor the idea or practice of controlling other beings in the course of everyday life" (Chisholm 1996: 178). Inuit "parents do not presume to teach their children what they can as easily learn on their own" (Guemple 1979: 50). The Yukaghir are Siberian cousins to the Inuit, and their model of childrearing emphasizes the autonomy of the learner because to "be a hunter, you must know everything yourself" (Willerslev 2007: 160). An egalitarian ethos also contraindicates the inherently hierarchical act of teaching (Lewis 2008).[31]

Deciding what another person should do, no matter what his age, is outside the Yequana vocabulary of behaviors. There is great interest in what everyone does, but no impulse to influence – let alone coerce – anyone. The child's will is his motive force. (Gray 2009: 507)

"Equality" may be said to be the paramount value of the Asabano and it is thus the mediating principle in interpersonal relations. Individuals both attempt to avoid infringing upon others, and are keen to ensure that their autonomy is not violated. (Little 2011: 149)

[Aka] respect for an individual's autonomy is also a core cultural value ... one does not impose his/her will, beliefs, or actions on others [including children]. (Hewlett and Hewlett 2013: 75)

---

[31] Borofsky notes from fieldwork on Pukapuka that, in status-conscious Polynesia, to seek instruction calls attention to one's inferior status (Borofsky 1987: 99).

In a learning situation [in rural Tahiti] ... to tell anybody what to do, is intrusive and taken as a sign of unjustified adult mood-driven irritability and impatience. (Levy 1996: 129)[32]

The relatively few restrictions placed on the young Okinawan child are an important basis for learning. By being able to participate freely, children learn what is going on in their village from day to day. (Maretzki and Maretzki 1963: 514)

The extraordinary efficacy of autonomous learning was demonstrated in an unlikely natural experiment. Cantel is an Indian community in the Guatemala Highlands that transitioned from total dependence on "simple farming technology not much removed from that of their pre-Columbian ancestors, to operating in their midst Central America's largest textile mill" (Nash 1958: 1). New workers learned to operate power looms in much the same way that they learned weaving at home.

The newly hired worker performs menial tasks[33] such as bringing material to the machine or taking finished goods off of it, but most of the time is spent observing the operations of the person running the machine. [The new worker] neither asked questions nor was given advice. When the machine snagged or stopped, she would look carefully to see what the operator did to get it back into motion ... This constituted her daily routine for nearly six weeks, and at the end of this time she announced that she was ready to run a loom ... and she operated it, not quite as rapidly as the girl who had just left it, but with skill and assurance ... at no time during her learning and apprentice period had she touched a machine or practiced operating ... She observes and internally rehearses the set of operations until she feels able to perform. She will not try her hand until she feels competent, for to fumble and make mistakes is a cause for *verguenza* – public shame. She does not ask questions because that would annoy the person teaching her, and they might also think she is stupid. (Nash 1958: 26–27)

The autonomous learner model is embraced across subsistence systems; it occurs across knowledge and skill domains, across gender and over the lifespan. I am not claiming that culture is transmitted to children in the complete absence of teaching, but that teaching is neither common nor essential to the process. The remarkable thing is that there are likely more vivid descriptions in the literature of adults spurning would-be learners than patiently teaching them. In *Playing on the Mother Ground* I provide an extended example, of mother Sua and daughter Nyenpu each weaving a fishnet. As the vignette unfolded, the main point seemed to be how little interest Sua had in getting involved in Nyenpu's weaving. Sua claimed that

---

[32] An interesting "work-around" for the prohibition on teaching is provided by the Fort Norman Slave, who hunt during severe winter weather and must traverse ice-fields. Fathers "instruct" sons about this dangerous environment (which comprises thirteen kinds of ice and multiple modes of travel) via a game-like quiz (Basso 1972: 40).

[33] See the apprenticeship discussion in this volume, Chapter 7, p. 287.

her stance was typical and replicated her own mother's attitude when she was learning net-weaving. Several other informants told me of approaching experts for help and being rebuffed (Lancy 1996: 149–150). Other ethnographers report similar tales. Reichard describes a Navajo girl who learned to weave in spite of her mother's repulsing her interest (1934: 38), which paralleled a case from Truk of a weaver/basket-maker whose kin were unsupportive of her efforts to learn their skills (Gladwin and Sarason 1953: 414–415), and a case from the Venda tribe where a potter is vehement that "'We don't teach. When women make pots some (children and others) come to watch, then go and try'" (Krause 1985: 95). The following was recorded in Khalapur, India:

A 6-year-old girl was trying to embroider a little piece of cloth. Her aunt and grandmother were nearby but did not help her. She threaded the needle after many tries and then followed the lines of a design, carefully counting the stitches and correcting her mistakes. After five minutes, her aunt and grandmother inspected her work and told her to take it all out because she was ruining the cloth. [Nevertheless] the girl continued to work and . . . correct her mistakes. [The observer felt] that she had done quite well for a first try. (Edwards 2005: 91)

A last, dramatic case comes from Japanese shellfish divers. One representative informant gave a detailed history of her gradual and entirely self-taught education in shellfish diving. On her first deep water dive with the adult women, her mother was present and she was asked by the ethnographer:

So your mother taught you how to find abalone? My mother! she said loudly, She drove me away! I tried to follow her to the bottom to watch, but she shoved me back. When we were on the surface again, she practically screamed at me to move OFF and find my danged abalone BY MYSELF. So we had to discard [one] cliché about how artisans learn. (Hill and Plath 1998: 212)

In fact, whether or not teaching occurs seems to be less about the difficulty of the to-be-learned skill or material and more about the emotional closeness between the expert and novice. Forming a teacher-pupil relationship rests on a foundation of filiality identified in theories of kin selection and reciprocal altruism (Dunbar 1998: 129). De Laguna found relevant variation in her ethnohistory of the Tlingit, with some women recalling close ties to mothers who taught them many things including basketry, and others who were rejected as students by their mothers and learned on their own (de Laguna 1965: 14; see also Hayden and Cannon 1984: 354). Even where investigators report high levels of teaching from *interview* surveys ("Who taught you to . . ."; cf. Hewlett and Cavalli-Sforza 1986), subsequent *observational* studies of the same phenomenon in the same society found teaching to be extremely rare (Boyette 2013: 91).

If we have all this evidence for culture acquisition sans teaching, why pursue a theory that assigns a critical role to teaching in the evolution and preservation of human culture and the successful rearing of children? Consider the data on which such claims are based. Those who seem to be advocates of this proposal draw entirely on lab experiments with captive populations, mathematical simulation or interview studies, studies with members of WEIRD (or moving toward WEIRD) societies, or fieldwork with non-humans, in particular meerkats (Thornton and McAuliffe 2006), cheetahs (Caro and Hauser 1992), and tandem-running ants (Hoppit *et al.* 2008).

6   Of marbles and morals

Introduction

[Play is a] form of buffered learning through which the child can make ... step-by-step progress towards adult behavior. (Roberts and Sutton-Smith 1962: 184)

From the perspective of Biyaka parents, the primary duty of young children is to play. In fact they believe ... that if children do not play, they will fail to learn anything. (Neuwelt-Truntzer 1981: 136)

One theme we've been pursuing throughout is the notion that high human fertility is facilitated by the child's relatively rapid transition from wholly dependent to semi-dependent status. Childhood, as a stage of development unique to our species, allows the child to develop slowly with relatively little attention from its mother, freeing her to bear another infant. However, being a child does not just mean that one can survive well with minimal care from adults; it also means, in a more positive sense, that one's life is filled with play activity. From the perspective of the harried parent, the child's deep engagement with playthings and playmates is a godsend. However, keeping busy turns out to be only one of a host of potential benefits conveyed by play. I see "play as providing a basic tool kit of activities among which various species, under varying environmental conditions, at varying points in the life-cycle, select to use, elaborate, and combine in particular ways to achieve particular ends" (Lancy 1982: 166).

We'll take a look at the many facets and potential benefits of play in this chapter, while acknowledging its ephemeral quality. We start with what might be the quintessential "pick-up" game – marbles – and consider its role in children's "moral" development. Next we consider several extremely common types of play – object play, locomotor play, and "rough and tumble" (R & T). We consider whether their ubiquity might signal the presence of evolutionary benefits. In a section entitled "Gamesmanship," we evaluate the notion that human intelligence may be primarily social in nature and that play exercises and/or telegraphs children's Machiavellian IQ. Play is, of course, affected by environmental and cultural factors. The composition of the play group and emerging gender-role differentiation are two areas where such factors are observed.

Play has also been analyzed as an avenue along which the traditional culture is passed on to the next generation. Even a casual observer will note children creating playlets that incorporate important cultural information, and, more subtly, we can tease out moral lessons from the folktales, songs, and games that children are repeatedly exposed to.

Cultural influences on play are also seen in the relative enthusiasm/disapproval adults display toward it generally, and, more particularly, toward play that may be aggressive and competitive as compared with more egalitarian interactions. In contemporary society, a philosophy has emerged that proposes, in effect: "Play is too critical a learning medium to be left to children." We examine the rise of parent-directed and parent-managed play. And, finally, we consider the "downside" of play, that is, we look at cases where society's valuation of the child – as cherub or chattel – leads to the *suppression* of play.

Marbles

Marbles is capable of infinite variation. (Opie and Opie 1997: 41)

I want to start this chapter with marbles because, as the great theoretician Jean Piaget discovered, the game captures so many developmental processes that it is like looking at the innards of a clock with its many gears and pinions. First we see the refinement of manual dexterity. Humans are tool users, and young humans, as a consequence, are object manipulators. In its most refined form, with perfectly polished and round orbs, marbles calls forth tremendous small motor skill and digital finesse. Then we see "gamesmanship" by which children manipulate each other to enhance both the quality of play and their own success. Lastly, we see the development of social understanding, of an appreciation of rules *qua* rules.

By at least the Roman era and probably earlier, children used knuckle-bones, which have faces or sides similar to dice, as projectiles to try and dislodge each other's stationary targets. In other words, the basic pattern of marbles, whereby a player shoots a hard object at one or more similar objects, trying to drive it or them out of a demarcated area, is probably quite old. The use of perfectly round, durable spheres must be more recent as technology found inexpensive ways to produce them, but animal vertebrae are still used where manufactured toys are not available (Casimir 2010: 51). The lengthiest treatment of marbles in English was prepared by the Opies, the greatest child folklorists of all time, and published in *Children's Games*

Figure 15 Schoolboys playing marbles in Marante Village, Sulawesi

with Things. They document three basic versions of the game, but the variation in rules of play is staggering.

To the uninitiated, a game of marbles seems anarchic. The leaping and shouting is partly caused by excited partisans cheering the players on, and partly by the calls and counter-calls that decide whether various rules can be brought into play or not. This is instant legislation. First it must be decided whether the game is to be played "Keepsies" or "Lendsies." If a boy finds his opponent's marble is obscured by a stone, stick, or lump, a shout of "Clears" (or "Clearsies") permits him to clear it away (Opie and Opie 1997: 42). Furthermore, for nearly every assertive claim by the shooter, such as those above, the non-shooting player can, if he's quick about it, offer a nullifying call so that calls of "Clearsies," "Kicks," "Changeys," are cancelled. Figure 15 depicts schoolboys playing marbles at the Marante village school, Sulawesi.

No wonder that Piaget saw marbles as a rich mine of clues to children's acquisition of moral standards. He was generally uninterested in the child's development as a social being, but his single foray in that direction aimed to elucidate what he called "moral development." In Piaget's view, for the child to develop morally, he would have first to acquire the notion that society is governed by rules and then to transcend that limited view by grasping that these rules can be arbitrary, anachronistic, and changeable. He must be able to juggle two rules that may be in conflict or to read nuances in a situation that lead him to question the applicability of a particular rule. Piaget saw the urban Swiss child's gradual development as a marbles player as the perfect natural experiment to view moral development unfolding: "Children's games constitute the most admirable social institutions. The game of marbles, for instance ... contains an extremely complex system of rules, that is to say, a code of laws, a jurisprudence of its own" (Piaget 1932/ 1965: 13).

Like the Opies, Piaget and his colleagues identify lots of variability in the rules and style of play (Piaget 1932/1965: 16, 17, 20). After documenting the primary dimensions of the game, Piaget begins to probe the players' cognitive representation of the rules.

> You begin by asking the child if he could invent a new rule ... Once the new rule has been formulated, you ask the child whether it could give rise to a new game ... The child either agrees to the suggestion or disputes it. If he agrees, you immediately ask him whether the new rule is a "fair" rule, a "real" rule, one "like the others," and try to get at the various motives that enter into the answers. (Piaget 1932/1965: 25).[1]

Piaget teases out distinct age-dependent styles in children's approach to marbles. Initially the child plays with the marbles as interesting objects with no game *per se*. By about age four, the child can play the game, knows how to make the right moves physically, and understands the necessity for turn-taking. "The child's chief interest is no longer psycho-motor; it is social" (Piaget 1932/ 1965: 45). He is able to imitate the model provided by a more mature player. But he really has no sense of strategy or of what to do to increase the likelihood of winning. Then, around age seven, players focus on winning, even though their grasp of the rules – as revealed through questioning – is still vague. By age eleven, there "is remarkable concordance ... when they are questioned on the rules of the game and their possible variations" (Piaget 1932/1965: 27). Nevertheless, the child still hasn't grasped rules *qua* rules. He still sees them as "imposed upon the younger children by the older ones ... as sacred and untouchable." But, by thirteen, boys understand the mutability of the rules (Piaget 1932/1965: 70). A very similar account is available from observation of Fijian marble players (Brison 1999: 112).

Piaget did not observe (or at least did not report on) episodes where novice players learned from those who were more expert. In fact, this is a rarely studied phenomenon – perhaps because in modern studies of children

---

[1] Interestingly, "Plato [thought] boys [should] be forbidden to make alterations in their games, lest they be led to disobey the laws of the State in later life" (Opie and Opie 1969: 6).

engaged in game-play, the players are usually of the same age and, hence, equally ignorant. But it is worth noting that, in learning to play marbles, even Swiss children follow the village learning model – no teachers.

Children in Gbarngasuakwelle learn games through a multi-phased process. First, they observe their older siblings at play. Next, they replicate what they've observed as closely as they can (drawing in the sand, manipulating stones, repeating what they've heard) but while still on the periphery. They attempt to join the game but are usually rebuffed as not yet ready. Once they are permitted to play, they are usually forgiven for violations, and better players may self-handicap. This attitude insures that play can proceed and that the novices will not be too frustrated. As their competence improves, learners will be chastised for rule violation – rather than being told what the rules are. At the last stage short of mastery, the expert players may then actually bend the rules in their own favor in order to remain consistent winners. Finally, the novice learns all the *official* rules and will "call" a rule violation, thus completely "leveling the playing field" (Lancy 1996: 112).

Furthermore, like Piaget with the Swiss marble players, I was able to plot very evident developmental trends within a particular Kpelle game and across the entire village game inventory. For example, for the dominoes-like game of *kwa-tinang:* "Younger boys seemed to memorize each configuration because on each trial they proceeded a little further ... Older boys showed signs of acquiring a mental map of the stones because they advanced in large jumps from try to try" (Lancy 1996: 105). *Kwa-tinang*, like many Kpelle games, utilizes stones, seeds, or other convenient counters or markers. Indeed, snapshots of village children often capture them "scavenging" for objects to incorporate into play activity.

In the next section, we will see that, even in the absence of manufactured toys, including lovely glass marbles, children seek out objects to manipulate and incorporate into their play activities.

Play with objects

The favorite pastime of [Aruacanian] boys eleven to fifteen years of age was spinning tops. Every boy owned a top and the cord with which he spun it – in all probability he had made both. (Hilger 1957: 101)

Piaget can also be credited with calling the attention of developmental psychology to the young child's fascination with objects. From an early age, infants are wont to grasp objects, mouth them, shake them, throw them, and examine them. Indeed the child's changing relationship to the physical world, her perception and manipulation of it, forms the backbone of Piaget's entire theory of cognitive development.

Among primates, play with objects is not common and, not coincidentally, tool-use is also rare.[2] However, among humans, the extent of the child's object play varies quite a bit. There are dangers inherent in free exploration by village infants and toddlers. Much of what they might discover lying on the ground is potentially dangerous. On the other hand, the child's tendency to play with and explore objects does have a practical side; for example, "if butchering was underway [in a Fore village], even toddlers could explore and manipulate the carcass, using whatever implements they could find" (Sorenson 1976: 198). Kammu (Laos) boys develop expertise in fabricating hunting weapons and traps by creating toys that gradually evolve into the genuine articles (Tayanin and Lindell 1991: 15). In many societies, including the Kammu, children are given scaled-down or cast-off tools to "play" with. "At about six years of age [Guara] boys are presented with a toy machete – made from a worn-out blade – cut to size" (Ruddle and Chesterfield 1977: 34). The archaeological record yields artifacts whose crudeness, small size, or inappropriate materials (e.g. a wooden "knife") suggest that toy tools and utensils were seen to afford learning opportunities for children (Mesoamerica – de Lucia 2010: 614; Arctic region – Kenyon and Arnold 1985). Figure 16 shows a boy from Ifaty Village, southwest Madagascar, with a model sailboat he has constructed.

"Safe" toys designed specifically for very young children tend to show up in the archaeological record when societies become more complex, as the frequent examples from Greece (Golden 1990: 270), Rome (Rawson 1991), the European Middle Ages (Mygland 2008: 91), and pre-contact Peru (Sillar 1994: 56) attest. The corpus of dolls and toys – including many with articulated limbs and inlaid eyes and teeth – recovered from upper-class homes in ancient Egypt is quite large (Wileman 2005: 31).

To encourage object play, we provide lots of toys, including safe, miniature tools, in various sizes, along with the dolls to use them. We also provide objects to play with that are specifically designed to facilitate the kind of cognitive complexity and flexibility that many assert is the *raison d'être* of object play (Power 2000). And, what is perhaps most remarkable, we sometimes intervene to "teach" our children how to use their toys or nudge them into more complex uses (Gaskins *et al.* 2007). I have found only one example of this in the ethnographic literature – a Wogeo father assisting his son with a miniature canoe (Hogbin 1946: 282) – and I am confident it occurs rarely. In research where the investigators created conditions designed to facilitate

---

[2] However, primates do play with objects and use tools in captivity, and they choose "gender appropriate" toys with great regularity (Kahlenberg and Wrangham 2010: 1067).

Figure 16 Child with sailboat in Ifaty, southwest Madagascar

their involvement, East Indian and Guatemalan villagers would not intervene in their toddlers' play (Göncü *et al.* 2000). It's hard to escape the conclusion that our "micro-management" of children's toys and play is driven by the inexorable demands of schooling.

In the USA, children have access to a huge array of store-bought toys as well as found objects and the child's environment has been safely child-proofed. No such conditions exist in village India. The few toys are either flimsy or fragile craft objects used for display; packing containers and the like are recycled quickly; and indoor areas are crowded and dangerous (Kopp *et al.* 1977: 436–437).

Environmental conditions and the absence of durable toys may limit object play in many societies, especially in comparison with the play experiences of contemporary children. For example, Luo children were observed playing with Vaseline containers, bottle tops, an old oil bottle, a tube of toothpaste, and old cassette tapes (Tudge 2008: 153). When we look at *physical* play, the situation is somewhat reversed. In the village there are few limits to high-energy, active play – especially of boys – while, in modern society, dangers associated with an urban environment and a more sedentary, indoor lifestyle may conspire to reduce active play sharply (Karsten 2003: 457).

Blowing off steam

[Bonerate] children love to play on the beach and in the water where they swim, dive, and splash water at each other. (Broch 1990: 102)

Chase play, for example, may reflect the operation of an evolved system for training predator-prey pursuit and evasion skills. (Barrett 2005: 217–218)

One attribute of childhood that is so commonplace that it passes largely unnoticed is that children are very *active* – especially boys. And most of this activity is recognizably play. Early scholars had trouble reconciling the apparently purposeless quality of play with its ubiquity. If you ask children what they're up to, the answer is likely to be "nothin'" or "just messing around." And yet, when we learn that "Marquesans ... speak of children as devoted to play" (Martini and Kirkpatrick 1992: 205), this sounds a familiar note. Why? Most answers to this question hinge on the fact that the child is in a state of rapid development – physically, emotionally, and intellectually. An early hypothesis claimed that "animals do not play because they are young, but they have their youth because they play ... [which] serves to fit them for the tasks of later life" (Groos 1898/1976: 76, xix).

Pellegrini has offered a modern account of this idea, and he stresses that males are generally more active than females of the same age and species. He claims that males' greater activity – observed from the prenatal stage onward – develops anatomical and behavioral systems that may prove advantageous later in male–male competition (Pellegrini 2004: 443). While most scholars have focused on the long-term developmental payoffs of active play, a more immediate benefit might be as follows: "If fat juveniles are more easily caught [by predators, then] to the extent that play behavior facilitates the loss of energy that would otherwise be stored as fat, it will be preserved by natural selection" (Barber 1991: 136).

In Rwanda's Parc des Volcans, the Mahoro mountain gorilla troop first habituated by Dian Fossey has several juveniles, and play – especially after the morning feeding session – is almost non-stop. One juvenile repeatedly twirled himself in a circle, falling down in apparent dizziness. I observed youngsters climbing up and down a slender, five-meter-high tree and exaggerating the swaying motion as they climbed, dangling from either hand or foot while grasping and waving large leaves they'd removed. Aside from solo locomotor play on the ground and in the tree, juveniles chased each other in games of tag and tussled in rough-and-tumble play – involving as many as three players at a time. They pulled each other off the tree, dropped, bomb-like, from the tree on top of their playmates, and wrestled in a rolling fur-ball. Trying to distinguish body parts among the entwined animals was impossible. In the space of forty minutes, the "jungle-gym" tree they'd been using had been utterly destroyed and the surrounding low bush had been flattened into a lawn.[3]

While this juvenile circus is in full swing, older troop members quietly feed, ruminate, and groom one another. As the Baldwins note, adults tend to be conservative and cautious – guarding lives and cultural traditions. The young are predisposed to explore, experiment, and "take risks since they are more expendable according to bioenergetic calculations" (Baldwin and Baldwin 1977: 368). Jane Goodall acknowledges that young chimps take real risks as they engage in games of aerial tag, and suggests that what they are learning about their environment offsets the costs, and further that, at an early age, their bodies can better withstand and recover from a bad fall (van Lawick-Goodall 1976a: 159). In the Middle Ages early childhood was referred to as the "age of concussion" (Heywood 2001: 97). However, even though there are risks in vigorous play, learning to evade capture in a game of tag is less risky than learning while being pursued by a predator (Barrett 2005: 217). These are other, subtler payoffs of active juvenile play:

The ontogenetic timing of play coincides with periods of maximal plasticity and responsiveness to experience in neurological development … play acts to promote adult competence in physical coordination, fighting, or food handling through its effects on the developing nervous system [, particularly] neuromuscular development. (Fairbanks 1995: 142; see also Fagen 1981)

M'buti children who live in the Central African rainforest are also partial to aerial play – as are children everywhere it seems: think *jungle gym*. By age four children are already adept at tree-climbing – a favorite pastime. As they grow stronger, they use vines to haul themselves up into the forest canopy, but the "idea is never just to get to the top, it is to know more about the tree" (Turnbull 1978: 183). Similarly, boys in Gbarngasuakwelle use a home-made *baling* to practice climbing palm trees. After some years of intermittent practice, some will be skilled enough to scale the entire trunk to harvest/tend palm nut and palm wine crops (Lancy 1996: 88).

In our society, various forces have combined to reduce the level of physically active play, but this trend is not necessarily shared with other post-industrial societies. In Sweden, children are sent out to play daily, regardless

---

[3] From my field notes, January 2003.

of conditions, as "There's no bad weather, only bad clothing." And, by comparison with Japan, American children's play is rather tame. Daniel Walsh describes his trepidation as he exposed his two children to the challenges of adapting to Japanese children's culture:[4] "Japanese preschools are, compared to contemporary American preschools, raucous places, filled with loud rambunctious kids who run, wrestle, hit, roughhouse, and climb on and over everything. Being *genki* – meaning exuberant, fit, strong, healthy, and physical – is highly valued. [The American children adjusted to Japanese expectations and, eventually, they] sat still less and exercised more" (Walsh 2004: 99, 102–103).

Aside from physical fitness and escape from predators, the give and take of playful interaction may serve social functions as well. One of the most commonly observed types of active play is characterized as "rough and tumble" (R & T) or play-fighting. This form of play has been heavily studied in the US and Europe and there is considerable speculation on its function.

Constructing the dominance hierarchy

Among [Pashtu nomads], play-fights were observed whenever a new household pitched their tent on the camping ground of the community ... boy(s) of the new household were invited to wrestle, and very soon, everybody knew the position of the new boy(s) in the rank order of the peer group. (Casimir 2010: 50)

R & T play – a special sub-type of physical/locomotor play – is widespread among juvenile mammals, particularly primates. Although subtle, there are clear distinctions between play-fighting and real fighting, including the use of non-verbal signals such as displaying a "play-face" to signal a non-aggressive intent (Blurton-Jones 1967). In the Mahoro troop, older juveniles handicapped themselves in order to play successfully with younger ones. In one pair I observed, the older player was more than twice the size of his partner but, nevertheless, consistently took the subordinate's role ("self-handicapping," from Fagen 1981). On the other hand, among peers, competition is keener and, while winners consistently relinquish their advantage so play can proceed, a dominance hierarchy or pecking order will be constructed through these bouts.

More generally, Weisfeld argues that competition – usually involving the display of physical prowess – is extremely common among the young. And the outcome of this competition is a linear ranking or dominance hierarchy (Weisfeld 1999: 55; see also Kyratzis 2004: 627). By age three, children's

---

[4] Fonseca describes Gypsy childhood as "rough ... the kids were tougher than our two, they had to be [as] ... the saying goes ... 'the child is not born with teeth'" (Fonseca 1995: 44).

cognitive development seems to allow them to compare their performance with that of others (Stipek 1995).

In Borneo, where inter-village warfare and head-hunting were once common, play-fighting may evolve into a "war with words," including taunts and insults between two groups from neighboring, hostile villages (Williams 1969: 82). In the Brazilian rainforest, where inter-group warfare is endemic,

> Xavante boys ... form two teams painted red and black, each with the symbol of his clan on his face. The two boys who will fight one another are chosen by the oldest boys of each clan. The children hit each other's arms with the roots of a strong grass until one of them gives up ... among the Camauiri, a turbulent form of play is the *Jawari*. One of the participants throws his spear towards a fence made of poles, trying to knock down the poles. The other players are lined up behind the fence and are not allowed to leave. As the "pitcher" knocks the poles down, the other players become easy targets and must then divert the spears, without moving their feet. Some are hurt during this game. (Gosso *et al.* 2005: 232)

In two Zapotec-speaking communities in southern Mexico, children from a village with high levels of adult violence spent significantly more time engaged in play-fighting than did children from the community where adult violence was uncommon (Fry 1987). And in a study Millard Madsen and I carried out in the Highlands of Papua New Guinea, a game (which Madsen had invented) that could be played cooperatively or competitively easily revealed whether the child players were from the same clan, distant, antagon-istic clans, or intermediate. Boys from the same clan always played coopera-tively, with each of two players taking turns winning a coin, and, vice versa, boys from potential enemy groups never made a cooperative move (Lancy and Madsen 1981).[5] And, in Africa, anthropologists have noted an elaboration of play-fighting, including the use of weapons, in societies where warfare was endemic or at least a vivid memory (Read 1960).

Interestingly, while parents rarely involve themselves in children's play, the exceptions can be found in societies where intra- and inter-community conflict is the norm and parents encourage violent play (Chapter 5, pp. 191–192).

Play-fighting can also be seen as the ontogenetic and historical precursor to certain types of *sport*. Simon Ottenberg has documented the high level of organization and ceremony associated with wrestling in Igbo (Nigeria) society. At the youngest grade (e.g. fifteen to eighteen = *Mkpufumgba*), participation is widespread, but gradually, at each higher age grade, the ranks of competitors are thinned. The importance of wrestling cannot be overestimated. "Wrestling is not only a sport, it is intimately associated with age organizations ... peer

---

[5] In an earlier study, Madsen had shown that suburban kids in the USA rarely played cooperatively while Mexican village children rarely competed (Madsen 1971).

group activity ... [and was formerly] ... directly related to warfare"
(Ottenberg 1989: 85, 86). Sport-style wrestling, where the winners of the
major competitions are treated as folk heroes and extremely attractive mates,
is also found in northeast Nigeria (Stevens 1996: 99). Of course, most of the
sports we think of as particularly Olympian – javelin, track, boxing, archery,
and, of course, wrestling – have their origin in combat or hunting. *Inzema* is a
Xhosa game in which boys in teams compete to spear a rolling gourd (Wilkins
2002: 36). A similar game, played in Botswana, has been statistically linked to
the degree of dependence on hunting for subsistence (Bock and Johnson
2004). "Aimed throwing" may contribute to the boy's physical development,
as "at puberty ... hormones stimulate specially primed cartilage cells in the
shoulder" (Parker 1984: 278).

R & T play and competitive sports serve as one of the primary means of
establishing rank among males (Pellegrini 2004: 441–442; Whiting and
Edwards 1988b: 289). But there are less obvious and perhaps even more
important play activities through which the dominance hierarchy may be
constructed, including make-believe (Goodwin 2006: 157) and games of
strategy.

Gamesmanship

Codes of social conduct ... regulate what is permissible during ... play, and ... these
codes might [point to] the evolution of social morality. (Dugatkin and Bekoff
2003: 209)

We evolved to become *Homo negotiatus*. (Rochat 2005: 714)

For me, personally, the quintessential game is not marbles but *mancala*.
"'Mancala' is an Arabic word that refers to a group of games often called
'count and capture' or 'pit and pebble' games [that] date back to ancient
times ... All mancala games involved scooping up playing pieces and dropping them around a board. Seeds were often used as playing pieces and the
move was called 'sowing'" (Wilkins 2002: 22). The Kpelle name for the game
is *malang*. I emulated the young men in the village and, volunteering as a
novice player, subjected myself to the withering scorn of older men who were
expert players. There's little doubt that, because older men are the experts and
own the boards, *malang* provides an excellent occasion to reinforce the
village's social order. Its popularity in Gbarngasuakwelle had diminished.
At one time, my informants said, you could tell a man's status from the size
and quality of his *malang* board. Nevertheless, there is no other village activity
that demands the same degree of complex place-keeping and arithmetic skill
as this game.

As a boy, the future *malang* champ passes through a lengthy curriculum of simpler games from a large corpus (Lancy 1996: 95–109). Many games involve hiding, guessing, and memory, or using seeds, stones, or bones as counters, projectiles, dice, and place-markers. In fact the Kpelle have an entire category of games called *Koni-pele* or stone play, and it includes at least ten distinct games of increasing complexity (Lancy 1996: 101–107).

However, aside from any physical or cognitive skills that may be enhanced during play, numerous observers have noted the honing of what we might call diplomatic skills. For example, "Word games are . . . contests of memory, wit and fluency . . . [that] practice skills of verbal combat that are highly important in the political arena" (Parker 1984: 282). Viewing children's games as forum for the development of social or diplomatic skill links to a revolution underway in our thinking about the *sapiens* part of *Homo sapiens*. One useful starting point is Richard Byrne's *The Thinking Ape*. He writes:

The essence of the Machiavellian intelligence hypothesis is that intelligence evolved in social circumstances. Individuals would be favored who were able to use and exploit others in their social group, without causing the disruption and potential group fission liable to result from naked aggression. Their manipulations might as easily involve co-operation as conflict, [and] sharing as hoarding. (Byrne 1995: 196)

The long-term success of hominims seems to derive from successful group living (Hrdy 2009). Humans are not large, speedy, or particularly efficient hunters. But they are very good at sharing the labor, sharing the fruits of their labor, cooperative care of the young, and banding together for protection from predators (Maestripieri 2007). Factors like climate are insignificant compared to the evolutionary pressure of group living, where the "core selective force was social competition" (Bailey and Geary 2009: 67). Successful individuals (in terms of inclusive fitness) are those who both "fit in" and can garner resources and support through diplomacy. Extrapolating from this argument, if children have social brains and, further, brains that need to be exercised to fully develop, games would be the perfect mental gym. Comparing across fifteen species of primates, observers found a statistically reliable relationship between cerebellum size and time devoted to social play (Lewis and Barton 2004; see also Fisher 1992). Still, humans have a more pronounced predilection for *gaming* than do other primates.

[Eighteen-to-twenty-four-month-old] children . . . engaged more spontaneously in all of the tasks, most especially in the social games whose primary goal was the interaction itself, whereas the chimpanzees had little interest in social games without a concrete goal. Related to this . . . children seemed to form a conception of how the game "ought" to be played ... children were so engaged socially that sometimes they even turned the tasks aimed at retrieving an object into a game ... when the adult partner ceased participating in the middle of the activity, the human children quite often attempted to reengage him. (Tomasello *et al.* 2005: 659–660)

Anthropologists have long speculated that core cultural values are transmitted to the young through games (Roberts *et al.* 1959). The role of game play in the promotion of particular dispositions will reflect specific cultural values. Wenger sees, in Giriama boys' play, opportunities to develop the talents and character associated with the role of *mwenye mudzi*, or patriarch (Wenger 1989: 102). Aymara boys in the Andes play marbles (girls play jacks) while herding their flocks far from the village. Ben Smith's careful analysis of these games illuminates the importance of *qhincha* (bad luck) in marbles. By confronting and enduring *qhincha* in the game, boys successfully fend off accusations of being feminine or homosexual. By implication, a boy who keeps his cool when something goes wrong (a pebble in the path deflecting his shot, a toddler tramping through the play area) demonstrates "*chacha*-ness" or "toughness," which represent masculinity (Smith 2010).

Note that we see Giriama *boys* improving their "gamesmanship," not girls, and one review shows that as males' facility with and engagement in games increase with time, girls' actually decrease. Girls tend to interact with other girls in rather sedentary ways. Relatedly, game facility does not predict girls' peer status. Instead of exhibiting competitiveness in their interactions with each other, girls express relatively high levels of positive affect and nurturance (Pellegrini 2004: 443). From the ethnographic record we learn that, compared with girls, boys play in larger groups, more competitively, and for longer periods.[6] Play bouts last so long, apparently, because of frequent disputes regarding the rules. Indeed, it almost seems that "the negotiation of rules was as important as the game itself ... [whereas, among] girls, the occurrence of a dispute tended to end the game" (Low 1989: 318).[7]

Candy Goodwin's insightful studies of contemporary American girls at play find considerable exception to these generalizations.[8] She observes both Hispanic and African-American girls who are intensely competitive in hopscotch and well equipped to contest not only the game itself but the rules of

[6] In November 2006, I observed numerous all-male play groups roaming throughout public areas in Shibam, a very traditional town in the Hadramwt, Yemen. This contrasts with the single group of four girls I observed, demurely playing cards on a "stoop" attached to the house.

[7] It is likely that girls engage in a cut-and-thrust contest for power discreetly away from the actual field of play. For them, the goal of the contest is getting picked early by one's friends. "A girl's current alliance partner is praised, while all the other girls are criticized" (Berentzen 1984: 80).

[8] The influence of girls' participation in sports, which has increased dramatically in the US (Hine 1999: 288) and perhaps elsewhere, may well contribute to greater homogeneity of play behavior across the sexes.

play – much like the marbles players described earlier. These feisty girls "patrol the boundaries of their play space from boys' intrusions, delimiting their territory" (Goodwin 1998: 39). She writes:

Conflict about rules and fouls . . . instead of breaching relationships . . . are a central part of the fun of playing. Rather than treating conflict and cooperation as a bipolar dichotomy, the girls build complex participation frameworks in which disputes, with their rich possibilities for cognitive organization . . . are embedded within a larger ethos of playfulness. (Goodwin 1998: 25)

In comparative research on children's gamesmanship in eastern Nigeria (Igbo) and the USA (Indiana), American players were almost twice as likely as Igbo players to argue for variance to the rules or an outright rule change when things didn't go their way (Nwokah and Ikekonwu 1998: 66) – budding attorneys all! On the other hand, throughout Nigeria, it is common for losers or those whose performance is sub-par to be smacked, pinched, or beaten by the other players – of both sexes. Observers note that "roughness of play in games teaches the child emotional self-control in public" (Nwokah and Ikekonwu 1998: 70).

Gamesmanship might play a role in children's success in the all-important public school environment; for example, "peer popularity . . . is predicted by the time [spent] playing games and teacher rated facility in games" (Pellegrini 2004: 445). Chick posits another payoff for the adept player in increased mating opportunities. He believes that successful child and adolescent players are advertising many positive but nascent qualities to potential future mates (Chick 2001). These might include the ability to negotiate and to show restraint and cooperation, and, perhaps, aspects of physical prowess that forecast future foraging success.

Key elements of the game experience are that the game has rules and structure, but these may be altered or stretched by players who're operating without adult supervision. That is, children must be free to construct successful gaming sessions without adult guidance or interference (in contrast to contemporary Little League baseball: Fine 1987). In this way rules can be bent, for example, to lower the threshold for participation by younger or less able players, or renegotiated so that play can continue even if one player wins consistently. A common strategy is to "self-handicap" (Boulton and Smith 1992: 436). Plentiful opportunities of this sort will nurture children's gamesmanship[9] or the ability to negotiate the complex social world faced by adults.

As widespread as competitive play of various kinds seems to be, it is not universal. That is, there are various cultural forces that may constrain opportunities to improve "gamesmanship." For example, Martini points out that

---

[9] For a longer and more detailed explication of how these processes unfold in the game of marbles, see Lancy and Grove (2011b: 490–491).

Polynesian children's extreme sensitivity to status leads them to *avoid* play that requires leaders or lengthy negotiation of rules or roles. Children who attempt to assert their authority are rejected in favor of consensus decisions (Martini 1994: 80).

The play group

Once they were walking they became the responsibility of older [Roma] kids, and they became part of the crowd scene . . . play was rough, such as Jeta's constant yanking and tweaking of all the little boys' penises . . . mostly it was okay; the kids were tough . . . they had to be (*o chavorro na biandola dandencar*, the saying goes – "the child is not born with teeth"). (Fonseca 1995: 44)

To build up one's reputation among peers, one needs worthy opponents, but they may not be readily available. The nature of play is affected by the species and age of the animals but also by the ambient "climate" for play and the composition of the play group. An example of what I mean by climate comes from a study of play in two contrasting Bedouin camps. In a homogenous camp, members coexisted peacefully, and children's play was varied and unconstrained. A second camp was more diverse, less harmonious, and "children were not permitted to roam freely or to enter the tents of neighbors" (Ariel and Sever 1980: 172). Even more severe constraints are routinely found in urban ghettos where mothers forbid their children to play outdoors or visit friends for fear of violence or moral corruption (Kotlowitz 1991).

And there may be constraints imposed on the *composition* of the play group. Margaret Mead noted in Samoa that toddlers only come into contact with those children watched over by *their* caretaker's friends. Thus the play groups of younger children are indirectly structured by the caretaker's peer associations (Mead 1928/1961: 42). However, a more powerful social influence on play is the *size* of the play group. In the "B" troop of mountain gorillas in aptly named Bwindi Impenetrable Forest, there were only two juveniles between one and four years of age, and one kept close to its mother. Not surprisingly, I observed only a few minutes of desultory, solo play as contrasted with the non-stop play described above for the Mahoro troop (see Sussman 1977 for a parallel case in two contrasting lemur species).

As part of a multi-site study of child development (Lancy 1983) in Papua New Guinea, we inventoried children's play. Many of our hamlet or village field sites were quite small. Consequently, the play groups we observed were inevitably of mixed ages, which had a ceiling effect on play complexity. Games all had to be simple enough to be played by toddlers – tag and hide and seek, as examples (Lancy 1984). Variability in play group size was associated with game complexity in a survey of childhood in six contrasting societies around the globe (Edwards 2005: 90; Whiting and Edwards 1988a). In a comparative study in Central Africa, gender and age segregation were less pronounced in smaller-population forager play groups than in the more populous farmer children's play cohorts (Fouts *et al.* 2013); however, conflict among players was rare in both communities (Fouts and Lamb 2009: 272). In such small communities, we should expect to see fewer effects of gender on play and, as predicted, girls and boys from !Kung forager bands were similar in their patterns of play (Blurton-Jones and Konner 1973). !Kung children played a great deal with members of the opposite sex and, in fact, "sexual play is what many adults remember most vividly" (Shostak 1981: 109). Lebou (Senegal) extended kin clusters lead to a relatively large population within a "family" compound, so play groups may be relatively homogenous in age, especially if composed exclusively of boys.

In Gbarngasuakwelle, toddlers were usually herded together in a crèche-like manner and supervised by one or two older siblings, freeing up many children – at any given time – from sib-care duties. Consequently, homogenous groups – of both males and females – were common. Players who were close in age and hence matched on maturity and size are more likely to engage in more complex and competitive games (Lancy 1996: 112–113).

In Gaskins' field studies in the Yucatan, she finds that close kin connections govern play group size, rather than the overall village population (Gaskins and Göncü 1992). She observes small, stable play groups tethered to the family compound. Older children, functioning as sib-caretakers (this volume, Chapter 4), are under an obligation, therefore, to insure harmonious relations prevail in the group, which means including even the youngest members in the play activity (Gaskins *et al.* 2007: 191). When play groups aren't closely scrutinized by adults, a different pattern may emerge, in which older players can be quite coercive and teasing is common (Grindal 1972: 37). In Rakiraki village (Fiji) children are charged with sib-care but free to express their feelings on the assignment: "The resentment of older children towards younger ones was evident in the way children teased and physically attacked younger children when there was no adult around to intervene" (Brison 1999: 109).

Girls, because they're responsible for sib-care, are more likely to play in mixed age groups (Bloch 1989). Among the Fore in the Eastern Highlands of Papua New Guinea,

Girls spend more of their time playing in the gardens and hamlet yards, often with infants and toddlers. They do not explore much beyond these arenas ... Boys, on the other hand, ranged much more widely in their explorations ... Much of their time was spent in ... more boisterous physical play. (Sorenson 1976: 191)

Friedl refers to Lurs boys in an Iranian village being "turned out in the morning like cows" (1997: 148). Girls, compared with boys, play less overall, play closer to home (Edwards 2005: 87), and transition from mostly playing to mostly working earlier (Lancy 2001b). Among the Inuit, at eight or younger "a girl was expected to interrupt her play activities to assist her mother with such tasks as cutting fresh ice ... and gathering moss" (Condon 1987: 55). Igbo boys' greater freedom to play mirrors the leisure enjoyed by men, who "spend many hours in ritual matters, political issues, and settling disputes ... while their wives do physical work" (Ottenberg 1989: 49).

In the next section, we'll see that play can be viewed as an informal means to transmit a variety of cultural information, particularly during make-believe. Make-believe play, introduced in the last chapter, is one of the most commonly described aspects of childhood in the archives of ethnography.

The universality of make-believe

[Igbo children] put grasshoppers, with their wings torn off, in these constructions, and pretend that they are people, creating scenes with them. (Ottenberg 1989: 96)

Adults everywhere seem to be at least mildly tolerant toward and amused by children's attempts to replicate adult society in their play. In Tapirapé (Brazilian) villages:

Boys sometimes played house and included little girls as wives. Adults roared with laughter when the children imitated quarrels between husband and wife [as well as] imitating copulation ... They even imitated the male masked dancers. On one occasion two small boys dressed in small versions of the "crying bird spirit" masks and danced about the village asking the residents for food. This was found amusing, and not at all sacrilegious. (Wagley 1977: 145)

Children's play appears to function as an oversize vacuum sucking up everything that happens in the village and transforming it into child-sized playlets. My sense is that, before the advent of television and manufactured play-sets, children incorporated the entire panoply of village life into their play. And this includes rare events. I once observed a group of boys re-enacting the passage of the president's motorcade, complete with siren-sounds and Liberian flags waving from the lead "vehicles" (Lancy 1996: 185). Harunobu created a woodblock print of a very similar scene in c. 1767–1768, with boys re-enacting a Daimyô procession.[10] Schieffelin (1990: 213, 217) observed and photographed Kaluli boys emulating their fathers serving as porters "on patrol." A seventeenth-century parent in England noted in his diary a "mock

---

[10] Suzuki Harunobu, c.1767–1768, *Children playing a daimyô procession*. Museum of Fine Arts, Boston. Available at http://educators.mfa.org/asia-africa/children-playing-daimy%C3%B4-procession-94370. Accessed January 8, 2014.

Figure 17 Crèche of Kpelle toddlers pretending to use a mortar and pestle

funeral staged by his daughters, aged eight and six. [They buried one of their dolls] with a great deal of formality" (Pollock 1983: 237).

Throughout much of Africa, children will be observed pretending to hull grain using a make-believe toy or scaled-down mortar and pestle (Lancy 1996: 85 – as in Figure 17) and, like target shooting, "practice pounding" is associated with a dependence on grain processing. Further, Bock and Johnson have found that children actually improve their skill through play practice: "play is an important factor in the development of adult competency" (Bock and Johnson 2004: 63).

In the Arctic "boys and girls play at building snow houses ... they borrow their parents' snow knives and make complete houses on a miniature scale" (Jenness 1922: 219). An active fantasy life is also indicated by the presence in archaeological sites in the region of "an extensive miniature material culture" (Park 2006: 56). None other than Franz Boas, one of the founders of modern anthropology, has written a vivid description of Baffin Island boys enacting an elaborate seal hunt – all in make-believe (Boas 1901: 111). The role of play, make-believe in particular, in children's acquisition of the characteristic adult skill inventory is discussed at length in the next chapter.

Meal preparation is a commonly observed theme. Esther Goody describes the richness and complexity of make-believe cooking in a village in north Ghana. Miniature kitchens are constructed, ingredients gathered, and soup made, all the while accompanied by singing and the construction of play scripts that mimic adult discourse. And, of course, the girls must insure that their play enfolds the younger siblings who are in their care. Boys have bit parts in these playlets as "husbands," and are limited to commenting on the flavor of the soup (Goody 1992). Gender roles are thus reinforced. On Wogeo Island, Hogbin observed this scene:

Wanai was now busily making mud pies and at this point begged Kalasika to build her an oven where these might be cooked. Gwa joined in the game, and, although no fire was kindled, the grubby mess was wrapped in leaves and put into the middle of a pile of stones. Wanai next made out that her water bottles were empty and told Naibula to fill them. "No, that's women's work," said Gwa. "We men don't touch such things. You go yourself." (Hogbin 1946: 276).

On Guadalcanal (Solomon Islands), Hogbin noted the transformation of make-believe as children became aware of and began to enforce the gendered division of labor: "boys leave the cooking and water carrying to the girls, who, in turn, refuse to help with the building" (Hogbin 1969: 38). In a Sri Lankan village, social rank is also rehearsed in these playlets; for example, older girls admonish their "assistants" that "You must serve the father first and a lot of food must be given to him" (Prosser *et al.* 1986: 184). Goody and others consistently note how make-believe meal preparation easily segues into for-real cooking. While domestic scenes are most frequently replicated in play, especially when girls are in charge, the entire panoply of adult society provides script material. From American slave autobiographies we learn that slave children created playlets around the theme of a slave auction (Alston 1992: 225–226). In civil-war-wracked Lebanon, Druze boys fill the intervals between shelling attacks with imaginative play:

Whenever there was a lull we would call our friends to come . . . and play together . . . Our favorite game was hide and attack. We make up machine guns and we had teams as armies so we throw bombs at them. We built barricades with chairs and pillows. (Assal and Farrell 1992: 277)

Given the conflict in Yemen, it is not surprising to find boys in Sana'a playing at mujahideen (Figure 18).

Make-believe reveals children's insight into the adult world. Araucania boys accurately mimic the speech and movements of drunken males celebrating fiesta (Hilger 1958: 106). Yanamamo boys pretend to "smoke" hallucinogens and then stagger around in perfect imitation of their stoned fathers acting as shamans (Asch and Chagnon 1974). The traditional Chaga wedding includes bride abduction, and "lifting of the bride" is a prominent part of the children's version of the wedding (Raum 1940: 251). Even more dramatic is the script used by Mehinacu (Brazilian forest dwellers) children when they play *ukitsapi*

Figure 18 Mujahideen play in Sana'a, Yemen

(jealousy). Boys and girls find new partners while their "spouses" are away. When the spouse returns from fishing, he discovers his wife in the hammock with her lover. Furious, he gives his wife a mock beating while the interloper takes off (Gregor 1988: 113). Arunta (aboriginal Australian foragers) children have been observed meticulously recreating gender-appropriate domestic scenes, including "adultery, with a boy running away with the 'wife' of another boy" (Williams 1983: 202). When Lepcha children play at marriage, it "always ends in simulated copulation" (Gorer 1967: 310).[11]

Also fairly common are descriptions of children – especially boys – dramatizing various ritual activities. Talensi (northern Ghana agriculturalists) boys "hunt" for mice, and after they've played with their captives for a while, they "sacrifice" the "dog"[12] on a miniature shrine and ask to be granted success in hunting (Fortes 1938/1970: 68). Mehinacu (Brazil) children produce an extremely accurate replication of the complete sequence of events from initial

---

[11] However, adults are not always tolerant of children's make-believe. Wogeo boys who carried out a simulated sacred initiation ceremony were thrashed when the outraged village elders found out (Hogbin 1946: 278).

[12] Mice are not considered appropriate prey for adult hunters, nor are they worthy sacrifices, hence they are transformed into "dogs" by the boys.

illness to the shaman's triumphant discovery of the culpable instrument of witchcraft (Gregor 1988: 114). In the socialization of future healers in the Kalahari and in Fiji, the process begins as early as five when little boys role-play the trance-inducing dance of the adult healer (Katz 1981: 62). Broch recorded five Bonerate girls between four and seven replicating a female possession-trance ritual. They took care to depict the act of walking on or stamping out "imaginary" embers. Only a few days earlier "a real possession-trance ritual had been conducted in a neighboring village" (Broch 1990: 107). Droogers reports on make-believe in a Wagenia (Democratic Republic of Congo) village:

A small group of ten to fifteen boys playing at initiation had adorned themselves with liana caps and raffia armlets. They were circumcised one by one. A slightly bigger boy, of about twelve, wielded a piece of bamboo with which he "cut" a piece off the penis bared especially for the occasion. Two others meanwhile beat out the rhythm that is normally played during circumcision, on a drum and tin. (Droogers 1980: 85)

Parenthetically, many an anthropologist has seen herself or himself reflected (unflatteringly) in the play of erstwhile subjects (Bascom 1969: 58). If make-believe is a popular daytime pursuit, then story-telling fills many a quiet evening. In the section that follows we will briefly review examples of folklore that serve to entertain children, but also convey important moral lessons.

The moral lessons in folklore

. It is a time of amusement, reflection and learning. (Ottenberg 1989: 91)

Folklorists have amassed whole libraries of tales, myths, and oral histories from pre-literate societies. And a significant portion of these materials will have a didactic character with children as the audience. Romans used Aesop's collection,[13] the English used Mother Goose, and the Kpelle have *Polo-Gyee*. *Polo-Gyee* may be "real" stories with fantastic elements (a talking fish) mixed in. The themes depict characters violating social norms and getting their just desserts, the language and events having a burlesque quality (Lancy 1996: 130–132). Other themes that appear in many folklore collections are the conflict that may arise between parents and children (Lowe and Johnson 2007: 163) and, of course, the evil stepparent (Geertz 1961: 37). One story on Java – known to all children – depicts two little girls: Brambang Abang (Red Onion) and Bawang Putih (White Garlic). "When Bawang Putih grew up,

---

[13] Wiedemann mentions that the tutor or *pedagogus* would be expected to use tales and fables in the curriculum (1989: 145).

she became a very good person, whereas Brambang Abang grew up stupid, unable to do anything useful, because all she had done all her life was play" (Geertz 1961: 43).

There are a few[14] cases in the literature of mothers or grandmothers telling stories around the hearth in the evening – one of the rare occasions when adults spend time entertaining or instructing children (Lancy 1996; Ottenberg 1989; Briggs 1970). On the Micronesian island of Chuuk, stories encapsulate the deeper history of the island's heritage, but "these tales represent valuable knowledge, and adults do not always share them easily" (Lowe and Johnson 2007: 153). Piaroa (Orinoco River foraging group) society features a

Wizard . . . who uses story-telling, especially episodes from the mythic past, to elaborate his moral lessons . . . the tales tell of characters whose out-of-control behavior leads to their own unhappiness and personal disaster, and sometimes to danger for others. (Overing 1988: 179)

Another unique and interesting collection of stories that might serve to "educate" children is found in the shadow puppet plays on Bali.[15]

The stories . . . are primarily drawn from the great Hindu epics, the *Mahabharata* and *Ramayana* . . . Children constitute the front rows of any audience, their attention being riveted on the servants who clown around and tell spicy, bawdy jokes . . . the system of morality, together with the history and cosmology represented in the plays, is . . . unconsciously adopted, and the molding of the individual to the social norms occurs . . . indirectly as a pleasurable "by-product." Adults place high value on their culture and are fully aware . . . that its continuity depends on its transmission to their descendants . . . Adults . . . explained that it is on the stage that such abstract ideas as rank, good and evil, or refinement and coarseness . . . are made tangible. (Hobart 1988: 118, 133–134)

Children draw on these shadow plays and religious ceremonies in their make-believe and this is explicitly encouraged (Mead 1964: 67), as shown in the photo in Figure 19 of boys parading in masks and costumes supplied by adults.

Proverbs and riddles also provide subtle lessons for children and adults as well. Riddles have been explicitly identified with the demonstration of cleverness and understanding of village "lore." For the Ngoni, riddles are "a test of intelligence and of memory" (Read 1960: 98). Proverb use among the Kpelle is

---

[14] Parents and grandparents patiently instructing youth via the medium of stories is more legend than reality. "Certainly it is not characteristic of this Ladino culture that the young gather around the knees of the old to listen reverently to a solemn exposition of the holy traditions and sacred memories of the people" (Redfield 1943/1970: 291).

[15] Children occupy the front rows during theatrical performances in Bengali villages. "Themes from these plays confirm the Brahmanical ethos [such as] . . . powerful mothers but passive wives" (Rohner and Chaki-Sircar 1988: 66).

Figure 19 Balinese boys parading in child-sized *Barong* costumes

common and, not surprisingly, there is a children's game called *kehlong* in which typical proverbial phrases are rehearsed in a paired association contest. Children who play and learn *kehlong* will still need further experience to decode the meaning of proverbs. They will gradually start to figure them out in their mid-to-late teens (Lancy 1996: 137–139).

Yup'ik (Inuit) children carve symbols on to a wet mud palette with a knife to illustrate the unfolding story. The lore conveyed in story-knife tales includes kinship patterns, gender roles, and community norms and values. Their tales have a more serious quality than those from Africa and are inevitably scary. Unfortunately, like so much of children's culture, this practice has been lost as modern media intrude into the village that once practiced subsistence fishing, hunting, and gathering (de Marrais *et al.* 1992). Aboriginals in central Australia constructed morality tales – an adolescent girl being beaten for her illicit liaison – using sand and leaves. But elders now lament that "Our children are not frightened anymore when we tell stories about spooky creatures in the dark. They ... have become used to seeing horrible images on the TV screen ... our society is like a jigsaw puzzle whose pieces have gone missing, one by one" (Tjitayi and Lewis 2011: 57).

In numerous African societies, children's play incorporates the always theatrical and sometimes sacred world of masked dance. In large villages, substantial cohorts of boys and, less often, girls form into voluntary associations to construct costumes, including masks, derived from adult models. They practice their routines of dance and song and, on appropriate occasions, perform for an appreciative audience in the village clearing. Adults are usually encouraging (whereas they may not encourage other forms of play). For example, "Each Igede village encourages young people to form children's music and dance associations to insure that the society of the future will have accomplished performers at funerals, New Yam festivals, and other ritual or social occasions" (Ottenberg 2006: 123).

There is some moral ambiguity here, as many of the masked figures are powerful entities that function to control social relations and individual behavior in the village. Their identity is shrouded in secrecy, and they are under the control of the most senior men. Nevertheless, among the Kuba (Central Africa kingdom), "some avenues are left open for the acculturation of the young boys into mask making and masquerade performance ... the grading of ... masks into a hierarchy allows certain masks to be accessible ... to children" (Binkley 2006: 113). Boys in the masking society will have opportunities to practice mask-making in the construction of reduced-scale masks. Or they may construct full-size but ritually impotent masquerade figures, which they wear during informal dance performances (Binkley 2006: 106).

In Mali, Bamana boys' masking is just the first stage in their developing understanding of the *Ndomo* ritual. Groups of young boys organize their own masked performance, and exhibit a surprisingly thorough understanding of how the performance is structured and an understanding of performance roles appropriate to men and to women at these events. However, while

boys understand that the rites, the masks and the various emblems are sacred, they do not fully comprehend *Ndomo*'s complex symbolism. The full meaning of the various ... masks, the sacred emblems, rites and songs ... [they] will learn [as] they are initiated into adult men's associations. (M. J. Arnold 2006: 61, 53)

These reports are largely retrospective, historical. Even in the early 1970s in a remote village, I found that I had to pull from people's memory playforms – especially those involving the kind of children's voluntary associations just described – to complete my inventory of Kpelle play (Lancy 1996: 107–108). This loss of children's culture, unfortunately, means that the question of just how much and what aspects of their culture village children acquire through song, story, riddles, and masked dancing will remain forever unanswered. The most I'm prepared to assert is that the lessons are predominantly moral ones (see Chapter 9, pp. 334–336).

How the cultural ethos shapes children's play

[When Lepcha] children play together it is always an imitation of adult life. (Gorer 1967: 309)

The very ethos of the culture may dictate the nature of play. In Israel, the *kibbutz* was created as a utopian alternative to the competition and status differentials inherent in modern society. Not surprisingly, a study of children's games revealed a bias toward egalitarian outcomes – no winners, no losers (Eifermann 1971). In Oceania, one finds examples of societies that are so egalitarian that, in children's play, "Competitiveness is almost never in evidence" (Hogbin 1946: 275). Among the Tangu of Papua New Guinea, children in teams play a game called *taketak*, which is designed – in keeping with local values – to end in a tie (Burridge 1957).

In small-scale, band societies, the play group, necessarily of mixed ages, must allow all players, no matter how inept, to participate; so the playing field is always level, so to speak, and supports the prevailing egalitarian ethos (Lancy 1984). !Kung children throw a weighted feather in the air and, as it floats down, they strike it with a stick or flick it back up into the air. The "game," called *zeni*, is played solo, and children make no attempt to compare skill or success (Draper 1976: 203). Aka foragers are highly egalitarian and Boyette notes the absence of R & T play and competitive games. Ndanga is a popular game in which "there is no winner in the game and there is no score kept" (Boyette 2013: 84). Baka society is notably egalitarian and sharing game is an essential value.

In one episode of play cooking, for example, an eight-year-old [Baka] boy shot a spider while hunting with a bow. He pulled apart the "game" and carefully shared the parts for three participants, including me, the researcher. He divided the eight legs into three groups and made up the difference with the cephalothorax, which he divided into two pieces. The abdomen was thrown away because it is "inedible." This episode makes clear that children [are cognizant of] adult food-sharing activities and mimic them in their play. (Kamei 2005: 354)

A few societies value harmonious relations among themselves and with outsiders. In these cases, R & T play is rare or attenuated. Children in Semai subsistence-farming communities in west central Malaysia, for example, rarely see aggression, and one of the few times an adult will intervene in children's play is to curb fighting. R & T play occurs but is extremely mild: "two children, often of disparate sizes, put their hands on each other's shoulders and wrestle, giggling, but never quite knocking each other over ... [and] pairs of children in the two- to twelve-year age-range flail at each other with sticks, but stop just before hitting each other" (Fry 2005: 68).

Another lens we can use to view the role of culture is the dolls children play with. One expects the toy collection to inevitably include dolls, but in the village, girls may play with *real* dolls. Bonerate "children have little need or desire to play with dolls ... they look after babies and toddlers" (Broch 1990: 110). Still, the doll is arguably the most widely found toy and the range of materials used and designs employed is immense (Ruddle and Chesterfield 1977: 36).[16] From rags tied into a shapeless bundle to high-tech baby dolls that produce a babble of baby-talk, wet themselves, and eagerly move their limbs, the variety is fascinating. While baby dolls seemed to have been a universal adjunct to Roman girls' play, lower-class girls had infant dolls that they mock-nursed, comforted, and cleansed while upper-class girls, whose future as adults would *not* include childcare, dressed and primped the ancient equivalent of Barbie (Wiedemann 1989: 149–150).

A young girl called Crepereia Tryphaena living in Rome around 150 BC had a thirty cm tall articulated ivory doll, which had moving joints at the shoulders, elbows, hips and knees, and a full trousseau including little gold rings, mirrors, beads, combs and bone and ivory jewelry boxes. This girl died aged around twelve, and her toys were placed in her tomb. (Wileman 2005: 36)

A doll from a second-millennium BCE upper-class Egyptian tomb displays the kind of hair-styling associated with a meticulously constructed wig belonging to a high-society dame. Roman boys had dolls (or should I say "action figures?") as well, such as a terracotta gladiator with articulated arms (Lancy 2008: 214–216). By the latter half of the nineteenth century, dolls were being employed to socialize girls in the trappings of bourgeois culture, such as fashion, etiquette, and polite gatherings like house calls and tea parties (Formanek-Brunell 1992: 114–116).

In the examples of make-believe discussed so far, children may seem to be creating a carbon copy, in miniature, of their society. However, as they repeat certain scenes over and over, they are exploring the sociolinguistic and psychological infrastructure of common social relationships found in their community. Hence, the anthropologist is not surprised to find two sisters role-playing sisterhood (Hardman 1980: 86). Children's make-believe does not slavishly replicate the scenes of village life. There is invention in the roles assigned, in the props used, in the script followed, but, importantly, children may "twist" the tale. That is, we do have a limited number of examples of children behaving like young social critics in their sometimes ribald and irreverent portrayals (Goldman 1998; Gregor 1988: 113; Hogbin 1970: 138).

---

[16] Young chimps "carry sticks in a manner suggestive of rudimentary doll play and, as in children and captive monkeys, this behavior is more common in females than in males" (Kahlenberg and Wrangham 2010: 1067).

This certainly suggests a very rich interplay between what children see, how they represent that information, and their re-enactments.

In Power's extensive review, he finds: "children's play in traditional cultures involves imitation of adult behavior in traditional roles and rarely involves fantastic transformations ... [or] character roles that the child will seldom, if ever, enact or encounter in life" (Power 2000: 272; see also Martini 1994). There "is little elaboration or introduction of variation or complexity during the course of [Mayan children's] play. Scripts and roles are repeated over and over, almost ritualized" (Gaskins and Göncü 1992: 32). In a comparative study of make-believe play, in several Brazilian communities, the authors found that, in a traditional Indian village, children had much less time for play, and play themes reflected village life, whereas in the wealthier, more urbanized samples, children's play was more extensive and creative – perhaps strengthening abstract and symbolic thought (Gosso *et al.* 2007). Other comparative studies underscore the class differences in play, with working-class children exhibiting far less fantasy play than middle-class children (Tudge 2008: 152).

In WEIRD society, children are expected to wrestle with emotional problems through make-believe. Indeed, this is often seen as the main function of make-believe, and there's an entire branch of clinical practice – play therapy – built on this assumption. However, this emotional loading is largely absent in village make-believe. Gaskins reports from her close observation of Yucatec Mayan children's play that intense emotional expression is absent. One reason may be that adults expect play groups to function harmoniously (Gaskins and Miller 2009). Mayan children are not absorbed in their own lives as they play. They also seem to have fewer traumas to deal with because they don't live in a neontocracy. For example, instead of feeling threatened by the arrival of a new sibling, children see the new family member as an allomothering opportunity. They have little access to fictional characters in storybooks, so while these characters populate Euroamerican children's play, they're absent from Mayan play (Gaskins and Miller 2009).[17]

For modern children, much of the "culture" may be hidden from view. Hence, television becomes their "window on society, their village square ...

---

[17] This contrast in childhood experiences may illuminate the classic case of child animism. One cornerstone of Piaget's (1929) theory of cognitive development posited that children are animists before achieving a fully grounded, rational understanding of the distinction between animate and inanimate. Margaret Mead (1932) tested this theory on Manus Island and found – neither in her observations of children at play nor in focused test queries – any evidence of animism among Manus children. On the other hand, the world of adults seems permeated by the actions of ghosts and other manifestations of animistic thought. Perhaps Piaget's children (his subjects) were animists because of the nature of their fantasy experiences with storybooks, toys and the ensuing make-believe.

what they see on the screen ... they incorporate into their [make-believe]" (Harris 1998: 210–211). Further, as Helen Schwartzman (1978: 25) argues: "children's ... play behavior does not always serve as a socializing ... activity ... it may ... challenge, reverse, and/or comment on and interpret the social order." In contemporary society, the transmission of culture occurs largely through formal institutions like school, church, and Little League. Consequently, play can be less conservative and there is no need to reproduce the culture in play. Our children engage in just as much make-believe as the children studied by anthropologists, or even more, but the scripts and purposes seem quite different. In Danish society, children's play, especially make-believe, is considered critical to the child's development, whereas Zapotec adults see it primarily as a means to keep children occupied and out of the way (Jensen de López 2005: 14).[18] In keeping with these differing views, village parents think nothing of diverting a child from play to carry out a chore, while Westerners lose sleep over the deleterious effects of television on make-believe play because it eliminates the need for children "to think up their own creative ideas" (Greenfield *et al.* 1990: 239).

Play is shaped by the ethos of society, as we've seen, and, in the next section, we'll examine the means and reasons for the *suppression* of children's play.

Suppression of play

The ideal [Zinacantecan] child is hardworking, obedient, and responsible; he does not waste his time in play. (Modiano 1973: 55)

Lion cubs are no different than domestic kittens. They're extremely playful, and yet, when their mother is off hunting, the cubs snuggle down into the high grass and remain utterly still – for hours. Upon her return, they burst out of hiding and gambol about her gleefully. Were they unable to suppress their playfulness in her absence, they would be spotted and carried off by any number of potential predators (Schaller 1976). The threat of predation is probably one of the greatest costs associated with juvenile play (Baldwin and Baldwin 1977: 384). And this example should suggest to us that there's often a downside to play – ignored by those who see it as a kind of universal elixir for a successful childhood (Lancy 2001b).

---

[18] This attitude seems to be almost universal in traditional societies. One striking exception occurs among the Ijaw of Nigeria, where adults pay a great deal of attention to children's make-believe, especially when it involves an imaginary companion. It turns out that they see small children as reincarnated ancestors and view make-believe as the child's interacting with the invisible representatives of the spirit world (Leis 1982).

While primates are quite playful, in general, those with a strictly arboreal lifestyle are less playful than those that spend quite a bit of time on the ground. And when food is scarce, juveniles must spend either more time foraging or more time resting; in either case, their playtime will shrink dramatically. This effect – of a reduction in play triggered by food shortage – has been demonstrated, empirically, for a wide range of primate species (Baldwin and Baldwin 1972) including humans (Barber 1991: 133). Not surprisingly, the death of the mother usually leads to a drop off in play (van Lawick-Goodall 1973).

Juveniles seem tied to their mothers by a kind of invisible tether, the length of which can be varied to fit the circumstances. "When the troop is quiet – such as during a general rest period – the infant leaves its mother and explores the environment" (Baldwin and Baldwin 1977: 349). Chimpanzee mothers in a captive colony give their young greater freedom to play and explore than do mothers observed in the wild, presumably because there are fewer dangers (Nicolson 1977). Howler monkey mothers monitor their children's play with peers and reel in the tether, so to speak, when the play-fighting gets too rough (Baldwin and Baldwin 1978). Squirrel monkey mothers seem to be extra vigilant for predation threats when their young are playing (Biben *et al.* 1989).

Tether-length is definitely a useful concept in observing human mother–toddler interaction (Broch 1990: 71–72). As Sorenson discovered in a Fore village, the infant's "early pattern of exploratory activity included frequent returns to the mother. She served as the home base, the bastion of security but not as director or overseer of activities" (Sorenson 1976: 167). For the forest-dwelling Chewong, the tether is shorter. Toddlers are discouraged from wandering away from proximity to adults with "loud exclamations ... 'it is hot,' or 'it is sharp,' or 'there are ... tigers, snakes, millipedes'" (Howell 1988: 163).

Of course, modern Euroamerican parents are often seen using an actual tether to control the behavior of their toddlers in dangerous urban environments. In the poorest urban ghettos, it is common for mothers to forbid their children to play outside the apartment, going so far as to lock them in when they're gone.[19] Even statistically "safe" neighborhoods may be *perceived* as dangerous by anxious parents with few offspring (Liden 2003: 128). Contrast these contemporary attitudes with earlier periods when children had much greater freedom to explore their environment, whether urban or rural (Heywood 2001: 97).

While mothers may be concerned for their children's safety, the public at large may frown upon play as disruptive of public order. Children's noisy play disrupted Parliament, so it was banned in the vicinity. In 1447, the bishop of

---

[19] Even within the apartment, the children are cautioned to stay away from doors and windows for fear of stray bullets (Kotlowitz 1991).

Figure 20 Street urchins

Exeter wrote decrying games of "toppe, queke, penny prykki" played in the cloisters, "by the which the walles of the saide Cloistre have be befowled and the glas wyndowes all to brost" (Opie and Opie 1969: 11). The addition of a football to the children's play arsenal was *not* welcomed by adults in Gbarn-gasuakwelle, as it introduced an element of mayhem in the middle of the village (Lancy 1996: 187). In the Sepik area of Papua New Guinea, Kulick found that foreign games picked up by the village children, such as marbles, were condemned by senior men as the "root of stupidity" (Kulick 1992: 177). In spite of prohibitions, children respond to an imperative and play in the streets, if no more suitable play space is available (Figure 20).

Contemporary children face a forest of obstacles to public play. This description of the gradual foreclosure of children's unsupervised play in rural Maine reflects this dramatic change in the nature of childhood.

A local pasture that served older generations as an amateur hillside ski area ... and a vacant wooded lot where boys acted out World War II battles and younger children looked for monsters [are] now filled with residential development[s] ... a whole network of shortcuts ("secret pathways") throughout the town is gone now, replaced by parking lots, a new bank building or, in some cases, "no trespassing" signs put up by recent in-migrants ... Busing cut children off from a prime connection to their ecology – the walk to school ... past interesting natural sites ... [lingering] to catch frogs at the pond, chase snakes, or bury and hold funerals for dead animals encountered along the way. (Beach 2003: 190)

Wooded areas have been posted and fenced off, as have schoolyards. Children's use of the latter facility is confined to supervised play on manufactured structures, rather than the trees and boulders that used to serve this purpose. New roads and increased speeds have blocked access to formerly foot-accessible public areas – such as the town "green." Beach's older informants recalled exciting and hazardous play experiences in and around barns, corrals, and agricultural equipment: "injuries and scars from their early years, evidence[d] ... physical adventurousness now probably less widespread among children" (Beach 2003: 191).

Parents restrict the play of their offspring not only to protect their investment; mothers may also see play as reducing the return on their investment. In Islamic areas of Nigeria, where women are sequestered,

children's street-trading activities facilitate the economic participation of women who trade through their daughters and pre-adolescent sons ... *mothers attempt to get more work out of children by prohibiting play*, which they perceive as a manifestation of indolence and hedonism that will be maladaptive in the future. (Oloko 1994: 211, emphasis added)

Among the Yucatec Maya, "the opportunity for play of any sort is relatively limited ... children as young as three or four are often given chores ... by age six or seven they are kept busy with work for long periods of time" (Gaskins and Göncü 1992: 31). Children in agrarian communities in Botswana – whose labor was in great demand – spent significantly *less* time playing, as did girls, children of junior wives, and children in school, than did children in communities that relied more on foraging (Bock and Johnson 2004: 81–82). The Baining deny the importance of play in childhood; children must instead aspire to work like adults (Fajans 1997: 168). They may "use a piece of bone to pierce the septum of the nose" as punishment and an active irritant if the child becomes too exuberant (Fajans 1997: 92). For a Kogi (Columbian farmers) child, "to be accused of 'playing' is a very serious reproach. There are practically no children's games in Kogi culture" (Reichel-Dolmatoff 1976: 278). Similarly, "play, or any behavior associated with idleness, is discouraged by the Guajiro (South American pastoralists)" (Watson-Franke 1976: 193–194).

In Laurence Wylie's ethnography of a farming village in France in the mid-twentieth century, children's only opportunity to play occurred on the walk home from school, as all but the very youngest had chores (Wylie 1957: 69). Going back further in European history, children were sent from home at an early age (as young as five) to toil as servants, pages, or apprentices in wealthy homes or were placed under the protection of better-off kin to "improve themselves." Opportunities to play would have been, consequently, quite limited. Those placed as oblates in monasteries had even less chance to be childlike: "according to surviving monastic/conventual regulations, [they] could be permitted to play for as little as one hour, once a week or once a month" (Shahar 1990: 197).

Play may be seen as a sign of waywardness. Bulusu' view play as naughty (*jayil*) and those who play "too much" as crazy (*mabap*) (Appell-Warren 1987: 160). Children may be scolded for getting dirty or telling stories they know aren't true (e.g. fantasizing) (Gaskins *et al.* 2007: 192). On Malaita Island, where children are expected to carefully observe and report on newsworthy events in the village, children's fantasy constructions are discouraged; they "are mildly reprimanded with 'you lie'" (Watson-Gegeo and Gegeo 2001: 5). Following the Protestant Reformation, many influential authorities condemned play[20] in general as well as specific kinds of play, such as solitary play or contact sports. Morality came to be equated with decorum and emotional restraint; "indulging children was a cardinal sin" (Colón with Colón 2001: 284). Similar sentiments were expressed by Chinese sages:

Huo T'ao had no tolerance for play ... as soon as a child is able to walk and talk, it must be taught not to play with other children. Children must practice treating one another as adults ... When [children] see each other in the morning, they must be taught to bow solemnly to each other. (Dardess 1991: 76)

Children who acted with adult seriousness and wisdom were upheld as models. (Wicks and Avril 2002: 4)

Early in the last century, moralists cautioned against the harmful effect on children of games of chance, theatrical performances, and itinerant story-tellers. Presumably these activities inflamed passions and awakened emotions better left dormant (Nasaw 1992: 22–24). Contemporary moralists are much more accepting of play in general, while nevertheless condemning commercially tainted dolls and video games that expose "innocent" children to premature glimpses of sex and violence. Playtime has been compressed as summer vacation and recess are eroded by the inexorable demands of schooling.

"Classic" children's pastimes, like marbles, have steadily declined in popularity (Sutton-Smith and Rosenborg 1961: 27), replaced by TV, computers, video games, and managed activities like sports and Boy Scouts. Quasi-public spaces that drew children in as ideal venues for exploring, make-believe episodes, and impromptu games are fast disappearing. Concern for children's exposure to violence and sexuality has led to restrictions on children's *physical* interaction with each other. These include a ban on R & T play in the school playground – perhaps the only available play space – and boys "smooching"

---

[20] In the West, the notion that play (frivolous) and training for adulthood (serious business) are fundamentally incompatible goes back at least to Plato and Aristotle.

girls prosecuted as "sexual harassment." But the major divide between children's play in the village and the current situation is the greatly expanded role of parents and other supervisory adults.

Parent–child play

[Sisala] parents regard an interest in children's play as beneath their dignity. (Grindal 1972: 25)

[For] middle-class parents ... teaching in pretend play consists of sharing conceptual knowledge about the world. (Vandermaas-Peeler *et al*. 2009: 95)

Noted child psychologist Jerome Bruner called attention to a mother playing peek-a-boo with her infant as the onset of a lengthy program to stimulate the child's intellectual development (Bruner and Sherwood 1976: 277). But cross-cultural surveys (Lancy 2007) of mother-infant relations challenge many assumptions like Bruner's about what is essential in childcare. An analysis of 186 archived ethnographies of traditional societies indicated wide variation in the amount of mother-infant play and display of affection (Barry and Paxson 1971). In a more recent comparative observational study, "Euro-American adults were much more likely than Aka or Ngandu adults to stimulate (e.g., tickle) and vocalize to their infants. As a result, Euro-American infants were significantly more likely than Aka and Ngandu infants to smile, look at, and vocalize to their care providers" (Hewlett *et al*. 2000: 164).[21] Play with infants also seems generally less common among agrarian societies; for example, an Apache (North American agro-pastoralists) "mother sometimes plays with her baby ... A father is not likely to play with a baby" (Goodwin and Goodwin 1942: 448). In hundreds of hours of close observation of parent–child interaction among Kipsigis (Kenyan) farmers, Harkness and Super (1986: 102) recorded "no instances of mothers playing with their children."

Other research shows that the *en face* position, in which the mother holds the infant facing her, is common in modernized societies but rare elsewhere, as is the tendency of the mother to talk with the infant (Field *et al*. 1981). Playing with (e.g. peek-a-boo), talking to, and stimulating the infant are all considered by developmental psychologists an essential in order to promote the mother-infant bond, but, again, some scholars now question the necessity for such bonding (Scheper-Hughes 1987b: 201). Among the Papel, with an infant

---

[21] In discussions with Barry Hewlett (Aka) and Hillary Fouts (Bofi) they affirmed (personal communications, February/March 2007) that, in their systematic observations of child-minding in forest foraging societies, parents rarely, if ever, play with their children.

mortality rate around 33 percent, mothers aren't supposed to talk to or get too emotionally tied to their infants (Einarsdóttir 2004: 73).

The pattern of infant–caretaker interaction that West describes on Fiji is quite representative with respect to who plays with the infant, how they do so, and why:

While mothers performed routine physical care of infants ... the playful interactions of the non-maternal caregivers ... or of relatives visiting ... were much more notable. Various persons, of all ages and either sex, greeted infants enthusiastically and often initiated playful slaps or clapping games, or engaged the infant in reciprocal vocal or (later) verbal routines [that] may have functioned to introduce infants to the significant others in the social matrix. (West 1988: 22)

Bakeman and colleagues studied carefully the nature of adult-child interaction among the !Kung, specifically seeking to test some of our Western assumptions about what is or isn't essential to the child's normal development. As on Fiji, they, too, found that "Non-mothers ... vocalized to and entertained infants more than mothers." In addition, they failed to see the parent–child interactions considered critical by psychologists for language development (Bakeman *et al.* 1990: 802, 806).

Among primates, play is universal, although, as we saw in the previous section, levels of play can be attenuated owing to hunger, predation threats, or the dangers inherent in the monkey's arboreal environment. Play between mothers and their young is almost non-existent – except among chimpanzees. At the Gombe Stream Reserve, Jane Goodall reported many episodes of mother–infant play (van Lawick-Goodall 1976b; Bard 1995), and Frans Plooij observed mothers playing with infants by tickling them vigorously. Infant chimps respond with laughter if they are being adequately but not excessively stimulated, or whimpering and crying if stimulated too much. During the second half of its first year, the baby interacts with others who also tickle it. Plooij asks:

Why is the chimpanzee mother providing her baby with what monkey infants get from their peers? One clue in the direction of an answer may be the group structure of chimpanzees. I observed that chimpanzee mothers spend most of their time alone with their babies. As a consequence it is the chimpanzee mother who has to give her baby this sort of interaction if he gets it at all. (Plooij 1979: 237)

Similar forces may promote mother–child play among humans. The small band of "Utkuhikhalingmiut [Inuit are] the sole inhabitants of an area 35,000 or more miles square" (Briggs 1970: 1). Aside from the almost total lack of other children to play with, the mother–child pair is isolated inside their igloo for days on end during the worst weather. Jean Briggs observed mothers talking to their children, making toys for them, playing with them, and encouraging their language development.

Further, there is every reason to believe that modern living conditions in which infants and toddlers are isolated from peers in single-parent or nuclear households produce a parallel effect. That is, like chimps in the wild, modern, urban youngsters *only* have access to their mothers as potential play partners. In Japan, the mother–child pair has become quite isolated, sequestered in high-rise apartment buildings. Male wage-earners are gone during the child's waking hours, drastically reduced fertility has eliminated sibling playmates, and three-generation, extended families are now rare (Uno 1991: 394–395).

If parent–infant play is spotty, parent–toddler play is virtually non-existent, even in societies where play with infants is observed. Among the !Kung, parents not only don't play with their children post-infancy, they reject the notion outright as potentially harmful to the child's development. They believe that children learn best without adult intervention (Bakeman *et al*. 1990: 796). The mother of a toddler not only faces potential conflict between childcare and work, she's likely pregnant as well. I would argue that the mother's greatest ally, at this point in the childrearing process, is the magnetic attraction of the sibling or neighborhood play group (Parin 1963: 48). The *last* thing a pregnant mother wants is for her child to see her as an attractive play partner. Even verbal play is avoided. From the Gusii perspective, the child may attempt to solicit the mother as play or conversation partner but will be ignored because, were the mother to respond, this would seem "eccentric . . . since . . . a child is not a valid human being until he reaches the age of 'sense'" (LeVine and LeVine 1981: 43–44) at six or seven. Interaction between Mexican children and parents "takes place in shared work activity rather than child-centered play" (Farver and Howes 1993: 350).

In spite of the dearth of evidence for mother–child play elsewhere, an American psychologist, in describing her methodology for studying the development of children's personality traits, explains, without qualification, that "Mothers were instructed to play with their children as they would at home" (Stipek 1995: 244). In another, similar experimental study with middle-class European subjects, the authors make the ridiculous assertion that children learn make-believe play through the patient teaching of their parents (Rakoczy *et al*. 2005: 71). Equally absurd are studies of parents "teaching" their children how to play with peers (Schütze *et al*. 1986; Waldfogel 2006: 43). The assumption that all mothers play with their children is so entrenched that, when middle-class mothers discuss their role, playing with their offspring – from birth – is usually central. For guidance they may turn to "How-to" books like *The Power of Parent–Child Play*. They will be introduced to Carol, a distraught mother comforted by the author, who weeps in relief after confessing: "I've always thought that something was very wrong with me, because I don't enjoy playing with my own kids. I fear they sense that and have already been damaged" (Sargent 2003: 109).

What explains this huge gulf between societies where mothers don't play with children and those where the absence of mother–child play is seen as an indicator of clinical abnormality (Trevarthen 1983: 151)? Why do well-educated Euroamerican and Asian parents invest so much of their precious time in activity – children's play – that parents elsewhere and throughout history have looked on as a welcome distraction, keeping children out of the way so they can do their work (Lancy 2007)?

Modern parents go to considerable lengths to bind their infants to themselves emotionally, and play is used as a means to this end.[22] This powerful attachment is fundamental to several parental goals that vary somewhat between the Western and Eastern hemispheres. In both areas, the mother is the child's first and most important teacher. She is directly responsible for insuring that the child is prepared for and strives to be successful in school (Stevenson et al. 1992). Asian mothers also use play, didactically, to socialize the child to restrain its own desires and adopt a cooperative and deferential attitude toward others (Sung and Hsu 2009: 436). Failure to do so brings scorn on the parents and humiliation for the mother (Haight et al. 1999). Until quite recently, Asian parents had a very direct stake in their child's success, as their future wellbeing depended on the caretaking zeal and largess of their grown children. Hence the mother works extremely hard to insure that her child will respond to her direction as teacher as well as to feel deep filial piety and gratitude toward both parents for the remainder of their lives and beyond (Lebra 1994; Kim and Choi 1994).

In the West, parent–child play emphasizes the development of narrative competence. Parents actively push children into realms of fantasy where a wide vocabulary can be brought into play and the child can experiment with hypothetical characters, relationships, and situations. These children are quite likely to be precocious in acquiring literacy and in their verbal interchange with others (J. R. Katz 2001: 71; Vandermaas-Peeler et al. 2009: 107). They learn to "talk like a book" (Martini 1995: 58). It should come as no surprise that this emphasis on "talking like a book" is central in the pedagogy of the most highly respected doyen of pre-school education in the US – Vivian Paley (Wiltz and Fein 1996). Concerned about their children's school success, middle-class mothers structure the child's play to promote concentration, self-discipline, emotional self-control, persistence in the face of failure, cooperation with others, and attention to adults (as teachers) as well as academic material

---

[22] Mother–infant play in East Asia is of unknown antiquity, but in the USA it has a short history. As recently as 1914, the *Infant Care Bulletin* of the US Department of Labor's Children's Bureau warned against the dangers of playing with a baby because "it produced unwholesome [erotic] pleasure and ruined the baby's nerves." However, from 1940 "Play, having ceased to be wicked, having become harmless and good, now becomes a duty" (Wolfenstein 1955: 172–173).

(Parmar *et al.* 2008: 163). The mothers carefully control the toy inventory to facilitate these lessons as well as expose their children to the artifacts of schooling, such as letters, numbers, colors, and "staying within the lines." It is not surprising, therefore, when researchers find broad commonalities in the play of children from educated, urban communities around the world (Roopnarine *et al.* 1994).

Middle-to-upper-class US fathers, while playing less with their offspring than do mothers, nevertheless behave as if this is a natural and appropriate part of their role – a view not shared in all industrialized societies. But fathers do play differently than mothers. "Mother's play ... tends to be more verbal, object mediated, and didactic, whereas father's play tends to be more physical, active and unpredictable" (Power 2000: 342). In other words, mothers play for the sake of the child, fathers for themselves.

Barbara Rogoff and colleagues have done extensive cross-national research that further underscores the very limited distribution of parent–child play. Their observations have been recorded at village sites in Guatemala, Central Africa, and India, and in middle-class homes in Taiwan, Turkey, and the USA. Only the middle-class, urbanized mothers routinely play with their children (Rogoff *et al.* 1991, 1993, Morelli *et al.* 2003). Even when village mothers were given novel objects, along with guidance and encouragement to play with their children, they persisted in the attitude that children should explore them independently while they did their work (Göncü *et al.* 2000: 322; Rogoff *et al.* 1993). Paradise records a scene that clearly reflects the prevailing attitudes:

[A Mazahua] woman is seated on the ground behind the produce she is selling, her legs stretched out straight in front of her. Two boys, a two-year-old and a three-year-old are playing on top of her legs. The older boy is lying on his back lengthwise along the woman's legs, the younger sitting astride him at his waist "galloping," both laughing ... The woman ... looks at what's going on around her and occasionally at the children on her legs ... with no change of expression ... as regards the play itself: she does not join in, her observance of it is intermittent, and she maintains an emotional distance. (Paradise 1996: 382)

In the USA, ethnographers have noted the low level, if not complete absence, of mother–child play in lower-class households (Ward 1971; Heath 1990; Lareau 1989). Similarly, in an industrial town in north central Italy, play is defined "as *una cosa naturale* (a natural thing)," precluding any involvement by adults in children's play. When asked to play with their toddlers as part of an assessment of child language, sample mothers refused or claimed they didn't know how to (New 1994: 130–132).

Not surprisingly, therefore, from a survey of the literature, we learn that children whose play is "guided" show higher levels of curiosity, greater interest in object manipulation, and more imaginative make-believe than village children whose caretakers don't think it appropriate to intervene (Power 2000). And, in US society, parents aren't the only adults who intervene to manage children's play, as we'll see in the next section.

The adult management of play

Many aspects of Little League baseball are structured by the demands and claims of adults – coaches, umpires, and parents. (Fine 1987: 15)

The idea that adults might intervene to structure and control children's play is tantamount to a contradiction in terms. Among the legion of play definitions, attributes like "voluntary," "purposeless," "child-centered," "autonomous," and "autotelic" are highlighted (Schwartzman 1978). Yet middle-class Euroamerican parents carefully manage their children's play – from birth (Power and Parke 1982: 162) – and there has been a steady increase in adult management of children's play (Sutton-Smith and Rosenborg 1961: 27) since the late nineteenth century (Guttmann 2010: 147). We now segregate players by age and tightly control the rules of engagement, so that "winners" are truly the best while practice and rigorous competition act as a grinding stone, constantly sharpening skills and building self-confidence. And, unlike the situation anthropologists working in the developing world describe, in our society, parents are avid spectators and impromptu coaches of their player/ children.

Boy Scouts, Little League, ballet, piano, and other forms of adult-managed play offer parents multiple benefits. As we've seen, doting parents can achieve, vicariously, those fifteen minutes of fame. They can also be assured that their children are acquiring habits of behavior and thinking that, if not leading directly to a lucrative contract in the big leagues, at least do no harm and undoubtedly contribute, in a general way, to life success. "One [beauty] pageant mom explains, 'I just want to see my daughters go somewhere in life. I didn't. I ended up having kids right away. I'm stuck at home now'" (Levey 2009: 204). Another benefit of enrolling one's child in a managed play activity is to segregate her from peers whose parents fail adequately to manage their free time and who might exert a "negative influence" on her. Mothers of rodeo queen aspirants justify this expensive and all-consuming pursuit: "keeping them on the back of a horse, keeps them out of the back seat of a car" (Raitt and Lancy 1988: 278). Lastly, and this by now has become a common refrain, children under the care of coaches, teachers, employers, and scout leaders – acting *in loco parentis* – free up parents from childcare responsibility and give them time to acquire resources for themselves and family members (Hofferth *et al.* 1991).

Nowhere is the adult's management of children's play more evident than in team sports,[23] Little League baseball in particular. But, before we review Gary Fine's ethnography of Little League, let's see what the *absence* of adult management might look like, as described by the Opies observing children playing in streets and fields in the first half of the twentieth century:

[Players] seldom need an umpire, they rarely trouble to keep scores, little significance is attached to who wins or loses, they do not require the stimulus of prizes, it does not seem to worry them if a game is not finished. Indeed children like games in which there is a sizeable element of luck, so that individual abilities cannot be directly compared. They like games which restart almost automatically, so that everybody is given a new chance. (Opie and Opie 1969: 2)

Also, when "one team outperforms another, players will often be re-rearranged to make the matchup more even … so that the game would not get boring" (Freie 1999: 91). In contrast, the Opies decry the fact that middle-class American children's "playtime has become almost as completely organized and supervised as their [schoolwork]" (Opie and Opie 1969: 16).

In the very competitive world of Little League baseball, a *laissez-faire* attitude toward rules has no place. There is an official rulebook, which runs to better than sixty pages, its existence precluding the negotiation of rules (Fine 1987: 20). The coach carries the burden of shaping the Little League experience to serve in socializing pre-adolescent boys: "coaches are expected to keep their players orderly and oriented to the serious performance of baseball, while displaying an emotional coolness" (Fine 1987: 31). Remarkably, a national survey suggests that children themselves *prefer* to have adults organize their lives. They think that organized youth activity is a good thing; the alternative is to hang out with friends suffering boredom because there's "nothing to do." And "three in four students agree that 'a lot of kids get into trouble when they're bored and have nothing to do'" (Duffett and Johnson 2004: 10; Luthar and Shoum 2006: 593).

[Youth baseball coach Sullivan] sometimes finds himself teaching children how to be kids. For a change of pace, he will try to get them to organize their own games, or he'll show them stickball or some other derivative form of baseball. "They can't do it very well," he said. "And they don't like it. They're like: 'If I'm going to play baseball, I want Sully around. I want to be in uniform and I want an umpire'" (Sokolove 2004: 84)

There is a growing backlash against the increasing takeover of children's play by adults (Gray 2013). Adult management of children's play denies children the opportunity to negotiate and construct joint activity with peers.

---

[23] In a recent study, team sports was the most popular extra-curricular pursuit (Kremer-Sadlik *et al.* 2010: 39).

So dependent are they on adult guidance that "children rarely attempt to join in each other's activity without the mother's prompting" (Budwig *et al.* 1986: 89). Returning to our discussion of the Machiavellian brain and the role of games as providing a mental gym to exercise and develop this brain, then the critical elements are:

rule-governed play, flexibility in applying the rules, and an absence of adult umpires. In short, children must be free to construct successful gaming sessions without adult guidance or interference ... curtailing play initiated by children seems likely to attenuate – if not destroy altogether – opportunities to develop the skills associated with gamesmanship. (Lancy and Grove 2011b: 492, 496)

It is ironic that adult concern for children's wellbeing and the desire to maximize the perceived benefits of play may, unintentionally, create social misfits such as bullies.

7 The chore curriculum

Introduction

"The child keeps on doing and doing, and then gets used to it" [is an expression] very often used [by Tapajós Indians] to talk about the learning process. (Medaets 2011: 4)

The Yukaghir (Siberian foragers) model of knowledge transferal could be described as "doing is learning and learning is doing." (Willerslev 2007: 162)

Nowhere are the gerontocracy and neontocracy perspectives further apart than on the issue of work.[1] Indeed, "the dissociation of childhood from the performance of valued work is considered a yardstick of modernity" (Nieuwenhuys 1996: 237). While we hamstring our children to keep them from working, fearing their loss of innocence and studiousness, the norm elsewhere is to open the pathway to adulthood. Indeed, even as the transformation of children into cherubs was well underway in the Victorian period, bourgeois girls "devoted much of their play time to sewing [various items] for church bazaars" because work was valued as a means to build character (Schorsch 1970: 142). In the village, we will see that, as soon as children can "help out" and make a contribution, they do so – eagerly, without coercion, and with minimal guidance. Children work in order to establish an identity. One's gender may be largely defined by the work one does. Recall from Chapter 2 the widespread notion of "delayed personhood." In many cases, escaping from this state of anonymity occurs through integrating oneself with the quotidian activities of older family members.

Anthropologists often note with some degree of awe how early the child begins to make a contribution to the domestic economy. On Rairoa, a four-year-old, outfitted with suitably sized container, may make as many as ten trips

---

[1] Anthropologists differentiate tasks ("work") that are incorporated into family life, and developmental in that children are learning while helping, from "labor." Labor for wages or to work off a debt may involve removing a child from its family and exposing him or her to arduous and unhealthy conditions, and it does not necessarily include opportunities for learning and advancement. In short, it is usually detrimental to children (Bourdillon and Spittler 2012: 9).

Figure 21 Sib-caretaker in Madagascar

a day carrying water from the community cistern to his home (Danielsson 1952: 121). I have often observed youngsters no older than five carrying and looking after infants, as Figure 21 from Madagascar illustrates (see also Ottenberg 1968: 80).

The term "curriculum" in chore curriculum conveys the idea that there is a discernible regularity to the process whereby children attempt to learn, then master and finally, carry out their chores. While the academic or "core" curriculum (of math, English, science) found in schools is formal and imposed on students in a top-down process, the chore curriculum is informal and emerges in the interaction of children's need to fit in and emulate those older, their developing cognitive and sensorimotor capacity, the division of labor within the family, and the nature of the tasks (chores) themselves. The primary theme of this chapter is the notion of children as workers – across foraging (hunting-and-gathering), pastoral, and farming societies. A complementary theme is the process by which children *learn* the trades of their particular society. In fact, children most often learn "on the job." Nevertheless, there are distinct regularities in this process that I've attempted to capture in the expression "chore curriculum" (Lancy 1996: 144, 2012a).

Prior to the modern era, education was not confined to a classroom or textbooks. It happened everywhere there were children to observe and emulate more proficient members of the community. Furthermore, as reviewed in the previous two chapters, the first evidence of the child taking on the role of pupil is usually found in object or make-believe play. So pervasive is this phenomenon that it is appropriate to refer to the earliest manifestation of the chore curriculum as the "play stage." If the play stage is nursery school, running errands can be construed as kindergarten. In errand running, the child, for the first time, is following explicit directions. Gradually, more demanding and complex tasks emerge in the chore curriculum consonant with the child's maturity and motivation. Among the universe of needed tasks, there are almost always one or two that are "just right" for a given child's age and strength. Furthermore, most realms of endeavor are conveniently and quite naturally graded in difficulty (Gaskins *et al.* 2007; Schildkrout 1990: 225).

We will explore a wide range of "learning to work" scenarios, which incorporate the almost idyllic process whereby bright-eyed, eager children take up the tasks of their elders and persist until mastery. Among well-documented task domains there are gardening, herding, gathering, hunting, fishing, and various handicrafts. In many cases, we will note that this process is unhurried and casual. Children may take many years to become proficient and productive. In other cases, we see evidence of adults pressing children to mature quickly and assume responsible roles.

A key issue in this chapter is the contrast between competence and productivity. Boys may become quite competent as foragers but, compared to their sisters, they don't add much to the family larder. They may, however, "step up" in times of crisis, leading me to speculate about the role of children as a "reserve labor force." The last two sections of the chapter present studies of craft learning including the informal processes found in the majority of cases and the, rarer, formal training of novices via an apprenticeship.

In the section that follows I want to make the case that children gain much of their social standing and identity through the work they do.

Work, gender, and identity

[When a Nuer boy] tethers the cattle and herds the goats ... when he cleans the byres and spreads the dung to dry and collects it and carries it to the fires he is considered a person. (Evans-Pritchard 1956: 146)

[In the eighteenth century] little girls of six could spin flax and comb wool ... the sawing and chopping of wood was a boy's industry. (MacElroy 1917: 89, 139)

So central is work in the lives of children that it is often constitutive of their identity (Mohammad 1997). In pre-modern Russia "our plowboy," "our herd boy," and "our nanny girl" were habitual terms parents used to address their children (Gorshkov 2009: 15). And, among the Tchokwe', "children are identified through the roles they assume [for example] *kambumbu* are children ... who help parents in the field" (Honwana 2006: 41–42).

In the Giriama language the term for a child roughly two through three years in age is *kahoho kuhuma madzi*: a youngster who can be sent to fetch a cup of water ... A girl, from about eight years until approximately puberty, is *muhoho wa kubunda*, a child who pounds maize; a boy of this age is a *muhoho murisa*, a child who herds. (Wenger 1989: 98)

Contrast this nomenclature with our commonly used expressions such as pre-schooler, kindergartner, sixth grader, and sophomore. In a neontocracy, the stage labels mark progress through the school curriculum.

Aside from terms that mark the child's developmental progression as a worker, we find numerous examples of adults turning these transitions into minor rites of passage, including these: a Kaoka boy's first pig (Hogbin 1969: 39); Wogeo families assigning a child their first garden plot (Hogbin 1946: 279); Hopi girls who've just mastered the art of corn grinding being "shown off" to visitors (Hough 1915: 63); a Vlach six-year-old being given his first shepherd's crook (Campbell 1964: 156); a Cheyenne boy's first bow and arrows (Grinnel 1923: 115); a Netsilik girl's first caught salmon and her brother's first goose (Balikci 1970: 45); and "When an [M'buti] boy kills his first 'real animal,' he is immediately acclaimed as a hunter ... [and honored by cicatrization] ... an operation performed ... by one of the 'great hunters'" (Turnbull 1965: 257). A !Kung adolescent who's killed his first large mammal earns a facial tattoo "so that anyone who glances at him can see that he is an experienced hunter" (Howell 2010: 36). A Murik Lakes (Papua New Guinea) girl's harvest from "clamming" is treated with respect and public acclaim (Barlow 2001: 87).

On the other hand, certain areas of work are considered inappropriate for children (just as certain tasks are reserved for males, others for females). The Kwoma actually prevent children from prematurely assuming more difficult chores because tasks are associated with rank, and moving to a more challenging assignment is tantamount to a promotion (Whiting 1941: 70). Koori (aboriginal) boys are not permitted to touch "real" hunting weapons (toy or scaled-down are OK), as that would demean the adult hunters who've earned the privilege (Basedow 1925: 86). Aka men do not eat game bagged by adolescents, as this would compromise their central role as decision makers "regarding hunting activity and the group as a whole" (Takeuchi 2013: 182).

Chores also play a major role in the differentiation of gender – especially before the appearance of secondary sex characteristics. Among the Kel Ewey Touareg, goats are tended by boys and girls, but only boys tend camels (Spittler 1998).[2] The Tarong equivalent of the camel is the *carabao* or water buffalo – tended only by boys (Whiting and Edwards 1988b: 224). In West Africa, weaving is the province of women among Akwete Igbo, but for the Baulè, males weave (Aronson 1989). Stereotypically, among Hadza foragers, girls forage and boys hunt (Marlowe 2010). Almost universally, girls are preferred as caretakers for younger siblings, and sons are conscripted for this chore only when a daughter is unavailable (Ember 1973: 425–6).[3] Should a boy *volunteer* to help out in the distaff arena, he's likely to be rebuffed,[4] no matter how earnest (de León 2005 cited in Paradise and Rogoff 2009: 117).

We also see a gap in productivity. In a series of observational studies conducted at village sites around the world, girls consistently spent more of their day doing chores, including sib-care, housework, and gardening. Boys spend relatively more of their time playing or just hanging out. Indeed, boys, in many societies, are defined as much by their freedom from work – relative to girls – as by the specific work they do. "These differences are seen from age three onwards" (Edwards 2005: 87). Boys range further afield, running errands, patroling distant fields, and hunting in the bush (Broch 1990: 145).

---

[2] Spittler has a very interesting discussion of the problem of an imbalance in the (Touareg) family. Daughters fill the son's role of camel-tending but not after they reach marriageable age, and likewise, boys – once they start to tend camels – refuse to tend goats "no matter how great the need of the family" (Spittler 2012: 77).

[3] In some cases, a shortage can be met by cross-gender role assignments. In a Luo-speaking community in Kenya, the shortage of daughters was community-wide and Carol Ember discovered that "Approximately half the boys in the community had been assigned 'feminine' work ... because the ratio of boys to girls ... was almost three to two ... at the time of the study" (Ember 1973: 425–426).

[4] I had a personal epiphany regarding the inadvisability of assigning boys as sibling caretakers in May 2007 as I stood on a busy street in front of the Registan in Samarkand. Two boys were pushing baby carriages in the street, just barely out of traffic. The street sloped downward and the lead carriage-pusher began a game of chicken, releasing his grip on the bar, then rushing after to grab it as the carriage rolled away on its own. This game was repeated with longer intervals between the release and retrieval.

To outside observers, boy's "work" often looks more like play while girl's work looks like – work. Observational data from the Tonga (southern Africa) indicate that: "Men spent twenty-nine per cent of their time in leisure and boys forty-seven per cent. These amounts are almost double those of women (sixteen per cent) and girls (twenty-six per cent)" (Reynolds 1991: 64). Close study of Hadza children's foraging illustrates the way in which girls "get serious" at an age when boys are acting rather frivolously, with significant consequences. From the age of ten, girls are gathering more food than they consume. Boys, on the other hand, concentrate on exciting but low-caloric-value foods such as honey and small game (Blurton-Jones *et al.* 1997). In more recent research, these findings have been augmented by the discovery that boys are excellent foragers but consume their catch on the spot rather than bringing it back to camp (Crittenden *et al.* 2013: 303).

Not only do girls begin the transition to working earlier than boys, but among the Giriama, their work:play ratio is higher (2:1) and they earn different assignments (maize-hulling vs. herding; Wenger 1989: 98–99). Generally speaking, a girl's working sphere coincides with that of her mother: the household, kitchen, nursery, laundry, garden, and market stall. (Paradise and Rogoff 2009: 113) depict a five-year-old Mazahua girl closely following her mother's lead in setting up an onion stand in the market – trimming, bunching, and arranging their onions. When invited to establish a satellite onion stand, "her excitement is unmistakable and she quickly takes the initiative in finding an appropriate spot and setting it up." Girls are literally in synch with their role models, as studies demonstrate a young Malian girl's ability to match the rhythm and stroke of an older partner in joint pounding of grain in a mortar and pestle (Bril 1986: 322).

Unlike the lock-step, standardized *academic* curriculum, the chore curriculum is highly elastic within and across cultures. A nine-year-old girl likely carries more of a burden for household tasks if she's the oldest of four children than if she's the youngest of four. She'll have less responsibility in a larger household (Munroe *et al.* 1984), where "many hands make light work." In an Iraqi Kurdish village, a nine-year-old girl has near-complete responsibility in the domestic sphere (Friedl 1992: 36), whereas in a Berber village in Morocco such a child would be eleven or twelve (Cross 1995: 70).

While girls seem firmly attached to their mothers and function from an early age as their assistants, boys are much less often in close proximity to their fathers.[5] Kerkenni (Tunisia) boys "do not socialize with their fathers or their fathers' peers. This would be disrespectful" (Platt 1988: 282; true also on Java – Geertz 1961: 107; Jay 1969: 68). And while many of a woman's

---

[5] Boys do provide substitute labor when possible, for example, taking over herding from the father, thus freeing him to do "socio-political" work (Juul 2008: 158).

burdens can be shared with a child, men's work tends to demand physical strength (clearing bush), finely honed skills (bow-hunting), or erudition – not attributes possessed by little boys. Fathers may find young sons a drag on their work effort and their association with a child may compromise their standing among peers (Kaoka – Hogbin 1969: 39). Little contrasts Asabano girls getting out their incomplete string bags to work on whenever their mothers are so engaged, with Asabano boys learning to make arrows, who must rely for guidance on older siblings or circumspect observation of men making arrows (Little 2011: 155).

In a fairly large number of societies, men reside separately from women and children. Boys are eager to be admitted to the sanctuary of the men's house or adolescent dormitory and begin to learn from other males (Kuba – Binkley 2006: 106). Kammu boys make this transition at five or six, and will then learn from observing and listening to men making and repairing hunting and trapping equipment and retelling the oral history of the tribe (Tayanin and Lindell 1991: 14). Similarly, when a Tapirapé (Brazil) boy became:

churangi (young adolescent) [and] moved from the family dwelling to the *takana* ... he was supposed to learn ... how to weave baskets, how to make a bow and straight arrows, how to fabricate the spirit masks that the men wore ... However, I never witnessed any express attempt ... to teach a young boy such pursuits. On the other hand, the *takana* was the place where adult men generally worked, and a boy had ample chance to watch them at it. (Wagley 1977: 149–150)

While fathers or older relatives keep their distance from boys, there are occasions when we do see tactical intervention to help the learner over a "speed bump."[6] There is a point in the Bamana farming curriculum when older boys struggle to master the art of planting millet. This involves a complex series of movements: use a narrow hoe to dig a hole in the furrow; tilt the seed-filled gourd attached to one's wrist just enough to spill three seeds into the hole; use the hoe to fill/cover the hole. A boy who's otherwise proficient may struggle with mastering this specific task until a father intervenes and carefully demonstrates (Polak 2011: 85). For Warao boys learning to make canoes – the *sine qua non* of survival – "there is not much verbal instruction ... but the father does correct the hand of his son [and demonstrates] how to overcome the pain in his wrist from

---

[6] These interventions are quite focused. A Butonese boy learning to make a complex trap may get help with a crucial step he's done incorrectly. But he can't expect anything that resembles instruction. If told anything at all it might be something like: "[If you do it that way] the trap will no longer be able to hear the fish call when he is in front of the trap" (Vermonden 2009: 213–214).

working with the adze" (Wilbert 1976: 323). On Tikopia, boys participate as uninstructed novices in house-building.

> Of specific instruction in technology I saw very little ... I did see, however, a cross-piece of wood lashed together with a sinnet braid in a complex style, specially prepared. This was a model of the *sumu*, the lashing used to fasten the roof-tree of a house to the supporting posts. The prevalence of gales ... makes a secure lashing important, especially for the large ancestral temples. When I asked the maker, Pa Niukapu, what the model was he said it was for his son – "that he may know how it is done." (Firth 1970: 89)

In WEIRD society, parents and adults generally take every opportunity to instruct children, even when they are patently unmotivated or too awkward and immature. The term "scaffolding" may be used to describe the process whereby the would-be teacher provides significant assistance and support so that the novice can complete a task that is otherwise well beyond his grasp (McNaughton 1996: 178). Elaborate scaffolding is rarely seen elsewhere (Chapter 5). No one wants to waste time teaching novices who might well learn in time without instruction. Play provides an alternative to adult scaffolding.

The play stage

> Nearly all of [the Mayan weavers in Nabenchauk] had done play weaving when they were little. (Greenfield 2004: 37)

> [Inuit] girls make dolls out of scraps of skin, and clothe them like real men and women. Their mothers encourage them, for it is in this way that they learn to sew and cut out patterns. (Jenness 1922: 219)

Ethnographic descriptions of work activity enacted in make-believe and object play are rich and varied, and even include archaeologists' reconstructions of childhood based on the discovery of miniature or crudely made artifacts and toys (de Lucia 2010: 614; Park 2006: 56–57). In the domestic sphere, we see children playing at food preparation, building houses, and making mats and furnishings (Hogbin 1946, 1969: 38). Edel recorded a great many instances of the play stage in Chiga childhood:

> Little girls strap bundles of leaves on their backs as babies, boys build little houses ... A little girl accompanying her mother to the fields practices swinging a hoe and learns to pull weeds or pick greens while playing about ... Playing with a small gourd, a child learns to balance it on his head, and is applauded when he goes to the watering-place with the other children and brings it back with a little water in it. As he learns, he carries an increasing load, and gradually the play activity turns into a general contribution to the household water supply. (Edel 1957/1996: 177)

When children re-enact activities they have witnessed, these are not just generic scenes but quite precise and thoughtful replications of complex systems. Sudanese children:

Acted out the social and work activities associated with agriculture [including variations such] as "tenancies" and one known as "bildat" or rain-fed subsistence fields. In "tenancies" they built ridges characteristic of irrigation in the area, planted the [appropriate] cash crops of cotton and groundnuts ... employed ... tools and equipment associated with mechanized cultivation and spent a good deal of time and energy carefully weighing and measuring their play harvests, distributing shards of "china money" differentially according to yield. In the subsistence version of the game, "bildat," children planted the traditional crops of sorghum and sesame complemented with legumes and vegetables. They did not construct irrigation ridges, but rather, sprinkled their crops with "rain." (Katz 1986: 47–48)

The smooth transition from the play stage to more productive work is evident in Hadza children.

[Young] children spend most of their time in mixed-sex play-groups in camp or just outside ... After watching 3–4-year-olds playing a while, one eventually realizes that children are not just playing but are actually digging small tubers and eating them ... Foraging simply emerges gradually from playing ... It involves a natural interest on the part of the young child watching older people forage and imitating them. Girls four–eight years old bring in 361 daily kcals, which is about twenty-five per cent of their requirements. Boys at the same age bring in only 277 daily kcals. (Marlowe 2010: 156)

A Kutenai (American Plains Indian) boy of two was given a toy bow and arrow to practice with. By three he was expected to be able to bag prairie chickens and by six to be making a significant contribution to the larder (Dawe 1997: 307).

Another arena where play leads to useful skill is in animal husbandry (Figure 22). In the Sepik region of Papua New Guiena, Kwoma children eagerly embrace the piglets they're given to protect, raise, and train (Whiting 1941: 47). Talensi boys are said to possess "a passionate desire to own a hen" (Fortes 1938/1970: 20). Touareg boys, who will eventually be responsible for the care of the family's camel herd during grueling treks, begin at four by caring for a goat. They play vigorously with their charges "as they would play with children" (Spittler 1998: 343).

Katz's comments – from fieldwork in the Sudan – are typical: "one of the most striking aspects of children's lives was the fusion between the activities of work, play and learning" (Katz 1986: 47; see also Polak 2012: 96). Gradually, however, the child is able to differentiate between playful and purposeful actions. Children exercise what psychologists (Wellman *et al.* 2001) refer to as a Theory of Mind (TOM) and can deduce another's goals and intentions and align themselves accordingly. This occurs as they move into the "errand stage."

Figure 22 Young shepherd, Ladakh

Running errands

"Run and fetch me" is one of the commonest phrases heard addressed to young children in Tikopia (Solomon Islands). (Firth 1970: 80)

Margaret Mead, reporting on her first field study in Samoa, provides one of the earliest characterizations of the centrality of work in childhood.

The tiniest little staggerer has tasks to perform – to carry water, to borrow fire brands, to fetch leaves to stuff the pig ... learning to run errands tactfully is one of the first lessons of childhood ... these slighter tasks are laid aside for harder ones as soon as the child becomes strong enough or skilled enough. (Mead 1928/1961: 633)

Running errands nicely illustrates key characteristics of the chore curriculum. Children, at least when they are very young, have a powerful need to become competent (White 1959), fit in (de Waal 2001: 230), strive for success

(Weisfeld and Linkey 1985), be helpful (Rheingold 1982; Warneken and Tomasello 2006), and emulate those more senior (Bandura 1977). Children stand ready to accept responsibility (Edel 1957/1996: 178), and the first assigned chore may be errand-running. "Between eighteen and thirty months of age ... the Guara child begins to act independently as a messenger ... Carrying water and firewood are the first daily chores regularly performed" (Ruddle and Chesterfield 1977: 31).

In Gbarngasuakwelle, a five-year-old girl gets to use a "cheater," a donut roll of cloth to help balance the small container she carries on her head. She proudly accompanies a group of five of her older sisters and cousins (containers matched to the size of each child) to troop down to the stream to fetch water for the evening's cooking and washing (Lancy 1996: 144). These milestones in the child's assumption of responsibility are widely acknowledged within the community (Landy 1959: 93) and happily anticipated by the children themselves.

Fetching and carrying is inherently staged (Zeller 1987: 544). A barely mobile toddler may be asked to carry a cup from its mother across an evening family circle to its father. The same toddler will tag along as an older sibling makes a longer delivery excursion, in effect serving as an understudy. Errands can vary by length and territory and between close kin and strangers, can involve loads of varying size and fragility, and can include an exchange of some kind, including a market transaction. Adults match their assignments to the child's level of skill and size (Broch 1990: 79), and each new assignment ratifies (and motivates) the child's growing competence (Wenger 1989: 98). "Praise and rewards were seldom given ... that [the Araucanian] parent was satisfied ... was enough reward. If a boy's conduct was outstanding, he was rewarded by being sent to a cacique with an important message, or with words of comfort to a family in which a death had occurred" (Hilger 1957: 77).[7]

Here is an example illustrating the complexity of the errand curriculum in rural Guatemala:

The simplest and earliest task for which children are given actual responsibility is the running of errands, transporting objects to or from people's homes or going to a local shop for a few cents' worth of goods. Considerably more difficult are the errands to the maize fields or other errands that require the child to go outside the community. Selling various items in the community may range in complexity from approximately the status of an errand to the cognitively complex task of soliciting buyers from anywhere in the community and of making change. (Nerlove et al. 1974: 276)

The stalwart little helper publicly advertises the quality of its upbringing and its worthiness as a potential foster-child, enhancing the family reputation

---

[7] In the Lower Tapajós, Medaets' (2013) informants willingly acknowledged how helpful and hard-working their children were but would never say that to them directly, as compliments were indicative of the intent to harm someone.

(Lancy 1996: 76). On the other hand, children are favored as errand runners because adolescents or adults seen in close proximity to neighbors' houses might be suspected of adultery, theft, or witchcraft. And boys are favored because their virtue isn't as fragile as that of girls. Learning to become an errand runner rarely entails teaching by an adult; children observe and replicate the process with only minor guidance from an older, sib role model.

Progress in the chore curriculum

My [Ngandu] mother forced me to go to the fields and to work hard all day. I came home sore and in pain ... But, I ask the same things of my girls. (Hewlett 2013: 70)

Pumé [forager] girls spend significantly less time in subsistence work than Maya [farmer] girls. (Kramer and Greaves 2011: 315)

Two central principles of the chore curriculum are the motivation of the child, which propels them up the learning gradient, and the nature of the task environment, which reduces the severity of that gradient by offering "steps" or grades. Motivation is always assumed but a "lazy" child will be chastised (Chapter 5, pp. 196–197). The steepness of the learning curve and number of intermediate steps may vary greatly. In the late 1970s, along with several colleagues, I undertook a comparative analysis of child development in nine contrasting societies – ranging from forest-dwelling foragers (Kiwai Island, Fly River) to swidden (slash-and-burn) horticulturalists (Kewa tribe, Southern Highlands) to maritime foragers and traders (Ponam Island, Bismarck Sea) in Papua New Guinea. A variety of evidence suggested that, unlike the highly standardized public school curriculum in place, the village curriculum ranged from fairly demanding to quite undemanding.

Children ... are expected to share or mimic adult responsibilities from an early age. For Kewa children this means digging and weeding in the garden, weaving *bilums* (netbags), carrying firewood and little else. On Ponam, by contrast, children are engaged in a host of multifaceted activities. They help to build and then learn to handle various size canoes, and they work various sections of the reef with different tools and techniques. They [learn to] make rope; work with wood; make a variety of traditional ornaments, costumes and *bilums*, and make various nets, spears and other fishing gear ... Furthermore, maritime ... gathering as a way of life is unstable and will change continuously in the direction of greater complexity [, while] Highlands sweet potato gardening and pig husbandry have persisted virtually unchanged for centuries. (Lancy 1983: 121–122)[8]

---

[8] Mention might also be made of the Australian aborigines who migrated to the island of Tasmania and whose tool inventory and cultural complexity shrank drastically over time (Henrich 2004).

Figure 23 Kewa boy digging in family sweet potato plot

From the Papua New Guinea study, we concluded that it would take much longer to master what an adult maritime forager knew than what an adult gardener might need to know (See Figure 23).

A third principle is demand. How rapidly the child learns and the amount produced will depend as well on the expectations of one's family for assistance. The !Kung made few demands on children to forage and provide food for themselves and others, but at least some children did so voluntarily (Howell 2010: 30; Konner in press; also true for the Aka – Boyette 2013: 88). Kramer compared gross levels of productivity as a function of age among Mayan farming children and their counterparts in two South American foraging groups. The Mayan children reached an equilibrium of producing as much as they consumed by thirteen, whereas foraging children took five to ten years longer (Kramer 2005: 135). The nature of subsistence plays a role. Hewlett and colleagues' (2011; Boyette 2013) long-term study of neighboring Ituri groups – Aka foragers and Ngandu farmers – illustrates this well. Ngandu children are expected to contribute to the domestic economy from an early age, and they are able to do this, in part, because the skills they will need are readily learned by the onset of adolescence. Ngandu subsistence relies heavily on children's desire to be compliant, less on their desire to achieve. This pattern is very typical in farming and herding communities (Hames and Draper 2004: 334; see also Kogel et al. 1983: 364).[9] By contrast, the Aka – like the !Kung but unlike another pygmy band, the Biyaka (Neuwelt-Truntzer 1981: 138, 147) – do not expect children to contribute greatly to the domestic economy. Nevertheless, by age ten, both boys and girls have mastered a large repertoire of, sometimes complex, foraging skills. "If need be … Aka ten-year-olds have the skills to make a living in the forest" (Hewlett and Cavalli-Sforza 1986: 930). Learning to make a living for Aka children seems to be driven less by the need to conform to family requirements than by the desire to achieve competence.

In the next two sections, I'll break down farming and foraging to reveal the steps or stages that the child must progress through in becoming fully competent.

Progress in the chore curriculum: farming

Jean de Brie … at the age of seven, was responsible for the care of the geese and goslings, at eight minding pigs, at nine helping a cowherd, by eleven in charge of eighty lambs and, at fourteen, 200 ewes in a medieval French farmstead. (Heywood 2001: 123)

Herding is, perhaps, the most evidently staged chore. The child first learns to care for a single, juvenile animal – as a pet. She or he helps cut and gather fodder and mucks out the byre. The child's progress is monitored. "Only after a [Chaga] boy has proved his reliability at herding goats is he preferred to

---

[9] An overview of the relatively demand-free forager childhood can be found on p. 69 in Chapter 2.

the work of pasturing cattle" (Raum 1940: 200). The Touareg boy progresses from a single kid (at three years of age) to a herd of goats (at ten) to a baby camel (at ten) to a herd of camels (at fifteen) to managing a caravan on a trek across the Sahara (at twenty). Preferentially, the aspirant herder interacts with and learns from herders who are slightly older, *not* adults. Adults are too forbidding to ask questions of or display ignorance in front of. Above all, it is a hands-on experience, as "The abstract explanation so typical of our schooling is completely absent" (Spittler 1998: 247).

Sisala boys learn herding from older brothers and cousins by tagging along when they graze the sheep and cattle (Grindal 1972: 29; see also Fulbe – Moritz 2008: 111). Ngoni boys work their way up from tending a goat to a calf, to sheep to a cow, to multiple cattle – all the while observing and discussing cattle with older brothers. The "cow curriculum" is quite extensive:

The Ngoni classified their cattle according to age, sex, coloring, size and shape of horns, whether castrated or not, whether in calf or not. Knowledge of the extensive series of names used for these "classes" of cattle was part of a herd-boy's A.B.C. By the time he was old enough to be told to drive certain cattle out of the kraal, designated by their class, he knew exactly which ones were meant. He could also use the cattle terminology to be precise in telling an owner about a beast which has strayed or one that had a sore hoof, or one that was giving an exceptionally good or poor flow of milk. (Read 1960: 133)

Still, it does appear that children can progress fairly rapidly through the herding curriculum.

[Tibetan] children as young as six or seven ... look after herds of goats, sheep, dzo, and yaks in the mountains ... a major responsibility since much of the wealth of nomadic families is invested in these animals. It can also be a very scary and lonely activity since wolves, snow leopards, and eagles regularly attack the sheep and goats. Using a slingshot to control the animals, boys at seven or eight years of age are considered to be effective herders. (Gielen 1993: 426)

Farming offers tasks as simple as chasing birds from the ripening crop (Grindal 1972: 29; Lancy 1996: 146) or plowing behind a team of oxen (Polak 2012: 105). The child is integrated into the chore curriculum at the appropriate stage (Orme 2003: 308). One sees a Guara trio working in the garden: "While the man makes holes with his digging stick, and his wife places seeds carefully in each hole, the child follows, using the feet to push the earth back over the hole" (Ruddle and Chesterfield 1977: 71). Fore girls learn to garden, entirely without instruction. Their make-believe gardening is followed by clumsy and even destructive attempts to emulate the gardening activities of their elders. Gradually, these efforts "more and more resemble the ... sustained gardening [that is] the basis of the Fore way of life" (Sorenson 1976: 200). Kwoma parents go further by actually setting aside an area of the garden for the child to work on their own – thereby protecting their own gardens from harm. Likewise, the child may be given their own scaled-down collecting calabash, hoe, or machete. Any produce from this mini-garden is "put in a separate bin in the family storehouse as the child's private property" (Whiting 1941: 46; see also Hogbin 1946: 279). Gardening is central to the childrearing model embraced by the Baining (New Britain Island, Papua New Guinea). They actively discourage play and introduce children to gardening as early as feasible (Fajans 1997: 92). This is true for the Guara as well and, in fact, they have adapted a fairly explicit curriculum to guide children's acquisition of their extremely complex and diverse subsistence system (Ruddle and Chesterfield 1977: 126).

By far the most thorough study of the planting curriculum has been undertaken, over many years, by Barbara Polak. She found that Bamana (Mali) children are very eager to participate in the work of grown-ups, and the grown-ups are eager for them to begin learning; but the children can do more harm than good, so their efforts have to be moderated. A seven-year-old is given a worn-out hoe that is smaller, lighter, and blunter than the one used by an older sibling (Polak 2012: 91).

Four-year-old Bafin has already grasped the meaning of sowing and is able to perform the various movements . . . he is entrusted with an old hoe as well as with some seeds so that he can gain some practice in this activity. However . . . he has to be allocated a certain part of the field where he neither gets in the way of the others nor spoils the rows they have already sown . . . As a rule, his rows have to be re-done. (Polak 2003: 126, 129)

Even half-hearted attempts are appreciated:

[At harvest] three-year-old Daole . . . begins to pluck beans from the tendrils. After he has filled the lid with a handful of beans, his interest fades. [He] carelessly leaves the lid with the beans lying on the ground and goes looking for some other occupation . . . Five-year-old Sumala . . . looks out for a corner not yet harvested and picks as many beans as will fill his calabash . . . [he] keeps on doing this for more than one and a half hours . . . Eleven-year-old Fase has been busy harvesting beans . . . since morning. He works as fast as . . . his father and grown-up brother . . . and only takes a rest when they [do] . . . Fase is fully competent . . . with regard to harvesting beans. He even takes on the role of supervising his younger brothers and checks their performance from time to time. (Polak 2003: 130, 132)

The Bamana illustrate Weisner's notion of "chains of support" in which each member of the family work group supports and guides those who are slightly less advanced on the competency scale (Weisner 1996: 308). Children not only gain in skill but assume greater responsibility for supervising the less skilled. And the parents intervene rarely but strategically. A mother, for example, might take note that a little one is getting tired – and in danger of carelessly damaging a furrow – so she sends him back to the village to fetch a gourd of water (Polak 2012: 100).

I want to emphasize that anthropologists would not consider any of these scenes to reflect child "labor." On the contrary, with few exceptions, we see work leavened by play. Indeed, "the separation of work and play (labor and leisure), which is characteristic of industrialized societies, is frequently absent in non-industrialized cultures" (Schwartzman 1978: 5). In a village near Kisoro, southern Uganda, I watched a curious game of tag. Four girls carrying infants held to their backs by a length of cloth chased each other around a cleared area. To "tag" someone, your baby had to touch their baby. Of course, if you ran or tagged too vigorously, your charge might start crying, ending your participation. Young Kipsigis (also in East Africa) shepherds play tag among their flocks while tree-climbers still keep a wary eye on their charges below (Harkness and Super 1986: 99). Further examples include:

[Great Whale Eskimo girls] like to go in groups to get wood and berries; the journey becomes a pleasant interlude. (Honigmann and Honigmann 1953: 40)

The [Chiga] herd-boy is learning the man's approach to work, relaxed and leisurely and broken by jokes or a song. (Edel 1957/1996: 177–178)

Foraging of the young is for the Zafimaniry an adventurous but not a serious form of activity . . . a form of play. Consequently the product of such activity, although it is very important nutritionally and economically, is not, nor in their evaluation should it be, taken seriously. (Bloch 1988: 28)

In the Sudan, children capture birds with nets and consume or sell their catch. However, bird trapping was pursued for its own intrinsic value and not for economic gain or to provide household subsistence. (Katz 1986: 48)

[On Madagascar, Mikea children] learn at their own leisurely pace. Their objectives when foraging may be primarily social and recreational. (Tucker and Young 2005: 169)

On the other hand, in many areas, this may be changing and children's contributions are becoming more critical. The robustness of the chore curriculum is amply demonstrated by its adoption as the village economy is modernized. By that I mean that the structure of the chore curriculum transfers to commercial farming. For example, in the Guatemala coffee industry, children make varied and critical contributions. The youngest plant seeds in small plastic bags to germinate new plants; they also collect coffee cherries that have fallen to the ground at harvest. Somewhat older children are responsible for weeding and spreading chalk. Twelve-to-fifteen-year-old boys are responsible for spraying urea as a fertilizer and assisting with the trimming, which may involve climbing plants to lop off branches with a machete. All help with harvesting and sorting the cherries. Agile boys are only too happy to climb into the branches to collect the fruit that adults cannot reach (Ruiz 2011b: 169–171; see also de Suremain 2000: 234).

The reader might well ask, "How is this different from the bean farming scenario described earlier?" I would say the main difference is that the coffee pickers can't choose *not* to participate, whereas there appears little compulsion in the children's involvement with bean cultivation. This is a representative statement: "Respect for the individual and his right to make work choices underlies Chiga treatment of young children" (Edel 1957/1996: 178). However, we must acknowledge that, in societies where traditional subsistence practices are very labor-intensive, where there are many mouths to feed, where taxes are levied, and where globalization reduces the value of adult labor, children's choices (and playtime) will be constrained. This is due to the fact that "parents exercise a considerable amount of coercive control over [their] time" (Bock 2002b: 211).

In several rural enterprises, including coffee growing and quarrying, children may receive no direct compensation for their work, but in other industries they may earn a wage, however meager. Children play a critical role in petty industries in Madagascar. Betsileo girls and women do the heavy labor of carrying stacks of sun-dried bricks (made from clay deposited in valleys) up a steep, zig-zag path to a ridge-top kiln (Figure 24, p. 272). The kiln is situated adjacent to a highway, facilitating the sale of the bricks. A standard load for a girl is ten bricks. Each round trip may take upwards of thirty minutes and, in a day, she will earn around US$1. Girls may be quite willing to take on these labors to earn pocket money, to help their families, and to pay for their education. Meanwhile, since the girls are earning money, their brothers are conscripted to do their "usual" chores such as infant-care (Figure 25, p. 273). In another Malagasy village, I found two boys, barely into their teens, working (without protection of any kind) with molten aluminum, melted down from recycled beverage cans and turned, in a mini-foundry, into aluminum cookware (Figure 26, p. 274).

A similar dynamic has been described in the Katanga area of the Democratic Republic of Congo. Families with as many as ten living children find they have no alternative but to employ their very young (age five and up) children in "artisanal" mining (André and Godin 2013). One of the reasons for the ease with which child "labor" has become a worldwide phenomenon of vast proportion is that it sits on a firm foundation of the ubiquitous chore curriculum.

To return to traditional subsistence patterns, the next section reviews children's acquisition of foraging (gathering, hunting, fishing) skill sets. The learning curve seems steeper in societies that depend entirely or primarily on foraging. For example, route-finding or navigation (Hill and Hurtado

Figure 24 Malagasy girl carrying bricks to the kiln

Figure 25 Malagasy boy as sib-caretaker

1996: 223) may be involved – skills unrequired for gardening or herding.[10] Still, the basic principles of the chore curriculum still apply.

Progress in the chore curriculum: foraging

When the [Buton] child practices angling on the reef flat, he is catching fish that are consumed by household members and this serves, at least in part, as his motivation. (Vermonden 2009: 218)

---

[10] Excepting, of course, long-distance movement of herds across relatively featureless landscapes, such as Sahara camel caravanning (Spittler 1998) and sub-Arctic reindeer herding (Istomin and Dwyer 2009).

Figure 26 Malagasy boys working with aluminum

In foraging, there is a range of graded tasks corresponding to the difficulty of the terrain and the challenge of finding and extracting edibles. For example, among the Biyaka, "gathering honey and termiting are considered too difficult (and dangerous) for children and are [not] practiced until late adolescence" (Neuwelt-Truntzer 1981: 138). With respect to terrain, we might contrast the !Kung with the Huaorani. In the former case, the terrain is extremely difficult and foragers face the threat of predation. Women cannot carry the extra water the children need to avoid dehydration (Howell 2010: 31). Hence, children are left behind in camp and don't begin their foraging careers until their teens (Hames and Draper 2004; see also Kogel *et al.* 1983). The terrain in the second case is somewhat more benign, and children as young as three are encouraged to join in (also true for the Aka – Hewlett *et al.* 2011: 1172; and Baka – Neuwelt-Truntzer 1981: 147), bringing their own small gathering basket (Rival 2000: 116). Earlier, the Hadza were cited, among whom even very young children successfully collect edible fruits and tubers (Marlowe 2010: 156). Hadza girls begin using the digging stick and carrying sack – primary tools for gathering – by age two but are only permitted to accompany adult gatherers from age eight, when their learning is enhanced through observing those more expert (Marlowe 2010: 80, 158). Similarly, children on the island of Mer in the Torres Straits can collect edible marine life from the shoreline and shallows. They can be seen "spearfishing with toddler-sized spears as soon as they begin walking, using them at first to spear sardines along the foreshore for bait." However while some types of collecting can be mastered quickly at an early age, others take more strength, and mature production levels are achieved later in childhood (D. W. Bird and R. B. Bird 2002: 262, 245).[11]

Hunting presents some unique challenges. Unlike so many other subsistence tasks where children are welcome to tag along, observe, and learn, they are a distinct liability on the hunt. Left behind because they are noisy, slow, and impatient (!Kung – Howell 2010: 30; Penan – Puri 2005: 233–234), "opportunities for observational learning [on Ache or Yora bow hunts] are limited" (Sugiyama and Chacon 2005: 259; see also Boyette 2013: 79). Effective hunting tools, such as the blow-pipe, "are difficult to make" (Huaorani – Rival 2000: 117). Hunting success may be dependent on strength, size, and stamina levels beyond the capacity of children (Gurven *et al.* 2006: 459).

But there are work-arounds for these problems. Recall the play stage: Hadza boys "get their first bows by about three-years-old and thereafter spend hours every day in target practice, often shooting at a gourd on the ground" (Marlowe 2010: 157; see also Hewlett *et al.* 2011: 1174). While adults might scorn small rodents, insects, reptiles, and birds as unworthy of attention, hunting them is little different in principle than hunting antelope. Boys thus can begin the hunting curriculum quite early – observing, tracking, and targeting these small creatures (Apache – Goodwin and Goodwin 1942: 475; Baka – Higgens 1985: 101; !Kung – Shostak 1981: 83). For tools, prospective hunters are typically given well-made but scaled-down bows and arrows (Cheyenne – Grinnel 1923: 114; Yanomamo – Peters 1998: 90–91), often by an older brother. A Huaorani boy is given a small blow-pipe to practice with at

---

[11] For a thorough discussion of the interaction of physical size and dexterity with experience and learning in the child's movement through the chore curriculum, see Bock (2010).

the same time he's encouraged to learn to make his own blow-pipe, so the complementary skills are learned simultaneously (Rival 2000: 117). While adult role models may not be available, older brothers seem quite happy to show off their skills for the edification of their juniors (Asabano – Little 2011: 155; Biyaka – Neuwelt-Truntzer 1981: 133; Penan – Puri 2005: 280). As the boys gain patience and discretion, they may be invited along on more casual "practice" sessions while observing the adult hunters (Puri 2005: 233–4). They justify their presence by taking care of the dogs (Inuit – Matthiasson 1979: 74) or some other auxiliary chore (!Kung – West and Konner 1981: 167). And boys are free to listen and learn as "real" hunters recount their experiences back in the village after the hunt (Tayanin and Lindell 1991: 14), even though – as noted for the Siberian Yukaghir – the hunters have no pedantic intent and make no adjustment for the rudimentary knowledge of the aspirant hunters (Willerslev 2007: 169).

So – as with bean cultivation – we can detect the stages of the hunting curriculum, as among the Apache:

[Boys of eight] started hunting . . . some small creature such as a bird or lizard [learning in company with] others of [their] own age on miniature hunting parties . . . By twelve . . . they were hunting quail, rabbits, squirrels, and wood rats, all of which could be used for food. At puberty the average boy was an accurate shot and knew all there was to know about hunting small game. When the occasional quail drives were held, old and young of both sexes joined, but boys were particularly active . . . it was not until after puberty, at fifteen or sixteen, that a boy was taken out on his first deer hunt by his father . . . or some other relative . . . youths . . . fetched wood and water for the camp and looked after the horses, at the same time gaining experience by being with skilled hunters. They received the less choice portions of the kill when the meat was divided – and they learned much of what they ultimately would know about hunting from observation without direct instruction. (Goodwin and Goodwin 1942: 475)

Still, fully adult prowess may only be achieved after years of actual hunting, during which the hunter learns "animal behavior . . . reading spoor, footprints, blood trails, wind and, stealth" (Marlowe 2010: 154; see also Blurton-Jones 2005: 107; Gurven *et al.* 2006: 463; MacDonald 2007: 391; Shostak 1981: 84).

Lastly, we might consider the closely related fishing curriculum. As with hunting, children may be considered a threat to the success of the enterprise and prevented from "tagging along" (Bonerate – Broch 1990: 85; Tapajós – Medaets 2011: 5). Yet they still manage to "pick it up." On the small, scattered islands of Micronesia, villagers enjoy a rich diet of marine products. Palauans name 300 distinct species, and can describe dozens of capture techniques.[12]

---

[12] Elsewhere in the Pacific, ethnographers have also recorded the huge information store a competent fisher must acquire and accompanying folk wisdom that may take years to master fully (Mandok Island – Pomponio 1992; Ponam Island – Lancy 1983; Wogeo Island – Hogbin 1946).

As Johannes documents, becoming expert may take years. On Tobia, boys began fishing at seven. Prior to the introduction of metal, fishhooks were precious and a boy first practiced with a baited line. Or the line would be looped and used to lasso small creatures in tide-pools. This long period of intense, small-scale exploration developed both dexterity and a broad knowledge of the marine environment. Working diligently, a boy might gradually master the art of making fishhooks from shell and bone. The final stage, reached in late adolescence, involved learning how to cast out beyond the reef crest to catch larger fish living on the outer reef slope. However, many specialized fishing techniques were considered private property, jealously guarded. Still, a young man was expected to attempt to "steal" them and advance in the fishers' pecking order (Johannes 1981: 88–89).

The Butonese (Sulawesi) fish with traps and youngsters can safely accompany trap-fishers, when they learn from observation. By eight they're trapping independently but still learning to make the traps, which also occurs via observation and self-initiated trial and error. This sequence – (1) observing; (2) then doing; (3) later, learning to make the materials; (4) learning to handle the boat; and (5) acquiring knowledge of where the best fishing grounds are – applies to all of the varied fishing methods practiced on the island. Fishers do not play the role of instructor, especially for particular, unique skill sets. Rivals attempted to learn tuna fishing from La Sidu "but he restricted access to it [because] ... being recognized as an expert in a fishing technique is a significant component of one's social identity within the village community" (Vermonden 2009: 220). A thorough study of Samoan youth learning to fish retells a, by now, familiar tale:

The observational and interview data suggest that learning how to fish occurs by observing the actions of an adult or more experienced adolescent at close proximity on several occasions, regardless of the fishing method employed. Older children (generally ten years or older) would then borrow the adult's fishing equipment and attempt to go fishing on their own without any adult supervision ... children observed were moderately skilled [with] one or more of these methods. When asked how they learned to do so, each indicated that they had at first observed the actions of a skilled fisherman and then had repeatedly tried to imitate their actions on their own, and with some practice, began to successfully catch fish. (Odden and Rochat 2004: 44–45).

The chore curriculum, then, is remarkably successful in moving children from a state of dependency to one where they are both self-sufficient and contributors to the domestic economy. From the foregoing, it should be obvious that the chore curriculum can be highly individualized. That is, slow and fast learners can be readily accommodated, as can those with latent talent in some areas only.[13] This flexibility also extends to the intensity of effort. Typically, kids are expected to be kids, to mix in play with their work (Danielsson 1952: 121). However, this great flexibility also facilitates accelerated transition through the chore curriculum toward self-sufficiency. What happens when children are forced to "grow up early"?

Children as a reserve labor force

This relative freedom may be curtailed, when, in the absence of a sister of the appropriate age, a boy may find himself conscripted for child care or other "women's work." (Ember 1973: 425–426)

Children ... were ... the most accomplished and versatile workers of the farming frontier. (West 1992: 30)

Scholars of human evolution, when they take note of children, see the prolonged period of dependency and the long-delayed onset of puberty and mating as providing a sheltered learning environment. Scholars reason that the human adaptive model requires the gradual acquisition of a large repertoire of increasingly more challenging skills. They offer an impressive catalog of the enormous variety of wild resources of which humans have taken advantage through a dazzling array of often Rube-Goldberg-worthy capture, collection, and processing strategies (Kaplan *et al.* 2000: 156). The implication is that children must be busy learning these survival skills for *years* prior to mastery. However, there has been a rapidly accumulating series of studies – of child foragers in particular – that show what we might call precocity in learning to forage. Many of these studies actually quantify the time children spend in learning and their productivity measured in kilocalories of food acquired. The Birds' work on Mer Island in the Torres Straits is representative:

Four-year old children ... don't really forage: they have knowledge of appropriate reef prey, but they are easily distracted and spend time pursuing items that are inedible or associated with extremely low foraging returns. They are also extremely slow and tire easily when the substrate is difficult to negotiate ... they may play the role of retriever in picking up [mollusks] spotted by adults ... The learning process involves little or no direct adult instruction [rather, by foraging] in groups with older children, observing intently their prey choice and processing strategies ... *by age six, children have become fairly efficient foragers.* (D. W. Bird and R. B. Bird 2002: 291, emphasis added)

---

[13] One important issue that has gone largely unexamined is the inevitable variation in "end-state." Spittler makes very clear from his studies of the Touareg that there is much variation in motivation and competency among adult herders (Spittler 2012: 79). But we really don't have descriptions of the social dynamics of "mediocrity" in child learners – outside contemporary schools (Chapter 9).

Children begin spearfishing with toddler-sized spears as soon as they begin walking [and those] that choose to invest in spearfishing practice *reach the same efficiency as the most practiced adult by ages ten–fourteen*. (R. B. Bird and D. W. Bird 2002: 262, emphasis added)

The Birds conclude: "How much experience do Meriam children need before they become efficient reef foragers? Evidently very little" (D. W. Bird and R. B. Bird 2002: 291). Other studies with similar findings include: young Martu children hunt (and survive on) goanna lizards (Bird and Bird 2005); Hadza four-year-olds gather (and eat) quantities of baobab fruits (Blurton-Jones *et al.* 1997); Zapotec children have a "precocious" command of ethnobotany (Hunn 2002); Ache girls match adult women's foraging returns by the age of ten to twelve (Hill and Hurtado 1996: 223); Samoan ten-year-olds fish successfully using a variety of methods (Odden and Rochat 2004: 45); "the knowledge and skill necessary for effective hook and line, net, and bow fishing seem to develop rapidly [in Yora children]" (Sugiyama and Chacon 2005: 257); !Kung boys are considered successful hunters and have been feted for bagging their first large mammal at least ten years before they marry (Shostak 1981: 84); and Kutenai boys at ten are able to bring down a bison calf with bow and arrow (Dawe 1997: 307). A survey of children's contribution to subsistence in sixteen communities across the spectrum of subsistence types showed great variation, from approximately one half-hour of work per day (!Kung) to 9.6 hours (Ariaal pastoralists). The variability within subsistence types was also wide:

Forager children show both high and low participation in economic activities, suggesting that children's work effort varies with factors other than whether a child is a forager, agriculturalist or pastoralist per se. (Kramer and Greaves 2011: 308)

These studies cast considerable doubt on the need for a lengthened childhood in order to learn subsistence skills (Blurton-Jones and Marlowe 2002: 199). We should also take note of the fact that while humans take many years to reach physical maturity, brain growth – critical for learning one's culture – is essentially complete by age seven (Bogin 1999: 130).

I believe that the solution to this apparent paradox lies in the elastic nature of human ontogeny (Bernstein *et al.* 2012: 398).[14] It is very clear from the

---

[14] The biological phenomenon is referred to as *phenotypic plasticity*. It represents the idea that organisms can change in response to environmental forces (West-Eberhard 2003: 34–35). "Evidence for plasticity and 'reserve capacity' is readily noted in primates as orangutans, gorillas and bonobos use tools with dexterity and sophistication in captivity but rarely use them in the wild" (King 1994: 121). Reserve capacity (RC) is also evident in the human growth pattern, in which the growing child overshoots the necessary capacity to begin reproducing (Crews 2003). And RC can "be channeled into trade-offs between greater growth, immune function, mating behavior, and/or reproduction and parental investment" (Bogin 2013: 34).

literature, as just discussed, that children can acquire subsistence skills quite early. It is also the case that their application of those skills in a significant way to support themselves and close kin may occur early or very late in childhood (Hewlett and Hewlett 2013: 77).[15] Under certain circumstances children might well ratchet up their productivity quickly and execute efficiently those skills they've been perfecting through playful work.

Many of those circumstances can be readily envisioned. Crittenden and colleagues found that variability in foraging effort by Hadza children was not simply a function of age but reflected individual motivation and family dynamics, such as a parent's disability (Crittenden *et al.* 2013) or death (see Bamana – Polak 2011: 142; Tonga – Bass 2004: 83; Yora – Sugiyama and Chacon 2005: 237). Less drastically, a mother suddenly burdened with a new baby will immediately shift some of her work on to her older children (Turke 1988). When the father is absent (military service, employment at a distance, trading), children's work should increase and we can expect to see a reallocation of role assignments, with boys assigned alloparenting duties (Stieglitz *et al.* 2013: 9). Similarly, when adolescents leave the household to pursue personal opportunities, we can expect to see younger children in the household take up the slack (Kim and Chun 1989: 176; White 2012: 81):

> In early industrialization the number of children working and the number working in factories both increased, while the age at which they started work decreased ... Older children were gaining independence [and leaving home] earlier, leaving younger siblings to augment family incomes. (Horrell and Humphries 1995: 485)

Recall the discussion in Chapter 2 of child circulation, whereby households with extra child workers donate them to households with too few.

We might also consider that children face trade-offs just as adults do. Trade-offs might be between work and play, between food acquisition and sib-care, between learning new skills and producing more, and between working for one's family and going to school (Bock 2002b, 2010; Clement 1997: 16; Obendick 2013: 105). Yora juveniles from the Peruvian Amazon tend to invest greater effort in fishing – in which they are quite productive – than in hunting, in which their productivity remains low until they've achieved adult levels of strength and knowledge of the forest (Sugiyama and Chacon 2005: 260).[16] Tsimané forager-horticulturalists of Bolivia are

---

[15] It is likely that Pleistocene foragers enjoyed much better nutrition than contemporary hunter-gatherers. The juvenile period may have been shorter (Blurton-Jones 2006: 252), and healthier, stronger, larger juveniles would have been able to capitalize on their skill set at an earlier age.

[16] Just the reverse seems to be true for Hadza boys, who invest more time in seeking out flashier foods than more mundane collecting: "running about in the woods trying to hunt and find honey is more fun than digging and picking and taking stuff home to mom" (Blurton-Jones *et al.* 1997: 306).

able to maintain very high fertility in part because of children's substantial contributions to the family food supply (Stieglitz *et al.* 2013: 2). On Victoria Island, Inuit boys who are first-born or early-born "produce more meat than later-born males [and] provide significant amounts of food to their parent's larders" (Collings 2009: 370). Quite recently in Tibet, there has been an explosion of demand for a worm-like fungus used in herbal medicine. "Children, with keen eyes and low-to-the-ground statures, are often the best pickers," and their schooling has been proportionally curtailed (Finkel 2012: 119).

The argument I'm making is that children, from an early age, acquire a level of skill in childcare, domestic service, foraging, and the like that they do not fully capitalize on, and this is particularly true in some foraging societies, such as the Aka and !Kung. This *reserve capacity* (RC) is analogous to the well-documented physiological RC (Bogin 2009: 567, 2013: 34). Collectively, we can see the children in a family or community as a *reserve labor force* that can be called into service. The ethnographic record yields several examples of culturally sanctioned reserve labor. On Palau, fourteen-to-fifteen-year-olds – who otherwise led pretty carefree lives – joined clubs. One of the functions of these clubs was to provide occasional community service (Barnett 1979: 32). Baining adolescents "are called upon to contribute to collective work parties, where a big job is done in one day" (Fajans 1997: 93), while Javanese youth are expected to work during the harvest, and their labor may be donated to a collective undertaking such as clearing irrigation ditches or house-raising (Jay 1969: 35, 69).

History is replete with examples in which an entire generation of children is conscripted. After the plague of 1348, much younger children were employed in Marseille, as they filled jobs previously occupied by older individuals who'd perished (Michaud 2007). In the 1960s, the Ik – who made their living as foragers in the remote north of Uganda – were forced from their hunting grounds by the creation of a national park. Unused to sedentary living and farming (and the land they were allocated was only marginally productive), they struggled to survive. Children were "put out" at three and forced to find their own food (Turnbull 1992: 135). Industrialization and urbanization through the eighteenth and nineteenth centuries created a demographic pattern whereby a single/widowed woman had to cope with a large brood, and her "children's ability to earn their keep provided the indispensable margin of subsistence" (Mintz 2004: 142). The youngest "scavenged for wood or coal ... scoured the docks for ... goods that could be used at home" or engaged in "pilfering" (Mintz 2004: 142). Diaries and ethnohistories record the experiences of Japanese children before and after World War II. They assisted in cultivating garden plots and begged in the streets. Entirely without guidance or encouragement, they learned to forage and brought home a wide array of edibles.[17] For example, one informant described how "she and the other village children came up with a novel way to fish for snails using a straw [and] mothers boiled the snails for dinner" (Piel 2012: 407).

Not only necessity but opportunity has led families to activate the reserve labor force. I discussed at some length in Chapter 2 the eagerness with which parents sought industrial employment for their children while resisting child labor laws and compulsory schooling. A striking but little-known instance of the reserve labor force played out in the North American West (Rollings-Magnusson 2009) during the "pioneer era." "In 1877, Curt and Mary Norton left their Illinois farm to homestead near Fort Larned in western Kansas, and with them came their eight children" (West 1992: 31). Very large families were essential for the enormous task of "taming" the frontier. Children willingly pitched in to help out wherever they were needed, and they were largely self-taught. From numerous diaries we can construct a picture of children farming, managing stock, hunting, fishing, marketing, transporting foods – largely on their own. And children also contributed to family survival through wage employment: "Nine-year-old Cliff Newland was hired to haul supplies every week to cowboys in line camps, a round-trip of seventy–five miles. Cliff knew that the pay – fifty cents a day – helped him and his widowed father pay for necessities on their small West Texas ranch" (West 1992: 37). Throughout much of the developing world, "street children" may share a portion of their earnings with families. In some rural villages in Bangladesh, these remittances constitute over a third of the family budget (Conticini 2007: 87).

Members of the emerging sect who called themselves Latter-Day Saints took this process a step further by promoting polygyny (multiple fecund wives regularly impregnated by a single patriarch), so anxious were they to populate the heretofore uninhabited (except by the native people, of course) inter-mountain West (Harris 1990: 196). But homesteaders in the nineteenth and early twentieth century did not have to depend entirely on their own fertility to increase the farm labor supply.[18] Known as the "largest children's migration in history," so-called "orphan trains" carried about 200,000 children (Warren 2001: 4) from orphanages and foundling homes in eastern coastal cities to families in the Midwest (Kay 2003: iii) and West. The orphan trains continued until 1929 (Warren 2001: 20), which indicates how very recently our fundamental conception of children as chattel changed to viewing them as cherubs.

---

[17] There is a body of research that supports the notion that children are "natural" foragers and do not need to be taught or even shown how it's done (Chipeniuk 1995: 492; Heth and Cornell 1985: 216; Zarger 2002).

[18] Two hundred plus years earlier children were swept off the streets of London and "deported to Virginia to provide labor, to sanitize London society, and to infuse the colony with the growth potential that these children embodied" (Barrett 2014: 162).

In the next section, we'll return to the survey of children learning the practical skills characteristic of their society; in this case, those of various crafts.

Learning crafts

The production of the flake axe from Hundvåg [Mesolithic era] shows signs of random, poorly planned knapping ... the edge was damaged by a succession of failed strokes, and finally the axe was discarded ... The knapper understood the concept of the production and the desired final shape, but lacked the practical skill needed to complete it. (Dugstad 2010: 70)

The view that one learns [Berber weaving] by simply being around weavers is pervasive. (Naji 2012: 374)

For the past hundred years in the West, ideas like a standardized curriculum in a state-supported school with compulsory attendance have been widely accepted as reflecting good economic and social policy. The state takes responsibility for insuring that every child – irrespective of his talents or his motivation – should be "educated" to some, officially determined, level. However, when first introduced, these ideas were strongly resisted. Parents may seek a greater return on their investment by putting children to work rather than sending them to school (Neill 1983: 48). A second objection is less obvious and that is the belief that, for advanced and less commonly practiced skills, children must be allowed to display the proper aptitude and willingness to learn before a skilled practitioner/teacher should take time to guide them. When a Conambo (Ecuadorian Amazon) potter feels the child has shown the appropriate motivation and level of maturity, she may incorporate the child's efforts into her own production, giving them a bowl to paint or taking one they've shaped and painting it for them (Bowser and Patton 2008).

I was surprised to discover that, in Gbarngasuakwelle, there is a gulf between the chore curriculum and what we might call the craft curriculum. The former is often compulsory – a child may be severely chastised or beaten for failure to complete appropriate chores satisfactorily. The latter is not only entirely voluntary, but children seem to be offered little encouragement in it. Indeed, they may be actively discouraged from trying to learn a craft or otherwise complex trade. I explored this issue at considerable length with my Kpelle informants in order to understand their perspective. First, they tend to treat craft skills as having some fungible value and, indeed, it is customary to make a token gift to an expert practitioner when seeking guidance or advice. Among the Coast Salish "certain skills are so highly valued that to try and emulate an expert without his or her blessing is treated as theft" (Barnett 1955: 110).

Second, there is the sense that the learner must go very far on her own observing, trying, and practicing diligently before an expert – even her own mother – will consent to critique or correct her handiwork (Lancy 1996: 149–150). And I don't think the Kpelle are especially callous or indifferent to aspirant craftspeople; I believe their perspective is quite typical. A Talensi cap maker told Meyer Fortes: "he learned his craft, as a youth ... by carefully watching [a capmaker] at work. When he was young, he explained, he had 'very good eyes'" (Fortes 1938/1970: 23). For girls learning crafts, self-guided, voluntary learning is usual:

A [Chiga] girl will ... take up the art of weaving baskets when and as it pleases her to do so. Her mother or sister will ... never say, "Make it tighter," or "Set the awl higher" ... they will not slow down the process or guide her hand. Should the beginner find the process discouraging and the trials unsatisfactory, she may abandon the whole effort, to renew it again at some later date, or perhaps to forget it altogether. (Edel 1957/1996: 179)

Meta, a young [Telefol] woman ... talked about the way in which she acquired looping skills. "I used to watch my mother ... making her *bilum* [string bag] One day ... while she went to the garden to work I took her *bilum*. I'd been watching her hands carefully and wanted to try myself. But I ... messed up her looping. I saw I'd done it all wrong and was frightened and put her *bilum* down. Then I ran away ... to hide in the bush. Later, when my mum came back it was really hard work for her to undo what I had done and she wanted to hit me." (MacKenzie 1991: 102)

But there is considerable variability in the acquisition process. Patty Crown's survey of twenty-five societies in which pottery making is an important activity found that in half the cases, children acquired their craft entirely through observation and practice. Puebloan girls in the southwestern US took the initiative to learn the craft, observing and imitating their mothers or other competent female relatives. Girls were discouraged from pursuing ceramics until they'd mastered all the "mandatory" chores associated with the domestic sphere. Adults spared little time to serve as teachers.

Questioning was discouraged, and if brief instructions were given, they were offered only once. Adults are quoted as stating that children understood the process more thoroughly when they learned through trial and error ... Learning apparently followed a sequence that mirrored the production process ... with the progression largely driven by the child's interest and skill level. There is no mention of children aiding adults in making or decorating pots. (Crown 2002: 109; see also Sillar 1994: 52)

Complementary surveys of Puebloan ceramics from museum collections fill in more details of the picture. Children seem to have started out in the play stage making toy figurines and vessels from clay.[19] Measuring fingerprints left on them, one can determine that the youngest artisans may have been four years old (Kamp 2002: 87). In a small number of cases, evidence of high and lower skill on the same vessel suggests joint adult–child production. In skillfully made vessels, children might contribute by doing the simpler part of the decoration, thus enhancing the adult's output. In well-made vessels with childish decoration, Crown avers: "The finished pieces were not enhanced by the child's contribution. Indeed, the degree of adult effort on these vessels suggests indulgence of young children or attempts to keep them occupied rather than instruction" (Crown 2002: 117).

In Africa also, pottery making is often practiced exclusively by women and, in at least one ethnic group in Cameroon, it is restricted to the wives and daughters of blacksmiths. In more conservative areas, mothers train their daughters via a formal apprenticeship that begins as early as seven and ends, with a ceremony, at about fifteen: "the 'newborn' potter is blessed by her parents in front of the community members and receives her own tools" (Wallaert-Pêtre 2001: 475). In effect, mothers benefit from their daughters' production until they lose them to marriage. However, culture change may dramatically impact this process. In another Cameroonian pottery-making area, many pottery-making traditions had disappeared as young women began producing ceramics *for sale*.[20]

Here, anyone can learn to make pottery, and [most of] the female population practices it. Training ... lasts an average of two years ... and no particular ritual marks the end of the learning period ... [Fali] potters were always ready to attempt new tasks, even if they knew they did not have the ability to succeed ... believ[ing] that something can be learned even through failure ... Personal gratification is important and overrides the judgment of other potters ... leading to a diversity of production and style. (Wallaert-Pêtre 2001: 476, 483, 489)

A strikingly parallel case has been documented by Patricia Greenfield and colleagues among Tzotzil Maya weavers in the Chiapas Highlands (Greenfield *et al.* 1995).[21] In this area, women weave, and, traditionally, mothers actively trained their daughters,[22] using methods handed down over generations, to

[19] There is evidence of a play stage in every area of craftwork (Huang 2009: 85).
[20] Nyarafolo pottery production has undergone a similar transformation (Köhler 2012: 118).
[21] No case of craft skill acquisition has been so thoroughly studied. Another interesting finding is that traditional weaving is undertaken in a kneeling position, so, from an early age, girls mimic the kneeling posture of older women as they care for babies and prepare food. This early and persistent posture facilitates a physical adaptation that maintains the ease with which kneeling can be sustained (Maynard *et al.* 1999).
[22] My sense is that the direct instruction observed earlier in Greenfield's work in Chiapas is rare. More typically, "children are not taught to spin or weave. Rather, they observe family members who have mastered these crafts and imitate them directly" (Bolin 2006: 99).

produce a limited repertoire of essential items. The approach recognized the need to create steps – by providing appropriately sized tools, for example – for the child to make a gradual ascent to mastery (Greenfield 2004: 49). The substitution of cheap, machine-made clothing for locally woven items, coupled with tourist demand for new products and innovative styles, led to the emancipation of young weavers.[23] They now master the art through their own trial and error, only occasionally seeking a mother's input. In fact, the mother may no longer be the primary role model, as girls are free to observe and emulate other women and peers (Greenfield 2004). It appears that young weavers also market their own products, and, perhaps, the fruits of their skill now accrue more directly to themselves rather than primarily augmenting their mother's output as in the past.

The staged character of the chore curriculum is also very much present in craft learning:

Infants and young children play by the loom. [Daboya] boys are . . . asked to run simple errands [and they] delight in constructing toy looms from sticks and bits of thread the men save for them, and weaving lamp wicks . . . When a boy is judged ready to settle down and work on a regular basis, he is assigned to, or chooses, a weaver to work with and learn from . . . bobbin boys divide their time between weaving and doing chores like laying warp and winding bobbins . . . Gradually he spends more of his time weaving, and carries out more of the stages in the production of the cloth he weaves, until [he is handed] a basket of sticks of thread and expected to . . . produce the finished cloth. (Goody 1982a: 70–71)

Whether or not adult experts make themselves available to potential novices depends on how critical the particular skill set is to successful adaptation in the society. For the Penan, basket-making is practiced by nearly every adolescent and adult in the community. And novice basket-makers are encouraged by experts to seek their help in learning "how to weave more complicated designs without error" (Puri 2013: 282). Among the Warao, a canoe is essential to a man's livelihood and boys quite naturally begin an informal apprenticeship in which the emphasis is on observing every step of the canoe-making process and participating as skill develops.

After several seasons of helping his father with the more menial tasks that accompany this third stage of the production process . . . [he] is eventually permitted to step into the boat and insert the cross-beams to spread the hull. The father still determines the right temperature of the water and he indicates how far up a particular cross-beam must be

---

[23] Studies suggest that young craftspersons do not readily innovate in design or technique without some outside demand for different products (Iranian weavers – Tehrani and Collard 2009: 289; Huron potters – Smith 2006: 71).

pulled to reach the maximum point of tolerance, but he remains on the ground and directs the operation from either end of the hull. (Wilbert 1976: 324)

In another South American group, the Baniwa, the equivalent of the Warao canoe is the grater board – an item of great utility and symbolism that yields the maker social capital. "Boys must learn the craft of grater-board making from their fathers ... because making the board is the first act of marriage" (Chernela 2008: 145). By contrast, pottery making in Nyarafolo society is entirely elective. "Passing on knowledge ... is an open and dynamic social process. Learning takes place in public spaces in the sphere of pottery-making women, and this means many women contribute towards learning" (Köhler 2012: 135). Girls must take the initiative to observe patiently, to help with menial or routine aspects and to practice diligently. A woman will chase away inattentive or disruptive girls so she can "get on with her own work." Women may occasionally offer direction but there is no explanation offered or instruction *per se* (Köhler 2012: 128, 131).

Apprenticeship moves further along the continuum toward the kind of formal training that is ubiquitous in modern society. As discussed in earlier sections of the chapter dealing with chores and crafts, children learn informally. They observe and participate in the flow of work as they are motivated and able. This remains true for most skilled work such as weaving and pottery, but occasionally, these skills will be transmitted via an apprenticeship.

Apprenticeship

One Japanese term for apprenticeship is *minari*, literally one who learns by observation. (Singleton 1989: 29)

In spite of the fact that [masters] do not deliberately organize most of the learning activities of apprentices, there is considerable structure to the educational process that apprentices go through. (Lave 1982: 182)

The ... apprentice [Tukolor weaver] learns ... not only the necessary skills in weaving ... but also the mystical and religious aspects of craft lore. (Dilley 1989: 190)

In a survey of traditional apprenticeship, I sought to distinguish children learning crafts informally from the more structured and formal apprenticeship. For my analysis, apprenticeship was defined as a formal, contractual relationship between a master and a novice, of a specific duration, which is designed to serve two ends: to provide cheap labor (by the apprentice; Stella 2000: 31) and/or fees to support the master's enterprise, and to afford the apprentice an opportunity to learn and receive certification for mastery (Lancy 2012a: 213–214). In the apprenticeship, youth continue to learn through a step-wise, observation/imitation procedure; there is very little explicit instruction by a master[24] and almost no verbal interchange. Occasionally, a master potter may correct an apprentice by grabbing his hands and shaping/moving them in the correct way (Gowlland 2012: 363). But an apprenticeship adds new elements. One such element is that parents are expected to pay a fee up front to induce the master to accept their child (Lloyd 1953; 38). In ancient Rome, a father wanting his son to learn the weaving trade would pay a fee *and* his son's room and board. The son was "bound" for a year, unable to leave his master for this minimum term (Shelton 1998: 111–112).

In a typical apprenticeship, the master will probably *not* be the boy's father, because a common ingredient is the verbal and physical abuse of the apprentice by the master.[25] A parent is considered incapable of imposing the required level of discipline (Coy 1989: 120; Aronson 1989). Tukolor "fathers prefer that another weaver ... train their sons ... since they feel that they will not exert enough discipline in training" (Dilley 1989: 188). Gonja (Ghana) believe that familiarity breeds contempt and that sons wouldn't show sufficient respect toward their fathers to learn from them (Goody 2006: 254). More generally, the hierarchical relationship between master and apprentice is of paramount importance. It is constructed from the high standing and *in loco parentis* power of the master on the one hand, and the youth, low standing, and incompetence of the apprentice on the other. The role of apprentice has been compared to that of a bondsman or acolyte (Ghosh 1992: 260). The master's knowledge is considered to have great worth and the apprentice trades his or her labor (Wallaert 2008: 187–188) and obeisance (Jordan 1998: 49) for access to that knowledge.

The master may be quite harsh in his or her treatment of the apprentice. For example, the apprentice Dii potter can expect to be punished (made to eat clay) and humiliated for any and all mistakes, to insure public acknowledgment that the failure lies with the apprentice and not the master (Wallaert 2008: 190–192). Indeed, some of the earliest legal tracts relating to youth address violence by a master against an apprentice. Rawson discusses the case of a Roman shoemaker who strikes his apprentice with a shoe last, knocking out his eye. The action was considered justified on the basis that the intent was instructional (Rawson 2003: 194). An apprentice from ancient Athens complains that he is "perishing from being whipped ... tied

---

[24] The single exception: training to become a long-distance navigator in the Carolines – a process I would describe as very academic although with a large hands-on component as well (Gladwin 1970; Lancy 2008: 257–259).

[25] An extremely well-known proverb from ancient Egypt is "The student has ears on his back," meaning that to get through to him, the master must beat him.

up [and] treated like dirt" (Golden 2003: 14). This attitude maintained the hierarchical relationship and insured that apprentices were highly motivated. Typically implicit but sometimes quite explicit in the pedagogy of apprenticeship is the notion that skills learned easily, without stress or discomfort, are devalued.

Menial work in the earliest stage matches the apprentice's ability level, provides a kind of pre-payment for the apprenticeship opportunity, and, most importantly, offers a measure – for the master to evaluate – of the apprentice's level of motivation (Gowlland 2012: 362). To become a potter in Japan, according to John Singleton, requires "a single-minded, wholehearted dedication to the craft ... talent is to be developed through persistence, it is not considered ... inherited or innate" (Singleton 1989: 29).

The staged character of the experience is illustrated in the Yoruba blacksmith apprenticeship:

He assisted ... by pressing the bellows in the forge and by holding some of the equipment, while the blacksmith beat a piece of iron into shape. After he had watched the master do some work, the apprentice began to heat metal and to make small knives ... The apprentice [next] learned how to make big knives and cutlasses when he reached the age of fifteen years, but by the time he became an adult (about twenty-one years of age), he had acquired highly technical skills to make instruments like hoes, traps, guns, lamps and umbrellas. (Obidi 1995: 376)

In Tanon's thorough study of the Dioula (Ivory Coast) weaving apprenticeship, what is striking is the severe restriction imposed on what the apprentice can and cannot assay, compared to the relatively open access to learning opportunities in the chore curriculum. The novice weaver is constrained to advance his skill in "baby steps" to reduce the likelihood of mistakes that an expert would need to rectify. Hence, while the ethnographer apprentice learns to weave in an intense period of rapid development (Tanon 1994: 34),[26] the native apprentice at eight is preparing bobbins; a few years later he's weaving plain white bands on a loom an expert has set up for him. A year or two later finds him weaving patterned blankets of larger and larger dimensions until, perhaps at eighteen, the "apprentice will learn to set up his first warp under the close scrutiny of his master" (Tanon 1994: 26).

It is likely that the costly material and equipment employed dictate a very careful allocation of tasks to the apprentice.

---

[26] The majority of ethnographic accounts of apprenticeship derive from participant observation, in which the anthropologist rapidly learns a skill that the apprentice is expected to take years to master. I find this a subtle affirmation of the argument made throughout the chapter regarding the undemanding nature of the village curriculum. There are exceptions to this generalization in the few pre-modern societies that include an extremely complex and varied food-getting technology (Inuit – Boyd et al. 2011).

Production processes [in a tailor shop] have logic and order to them, and these shape apprentice learning activities ... it is more costly to make an error when cutting out a garment than when sewing it. Apprentices learn to sew garments before learning to cut out garments ... [they] work on small garments that can be made of scraps before items that take more, or more expensive fabrics ... [they] start on simple garments and gradually move on to more complicated ones. (Lave 1982: 181–183)

In the art of Japanese sushi making, the apprentice is forbidden to even touch the utensils, rice, fish, or other ingredients for the first few years of his training. He is allowed only to carefully observe the Sushi master and wash the dishes, until one day the master suddenly gives him permission to attempt his first sushi. It is no exaggeration to say that the apprentice produces exquisite sushi from the start. (Matsuzawa *et al.* 2001: 573)

One of the most interesting aspects of apprenticeship is the understanding that the master's expertise is at least partly due to his or her knowledge of secrets or lore and that this information is not willingly passed on to apprentices. The African blacksmith, in particular, is invested with special knowledge and may be empowered to perform certain rituals (Lancy 1980b). Peter McNaughton (1988: xvi), who served as a blacksmith's apprentice in Mali, describes the craft as floating "on a sea of secret expertise." Tukolor weaving lore "called *gandal* ... can be used ... to protect the weaver from spiritual forces associated with the craft and ... as a means of defense against the malicious intention of other ... weavers" (Dilley 1989: 195). None of this lore is freely given to the apprentice and a truly worthy apprentice, is expected to "steal" as much of these more subtle aspects of the craft as he can winkle out (Gladwin 1970: 72; Herzfeld 1995: 131; Jordan 1998: 56; Marchand 2001: 119). Indeed, he may hang on, continuing to work, gratis, in hopes of discovering vital secrets (Bledsoe and Robey 1986: 216).

To understand the distinct aspects of the apprenticeship – compared to other processes underlying the acquisition of particular skill sets – we must use two lenses: pedagogy and sociology. From the perspective of pedagogy, apprenticeship does not appear unique. Craft mastery includes, as we've seen: a play stage; observation of an expert at work and imitation by the novice; a laddered or staged sequence of sub-tasks; a great deal of trial and error; the demonstration of diligence and motivation on the novice's part, to attract the attention of the expert; and little or no verbal instruction or even structured demonstration by the expert. This suite of characteristics can be found in the informal transmission of crafts as well as the formal apprenticeship. This isomorphism helps us to understand why some anthropologists who've focused on apprenticeship have considered it as just another variation on the village-based informal learning – contrasted with schooling – pattern (Greenfield and Lave 1982; Singleton 1989). They have attended to the pedagogy of apprenticeship, ignoring the sociology.

The master's high standing adds another dimension to apprenticeship that comprises the inherent sociology. There is an economic aspect to the master's rank. Apprenticeship tends to be associated with more complex skill/valuable products vs. less complex skill/less valuable products, e.g. wheel-thrown (Singleton 1989) vs. coil-built pottery (Bowser and Patton 2008), superior- vs. inferior-quality stone beads (Roux *et al.* 1995), and metal tools (Obidi 1995) vs. floor mats (Lancy 1996). Apprenticeship usually implies an expensive infrastructure such as the blacksmith's forge, a tailoring shop with sewing machines, a large complex loom for large-scale textiles, or a potter's wheel and kiln (Gowlland 2012: 362). In Accra, "a sewing-machine [is] a substantial capital investment which inhibits widespread entrance to the trade" (Peil 1970: 139). Such expensive infrastructure precludes opportunities to "pick up" the necessary skills.

The crafts transmitted via an apprenticeship are/were of considerable economic significance compared to other crafts. These workshops produced critical goods of a refined quality. It was, therefore very much in the economic interest of masters to limit access to the craft, controlling the training to insure high, uniform standards and to limit competition. In more populous towns or cities with multiple practitioners of particular crafts, we can expect them to band together in guilds (Lloyd 1953). Guilds, historically, served the masters' needs at the expense of the apprentice (Kaplan 2007). Ethnographers and historians both stress the conservative nature of craft production when a formal apprenticeship is indicated. This suggests that these craftspersons must expect stable market conditions with little demand for innovative products. Where change and innovation are the rule, novices learn informally from multiple experts rather than a single master.

The craft master usually commands political and religious expertise or spiritual power above the ordinary. Indeed, many societies treat their most prized crafts as imbued with the divine (Stout 2002: 700). Among the Kpelle, the blacksmith is inevitably a respected diviner and ritual specialist (Lancy 1996). High craft skill combined with spiritual and social potency usually signal the necessity for esoteric cultural knowledge and folklore unique to the profession. To acquire this lore, and the high standing that it affords, the apprentice must bind himself to a master in a very formal apprenticeship.

The apprenticeship must shape aspirant craftspersons to enter an exalted profession. The process of socialization begins in the careful selection of the apprentice and the formal agreement, sealed with a fee or gifts. Where the informal crafts novice is free to abandon the pursuit (Edel 1996), the new apprentice is doubly obligated, to the master and to his own family, to conform to the demands of the apprenticeship. The apprentice's lack of autonomy to pursue particular avenues for his or her further development, such as assaying more challenging products – absent the master's approval – reinforces a psychological sense of dependency. The existence of important lore or "deep knowledge" that the apprentice is aware of but unable to access in any legitimate way can reinforce a sense of commitment and loyalty. In short, the socialization goals of apprenticeship are almost synonymous with the "Bush" school or adolescent initiation rite (Chapter 8), and, as I have argued previously, the primary purpose of this institution is indoctrination (Lancy 1975).

Apprenticeship addresses the need for those whose high social standing and wealth stem from the mastery of a relatively scarce and valued trade to transmit their knowledge and skill to the rising generation. At the same time they must avoid exposing themselves to the reputation- and income-reducing effects of potentially irascible youths in their midst. We see in the pedagogy of apprenticeship well-established practices that serve effectively to transmit the entire cultural repertoire down the generations. The socialization practices found in apprenticeship add a number of attributes to the mix and are designed to carefully integrate the youth into a closed fraternity or, failing that, to eject and effectively bar the failed aspirant.

8   Living in limbo

Introduction

Sexual ... repressions are quite unknown ... On moonlit nights young [Rairoans] ...
assemble in some glade in the palm forest for singing, dancing and amorous games.
(Danielsson 1952: 123)

Circumcision begins the process of separation from the old status known in Mende
as *kpowa* ... "fool, or stupid one" ... into the new status of responsible, informed adult.
(Day 1998: 65)

In humans, adolescence is associated with dramatic physiological change,
notably puberty and a rapid growth spurt (Bogin 1994). First menses is often
treated as an important milestone, sometimes triggering an elaborate series of
rites to mark the change in a young woman's status. Other physiological
markers may be treated as culturally salient.

The period of youth on Vanatinai begins at about age fourteen, or when the signs of
puberty ... are visible to onlookers. For a girl that is when her breast buds are noticeable,
"the size of betel nuts," and for a boy when his voice begins to change ... The term ...
for young females is *gamaina*, which translates literally as "child female." (Lepowsky
1998: 128)

But societies vary in the alacrity with which they crown the achievement of
biological maturity with the status of social maturity. In the West, the long
hiatus between puberty and marriage/family formation has spawned an entire
youth culture (Harris 1998: 275). And this culture has become so attractive that
Hine claims: "Ours is a culture that is perpetually adolescent: always becoming
but never mature" (Hine 1999: 10). Fernea, writing in the early 1990s, claimed
that by contrast, in the Muslim Middle East, "adolescence, as perceived in
modern Western thought, scarcely existed" (Fernea 1991: 453). In rural
Morocco, marriage follows soon after puberty and, with this rite of passage,
adulthood is conferred (Davis and Davis 1989: 59). Similarly, "Rural India
lacks an adolescent culture. The burden of adult responsibilities falls quickly
on young people" (Deka 1993: 132). Copper Inuit girls "would often be

married and performing many adult roles even before reaching sexual maturity" (Condon 1987: 67). The following analysis of adolescence in a Chinese fishing village fits thousands of villages around the globe:

> Problems of adolescent adjustment appear to be minimal, especially for boys ... children grow up with a clear idea of exactly what their place in the socio-economic system [will] be ... the necessary skills ... acquired gradually and at home; marriages ... arranged when the children were about sixteen years old ... the ceremony of marriage conferred adulthood publicly and without any doubt [giving] adolescent sexual activity both limitation and legitimation ... there were virtually no alternatives offered to adolescents, no choices they could make ... no sharp discontinuities at any stage. (Ward 1970: 115)

In most societies, however, a discernible gap appears between puberty and the age at which young people are considered competent to create a family and household, thus affording an adolescent period – however brief (Schlegel and Barry 1991: 18). Age of menarche or the onset of puberty ranges from twelve among wealthy, well-nourished Westerners through fourteen in poorer but reasonably well-nourished populations (Egypt) to seventeen in the least well-nourished areas (Nepal, Central Africa, New Guinea Highlands; Eveleth and Tanner 1990: 170). Further, during the past hundred years, with improved nutrition, the onset of menarche has steadily advanced (Goldstein 2011) – in Japan, for example, by a year each decade from 1950 onward (Eveleth and Tanner 1990: 171).

Adolescence is also affected by the nature of the subsistence system. In the previous chapter I noted that, in agrarian societies, children's economic contributions may be significant, childhood is curtailed, and adolescence might be brief. However, among foragers, children may not become nutritionally self-sufficient until their late teens, so one sees a distinct adolescent period (Hewlett 1992: 229–230). !Kung foragers don't reach puberty until their late teens and males rarely marry before their mid-twenties (Howell 2010: 31). However, we are unlikely to find a society that supports an adolescent period as long as that found among the modern executive class, typically a decade at least. Since the mid-1970s, the number of offspring aged over twenty still living at home has increased dramatically (56 percent of adolescents aged eighteen to twenty-four are living with parents in the USA; cf. Fry 2013). Demographers label this group "emerging adults," suggesting that, while they are biologically and legally adult, they are "unmarried, financially dependent and still being cared for by their parents" (Armstrong 2004). Similarly, Japan is now experiencing rapid growth in the population of "parasitic singles." By staying at home, older children save the cost of rent and continue to enjoy their mother's devoted service (Kingston 2004: 274).

A contemporary teenage "couple" is biologically capable of conceiving and bearing a child, and our legal system can confer legitimacy on their union.

Wealthy Western nations can insure that this young family has a roof over its head and doesn't starve. And, of course, the teenagers[1] themselves are driven by powerful forces to create and consummate sexual unions. Yet all these forces must somehow be held in check, particularly during the ever-lengthening "student" years (Arnett 2002: 321). This is incendiary material awaiting spontaneous combustion. And yet, it doesn't happen that often, because many societies go to enormous trouble to insure that teenagers are not giving free rein to their libidos. The result: a significant segment of the population lives in a state of limbo – neither child nor adult.

Hangin'

Many young Tongan boys are eager to move into the boys' huts, to be associated with the older boys, and to experience their comparative freedom. (Morton 1996: 112)

In most societies, boys and girls mingle freely during childhood until the pre-teen years. The Fore of Papua New Guinea are typical: "Up to about the age of seven years, the activities of both boys and girls were much the same" (Sorenson 1976: 191). However, at the beginning of middle childhood, children spontaneously segregate. "First the girls and then the boys show a decided preference for same-sex playmates during this 'gang stage'" (Weisfeld 1999: 113; see also Wilder 1970: 230). Also, from a very wide range of primate studies comes the common observation that juvenile males form a distinct subset of the troop. Juvenile females are attached to their mothers, eagerly seizing opportunities to allomother their younger siblings and groom high-ranking females (Baldwin and Baldwin 1977: 364), which might be future allies when they have offspring of their own. But the young males, chased away by higher-ranking males and females, find security and entertainment (they're play partners) in hanging out together (Mitchell 1981). Mature males want to protect their breeding rights, and females want to protect their young from the boisterous attentions of their clumsy older sons; hence, the juveniles form what amounts to an outcast cohort or gang. For their part, the young males don't seem to resent their outcast status; on the contrary, they relish it. Similarly, the literature on human adolescence is replete with cases like these:

[Ache] males of this age . . . often engage in obnoxious or high-risk behavior in order to gain attention. Although they often swagger in an exaggerated manner when among age mates or women and children, these adolescent boys also show clear signs of intimidation when fully mature adult males are present. (Hill and Hurtado 1996: 226)

---

[1] The term "teenager" dates only from World War II (Hine 1999: 223).

[Warao] groups occasionally form one-sex gangs and roam through the territory giving expression in various ways to adolescent *Sturm und Drang* [and this does] not make their parents happy. (Wilbert 1976: 325)

Young [!Kung] men are . . . referred to as "the owners of the shade" . . . and they may be resented by the older generation. (Howell 2010: 36)

Out of the range of parental authority, adolescents often revel in their independence, cultivating in-group norms, slang expressions, distinctive clothing styles, and so forth to further separate themselves from adults. If they have some disposable income, they can further isolate themselves in cars and other settings. A favorite ploy is to retreat behind a sound barrier of "music" that is insufferable to adults. The same adolescents often engage in a variety of delinquent behaviors, as though they have adopted the adolescent culture in favor of the adult one. (Weisfeld 1999: 106)

[Early medieval] Ireland suffered from the activities of gangs of lawless young warriors . . . They lacked the wealth to establish their own families, so they joined the *fian* . . . At around twenty years of age, often on the acquisition of an inheritance through the death of older male relatives, a young man would finally join the group of married property owners. (Crawford 1999: 162)

While societies may try and restrain this "anti-social" behavior, it may be accepted philosophically. In North America, the ultraconservative Amish sect permits males to "run wild" (*Rumspringa*) for a brief but necessary interlude just prior to marriage (Hostetler 1964: 192). One solution, in much of the Pacific and in parts of Africa (Read 1960: 94) as well, is to segregate adolescent males in dormitory-like accommodations. Among the Hopi, boys move into the *khiva*, or men's house (Schlegel and Barry 1991: 70). Other societies where boys, especially,[2] leave their homes to reside with other adolescents and/or senior males include the Tapirapé (boys move to the *takana*; Wagley 1977: 149); Igbo boys move to the bachelors' house (Ottenberg 1989: 49), Ngoni boys move to a dormitory (Read 1960: 94), Wogeo boys move into what Hogbin (1970: 103) refers to as a "clubhouse," Trobrianders move to the *bukumatula* (Malinowski 1929), and in the Sepik River area of Papua New Guinea, it is the *Haus Tambaran* (Tuzin 1980).

Even though these adolescent male associations may be referred to in the literature as "gangs" (Howard 1970), this may be misleading. While given a great deal of freedom, young Rotuman males, for example, "form the nucleus of communal labor in every village" (Howard 1970: 66–67). That is, while they hang out and have fun together, Rotuman youth also relish the solidarity

---

[2] One reason that boys are much more likely to be removed from their homes than girls and subjected to severe pain and privation during initiation – aside from toughening them up to be warriors – is the very widespread notion that boys cannot grow into men without the systematic removal of female essence acquired during gestation, birth, and infancy.

of working collectively for the community. Adolescent male associations can coalesce into civil defense forces on fairly short notice, as apparently happened on a regular basis in medieval Europe (Mitterauer 1992: 164).

Scholars have explored the adaptive value of such adolescent male groups. Proposed benefits of adolescent "dispersal" include "that the likelihood of close kin mating is reduced" (Schlegel and Barry 1991: 20). Another possibility occurs in societies where hunting is cooperative, a situation found among chimpanzees as well as among many human groups. In these cases, the close fraternal relations within a cohort of young males just might establish the coordinated reflexes that will yield significant caloric payoffs in adulthood (Sugiyama and Chacon 2005). Field experiments with chimpanzees in the Bossou forest of Guinea established that juveniles are less conservative and neophobic than adults and have been observed discovering and spreading useful innovations (Matsuzawa et al. 2001: 569–570; see also Whiten et al. 1999: 284). Successful hunting or, indeed, the opportunistic discovery of new food sources may be inherently risky. The juvenile group, human or non-human, travels away from "camp" in search of adventure, where they may find food – or a predator may find them.

Dozens of studies have documented the heightened likelihood of sensation-seeking (Zuckerman 1984) or risk-taking by adolescent primate males in groups. Demographers have identified an "accident hump" in mortality curves for male primates, including humans, during puberty (Goldstein 2011). As an example, sub-adult "vervet monkeys are more likely to approach humans in the field and also approach strange males, enter a new area, or approach novel objects than were younger monkeys or adults" (Burghardt 2005: 390). Among Japanese macaques, the adult sex ratio is five females to one male, and this is attributed entirely to males lost to risky behavior (Fedigan and Zohar 1997). Playful, rapid locomotion through a terrestrial environment, just like high-speed driving at night on winding roads, can have fatal consequences. Male-on-male fighting can result in injury or death (Walter 1987: 359). However, potential payoffs to the risk-taker include enhanced social rank and increased mating opportunities (Ellis 2013: 61; Geary 1998: 63). Several studies have documented the relationship between an adolescent male's standing in the peer group (place in the dominance hierarchy) and athletic prowess, physical attractiveness, and appeal to the opposite sex (Weisfeld 1999: 215).

Among contemporary adolescents, the costs of risky endeavors abetted by peers may be more evident than the benefits. Lives are cut short or blighted by substance abuse, STDs, vehicle accidents, suicide, and, notably, homicide. This last is a particular problem in the USA because of the lack of restrictions on firearm purchase, storage, and use, and "what might be a fist fight between young men in London or Paris, easily becomes murder in Chicago or Washington, D.C." (Arnett 2002: 331). Research portrays US adolescents as not too concerned with family needs. "Instead, their focus is on who they are, how attractive they are ... and how it all looks to their peer group" (Sax 2005: 133). Worse, peers can override the guidance of parents and teachers. Studies document that peer influence can enhance or depress academic performance (Kindermann 1993). Among African-Americans, Signithia Fordham and the late John Ogbu have shown how bright, academically talented students are harassed by their peers – who accuse them of "acting white," of being "brainiacs" or "gay." And these efforts are often successful: capable students do reduce their effort to avoid outshining their peers academically (Fordham and Ogbu 1986; Ogbu 2003: 105).

In the next section, we'll see that the attributes of male adolescence that may make young men a burden to their communities become distinct assets in warrior societies.

Creating warriors

During the period of seclusion [Sebei boys] engaged in stick-fighting duels and practiced spear throwing and other military arts. (Goldschmidt 1986: 105)

Powhatan boys were trained from early in life to be stoic warriors who could withstand multiple hardships. Boys were initiated from ten to fifteen years of age ... held deep in the forest ... by older, initiated men, who subjected the boys to beating and forced them to ingest an intoxicating but dangerous plant. (Markstrom 2008: 161).

Contemporary industrialized society would appear to dictate a lengthy period of adolescence as youth take ever longer to complete the preparation necessary for successful adulthood, including adequately paid employment.[3] But in the pre-modern world, male adolescence also extended well into the third decade in societies that depended on maintaining what was, in effect, a standing army. The best known of these societies was that of the Spartans, who left nothing to chance in preparing the *ephebos*, including putting to death all but the most robust infants. Intense training began at seven when boys were transferred from their homes to a dormitory, remaining until they were twenty. Boys were exposed to extremes of physical endurance, and their emotional toughness was fostered by "a process of hazing and ridicule" (Sommerville 1982: 24–25).[4]

---

[3] Indeed, in the USA, even a college degree is no guarantee of competence in an increasingly information-rich and complex society (Baer *et al.* 2006).

[4] Until fairly the 1970s, elite English boarding schools (and their US counterparts) for males weren't all that different in terms of the constant hazing of younger by older boys, the emphasis on physical deprivation and removal from family, and daily engagement in team sports. This is probably what prompted Arthur Wellesley, the duke of Wellington, to remark: "The battle of Waterloo was won on the playing-fields of Eton."

Parents cheered on their sons during flogging competitions. "If a boy perished during such a competition without making a sound, he died a hero" (Peisner 1989: 120). As noted above, a significant element in Spartan training was the removal of the boy from his home (Shapiro 2003: 107).

Inca society was similar to Sparta in its determination to turn well-born boys into fearless warriors. After years of rigorous training that included, for example, carrying "heavy loads of firewood to build their strength," they were put through the culminating tests during the great *capac raymi* festival. Aside from marking the transition to adulthood, the ceremonies tested the boys' resistance to suffering through fasting, running long, arduous marathons, and sleeping on the ground in the high mountains. Those who persisted had their earlobes perforated in the *tocochicoy* rite and received the large ear-plugs characteristic of South American warriors. Finally, the last test was a footrace down from the mountain, which usually resulted in a few crippling injuries as all sought to become the "first boy to reach the bottom and drink the *chicha* proffered by the girls" (Shein 1992: 77).

Exclusion from the domestic society of the village and/or home (Gregor 1970: 243) may be a critical element in effecting the "separation" that van Gennep (1908/1960: 62) identified as the first stage in the rite of passage. In the past, Kpelle pre-adolescents in same-sex cohorts were dramatically removed from the village by masked figures and sequestered for months or years in specially constructed villages in the bush (deep forest) to enforce a transition from "carefree" childhood to responsible adulthood (Erchak 1977). A similar fate awaited neighboring Temne boys:

From the time of capture ... boys were in *kabangkalo* [where they] were scarified and [subject to] flogging, withholding [of] food, extra work, supporting a heavy weight for a long time and so on. (Dorjahn 1982: 39–40)

To the present,[5] pastoralist societies in Africa are noted for their ready willingness to attack neighboring groups in raids to secure cattle and women. In turn, we frequently see the creation of distinct warrior subcultures into which young men are inducted (Gilmore 2001: 209). Among the Dinka of the Sudan, boys were initiated between the ages of sixteen and eighteen and given gifts of well-designed spears symbolizing the military function of youth (Deng 1972). The pastoralist Masaai are also notorious warriors. The process of joining the warrior elite, becoming a *Moran*, begins with a rite of passage.[6] The principal test

---

[5] What drives conflict in Northern Kenya? *IRIN Humanitarian News and Analysis.* UN Office for the Coordination of Humanitarian Affairs. December 18. Available at www.irinnews.org/Report/ 87450/KENYA-What-drives-conflict-in-northern-Kenya. Accessed October 5, 2013.

[6] One study found a close association between the effort invested in rites of passage for boys and the importance of promoting a warrior mentality (Sosis *et al.* 2007).

of a boy's worthiness is the circumcision, during which a "flinch or even the bat of an eyelid as primitive razor sears into flesh is interpreted ... as a desire to run away and [this loss of] honor ... can never be redeemed" (Spencer 1970: 134).

After the circumcision ceremony, the initiates spend a period ... under strict ritual prohibitions [in] close company with other initiates. These prohibitions end with a further ceremony at which the initiates formally become *Moran*; they start to grow their hair, and to plait it and embellish it with red ochre. This is the first of a series of ceremonies known as *ilmugit*, and the initiate vows ... not to eat any meat seen by a woman [, rather] meat of the bush where the *moran* belong and where they share one another's company [while avoiding that of] young ... women. (Spencer 1970: 137)

Not surprisingly, the *Moran* are looked on with awe, especially by young boys. They are admired and feared but, at the same time, their physical and social isolation from the community insures that older men can maintain their control over access to the tribe's young women. They decide when and whom a *Moran* will finally, at age thirty to thirty-five, be allowed to marry.[7]

In Polynesia, boys became men during lengthy rituals, including circumcision, which demonstrated their courage. Before they rejoined society, they would be tattooed extensively. This, like the Moran's unique hairdo, made their new status obvious to all. Indeed, on Tonga, males who'd not yet been cut did not take meals with the household and "would be spurned by the girls ... teased that they [were] unclean and still young boys" (Morton 1996: 112). Uncircumcised Dowayo (Highland Cameroons) males "are accused of emitting the stench of women ... they cannot participate in all male events; they are buried with women" (Barley 1983/2000: 74).

The warrior societies native to North America employed a number of similar tactics to prepare young men for the rigors of armed conflict. The Creek inflicted bloody wounds to punish mischievous boys, but also "the profusion of blood ... served to convince the child that the loss of it is not attended with danger, or loss of life: that when he becomes ... a warrior, he need not shrink from an enemy" (Swanton 1928: 363). Navajo boys were awakened in the middle of the night and made to roll naked in the snow (Leighton and Kluckhohn 1948: 56). Among the Plains Indians, aspirant warriors were sent off to fast in the wilderness as part of their "vision quest" (Delaney 1995). Indian youth attached a boulder to their bodies with hooks, dragging it considerable distances to demonstrate courage and endurance.

Initiation rites provide opportunities to develop *and* display the attributes of a warrior. Gisu initiates are deemed worthy of warrior status if they

---

[7] In Western Australia, a protracted series of initiation rites slows the Ngaanyatjarra's progress to adulthood, and young men are kept from marriage until their third decade, while girls are married at puberty (Brooks 2011: 190).

unflinchingly endure the "fierce, bitter and terrifying" *Imbalu* ordeal. But the boys can also display their ferocity and worth by dancing non-stop, day and night, while wearing an elaborate costume that includes "a headdress made from the skin of a colobus monkey and long tails decorated with cowrie shells which hang down [their backs] and swirl in the dance" (Heald 1982: 20).

Another bastion of the warrior cult can be found in Papua New Guinea (Reay 1959; Strathern 1970). Gil Herdt, working among the "Sambia," has contributed much to our understanding of the shaping of boys into misogynist warriors. Elaborate rituals and rites of passage separate boys from their mothers and make them "manly," teaching them to despise and lord it over women and enemy tribesmen. The first stage in this initiation includes days of hazing, fasting, beating, sleeplessness, and sudden surprises. This is followed by forced nose-bleeding to remove female contaminants.

The first boy is quickly grabbed. He struggles and shouts but is held down by three men ... before [he] can catch his breath the initiator rolls up cane-grasses and, as the novice's head is held back, pushes them down repeatedly into the boy's nose. Tears and blood flow as the boy is held ... then another boy ... is grasped and bled. One lad tries to run away but is grabbed ... he is ... bled harder and longer than the others ... Another boy is penetrated until blood flows profusely; and after each instance of this, the collectivity of men raise the ritual/war chant. (Herdt 1990: 376)

Similarly, among the Mende of Sierra Leone:

Each boy is seized in turn by a number of the men ... stripped naked and his clothes kept to wipe away the blood which flows from the cuts. Then he is thrown roughly on to the ground, and the appropriate marks are made, either by a hook, which raises the skin, or by a razor. If he shows fright, or tries to run away, his head is pushed into a hole, which has already been dug for the purpose. During the operation, the "spirit" plays loudly on his pipe and there is a clapping of hands, which drowns the noise of the boys' cries and prevents them being overhead by passers-by, especially women and children. (Little 1970: 214)

One element that looms large in the training of male adolescents in much of Africa and Papua New Guinea is misogyny, as noted above. There is a distinct focus on teaching boys to feel superior toward and contemptuous of women. The "text" of many messages conveyed to initiates is replete with references to women's physical weakness relative to men and their power to pollute through menstrual and puerperal blood. Another tool in the men's arsenal is the use of "secrets," including sacred terms, rituals, locations, and objects such as masks. These "secrets" are denied to women on pain of death.[8] For the Arapesh (Sepik Region), "initiation ceremonies [include] an ordeal

---

[8] During fieldwork in Gbarngasuakwelle one evening, I had gathered a small group consisting of a woman and three or four children in order to record folktales. A bell rang (although I didn't

followed by the novices being shown the secret paraphernalia ... flutes, frims, paintings, statues, bullroarers" (Tuzin 1980: 26). Denying female access to powerful spirit forces aids in maintaining male hegemony. A Mehinacu girl "cannot learn the basic myths because the words 'will not stay in her stomach'" (Gregor 1990: 484). Wagenia "women and girls belong to the social category of the non-initiated, from whom the secrets of initiation were carefully concealed" (Droogers 1980: 78). Among the Igbo of southeastern Nigeria, boys are moved through a series of ceremonial stages that simultaneously distance them from women and bind them to senior males. From an early age, boys are gradually invested with the trappings of their authority, including boys' masquerades, their transfer to the boys' house, and various rituals – all of which were forbidden to females (Ottenberg 2006: 117–119).

We might also want to briefly look at the training of warriors in more complex societies. In Japan, the preparation of Samurai included puberty rites featuring severe ordeals (Sofue 1965: 156–157). During World War II, the training of suicidal *kamikazé* pilots involved *seishin kyoiku* – rigorous physical and spiritual training to build character (Rohlen 1996: 50). The Hitler Youth and the Soviet Young Pioneers both capitalized on the idealism and fanaticism characteristic of adolescence (Valsiner 2000: 295; see also Kratz 1990: 456). During the Cultural Revolution, Chinese authorities used the naturally "anti-social," rebellious nature of adolescents in recruiting, training, and then setting them loose as "Red Guards" to destroy bourgeois, Western, or intellectual elements of Chinese society (Lupher 1995). Today, Muslim terrorist organizations easily recruit male and female adolescents to serve as suicide bombers. Again, there are fundamental biological and psychological aspects of adolescence that render them susceptible to group-think mentality. Normal standards of human decency are suspended, allowing them to commit crimes in the name of the group.

Spencer's observations on the Masaai have wide applicability: "brainwashing for religious and political ends can be effectively done by finding a 'sore spot' in the victim's experience and working away at it" (Spencer 1970: 149). Don Tuzin provides a vivid illustration of the use of such psychology by Arapesh males to enthrall initiates in the *Falanga* rite:

Immediately following [the ordeal], the initiators drop their razors, spears, cudgels or what have you, and comfort the boys with lavish displays of tender emotion. What resentment the latter may have been harboring instantly dissipates, replaced

hear it) and my informants almost literally turned white with fear and immediately raced to their homes, warning me to douse the lantern and go to sleep. I learned the next day that the bell had signaled the imminent arrival of a masked "devil" in the village, to look upon whom would mean instant death for anyone other than males already initiated into the Poro secret society (Lancy 1996: 99).

by a palpable warmth and affection for the men who, moments before, had been seemingly bent on their destruction. As their confidence recovers itself, the novices become giddy with the realization that they have surmounted the ordeal. (Tuzin 1980: 78)

As we've seen, many initiation ceremonies include contests or military-like exercises that were central to the preparation of warriors. And these have given us much of our modern repertoire of organized sports. Cudgel fighting was common among East African pastoralists (Read 1960: 95). Xhosa informants suggested that, while cudgel games are now "just a sport," earlier they were considered central to a warrior's training – true for the Zulu as well (Edgerton 1988: 179). Still, "a *mtshotsho* boy who fights well and fearlessly will be admired [and] respected" (Mayer and Mayer 1970: 168). In West Africa, cudgel fighting gives way to wrestling, which seems to have transitioned smoothly from its role in warrior training to become a popular sport (Ottenberg 1989: 85–86; Stevens 1996). In East Asia the "martial arts" have also evolved from warrior training into competitive sports (Donohue 1994).

In the absence of a warrior subculture and the energy-absorbing pursuit of athletic glory, adults may yet feel the necessity of curbing or taming their obstreperous and "self-centered" adolescents. Canela tribesmen from Brazil publicly chastise and humiliate wayward youth.

A senior male might call his "nephew" to stand before the assembled village while he stomps on the youth's insteps, yank[s] him off the ground by his sideburns, and give[s] him a blistering lecture, describing his shameful infractions for all the women to hear . . . [rakes] the . . . youth's legs with rodents' teeth until they bleed. . .forces pepper into his mouth, and . . . draws back his foreskin for the assembled men and women to see the glans of his penis. Girls who had violated the norms of sexual and dietary restraint [are] shamed in this ceremony by having their leaf aprons torn off and their genitalia exposed. (Crocker and Crocker 1994: 37)

The Hopi of the southwestern USA were not known as particularly warlike, especially compared with their Navajo neighbors. But male initiation could be quite severe. In Don Talayesva's autobiography, he confesses to being quite "naughty" as a boy. So, when he was initiated into the *Katsina* society with his age group, his father arranged for him to be taught a lesson by having the Whipper Katsinas give him extra blows with the sharp-spined ocotillo whips to "drive the evil from [his] mind, so that he may grow up to be a good and wise man" (Simmons 1942: 80). "When [a Chaga] adolescent flouts parental authority and has become a cause of public annoyance, father and mother agree that he should be curbed by the *kisusa* rite" (Raum 1940: 303). Tapirapé young men who were "known to be having sexual relations, or [were] getting too imperious [, were] scratched over [the] thighs and arms with the teeth of the agouti until the blood flowed freely" (Wagley 1977: 151).

In a few societies, male adolescents are tamed not through a military-like boot camp, but rather through strict religious practices. All Mormon males are expected to marry after completing two years of missionary service, proselytizing their faith. In India, high-caste youth go through the lengthy *upanayana* rite during which, with shaved heads, they wander as ascetic, begging monks (Rohner and Chaki-Sircar 1988: 85).

[In the Middle Ages] the chief means of controlling adolescent passion and preparing the youth for the responsibilities of adulthood was . . . fatigue of the body through fasts, prayers, vigils and manual labor [while the] primary virtue which [was to] be encouraged in adolescence [was] shame. (Goodich 1989: 109–110)

Interestingly, the initiation process for girls may also resemble a monastic experience. "During the [seclusion] period [a Tlingit girl] thirsted and fasted, sitting as immobile as possible with her fingers laced together with string" (de Laguna 1965: 20). Guajiro (montane Venezuela) girls are secluded for up to five years (depending on the family's means) in a nearly lightless hut. "If the girl cries she will be severely criticized for her childish attitude and reminded of her new status as an adult woman who must exercise self-control" (Watson-Franke 1976: 197). Seclusion at first menses, accompanied by emotional and physical restraint, is also found in the Pacific (Lessa 1966: 102); among North America forest foragers (Markstrom 2008: 79); in Amazonia (Gregor 1970: 243); in Cambodia (Smith-Hefner 1993: 145); and in southwestern USA (Markstrom 2008: 131), among others.

Clearly, one central goal of adolescent initiation is to curb and channel emerging sexuality. In the section that follows, I will show that the inherent conflict that arises when youth exist in the limbo of sexual desire arising in a pre-adult body and mind is as much a matter of culture as one of nature.

Sexuality

[!Kung] children play at sexual intercourse so frequently and consistently that there is . . . no "virginity" to be lost. (Howell 2010: 29)

Tales are told . . . with great relish, of the hazardous courting expeditions . . . when a [Uduk] boy went "weasel-crawling" to exchange endearments with his sweetheart through a small hole in the wall of her hut. (James 1979: 136)

It is clear that when no property accompanies the marriage, virginity is of little interest. (Schlegel 1991: 725)

In 1904, G. Stanley Hall published the first comprehensive treatment of adolescence. This work was to have enormous influence on psychology and on anthropology as well. Ironically, rather than seeing the "problems" of adolescence as due to delayed or thwarted sexuality, Hall, rather puritanically, saw modern society as creating a "hothouse atmosphere" in which sexual "ripening" was accelerated. Nevertheless, he argued that adolescence was universally a stressful period fueled by the individual's emerging sexuality. Urged on by her mentor, Franz Boas, Margaret Mead took up this gauntlet and traveled to Samoa to study adolescence in a "primitive," non-Western society. Mead concluded that Hall was wrong – adolescent stress was culturally constructed rather than biologically based – because Samoan adolescents were relaxed about sex and everything else. This single negative instance, Mead argued, was enough to undermine Hall's universality claim (Mead 1928/1961). Mead, in turn, was challenged – posthumously – by Derek Freeman. His work, *Margaret Mead and Samoa: The Making and Unmaking of an Anthropological Myth*, embroiled American anthropology for years. Freeman offers a multilayered and thorough documentation of adolescent stress and restricted sexuality in Samoa, beginning with the earliest travelers' reports from the islands. Far from the easy and casual approach to sex described by Mead,[9] Freeman describes an ancient and still powerful "cult of virginity," present in Samoa and throughout western Polynesia:

Taupous, or ceremonial virgins, occupied positions of great social importance and virginity at marriage was very highly prized ... young chieftains would vie for the special prestige associated with the deflowering of a *taupou* ... in public ... If no proof of the bride's virginity was obtained, she was sorely abused by her friends, called prostitute ... exposed as a non-virgin, her brother, or even her father ... rushed upon her with their clubs, and dispatched her. (Freeman 1983: 227, 229, 231)

Freeman goes on to describe the less spectacular but nevertheless pervasive restrictions on adolescent sexuality brought to Samoa by the Victorian-era Christian missionaries, who, for example, hounded the Samoan women, appropriately dressed for the climate, into wearing chaste, full-body-covering *mumus*. Margaret Mead might have had better luck in working with Quechua speakers in the Vilcanota Valley of Peru. Long-term ethnographer Inge Bolin concludes that adolescent anxiety is rare because a "degree of promiscuity is not frowned upon until marriage or a firm commitment has been made" (Bolin 2006: 142). In the Massim area of Papua New Guinea, including the Trobriand and Vanatinai Islands, where matrilineality prevails, adolescent sexuality is considered healthy and normal. Adolescents are expected to become distracted and preoccupied by their physical appearance and sexual attractiveness, and adults willingly share their love potions with them (Lepowsky 1998: 133).

---

[9] Alice Schlegel suggested to me that Freeman focused mainly on aristocratic Samoan culture while Mead may have been interacting primarily with very low-status girls with consequently different mores (personal communication, November 2005).

Aka adolescents are expected to initiate sexual activity when they feel so inclined, and they feel no strong need to separate or break away from their parents (Hewlett and Hewlett 2013: 94).

The "Red" Xhosa in southern Africa are also quite "liberal." Sex play is tolerated in childhood, and *metsha*, or external sexual intercourse, is encouraged in adolescence. Indeed, girls who spurn sex are thought to become stiff and eventually turn into witches. And "a male who has not had sweethearts – an *isishumana* – is unlikely to enjoy prestige in the youth organization" (Mayer and Mayer 1970: 175). As a result, youth "problems" are minimal, and "traditional" girls – because they practice *metsha* – are less often pregnant than "School" (Christian) or urban Xhosa girls (Mayer and Mayer 1970: 163).

A surprising number of societies, including the prim and proper Balinese, tolerate sexual play among very young children (Covarrubias 1937: 137; see also the Sebei – Goldschmidt 1986: 97). The Muria from central India move their children into a dorm-like structure from late childhood to the end of adolescence. This *ghotul* is coeducational, and girls and boys are encouraged to form short-term but mutually satisfying relationships. In effect the Muria seem to be bowing to the inevitable (Elwin 1947). Similarly, in the Nicobar Islands, boys and girls have the sexual freedom to find a good match, and these unions are fully legitimated by their families and the community (Mann 1979: 99). In Tamang communities in the Himalayas, adolescents are expected to enjoy sexual relations discreetly during celebratory occasions such as night-long shamanistic rituals and community-wide dances (Fricke 1994: 102).

Among the Ache, a girl may have as many as four different sexual partners before menarche (Hill and Hurtado 1996: 225). The Yuqui, another group of South American forest dwellers, believe that "it is only by having intercourse with a ... number of men that [a girl] is able to achieve sexual maturity, or ... to be able to bear children" (Stearman 1989: 93). Similar beliefs, while not common, are found scattered around the globe and include, for example, the Lepcha of Sikkim (Gorer 1967: 175). Jane Lancaster surveys research showing that humans are sub-fertile for at least two years after first menses. Hence, "although sexual activity almost invariably follows menarche, the likelihood of pregnancy is very low for the first few years" (Lancaster 1986: 25). She also identifies possible benefits of premarital promiscuity, including the development of strategies to attract a mate and the ability to discern the value of potential future spouses (Lancaster 1984).[10]

In broad areas of Papua New Guinea, including the Highlands and the Sepik, it is male reproductive potency that must be developed. There is

---

[10] Perhaps as a result of under-nutrition, "too-early" pregnancy does not appear to be a conspicuous problem among societies where sexual relations begin at the onset of adolescence, or earlier.

the "conviction that maleness, unlike femaleness, is not a biological given. It must be artificially induced through secret ritual" (Herdt 2001: 165). One impediment is the boy's femininity, acquired as he is born of, nursed, and raised by women: men and women live apart and fathers are not involved in childcare. The Anga of the Eastern Highlands counter this threat by a rite in which eight-to-twelve-year-olds are smeared (by their mother's brother) with red pandanus seeds and red ocher (representing blood) and pushed through narrow structures decorated with red leaves representing the uterus and vulva. The drama continues through the ritual daubing with yellow mud, (repeating a rite practiced with newborns) and the boys are now reborn as males, capable of reproduction (Bonnemere 2006). Elsewhere in Papua New Guinea, sexual maturity may be enhanced by forming a homosexual relationship with an older man, such as among the Keraki (Williams 1936). The pattern of sexual relations between boys and slightly older men is carefully scripted to enhance the boy's physical maturity, primarily through the ingestion of semen during fellatio. Due to the low-protein diet, children reach puberty very late and women, with the greater demands imposed on their bodies by hard physical labor (men are politicians, hunters, and warriors) and childbearing, waste early. To avoid this fate for their sons, men take great pains to encourage the growth of strength, courage, and masculinity in boys via special taboos, initiation rituals, and homosexual relations (Gray 1994). These practices are by no means rare, as Creed notes: "the practice of homosexuality in New Guinea is widespread, highly structured, and culturally regulated" (Creed 1984: 158).

Canela (Brazilian foragers) society occupies a kind of middle ground between *laissez-faire* and restrictive. Young men can expect to draw sexual satisfaction and strength from intercourse with much older women – as contrasted with the alleged strength-depleting effect of sex with their peers. Adolescent girls, on the other hand, should copulate with older men to gain strength and vitality (Crocker and Crocker 1994: 33–34).

While a relaxed attitude toward pre-adult sexuality may be the rule in foraging (Hewlett and Hewlett 2013: 88) and some pastoralist societies,[11] it is seen as problematic in more complex, patriarchal societies (Hotvedt 1990; Barry 2007; Broude and Greene 1976).[12] A woman's value as a provider may be diminished, thus enhancing her value as a breeder. Consequently, others control the young woman's sexuality, as a means of confidently verifying the paternity of her offspring. Virginity is a key factor in a daughter's marriage-ability, and it behooves families to guard it vigorously: "a [Rotuman] girl's sexuality was 'owned' by her local kinship group; it was they who benefited

---

[11] Nor is this parental and community tolerance extended only to heterosexual relations among pre-adults (Blackwood 2001).

[12] For a discussion of adolescent sexuality in antiquity, see Lancy (2008: 291).

by a favorable marital transaction" (Howard 1970: 72).[13] Among the Gebusi, living in an area of Papua New Guinea bisected by the Fly River, "adult kinswomen ... adopt a strong protective relationship towards adolescent girls in regard to male sexual conduct" (Cantrell 1998: 96). An extreme case is provided by the Guajiro pastoralist peoples of northern Colombia. From toddlerhood, girls are warned to keep their distance from all males and told that sex is evil. Later, they will be severely scolded for conversing with boys and, if a girl persists, the "mother may place the tip of a hot branding iron on [her] vagina [as] a convincing object lesson" (Watson-Franke 1976: 151).

The rationale for this repressive treatment lies in the fact that the groom and his kin must assemble bride-price in the form of livestock and jewelry, which is seen as "purchasing ... the bride's sexual integrity for the exclusive pleasure and delight of her husband" (Watson-Franke 1976: 153). Similarly, in Turkey, separation of the sexes and women's limited power are justified in the name of honor (*namus*). *Namus* requires that "men control the sexuality of their women ... wives, daughters, sisters, and other female relatives" (Kagitçibasi and Sunar 1992: 78). Girls are prevented from going very far in school in much of the Muslim world, ostensibly to prevent them from forming even the most fleeting relationship with a boy (Davis and Davis 1989: 61; Prothro 1961: 15; Williams 1968: 49). Attitudes are gradually liberalizing, but in "tribal" regions of Pakistan and Afghanistan, opposition to schooling for girls (and the threat of their emancipation from male dominance) leads to frequent atrocities.

One aspect of the large complex of customs surrounding young women's sexuality that has become a *cause célèbre* is clitorodectomy.[14] In spite of very widespread and persistent international condemnation of the practice (Rahman and Toubia 2000), it shows no signs of abating and, indeed, is most vigorously defended by the very women who have been "mutilated." Originating in Egypt,[15] it is still practiced on the majority of Muslim and Christian Egyptian girls. It is also common throughout much of Africa and in areas where Muslims are in the majority, affecting upwards of 100 million women (Matias 1996: 2). The most commonly voiced rationale for clitoridectomy is to curtail the woman's sex drive, reducing the risk that she will fornicate or be tempted into adultery.

Restrictive attitudes regarding women's sexual activity often go hand in hand with the contrasting expectation for young males to display machismo through conquests. Sebei (East African pastoralist) youth "will bleed their

---

[13] See Caldwell *et al.* (1998: 143).

[14] Information from Equality Now. Available at www.equalitynow.org. Accessed April 26, 2013.

[15] Evidence for circumcision rites is found in various Egyptian sources beginning with a scene of ritual (male) circumcision from a sixth-dynasty (twenty-fourth-century BCE) tomb (King 2006: 48–49).

penises with a thorn 'to make them sharp,' so they can penetrate a virgin" (Goldschmidt 1986: 105). Among the Lepcha, "Almost all boys and young men get their first real sexual experience and training from an older married woman" (Gorer 1967: 161). Boys in Guajiro society are expected to be sexually aggressive as long they are discreet and bring no shame on their families (Watson-Franke 1976: 152; see also Lewis 1961: 38). Rotuman boys "are expected to pursue sexual gratification . . . whereas girls are discouraged and in most cases closely guarded" (Howard 1970: 71). While this imbalance almost inevitably favors males, rare cases where women are expected to initiate sexual contact while men are shy and intimidated by sex do exist (Kaulong – Goodale 1980: 135).

Interestingly, adolescent sexuality in the USA has become a battleground, due, I believe, to the conflicting dictates of the dominant neontocracy – keep the kids happy – and lasting vestiges of the gerontocracy. We indulge children's fantasies with Barbie and her wardrobe of sexy clothes and permit very young girls to use make-up, so that by "fourth and fifth grades some girls own their own cosmetics" (Thorne 1993: 148). But, in Mormon Utah, for example, little is known about adolescent sexuality and the causes of teen pregnancy because state law explicitly prohibits agencies from questioning minors regarding sex. This prohibition is based on the fear that, by questioning teenagers on this subject, an otherwise dormant and unconscious interest will be activated. In Hindu communities in the USA parents go to great lengths to inculcate values imported from India. But many young women resist parental dictates to dress modestly, preferring to assimilate. With contempt, one informant asserted: "Nobody really takes chastity seriously anymore" (Miller 1995: 74, 76). As a result of this ambiguity, "No clear mores currently exist in US society concerning the sexual behavior of unmarried young people in their teens" (Arnett 1999: 320).

Ultimately, societies where the transition between childhood and adulthood is brief and uncomplicated are in the minority. In the majority, youth are "aided" in making the transition through a rite of passage.

Becoming a woman

Adolescents must be respectful; and they must accept parental control. (Edel 1957/ 1996: 183)

The *kufar* for [Ulithian] girls has two aspects: the physiological coming of age and the sociological attainment of adulthood. (Lessa 1966: 102)

In more than half of the societies in the ethnographic record, adolescents must pass through an initiation process (Schlegel and Barry 1980: 698), and this proportion climbs to two-thirds if we include any type of ordeal (Schlegel and Barry, 1991).[16] Aside from preparing warriors, as noted earlier, initiation, in many but not all cases, certifies adolescents as ready to begin mating and forming their own family (Vizedom and Zais 1976). And this theme is particularly evident in girls' initiation rites.

Among pastoralist groups, such as the East African Sebei, a girl's circumcision may carry much the same meaning as a boy's – admission to adult status – not as a deterrent to sexual pleasure.[17] As such, girls eagerly submit to the ordeal, and despite the absence of sanitary conditions, deaths from the operation are rare. "The dominant theme of the initiation rite is that of an ordeal – trial and proof of maturity" (Goldschmidt 1986: 95–96). Goldschmidt, however, makes clear that the youths themselves press adults to sponsor the initiation rites.

Among West African Mende farmers, the girls' initiation is organized by the Sande women's secret society (boys' initiation by the male equivalent – *Poro*):[18]

Girls first go through a portal, into a cleared place in the forest ... ritually separated [for two to three years] from the social context in which they were girls. One of the most dramatic ritual elements ... is clitorodectomy ... Sande women explain that this makes women "clean" [also] the pain ... is a metaphor for the pain of childbirth ... Womanhood is symbolically achieved in clitorodectomy and confirmed, under the midwife's hand in childbirth. [Another] important element in the ritual process of Sande initiation is fattening. Beauty, prosperity, health and fertility are explicitly linked to fatness ... The opposite of fat is ... dry, connoting among other things a dry and barren uterus. (MacCormack 1994: 111–112)

Those on the threshold of adulthood may experience various forms of, sometimes painful, body modification other than circumcision. Abelam (agriculturalists of the Sepik Region, Papua New Guinea) girls are "scarified at their first menstruation ... standardized patterns are cut on their breasts, bellies, and upper arms" (Hauser-Schaublin 1995: 40). Mehinacu and Canela nine-year-olds have their ears pierced to hold wooden plugs (Gregor 1970: 242; Crocker and Crocker 1994: 116). Tapirapé boys acquire a prominent lip plug (Wagley 1977: 149). Young Tapirapé women, just prior to their first pregnancy, pass through a rite that includes decorative scarification:

[16] There is, however, a paradox here. Despite their uniqueness and interest for anthropologists and their commonality, initiation rites – with a few exceptions – are not well documented. By their very nature, the rites are conducted in considerable secrecy and it is the rare ethnographer who's become a *participant* observer of the process (Bellman 1975).

[17] Not surprisingly, given the privation and pain that usually accompany initiation, parents are rarely involved with the initiation of their own children (Hotvedt 1990: 167–168).

[18] Historically, *Poro* prepared Mende youth to become warriors, defending the village and raiding neighboring villages to capture slaves (Rosen 2005: 64).

This traditionally consisted of a quarter-moon design on each cheek and a half-moon design under the chin ... only women who carried that design on their face were truly beautiful. The design was drawn in charcoal and then cut into the face with crisscross lacerations using the sharp incisor teeth of the agouti or paca ... into these wounds ginipap juice was rubbed so that it would become permanently black. (Wagley 1977: 163)[19]

The teeth are often subject to modification. Aka youth have their incisors filed to points (Konner 2005: 51). Adolescent Japanese girls, during the Tokugawa period, had their teeth blackened (Sofue 1965: 156). Balinese children have their teeth filed and blackened during their coming of age ceremony, as follows:

The patient is laid on ... offerings, the head resting on a pillow which is covered with ... one of the magic cloths ... The body is wrapped in new white cloth and assistants hold down the victim by the hands and feet. The tooth-filer ... inscribes magic syllables (*aksara*) on the teeth about to be filed with a ruby set in a gold ring. The filing then proceeds, taking from fifteen minutes to a half-hour, endured stoically with clenched hands and goose-flesh, but without even a noise from the patient. (Covarrubias 1937: 135–136)

A common rationale for the girl's rite is the theme of "fattening," as mentioned above for Sande initiation – to prepare for the rigors of childbearing (Schlegel and Barry 1980: 698). Girls are held in seclusion and kept well fed so that they "fill out," and thus display their readiness for mating (Gleason and Ibubuya 1991; Ottenberg 1989 : 12). Paiela (Papua New Guinea Highlands) girls are aided by an array of magical plants and procedures to enlarge their breasts (Biersack 1998: 74–75). For the Bemba of Zimbabwe, the girls' initiation process, *chisungu*, is replete with the imagery of mating and reproduction:

Women ... snatch at a *mufungo* bush for leaves ... [which] they fold into cones to resemble small conical fish traps. They sing a song about setting fish traps and ... pretend to catch each other's fingers in the leaf traps ... The traps and fingers represent the female and male sexual organs and a song "The fish has many children and so will the girl" is sung. (Richards 1956: 65)

Also in southern Africa, Chewa girls go through the *chinamwali* initiation in which they dance around various clay figures, including a python "that is thought to be in control of fertility of the land and human beings" (Yoshida 2006: 234). Hadza initiates dance and sing publicly, their nude bodies shiny with animal fat. At intervals, the "girls would give chase to older teenager boys and try to hit them with their fertility sticks (*nalichanda*)" (Marlowe 2010: 56).

---

[19] In addition to visible symbols, nomenclature may also accompany the change in status. Tapirapé girls are *kotantani*, becoming *kuchamoko* after their first menses (Wagley 1977: 150).

While these examples showcase the positive aspects of a woman's emerging fertility,[20] for many societies, menstruation, intercourse, pregnancy, and child-birth are seen as potentially harmful to the community. For the Ndu of the Sepik area of Papua New Guinea, women's *narandanwa* rites are episodic and designed to "detoxify" the pollution accompanying these physiological processes (Roscoe 1995). Another common theme of women's "coming of age" rites is the role of the woman as provider.[21] A Hopi girl's first menstruation signals the onset of ritual events, such as the corn-grinding ceremony when her hair is reshaped into the "butterfly whorl" style. At the same time, her tether is shortened and she will now be expected to remain in close proximity to her mother and apply herself to learning all aspects of the woman's domestic repertoire (Schlegel 1973: 455–456). For the Makiritare peoples of the Orinoco basin,

the *ahishto hiyacado* is begun with the first signs of ... menstruation ... the whole village is alerted ... inside a *conuco* beside the village .... the women simulate all the tasks the girl will be responsible for during her lifetime inside the garden ... some elders gather around her and ... start singing songs to encourage her to be a hard worker. (Guss 1982: 264)

As these examples suggest, initiation rites aren't only (or, in some cases, even primarily) for the "benefit" of the initiate. For the Rauto of Papua New Guinea, the initiation rite – like costly weddings in some strata of contemporary society – is seen as an opportunity to acquire and display wealth and status: "The menorrheal rites cannot begin until the girl's family has amassed sufficient wealth in the form of pigs, taro, and shell valuables to pay for the ritual services that will be provided" (Maschio 1995: 137). A second example is the Japanese maiden's "coming of age" ceremony, the focus of which will be her expensive kimono, make-up, and accessories – conspicuous display designed to enhance her family's public image (Goldstein-Gidoni 1999). For Baka foragers, "initiation takes months of preparation by the whole camp" (Higgens 1985: 102). One way to view the parents' support for initiation rites is that they are enhancing their child's connectedness to the extended family and community. And, given the essentially cooperative nature of human

---

[20] Somewhat ironically, while adolescent initiation ceremonies signal the youths' readiness for mating, they may also signal a broader segregation of the sexes. That is, in many cases, girls and boys have been free to associate but initiation begins a rapid process whereby, once married, men and women live in separate spheres with different role assignments, recreational pursuits, and even, in many cases, residence. This pattern is not uncommon, and has been most thoroughly described for the Kipsigis (Harkness and Super 1985: 222).

[21] In the case of foraging societies, a young male's demonstration of his ability as a provider is noted – such as an Inuit's youth's first caribou or seal – but not necessarily with a full-fledged initiation ceremony (Condon 1987: 56).

reproduction, the more allies the young men and women have in their quest to marry, establish a household, and raise children, the better (Bogin 2009: 513).

In a few cases, the initiation follows or occurs almost simultaneously with parenthood. In certain Ijo (Nigeria) villages the clitorodectomy, which "initiates" the process of becoming a woman, is performed in the seventh month of pregnancy.[22] Following delivery and recovery, the new mother dances in "the *seigbein*, a twelve-day celebration of the ancestors and a purging of bad spirits from the town" (Hollos and Leis 1989: 75). This completes the process of becoming an adult. For a young Hausa woman, adult status (*màcè*) is conferred only after her first child has his or her naming ceremony (Faulkingham 1970: 166). For the Sambia, adulthood (*aatmwunu*), for both sexes, is not conferred until two pregnancies have been brought to a successful conclusion. However, ceremonial recognition of the man's potency continues through the fourth birth, after which "there is no reason to belabor what is by now obvious: a man has proved himself competent in reproduction" (Herdt 2001: 164). In Thailand, "land is often given to a couple at the birth of their first child, rather than on marriage, as it is parenthood and not marriage that is a sign of the couple's maturity" (Montgomery 2001a: 60). On Vanatinai Island, neither marriage nor the birth of a child is sufficient to claim full adult status, which is only conferred once the individual (in their late twenties) has settled into a "stable" marriage (Lepowsky 1998: 127).

Marriage *per se* may not always be treated as an important rite of passage. But, like the initiation ceremony, a primary function of marriage may be to curtail the uncivil activities of adolescents – sexual promiscuity, in particular. Earlier, I noted the way in which the transfer of property at marriage might be used to add weight to the prohibition on adolescent female sexual activity. But unruly male adolescents can also be brought to heel by the threat by kinsmen to withhold support for their marriage.[23] Among the Kaugel of the New Guinea Highlands, young men who fail to fall into line and demonstrate the proper deference accorded to senior members of the tribe risk permanent bachelorhood, as they can't possibly acquire on their own the enormous resources required to make an adequate bride-price payment (Bowers 1965).

---

[22] "None of the female subjects, regardless of their future plans and aspirations, voiced any objection to the procedure, and most of them eagerly looked forward to it as to a graduation ceremony into adulthood. The clitoridectomy fees are paid by the father of the woman's unborn child, which established the paternity of the child" (Hollos and Leis 1989: 125).

[23] Although this doesn't seem to be discussed much in the literature, adults customarily make critical decisions in the lives of adolescents – allocating them land, paying their school fees, donating their service to organized religion, sending them off to soldier or labor or apprentice, and pairing them with a spouse. These decisions strike me as closely parallel to the decision making that occurs upon the birth of a child, discussed in Chapters 2 and 3. That is, the parent is acting strategically to maximize both genetic and material returns from their offspring.

Schapera (1930) describes a parallel case in southeastern Africa where senior Tswana men own the cattle that junior men need in order to acquire a bride.

Marriage arrangements

A [Bakkarwal] girl must be engaged before she reaches menarche and becomes nubile. In principle the earlier the better, for her and for all others, since the chances of her becoming sexually dangerous to herself and to others must be minimized. (Rao 1998: 121).

If the [Hadza] couple continues to be together for perhaps a week or a few weeks, they ... are then considered married. Marriage involves no ceremony, but is defined by cohabitation. (Marlowe 2010: 170)

While we've seen wide variation in the treatment of adolescent sexuality and variation in how closely or loosely adolescents are bound to their natal families, there is far less autonomy when it comes to marriage. A few societies may let youngsters select their own mates. For instance, among the Tapirapé:

There was no marriage ceremony, nor a bride price. When a young man reached an understanding with a young woman he would carry a load of firewood across the village plaza and deposit it at her family dwelling. This was a public announcement of his union with the girl. He then moved his hammock next to hers and became an economic participant in her household. First marriages between young men and young women were proverbially brittle – almost trial marriages. (Wagley 1977: 157)

More commonly, "matchmaking" is done by one's kin. An important factor to consider is that, depending on inheritance and residence patterns, a family will, in marriage, be losing or gaining a potentially valuable worker (Schlegel and Barry 1991: 106). In Mayan farming communities, adolescents are kept from marriage until relatively late (nineteen for females, twenty-two for males) as their contribution to the household economy is so valuable (Kramer 2005). More typically, Moroccan mothers eagerly play matchmaker to marry off their sons to girls who'll be good homemakers and responsive to their mother-in-law (Davis and Davis 1989: 77). The term "daughter guarding" has been coined to describe a process whereby a girl's parents monitor her associates closely to prevent her from making a bad match or diminishing her prospects by unchaste behavior (Flinn 1988: 195; see also Wilder 1970: 230). "Traditional" Javanese avoid this problem by marrying "off pre-pubertal daughters ... and it [becomes] her new family's concern ... to keep her away from other men" (Geertz 1961: 56).

Typically, a [Datoga] daughter is supported by her family in the quest to place her with a man with "prospects" from a "good" family (Sellen 1998b: 330).

They usually want the best for their son or daughter and their grandchildren, but a marriage might also be used to acquire or distribute social capital. An Arapesh father may arrange bride-price to acquire for his son the daughter of someone to whom he owes a favor (Leavitt 1989: 308). I would venture that there are societies where parents – especially fathers – spend far more time in negotiating the details of their offspring's marriage (dowry, bride-price, housing, land tenure) than they ever did in childcare. "If the [Vlach] father does not arrange an honorable and successful marriage for his daughter, his reputation in the community is diminished" (Campbell 1964: 159). It is in the best genetic interest of parents to make a good match for their offspring to increase the likelihood of getting well-cared-for grandchildren who will survive to carry their genes into the next generation (Blurton-Jones 1993: 406). The girls in Figure 27 are being readied for an "arranged marriage."

It is also rare for a society to treat pregnancy out of wedlock with equanimity. Non-mainstream communities in North America where marriages are tentative and somewhat optional provide exceptions. In a poor Black community in North Carolina, "from 1969 through 1986, no girl ... completed the teenage years without having at least one baby. The particular father ... mattered little ... the neighborhood seemed glad to have a child" (Heath 1990: 502). In Holman, a remote Inuit community with plentiful resources, a teenage girl can be assured both that her own family will assist in rearing her child and that extended family members would come forward offering to adopt should she decide to give up the baby (Condon 1987: 98). Likewise, in poor white Appalachian mountain communities, pregnancy in one's teenage daughter or a son's impending paternity may be seen in a positive light. The hope is that caring for a child will have a maturing effect (Fitchen 1981: 128).

More commonly, marriage is viewed as a tension-laden piece of diplomacy where the marriageable daughter courts disaster for herself and her family. In matrilineal Hopi society, young men are reluctant to leave the comfort and ease of their family home to labor long and hard on behalf of their wife's family. Luring a good son-in-law into the family is unlikely if one's daughter is lazy or promiscuous (Schlegel 1973: 457). Among the Bajau fishermen of the Sulu Sea, whose dwellings are their boats, a girl may enjoy discreet sexual relations, but if she's perceived as too free with her favors, she will be "unable to command a high bride-price and may have to settle for a less desirable mate" (Nimmo 1970: 255). In patrilineal Teso (Uganda) society, a post-pubescent girl who isn't married is a source of anxiety to her father because on her reputation rests "his hopes for bridewealth cattle ... that he will need in order to marry [off] his sons" (de Berry 2004: 56).

Societies treat marriage much more seriously when there is wealth accumulation (agro pastoralists versus foragers) and the distribution of that wealth through bride-price or dowry, and/or subsequent inheritance. Adults, particularly males,

Figure 27 Brides-to-be, Luang Prabang, Laos

exercise tight control over mate selection (Apolstolou 2009: 46). Marriage is viewed as an opportunity to secure a "good" match for one's offspring or to endow them with family wealth – to aid in their household formation and the creation of a suitable home for grandchildren. Alice Schlegel, in a brilliant study, explicates this phenomenon. Societies that dower their daughters need to guard against ne'er-do-well, social-climbing males (exemplified by Wickham in *Pride and Prejudice*) who would advance their fortunes through seduction; hence, a premium is placed on female chastity before marriage (Schlegel 1991: 724).

Finally, there are a number of societies that value premarital chastity so highly that, at the earliest sign of puberty, daughters are married off (Whiting *et al*. 1986: 287).

However, as the next section reveals, rapid social change is having a dramatic impact on these customs – rites of passage, in particular. For example, the availability of wage employment permits adolescent males to finesse the approval of senior males by acquiring resources to marry and start a household of their own without the seniors' assistance (Caldwell *et al*. 1998: 139).

Adolescence and social change in traditional societies

By handing over [Teso] girls to soldiers, the middlemen destroyed the claim of their fathers for bridewealth. (de Berry 2004: 56)

None of the [Lurs] women weavers of nomadic-style tribal rugs and flat weaves used locally has young apprentices; their skills and products are considered old-fashioned. (Friedl 1997: 4)

There is no longer a defined pathway, clearly articulated with the goals of later life, for the [Ngaanyatjarra] "youngfellas" to follow. (Brooks 2011: 196)

As discussed earlier for chimpanzees, juveniles are often found along the leading edge of social change and innovation. In Sadolparo village in India, the Garo people practice an "animist" faith called Sansarek. However, the Christian church service is entirely populated by adolescents who reject and admit to being ashamed of Sansarek (Stafford and Nair 2003; see also Robbins 2004: 138). Earlier, we noted that adolescent males are expected to roam more widely, beyond the family pale. And, in recent history, that has often meant that they are the first members of the village to venture forth to the big city or commercial enclave (plantation, mine). Returning, they bear gifts and radical ideas.[24] Less frequently but still in significant numbers, adolescent females

---

[24] No doubt in the first wave of urbanization, adolescents chose to migrate – often against the wishes of their families. Today, in much of the Third World, overpopulation and the declining productivity of rural farms means that adolescents are compelled to migrate because they cannot support themselves through agricultural labor.

migrate to urban areas in search of schooling and/or employment as sex workers (Rubenson *et al.* 2005). Youth also may serve as conduits for change; for example, girls or young women may be the first to adopt new designs in textiles (Greenfield 2004). Young Telefol women "have been quick to master the non-indigenous ... method of working multicolored designs into the fabric of the *bilum*" (MacKenzie 1991: 106). Aboriginally, the Matses of Peru dwelt in the deep forests of Amazonia but gradually moved to more accessible sites along major watercourses. Matses boys were in the vanguard in exploring and exploiting riverine resources – fish, in particular. Their rapidly acquired competence lowered the barrier for adult engagement with this unfamiliar and previously avoided ecology (Morelli 2011).

Clearly, vestiges of urbanization will find their way to the hinterlands, and adolescents are often the quickest to adapt and respond. "Settlements" provided for forest-dwelling tribal people in South America often incorporate medical facilities, schools, commercial outlets, and foreign religious institutions. Some Ache were induced to settle on a reservation and younger tribesmen adapted more rapidly to the changed circumstances. As a consequence, "the traditional power structure was turned upside down ... young men [acquired] more wives and children than they had been able to acquire in the forest" (Hill and Hurtado 1996: 53).

Adolescents may be particularly susceptible to the pressure or enticements of modern institutions including, cities, schools, churches, plantations, and factories. In villages on Dominica, parents regret that "children have become ruder and developed bad or negative attitudes from watching television" (Quinlan and Hansen 2013: 268). China has witnessed a dramatic change in rural society as adolescents flee from the stultifying control of traditional authority figures (Grier 2006: 482) to take advantage of new employment opportunities in huge industrial enclaves that have sprung up (Stevenson and Zusho 2002: 141). In Paraiba, Brazil "young people want to leave the mountains ... despite stereotypes of being 'rooted to the land,' [they] covet jobs in the city and leave with no intention of returning" (Kenny 2007: 113).

Among the Kamea (Papua New Guinea), "It was inconceivable for an uninitiated youth to take a wife. The men's cult taught young men how to behave in the presence of women and how to avoid being contaminated by the polluting sexual substances of their brides-to-be" (Bamford 2004: 42). Initiation and other "pagan" practices have been suppressed and driven underground by Christian missionaries. Hence, young men no longer can advertise their initiated status by wearing a bone inserted through the nasal septum (Bamford 2004). Bumbita Arapesh youth may no longer experience initiation into the Tambaran cult, which will impair their ability "to produce thriving and abundant crops of yams," the staple food (Leavitt 1998: 186). In a remote area of the Highlands, Aletta Biersack has documented the breakdown of the lengthy and elaborate bride-price negotiation/display as young Paiela men bypass these traditions in obtaining wives. She warns: "What drops out of the picture with a loss of these practices is not just . . . ritual . . . but . . . the very social order that the ritual was meant to construct and maintain" (Biersack 1998: 87). In Africa, acculturation has diminished the importance of initiation, including:

> Vaginal inspection . . . and infibulation, cultural practices that were powerful sources of sexual control in adolescents as they marked specific developmental transitions . . . traditional education through initiation rites, chaperones, folklore, the orientation of adolescents to acceptable sexual behaviors by grandparents, through oral traditions, seems to be losing its relevance rather rapidly. (Nsamenang 2002: 84–85)

The breakdown of the village social structure is evident (Brooks 2011: 196). In Gbarngasuakwelle, young men returning from the town imported playing cards and the Ludo board game, eschewing the traditional *malang* game. Since senior males are the acknowledged masters and own the often intricately carved *malang* boards, this change effectively closed off yet another opportunity elder males used to assert their superiority over the young (Lancy 1996). In Guinea, as in much of Africa, young men are beholden to their seniors for the resources required to secure a bride and establish a family. In a gerontocracy, the young are at the beck and call of seniors, but young Guineans, in joining the defense forces, acquire capital and free themselves from these obligations. On the downside, they may also forego the extended kin ties that support allopaternal care of their offspring (Vigh 2006: 46, 53).

Throughout much of contemporary Papua New Guinea, young males are referred to in Melanesian pidgin as *bikhet* (="big head", or, in an urban context, *rascal*). Christian missions offer them the opportunity to escape the restrictions imposed by traditional rites associated, in the Sepik area, with the men's *Haus Tambaran*, without successfully socializing them to embrace Western/Christian values. Similarly, in attending government schools, young males signal their abandonment of the traditional agrarian economy without actually learning enough to secure a job in the modern economy. In short, they have been led to believe they are superior to the senior men, yet bring no significant resources to the community; hence – *bikhets* (Leavitt 1998; for Java see White 2012: 95). Sedentarization of Inuit bands has led to conglomerations of adolescent males who now represent a "serious social problem" (Konner 1975: 117). More generally, delinquency in the village can be linked to the loosening of ties between adolescents and adults, including members of one's lineage. Where kin ties are strong, adults other than parents also exert a restraining influence (Schlegel 2000b).

When men migrate from the village, their absence leaves women, and especially children, with a greater burden (Honwana 2006: 81; LeVine 1966: 188). Not surprisingly, women may become eager to follow the men's lead and escape rural poverty. In Sri Lanka, young village women are able to earn regular wages in the garment industry in Colombo, but they risk being labeled *Juki Girls* and deemed unfit for marriage (Lynch 2007: 107). The decline in subsidized agriculture in China just as factory employment is expanding in the cities has led young women to trade close parental control and the boredom of the village for freedom, big-city bright lights, and a meager wage (Lee 1998). Traditional matchmaking and family formation, naturally, go by the board as "heterosexual dating has become increasingly frequent in China" (Stevenson and Zusho 2002: 149). Farmers, of course, now find it extremely hard to find a spouse.

While young men everywhere enjoy greater freedom to exploit opportunities outside the constraints of village life, both legal statutes and vigilante justice combine to deny young Muslim women opportunities for independence, and the traditional patriarchy is maintained. Elsewhere, such as in Barbados (Stoffle 1977), barriers, are falling. Pregnancy may not be seen as an impediment (Sinhalese – Caldwell *et al.* 1998: 141), as the baby can, sometimes, be placed with relatives in the village (Hollos and Leis 1989: 73). The relevant large-scale demographic trends in Africa show the age of marriage rising, as adolescent women seek education and employment in lieu of marriage; however, the age of first pregnancy is not appreciably rising, perhaps due to the non-availability of contraception (Bledsoe and Cohen 1993).

A shift has begun whereby employers are preferentially hiring women, who are more reliable and cheaper than men.[25] In Costa Rica, the decline in coffee prices has eliminated a reliable source of employment for rural men while women's employment in manufacturing has increased dramatically. Hence men find themselves unable to fulfill the traditional breadwinner role and are, in effect, unable to achieve adult status (Mannon and Kemp 2010: 11). If young men cannot find the means to support a family while women can earn a living and care for offspring, perhaps with the assistance of their mothers, it follows that the nuclear family will decline in importance. More ominously, poverty and civil strife may sweep adolescents into the ranks of impromptu militias. One well-studied case is Tajikistan, where overpopulation has created a huge cadre of unemployed youth who periodically go on the rampage (Harris 2006: 29).

---

[25] A parallel phenomenon may be occurring in education. In a long-term study in a Javanese village: "girls previously lagged behind boys in access to secondary education, they have now caught up, and now girls up to age eighteen actually spend more time in school and home study than boys" (White 2012: 91).

Disaffected African students, their hopes for white-collar jobs dashed by stagnant economies, are easily recruited as "rebels" (Lancy 1996: 198) and street rioters (Durham 2008: 173). Terrorists and rebel armies capitalize on the peculiarities of adolescent psychology, brought on in part by "living in limbo," to create pliable fanatics (Rosen 2005: 157). Rosen also notes the continuity between traditional Mende warrior training, described earlier in this chapter, and the recruitment and training of child soldiers.

The RUF [Revolutionary United Front] also made use of ... Poro-like rituals. RUF recruits were often sworn to secrecy and took oaths of loyalty, the violation of which was said to result in the magical death of the violator ... many fighting groups seized on these powerful symbols as a means to organize and control youth ... [who willingly] ... brought opponents before youth-run kangaroo courts, and hacked men and women to death with machetes. (Rosen 2005: 72, 78)

A similar process unfolded in the long civil wars following Portugal's exit from its African colonies. A seventeen-year-old from Angola recalled:

We all had to drink two spoons of blood each. They told us that this was important to prevent us from being haunted by the spirits of the people we might kill ... Echoes of traditional religious beliefs and practices are audible in these testimonies. Militia commanders deliberately used features of local peacetime initiation rituals in the initiation of recruits into violence in order to make soldiers fearless and to mystify the taking of life. (Honwana 2006: 62)

Initiation rites in the socialization of young rebels, unlike traditional rites, do "not facilitate their social transition into responsible adulthood" (Honwana 2006: 63). Similarly, in the Salvadorian civil war, young soldiers "were not given a chance to practice and learn how to be *campesinos*, dedicated to subsistence agriculture ... and the lack of preparation for a new, adult peacetime identity led many youth to choose the negative identity of ... *marero* [delinquent/gang member]. (Dickson-Gómez 2003: 344–345)

In the developed societies, remote rural and impoverished urban enclaves foster the same sort of anomie – with comparable results. Adolescent males living in run-down US inner cities are extremely likely to be incarcerated, infected with HIV/AIDS, or addicted, or end their lives as homicide or suicide victims (Rose and McClain 1990).[26] Similarly, adolescent males living on Indian reservations suffer mortality and suicide rates three times the national average. On Red Lake Reservation (North America), the locus for a devastating mass murder/suicide by a despondent teenager in 2005, a third of those

---

[26] "Youth Challenge" is a program run by the US National Guard to rescue inner-city dropouts. Recruits – just like their counterparts in the military – are subject to an ordeal of rigorous discipline. They are weaned from drugs and crime and socialized to the mores of the dominant society (Eckholm, 2009).

eligible aren't in school, and gang violence and drug abuse are endemic (Harden and Hedgpeth 2005). Parallel conditions prevail among Australian Aboriginal populations in contemporary Australia. Political and economic forces are combining to create conditions in which adolescent limbo threatens to become a life-long state. The agricultural economy, whether small-scale village-based farming or plantation-scale agribusiness, is in stagnation or decline. Manufacturing is migrating "downward" from wealthy nations in Europe, Asia, and North America to rapidly modernizing countries. But this spreading wage economy is hardly penetrating the poorer countries, including most of Africa, Oceania, and large sectors of the Western hemisphere and Southeast Asia.

Modern economic forces have created two very different kinds of adolescence. We've just been reviewing the fate of individuals who, as a result of economic insecurity, seem not to be able to exit adolescence and cross the threshold into community-supported family formation. In the concluding section, we will consider individuals who must remain in adolescence to take advantage of economic opportunities that are only available to the well-educated.

Adolescents as students and consumers

Students in secondary school learn about a life state called adolescence, so for some school has "created" the concept as well as the expectation of behaviors associated with it. (Davis and Davis 1989: 59

Today ... people [in Madagascar] unequivocally associate youth with fashion. (Cole 2008: 101)

The internet has become an alternative space for Iranian youth. (Khosravi 2008: 157)

In the Philippines, there is a growing gulf between urban, educated adolescents and their lower-class or rural counterparts. Relative to the latter, the former are delaying marriage and family formation, as children are seen as an economic liability (Santa Maria 2002: 184). Surveys show that, where the pathway from school to wage employment is relatively secure, "parents are found to work harder and longer hours to replace the loss of children's labor" (Larson and Suman 1999: 708)." However, in White's long-term study in the Javanese village Kali Loro, he finds that, for contemporary youth, schooling has become a form of consumerism. That is, the economic payoff is very chancy, yet, in spite of the fact that students don't enjoy schooling – of low quality, and teaching is uninspired – they persist through secondary school. They do so to sustain the self-image of being modern and "with-it" and to postpone the day they'll assume the role of a typical villager "scratching a living in various kinds of manual work" (White 2012: 94).

Students' contribution to the household may diminish, while parents may need to pay school fees and equip children with uniforms and school books and/or tools. In Morocco, "it cost ... 400 dirhams ($66) each year to attend school, which is about what a woman would earn working as a field labourer ... for a whole month" (Davis and Davis 1989: 62). In "some countries, such as Egypt, private schools have become more numerous and popular among those who can afford them, as public schools become more crowded and less effective" (Booth 2002: 223).

The expectation, of course, is that for students, schoolwork equals "chores."

Schoolwork fills close to half of waking hours among Korean adolescents, a third of waking hours for a sample of Japanese adolescents and samples of adolescents in an elite Italian high school ... In East Asia, the school day is 8 hours long, and students attend an extra half day on Saturday ... homework was found to take ... 2.5 hours per day for samples of Polish, Romanian, and Russian adolescents ... 3.0 hours per day among Korean high school students ... in Taiwan ...11th graders report spending an average of 3.7 hours per day on homework. (Larson and Suman 1999: 712–713)[27]

However, besides schoolwork, it is common for adolescents to be provided with supervised extra-curricular activities. In East Asia, music lessons and practice are the norm. In Europe and the USA, competitive athletic activity soaks up adolescents' time and their parents' euros/dollars (Kremer-Sadlik et al. 2010).

While the need to engage in the decades-long apprenticeship known as formal education is the most important factor in the creation of modern adolescence as a distinct life-stage, the *culture* of adolescence is largely a product of the discretionary income of youth. In the USA, youth "spend about $100 billion a year, just on things for themselves. Two thirds of this comes from their own earnings, the rest from their parents" (Hine 1999: 23). This commercial culture has been taken up, in varying degrees depending on income, around the globe. "Japan has emerged ... as a competitive producer of cutting-edge 'cool' goods in the tough market of global youth culture" (Allison 2008: 180). In the Solomon Islands:

Young people, either school-leavers or drop outs without any marketable skills, come to town, lured by the "lights" of Honiara: cinemas, shops, crowds, sports games,

---

[27] The USA is anomalous in these surveys because figures for schoolwork and homework are much lower than in other modern, post-industrial countries. This is at least partly because admission to two- and four-year post-secondary institutions (which educate and credential one for the workforce) is comparatively more liberal.

big markets, take-away food, etc. They are drawn by the desire to experience it all, or at least to see it all. (Jourdan 1995: 211)

In South Africa, "Coca-Cola kids [have] embraced Western values of individualism, competition, and materialism ... In rural north China, intergenerational squabbles have emerged over young people's embrace of materialistic values, their display of new clothes, leather shoes, expensive cigarettes, and cassettes" (Gibbons 2004: 258). In a Javanese village, children are eager to take advantage of "three newly installed PlayStation kiosks" (White 2012: 93). "St. Valentine's Day has sprung up as a day of celebration, a 'sweetheart's day,' spreading rapidly through the college-preparatory schools of cities and towns all over Poland" (Schlegel 2000a: 80). Youth in Kenya are choosing to adopt a national identity and, in the process, willingly violating kinship and age cohort principles of their (Gusii) tribe (LeVine 2011: 428).

In the Muslim world, two potent movements, aided and abetted by social media, contest for the allegiance of youth. One stream flows "towards the mosque and Islamism, the other towards the West" (Schade-Poulsen 1995: 82–83). While young mujahideen and suicide bombers make headlines, youth also are at the forefront of change tugging their societies toward Western fashions and values. The "airwaves of Morocco are filled with songs of romantic passion [while] upper-class youth in ... Casablanca may live lives similar to Americans, with dating and discos" (Davis and Davis 1989: 133, 209). Tajik girls link themselves to boyfriends, in defiance of family and custom, in the hope of having some control over whom they'll marry (C. Harris 2006: 108). "In Algeria ... a new musical style ... called raï came into being ... using Western instruments and mixing local popular songs ... with ... American disco" (Schade-Poulsen 1995: 81). In Iran, the younger generation has become "Americanized," and "they criticize and reject not only political Islam but also Islamic traditions in general, which were unquestionable for their parents' generation" (Khosravi 2008: 126–127).

These changes in the lives of adolescents suggest that they will continue to live in limbo. The Mardu of Central Australia live in one of the poorest regions of the country. Jobs are scarce and, because they "have not embraced schooling with much enthusiasm or success" (Tonkinson 2011: 219), employment elsewhere is unlikely. Nevertheless,

Mardu adolescents and young adults are keen consumers of global youth culture. They enjoy many of the same products and pastimes as their peers in Australia and elsewhere. Many drink alcohol, and some indulge in recreational substance use; they wear clothing that mimics the styles of hip-hop and sports stars. In their homes they watch television and DVDs, listen to CDs, and play electronic games. (Tonkinson 2011: 218)

As Kincheloe notes, digital – especially social – media allow children to "negotiate their own culture," but it is a culture that is dependent on resources provided entirely by adults. In order to obtain the means to become truly independent agents, children must subject themselves to the authoritarian culture of family, school, and employer. This paradox "has placed many children in [a] confusing and conflicting situation" (Kincheloe 2002: 78; see also Arnett 2002: 312; Lancy 2012b).

9   Taming the autonomous learner

The reluctant scholar

A diller (unwilling scholar), a dollar, a ten o'clock scholar! What makes you come so soon? You used to come at ten o'clock, But now you come at noon. (Mother Goose nursery rhyme, *c*.1760)

To teach *hanzi* [Chinese characters], reading aloud and reciting texts are the most basic methods ... [reflected in an] old Chinese saying: "If you read a text for a thousand times, it will be understood." (Wang *et al* 2009: 400).

Camilla Morelli (2011, 2012) has been a recent participant observer – with a focus on children – in a transitional community of Matses Indians in the Peruvian Amazon. She marvels at how facile and active the Matses children are in the natural environment, compared to what she feels is her own ineptitude. She is cowed by three- and four-year-olds who competently paddle and maneuver canoes on the wide river. She observes young boys nimbly catching and handling enormous catfish (Figure 28). And then she is struck by the painful contrast between the children's mastery of their natural surroundings and the great discomfort and incompetence they display in the classroom. She summarizes the dilemma as "learning to sit still." Somehow Matses children must suppress their spontaneous inclinations, which serve them well in learning their culture, and adopt a pattern of behavior and cognitive engagement that is completely novel. In the classroom they can't sit still, they can't remain silent. These children display the symptoms of what, in the context of a typical US classroom, would be labeled a "disorder."

Chaga peoples in rural Tanzania feel that schooling – especially too much reading and writing – is driving children "to the brink of hysteria" (Stambach 1998a: 497). Moving north to the Sahara, Touareg boys aspire to sleep under the stars on a camel caravan. Touareg homes:

Contain neither chairs nor tables ... people sit or lie on a mat, and constantly change their position ... sitting on a chair is the most unnatural thing in the world. And apart from the schoolchildren, no one stays inside a closed room [because] a closed room is like a prison. (Spittler 2012: 68)

326

Figure 28 Matses boy with catfish

In Elementary schools in Denmark, Danish kids are "calm" while immigrants are "wild." Teachers use scolding and guilt to tame the wild ones (Gilliam 2008).

The story of childhood that has unfolded in this book contains many scenes, but classrooms are conspicuously absent. Children across cultures and through time have managed to grow to adulthood and learn to become functioning members of their society without the necessity of schooling. Jump to the twenty-first century and we find a world where childhood without schooling is unthinkable. The ubiquity of schooling belies the fact that it is a costly investment (for nations, for families, and for children) that often pays little or no return. The central theme of this chapter is the "strangeness" of the modern practice of schooling. I use the term "strange" because, in a survey of childhood across history and culture, the suite of practices and teaching/learning abilities associated with modern schooling is largely absent (Azuma 1981: 25). I will argue that successful schooling rests on firm cultural foundations associated with Western and East Asian societies (Tyson 2002: 1183; Li 2012), but extremely rare elsewhere (Tudge 2008: 153).

Examples of this mismatch abound. From seventeenth-century Holland (Durantini 1983: 152–154) to eighteenth-century Japan (Kuroda 1998: 42), we can find a popular genre of painting the Dutch called "unruly school scenes." As soon as the teacher's attention was focused elsewhere, groups of students would "play up" and chaos would ensue. In rural Ghanaian villages, boys are eager to trade the strictures of the classroom for the freedom of the herder. And their parents, who see that schooled individuals have not gained any economic advantage, do little to encourage their young scholars (Goody 2006: 245; see also Ofosu-Kusi and Mizen 2012: 279). Among Zinacantecans, the brightest, most able children are kept at home to work and learn while the "stupid ones go to school, so the teacher can make them smart" (Greenfield 2004: 66). The Touaregs, famous desert caravaners studied by Gerd Spittler, refused to send their children to a new school even though attendance was compulsory. Some even went so far as to purchase potions from the shaman to make them appear stupid (Spittler 1998: 16, 33).[1]

On an Indian Reservation in the US, children are viewed as being inattentive because they don't gaze at the teacher when she is speaking, and yet averting one's gaze in the presence of adults is "proper" behavior in the village (Phillips 1983: 101, 103). "As soon as Huaorani children are placed in the school context, they become shy, quiet, and reserved ... [because those who] have forgotten something, have their ears or hair pulled" (Rival 2002: 153). Mazahua children regret their loss of autonomy in the classroom, where they "are rarely allowed to take the initiative" (Paradise and de Haan 2009: 200).

---

[1] From more recent fieldwork, Spittler reports that the cross-desert caravaners are now challenged by border authorities, tax assessors, and merchants and find that knowledge of French and some level of numeracy and literacy are essential to their trade. So they have become more sympathetic to schooling (Spittler 2012: 70).

The accoutrements of schooling or formal education – teachers, class-rooms, books, chalk boards – weren't needed as children learned their culture without such aids. On the other hand, the village is not completely free of formal institutions with socializing functions, the apprenticeship (discussed in Chapter 7) and "Bush" school (Chapter 8 and below) being widespread exemplars. More importantly, at least one of these institutions probably gave rise to the earliest schools. That is, schooling can be considered to have evolved in at least two steps. It used to resemble the apprenticeship, with attention focused on the master/teacher who grudgingly shared what he knew while enforcing obedience and menial labor from apprentices/students. In keeping with the shift to the neontocracy, schooling has become universal, egalitarian, student-centered, and free of punishment – corporal and otherwise. Teachers and parents have become partners in the careful and diligent nurturing of each child's potential from infancy. This more recent version of schooling has yet to penetrate most of the traditional communities typically studied by anthropologists.

Another theme that runs through this chapter is *resistance*. Schools have encountered resistance from pupils who struggle to "sit still" or to meet the teacher's gaze; from parents who'd prefer their children to be working and who reject their assigned role as "under-teacher," prepping and supporting their child's schooling; from patriarchal societies that impose limits on the choices available to women; and from the general public because of the very poor quality of instruction and the coercive atmosphere. Even as societies modernize and the character of schooling changes, resistance is very much in evidence. In the US and, to a lesser extent, in Europe, significant numbers of students strenuously resist engagement with academic subjects and the concomitant mental effort. Hereafter follows a review of the culturally constructed and preserved strategies employed to prevent or overcome student resistance to the now very necessary institution of schooling. And, lastly, we consider how being schooled changes the way people deal with information.

The rise of schooling: First the stick, then the carrot

[Ben Johnson noted in the late 1500s that the] schoolmaster spent his days sweeping his living from the posteriors of little children. (Lyon 2009: 24)

Children were likely to look for any means of subverting or escaping from such regimes. (Cunningham 1995: 105)

Schooling has its origin in the apprenticeship. I make this claim largely on the basis of the many parallels between the character of the apprenticeship (Lancy 2012a; this volume, Chapter 7, p. 287) and the earliest schools. The first students, like apprentices, were drawn from a select group because there were fees involved and specific prohibitions on students from the lower class or peasant communities (Bai 2005: 159; Orme 2006: 131). From school records, the earliest scribes were noted as the offspring of such luminaries as governors, senior civil servants, and priests (Saggs 1987). Corporal punishment is also essential to the conduct of schools – as it is to the apprenticeship.

The oldest known classroom and pedagogical material were found in Mesopotamia. The *edduba* or Tablet House from the third millennium BCE excavated at Mari had two rows of benches for the students and many discarded tablets. The clay tablet facilitated instruction because it could be easily erased and reused and was much less costly than the writing media used elsewhere in antiquity. Kramer notes that the schools were "uninviting," the lessons were dull, and discipline was harsh (1963: 243). One poor novice describes his experience: "My headmaster read my tablet, said: 'There is something missing,' caned[2] me. 'Why didn't you speak Sumerian,' caned me. My teacher said: 'Your hand is unsatisfactory,' caned me.' And so I began to hate the scribal art" (Kramer 1963: 238–239).

In Greece "The teacher's badge of authority was the *narthex* ... the stalk of the giant fennel [, which had] the capacity to hurt more than a hard stick" (Beck 1975: 35). The instrument of instruction in the Greek home was a sandal, but this disciplinary tool was also part of the teacher's arsenal (Beck 1975: 44). The Roman "schoolmaster's didactic tool of choice was the ruler or the whip: it enabled him to keep order amidst the rowdy crowd with which he was confronted on a daily basis" (Laes 2011: 124). In Renaissance Italy: "Under the rod of a master, the students would achieve 'the splendor of learning'" (Grendler 1989: 13). Even as schools evolved to more closely resemble contemporary practice, the teacher remained a remote and formidable authority figure, much like the master potter or blacksmith. In Britain the master is depicted perched at his elevated desk "grasping the birch – a bundle of twigs – that formed his badge of office" and used "to punish indiscipline and inability to answer" (Orme 2006: 144). A teacher in Britain in the 1590s "laments that children are afraid to come to school and wish to leave as soon as possible because of the severity and frequency of the whippings" (Durantini 1983: 125). In nineteenth-century France the teacher relied upon "leather and wooden rods thick enough to injure a child, or at the very least to put his hands out of action for a considerable time. The teacher was therefore a daunting figure for young children" (Heywood 1988: 65). These practices grew out of the belief that children would not naturally accept the role of student. Greek

---

2 The specific cuneiform sign is an amalgam of the signs for stick and flesh (Kramer 1963: 237).

disciplinarians could cite injunctions in Plato's *Protagoras* that assigned them the duty of straightening children like a piece of bent wood.

Sumerian students as young as seven endured a many-year-long curriculum beginning with the menial tasks, also characteristic of the apprenticeship. The students spent tedious hours every day copying over and memorizing long lists of names, technical terms, legal phrases, and whole dictionaries (Saggs 1987). Fragments of *ostraca* or pottery shards from Egypt show similar endless copying of prescribed texts. And the number of errors in the texts suggests that many scribes may have been mere artisans, and not actually literate (Strouhal 1992: 35–37). Students often learned in a language that was not their mother-tongue or even one they'd not heard spoken. European schools employed Latin exclusively, so students learned to recognize words and pronounce them, but they could not understand what they read unless they were told (Orme 2006: 59; see also Reynolds 1996: 10). In thirteenth-century schools, "each student daily had to memorize a poem or story and recite it. When they did poorly they were beaten" (Gies and Gies 1987: 210). Unlike the chore curriculum, the early school curriculum made little allowance for children learning through play, at their own pace, or through their own motivation and initiative. As schooling spread in Japan, "curricula were geared towards the eventual mastery of classical texts [and] there was little recognition of the fact that 'the child' was the primary target of schooling" (Platt 2005: 969). Autonomous learning was also thwarted because the school, like the initiation ritual, exercises complete control over access to knowledge (Lancy 1975: 378).

Education in Asia has its origins in the almost messianic teachings of Confucius (K'ung-fu-tzu, 551–479 BCE). The net effect of Confucianism was to create in China the earliest meritocracy: a government run by learned and morally sound bureaucrats. Hence, formal education in East Asia has a much longer, if no less checkered, history (Zheng 1994) than it does in the West. The cornerstone of this system was the imperial examination for entry and placement in the civil service (Kinney 1995: 18–19). In the late fourteenth century CE, for example, exams lasted from twenty-four to seventy-two hours and were held in spare, isolated halls. Each candidate was issued an ID number and his answers were rewritten by a scribe so that the examinee's calligraphy wouldn't reveal his identity to the exam reader. This system gave rise to what is today called "examination hell."

As in the apprenticeship, those who survived the ordeal of schooling could expect a secure economic future. Because of these status and pecuniary considerations – "Education was one way to lay claim to being a gentleman" (Lyon 2009: 25) – and the desire of senior scribes to protect their monopoly, students were humiliated, beaten, and generally awed by their masters. A primary goal of early schooling was to contain the child's natural exuberance and curiosity and create "a pious, disciplined, obedient, and teachable child" (Cunningham 1995: 48). Similarly, the "purpose common to the education of medieval clergy and nobles, as it was to that of apprentices, was the inculcation of self-control and of respect for authority" (Gies and Gies 1987: 217). Monks in an Anglo-Saxon monastery were charged with maintaining strict discipline so that "playful youth ... should find no outlet for their exuberance" (Crawford 1999: 147). And as teachers today attempt to recruit parents as partners, in the past "pedagogues advised fathers to 'chasten' their children, that is, to reprimand and instruct them" (Alexandre-Bidon and Lett 1999: 63).

The atmosphere in early classrooms was grim.

[Roman] teachers met their students outdoors and held classes on the sidewalks or in piazzas. There were, of course, many disadvantages for the students, and traffic noise and street crowds must have been very distracting, and inclement weather was surely a problem. However, sidewalk schools avoided rent and lighting costs. (Shelton 1998: 103–104)

Elizabethan classrooms were big drafty spaces, often converted from chapels; they were noisy and dirty, freezing in the winter, and dark at both ends of the school day. (Lyon 2009: 22)

The only seat, which constituted the single piece of schoolroom furniture, was reserved for the master. This was "the chair." From this chair, he towered above his students who were seated on the floor, cross-legged, reading or writing on their knees. (Alexandre-Bidon and Lett 1999: 12)

Schools in New England colonies were small and uncomfortable with few furnishings and books. Many teachers were poorly prepared and most were intense disciplinarians, dealing out harsh punishment for infractions. (Frost 2010: 36)

The lamentations of passionate critics provide another window on the nature of schooling. These critics believed that the reluctant scholar problem could be solved by making schooling more like the experiences of the unschooled child, mixing in play, letting the child make choices, rewarding curiosity and independent learning. The fact that these pleas continue to appear over nearly two millennia suggests how enduring and intractable were the earliest ideas about the nature of schooling.

[In the first century CE] Quintilian believed that learning through play was to be cultivated from an early age. (Rawson 2003: 127)

[A fifteenth century Chinese philosopher] disapproved of the curriculum in the Ming [Dynasty as] children were forced to recite phrases and sentences and imitate civil service examination papers every day .... Wang Yangming [recommended instead that school] children be "happy and cheerful at heart." (Bai 2005: 50)

[Erasmus in the early sixteenth century wrote] that a constant element of enjoyment must be mingled with our studies so that we think of learning as a game rather than a form of drudgery ... Schools he lamented [were] torture-chambers; you hear nothing but the thudding of the stick, the swishing of the rod, howling and moaning, and shouts of brutal abuse. (Cunningham 1995: 44–45)

At the middle of the sixteenth century the Jesuits began opening schools with a more liberal approach that included, for example, some instruction in the vernacular. But the Jesuit order was suppressed by the Pope in 1773 and all the Jesuit schools (save a few in Russia) were closed. (Farrell 1970)

The idea that school should *interest* children was considered a radical new pedagogical philosophy in the United States of the 1840s ... It contradicted schoolmasters' prior assumptions that only a sense of duty or the master's cane would motivate learners. Yet it had become important to maintain students' interest at least in part because the interested student was an *attentive* student. (Anderson-Levitt 2002: 82)

It wasn't until well into the twentieth century that these reformist principles finally took firm hold of schooling in the West, and they are just now gaining traction in China (Kipnis 2001: 10–11). Pre-school education – with play as a central element of the pedagogy; child-centered instruction; teachers who strive to "get down to their pupils' level" (literally and intellectually); a concern for the child's sense of wellbeing; tailor-made curricula; the cessation of corporal punishment; materials designed to arouse interest and motivation; and aggressive policies to prevent drop-outs are all of recent vintage. These are among the attributes of modern schooling in post-industrial society, which set the institution apart from earlier schools. The character of early schools was adapted to the gerontocracy, whereas the neontocracy gave birth to contemporary ideas about education.

If the symbol of early schooling was the stick, then the current symbol should be a carrot. The greatest problem facing schools in the USA seems to be persuading students that they should want to be there. In the popular press, this is a typical headline: "Across the USA, education experts are reimagining the school day to make it more engaging, effective and fun."[3] On the same day that the headline appeared, the cover of a similar publication displayed a picture of a friendly looking red-and-white robot, with this headline: "Meet your child's new teacher: Projo the robot is just one of the exciting innovations helping kids succeed in school."[4]

In spite of its painful history, schooling, in the latter half of the twentieth century, began to be looked on as the cornerstone of modernization and

[3] *Parade Magazine.* Available at www.parade.com/62420/michaelbrick/three-cheers-for-school-building-a-better-school-day. Accessed August 11, 2013.
[4] *USA Weekend.* Available at www.usaweekend.com/article/20130809/LIVING/308090008/Six-innovators-offer-a-fresh-perspective-on-learning. Accessed August 9, 2013.

progress.[5] As Chinese influence permeated Asia, and Western culture was imposed on the "New World" and "Global South," schooling, with set curricula and designated teachers and classrooms, slowly penetrated every corner of the globe. However, as we will see, the kinder, gentler pedagogy of the West has yet to take root in most rural schools in less developed countries.

As I've discussed in several earlier chapters, non-elite children before the modern era learned what was essential largely through informal means. But there is one traditional institution that employed quite formal and routinized procedures to transform all youth of the appropriate age. Like early schools, it shares many attributes of the apprenticeship. This is the initiation rite – introduced in the previous chapter. It has only rarely been analyzed as an educational institution.

"Bush" schools

Formal education in the initiations is minimal, as it is only occasionally desirable in everyday Afikpo life. There really is no "school in the bush," the specific knowledge that the boys acquire is not extensive. (Ottenberg 1989: 237)

Compliance with the traditional wisdom enshrined in the formal songs and dances of the elders is a sure sign that one "understands." (Maxwell 1983: 58).

I earlier referred to the "strangeness" of schooling as an institution with few historical or cultural antecedents. One possible antecedent is the initiation rite for youth. These varied customs have been referred to as "bush schools." However, the emphasis seems to have been on indoctrination, not education or training (Lancy 1975). Chisungu, the lengthy girls' initiation in Bemba (Zimbabwe) society, includes "rites representing hoeing, sowing, cooking, gathering firewood ... but, instruction, in the European sense, was quite unnecessary in such subjects" (Richards 1956: 161). By highlighting women's traditional occupations the goal was not skill-training, as the girls were likely quite proficient already, but affirming gender identity. A similar form of moralistic instruction may be found in male rites:

The [Gisu] circumciser gives [the initiate] food, fire, a hoe, a knife, a drinking tube and other utensils of adult life. As each item is handed to him the boy is told both of its proper use and of its misuse, for example, "Kindle this piece of firewood and as you kindle it I say, 'Do not go and burn down the houses of your neighbors. I have made you kindle it so that your wife can cook for you and you can heat water and make tea

---

[5] Econometric analyses show that schooling, *per se*, has little modernizing influence – at least on the economy. Rather the spread of market activity prompts the transition to modern institutions (Baten *et al.* 2009: 806).

for yourself' . . . I give you this drinking tube to hold and say, 'Drink beer and brew it. Do not get drunk and quarrelsome so that you are always fighting'." (Heald 1982: 23)

Adolescents are perceived to need a degree of "packaging" to reorient them from the peer group to the larger community, to reinforce their respect for authority (Edel 1957/1996: 183), and to ready them for the responsibility of family formation (Marlowe 2010: 56).

Although detailed descriptions of initiation rites are rare, a set of pedagogical principles can be extracted from cases in the ethnographic record. First, all initiation rites involve some element of body mutilation ranging, mildly, from tattooing (Markstrom 2008: 132) to scarification (Wagley 1977: 163) to the excision of the genitalia (Arnold 2006: 50). The Papua New Guinea Highlands and Sepik regions are particularly noted for the pain and utter terror associated with the process (Herdt 1990: 376). Typically, the child is symbolically killed by a monstrous figure and then resurrected or reborn (Higgens 1985: 103). In addition to painful injury, other anxiety-inducing treatments include forcible removal from one's home (Dorjahn 1982: 40), confinement or seclusion in a strange place for an extended period (de Laguna 1965: 21), and physical ordeals such as bathing in ice-water and running or dancing until exhausted (Markstrom 2008: 131–2). "The dominant theme of the initiation is that of an ordeal – trial and proof of maturity" (Goldschmidt 1986: 95–6). Consequently, as in the apprenticeship (Lancy 2012a: 117), parents tend not to be involved in their child's initiation.

A second common element is that the rites constitute an induction into the prevailing social order (Markstrom 2008: 262).[6] For example, in the Bonerate circumcision ritual, "novices are formally introduced to the ideal standards of conduct to which adults should conform," including the appropriate display of shame and respect for others and acute awareness of their social position (Broch 1990: 137–138). Rites for girls emphasize subservience to senior women and obedience to one's future husband (Richards 1956: 103) and those for boys, subservience to senior men and dominance over women (Tuzin 1980: 26). The youth is forcibly weaned from the "bad influence" of the peer group (Rao 2006: 59) or the mother. Didactic instruction in the "lore" of the society is not evident. On the contrary, the initiation rite is an opportunity to impress upon young people their ignorance and powerlessness. "In Kpelle society, secrecy . . . supports the elders' political and economic control of the youth" (Murphy 1980: 193). Similarly, for Ngaanyatjarra aboriginal youth, "knowledge had to be prized from [the elders] bit by bit, and with a lot of effort" (Brooks 2011: 207).

---

[6] There is a strong suggestion in the research on neurological changes in adolescence that the brain is shifting gears from task mastery to mastering the complexities of adult interpersonal relationships (Blakemore 2008).

Male initiation has been thoroughly described for the Baktaman of Papua New Guinea. There are several initiation stages stretching over the entire period of adolescence and early adulthood. Barth's analysis reveals that the initiation rites aren't so much about transmitting cultural knowledge as about senior males controlling those more junior. Whereas the youth has, to this point, been able to learn from overhearing or observation in relative autonomy, the information conveyed in the initiation is secret and tightly controlled. "Much of the more highly valued information is cast in codes known only to a few members of the community" (Barth 1975: 18). And this is to be expected, as "knowledge is power everywhere in Melanesia" (Lepowsky 1993:75).

Especially in the initial stages, boys are subjected to a stressful ordeal:

Water and fire are also used for torture, reinforcing the basic messages of earlier initiation: that those forces are powerful and dangerous; sacred knowledge is costly and must be paid for with hardship and its value thus confirmed. (Barth 1975: 66)

As information is transmitted to the initiates they are warned, on pain of death, to maintain the secrets, but then, at a later stage, they learn they've been deceived.

Sometimes, statements and promises have been made that were immediately exposed as lies by the next ritual act; sometimes information was made vaguely suspect by hints or evidence that it was rendered false or grossly incomplete by further secrets. Even the central revelation of one initiation – e.g. the showing of the bones to second degree novices – was shown to be largely a hoax in a latter initiation. (Barth 1975: 81)

The primary point of these exercises seems to be to maintain and enhance the power of senior men over women and younger men. The knowledge conveyed has no practical purpose and the process of conveying that knowledge is carried out with "a view to retaining privilege for the seniors" (Barth 1975: 219). And this view – of knowledge as something grudgingly transmitted to youth in a way that protects and enhances the hegemony of seniors – is common (Brooks 2011: 207; Dorjahn 1982: 47). In spite of "instruction" in the initiation rite, youth are clearly not acquiring much declarative knowledge, nor learning practical skills during what is mainly a religious experience. This point holds, generally, for the processes underlying the religious indoctrination of youth (Mithen 1998: 101; Pagel 2012: 156).

Close cousins to the "Bush" school are Kuttab schools, which have been around a long time and are found wherever Islam has taken hold. Instruction consists primarily of reciting and ultimately memorizing the Qur'an, for which literacy is not essential (Fernea 1991: 452). These schools aim to indoctrinate pupils in a specific moral code (Moore 2006: 113). Similar emphases on rigid discipline and memorization of texts are found in religious schools serving Hindu (Broyon 2004) and Coptic (Levine 1965: 267) students. There has been a growing resistance to secular education and outright conflict between public schools and Qur'anic schools in some Muslim areas, such as northern Cameroon (Moore 2006: 114).

We can also find a few examples of school-like settings for acquiring particular skills or areas of expertise, such as instruction in the traditional Balinese gamelan percussion instruments. However, to a Westerner, although there is a classroom and a teacher, it does not look like "education." The teacher models correct performance; otherwise it is up to the pupils' initiative. He "explains nothing, since for him there is nothing to explain. If there are mistakes, he corrects them" (McPhee 1955: 89). Observing a dance class for girls on Bali in 2011, I was struck by the almost total absence of verbal instruction. Expert dancers modeled correct movements and, occasionally, would physically shape a novice's posture or stance. In Yemen, the training of a master builder is long and demanding as there are many skills to be acquired. Nevertheless, Yemeni minaret builders disavow any reliance on teaching, as we understand it (Marchand 2001: 219). These cases suggest that a key difference between "Bush" schools (and other traditional practices to train or indoctrinate the young) and schooling is the use of verbalization in the latter and its absence in the former (Rogoff 1981: 277–278).

Just as we can find antecedents for the earliest schools in the apprenticeship, so too, we find that, as schools are introduced to formerly school-less communities, they much more closely resemble medieval schools than they do modern, progressive institutions. Bare, drafty classrooms, rote memorization, a scarcity of teaching materials, corporal punishment, unintelligible teachers, menial labor by students, the underrepresentation and exploitation of girls – all harken back to the dawn of schooling in the West.

Village schools

[Teachers in Guinea believe] "Il faut suffrir pour apprendre" = to learn one must suffer. (Anderson-Levitt 2005: 988)

The image of the "dirty" village child or "primitive farmer" [is juxtaposed with] looking "proper" and "smart" in a school uniform. (Meinert 2003: 189)

On every continent, it is now unusual not to see an example of Western- or Asian-inspired public schools in every village. But a closer look doesn't inspire confidence. Even a casual observer will note the crowding, the lack of materials, the teacher droning in a language the pupils aren't following very well, and his clear preference for chastisement over praise (Borofsky 1987: 94). A massive international investment in human capital has yielded a low return, and we will examine some of the reasons why that's the case. Alber refers to children in Tebo village (Benin) dropping out because

Figure 29 Turkmen camel herder

fieldwork is preferable to the boredom and the "despotic" abuse by teachers (Alber 2012: 169). In Ghana, "many boys are eager to escape schooling to the freedom of the herdboy's life" (Goody 2006: 245). Eveny (Siberian pastoralists) adolescents may be responsible for the entire reindeer herd (compare the Turkmen camel herder in Figure 29), and they drop out of school because they resent the novice role they must play there (Ulturgasheva 2012: 119).

In the late 1960s, I had the opportunity to observe village schools in Liberia serving children of the Kpelle tribe. One in Sinyée – a village near a major road, hospital, and mission-run liberal arts college – was well constructed and equipped. The building, contents, and teachers all represented investments by the Liberian and US governments – USAID funded the buildings, and the US Peace Corps supplied hundreds of teachers. The goals were primarily to promote improvements in the quality of life at the village level, including enhanced health, agricultural production, and entrepreneurship. Secondarily, there was the desire to build an educated workforce that would provide the human capital upon which a modern economy could be built.[7] And, third, as in much of postcolonial Africa, nationalism rarely went beyond the capital, as tribal groups in the interior were largely in ignorance of the national government – beyond worshipful regard of the reigning president. Schools

[7] At that time, Liberia's economy, while robust in dollar terms, was considered fragile, as it depended on the extraction of non-renewable resources (iron, old-growth timber) and production of raw commodities (rubber) with zero in-country manufacturing or secondary production (Clower *et al.* 1966). Little has changed (Gay 2014).

were to foster the Liberian identity.[8] These initiatives, with the same objectives, were undertaken with great fanfare and optimism in the so-called "Third" or "Underdeveloped" World from the early 1960s to the 1990s, only to fail in Liberia and elsewhere. The goals were perfectly reasonable, but the means provided to achieve them were patently inadequate (Kilbride *et al.* 2000: 139; Lord 2011: 98).

I did not observe a great deal of learning in the Sinyée school (see also Gay and Cole 1967: 35) and felt that conditions were more akin to those of the "Bush" school described earlier. Aside from the severe problem imposed by pupils' near-zero knowledge of English, which was the language of instruction (compare medieval students learning in Latin), I saw "no books in Kpelle homes to learn from, no library, no 'Sesame Street,'" (Lancy 1975: 375). Parents, almost all of whom were illiterate, could not prepare or support their children's learning of academic subjects. Aside from the lack of village literacy, mathematics does not exist to a villager who sees instead a series of discrete problems and discrete solutions (Gay and Cole 1967).[9] One very general principle might be, "keep it simple."[10] Traditional means of measurement and counting are often among the first casualties of outside contact, when measurement tools are abandoned in favor of more efficient foreign methods (Lancy 1983: 109). Another finding is that the math used to solve everyday problems – especially the calculations employed by urban street sellers – does not transfer to school math (Saxe 1990; Rampal 2003). And, in spite of hundreds of attempts (Demmert and Towner 2003) to alter the curriculum to create bridges between village and school ways of thinking, the successful efforts have been rare and costly (Lipka *et al.* 2005).

A decade later I found a scenario similar to that of *c.* 1960–1970 Liberia in Papua New Guinea. In the Gapun village school, for example,

Children learn very little during their first two or three years ... due ... to their inability to cope with instruction in English ... Outside of school ... literacy skills are almost never used ... after they leave school at ages fourteen to fifteen, many of these young people may never read and will almost certainly never write again. (Kulick and Stroud 1993: 32)

---

[8] For a thorough treatment of the Ghanaian government's use of the schools to create a national identity, see Coe (2005).

[9] Much the same argument has been made for biology. "Children and adults do not seem to construct uniquely biological causal mechanisms for their everyday experience ... most children and probably even adults do not develop a 'folk-biology' unless given science input" (Au and Romo 1999: 396).

[10] As examples, Ghanaian "[fish-]sellers probably do not utilize all supply and demand information and do not combine such information to arrive at an overall assessment of market condition because, like all other decision makers, they avoid complex calculations" (Quinn 1978: 214). And in Liberia, I found that imprecise and limited measurement led to the construction of houses that only approximately reflected regular geometric shapes (Lancy 1996).

The failure of village schools in promoting literacy and other "modern" modes of thinking led to a shift in emphasis. Universal primary education – considered by the United Nations the *sine qua non* of modernity – was now embraced as a means to promote *rural development*. This was not a message that parents wanted to hear (Lancy 1979). But this redefinition of purpose has continued to be adopted in many areas of the Third World, provoking a similar response. In Uganda in the late 1990s, top-down attempts to "ruralize" or "vocationalize" the curriculum were resisted (Meinert 2003). At the local level, people continued to view the school as preparing students for non-rural, upwardly mobile futures.

In the intervening years, there has been relatively little change in rural classrooms in Papua New Guinea. For example, among the remote Asabano people, Little reports:

Children are forced to practice their reading skills with instructional bread-baking booklets that came free with the purchase of bags of flour in some distant town, many years ago ... the community has experienced difficulty in keeping an instructor for their school ... as [they] are loathe to journey to such a remote location ... the teacher ... moves between three different structures [for the different grades] ... students ... thus spend the majority of their day in a classroom without the presence of a teacher ... families are often unable to pull together enough funds ... and so children often attend school for a year, take a hiatus, return for a year, and so forth. [Consequently, each grade has] students of all ages and cognitive abilities. (Little 2011: 160–161)

As we travel around the globe, these and other problems emerge as anthropologists look at the school in the village. In Chillihuani village, where hamlets are dispersed[11] over a valley running from 3,800 to 5,000 meters, children's attendance at school is limited by the harsh climate and the great distance they must cover during the journey from home to school (Bolin 2006: 85). The monolingual Quechua-speaking children struggle with Spanish as the language of instruction. The classroom is so overcrowded that many must sit on the floor. In spite of a sympathetic teacher locally, Bolin notes that, generally, Indian children suffer harassment and other forms of abuse at the hands of mestizo teachers and students (Bolin 2006: 87).

In the schools in the Chiapas Highlands of Mexico, students were beaten and made to kneel on pebbles or fruit pits to drive lessons home. It is no wonder that "Indian parents did all they could to save their children from the

---

[11] This is a fairly common pattern, as homes may be located adjacent to farms. In Yemen, I observed children walking up to four miles to school, and they made the round trip twice each day so they could join their families for the main meal at noon. With recess and various other non-academic activities, I estimated the "instructional" day to be about three hours long for Yemenis through the sixth grade.

terrible fate of attending school" (Modiano 1973: 87). In Central Africa, "pygmy" school children are harassed and bullied by children from more powerful Bantu tribes, and government officials speak of them with evident racism and contempt. The obstacles they face mean that, according to a sympathetic teacher: "They sometimes take three to four years to complete a single year of normal schooling" (Raffaele 2003: 132). In Bangladesh, village children begin schooling quite late – on their own initiative – and their attendance is erratic. Hence, by adolescence, the average child has completed only three years of education (Nath and Hadi 2000). On Malaita Island in Melanesia, the teacher corps is poorly trained, is not fluent in the language of instruction (English), and turns over frequently. Materials are outdated and full of culturally inappropriate references. Children "memorize the singsong phrases required of them for oral recitation without understanding what the sentences mean" (Watson-Gegeo and Gegeo 1992: 18–19).

Anthropologists have documented the inadequacy of village schools (Barnett 1979: 8) as well as the lack of compatibility between schooling practices and traditional beliefs. For example, in most societies, parents tend to assume children will learn their culture autonomously – without being taught. This dictates a posture of "noninterference" in their children's schooling (Deyhle 1992: 40; Levin 1992: 67; Matthiasson 1979: 77; McCorkle 1965: 74). On Pulap Island (Micronesia), Flinn observed the following incompatible culture mix:

Although the educational system ostensibly derives from an American model ... many aspects nonetheless continue to transmit Pulapese culture ... the atmosphere at the school is very lax and permissive to an American observer ... The cupboards and shelves of the classrooms are in disarray ... The bells marking the periods ring at haphazard times – resulting in periods of irregular and unpredictable length and a recess that lasts two or three times the designated length ... Much of the seemingly chaotic behavior is consistent with other aspects of life on Pulap. No one follows a clock or is concerned with tardiness, and no island event scheduled for a particular time ever begins at that time. (Flinn 1992: 52)

Moore observed another variation on the clash of cultures in Cameroonian village schools between the modern, constructivist teaching methods practiced in the West and now promoted by the Ministry of Education and teachers' adherence to a traditional, authoritarian teaching style that stressed discipline and rote memorization (Moore 2006: 115; for a similar situation in Guinea, see Anderson-Levitt and Diallo 2003). Parents are not necessarily opposed to the authoritarian style of teaching that is so prevalent. Failing to see any direct utility in school subjects, they may view classroom lessons as the imparting of powerful secrets that will transform their children, much like the initiation rite. Teachers may be viewed as modern incarnations of the respected ritual leaders and elders whose powerful knowledge was closely guarded (Bledsoe and Robey 1986: 218; Macedo 2009: 181).

The Mende have situated formal education within local authority structures of obligation and mystical agency. They maintain that, since valued knowledge is a key economic and political commodity, teachers, as its proprietors or 'owners,' can demand ... compensation from those who benefit from it ... before their new knowledge and skills can bear fruit, children must display gratitude to their benefactors through labor, remittances, and unquestioning loyalty[12] ... Children who did not earn knowledge through blessings may find their knowledge a liability rather than an asset. Those who display a precocious fund of knowledge (not acquired from a teacher) are either ignored or regarded with acute suspicion. (Bledsoe 1992: 182, 192)

Schooling has had a particularly difficult time taking root among nomadic tribes (Juul 2008: 153; Ulturgasheva 2012: 76). These people have a history of being exploited and marginalized by "outsiders," including state organizations. They have not been eager to enroll their children in school, and governments, in turn, have been unwilling to set aside the policy of using fixed locations for schools as a means to sedentarize and manage the nomads. One group that has gradually embraced schooling is the Harasiis community, which migrates through the Empty Quarter of southeast Arabia. Although only a fraction of the children sent to elementary school (from 1994) eventually graduated from high school, those that did earned salaried employment, and this success has sustained schooling in "the heart of the desert" (Chatty 2006: 227). Rabaris nomads of the Hindu Kutch in Gujarat India have effected a compromise whereby one son is left to live with relatives in the village to attend school and – it is hoped – get a job eventually while the rest of the children are integrated into the pastoral lifestyle (Dyer and Choksi 2006: 169).[13] As discussed earlier for Papua New Guinea and Uganda, the Indian government would like to use schooling to "modernize" scheduled tribes without altering their mode of subsistence, but schooled Rabaris can be expected to abandon pastoralism and to join the growing population of urban immigrants (Dyer and Choksi 2006: 171).

For children of the Shipbo tribe in Peru, schooling leads them into a kind of twilight zone, because it keeps "them from learning their environment and own culture, [yet gives] them only minimal skills for life in town" (Hern 1992: 36). While in school they are removed from opportunities to observe and emulate their elders – who will not stop to remedy this loss by actively teaching them. Among the Cree, because parents don't see themselves as teachers, they take

---

[12] Note the parallel with the apprenticeship (Chapter 7, pp. 287–292).
[13] This seems to be a common strategy, practiced by Sudanese (Katz 2004: 66) and Benin farmers (Alber 2012: 184), as examples.

no special pains to alter their foraging behavior to accommodate children's school attendance. They could schedule bush collecting trips for weekends or holiday periods so children could accompany them and continue to learn from observation, but they do not. As a result, traditional subsistence knowledge is not being passed on (Ohmagari and Berkes 1997). Similarly, "Young Lacandones (rural Mexico) tend to know much less about the forest than their fathers" (Ross 2002: 592). And the Chewong aver that "'We wait for [them] to come and ask us how to make a basket, or how to say a spell.' If no one asks, then they believe that the knowledge will die out" (Howell 1988: 162).

Their heads will be turned, their attention diverted from the village – where their future might be secure – to the town, where the poor quality of their education hobbles them. Nsamenang characterizes all of Africa in these terms; for example, "the school system in much of Africa has so spiraled out of control that it mainly churns out unemployed youth who can read and write but who are totally dependent and cannot even create or utilize local knowledge" (Nsamenang 2002: 91).

As depressing as these scenes are[14] – and they could easily be multiplied – we must bear in mind that, from the child's perspective, school may look quite different. If the alternative is lugging around a cranky baby brother or weeding the garden or sticking around home all day helping mother, then spending a few hours in the company of peers, even under otherwise adverse circumstances, might not seem so bad. In Guinea, for instance, "Students wanted to be in school and certainly preferred school to being home, where they would have to do chores. That is why the big punishment was to be 'bani' (banished), turned away from school" (Anderson-Levitt 2005: 988). Schooling may be the lesser of two evils. Furthermore, in my conversations with village students in Liberia, Papua New Guinea, and Trinidad, the males, at least, freely expect that this reprieve from farm labor will be permanent. They expect to follow the yellow brick road of public schooling right to a well-paid white-collar job in the capital city.

However, the majority discover that the road ends well short of their goal. In Zawiya, Morocco, for example, fewer than 3 percent of the age cohort

---

[14] It's worth remarking that learning can occur under what appear to be very adverse circumstances. Some readers no doubt shared my experience of attending a one-room, multi-graded primary school with no plumbing and little heat. European immigrant children, especially working-class Jews in New York in the early years of the twentieth century, attended horrible, overcrowded schools. There was no accommodation for non-English speakers; in fact, students were punished for using Yiddish by having their mouths washed out with (kosher) soap. In spite of achieving successful integration and even prosperity, as adults, the Jewish students still recalled their suffering and acute embarrassment (Berrol 1992: 45, 54–55).

completes high school, and even college graduates face poor job prospects. This has led to "increasing frustration and cynicism" (Davis and Davis 1989: 141–142). This malaise is by now quite widespread. Universal primary schooling has created "an avalanche of failed aspirations throughout the third world" (LeVine and White 1986: 193) and village schools find themselves "in the business of producing failures" (Serpell 1993: 10). Particularly in Africa, frustrated "school leavers" of the 1960s and 1970s became the brutal "rebels" of the 1980s and 1990s (Coulter 2009: 42–43; Honwana 2005; Rosen 2005: 80; Utas 2005).

A significant factor in a parent's decision to send a child to school is whether the child can be spared from chores. This is more likely to be true for boys (whose chore assignments are often lighter) and for children with several siblings old enough to do chores. Of course, with the increasing pressure of *compulsory* school attendance, this decision may be taken from parents, with predictable consequences:

Traditionally, small boys do guarding and herding but nowadays they must be sent to school. The result is that cattle are allowed to wander about the fields and inflict great damage on the crops. (Barley 1983/2000: 58)

Aside from the opportunity costs of lost labor and the real costs of school fees, uniforms, and materials, another important factor in gauging a community's commitment to schooling is the potential return on the investment. As we will see in the next section, the return may be zero.

Schooling and investment

German settlers in Pennsylvania opposed education on the ground that it would make children lazy and dissatisfied with farm work. (MacElroy 1917: 59)

Lu You called village schools *dongzxue*, or winter schools, because sons of farmers were sent there only in winter. (Bai 2005: 25)

It is difficult to say precisely when [Ghanaian] children become net economic assets to their families, but education delay[s] that transition. (Lord 2011: 102)

As discussed in Chapter 2, in most of the world, children have no intrinsic value but have great potential worth as future workers and as caretakers for their elderly parents. The introduction of schooling into the traditional society may not, therefore, be embraced with unbridled enthusiasm, as it implies both direct costs and the opportunity costs associated with the loss of the child's labor. In this section we'll learn how canny parents carefully assess the costs and benefits of their children's schooling.

We can detect a movement to extend basic schooling to all children from the period of the Protestant Reformation. Nevertheless, "If the school came to loom increasingly large in the lives of young people, it did so in an extremely long, drawn-out process" (Heywood 2001: 161). One reason is that, whenever possible, children were employed. In sixteenth-century Portugal, schooling was viewed as "useless to the future of their children, because as peasant, fisherman, or shepherd they would not need it" (dos Guimarães Sá 2007: 31). Somewhat later:

The literacy rates of textile, metal, and transport workers declined in the late eighteenth century, as these occupations did not require advanced reading or writing skills. Additionally, the demand for child labor disrupted education, as children in the factories had fewer opportunities to attend school. (Graff 2011: 42)

Even today in Fez, Morocco, successful craft industries like leather-working prefer to admit unschooled boys to their workshops, as school-transmitted knowledge is "a handicap or at best a waste of time"; hence boys' attendance at school has declined (Schlemmer 2007: 114). In southern Morocco, a girl becomes a competent weaver with little or no investment; she just needs to pay attention to females who're weaving. Schooling is seen as requiring a much greater investment and is perceived as a "drain on female human resources for the household" (Naji 2012: 377).

The earliest rural schools – and many today – were pretty casual affairs. Schools on Java were open only a few hours a day, but still they closed often to permit children seasonally extra time for farm-work. After the third grade their education was complete (White 2012: 89). In rural areas, children are or were kept from school whenever there was farm-work to do (Cunningham 1995: 83) and, even in Europe until the 1920s, "the primary school perched uneasily in the village, as it struggled to insert itself into the mainstream of rural life" (Heywood 1988: 61). Girls in Botswana farming communities – who can free their mothers to work in fields by doing household chores – are less likely to be sent to school. In herding societies, boys are preferred as livestock tenders, and are, hence, less often sent to school than their sisters (Bock 2002b: 218). In impoverished and land-poor Guatemalan villages, children's schooling is pre-empted by their employment in quarrying and coffee industries (Ruiz 2011a, 2011b; see also André and Godin 2013; Stambach 1998b: 193). Students may need to work to earn the funds to pay for their schooling (Bass 2004: 99; Hilson 2010: 463). While rural children may be able to attend school, outside the classroom, they're afforded little opportunity to study (Akabayashi and Psacharopoulos 1999: 122; Martin 2012: 205).

Parents' views on the value of schooling are more varied than children's, if not more sophisticated. Working for the Ministry of Education, I traveled widely in Papua New Guinea during a period (1976–1980) when the number of school places was expanding even as the number of new salaried positions was shrinking rapidly. In the civil service sector (including schools), the transition from Australian expatriate staff to native replacements was nearly complete and the only paying jobs in the private sector were for unschooled workers on plantations and in mines. I had numerous conversations with parents whose generation was the first in the region to learn of the outside world. They were convinced that, by attending the rudimentary (in every sense) school in the village, their son would travel the *rot bilong mani* (road to riches) to a life of ease – just like the *whitpela*. When I asked if they were taking special pains on weekends to insure that their children in school would "catch up" on what they were not learning about village life, they responded, in effect, "What for? They won't ever live in the village."[15] Other sites that I visited had had a longer period of association with schooling. There I met adults, now sadly wiser, who angrily denounced the *bikhets* (big-heads) – school leavers who had returned to the village without jobs, and without any appreciation for or tools to succeed in village life. In fact, Ali Pomponio and I took advantage of the gradual spread of public schooling in Papua New Guinea – from coastal areas inland – to systematically compare parental perspectives. In the Southern Highlands where children had only recently gained access to schooling, Imbonggu parents willingly paid school fees and sent the majority of their sons to school, eagerly anticipating the eventual windfall of remitted wages when their children became salaried civil servants. In the Siassi Islands, parents had enjoyed such a windfall from their children, who were among the first to gain access to secondary education in the 1960s and who did find ready employment in government jobs that were opening up. But, by 1979, the expense of sending children through to secondary school had climbed, while the returns had declined: graduates were no longer finding jobs. Hence, enrollment in local elementary schools had dropped dramatically as parents recognized that schooling was no longer a good investment (Pomponio and Lancy 1986: 45–47).[16] They realized that they would achieve a greater return from their children if they kept them busy in gardens or collecting on the reef (Pomponio 1992).

[15] While village parents around the world seem eager to send their children off to earn their fortunes, studies of Native American communities in the US present a very different picture. Here, parents strenuously resist any notion that their children will use schooling as an "exit" strategy to move away from family and the reservation. This "resistance" is cited as one of the major causes of very low academic success by Native American students (Deyhle 1991: 294, 1992; Condon 1987: 162). Other North American examples of resistance to the demands of the school ethos include the Amish (Hostetler and Huntington 1971/1992: 3) and Hopi (Simmons 1942: 100).

[16] A similar pattern can be found on Rotuman (Howard 1970: 63), Malaita, (Watson-Gegeo and Gegeo 1992: 17), and Ponam islands (Carrier 1981: 239), as well as in Africa (Grindal 1972: 92).

Elsewhere, in *expanding* economies, the investment may pay off. Villagers in China invested heavily in children's schooling, which took precedence over other obligations, including chores and religious ceremonies. The older children who were sent away to get an education were expected to become the "'backbone of support' for their siblings who remained in the village" (Obendick 2009: 106). Migrating from the village to seek employment before completing one's education is now discouraged and school teachers are held up as models for students to emulate (Stafford 1995). In Shandong, zeal for schooling – village students outscore urban students on national exams – comes from the desire to escape the stigma of being a peasant (Kipnis 2001: 17).

A common theme in the narratives gathered by ethnographers is that the school has little to do with traditional village life (Nieuwenhuys 2003: 106). Among the Inuit:

Children who previously spent their days helping parents with hunting, trapping, fishing, skin preparation, and general household chores now spend much of the day in an institutional setting learning skills unrelated, and sometimes antithetical, to those emphasized at home. (Condon 1987: 157)

If parents[17] believe their children have economic opportunities outside the village that education can help them realize, they'll send them to school, buy the uniforms and books, and pay the fees. Otherwise, they'll refuse to make these sacrifices (Akabayashi and Psacharopoulos 1999). Yemeni adolescent boys are "actively discouraged by parents and peers from pursuing studies as there were no perceived gains and prolonged education was viewed as an impediment to early marriage" (Marchand 2001: 102). Similarly among the lowland Maya, there are no jobs that require schooling, while maize cultivation is learned easily by everyone. Sending children to school seems like a bad bargain (Kramer 2005: 38; see also Barber 2002: 364).

Parents who do hold aspirations for their children may elect to send children to serve in the households of distant kinsmen, in hopes that they will gain access to superior urban schools. This example is from Liberia:

Many children must support themselves through school as wards in the households of people who live near schools. Parents realize their children may be overworked, underfed, or beaten in other people's households but they hope for a minimum of mistreatment in exchange for a chance to have an educated child. The potential income from an educated child with a good job warrants the risks involved. (Bledsoe 1980a: 35)

---

[17] I use the term "parents" for convenience. In my reading of the literature, the decision to send a child to school, and provision of the source(s) of funds to do so, is just as diffuse a responsibility as any other aspect of childrearing, as discussed in Chapter 4.

Zambian students may need to migrate independently to urban areas to continue their education beyond the primary grades. They must fend for themselves to provide shelter, food, and schooling expenses (Bass 2004: 119). But many fail. Kenny finds children on the streets of Brazilian towns who are "too hungry to go to school" (2007: 89).

Such risky strategies are motivated by the growing disparity between rural and urban schools (Leinaweaver 2008a: 63). In the Solomons:

The poor quality of teaching and the lack of resources in most rural schools guarantee that few children will pass the examinations for admission into secondary school. Those who do are most often channeled into a vocational rather than an academic secondary school. The majority who fail their exams return to the village, work on the plantations, or seek low-level jobs in town, often with a strong sense of defeat. Children of the urban elites attend well-endowed urban public or private schools, thereby guaranteeing that the elite group will perpetuate itself in the next generation. (Watson-Gegeo and Gegeo 1992: 20)

Pervasive economic woe is no impediment to the creation of "haves and have nots," as shown in a comparison of urban private and rural public schools in Ethiopia (Poluha 2004). In places as different as Egypt (Booth 2002: 223, 226),[18] rural Senegal (Juul 2008: 157), and Micronesia (Falgout 1992: 39), aspiring parents are allocating scarce funds to send their children to private schools (see Figure 30). Hardly upscale, they are, however, superior to the available public institutions. In Pakistan, public and private resources are being redirected toward private schools as "a strong wealthy modernizing elite continues to impose its goals on a relatively poorer, traditional mass of common people" (Jalil and McGinn 1992: 105). In Tanzania, the proliferation of private schools has "served further to differentiate wealthy communities from poor" (Stambach 1998b: 196). In Morocco, religious fanaticism has "Islamized" and "Arabized" the public school curriculum, handicapping students as they advance from secondary to tertiary schooling. Meanwhile, the Moroccan middle/upper class entrenches its position by enrolling children in private schools where French and economically relevant subjects are the foci (Boum 2008: 214).

On Tonga, classrooms are crowded and most schools have an acute shortage of teachers and educational resources. Despite the high value placed on education, teaching is a fairly low-status profession, and the working conditions are poor. With more generous funding, Mormon and Seventh Day Adventist schools – with their sports facilities, new buildings, modern equipment and textbooks, and extra-curricular activities for students – provide a sharp contrast

---

[18] Also in Egypt, at least some public schools display very uneven distribution of resources, with high-achieving students served in a section of the school with clean, modern facilities compared with the remainder (Saad 2006: 92).

Figure 30 Malagasy student in a Ranohira private school

to the public schools. Families who've enjoyed economic benefits from schooling in the past are able to meet the cost of school fees and other school-related expenses through remittances from overseas relatives (Morton 1996: 39).

In the upper echelon of Mexican society, maids and house-boys replace the labor normally provided by children of the household. In turn, the privileged children "consider themselves above any manual labor and above those who must perform it ... their time should be spent in schooling and in entertainment" (Modiano 1973: 85). In São Paulo, the poorly paid girls who serve as maids can attend school only after completing their round of household duties (de Oliveria 1995: 260). In Bengali villages, the labor of low-caste families provides the added wealth and leisure that permit high-caste children to succeed in school, often with the aid of paid tutors (Rohner and Chaki-Sircar 1988: 75; see also Skoufias 1994: 344; Ullrich 1995: 177). Just as in the US (Coll and Marks 2009: 110; Pugh 2009: 191) and England (Buckingham and Scanlon 2003: 150), the careful selection of the school one's children will attend has become one of the means for upwardly mobile families to join "an international middle-class culture" (Fiji – Brison 2009: 316; see also Kashmir – Rao 1998: 109; Tahiti – Levy 1996: 129).

However, greater wealth is not always a guarantee that children will be sent to school. In some cases, such as in Howa, the Sudan, villagers with access to more resources, including land, are able to make greater use of their children's labor and earn a more immediate return from them than promised by schooling (Katz 2004: 65).

The provision of resources by the central government to villages to "educate" children has usually been inadequate in terms of preparing students to enter the wage sector. Worse, it has not even insured that some segment of the village is sufficiently educated to take on the multinational corporations. Pomponio documents the ease with which rural Papua New Guineans are hoodwinked into giving away precious natural resources (old-growth timber) for a pittance (Pomponio 1981; see also Solomon Islands – (Watson-Gegeo and Gegeo 1992: 19). Pandya describes the Indian government's institution of a public school in an Ongee (Andaman Island) village. In a multi-year account, we learn how the community struggles to find something useful or meaningful in the curriculum that's been imported *in toto* from Hindu-speaking, urban India. After twenty years, "five boys who had been in the school off and on for about eight years ... could not read or write" (Pandya 2005: 400). The villagers are effectively mute, as the forest – their home and their livelihood – is rapidly cut in large-scale logging.

It's a necessary first step for parents to acquiesce to their children's schooling and find funds to cover the inevitable expenses, even to the point of paying for private schooling. But, in the modern Western and Asian societies where schooling is associated with employment, a cornerstone of current theories of education and child development is the necessity for parents to involve themselves directly in their children's education, virtually from birth.[19] Schooling, generally, and academic literacy, in particular, call upon numerous skills and a mindset that do not seem to emerge naturally in the course of the child's development. Unlike social learning and make-believe play, which do come to the child's aid as marvelous systems for acquiring his or her culture, the tools to decode and absorb school subjects must be inculcated by a patient teacher, perhaps over several years prior to the start of school itself. The evidence we've seen so far suggests that this may be another of the obstacles on the road to success for village children (Alber 2012; Harris 2006: 91).

---

[19] In a large-scale survey undertaken in the US, "Mothers ranked teaching as their most prominent strength" (Strom *et al.* 2004: 681).

Parents as teachers

An [Aymara] mother feels proud when her child shows her what it has done independently, without further instruction ... Parents tend not to impose their own desires on a child's activities as is done in school, but rather wait for the moment when the initiative comes from the child itself. (Arnold 2006: 121)

The school failure experienced by high-risk youth may be attributable to inadequate preparation for the transition to literacy in the early years. (Snow and Powell 2008: 26)

One of the major themes of Chapter 5 is that village adults rarely see the necessity of teaching children; rather that children are expected (and rarely fail to meet that expectation) to observe and emulate the behavior of more competent community members, practicing until they, too, are competent. In the concluding section of Chapter 4, I contrasted the intensive and elaborate language socialization employed by modern, middle-class mothers with its absence elsewhere and linked this to the need to prepare the child for school. A perfect illustration of this contrast can be found in dinner-table conversations.

Dinner table conversations offer rich opportunities for extended discourse [as] every member of the family should contribute to the conversation [, which] provides rich information to children about the meanings of words ... The more children are exposed to extended discourse during mealtime conversation, the more chances they have to acquire vocabulary, understand stories and explanations, and know things about the world. Because these are capacities that are drawn on heavily in school but are typically not much attended to in preschool or primary classrooms, children who have had the chance to acquire them at home have an important advantage in pursuing academic success. (Snow and Beals 2006: 52–55, 64)

In the village, children at mealtimes may be ignored; Or they may be the passive recipients of didactic lessons in manners, or expected to carefully "overhear" conversations that may contain important maxims they should internalize. They are *not* expected to participate in these conversations (Chapter 5, p. 184; Ochs and Izquierdo 2009: 395).

When [Tongan] children are present during adult conversations they are expected to remain silent ... adults either ignore them or treat them with impatience or anger ... Children who interrupt or offer advice to adults without being asked may be accused of being *fie poto* (thinking themselves clever) ... Even at mealtimes when, in most households, the whole family sits together, the adults do not usually include the children in their conversations. (Morton 1996: 166, 90, 170; for comparable observations from Tanna Island, see Lindstrom 1990: 114)

Village parents are more likely to serve as role models than as teachers.[20] And, as children transition from observing to participating, parents may willingly accommodate them as partners, to "create room" for them (de Haan 2001: 188; Ulturgasheva 2012: 117). There is very little talk of any kind and, importantly, "The emphasis is not on how an individual performs [as it would be in the classroom] but, rather, on what gets accomplished" (Paradise and de Haan 2009: 196). This contrast between adult–child language interaction patterns in the village and those found in schools and the modern societies that spawned them has received a great deal of attention. Susan Phillips and others have shown that Native American children use patterns of communication at home that are different than those expected in the classroom and this accounts in part for their failure to meet the school's academic expectations (Phillips 1983).[21] Cazden discusses the conflict that arises in US public schools when children are asked to "share" or "show and tell" a personal narrative. While middle-class children have no difficulty with this rhetoric, poor African-American children have had little exposure to or practice with it. In fact their stories tend to be episodic. Teachers are less accepting of episodic narrative and try to steer children around to topic-centered narratives because they want the child to "construct an oral text that is as similar as possible to a written composition" (Cazden 1988: 14; Michaels and Cazden 1986: 136). In a Tongan classroom, teachers may well expect students to volunteer information, ask questions, or eagerly answer the teacher's academic questions. In a Tongan village, children are to learn through observation alone (Morton 1996). While Samoan teachers might praise a pupil, "family members rarely issued praise" (Ochs and Izquierdo 2009: 398). In Kenya:

Gusii mothers ... expected their infants and toddlers to comply with their wishes ... They rarely praised their infants or asked them questions but tended to issue commands and threats in communicating with them ... many of the interrogatives were rhetorical questions that have the force of commands or even threats: "Why are you crying?" or "Do you want me to beat you?" (LeVine 2004: 156)

These village norms have real consequences in terms of the mindset children bring to the classroom, as demonstrated in an ingenious experiment. Mayan children were compared with middle-class American counterparts in an origami-folding task. The village-reared children were much more attentive to the demonstration and to the activities of others in the setting, especially

---

[20] And not just village parents; urbanized "Japanese mothers want to avoid direct teaching when possible, and tend to model behavior ... rather than [use] verbal instruction" (Azuma 1981: 25).

[21] Another study that documents differences between village and school participation rules was undertaken on Kosrae (Michalchik 1997). For a discussion of the *congruence* between home and school in middle-class society – in Italy and the USA – see Sterponi and Santagata (2000).

adults. Unlike the Anglo children, they did not seek additional information to aid them in completing the task (Correa-Chavez and Rogoff 2005: 9).[22] Parallel results were observed in a study comparing native Hawaiian and Haole (Anglo) students, in which the latter were much more likely to request adult assistance and, consequently, were more successful at the task (Gallimore *et al.* 1969).

Village parents may use punitive means to shape children's behavior (Chapter 5, p. 196), a tactic at variance with modern notions of appropriate teacher behavior (Wolf 1972: 68).[23] Observers of children in urban slums also see adults imposing harsh discipline. A mother in a favela of Rio de Janeiro knows "intuitively that in order for her children to survive, toughness, obedience, subservience, and street smarts are necessary; otherwise, the child can end up dead" (D. Goldstein 1998: 395). An observer in Sweden would see something quite different with parents striving to "enter and understand the child's world ... to ensure their children's participation in decision making" (Dahlberg 1992: 132–133).

Western parents emulate modern teaching practices[24] in offering children inducements and praise or a show of excitement – behavior absent in village mother–child relations (Rohner and Chaki-Sircar 1988: 77). Such praise "may serve to motivate children to engage in activities in which they otherwise might not choose to participate" (Rogoff 2003: 306–307). As noted in Chapter 5, children want to learn their culture and may need no more than the occasional tongue-lashing to remain diligent in their pursuit of adult competence. But school subjects are often of far less interest and children require incentives to raise their motivation to adequate levels.

Another source of conflict noted by many anthropologists is the school's emphasis on individualism, on students taking individual responsibility, on earning *their* grade, on paying attention to the teacher and not their peers. This contrasts with a village emphasis on collectivism, especially where children are concerned. "Children are more likely to be trained to become people like us, rather than a person like me" (Ritchie and Ritchie 1979: 65). Here is a concrete manifestation of this attitude at work in Poomkara (south India) village:

---

[22] In a parallel study in the US, groups of children whose immigrant mothers were relatively well or poorly educated behaved differently when shown how to make origami figures. The latter group relied solely on observation whereas the former sought additional information through questioning the teacher (Mejia-Arauz *et al.* 2005).

[23] In rural Morocco, beating as a form of "instruction" is still accepted at home and in school (Nutter-El Ouardani 2013: 115).

[24] And schools expect them to, as shown in studies from Norway and France (Liden 2003: 127; Wylie 1957: 60).

Children could be everywhere in the house but could claim none of the spaces as theirs ... Schoolbooks were often simply stuck under the palm roof and children's clothes hung on a rope. Children did their homework sitting on the same mat on which they slept at night. Even this mat was often shared with others. (Nieuwenhuys 2003: 103)

This vignette also suggests that village parents don't feel much need to make adjustments in domestic arrangements on behalf of their schoolchildren. "The Navajo way is that you are in school all day ... at home you have other things to do; haul water, chop wood, help with the children" (Deyhle 1991: 288). In post-industrial society, by contrast, there are warehouses full of child-specific furnishings, many of which explicitly wear an "educational" label (Sutton-Smith 1986: 33). Here's an interesting Japanese invention:

The home-study desk bought by most parents for their smaller children symbolizes the hovering care and intensity of the mother's involvement: all models have a high front and half-sides, cutting out distractions and enclosing the workspace in womb-like protection. There is a built-in study light, shelves, a clock, electric pencil sharpener and built-in calculator. [One] popular ... model included a push button connecting to a buzzer in the kitchen to summon mother for help or for a snack. (LeVine and White 1986: 123)

In comparative studies with the Maya that have focused on this wide cultural divide, mothers and children with more schooling readily adopted the roles of teacher and student in an experimental learning context whereas those with little or no schooling acted as if the child would learn autonomously through exploration, observation, and imitation/practice alone (Chavajay 2006; Correa-Chavez and Rogoff 2005; Göncü et al. 2000; Maynard 2004b; Mejia-Arauz et al. 2005). Other findings of this dramatic shift in models of childrearing come from the Inuit (Crago 1992: 498). Similar change has been documented in Tahiti and Nepal, where acculturated parents adopt "modern" childrearing practices that emphasize school readiness and developmental milestones as compared to the *laissez-faire* practices of their "old-fashioned" village counterparts (Levy 1996). In a recent survey of villagers in Fiji that had had over 100 years' exposure to schooling and missionary activity, parents freely claimed to have "taught" children much of what they knew (Kline et al. 2013).[25]

There have been a number of surveys since the 1960s that provide additional support for the idea that schooling may change childrearing practices. LeVine and colleagues aggregate results from several countries with large low-income populations that support the notion that even a few years of schooling can

---

[25] If anything, missionary efforts may be more powerful than exposure to schooling in persuading village parents that they should teach their children (Little 2011; Sprott 2002: 226).

"modernize" women's approach to their own fertility (reducing it), improve their ability to keep their offspring alive and healthy, and lead the women to "internalize the teacher role from their experience in Western-type schools and use it as mothers" (LeVine *et al.* 2012: 139).

On the other hand, the transition from gerontocracy to neontocracy is neither swift nor automatic. De Haan carried out an important study in a transitional Mazahua (Mexico) village in which sets of teacher–child and mother–child pairs were observed after being told to teach the children two tasks that involved building/expanding a market stall. Mothers did not explain the tasks, the procedures, or the child's role. They assumed the child would figure all this out on their own and readily mesh with the parent's activity. By contrast:

Teachers would, before anything else, try to form the child's attitude to the activity. They would make clear that the child was supposed to be attentive to the teacher ... in order for learning to take place the child was going to be *told what to do* and the teacher was responsible for telling the child. (de Haan 2001: 186–187, emphasis added)

While the parents focused on completing the task, teachers focused on making sure the child understood each step in the process and had had sufficient practice and feedback to reach full competence in each sub-task, before proceeding to the next. In effect, "completion of the task was 'given up'" (de Haan 2001: 187).

Schooled parents may acknowledge the value of teaching in interviews or in an experimental setting, but numerous ethnographic accounts describe the absence of school preparedness activity (e.g. "lessons," bedtime stories, dinner-table conversations) in poor and/or acculturating communities (Valdez *et al.* 2007: 83). In spite of their own schooling, parents may make limited use of literacy, especially in interacting with children (Rojo 2001: 63–64). The linguistic anthropologist Shirley Brice Heath conducted a long-term ethnographic project with families in the Piedmont region of the US in the 1970s. Her goal was to understand how different communities interact with literacy, especially where children were concerned. In a poor African-American community, "Tracton," use of books (other than the Bible) and printed material was limited, and parents did not engage in elaborate conversations with their young children, nor did they see it as their responsibility to act as the child's first teacher. She recorded sentiments that echo those recorded by anthropologists in villages throughout the world.[26]

---

[26] And in history, as well. In Dickens' vivid narrative, we hear Sam Weller's (Mr. Pickwick's young man-of-all-work) father proudly claim credit for his son's perspicacity: "I took a good deal o' pains with his eddication, sir; let him run in the streets when he was very young, and shift for hisself. It's the only way to make a boy sharp, sir" (Dickens 1836/1964: 306).

He [her grandson] gotta learn to know 'bout dis world, can't nobody tell 'im. Now just how crazy is dat? White folks uh hear dey kids say sump'n, dey say it back to 'em, dey aks 'em 'gain 'n 'gain 'bout things ... He just gotta be keen, keep his eyes open ... Gotta watch hisself by watchin' other folks. Ain't no use me tellin' 'im: "learn dis, learn dat" ... He just gotta learn ... he see one thing one place one time, he know how it go, see sump'n like it again, maybe it be be same, maybe it won't. He hafta try it out." (Heath 1983: 84)

In a nearby, predominantly white, middle-class community, "Maintown," Heath sees a different picture. Here homes are saturated with literacy as are the lives of children – from an early age. Aside from bedtime stories, which appear to be a nearly foolproof strategy to enhance children's learning to read (Lancy 1994), in Maintown:

As early as 6 months of age, children are introduced to books and information derived from books. Their rooms contain bookcases and are decorated with murals, bedspreads, mobiles, and stuffed animals that represent characters found in books ... Adults expand nonverbal responses and vocalizations from infants into fully formed grammatical sentences. When children begin to verbalize about the contents of books, adults extend their question from simple requests for labels ... to ask about the attributes of these items ("What does the doggie say?" "What color is the ball?"). (Heath 1982: 52)

Heath's results have been replicated in the southern US and in several European countries (Tudge 2008: 153, 168). McNaughton has found directly parallel results working with Pacific Islander and *pakeha* (Anglo) communities in New Zealand (1996: 194–195). On US Indian reservations, where only one-third of the population completes high school, parents pay little attention to their children's schooling: "This noninterference approach is typical of some traditional Northern America Cheyenne parents who allow adolescents more freedom in making decisions than is characteristic of American middle-class culture" (Ward 2005: 124). Lareau's cross-class comparative ethnography identifies similar attitudes from a typical US working-class community. Mrs. Morris, a mother from Colton, saw her son Tommy's education begin-ning when she "turned over responsibility" for him to the school. Afterwards, she remained largely in ignorance of his progress and was surprised to be called to the school and informed that he was doing poorly (Lareau 1989: 41; see also Ogbu 2003: 236). Teachers refer to mothers like Mrs. Morris as "'dry-cleaner parents' who drop their rambunctious kids off in the morning and expect them to be returned at the end of the day all clean and proper and practically sealed in plastic" (Gibbs 2005: 47).

The routines that middle-class parents employ to insure school readiness, including, especially, involving children with books and literate speech, have been referred to as a form of "cultural capital" (Bourdieu 1973). "In this view, home preparation is seen as essential, making it difficult for low-income children, who don't receive such preparation, to succeed in school, even if teaching is adequate" (Martini 1995: 50). Also, knowing how to approach and talk to authority figures – teachers in particular – is part of the portfolio of cultural capital not readily available to members of the proletariat: "The McAllisters, like other poor and working-class families, display caution and at times distrust towards individuals in positions of authority in dominant institutions" (Lareau 2003: 157). Cultural capital includes familiarity with the "high culture" that is the foundation of academic education.

[Poor, rural Applachian families] don't routinely take their children to libraries, museums, or other cultural institutions. Children, therefore, lack the "mental pictures to go with the words in . . . school books." (Fitchen 1981: 142)

Of particular significance is the gap in the amount of pre-school language stimulation between lower- and middle-class homes. In one comprehensive study, children of professional parents were exposed to three times as much verbal stimulation as those of parents on welfare, and the children's own vocabulary was twice as large. Vocabulary, in turn, is highly predictive of school success (Hart and Risley 1995: 90).

In this section, many conflicts between village – or lower-class (Lareau 2003: 3) and immigrant (Coll and Marks 2009: 91) communities, – strategies for enculturation and the ethos of the public school have been enumerated. Villagers have access to well-developed cultural routines to replicate themselves and raise well-adjusted, productive community members. But they lack, and seem unprepared to easily acquire, student readiness and support routines that are often assumed by school authorities to be already in place.

An educated woman

Roman men did not appreciate well-educated women. (Colón with Colón 2001: 105)

[In post-industrial society] women are coming on much stronger, often leapfrogging the men to the academic finish. (Lewin 2009)

To this point in the chapter, students have been boys explicitly or this has been largely assumed. That is because girls have rarely had access to schooling. That imbalance is beginning to disappear. In ancient Egypt, some girls were, taught to read and write, and the hieroglyph for scribe is found from the Middle Kingdom (beginning of the second millennium BCE) with the determinative for female added. No such practice existed at the time in Mesopotamia (Colón with Colón 2001: 28). In classical Greek society, girls did not go to school, and the extent of any education they may have encountered in the homes of their parents was probably limited. Girls were referred to as *pais* (child) until they married, whereas boys left that inferior (slaves were also *pais*) state when they came of age (Golden 2003: 14). These views clearly made the idea of education for women unthinkable.

Some Roman girls attended school; however, because they were married in their teens, their studies were limited compared with those of boys. As in Greece, the few well-read and erudite Roman women were likely to be courtesans (Shelton 1998: 105). This was true in China as well, where it was understood that, in a properly run household, females were not only segregated from males but excluded from cultural events and intellectual life as well. Exposure to and training in the arts and literature were available only to courtesans (Dardess 1991: 83–84).

In the early modern era (the eighteenth and nineteenth centuries), schooling for middle- and upper-class girls became the norm, but was aimed primarily at preparing them for society and to insure their virtue. Unlike boys, they weren't taught Greek or Latin or other "higher" subjects designed to prepare students for employment and/or leadership (Pollock 1983: 251). This attitude persists today. In modern, well-off communities, while boys are expected to excel and use college as the means to an outstanding career, many girls pursue post-secondary schooling to make themselves a more attractive mate and more competent mother.[27]

In the village, the impediments to boys' education are trebled for girls. In Turkey, as in so much of the world, "A girl is regarded as the 'property of strangers,' since when she marries she will contribute to the welfare of her husband's family, not her own" (Kagitçibasi and Sunar 1992: 77). This equation nullifies any profit parents might find in sending daughters to school. A second and related issue is the need to keep daughters chaste to preserve their value as wives. Girls on Madagascar are withdrawn from school at puberty, no matter how well they're doing, "because their parents are so fearful of their involvement in what is assumed to be a highly sexualized urban world" (Sharp 2002: 227; see also C. Harris 2006: 105).

Third, numerous anthropologists have observed the discouraging treatment of schoolgirls – by boys and teachers. Girls – but not boys – may be expected to clean the classrooms. In Nigeria, the sexual harassment of female students, from primary through university, has reached epidemic proportions (Houneld 2007).

Fourth, girls are perceived as much more useful adjuncts to the household. They are preferred as child-minders and as their mother's helpmates in farming and the domestic sphere. While Ijo girls may now go to school, this has hardly

---

[27] This would be the perspective of the majority of young women in Utah who belong to the LDS (Latter-Day Saint or Mormon) church. See also Holland and Eisenhart (1990) and La Russo (1988: 145). However, I believe that these cases are vestigial. The majority of middle-class women, in future, will aspire to professional careers.

lessened their contribution to the household, while boys may roam about the village – as they always have – after school (Hollos and Leis 1989: 70). Spending a great deal of time just getting to and from school has a disproportionate impact on girls' schooling, leading to "late entry of girls into school, frequent and prolonged absenteeism, and dropping out" (Mungai, 2002: 34). It is extremely rare to find village parents providing the same level of support for girls' and boys' schooling (Bolin 2006: 108). In Nepal, girls are forced to leave school early, and Sarah LeVine found that they spoke of their truncated education with convincing bitterness.[28] Regardless of academic talent, many had been pulled out of school to work in the house and on the family farm, or to work as domestic servants or as laborers on construction sites. Their parents, to whom they give their wages, sometimes use the money to pay their brothers' school expenses (LeVine 2006: 37).

However, even with limited schooling and a low level of literacy, Nepali young women are distinguishable from their unschooled or less literate compatriots. They are more savvy when it comes to their own and their children's health care (see also Lee and Mason 2005) and are more effective at supporting their own children's formal education (LeVine et al. 2004: 875). Indeed, private schools in India deny admission to students whose mothers aren't educated for just these reasons.[29] In Central India, the "modern" view is that girls should complete five years of schooling, as brides-to-be are expected to have some education but more than five years would be too much, as "parents did not want a daughter-in-law who was overly *parhai-likhai*, who may be able to read but not to cook" (Froerer 2012: 349).

For years, worldwide surveys have shown that children's prospects are improved if their mothers have been schooled (LeVine et al. 2012: 21; Schultz 1994), and anthropologists are trying to uncover more specific reasons for this relationship. For example, schooled mothers may make more effective teachers of their pre-schoolers, adopting more school-like modes of discourse with them (Mejia-Arauz et al. 2005: 290). The effects may be broader, as academic literacy may confer a range of communication skills such as taking information from radio broadcasts or better articulating a child's symptoms to a medical clinician (LeVine et al. 2012: 122–123).

In the West, gradual social change has elevated the status of women, and schooling has been instrumental in this process.[30] In Finland, for example, the majority of adult women are wage-earners and have slightly more education

---

[28] Of course, as we know from the headlines, girls in Pakistan and Afghanistan risk their very lives in pursuing schooling (Anonymous 2013).

[29] Anita Rampal (personal communication, April 2004).

[30] Reports of progress in girls' education have surfaced from India (Roopnarine and Hoosain 1992), Korea (Cho 1995: 160), and Pohnpei (Falgout 1992: 40).

than men (Husu and Niemela 1993: 61). On Java as well, girls have overtaken boys at least through secondary school (White 2012: 91). And among the Chaga, a relatively prosperous rural enclave in Tanzania, young women are so successful as students and, later, wage-earners that they are forgoing marriage (Stambach 1998b). Educated African women who do marry have fewer children and are less likely to be in a polygynous household (Hollos 1998: 255). There is, in fact, diverse evidence that the "information society" may favor female students.[31]

In the next section, we'll discuss the continuing resistance (d'Amato 1993: 188) to academic learning even in societies where schooling is seen as essential for successful adaptation to employment.

Resistance to schooling

Someone said that his classmates would rather have "freedom than calculus." (Ogbu 2003: 21)

Senior year, he explained, was "kick back time." (Gibson 1987: 288)

The idea of the richest nation on earth inhabited by so many students not wanting to learn really threw me for a loop. (Li 2012: 7)

Beginning with the Matses boys who'd "rather go fishing," this chapter has described the unpropitious life history of schooling. Whether we look at clashes with children's natural exuberance and curiosity, with customary social interaction patterns, with parental expectations for a return on their investment, or with traditional prescriptions for the role of women, we can see manifold examples of schooling's promises going unrealized. Collectively, we see much evidence of "resistance" to the change that schooling represents, to its methods, to the loss of children's labor, to the alteration in children's self-image, and to their lost autonomy, among others. What is quite remarkable, however, is that, in some of the most economically advanced nations in the world, resistance to schooling is very much in evidence.

In a historical survey of public schooling in the US the authors argue: "if quality education is taken to mean a strong academic curriculum taught by engaged, engaging, and well-educated teachers in schools committed to the promotion of intellectual development, we simply cannot locate much of it in the past" (Kantor and Lowe 2004: 6). Contrast this state of affairs with China,

---

[31] Another reason that girls may do better than boys in school is that they are easier to "tame." That is, girls take on the subordinate role of mother's helper and apprentice from an early age. Hence, they may more readily adapt to the subordination and focused attention required in the classroom.

where "The sea of learning knows no bounds; only through diligence may its shores be reached" (Ho 1994: 296). Jin Li has carried out an interesting analysis of the terminology employed in China and the US to discuss teaching and learning. Vocabulary that was prominent in Chinese discourse on education – hard work, effort, persistence, desire, and passion – is absent from comparable American discourse (Li 2003: 261–262). Schooling in Asia seems never to have strayed far from the Confucian verities, whereas in the US student intelligence, whether inherited or acquired, has rarely been the cornerstone of respected pedagogy, as one critic of "multiple intelligences" points out (Gottfredson 2004: 42, 45).

Even as the US embraced universal primary and then secondary education, schools were early transformed into institutions that were shaped as much by youth culture (itself a by-product of the neontocracy) as by high educational goals and expectations (Consnoe 2011: 22; though this was much less true in Europe – Milner 2006: 152). Muncie, Indiana – a typical American town – was profiled by the Lynds in the mid–1920s. To the citizens of "Middletown," high school was represented by dances, dramatics, and other interests, but:

The "Bearcats" ... basket-ball team ... dominate the life of the school. By contrast, teachers, learning, and the content of books weren't particularly valued; instead, education, appears to be desired ... as a symbol ... it is not primarily learning, or even intelligence, as much as character and good will which are exalted. (Lynd and Lynd 1929: 213, 219–220)

In Best's report, we learn that, from the end of winter, the "prom" (fancy dress dance) becomes the focal point of student life. It is seen as a welcome "break in the monotony of ... what are often considered mundane [secondary] school routines" (Best 2000: 18).[32] While students can achieve "success" in school through athletics, political and social leadership, and good looks, academic success may be a mixed blessing. Children who seem conspicuously committed to the academic opportunities offered in school are scorned as "nerds." And this pejorative view is echoed elsewhere:

In Britain, the equivalent term for nerd is *swot*, in Germany – *Schreber*, in France – *bouttoneux* ... The key defining attribute is the boy is intellectually curious and makes an effort to pursue his interests (especially science, math, and technology, or else subjects that the rest of the peers find too complex and difficult to comprehend); above all, he is a high achiever in those subjects. (Li 2012: 189)

---

[32] And it is likely that the character of schooling will continue to shift away from an academic emphasis to a social emphasis, given the rapid expansion of digital culture and social media (Bauerlein 2009: 9).

Rather than be scorned as a "nerd," students resist efforts to enforce academic standards and they redefine the value hierarchy by joining and supporting "cliques" (Milner 2006: 40–43). Some of the most popular include: Bandos (band members, musicians); Stoners (conspicuous drug users); Skaters (skateboarding fanatics); Hackers (also known as computer geeks); Grunge (emulators of prison inmates – Hemmings 2004: 21); and Airheads (Barbie-like mannequins). However, the Jocks are both ubiquitous and paramount (Canaan 1987: 388). Middle-class American parents do what they can to divert their children to "safe" cliques (Jocks vs. Stoners). They invest heavily in their children's sports activity, dance classes, and organized social groups like Boy Scouts. Investments in their appearance, such as orthodontic braces, "cool" clothes, and a respectable car, may be substantial as well. The net effect is to increase the likelihood their child will, at the very least, fit in (Chang 1992: 111; Gibson 1987: 289; Grove 2009); better yet, be popular; and, at best, earn an athletic or leadership scholarship.

In a study of six ... high school classes ... athletic ability and attractiveness were significantly correlated with popularity, leadership, and dominance ... Attractive, athletic boys were also ranked as desirable dates and party guests by girls. A boy's intelligence had little or no effect on any of these measures of social standing. (Weisfeld 1999: 215)

Particularly among (non-Asian) minority students in the USA, athletics are seen as a far more promising avenue to popularity than good grades: "Black students invested so much time in sports that they had little time for their academic schoolwork" (Ogbu 2003: 156). Among Northern Cheyenne, some students whose low grades rendered them ineligible to participate in school sports transferred to another school with lower standards (Ward 2005: 137).

Anthropologists who have carried out in-depth studies of high schools with predominantly minority students have discovered that the antipathy toward "good" students has generalized to become a condemnation of anyone who "acts white." In a mostly black high school in Washington, DC, Signithia Fordham asked her informants to identify attributes that would indicate a student was "acting white," and should, therefore, be ostracized. Among the many items were included "speaking standard English[33] ... going to the opera or ballet...spending a lot of time in the library studying ... reading and writing poetry" (Fordham and Ogbu 1986: 186). They document the powerful effect of peer pressure as students who had been doing well academically lessen their effort in order to fit in. "Because his friends are critically important

---

[33] They "lease" rather than attempt to gain "ownership" of Standard English (Fordham 1999).

to him and his sense of identity, Max ... holds on to them at the expense of his academic progress" (Fordham and Ogbu 1986: 189).[34]

In a racially mixed high school on the Utah–Arizona border, Navajo students are stigmatized because they are Indian, and they are not represented among the respected cliques. So they forge their own clique based on dedication to and success at breakdancing. The "Breakers" set themselves defiantly apart from the Jocks and Preppies.[35] According to ethnographer Donna Deyhle, the creation of a distinct clique with all the accoutrements, including dress, allowed the Navajos "a means for expressing success in an otherwise indifferent or negative school and community environment" (Deyhle 1986: 112).

Even Asian students may find themselves drawn inexorably to peer associations that are antithetical to school values if their parents lack the cultural capital to insure their early success (Lew 2004: 304). In a very important study in an urban, multi-class, multi-ethnic school, Goto found a multiplicity of cliques illustrating the interplay of ethnicity and social class we've been discussing. The Nerds were hardworking, serious, ethnic Chinese students. Normal People were those who were doing well academically but who took pains to hide it in order to fit in. Homeboys were the black and Hispanic students who resisted conformity to school requirements. Last were the Wannabes: Cambodian and Vietnamese students who could not keep up with the Nerds, so they sought acceptance by the Homeboys (Goto 1997).

The academic resistance displayed among students in their distinct cliques is also evident in the classroom. From non-white Homeboys to white Stoners, anti-intellectual students constantly disrupt lessons by talking and fooling around (Willis 1977: 13). They complain, lobby teachers for easier assignments, and provide a colorful array of excuses to escape even these obligations. Beleaguered teachers make "huge concessions or surrender

---

[34] Remarkably (given how recently secondary schooling arrived on Manus), Peter Demerath discovered a precisely parallel case of resistance in a Manus Island (Papua New Guinea) high school, where academically committed students were accused of "acting extra" (2000: 197).

[35] The obvious question here is what is the chicken, and what is the egg? Do ethnic minority students form themselves into anti-academic cliques because the dominant society damns them to failure in the form of teachers' racist attitudes, culturally biased curricula, and testing and grading policies that undermine their self-esteem? Or is academic failure a result of students willingly opting out of the academic demands of school culture to join a more comfortable "Breakers" or "Homeboy" clique? Deyhle would, I suspect, vote for the former, while the late John Ogbu was increasingly moving toward the latter perspective. From a study set in a middle-class black community, he noted, for example, "In our observation of more than 100 classroom lessons from elementary through high school we did not record a single instance of cultural barriers preventing a student from learning the subject" (Ogbu 2003: 38).

altogether[36] to students who spend entire class periods cavorting with their friends" (Hemmings 2004: 45–46).[37]

From their origins in the apprenticeship model and from sparsely equipped, overcrowded, chaotic sheds or huts, schools have evolved to become much more comfortable, student-centered, and student-friendly. Teachers are trained to use the most effective methods and modern materials – often delivered interactively via the computer. We have ever more precise ways to measure student progress and to remediate any deficit. Nevertheless, by any number of measures, students are falling short of the standards set by oversight bodies, college admission criteria, and employer needs (Crain 2008; Lancy 2008: 347). For example, in the annual assessment of US secondary school students' mastery of the knowledge required to succeed in college – without remedial instruction – only 25 percent of secondary students met this criterion, and the percentage is shrinking (ACT 2013). Unfortunately, the social capital that students acquire in secondary school – via breakdancing, being chosen prom queen, quarterbacking the football team, and grunge band membership – rapidly loses its value once they've left the school. Hence, for a significant segment of the adolescent population, school provides an – increasingly expensive – custodial function without serving any significant educational function (Caplan et al. 1991: 157).

But what about "successful" students? If the cultural and natural human biases are poorly adapted to the school or academic environment, how can these biases be overcome? Such success has been demonstrated rather dramatically by a segment of the population: immigrants from less- to more-developed countries. Students succeed in spite of facing the additional challenge of adapting to a new culture.

Preventing resistance

Ideas about schooling (internal working models) migrate with . . . parents to the United States. (Roopnarine et al. 2004: 332)

It would not be an exaggeration to say that most of these high-achieving students lived hyperscheduled lives. (Demerath et al. 2008: 285)

Schooling in the West, particularly in the USA, has evolved into an institution much like the shopping mall, with environments and experiences to fit every

---

[36] These tactics are also used on parents: "Children repeat their demands insistently until they succeed, their parents yielding out of weariness" (Montandon 2001: 61).

[37] Not surprisingly, "managing student behavior" is cited as one of the three biggest challenges facing secondary school teachers (Goodwin 2012).

taste. Because of the myriad non-academic opportunities, "Jocks" and their parents, for example, report great satisfaction with the school – in spite of mediocre academic results. Still, charter, magnet, and private schools serve the needs of parents and children who ardently pursue academic success (Coll and Marks 2009: 111). That is, there are niches within the larger system of education where Nerds actually fit in. One excellent example is the "Bee."

The most noteworthy aspect of the Scripps (US) National Spelling Bee in 2004 was that a child of Indian immigrant parents did not win it. Indians had won the coveted prize in four of the previous five years, and, won in six of the eight succeeding years. Thirty of the 249 finalists in 2004 were Indian-American (who constitute less than 1 percent of the population) and Akshay Buddiga was the runner-up. His older brother Pratyush had been the big winner in 2002, correctly spelling "prospicience" to take the prize. Pratyush's accomplishment was all the more remarkable given the fact that at his public middle school in Colorado Springs, he was teased almost daily for his dark skin, Indian heritage, uncircumcised penis, and nerdiness. Upon returning to school following the contest, he expected to be beaten up in gym class. These extraordinary "overachievers" are featured in the marvelous documentary *Spellbound*, made about the lives of participants in the 1999 National Spelling Bee. For example, Neil Kadakia's performance was assisted by the efforts of a thousand Indian villagers his grandfather had paid to chant on his behalf. Perhaps more practically, he was aided by the hundreds of hours of training overseen by parents. One of the highlights of *Spellbound* is Neil's father's detailed explication of the complex and intense regimen they had developed for Neil (Blitz 2002).

The spelling-bee success of first-generation east Indian students is the tip of a large iceberg that anthropologists have been examining since the late 1980s. One of the first studies was carried out by Greta Gibson, who focused on a community of Sikh immigrants from the Punjab (northern India) living in a working-class town in California. The Punjabis chose to work just as hard as they had as farmers in India, but in the USA, they have been able to experience significant upward mobility. There were opportunities for factory employment, and by living frugally, they acquired farmland (particularly orchards) with their savings. Pushing their children to excel in school, the graduates found high-paying jobs in technical fields and shared earnings with the family.

Punjabi teenagers experienced a great deal of conflict in school centered on religion, values, dress, customs, and lifestyle. They were subject to racist taunts and had to communicate and learn in what was for them a second language. Nevertheless, on a variety of measures of academic success, Punjabi students did better than Mexican-American and Anglo students. "Parents were not naive about the difficulties their children faced in school.

They simply brooked no excuses for poor performance" (Gibson 1988: 293).[38] They couldn't blame teachers or the "system." If students fell out of line, parents forced them into early marriage and/or put them to work in fruit orchards. The primary method by which Punjabi parents facilitated their children's success was by insisting that they conform rigidly to the academic demands imposed by the school. And the children implicitly accepted their parents' views. They worked hard, did homework before watching TV, stayed out of fights, and obeyed and respected their teachers. Students did not want to follow their parents into the orchards but aspired to well-paid white-collar professions. Punjabi parents declare that "American" kids have too much freedom and too little responsibility. The Punjabi children weren't permitted to participate in extra-curricular activities such as sports, to hold jobs, or to date – since marriages are arranged. By contrast, only 12 percent of the Punjabi students' Anglo classmates took college prep courses, and parents and students seemed to share a low estimate of the value of schooling.

Similarly, principals observed that the Mexican American children seemed to have less sense of purpose and direction in school than the Punjabis ... Mexican American parents ... looked to the schools for assistance in helping children develop and maintain their Spanish skills, while the Punjabi parents favored all-English instruction. (Gibson 1988: 107)

This and other evidence from Gibson's study suggest that parents in the three groups view schooling quite differently. They convey their differing values to their children and to the school authorities, and these values significantly influence student–school interaction patterns. Gibson's findings closely parallel those found in an ethnography of Southeast Asian "boat people," who escaped after the fall of Saigon in 1975 (Caplan *et al.* 1991; Finnan 1987). As is illustrated by her title, *Accommodation Without Assimilation*, Gibson (1988) showed that, contrary to the prevailing views of native minority groups (e.g. "Ojibwe students ... interpreted academic success as tantamount to assimilation"; Hermes 2005: 46), East Indian students *do* succeed academically without assimilating to the dominant culture.

Meanwhile, evidence accrues that other immigrant groups with high aspirations also import some successful strategies for insuring their children's academic success. Southeast Asian (MacNall *et al.* 1994: 53), Caribbean (Coll and Marks 2009: 121; Roopnarine *et al.* 2004: 332), Central American

---

[38] This general attitude is what propels Asian students to success in spite of poorly endowed school systems. For example, Korean students outperform US students by a wide margin on objective tests of achievement, despite the government spending less than half the funds and despite much larger class sizes. One of the clues to understanding these differences is that "guilt in Korea has a positive aspect ... that promotes filial piety [and] achievement motivation" (Park and Kim 2006: 424).

(Suarez-Orozco 1989), and Russian (Delgado-Gaitan 1994) immigrant students have vaulted over their neighbors whose US ancestry may go back many generations (Ogbu 1987). Indeed, in Hemmings' ethnography of three high schools, recent immigrants, who may come from diverse points on the globe, form a distinct clique based on shared values. One informant told her that:

Her best friend was Japanese-American. The two were inseparable, often walking arm-in-arm through the hallways. Her other friends included a Pakistani Muslim girl, a Russian immigrant, and a girl from India. Christina said the girls had become close friends because they came from families that were different from those of preppies. "Our families are really, really strict about things. Like we're not allowed to go on dates and church is the center of our lives." (Hemmings 2004: 29)

One way to understand the immigrant groups' approach to schooling is to refer again to the relationship between schooling and investment. Their view of the role of children is characteristic of the gerontocracy. Parents recognize the enormous economic potential that resides in their children. They have left behind in their native land schools that do not prepare children adequately for the limited professional job market. They have emigrated to a country with much better schools – largely free or low-cost – with the distinct promise of lucrative employment following on successful progression through college. While they are unwilling, perhaps, to invest in their children's sports equipment or prom gowns, they will invest heavily in after-school tutoring academies such as Kumon (Levey 2009: 202) and other opportunities to "push" their children to the top of the class, positioning them for generous scholarships at the tertiary level. A mother with a son enrolled in Kumon stresses the application of a strong work ethic (*vide* chore curriculum) to schooling. Mothers interviewed at Kumon classes thought that:

Children need to be learning . . . skills and . . . acquiring capital at a young age. A mom explains, "He knows that he is supposed to work. He's going to be in *first grade now*, so I always tell him that you have to work more hard." (Levey 2009: 209)

Immigrant families seem acutely conscious of the peer pressure facing their children. Early Jewish immigrants, in particular, cloistered their children in their homes because they were afraid they would "fall prey to the social influence of Gentile friends, particularly those from poor, immigrant families with rural origins in which parents did not value education" (Blau 1969: 65). Immigrant families enforce a model of adolescence – lacking jobs, money, sports, romance, sex, music, "hanging out," and cars – completely at odds with mainstream American values. Where native US parents and teachers measure success in school by social criteria such as popularity, immigrants consider academic advancement to be the school's *raison d'être* (Gibson 1987: 289).

Non-migrant or native families have developed an alternative suite of cultural practices to overcome children's resistance to academic subjects. The most conspicuous element in this strategy may be "'helicopter parents,' who hover over the school at all times, waiting to drop in at the least sign of trouble" (Gibbs 2005: 44). Another element would appear to be the tight structuring of the child's schedule of activities. Helicopter parents "hover" at home, too! Idleness is seen by parents and children (Duffett and Johnson 2004: 10) as the greatest deterrent to schooling success. Investigators report frequent, lengthy bargaining between parents and offspring in which the parent offers a desirable activity or pastime (social media) in trade for a less desirable one (piano practice) (Wingard 2007: 86). Similar strategies may be employed by teachers in "better-quality" schools. That is, teachers grant students a great deal of authority and choice in return for their commitment to maintaining high grades in a rigorous curriculum (Demerath et al. 2008: 275). In the upwardly mobile communities where "pushy" parents rule, the Mom Taxi is likely to be driven by the father: "[Mr. Tallinger] stays behind to take the children to school and to attend 'donuts with Dad,' an event sponsored by the parent–teachers organization" (Lareau 2003: 51). This finding of heightened involvement by fathers in their children's education has emerged in several studies, including those of middle-class African-American (Roopnarine et al. 2005), Caribbean (Rooparine et al. 2006), and Indian (Verma and Saraswathi 2002: 109) communities. On the other hand, research indicates that children with non-involved fathers may "fail at school, develop behavioral and emotional problems, get into trouble with the law, engage in early and promiscuous sexual activity, or become welfare dependent later in life" (Horn 2003: 129).

Sometimes the helicopter parent is more concerned about preventing downward social mobility. "Attentive parents study the faculty like stock tables, looking for the best performer and then lobbying to get their kids into that teacher's class" (Gibbs 2005: 46). Mothers are intimately aware of their children's progress in school. As Lareau notes, "parents' activities shape the degree to which children receive a 'generic' or a 'customized' educational experience" (Lareau 1989: 123). Mrs. Harris observes Alan's (lack of) progress in spelling as she serves a volunteer stint in the classroom. She asks for and is granted spelling materials to work (successfully) with Alan at home. Another family found out that their son needed occupational therapy for fine muscle control, which they willingly paid for, and the child experienced "dramatic improvement in his posture, his handwriting, and his motor coordination in soccer" (Lareau 1989: 117). Indeed, this is one of Lareau's most striking findings, that "the most intense family–school relationships were not for the highest achieving students in upper-middle-class families. These occurred in families whose children were at the bottom of their class" (Lareau 1989: 129; see also Pomerantz and Moorman 2007).

Where helicopter parents and nerds are outliers in the USA, in East Asia they represent the mainstream cultural pattern. Japanese mothers cannot "leave education to the specialists"; they willingly purchase an annual set of books from traveling salesmen to "keep abreast of what is currently in the curriculum" (Hendry 1986: 25). The short summer break is a critical time for Japanese children as schools and parents worry about a loss of momentum. "Parents feel that ... vacation or not their children must work equally hard not to miss out and fall behind the competition" (Benjamin 1997: 98). The mother's role in her child's education is firmly established in *yochien* (nursery school), where she is given very strict guidance on the preparation of the child's Obentō lunch. This time-consuming effort goes to produce a meal that is as much about indoctrination (for mother and child) in what it means to be a Japanese student as about sustenance (Allison 1991: 10). Elsewhere in Asia:

Chinese parents are immensely involved, focused, and willing to apply a variety of incentives and punishments to get their child to focus on his or her studies to earn the highest class mark. (Jankowiak *et al.* 2011: 158)

[Korean mothers] think of their children's scores as their own ... [they are ever vigilant] in order to prevent their children from collapsing or falling behind in the war. (Cho 1995: 151)

Helicopter parents aren't just concerned with choosing a "good" school and good teacher; equally important is the careful screening of the child's peers (J. R. Harris 2006: 233). Alex Williams is a young African-American male who is the subject of Lareau's ethnography. He belonged to an all-black church, and he had regular opportunities to form friendships with other middle-class black children. His parents carefully scrutinized his social environment, always seeking, as Ms. Williams said, to keep him in the company of individuals who were also "cultured" (Lareau 2003: 132–133). Comparable results have been reported by Tyson (2002: 1183) from her study of middle-class black families who'd clearly acquired (and utilized) the requisite cultural capital to insure their children's academic success. Ogbu found that black high school students who successfully resisted peer pressure and took Honors and AP classes – earning good grades – were bolstered by the close supervision of parents and through carefully choosing a few like-minded friends (Ogbu 2003: 216–217).[39]

As they transition from one set of peers to another, subtle changes occur in students' attitudes toward and performance in school (Kindermann 1993).

---

[39] Japanese schools have an explicit program to create classroom groups and shape them so that peer pressure is aimed at motivating members to succeed academically. In this way, parents, teachers, and peers are all working in consort to prevent academic failure or malaise (Benjamin 1997: 53).

A parent's knowledge of this phenomenon is, again, part of the stock portfolio I've been labeling "cultural capital." In selecting their homes on the basis of an assessment of school quality, middle-class families are also, as a bonus, insuring that their children's neighborhood playmates will share the values they espouse (Lewis and Forman 2002). In working-class communities, children "have more autonomy from adults than their middle-class counterparts" (Lareau 2003: 151). Working-class parents with high aspirations for their children, such as Kusserow's informant Lisa, speak of "the pull of the wrong crowd" and how individualism and strong self-esteem help a child "resist that and get above it all" (Kusserow 2004: 63). Another one of Kusserow's informants, Ellen, offers a similar perspective.

Ellen described herself as not necessarily from a "lower-class" background ... she decided to send [her kids] to a Catholic school not because it was better academically than the public school, but because the Catholic School had "a better class of people in it." "For some reason I do feel that in the Catholic school there's more mothers [or] better families ... that do care more." (Kusserow 2004: 76)

Anthropologists have been at the forefront of efforts to problematize schooling. That is, while educators and psychologists are preoccupied with analyzing and remediating *failure*, anthropologists have documented the many conflicts between schooling and alternative (and probably more "natural") routines for preparing children for their adult roles. Given the many conflicts discussed in this chapter we should, perhaps, *expect* to see schools fail for the majority (Loveless 2010).[40] The widespread reporting of academic cheating even at the most prestigious and selective schools and universities (McCabe *et al.* 2012) is a sobering reminder of how difficult it is for humans to adapt to schooling. *Successful* academic progress and mastery then become the more compelling objects of inquiry. As yet, however, few (Demerath *et al.* 2008; Gibson 1988; Kusserow 2004; Levey 2009; Pugh 2009) studies have probed the cultural foundations of schooling *success*.

From the foregoing we can discern two broad strategies. First, throughout East Asia and among immigrants to the US from various regions of Asia, including India, we see a model that creates a moral imperative for the child

---

[40] Unlike the US, where students continue in school in spite of mediocre to poor academic success, Germany does a much better job of matching publicly provided training to the needs and inclinations of children and the requirements of employers. Where the US education system is almost entirely academic, "vocational education ... leading to the acquisition of a training certificate absorbs the majority (about 70%) of German youths" (Mortimer and Krüger 2000: 487). The US system has resisted change in part because of the neontocracy, in which children can never be seen as poor or unpromising scholars. In Germany, "signs of failure are much more visible and clearly definitive as German youths move through the educational structure" (Mortimer and Krüger 2000: 479).

to become a good student. The imperative includes such ideas as the child's filial devotion to parents and family; respect for the teacher and the academic curriculum; hard work; sacrifice and suffering; a sense of being in a race in which only a few will be winners; the mother's deep commitment to the child's success, including vigilant monitoring of homework; and investment in costly supplemental, private instruction (e.g. Kumon). This moral imperative is supported by the careful cultivation of shame and guilt (Fung 1999). Children are made aware of the enormous sacrifice made on their behalf by family members and that to fail to reciprocate by wholeheartedly embracing their schoolwork is tantamount to a betrayal. The idea that shame and guilt are necessary and very positive human attributes dates to Confucius (Li 2012: 40). By contrast, this is a typical assessment of the US perspective: "As a society we are attracted to innate traits, to talents, giftedness, and effortless achievement, because this fits in so well with the ideal of the individual genius, a more appealing idea than hours of practice, struggle, and hard work" (Gross-Loh 2013: 105).

The second strategy to overcome resistance is associated with the neontocracy, primarily middle- and upper-middle-class culture in the West. I will borrow Lareau's (2003: 132) very apt term "concerted cultivation" to label this strategy. The basic idea is that the child is a project, an opportunity to create a unique, "special" individual. Unlike the first strategy, the focus is not exclusively (or even primarily) on academic (or musical) success but on creating a well-rounded person whose rare talents (e.g. sports, dance, music, foreign language, theater, rodeo) have been identified and *cultivated* – spending up to $1,000 a month on extra-curricular activities in Pugh's (2009: 85) sample. In addition, there is the perceived need to engage the child in discussion and verbal interchange from an early age. In fact, teaching speechless babies to "sign" has become very popular and allows parents to accelerate vocabulary development. From the promotional material:

Considering how slowly babies learn even easy words like *ball* and *doggy*, let alone difficult words like *scared* or *elephant*, many months are lost that could be spent having rich and rewarding interactions, both for the child and the parent. (Acredolo and Goodwyn 2002: 3)

As noted by Li, being a facile and fluent speaker has been valued in Western society since the Greeks, but never more so than today (Li 2012: 277). And we can readily imagine how participating in demanding, highly structured activities like sports, together with verbal fluency, all-roundedness, and standing with peers, would all contribute to successful – if not National-Spelling-Bee-caliber – performance in the relatively undemanding public school academic program. There are, of course, some elements common to both resistance-defeating strategies, such as the aggressive management of the make-up of the child's peer group. But the point is that parents who employ one or other of these strategies generally see their children make at least satisfactory progress in school through the tertiary level, while those who do not may find their children successfully resisting the culture of schooling.

The schooled mind

Teaching literacy (as well as mathematics) in Western schools involves the teaching of arbitrary symbols (letters, words, numbers) and the rules for applying them to specific cases. (LeVine *et al*. 2012: 51)

The use of taxonomic categorization has been found consistently for [individuals] with more than a fourth-grade education. (Rogoff 1981b: 250)

The blow-gun is a sophisticated and complex hunting tool that is correspondingly difficult to make. Everett describes his careful observation of several instances where a Pirahã boy, diligently observing his father, learns the many necessary steps. The learning process unfolds with almost no verbal exchange (Everett 2014). In contrast, learning in the typical village classroom involves a great deal of talk – mostly by the teacher – and very little doing. We have two very different approaches to the transmission/acquisition of culture, reflecting the contrasting nature of the material to be learned. Schools transmit declarative information that must be represented in language whereas children in the village are learning procedures – how to *do* things. Even in domains where instruction or explanation seems warranted, they are absent:

I hardly ever saw [Yukaghir] children having things explained to them, especially with regard to spirits and ritual practices. The transmission of such knowledge consists largely of hands-on training in specific ritual techniques ... very little knowledge about spiritual beings is explicitly transmitted between generations. (Willerslev 2007: 161, 173)

The distinction between declarative and procedural information has implications for determining the default mechanism underlying the child's acquisition of her culture (Thornton and Raihani 2008: 1823). Declarative information may be best conveyed by teaching or another top-down, highly structured process, whereas procedural skills may be best acquired through a bottom-up, learner-initiated process (Bjorklund 2007: 192). For example, Wyndham's study of Rarámuri ethnobotany found that even very young children may be knowledgeable about plants and their uses, while neither children nor most adults were particularly fluent when it came to plant names (2010: 87, 96).

    And the language used in schools is profoundly different than that used in vernacular or colloquial conversation. For example, a common rhetorical device in the classroom is for the teacher to ask a pupil a question that the teacher already knows the answer to. This is not done in normal discourse (except, of course around the dinner table in WEIRD society). Not only is the school's curriculum transmitted orally, it is also represented in written form. This is because "complex information transmitted through written instructions has lower rates of error than if it were transmitted verbally or if the recipient is able to only watch someone perform an activity" (Erkens and Lipo 2007: 247). Drawing on a wide range of research, LeVine and colleagues (2012) are convinced that intensive immersion in a sea of novel, sometimes abstract words and ideas – spoken, read, and written – changes the way people interact with the world.

The sheer volume of information transmitted through verbal, written, and pictorial media provokes cognitive change in students (Lancy 1983: 112–116, 1989: 17). However, with one important exception (Bruner 1966), most early theories of cognitive development in children failed to take into account the impact of schooling. Although Jean Piaget's theory of cognitive development is notably comprehensive and enduring, its universality was cast in doubt by researchers who tried replicating his Genevan results outside the West. Greenfield (1966: 234) found that Piaget's milestones for cognitive development in the "concrete operations" stage are met only by children with four or more years of schooling. This finding was extended and replicated by many other studies (e.g. Cole *et al.* 1971; Lancy 1983; reviewed by Rogoff 1981b) in the ensuing years. Schooling (that endures for at least four to six years) shapes cognition in a variety of ways, but above all it leads to a more analytic approach to information and problem solving:

Analytic thought involves a detachment of objects from contexts, a tendency to focus on objects' attributes, and a preference for using categorical rules to explain and predict behavior. (Henrich *et al.* 2010: 72)

Goodnow offered a further enumeration of the kinds of information-processing imperatives that schooling introduces in children's lives. These include finding patterns or universal rules, "sets," and "things that go together." The school expects "complete*"* answers that take all the available information into account and general, more inclusive solutions (Goodnow 1976). Contrast can readily be drawn with, for example, a Nepali village where the "hardness of directly perceived, unchallengeable, fixed reality is a powerful force for social stability" while analytic, logical, verbal thought would be "subversive and transformative" (Levy 1996: 136).

One very important milestone in our understanding of the effects of schooling on thinking was the work of Alexander Luria in Soviet Central Asia in the 1930s – finally made available in English in 1976 due to the efforts of Michael Cole. Luria conducted interview-style testing of unschooled peasants.

In the first example we can see the villager reasoning from personal experience (or lack thereof) and inability or unwillingness to apply a general rule.

Problem posed: "In the Far North, where there is snow, all bears are white. Novaya Zemlya is in the far north and there is always snow there. What color are the bears?" Response: "We always speak of only what we see; we don't talk of what we haven't seen." (Luria 1976: 108)

In another problem, men and women were asked to sort and group various kinds and colors of weaving yarn (Uzbekistan is noted for its carpets). The male response was "men [not being weavers] don't know colors and call them all blue." The women refused to impose any grouping or organization – something educated Uzbeks did quite easily – exclaiming that "none of these are the same" (Luria 1976: 25, 27). In a fishing community in Sulawesi, Vermonden found directly parallel results, with fishers resistant to discussing marine life more generally; they eschewed speaking of types of fish or of considering different ways of grouping them. Their thinking was governed by their practice (true also for Penan hunters – Puri 2005: 280 – and South American and African subsistence farmers – Henrich *et al.* 2010: 72).

Expertise does not consist in trying to master the largest repertoire of fishes but, rather, focusing on the fishes the fisherman interacts with ... practice not only shapes which species a fisherman is interested in, but information provided for each fish also differs depending on a fisherman's specialization. (Vermonden 2009: 215)

Had Vermonden's informants been schooled, they might have used broader and more inclusive organizing principles and been able to display a more encyclopedic knowledge of fish.

In addition to the increased memory/information load that seems to be driving the search for efficiency of thought and reasoning, a second factor is the criticality of the information. Individuals will use more efficient, analytical procedures if there are negative consequences for failure to acquire the information. In schools – but rarely in villages – there are penalties for failure or slowness to learn.[41] Recall the ubiquity of "instruments of correction" – discussed earlier in the chapter – used on "dunces" as well as "miscreants." In contemporary village schools, wrong answers may provoke hazing from peers, a tongue-lashing from the teacher, and withdrawal of parental support for continued schooling.

It's not just that villagers lack the subtle cognitive training that leads to more analytic strategies; they may have a worldview that dictates an alternative way of perceiving and parsing their surroundings. Certainly Luria's peasants preferred to focus on the practical rather than conceptual relationships among

---

[41] In the village, failure to *perform* (e.g. lack of dependability) may be punished.

items in the categorization tasks that were set for them. In research in Papua New Guinea, we found that achievement of Piaget's concrete operations and similar cognitive measures of efficient thought was uneven and varied by culture (nine contrasting societies were sampled) and by whether the child had had five to six years of schooling (Lancy 1983). In some cases we took the local perspective. Melpa (Western Highlands) unschooled children "failed" the tests, particularly those that required the application of a (more efficient) taxonomizing strategy in grouping and organizing an array of local objects. This included Inhelder and Piaget's (1964) "class inclusion" task. However, when we turned our focus to adults, men and women showed a disinclination to acknowledge the nesting that occurs in a taxonomic array, translating opportunities to respond taxonomically into pairing or "making twos" – the most compelling and pervasive (found across all conceptual domains including kinship, counting, color classification, etc.) Melpa means of organization. Functional relationships as preferred by Luria's Uzbeks played a small role as well. In further experimental studies we were able to demonstrate that this powerful preference for pairing did "block" any tendency to taxonomize, thus undermining the class inclusion concept (Lancy and Strathern 1981: 788).

It is important to acknowledge that the transformation from reliance primarily on social learning to reliance on schooling and rational, scientific thought is by no means achieved in all individuals who happened to be schooled – even through the tertiary or college level. "Primitive" thought persists in "modern" society. This is because "to get the benefits of social learning, humans have to be credulous ... accepting the ways that they observe in their society as sensible and proper, and such credulity opens up human minds to the spread of maladaptive beliefs" (Boyd and Richerson 2006: 468).[42] As Nobel laureate Herb Simon (1956; see also Edgerton 1992: 201; Sober and Wilson 1998: 241) brilliantly deduced, we are more often "satisficers" than optimizers. We muddle along, like Lévi-Strauss' (1966) *bricoleur* doing a good enough job to get by (see also Barrett *et al.* 2002: 278). The Pirahã are an Amazonian tribe that manages very well in spite of lacking "numerals, counting and most terms for quantitative comparison" (Everett 2005: 622). Humans are also disposed to seek "cognitive closure" because of the "drive to attain group consensus in order to reduce insistencies, ambiguities, and uncertainties in beliefs" (Richtner and Kruglanski 2004: 117). We follow the herd and most of the time we don't think at all about what we're doing – we're on auto-pilot (Bargh and Chartrand 1999: 464). This acknowledgment of individual fallibility helps us understand the persistence of maladaptive practices and why culture change is rare (Boyd and Richerson 1996). For example, Efe archers eschew

---

[42] Widely held but maladaptive beliefs in US culture include the idea that individuals need to be able to carry loaded firearms in public for "protection."

borrowing net hunting from their fellow pygmies who practice it, even though they know it would lead to larger game catches. Their territory in the Ituri forest is conducive, but they feel the effort of making the nets would be too great (Bailey and Aunger 1989). The Mapuche of Argentina encounter frequent periods of hunger and starvation, yet refuse to catch and eat fish in the lake because "Mapuche eat only animals with fur. No fish!" (Politis 2007: 339). This dogged resistance to evidence and change is legion in human society (Edgerton 1992); one has only to think of "well-educated" smokers, climate change deniers, and Ponzi scheme victims.

In short, while we embrace the idea that schooling can be of great benefit to the individual, her family, and society at large, the glass may always seem half empty. Students may resist the physical and social constraints imposed by schools. "Good" teaching may be a rarity. Parents may lack the cultural capital to shape the child to the demands of the school. Even students thoroughly socialized to the student role may resist intellectual engagement and become "in-school dropouts." Governments – even the wealthiest – may not provide adequate funding.[43] There may be a poor fit between the curriculum and the requirements of the job market. And, lastly, while schooling may promote an analytic way of looking at the world, thinking analytically is taxing and most people, most of the time, would rather not be bothered (Shweder 1984: 36).

---

[43] I am thinking specifically of the US failure to fund pre-school education (Lancy 2008: 350–351).

10   Too little childhood? Too much?

Introduction

The global distribution of resources ... means that some children must work to ensure household survival whilst others can over-consume. (Holloway and Valentine 2000: 10)

Previous generations of ethnographers have described the successful adaptation of children to societies that are themselves successfully adapted to their environment and material circumstances (Korbin 1987b). But, as these patterns of cultural adaptation are stressed by global forces that overwhelm local coping strategies, the lives of children are adversely affected. Anthropologists are prominent in the corps of concerned observers working to understand the contexts in which contemporary children live and to offer ideas to improve their lot (Schwartzman 2001: 15).

We will see that the distinction posed at the outset between cherubs, chattel, and changelings continues to apply in the present and into the future. In the neontocracy, the elevation of children to god-like cherubs, and corollary expense, show no signs of slowing. Among the poor, parents continue to seek the means to divest themselves of unwanted changelings or to convert their offspring to usable chattel. Indeed, Olga Nieuwenhuys simultaneously condemns the export of the "modern" model of childhood (Nieuwenhuys 1996: 242) – turn them all into cherubs – *and* the globalization that turns underprivileged children into chattel on behalf of their wealthy counterparts. She argues that poorly paid children's labor in developing countries is, effectively, a subsidy, which keeps the cost of goods purchased on behalf of First World children artificially low (Nieuwenhuys 2005: 178).

In this chapter, we will visit several "flash-points" in the contemporary crisis of childhood, beginning with the family where supporting social mechanisms are imperiled. Unlike the casual process by which children proceed through a chore curriculum, described in Chapter 7, we now see a degree of urgency – children must begin earning their keep earlier and earlier (Campos *et al.* 1994: 323). We will see children divorced from the comforting confines of family and village, migrating, often involuntarily, to work on plantations, in factories, or in mines, or to the urban jungle. The ties that bind children to parents and community may be sundered by migration or the death or incapacity of one or both parents. Increasingly, observers identify self-sufficient children, especially in urban areas, surviving independently from family. However, as they are caught up in urban crime or free-roving militias, children hover on a razor's edge of moral ambiguity: one minute they're victims, the next, aggressors (Machado Neto 1982: 534).

Briefly focusing on privileged children, we note that they suffer from a cultural pattern of overprotection and indulgence. Parents seek to maintain children in a state of innocence and dependency as long as possible. Images of college students going to sleep clutching teddy bears suggests how successful their parents have been. Childhood now represents an enormous marketplace for consumer products. This ironic contrast between shrinking and expanding childhoods is well represented by images of malnourished slave children in Côte d'Ivoire harvesting the cocoa beans that will be processed into the chocolates consumed by obese children in the West (Chanthavong 2002). The chapter concludes with a catalog of the major conclusions that might be drawn from this volume.

Childhood curtailed

The child labor pool [in Pakistan] is all but inexhaustible, owing . . . to a birth rate that is among the world's highest. (Silvers 1996: 81)

Most street children are simply "excess" kids. (Scheper-Hughes and Hoffman 1998: 362)

Tanzania is, by African standards, a relatively prosperous and stable country. And yet, the major cities and towns are flooded with children who have left home and/or are barely connected to their families. Estimates from 2012 place the number of street children in the country at 300,000 (Wagner *et al.* 2012: 37). Interviewing children in Dar es Salaam revealed that their childhood – when others care for them – had been truncated. Justin left his village at six because, at the end of a day of herding and school, "they usually had eaten all the food" (Wagner *et al.* 2012: 40). The first sign of the child's changed status usually arises in a conflict over playing versus working (Evans 2004: 76). The conflict escalates from there.

"Home," for Peter, was characterized by a lack of food, clothing, opportunities for education, love or care, and indeed, familial ties with his alcoholic mother had already become tenuous long before Peter stayed on the street . . . Juma's "father" had four wives . . . and twenty-three children . . . When Juma's father chose to de-emphasize the relationship [with Juma's mother], due to demands on scarce resources, tensions, and conflict of interest with his other more favored wives and children, [led to] Juma's mother and her children [becoming] marginalized. (Evans 2004: 75, 83)

The conditions that foster the birth and development of healthy children are very well understood. However, the number of children born into adverse circumstances is rapidly increasing, relative to those born into favorable circumstances (Gielen and Chumachenko 2004: 91). For example, in much of Africa, the fertility rate (births per woman) is very high (5.9 in Nigeria) while the adult death rate, from HIV/AIDS, malaria, and TB, is also extraordinarily high, leaving children to be raised entirely by other children (Gielen and Chumachenko 2004: 87). Traditional means to limit family size, including infanticide and the post-partum sex taboo, have been suppressed by outside moral authorities that may also oppose modern methods of contraception (Miller 1987). The resulting overpopulation in the countryside pushes villagers into urban areas; squalid slums are the fastest-growing housing category in much of the world[1] (Strehl 2011: 45). The cosseted security of a village childhood is exchanged for the bare survival of an urban scavenger.

Ironically, while parents in wealthy nations express concern about whether they can "afford another child," in poor nations like Burkina Faso parents feel almost no responsibility for the wellbeing of their children:

There are no perceived disadvantages in having lots of children. Children are never seen as a drain on resources. The availability of food is believed to be purely a product of the God-given fortune of the child, and nothing to do with the level of resources available within the household or the number of mouths to feed [because] "every child is born with its own luck." (Hampshire 2001: 115)

In Fransfontein, a rural area of Namibia, Julia Pauli finds that the breakdown of traditional marriage and family structures characteristic of impoverished urban areas is spreading to villages. She uses the term "multiple parenthoods" to describe a phenomenon whereby children may never know their father, and their mother may play a minor caretaking role in their lives. Since Pauli's main informant had had ten children by at least five partners, any one of her children might discover dozens of "siblings" – offspring of their fathers. Hence children must participate in elective families, forming kin-like ties on a fraternal basis. Like street children – their urban counterparts – the children of Fransfontein find that peers are preferred as nurturers, compared to often harsh and exploitative adults (Pauli 2005).

[1] State of the World's Cities Report (2006–2007) Brussels, Belgium: United Nations Human Settlements Programme. Available at www.unhabitat.org/pmss/listItemDetails.aspx?publicationID=2101. Accessed October 10, 2013.

In some communities, such as the Shipibo Indian village of Manco Capac in the Peruvian Amazon, people are desperate for contraceptives – which they've heard about but cannot obtain. Hern's informant:

Chomoshico was nearing the end of her eleventh pregnancy. She already had seven living children. Neither she nor her husband wants more. "Enough. Clothes cost," they told me. "I'm tired of having children," she said. "I almost died with the last one." Her husband has tuberculosis. In the same village, a few weeks before, a young girl died on her thirteenth birthday trying to give birth to twins. And in that girl's natal village, just up the river, I had just seen my first case of frank starvation among the Shipibo Indians, with whom I had worked . . . since 1964. (Hern 1992: 31)

There are reports of relatively educated (LeVine *et al.* 2004: 875) or urbanized women eagerly seeking opportunities to limit births (Pickering 2005), especially where high fertility is seen as hampering economic opportunities (Kress 2005). However, lack of funds and/or ideological opposition may severely limit the provision of women's health services, which means that relatively few women are in a position to plan or reduce their pregnancies. Egypt is being crushed under the weight of its enormous population: 62 percent of its citizens are under fourteen (Gielen and Chumachenko 2004: 88). But high fertility is a cornerstone of Muslim ideology. Unlike many of its neighbors, Egypt has many well-educated women who can be expected to limit fertility and to raise healthy, well-educated children more effectively (LeVine *et al.* 2012). However, these women are spurned by educated males who prefer less well-educated wives (Ahmed 2005: 157).

A family with too many mouths to feed with the available resources is a maelstrom of tension. Alcoholism and abuse of women by men and of children by adults becomes the norm (Martini 2005: 134). Consider that thousands of street children in Angola, Congo, and the Republic of Congo had been branded as witches and cast out (if they survived the preceding abuse) by their families, as a rationale for not having to feed or care for them (La Franiere 2007; de Boeck 2005).

Studying families and children "in pain" is difficult for the anthropologist. Wolseth writes passionately about the anger he feels watching one of "his" Santo Domingo street kids contract for sex with a wealthy white foreigner (Wolseth 2010: 423). Philippe Bourgois writes:

When the shrieks of crying children rose through the heating pipes in my tenement in East Harlem, New York, I fretted: Was I ethnocentrically misreading the . . . aggressive childrearing practices of my second-generation Puerto Rican immigrant neighbors? (1998: 331)

In spite of the ill-treatment, children may well be valued as chattel. From an early age, children can aid their parents with homemaking, and through their assistance to older family members employed in commercial agriculture and rural industry (Chapter 2, pp. 61–63). Indeed, they may well be able to obtain wages and other resources on their own: "In the lowest castes, children become laborers as soon as they can walk" (Silvers 1996: 81–82).

Children as breadwinners

[In Mexico] the more working children a family has, the more money can be put aside. (Bey 2003: 291)

His earnings helped support his infirm mother and six siblings. His father was in prison for murder. (Kenny 2007: 76)

Children have always been expected to assist their families but, in many contemporary families, such assistance may come at a high price (Rurevo and Bourdillon 2003: 23). Heather Montgomery studied Baan Nua, a type of squatter community in Thailand that is becoming more and more common. Forced off the land because of crowding in their rural homeland, adults find that the surest source of income is through the prostitution of their children, nearly half of whom had been so employed (Montgomery 2001b: 72). In Ho Chi Minh City, girls in their later teen years join the ranks of prostitutes to earn a respectable income and to help support their families (Rubenson et al. 2005). An inexhaustible labor supply depresses factory wages in India, and families can only make ends meet if all able-bodied members are employed (Nieuwenhuys 2005: 178).

In southern Mexico, rural Mixtec are too numerous to all make a living off the land and earn enough cash to meet burgeoning needs for new expenses like electricity, clothing, and taxes. There is mass migration each year to the agribusiness-controlled croplands (growing, for example, tomatoes) in the north. "Any worker, whether, man, woman or child, is paid twenty-seven pesos per day." Children's productivity is comparable to an adult's even considering that they "are put to work before the permitted age of eight [using] forged papers" (Bey 2003: 292).

In northern Ghana, Talensi farm plots grow smaller as the population increases. Neither the soil nor the climate permits an increase in production. The specter of starvation has been lifted by the low-wage employment of the community's children in the nascent gold-mining industry. For example, Nangodi:

is a highly impoverished community that is infested with blackflies ... parents ... blinded by blackfly bites ... depend on their children for income; they crush rocks, and process and sell gold in order to purchase tomatoes and peppers for cooking. (Hilson 2010: 459)

Figure 31 Suitcase makers in Kashgar [China]

Recall the discussion in Chapter 5 (p. 278) of children as a "reserve labor force," and it would certainly seem that many communities have had to activate that reserve. As Kenny recorded (1999: 375): "In many households in low-income communities ... it is children who put the food on the table." And children generally respond positively to these family needs. In El Salvador, children "expressed this feeling of greater responsibility for their older and traumatized caretakers" (Dickson-Gómez 2003: 335). Thai children claim they've "become and remain prostitutes out of duty and love to their parents" and strenuously resist attempts to remove them from their parents' custody (Montgomery 2001b: 82).

In spite of numerous international agreements and the existence of many watchdog organizations, children are employed (as in Figure 31) because rural villagers may have few other options available.[2] In Peru, where children must

[2] "Generally, international campaigns to stop child labor have not resulted in children going back to school and improving their situation. The more likely result is that they are forced into work that is more poorly paid and more dangerous than what they were doing before" (Bourdillon 2000: 15; see also Reynolds *et al*. 2006: 291–292).

be sixteen to work in commercial agriculture, younger employees use false identity cards. Or they may seek employment on smaller-scale plantations, which do not produce for the export market directly and "are less subject to monitoring by the labor inspectors" (van den Berge 2011b: 153). Employers are eager to hire children because, aside from their lower wages, minors follow directions and work without complaint. Parents are supportive because children's earnings are critical when there may be only one employable adult whose low wage can't support the whole family (van den Berge 2011b: 156–157).

Of course, many families find that, even with all children working, they can no longer survive as farmers or foragers. The whole family or some members migrate to the exploding urban slums. Everyone, including each child, is constrained to be opportunistic. In one interesting study, investigators found that children follow the "optimal foraging model," meaning that they partition the ecology (in this case, selling to occupants of slow-moving or stopped cars at a busy intersection) to achieve maximum payoff (Disma et al. 2011: 373). In effect, children transfer foraging skills to the city. Many children who're making a living in the streets return in the evening to the squatter settlements where their families live. In Mexican cities, there are deeply rooted economic niches for children. For example, they assist store patrons to carry their purchases to their vehicles or clean windshields in return for tips. They sell newspapers on the street corner; others perform magic and circus-type acts in public. Parents may carefully orchestrate children's work (Taracena and Tavera 2000). In Quito, I observed "chiclé" (literally Chiclets[tm] or other small hard candies) sellers at traffic intersections. Children of seven to nine seemed to behave like sellers, quickly moving on if rebuffed. Younger children of four to six acted more like beggars; if rebuffed, they'd hold their palm out and beg in a whining tone. They tended to be filthy and dressed poorly, but I observed that the (I presume) older brother who hovered nearby with back-up supplies of candy was clean and well dressed. The overall picture was that whole families "worked" particular locations, with mothers selling crafts and trinkets from a relatively fixed location, while child sellers were more mobile.

Immigrants from Latin America depend heavily on the economic contributions of their children, who are involved in selling food, clothes, or other merchandise alongside adult street vendors; helping their parents to clean houses ... cleaning tables in a pupusera ... In one family, the five children (ranging in age from four to twelve) spent several hours each evening putting price stickers on "Barbie" sunglasses that were sold ... they told me, in Toys 'R' Us ... [Also] ... parents in Pico Union take it for granted that children should use their English abilities [and] literacy skills to translate for them [and cope with the] ... complex English literacy demands for daily life in Los Angeles. (Orellana 2001: 374–376, 378; see also Orellana 2009)

In contrast to these scenes of the survival of family life in the face of adversity, numerous observers report conflict between poor children and their parents. This conflict arises because of the harsh treatment meted out by poor, stressed-out parents and their appropriation of the child's income (Verma and Sharma 2007: 194). Another source of conflict arises from the child's thwarted aspirations for agency (see below). While the child may have assumed much of the parent's role in caring for younger siblings, cooking and taking care of the household, and/or earning a wage that supplements or is larger than that of the nominal "head of household," he or she is still treated like a child (Kenny 1999, 375, 379; 2007: 71, 74). Hence, the forces that loosen family ties include not only the immigration of family members for economic reasons, the threat of armed conflict, and fatal illness such as AIDS but, also, internal family discord that weighs heavily on the child.

Children without parents

The extended family system [is] breaking down ... people cannot afford to look after their kin. (Mapedzahama and Bourdillon 2000: 39)

It is not uncommon ... to find children [in Zimbabwe] as young as ten or eleven heading entire households due to the death of both parents and the absence of relatives to look after them. (McIvor 2000: 173)

Living with one's family can be one of the riskiest locations for a child ... where abuse is more abundant than food. (Kenny 1999: 384)

From a child's perspective, whether living in a fully industrialized or economically undeveloped country, poverty is synonymous with single-parenthood. Even where fathers are present, they may not be a positive force in the child's life – e.g. a Russian boy told by his alcoholic father not to come home without a bottle of vodka (Fujimura 2003). Although father absence may have relatively little direct impact on young children, adolescents clearly miss the restraint imposed by the family's moral guardian. Draper and Harpending (1982) argue that the father's presence in the household models the value of enduring pair-bonds and conveys an expectation of long-term investment in one's offspring. Children in families without fathers have teenagers who join gangs (Vigil 1988: 426) and/or become parents. Teens make poor parents, as demonstrated in studies from developing and industrialized societies (Elster and Lamb 1986: 184; Gelles 1986: 347).

Internationally, teenage parenthood will continue to rise, but the large number of children growing up in single-parent households is now overshadowed by the growing cadre of orphans. We have seen in Chapter 3 that communities take steps to insure there won't be too many children for a given set of parents or the community as a whole to nurture, but HIV/AIDS has overwhelmed these coping mechanisms as high fertility, discussed earlier in the chapter, is coupled with unprecedented (since the Middle Ages) adult mortality. (Bock and Johnson 2008) describe the insupportable burdens on grandmothers in many Botswanan families that prevent them from standing in for their ill or decreased daughters.

The number of children who have lost one or both parents has reached plague dimensions. "UNICEF estimates ... more than twenty-four million orphans in sub-Saharan Africa ... Uganda alone [has] two million ... nineteen per cent of [the population]" (Oleke *et al.* 2005: 267). Even when these children are absorbed into the homes of relatives, they fare badly compared with their peers whose biological ties to the family are stronger. They don't eat as well, they're assigned more chores, and they're less likely to be enrolled in school (Case *et al.* 2004: 6). Nevertheless, it has been argued that the traditional *laissez-faire* childrearing mechanisms – described in Chapter 5 – actually help prepare children better to cope with the disruptive effects of war, pestilence, and famine (Mann 2004: 8–9). Indeed, studies of Somali refugee families indicate that children's resilience allows them to withstand adverse conditions better than adults (Rousseau *et al.* 1998).

Although "AIDS orphans" have attracted the most attention, another group of children growing up without their parents have been left behind in the village when their parents migrated for employment. The US and Canada, for example, have adopted immigration policies that, effectively, invite mothers from the "south" to leave their own children to travel north to work in domestic service (Katz 2001). Heather Rae-Espinoza (2006) has studied these bifurcated families split between Ecuador and the US, and she also finds that the "It takes a village" model is severely strained in the face of too many children per adult caretaker.

Another contemporary crisis that separates children from parents is the trend to recruit/abduct children for use as soldiers in civil conflicts. The many violent internal conflicts in Southeast Asia, the Middle East, and Africa have not spared children.[3] In northern Uganda the Lord's Resistance Army has abducted 18,000 children and turned many of them into willing soldiers. When captured or "rescued," these children pose a dilemma for society. Should they be treated as victims or perpetrators (Mawson 2004: 131)? In Cambodia, the Khmer Rouge consistently used children as informers and enforcers, thus provoking general paranoia and abuse of unattached children (Boyden 2004: 242). In Colombia, one-third of the

---

[3] In 1998 it was estimated that up to 300,000 children were actively involved in armed conflict. Information from www.child-soldiers.org. Accessed July 8, 2013. It is important to note that finding children among the ranks is hardly a recent development (Rosen 2005: 5).

population is younger than eighteen. Roughly half of them are "internally displaced persons (IDPs)" who find a home and improved living conditions in the sheltering embrace of the armed forces or rebel militias (see Figure 32). "For many children ... joining a fighting force is a matter of survival. It renders the distinction between forced and voluntary recruitment academic" (Geisler and Roshani 2006: 1). And children become enthusiastic combatants: "Armed children and youth spread unspeakable fear throughout Sierra Leone. They were responsible for thousands of murders, mutilations, and rapes, and for torture, forced labor, and sexual slavery" (Rosen 2005: 58).[4]

As hostilities end, the survivors may not be able to return to and reintegrate into their community or even their family. They are in an anomalous position as victims who became aggressors. "The possession of guns and a license to kill remove them from childhood. But child soldiers are still physically and psychologically immature; they are not full adults who are responsible for themselves" (Honwana 2006: 3; see also Coulter 2009: 57). In El Salvador, and likely elsewhere, demobilized "rebels" receive insufficient "respect, solidarity and support" in their home community. They migrate to urban areas to join urban gangs, where "violence takes a huge toll" (Dickson-Gómez 2003: 332).

As childhood is curtailed and children shift from dependants to laborers (or soldiers), the social contract that constitutes "family" may be abrogated. Children may, effectively, orphan themselves. Whether given a push by their parents (Khair 2011) or not (Whitehead *et al.* 2005), children are readily leaving for the city to seek employment – as vendors or domestics in Mumbai, for example. Some see themselves as searching for adventure in the city, and a wage of 25 cents an hour puts spending money in their pocket where before there was none. When interviewed, they don't seem too eager to rejoin the bosom of their small-town or rural families (Iversen and Raghavendra 2005) or to enter the dubious comfort of a government-sponsored facility. Children may be driven away by physical abuse (Kovats-Bernat 2006: 49) or when they perceive that the bounty they bring home goes unappreciated by self-centered, addicted parents (Kenny 2007: 68). As "street children," they may find more calories foraging in public than they will "at home" (Aptekar 2004: 379; Davies 2008: 326; Disma *et al.* 2011: 374; Kenny 1999: 381; Kovats-Bernat 2006: 118).

While there may be a significant cadre of researchers and aid workers whose attention is focused on children without families, it is uniquely the task of

---

[4] For a vivid and probably accurate portrayal of child soldiers in Sierra Leone, see the film *Blood Diamond* (2006). Ironically, children orphaned by civil war and AIDS in Mozambique served as extras during the filming.

Figure 32 Soldier boy in Yemen

ethnographers to capture the "big" picture. Anthropologists are interested in documenting the culture that is constructed and sustained by children whose "family" is synonymous with peer group.

Street culture

Street children ... a centuries-old problem ... behaved like "tribes of lawless freebooters." (Cunningham 1995: 145)

"The best thing that ever happened to me is to become an adult and manage my own life." – Jorge, age 12. (Kenny 2007: 63)

Figure 33 Siblings in Srinagar

By far the most commonly abused drug among them is also the cheapest to acquire: siment, a cobbler's glue, the vapors of which are inhaled through the mouth and nose. (Haiti – Kovats-Bernat 2006: 42)

Overpopulation, along with economic stagnation or decline, drives children from their homes even in the wealthiest countries, as documented in the US following prolonged depressions during the nineteenth (Riis 1890/1996) and twentieth centuries (Minehan 1934). Then there's the push to "modernize" the economies of poorer nations: to take the Cuban case, one result has been the emergence of street children in Havana (Mickelson 2000; see also Kilbride *et al.* 2000). So we might say that street kids have existed as long as there have been streets. But we want to treat these children as something more than statistics. They are able to survive under adverse circumstances and create many of the elements of family and community.

Lewis Aptekar (1991) has conducted fieldwork with street children in many cities and finds that, in the absence of parents, siblings do a more than adequate job of caring for their young kin (Figure 33) – as we saw in Chapter 4 (pp. 136–138). Studies of AIDS orphans in South Africa similarly reveal the "dexterity young people bring to bear in drawing on networks of kin to reconfigure a sense of place for themselves" (Henderson 2006: 322).

Obviously, one of the first concerns for a new street kid is sustenance. There is an amazing array of economic niches available. Children may aid drivers in finding a place/parking their car and then guard it from traffic police and thieves (Chirwa and Wakatama 2000: 55). They sell candy, cigarettes, and newspapers to passers-by, and they "mine" the urban dump for saleable items.

[Makutano, Kenya] children know the restaurant employees well and have formed special relationships with them, ensuring that leftovers are reserved for them and that they come at the right time each day to pick them up. Attending church each Sunday is a further resource for a good meal. (Davies 2008: 318)

[Caracas street kids] go in groups [to a pizzeria] and first ask for soup. If they did not get it, they would start jumping around and screaming. The waiters would grow tired of this and finally give them food. (Márquez 1999: 47)

Young porters at the [Lima] fruit market carry weights between 200 and 400 kg on their trolley ... At the vegetable market, children of about seven years old and up are found selling discarded vegetables ... for lower prices. They may earn between five and ten sol (2.50–5 Euros) during a working day. (Ensing 2011: 24)

Children who make music and ambulant candy sellers hang around [Cusco] bus stops and bus stations where they can be seen jumping from one bus to the other. (Strehl 2011: 46)

Young women [in Brazil] have sexual relationships with foreign tourists [as] one strategy among many for dealing with poverty ... It is often one of the only available economic niches open to poor females. (Kenny 2007: 85)

[In Nairobi] children can beg up to the age of fourteen years, when they no longer look "innocent." (Kilbride *et al.* 2000: 70)

Boys [in Freetown, Sierra Leone] also serve another clandestine purpose, acting as the conduit for bribery between taxi, *podo-poda*, and *okada* riders, and the traffic police officers. (Lahai 2012: 52)

[In Kampala, Uganda] young men with bundles of bank notes make their money by breaking down their customer's larger notes into smaller bills for a commission. (Frankland 2007: 43)

The culture of the streets also incorporates a sort of "chore curriculum" (Chapter 7). That is, fieldworkers observe a step-wise progression from relatively untaxing work undertaken by the very young to sophisticated "business" undertaken by veterans (Visano 1990). Children rapidly learn to beg, for example.

Begging styles typically include not only verbal requests but also holding a hand out, pouting, exaggerated smiling, and less frequently, threatening gestures with the face and hands ... [S]treet children successfully beg from a full range of givers. (Kilbride *et al.* 2000: 70)

Because there is vertical differentiation in the street economy, older residents are willing to train new recruits (Wolseth 2009), teaching them "the tricks of the streets" (Márquez 1999: 64).

[Older boys in Ouagadougou assisting younger kin to adapt to street life] spent the first couple of days introducing the newcomers to the secrets of shoe-shining. The younger boys were shown how to shine shoes, in which neighborhoods they could expect to find most customers, how to approach them with the deference required in customer dealings, especially while awaiting the standard payment of 50 Fcfa (€0.08) per pair of shoes. (Thorsen 2009: 311)

Other simple tasks suitable for the very young include guarding cars, scavenging for discarded plastic bottles and charcoal to sell, and running errands (Davies 2008: 318). Children work their way up to more lucrative and sophisticated means of earning a living, "forming discrete occupational geographies that make up the nodal points in the networks of the urban economy" (Frankland 2007: 43). Informal sales through unlicensed marketing range from children's toys to hard drugs. Kampala street sellers may be well dressed and fluent in several languages. They may serve as "pilots" or guides leading foreigners to the market "or directing European sailors and soldiers to prostitutes" (Frankland 2007: 43). Sex work seems also to be graded, as girls begin by exchanging sex for food and favors from other street kids, and go on to exchanging sex with tourists for gifts or money (but without fixed fees) and then to full-fledged prostitution (Kenny 2007: 85). Then they may earn more than their male counterparts who are occupied as street sellers and porters (Conticini 2007: 85). Eventually, street "kids" age out. In Caracas, older youths earn the label *malandro*. These youths take pains to dress well and blend in, earning a living from theft. They "would not be seen as 'street children' causing mischief, but as *malandros* committing serious transgressions. They have outgrown their cute rascal image" (Márquez 1999: 53).

Inseparable from the need to make a living is the need to fit in (recall discussion of drives to become competent and fit in from Chapter 5, p. 173). As they do in the village, children in the streets attend to the actions of role models – others near them in age – from whom they can learn the culture. "A honeymoon period exists in which kids transition from household ... ties to street ties, often with the help of a close friend or family member who is already on the streets" (Wolseth 2010: 432). This assistance may extend to the older patron "setting up" the newcomer as a beggar or sex worker, or introducing and initiating the child into an informal, roving band (Hecht 1998). Newcomers may be sent to make drug purchases (their youth shielding them from police surveillance), and "through such services and errands, kids gain not only valuable street information but also increased status and reputation within their group" (Wolseth 2010: 436).

The street children in Makutano [Kenya] recognize a single leader *kichwa* [who] regularly arranges small jobs for [them] ... The *kichwa* further acts as an arbitrator and an organizer in a variety of situations. He ... is able to argue for a certain degree of respite from police harassment . . . [the informal group is also supported by] "chumship" where [the formation of a] dyad . . . involv[ing] a younger child forming a close personal attachment to an older, more established street child . . . aids the process of integration into the group. (Davies 2008: 316–317)

Small groups and dyads evolve into socially constructed "families." Terms like "brother," "sister," "husband," and "wife" are adopted by partners in long-term relationships. The use of socially constructed "'fictive' . . . kin terms among street children serves to resemble biologically based interdependent family relationships" (Kilbride *et al.* 2000: 83). The qualities that may be lacking in their natal families can be found in street families, including the sharing of food, money, and housing, the open display of affection, and care provided for sick members (Davies 2008: 317). Shelters and other public facilities may be shunned because they provide little comfort beyond the bare necessities of survival. However, the shelter may be seen as a temporary sanctuary in which to evade police or an "enemy," or when ill or suffering extreme privation (Ayacucho – Leinaweaver 2007: 377; Caracas – Márquez 1999: 156; Moscow – Stephenson 2001: 532).[5]

New arrivals will learn the unique language or slang used on the street (Vigil 2003). Makutano's street kids use invented terms for glue, radio, intoxication, to beat someone, and "ex" street children, among others (Davies 2008: 323). In Belo Horizonte "members of a *turma* create a private language using code words, gestures, and letter substitutions" (Campos *et al.* 1994: 328). Clothing also sets them apart. Typically they look like ragamuffins as an aid to begging or avoiding police, who spurn them as too smelly and dirty to transport to jail (Márquez 1999: 47). In Makutos, children affect too-large clothing, particularly overcoats where they can stash their possessions. The big coats "act as a symbol of identity and cohesion" because "normal" children don't wear them (Davies 2008: 323). In Santo Domingo, street kids broadcast their success by wearing "flashy" clothes (Wolseth 2010: 422–423).

The street child belongs to a "family" and the family, in turn, can usually claim a territory[6] – particularly to spend the evening/night. Children may gravitate to the most trash-strewn, polluted, undesirable areas just because adults avoid them and the youth can remain unmolested (Beazley 2008: 243; Davies 2008: 321; Márquez 1999: 44). Kids may be attracted to rather lawless neighborhoods, such as Moscow's *Arbat*, where they can pursue their largely illegal lifestyle without being hassled by merchants and the police (Stephenson 2001: 538). A cemetery may be the ideal home base. In Port-au-Prince, Haiti:

---

[5] Many street kids maintain ties with and continue to send resources to their biological families as a kind of insurance policy (Conticini 2007: 88; Kovats-Bernat 2006: 109).

[6] Territory or a "hood" is essential for a gang but also characteristic of more informal groups.

Each night, Ti Amos follows Bèl Marie and the other girls with whom she sleeps to their meeting place at the entrance to the cemetery. There they gather together the day's take of food and money so that it may be shared. She tells me they often sniff glue after eating to help them *bliye lamizè-nou* [forget their misery] and go to sleep. (Kovats-Bernat 2006: 65)

The society of the streets is also divided, as children make many of the same social distinctions that adults do among age, gender, and lifestyle. The last includes a child's sexual and drug activity (with glue sniffers at the bottom of the hierarchy; cf. Márquez 1999: 39). The society is highly gendered in that there are far fewer girls than boys and they have fewer economic niches they can exploit (Kovats-Bernat 2006: 42, 38). One's "occupation" also contributes to stratification, with "scavengers" ranked above beggars (Kenny 2007: 67). In Santo Domingo no one wants to wear the label of *palomo*, which is reserved for kids who beg and scavenge in dumpsters, sniff glue, and look and smell filthy (Wolseth 2010: 423).

Despite this evidence of successful adaptation to a parent-less, urban existence, one should not over-romanticize the life of street children. They are vulnerable to a whole host of threats, from traffic to bullies to STDs. They are resented by adults competing in the same economic niches (Ensing 2011: 25). Merchants who deplore their begging and petty theft from customers almost universally condemn them. Their very presence is a deterrent to public access to commercial establishments (Kenny 2007: 102; Márquez 1999: 37). In Nairobi, youths threaten to plaster feces on passers-by unless they're paid off (Droz 2006: 349–350). Such blatant anti-social activity, in turn, creates a climate that justifies children's "elimination" by death squads, funded by the business community (Stephens 1995: 12) to clean up this "blemish on the urban landscape" (Scheper-Hughes and Hoffman 1998: 353). Short of murdering them, governments may try and drive rural children out of urban centers by denying them schooling and social services because they lack a residence permit (Burr 2006: 67). Even if their behavior remains within the law, they can expect to be harassed by the police (Kilbride *et al.* 2000: 77; Strehl 2011: 50).

They are not safe from each other. Boys assault girls for invading "masculine space" (Beazley 2008: 236–237). Gangs "set up a strict code of loyalty and honor, punishing norm breakers harshly and allowing no recourse to a higher authority" (Campos *et al.* 1994: 328). Even in informal groups, the same children might at one moment behave altruistically and, at another, "fight ferociously over a pair of shoes or a sleeping space" (Márquez 1999: 45). In spite of their independence and self-sufficiency, they are children, after all.

In Port-au-Prince, children engage in *lage domi*: ritualized sleeping wars ... considered by street youths to be a final solution to long-festering animosities that repeatedly emerge ... The final violent act is usually a blow ... while the victim sleeps ... Nadès received a slash to the bottom of his feet, which he avenged by burning the foot of his tormentor with molten plastic. (Kovats-Bernat 2006: 130–5)[7]

The study of street children can tell us a great deal about the capacity that children have to survive against very great odds. They display a remarkable degree of plasticity in developing competencies with little or no adult guidance or supervision. But, as discussed in Chapter 7, this kind of hurried rush to maturity is not the norm. It arises in times of crisis such as war, famine, and plague or when families see economic opportunity in the employment of their children. The plight of children doing an adult's work or living rough in the city should be cause for an international outcry. Concern has been muted, perhaps because the long-term threats of human-induced climate change, civil and sectarian strife, and political corruption seem more compelling.

Children's agency

In recognizing the agency of youth ... anthropologists are engaged in an act of liberation, restoring to those who seem powerless their individual rights to act effectively upon the world. (Durham 2008: 151)

In insisting on granting all children the agency to express opinions and enable them (materially) to fulfill their own needs and desires, agency advocates are ignoring the role traditionally assigned to children and behaving in a profoundly ethnocentric fashion. (Holloway and Valentine 2000: 10)

Many contemporary anthropologists see the problem of laboring and street children as an absence of agency. They aren't granted authority over their own lives or status and influence in society (Alanen 2001: 21). Their "voices" aren't being heard by those in power (Kellet 2009). But this perspective fails to take into account that the most significant insight gained from using anthropology's lens to study children is to appreciate their relative value. Our society is a neontocracy where kids rule and we honor (some might say "indulge") their views and desires (Dahlberg 1992: 132–133; see also the discussion in this volume, Chapter 2, pp. 70–74). Because most societies look more like a gerontocracy, as the quote earlier (p. 382) from Thailand suggests, children are the least important members of the community. At an early age, they display many liabilities and no assets. As fetuses and then neonates, they endanger and deplete the wellbeing of women, who are the workhorses of

---

[7] Since this was written, Kovats-Bernat has found that a more recent flood of handguns into Haiti (probably from the plentiful supply in the US) has dramatically increased the likelihood that these conflicts will end in death (Kovats-Bernat 2013: 195).

most communities. Children lack the strength and skill of adults and the wisdom of the elderly. So why grant them agency or authority?

On the other hand, we must readily acknowledge that if agency is viewed as freedom to take the initiative, then the children discussed here have it in spades – in marked contrast to our cherubs (next section).

These children hop on buses and ride them for free, know that hustling counts and is rewarded economically, and spend the better part of the day in an urban, informal labor market, amid the dangers, excitement, sights, sounds, and stimuli of life. (Kenny 1999: 379)

Once on the street, children experience a sense of freedom that they do not enjoy in the home, and increasingly spend less and less time within the fold of the family. (Kovats-Bernat 2006: 108)

However, if agency = efficacy, authority, and power, then a paradox is immediately apparent. While children may resent the lack of status and authority in their homes and communities, in the street, they become acutely aware of the advantages of lowly status. "Granting them 'agency' means they are legally responsible for the crimes they commit, in which case, they are confined to prison, e.g. with zero agency" (Lancy 2012b).[8] In Márquez' study of street kids in Caracas she found:

that the youngsters are fully aware of the sanctioned opinion that defines them as minors not entirely capable of being responsible for their actions ... They know that being younger than eighteen gives them, if nothing else, a certain impunity; they know that regardless of the nature of their crime, most often they will not be treated as adult prisoners. (Márquez 1999: 111)

If the essential ingredient in a campaign to extend agency to at-risk youth is enhanced choice and respect for their decisions and views, how do we respond when they chose to use drugs, steal, prostitute themselves, or join a gang (Reynolds *et al.* 2006: 192)? Or when they reject the "healthy" choices we offer, such as residence in a public orphanage, in favor of the friendships, freedom, and money they find on the street (Fujimura 2003, 2005)? On the other hand, Susan Levine deplores the conundrum facing reformers who would ban "child labor" and thereby deny children the agency to earn a wage to support themselves and pay for their schooling (Levine 2013).

As Kovats-Bernat astutely notes: "The agency of street children in Port-au-Prince has always been and continues to be mediated by the structural

---

[8] Hecht (1998: 143) notes that the legal limbo street kids occupy can be deadly. Since they aren't prosecuted for the crimes they commit, the public tolerates extra-judicial "solutions" to the problem.

conditions in which they live" (Kovats-Bernat 2006: 183). Only by changing the conditions that underlie their birth can we significantly improve the futures of children now destined for the streets. Programs to promote child welfare must take the low value attached to children into account and insure that any government intervention or change in their legal status leads to increased value added to children, rather than decreasing it. For example, parents cannot be expected to relinquish their children's labor and pay school fees unless there are jobs available to those who complete school successfully (Demerath 1999; Levine 2013; this volume, Chapter 9, p. 367). If there are no jobs requiring literacy or more advanced schooling or if the quality of education provided is so poor that students can't meet the hiring criteria, then establishing public schools in the village or barrio becomes a meaningless gesture of "modernization," or "development."

All members of the child's extended family can step forward to serve as primary caretaker should the need arise. Out-migration by parents shouldn't, therefore, have an enormous impact on children. But the system is quite complex, as non-parental caretakers expect some form of reciprocity. The latest figures show that women are now as likely to be migrants as men, and, while they are much more likely than men to send remittances home to the village (Alcalá 2006), their absence must have an impact on the quality of childcare. In short, it is regrettable that village children may benefit *either* from the modern economy *or* from parental care but not both. "Fair trade" in the garment industry, for example, might mean factory workers were paid enough to house, support, and *live with* their children.

If we believe the economic and social infrastructure is collapsing in many Third World countries and among poor communities in the developed countries, then one evident consequence is that there will be "surplus" children (Jacquemin 2006: 391). The most expeditious intervention that can be made to redress this collapse is through massive inputs to programs that facilitate protected sex and fertility reduction. Basically, in spite of drastic declines in rural economies and the rise of adult mortality and disability, the birth rate remains high. There are, consequently, too many children for the available supply of food, caretakers, or decent schools. Obviously, in the absence of artificial population-limiting mechanisms like contraception, the population will be reduced through other means, including diseases like malaria and child maltreatment or "selective neglect" (Korbin 1987a: 36). Economic inducements for adults to limit fertility may be a better way to allocate historically inadequate resources than to try and ameliorate children's suffering through interventions of dubious value (Márquez 1999: 56).

For children, there is no *détente*. While traditional forms of village warfare tended to arrive at a stalemate and children were relatively unaffected, today children are both the primary victims and, often, the primary perpetrators of armed

violence. Attempts by the superpowers to separate and/or equalize warring fac-
tions largely fail until the carnage reaches holocaust proportions. The only
diplomatic policy that will favor children is disarmament, starting with a total
ban on land mines.[9] All lethal weapons should be treated as we treat opium, as
inherently harmful to all humans and worthy only of contraband designation. The
cherished US "right" to bear arms is nothing more than a lottery with constantly
improving odds that winners – often children – will get wounded or killed.[10]

While we can discuss improvements in our interventions with children in
the Third World, the First World will continue to play a minor, if not negative,
role in children's lives throughout the world until we confront our own
ethnocentrism. Even though we recoil from discussions of children as chattel,
our current policies, in fact, turn children into commodities with a precise
dollar value. Effectively, we embrace the notions that anyone can have a
child, everyone can have as many children as they want, infertility can be
circumvented, and the fetus is human and deserves whatever measures are
available to keep it alive, regardless of any handicaps or defects it may harbor.
The net result of our mindset is that the *marketplace* decides the fate of
children. In poor countries, food shortages mean many potentially sound
children will suffer malnutrition and neglect. Wealth in the "North" that might
be sent "South" to vaccinate, educate, and feed these children is, instead,
spent at home on expensive technologies and caretakers to keep alive children
whose quality of life is non-existent. While sick, premature babies born to
the well-off will survive through "miracles" of modern medicine, the poor
will lose their otherwise healthy children to preventable diseases. The rich
will purchase their way to parenthood, regardless of their biological or
psychological "fitness." Poor people nurture their employer's children while
neglecting their own. Children working for low wages in impoverished
countries will produce clothes and toys to enrich the lives of children in
developed countries whose parents are grateful to find "bargains" for them
at WalMart.

Overprotection

Americans [are] eager to protect children from dirty words and pornography but not to
shelter them from consumer desire. (Cross 2004: 185)

---

[9] International Coalition to Ban Landmines. Available at www.icbl.org/intro.php. Accessed
August 12, 2013.
[10] "The movement of illegal guns in America: The link between gun laws and interstate
gun trafficking." New York: Report commissioned by Mayors against Illegal Guns. Available
at www.mayorsagainstillegalguns.org/downloads/pdf/trace_the_guns_report.pdf. Accessed: August
15, 2013. See also Coalition to Stop Gun Violence. Available at http://csgv.org. Accessed
August 12, 2013.

Plumbing the depths of children's desire [is] good parenting. (Pugh 2009: 112)

Parents ... infantilize their children by overprotecting them and assuming them incapable of handling any challenge. (Marano 2008: 83)

It is no small irony that the enduring image of Third World children as fending for themselves in an urban jungle is juxtaposed with an image of First World children as smothered by over-solicitous parents and governments. While Third World children are being sold to slavers, swallowed up in brothels, and snuffed by death squads, First World parents' fears of harmful strangers and other threats are magnified to an irrational level (Best and Horiuchi 1985; Shutt *et al.* 2004; Glassner 1999; Welles-Nyström 1988: 76).[11] In suburban UK neighborhoods, play is discouraged because parents are concerned about children "getting in with the wrong crowd" (Clarke 2008: 255). In Japan, by contrast,

Parents realistically do not worry about their children being kidnapped, accosted, or molested, either by adults of by older children [, or] worry about their children getting hurt in traffic ... play was more unsupervised than many American children enjoy. (Benjamin 1997: 35, 92)

In the US, the typical "recess" during the school day to allow children to blow off steam in free play has been eliminated or sharply curtailed or is now subject to adult control and management. These changes were motivated by exaggerated concerns for children getting hurt, teasing or bullying each other, or getting abducted (Smith 2010: 201).

Clarke notes that parents use toys as the mean to compensate children for the withdrawal of freedom. Children forgo exploring their environment (many areas of the home are off limits as well) in return for richly furnished indoor play. In the process, parents are cultivating avid consumers as well. Shelly (ten years) complains about a gift from her Aunt:

"I got Care Bear pajamas [laughing] from my aunty! I pretended I liked them when she was there but then I got my mum to take them back [to the shop]" ... Eleven-year-old Philip was much happier with his Auntie's gift because he informed her exactly what brand of microscooter to buy: "I wanted a Huffy because they're the best at the moment and so I gave her the product code number and price and everything in case she got it wrong." (Clarke 2008: 257–258)

In Thailand, there is "no concept of any golden age of childhood ... children are pitied because ... they are everybody's *nong* (younger sibling/inferior)" (Montgomery 2001b: 59). For the Ifaluk, conspicuously happy children are a

---

[11] Fass argues that these irrational fears blind us to the real threats contemporary American children face from inadequate medical care, poor schools, and unhealthy lifestyles (Fass 1997).

cause for concern and may require suppression (Lutz 1988). In contrast, we embrace the "myth of childhood happiness . . . [which] flourishes . . . because it satisfies the needs of adults" (Firestone 1971: 31). So, when our children are unhappy – an unacceptable state – we seek medical assistance, resulting in a tripling of youth on anti-depressants since 1993 (Zito *et al.* 2003).

Our need to keep our children happy grants them enormous license. China's one-child policy has led to the proliferation of "Little Emperors," who are indulged in their craving for junk food to the point of obesity and heart disease (Chee 2000). In the US, obesity is rapidly increasing, in part because parents consider it too risky to let their children "run around" the neighborhood (Seiter 1998: 306). A study conducted in the UK, for example, showed a dramatic decline since the mid-1990s in the number of unaccompanied children permitted to cross the street, go to the cinema, or use public transport (Qvortrup 2005: 8; see also Karsten 2003; Skenazy 2009). Contrast this attitude with that of the Swedes, for whom, as we have seen, there is "no bad weather, only bad clothing," and "even crawling infants are encouraged to explore nature. In the summer . . . babies and young children spend days at a time completely naked, running around the grass or beach" (Welles-Nyström 1996: 208).

WEIRD children are protected from the need to work. They do no chores and even the burden of maintaining their own considerable domestic space and possessions is lifted from them. Not surprisingly, they don't volunteer, either (Wihstutz 2007: 80; see also this volume, Chapter 2, pp. 71–73). As far as "fitting in" to the family is concerned, children are given a free pass. As recent as this phenomenon is, it is difficult to assess the likely negative consequences in terms of the development of responsibility, empathy, and pro-sociality. However, the creation of "Little Emperors" in China "has produced significantly less trusting, less trustworthy, more risk-averse, less competitive, more pessimistic, and less conscientious individuals" (Cameron *et al.* 2013: 1).

Overprotectiveness may have other negative consequences. In the mid-1990s, a handful of tragic cases prompted governments in North America to require children's toys and clothing to be fireproof. Now, the widely used fire-retardant in children's products (a chemical which "migrates" into the atmosphere) is being blamed for the enormous spike in children's hyperactivity (Maron 2013). The growing incidence of child asthma, eczema, allergies, and chronic illness is now being blamed on our tendency to shrink-wrap our kids in a too-clean environment. We prevent them from exposure to bacteria-rich and tolerance-inducing dirt, manure, animals, and plants. Amish farm children have a far lower incidence of allergies than do non-farm children (Holbreich *et al.* 2012).

Where parents, historically, used threats of the bogeyman to restrain children's behavior (Chapter 5, p. 195), modern parents go out of their way to eliminate fears of "monsters" and such (Beals 2001: 77). Hallowe'en was, in the recent past, an opportunity for children to experience the supernatural, encounter fear, and take risks. Parents acknowledge that Hallowe'en is no longer "scary," recalling fondly the high jinks and excitement of their own unsupervised trick-or-treating. But they are reluctant to expose their children to "danger" or anything frightening. A mother who took her child on a Hallowe'en hay-ride "which turned out to be scarier than expected regretted her decision" (Clark 2005: 195). Hallowe'en is now just another occasion for a parent to make her child happier by willingly spending hundreds of dollars on his or her chosen costume (Pugh 2009: 84–85).

In school, we are so anxious to protect children's self-esteem that we shower them with praise and withhold appropriate negative feedback. Results may be the opposite of what we intend – frequently praised children lose motivation and persistence (Baumeister *et al.* 2005; Mueller and Dweck 1998). In the USA, "thought police"[12] protect children from exposure to information about sex. For example, Hinc (1999: 23) describes parent–teacher association (PTA) members in North Carolina diligently excising portions of the ninth-grade health textbook that discussed sex, contraception, and AIDS; so, in ignorance, teenagers get pregnant and contract STDs (Arnett 2002: 317). US students may also be protected from scientific information that runs counter to holy scripture, so they are, by international standards, scientifically illiterate (Zimmerman 2002).

But the number-one scapegoat for all that troubles the youth of our society is the popular media (Sternheimer 2003: 63). Innumerable watchdog organizations aggressively work to sanitize popular music, TV, cinema, the internet, and video games (Giroux 1998: 270). However, and in spite of millions of research dollars expended, there is little evidence of lasting harmful effects of media on children (J. Goldstein 1998). The most significant effects relate to the rise of sedentism and consumerism. For example, the decline in national park visitation tracks perfectly the rise in video game use (Nielson 2006). And in a study of children's "Letters to Santa ... children who watched more television ... were more likely to request not only more branded goods, but also more items generally ... For most toy companies, it is only about profit. The role of children is a clear one: they are cash cows to be milked" (Clark 2007: 165).

So we close this section with a pair of images, of an American child – with an allowance to "invest" – engrossed in conversation with a parent as they consider the relative cost and merits of several soccer balls in the sports store[13] and, halfway around the world in India (Figure 34), of another child who labors to meet her football-stitching quota[14] (Palley 2002).

---

[12] Islamic countries are also noted for the employment of moral guardians to monitor school curricula (Jalil and McGinn 1992: 101; Kaplan 2006).

[13] Actual event recorded by the author in August 2006.

[14] Child labor in India. Available at www.indianet.nl/ka_f_e.html. Accessed August 8, 2013.

Figure 34 Football stitcher from Gandhi Camp

What have we learned?

Throughout the book, I have drawn contrasts between the childhood that is depicted in our common understanding (and, to a great extent, in the pages of child development texts) and what one sees in the ethnographic and historic records. We can summarize these discussions through a series of polemical comparisons[15]:

- In our society, the child's wellbeing is paramount; its needs trump the desires of other family members.

---

[15] These dichotomies do not capture all the cross-cultural variability discussed in this book, needless to say. Chapter 3 details many interesting differences between middle-class US, French, and East Asian childhoods, for example.

- – Not so elsewhere; children are the lowest-ranking members of the community and are treated accordingly, being fed on leavings from the adult's meal, for example.
- Every child is invested with tremendous inherent worth. We spend millions in enhanced reproductive techniques and millions more on keeping alive even the highest-risk neonates.
- – Since the dawn of mankind, humans have abandoned or disposed of surplus or defective babies. Girl babies are especially vulnerable to population-limiting choices. Societies develop elaborate customs that legitimate and dignify these practices, such as treating an anomalous infant as a changeling. As these practices were, eventually, condemned by moral authorities, unwanted babies were consigned to institutional care, where the majority perished.
- From the moment of birth, if not before, we have assigned a high value to the child and make investments of time and resources accordingly.
- – Historically the newborn may have been little valued or viewed as having value except in the future as a helper and, later, the caretaker of aging parents.
- The baby is treated as a sentient being from birth, a worthy object of speech and capable of communicating non-verbally. Indeed in East Asia and among the Western elite, the fetus may be seen as capable of responding to speech and music.
- – More commonly the infant provokes mixed emotions and ambiguity. High infant mortality and threats to the mother's life cast a pall. The infant – lacking hair, speech, pigmentation, motor control, and continence – is not seen as a person. Personhood may be delayed for months or years. But babies aren't just non-persons. Elaborate theories exist that account for the liminal state of the infant and prescribe appropriate treatment, which extends to the methods for interring a stillborn or deceased child.
- Each child is a treasure with great emotional value to the new parents. The family fully expects to provide care and resources to each child well past puberty. Our society sees children as precious and innocent, needing protection from the world of adults and exploitative labor.
- – With the significant exception of nomadic foraging peoples, children are considered chattel, the property of their parents. As such they can be sold or donated to another family or to the church. More commonly there is the expectation that the child will participate in the household economy as their maturity level permits. Children of age ten may be doing a "full day's work." In many agrarian societies, the child is able to provide a surplus of calories or "return" on its parents' investment. Adults may celebrate the child's accomplishment – as a worker. In early industrialized societies,

children were employed – to enhance the family's earnings – from an early age. Childhood might be described as "brief."

- Most modern societies embrace the ideal of limited fertility so that one can "afford" the high costs of raising (few) children.
- – In the past and in much of the world that still practices subsistence, high fertility – especially the production of males – is highly valued, even if children may not be. Childless individuals may be scorned.
- The modern "ideal" family features the biological parents and their children cohabiting under one roof. The parents, faithful to each other, cooperate fully in the household economy and share the great burden of childrearing.
- – Studies of human reproductive patterns and the notes of anthropologists reveal that men rarely commit to life-long monogamy, may not reside with their wives and offspring, and, hence, may have virtually no contact with their children. The "nuclear" family is relatively rare; far more common are large extended families and households composed of mother and offspring. Polygyny, or families composed of a husband and two or more wives, is extremely common – at least as a cultural ideal.
- Unthreatened by mother or infant mortality, we celebrate the child's birth with baby showers, redecorated nurseries, open houses, and christenings.
- – More commonly, the mother and baby are in a liminal state, vulnerable to infection and other medical crises as well as potential harm to and from others. Birth and the post-partum period may be characterized by secrecy and seclusion.
- We regulate many aspects of our infant's and young children's lives, including creating a unique environment for them – cribs, nurseries, high-chairs. We regulate where and when they eat and sleep. On the other hand, we make many adjustments in our schedule of activities to insure the children are kept stimulated and engaged.
- – More typically, no separate eating or sleeping arrangements are made for children. Infants sleep with their mothers and are fed on demand, around the clock. Toddlers feed opportunistically and/or when others are eating. Although there may be special "weaning" foods, the child quickly transitions to the same diet as everyone else. The infant's basic needs are taken care of promptly, but otherwise they rest undisturbed.
- We treat the child's illness as strictly a *medical* problem. Modern vaccinations and treatments have reduced infant mortality to insignificant levels.
- – In the village, illness may originate in supernatural forces or familial discord that must be diagnosed and placated before the child can get well. The lack of vaccinations, folk medicaments that often do more harm than good, and chronic infection and malnutrition maintain infant mortality at high levels.

- Sex and biological relatedness have become far less critical in judging a child's value to its parents. Girls are welcomed and the adoption of non-related children is common.
- – In more traditional communities, relatedness and sex remain important criteria in determining whether the newborn is celebrated or disposed of. Children are adopted by kin, only rarely by unrelated individuals.
- Hygienic and fully nutritious formula has made it possible to nurture all infants, including multiple and premature births.
- – But most babies can only be sustained by frequent, round-the-clock nursing and/or the maintenance of the post-partum sex taboo, both of which reduce the chance of another pregnancy. Early weaning due to the mother's pregnancy or the use of unsanitary supplemental feeding lead to the nurse-ling's illness, malnutrition, and death.
- In the West and in East Asia one commonly finds selfless mothers who lavish attention and instruction on their young well into adolescence.
- – In traditional societies, mothers pass off their infants and toddlers to sibling or granny caretakers. The mother's energies are, preferentially, devoted to subsistence or commercial activity and to preparing herself for the next birth.
- Also in the developed societies, there is the presumption that, to mature successfully, children require intellectual stimulation from birth – or even in the womb. Their caretakers aim to "optimize" the child's development to maximize their accomplishments.
- – Children are believe to be without sense or the ability to learn until at least their fifth year. They are, in effect, unteachable. In lieu of stimulating and engaging babies, childcare methods emphasize keeping it in a quiescent state to reduce risk and the burden of care. Swaddling, carrying the child in a sling, and using a cradle aid this effort.
- We have very low expectations for our children to assist us in our work, household duties, and care of family members. They are free to play or attend school.
- – Village children eagerly participate in "chores," particularly the care of younger siblings – a role that little girls relish.
- We don't expect grandparents to be involved in childcare, particularly where they don't reside with or near the family.
- – Grannies play a critical role in childcare, particularly of recently weaned children.
- We *do* expect fathers to participate in childcare.
- – Fathers rarely contribute to childcare, and there may be specific prohib-itions on any close contact between fathers and their offspring. In fact, even where "fatherhood" is valued, fathers may have little involvement in domes-tic life, including childcare.

- While we think babies are "adorable," even "terrible two-year-olds" can be "cute."
- – Many societies practice "toddler rejection," whereby the recently weaned and cranky child is banned from the breast and sent to grandma's or to play with older siblings. The recalcitrant child may be treated harshly by all and sundry, in spite of dramatic tantrums.
- There is considerable anguish and debate – at least in the US – regarding the role of professional child-caretakers. Claims are made about the harm done to children being cared for by someone other than the child's mother.
- – Historically, women have always availed themselves of professionals – if they could afford it. These included wet-nurses, nannies, pedagogues, and tutors.
- Annually, there is a flood of volumes and new websites devoted to authoritative, "scientific" coverage of the child's development and appropriate, necessary parenting practices.
- – Many, if not most, of these ideas are novel and untried from a historical and cross-cultural perspective. Many modern "solutions" may cause unintended, negative outcomes.
- Our recent history shows formal schooling starting in early childhood and lasting into adulthood. Teaching the young is seen as both essential and extremely challenging.
- – Throughout the ethnographic literature, formal schooling is virtually absent. Children are supposed to learn the culture through observation and imitation. Teaching is seen as unnecessary and a waste of an adult's precious time.
- We invest a great deal of time in socializing our children and we do this through conversations. The intent is to instruct children by precept and persuasion. Corporal punishment is seen as a retrograde strategy for socializing the young and may be prohibited by law.
- – Relatively speaking, adults avoid interfering with children's autonomy, expecting them to *want* to fit in and learn their culture. If the child deviates from expectations, brief and sometimes harsh directives are used to correct. Other harsh correction tactics may include frightening the child or corporal punishment. Parents who don't discipline their children are pilloried.
- Much of adult culture, including work, food acquisition, sex, and entertainment, is restricted. Children are perceived as too young, uneducated, or burdensome to be readily admitted to the adult sphere. On the other hand, parents take special pains to spend "quality time" participating in the child's world. Dinner-table conversations, for example, at least in the US, may be child-rather than adult-centered. Parents "play" with their children in a great variety of contexts (make-believe, games, "roughhousing").

- – In the village, adult lives are an open book to be read off and learned. The children's world is generally devoid of adult participation. Adult–child "conversation" would be unseemly. Children are tolerated in adult company if they remain undemanding and unobtrusive. Children learn a great deal from observing other family members as they work, prepare and eat meals, and do craft-work. An exception to this pattern may be found in hunting-and-gathering societies, where very young children may be unwelcome on foraging and hunting expeditions.
- Children require stimulation and instruction from infancy. The roles of parent-teacher and child-student are established early and maintained until puberty and beyond.
- – Infants and toddlers receive little attention from adults and no instruction *per se*. Children are avid spectators and this trait is considered the basis for the child's acquisition of her culture. Instead of focusing attention only on one's (parent acting as) teacher, village children display a broad awareness of all that's going on around them. Children are seen to acquire "sense," or the ability to learn from example and to adjust behavior in accord with adult expectations, around the age of five to seven. "Intelligence" is conceived of not as cleverness and verbal knowledge but as compliance and awareness of the expectations of others. It is the ability to be a positive contributor to family life and subsistence. "Independence" doesn't mean having one's own opinions and possessions but being self-sufficient and not making requests of others.
- The average child in the neontocracy has access to lots of safe and "educational" toys but may lose interest in them quickly. Toys are subject to fashion and fad.
- – In the gerontocracy, the very young play mostly with found objects – often tools and utensils. These may include sharp knives and other "dangerous" items. While the risks are acknowledged, the assumption is that the child will only learn to use the object by using it, clumsily at first but then with greater precision.
- Make-believe play is valued as a learning medium in nearly all cultures. In ours, parents become actively engaged with children's make-believe in purchasing or making appropriate props, in guiding the child's development in make-believe and fantasy, in linking make-believe to reading, books, and stories, and in using the medium pedantically to teach moral and other lessons. When we don't intervene to guide play, our children have a tendency to become bored.
- – Village parents get involved in make-believe only to the extent of donating materials, including miniature or cast-off tools. Otherwise, they keep their distance. Boredom seems unknown.

- We are leery of our children's peers, fearing their "bad influence." We isolate our children in the home and carefully select peers to invite for "play-dates" and "sleep-overs" and by choosing particular schools, associations, and sports teams to enroll our children in.
- – Village children are incorporated into the neighborhood peer group from a very early age. They spend far more time in the company of, being cared for by, and learning from peers than parents.
- In the neontocracy, children have very high standing – from birth. Especially in the US, the child is given an almost inexhaustible supply of social capital and does very little to earn it. Deference to strangers, those older, kin, and parents is either not expected at all (in the US) or inculcated at a relatively late age. The same would be true for behavior in public places.
- – In the gerontocracy, children occupy the lowest rank and must early on – often via explicit instruction – learn to behave correctly with others, including, especially, sharing. Correct kin terms and terms of address that reflect relative rank are drummed into the very young. Many post-industrial societies, such as France, Japan, and Korea, still socialize children in good manners, including table manners, and proper speech and behavior toward others – particularly adults.
- Aggressive behavior by children, including verbal aggression, is tolerated less and less. Such behavior is considered harmful to the less aggressive, less popular children.
- – Cross-culturally, there is great variability in the tolerance for aggression. This ranges from societies that actively promote aggressive behavior – of future warriors – to those that suppress this behavior in keeping with a low-conflict, egalitarian ethos. However, most societies tolerate and expect children to engage in rough, boisterous play and verbal dueling and teasing.
- Contemporary values in modernized societies stress the malleability of gender roles: girls are encouraged to pursue everything from contact sports to careers in politics.
- – More typically, we see: extremely rigid management of the development of gender roles, whereby the daughter becomes a full-time assistant to her mother, and boys may endure a painful initiation to divest them forcibly of any feminine traits acquired from their mothers.
- Our childrearing manuals admonish us that children have a need and right to play. The experts fret that childhood is "hurried," play opportunities curtailed.
- – Parents in a gerontocracy see much less value in play, aside from keeping children busy and out of the way. Play is often seen as antithetical to the child's fulfillment of its role as a productive contributor to the household.

- Play in the West (especially in the US) has rapidly changed. There is much greater adult involvement in children's play, ranging from the infant exploring novel objects (guided by a parent) to children participating in football (soccer) that is managed by parents, coaches, and referees. Rules are designed to be learned and then adhered to.
- – Traditionally, children's play is unmediated by parents, coaches, strict rules, structured playing fields, or "regulation" equipment. Children have free rein to utilize the traditional accoutrements of game play – customary rules, home-made marbles, chalked lines on sidewalks, scavenged play materials, the language of the game, etc. – and to modify them as the occasion warrants. This ad hoc process facilitates the development of "gamesmanship," or the ability to manipulate social relations during play to maximize the satisfaction of the players as well as the payoffs to the "best" players. "Best" might here mean not just a consistent winner but someone that others are eager to play with.
- There is also much greater solitary play, as families are smaller and neighborhoods are "dangerous." Much of this play is now conducted via electronic media. Television has spawned a menagerie of related progeny.
- – The quintessential play experience takes place within an enduring and ubiquitous neighborhood play group. The composition of the group might be mixed with respect to age and gender, at least for children five and under. The children's play space was/is the community as a whole, considered safe under the watchful attention of older neighbors. All play is active and profoundly social.
- Contemporary children's make-believe is heavily slanted toward fantasy. Fantasy elements are inserted into play via TV programs, children's books, fantasy-themed toys, and parents' coaching of make-believe play.
- – Make-believe in the village, lacking these fantasy sources, is firmly rooted in the real world that children can readily observe. There are few or no taboo subjects; children may act out relations between the sexes and religious rites. Inventiveness is evident in the construction of scripts, the scavenging of props, and the assignment of roles and personalities to players. Some of the most memorable play episodes recorded by anthropologists show children successfully parodying adult behavior and discourse.
- In the neontocracy, children are the recipients of care. They are relieved of the burden for their own care and the care of others. To prolong innocence we deny them opportunities to "pitch in" and help out, redirecting their energy from altruistic work to self-centered play. They learn this lesson well and remain unhelpful and dependent well beyond puberty.
- – In a gerontocracy, we see the very early emergence of the desire to be helpful, to become competent and to fit in. All family members project the expectation that the child will strive for independence and self-sufficiency

and will seek and find chores that are helpful. Play tracks work very closely and they are complementary rather than antithetical.

- In the family context, the roles of mothers, fathers, and children tend to be quite different. Each operates separately, in a distinct sphere of activity. The kitchen is the mother's domain, father owns the "den," and each child occupies his or her bedroom.

- – Village family members participate in many of the same suite of activities, in the same physical spaces (fields, garden, kitchen). Differentiation occurs in terms of more specific tasks or sub-components of the tasks. These may be identified as male or female responsibilities. They may be broken down into easier or more complex tasks apportioned on the basis of maturity and competence (sweeping the floor vs. doing the laundry).

- Since G. Stanley Hall published his monumental work on adolescence in 1904, the educated public in the West has accepted several broad generalizations about the nature of adolescence. These include conflict over sexuality, a "generation gap," and a difficult or even traumatic transition to adulthood.

- – Such generalizations have been challenged by anthropologists, beginning with Margaret Mead's classic *Coming of Age in Samoa* in 1928. We discover many societies where sexual relations begin early and without drama. Similarly, adolescence may be quite short, as mature, hard-working children move, seamlessly, into their adult roles. Adolescent–parent conflict is not even the norm in all post-industrial societies. In East Asia, children are raised to respect and appreciate their parents, sublimating their will to theirs. This successful cultivation of filial affection and, later, responsibility carries right on through adulthood. Anthropology also confirms the existence of very widespread and likely inherited commonalities such as heightened risk-taking, sexual desire, and the tendency for adolescent males to cluster in "gangs."

- In WEIRD societies, intervention may be necessary to resolve adolescent psychological conflicts and disabilities. Suicide rates spike. Counseling and psychotropic drugs may be prescribed to reduce stress and "acting out" behaviors.

- – Elsewhere, the "problems" of adolescence are considered largely behavioral. Dramatic, painful, and demanding initiation rites may be "prescribed" as the remedy to correct anti-social behavior and bring youth into line with adult expectations. A significant element may be to indoctrinate initiates for their new roles as young adults. As such, they gain opportunities such as marriage and the resources to form a family. But they also lose their autonomy and must now display proper subordination vis-à-vis older community members.

- In the West and, increasingly around the globe, marriages are "love matches." Couples find each other, and declare their love, and the family and society "bless" the union.

- – Across the ethnographic record we see two broad patterns. In one, youth are free to experiment sexually and couples may engage in trial marriages, which go unrecognized until the couple "settles down" monogamously, establishes a household, and starts bearing children. Marriage *per se* may be a minor rite of passage compared to bearing children, which is more significant. In a second pattern, characteristic of more complex and stratified societies, marriages are arranged. This arises because wealth and property will be transferred across families and/or down a generation. Since kin have a stake in enlarging the polity through adding new members (via marriage and childbearing) and are loathe to lose valuable individuals and goods to "unsuitable" parties, marriage is tightly controlled.

- We believe that "child" and "student" are virtually synonymous. We have assumed that the cognitive infrastructure that undergirds successful school learning is hard-wired (following Piaget). When our students perform poorly in school and/or seem reluctant to participate in the schooling process, we blame teachers, curricula, peers, and nefarious "disabilities."

- – In reviewing the anthropology of childhood, this assumption can be turned on its head. Children seem very ill-suited to the role of student. They are normally active, autonomous learners. Being confined to a classroom and being forced to attend to the dictates of a teacher seem almost like punishment. In the village, children learn by doing and there's a direct payoff for their effort in terms of increased agency. The learning of declarative information and employment of analytic strategies in processing information are rarely required. Far from appearing automatically, the cognitive skills associated with academic thought must be cultivated through schooling. By the same token, adults do very little "teaching" and their "methods" include, prominently, scare tactics, orders, and corporal punishment – hardly a model pedagogy.

- In another line of evidence, the "strangeness" of schooling is borne out by the tremendous "resistance" revealed by the dominance of non-academic activity in US schools and the disengagement from intellectually challenging material on the part of the student majority. Add the great number of drop-outs or school leavers in other countries where continued enrollment is contingent on performance. In examining successful students in the US and elsewhere, we become aware of the enormous cultural capital (for example, the "bedtime story" routine) needed to insure a child's academic success. While tactics may vary cross-nationally, common to all is the deep commitment of parents to the careful cultivation in each child of a positive and prepared approach to academic work. Taking everything into account, one can readily build an argument that children *should* fail as students.

- In a neontocracy, adults are eager to "empower" children by teaching them what they know.
- – In a gerontocracy, the opposite occurs: adults withhold knowledge from youth to maintain their own power and hegemony.
- Currently, the role model for "teacher" is the WEIRD parent patiently and lovingly guiding the child's fledgling efforts at understanding. Lessons are fitted carefully to the learner's interests and level of ability, as in Vygotsky's "Zone of Proximal Development." This implicit model may not be acknowledged but finds its way into programs to train teachers in "constructivist" teaching, for example.
- – A review of the history of schooling suggests that, until recently in the West and Asia, and continuing as the case in the Third World, we must look to the apprenticeship for the origins of the classroom model. As masters lord it over cowed apprentices, teachers exercise dictatorial control, enforced by frequent physical punishment. Classroom lessons are as boring and repetitive as the menial tasks undertaken by apprentices. Students are expected to see themselves as fortunate that resources have been invested in order to afford them the economic advantages of (a trade or) education. Failure is laid squarely at the student's door.
- Given the predominance of "standards" and "standardized" in discussions of contemporary schooling, there may be the perception that schools are as mechanized as factories. The impression is created that managers – by imposing standards, principles, and rules – will produce the desired outcomes in terms of teacher and student behaviors.
- – From the studies of anthropologists it is patently clear that the results of schooling are almost wholly dependent on the surrounding cultural context. The child's home experiences, the local community's expectations for the school, economic opportunities post-schooling, and the funding available (to pay teachers, for example) are among the many factors that contribute to the mix. The primary contribution that child psychology makes to these outcomes is the cumulative nature of the skills and knowledge transmitted through the curriculum. That is, children who are academically able in kindergarten will be academically able as college freshmen.
- We believe that the child's "normal" state is one of happiness and act vigorously to alleviate any symptoms of unhappiness.
- – Given the child's low status, lack of skills, and resources, why should she or he be happy? Consider also the likelihood of malnutrition, infection, and chronic illness. Unhappiness is to be expected, and when we see village children who are obviously joyful in spite of all, we marvel at their resiliency. Would that we acknowledged such resiliency in our overprotected (and medicated) cherubs.

References

Aamodt, Christina (2012) The participation of children in Mycenaean cult. *Childhood in the Past* 5:35–50.

Abelow, Benjamin J. (2011) The shaping of New Testament narrative and salvation teachings by painful childhood experience. *Archive for the Psychology of Religion* 33:1–54.

Achpal, Beena, Goldman, Jane A., and Rohner, Ronald P. (2007) A comparison of European American and Puerto Rican parents' goals and expectations about the socialization and education of preschool children. *International Journal of Early Years' Education* 15:1–13.

Acredolo, Linda and Goodwyn, Susan (2002) *Baby Signs: How to Talk with Your Baby Before Your Baby Can Talk*. Chicago, IL: Contemporary Books.

ACT (2013) *The Condition of College and Career Readiness – 2013*. Iowa City, IA: American College Testing Service. Available at www.act.org/research/policymakers/cccr13/pdf/CCCR13-NationalReadinessRpt.pdf Accessed August 8, 2013.

Adamson, Peter (2007) Child poverty in perspective: An overview of child well-being in rich countries. *Innocenti Report Card 7*. Florence: UNICEF Innocenti Research Centre.

Adriani, Nicolaus and Kruijt, Albertus C. (1950) *The Bare'e-Speaking Toradja of Central Celebes*. Amsterdam: Noord-Hollandsche Uitgevers Maatschapp ij.

Afsana, Kaosar and Rashid, Sabina F. (2009) Constructions of birth in Bangladesh. In Helaine Selin and Pamela K. Stone (Eds.), *Childhood across Cultures: Ideas and Practices of Pregnancy, Childbirth and the Postpartum*. pp. 123–135. Amherst, MA: Springer.

Ahissou, Virgile and McKenzie, Glenn (2003) Child laborers rescued from quarries. Associated Press, October 17. Available at www.seattlepi.com/national/article/Child-laborers-rescued-from-quarries-1127185.php. Accessed October 5, 2013.

Ahmed, Ramadan A. (2005) Egyptian families. In Jaipaul L. Roopnarine and Uwe P. Gielen (Eds.), *Families in Global Perspective*. pp. 151–168. Boston, MA: Allyn and Bacon.

Ainsworth, Mary D. (1967) *Infancy in Uganda: Infant Care and the Growth of Love*. Baltimore, MD: Johns Hopkins University Press.

Akabayashi, Hideo and Psacharopoulos, George (1999) The trade-off between child labour and human capital formation: A Tanzanian case study. *The Journal of Developmental Studies* 35(5):120–140.

412   References

Akhtar, Nameera and Gernsbacher, Morton A. (2008) On privileging the role of gaze in
    infant social cognition. *Child Development Perspectives* 2:59–65.
Alanen, Laeena (2001) Explanations in generational analysis. In Leena Alanen and Berry
    Mayall (Eds.), *Conceptualizing Child–Adult Relations*. pp. 11–22. London: Routledge.
Alber, Erdmute (2004) "The real parents are the foster parents": Social parenthood
    among the Baatombu in Northern Benin. In Fiona Bowie (Ed.), *Cross Cultural
    Approaches to Adoption*. pp. 33–47. London: Routledge.
    (2012) Schooling or working? How family decision processes, children's agencies
    and state policy influence the life paths of children in northern Benin. In Gerd
    Spittler and Michael Bourdillon (Eds.), *African Children at Work: Working and
    Learning in Growing Up*. pp. 169–194. Berlin: LitVerlag.
Alcalá, Maráa José (2006) *A Passage to Hope: Women in International Migration*.
    New York, NY: United Nations Population Fund.
Alexander, Richard D. and Noonan, Katherine M. (1979) Concealment of ovulation,
    parental care, and human social evolution. In Napoleon A. Chagnon and William G.
    Irons (Eds.), *Evolutionary Biology and Human Social Behavior:
    An Anthropological Perspective*. pp. 436–453. North Scituate, MA: Duxbury Press.
Alexandre-Bidon, Daniéle and Lett, Didier (1999) *Children in the Middle Ages:
    Fifth–Fifteenth Centuries*. Notre Dame, IN: University of Notre Dame Press.
Allison, Anne (1991) Japanese mothers and Obentōs: The lunch-box as ideological
    state apparatus. *Anthropological Quarterly* 64(4):195–208.
    (2008) Pocket capitalism and virtual intimacy: Pokémon as symptom of
    postindustrial youth culture. In Jennifer Cole, and Deborah Durham (Eds.),
    Figuring the Future: Globalism and the Temporalities of Children and Youth.
    pp. 179–195. Sante Fe, NM: SAR Press.
Allison, Marvin J. (1984) Paleopathology in Peruvian and Chilean populations. In Mark
    N. Cohen and George J. Armelagos (Eds.), *Paleopathology at the Origins of
    Agriculture*. pp. 531–558. Orlando, FL: Academic Press.
Alston, Lester (1992) Children as chattel. In Elliot West and Paula Petrik (Eds.),
    Small Worlds: Children and Adolescents in America, 1850–1950. pp. 208–231.
    Lawrence, KS: University Press of Kansas.
Altman, Irwin and Ginat, Joseph (1996) *Polygamous Families in Contemporary
    Society*. Cambridge: Cambridge University Press.
Altmann, Jeanne (1980) *Baboon Mothers and Infants*. Cambridge, MA: Harvard
    University Press.
Altorki, Soraya (1980) Milk-kinship in Arab society: An unexplored problem in the
    ethnography of marriage. *Ethnology* 19(2):233–244.
Ames, David W. (1982) Contexts of dance in Zazzau and the impact of Islamic
    reform. In Simon Ottenberg (Ed.), *African Religious Groups and Beliefs*.
    pp. 110–177. Meerut: Archana.
Anderson, Kermyt G., Kaplan, Hillard, Lam, David, and Lancaster, Jane B. (1999)
    Paternal care by genetic fathers and stepfathers II: Reports by Xhosa high
    school students. *Evolution and Human Behavior* 20(4):433–445.
Anderson, Kermyt G., Kaplan, Hillard, and Lancaster, Jane B. (2007) Confidence of
    paternity, divorce, and investment in children by Albuquerque men. *Evolution and
    Human Behavior* 28(1):1–10.
Anderson-Levitt, Kathryn M. (2002) *Teaching Cultures: Knowledge for Teaching
    First Grade in France and the United States*. Cresskill, NJ: Hampton Press.

(2005) The schoolyard gate: Schooling and childhood in global perspective. *Journal of Social History* 38(4):987–1006.

Anderson-Levitt, Kathryn M. and Diallo, Boubacar Bayero (2003) Teaching by the book in Guinea. In Kathryn M. Anderson-Levitt (Ed.), *Local Meanings, Global Schooling: Anthropology and World Culture Theory*. pp. 75–97. Basingstoke, UK: Palgrave Macmillan.

André, Géraldine and Godin, Marie (2013) Child labour, agency and family dynamics: The case of mining in Katanga (DRC). *Childhood*, June 13.

Anonymous (2009) Child slavery in Jaintia Hills indicates poor human rights standards in the region. *Asian Human Rights Commission News*, November 20. Available at www.humanrights.asia/news/ahrc-news/AHRC-STM-228-2009/?searchterm=. Accessed October 5, 2013.

(2013) Shot Pakistan schoolgirl Malala Yousafzai addresses UN. *BBC News Online*, July 12. Available at www.bbc.co.uk/news/world–asia–23282662. Accessed July 12, 2013.

Anonymous Venetian Diplomat (1847) *A Relation of the Island of England*. Translated by Charlotte A. Sneyd. London: Camden Society 37:24–25.

Ansar, Sarah F. D. and Martin, Vanessa (2003) *Women, Religion and Culture in Iran*. London: Curzon.

Apicella, Coren L. and Marlowe, Frank W. (2004) Perceived mate fidelity and paternal resemblance predict men's investment in children. *Evolution and Human Behavior* 25(6):371–378.

Apostolou, Menelaos (2009) Sexual selection under parental choice in agropastoral societies. *Evolution and Human Behavior* 31: 39–47.

Appell-Warren, Laura P. (1987) Play, the development of Kakada', and social change among the Bulusu of East Kalimantan. In Gary Alan Fine (Ed.), *Meaningful Play, Playful Meaning*. pp. 155–171. Champaign, IL: Human Kinetics Publishers.

Aptekar, Lewis (1991) Are Colombian street children neglected? The contributions of ethnographic and ethnohistorical approaches to the study of children. *Anthropology and Education Quarterly* 22(4):326–349.

(2004) The changing developmental dynamics of children in particularly difficult circumstances: Examples of street and war-traumatized children. In Uwe P. Gielen and Jaipaul L. Roopnarine (Eds.), *Childhood and Adolescence: Cross-Cultural Perspectives and Applications*. pp. 377–410. Westport, CT: Praeger.

Ariel, Shlomo and Sever, Irene (1980) Play in the desert and play in the town: On play activities of Bedouin Arab children. In Helen B. Schwartzman (Ed.), *Play and Culture*. pp. 164–174. West Point, NY: Leisure Press.

Ariès, Philippe (1962) *Centuries of Childhood*. Translated by Robert Baldick. New York, NY: Alfred A. Knopf.

Armstrong, Elizabeth (2004) Lost in transition? Young adults take longer to become emotionally and financially independent. *The Christian Science Monitor* 96(72):15.

Arnett, Jeffrey J. (1999) Adolescent storm and stress, reconsidered. *American Psychologist* 54(5):317–326.

(2002) Adolescents in Western countries in the 21st century: Vast opportunities – for all? In Bradford B. Brown, Reed W. Larson, and T. S. Saraswathi (Eds.), *The World's Youth: Adolescence in Eight Regions of the Globe*. pp. 307–343. Cambridge: Cambridge University Press.

Arnold, Denise Y. (2006) *The Metamorphosis of Heads: Textual Struggles, Education, and Land in the Andes*. Pittsburgh, PA: University of Pittsburgh Press.

Arnold, Mary Jo (2006) Ndomo ritual and Sogo bo play: Boy's masquerading among the Bamana of Mali. In Simon Ottenberg and David A. Binkley (Eds.), *Playful Performers: African Children's Masquerades*. pp. 49–65. Brunswick, NJ: Transaction Publishers.

Aronson, Lisa (1989) To weave or not to weave: Apprenticeship rules among the Akwete Igbo of Nigeria and the Baulé of the Ivory Coast. In Michael W. Coy (Ed.), *From Theory to Method and Back Again*. pp. 149–162. Albany, NY: State University of New York Press.

Arriaza, Bernardo T., Cardenas-Arroyo, Felipe, Kleiss, Ekkehard, and Verano, John W. (1998) South American mummies: Culture and disease. In Aidan Cockburn, Eve Cockburn, and Theodore A. Reyman (Eds.), *Mummies, Disease, and Ancient Cultures*. pp. 190–234. Cambridge: Cambridge University Press.

Asch, Timothy and Chagnon, Napoleon (1974) *Children's Magical Death*. Watertown, MA: Documentary Educational Resources.

Assal, Adel and Farrell, Edwin (1992) Attempts to make meaning of terror: Family, play, and school in time of civil war. *Anthropology and Education Quarterly* 23(4):275–290.

Associated Press (2010) Pope urges respect for embryos. *Bloomberg Businessweek*, November 27. Available at www.businessweek.com/ap/financialnews/ D9JOKCE00.htm. Accessed January 12, 2013.

Ataka, Yuji and Ohtsuka, Ryutaro (2006) Migration and fertility of a small island population in Manus. In Stanley J. Ulijaszek (Ed.), *Population, Reproduction, and Fertility in Melanesia*. pp. 90–109. Oxford: Berghahn Books.

Atran, Scott and Medin, Douglas (2008) *The Native Mind and the Cultural Construction of Nature*. Cambridge, MA: MIT Press.

Atran, Scott and Sperber, Dan (1991) Learning without teaching: Its place in culture. In Liliana T. Landsmann (Ed.), *Culture, Schooling, and Psychological Development*. pp. 39–55. Norwood, NJ: Ablex.

Au, Terry Fit-fong, and Romo, Laura F. (1999) Mechanical causality in children's "folkbiology." In Douglas L. Medin and Scott Atran (Eds.), *Folkbiology*. pp. 355–401. Cambridge, MA: MIT Press.

Aunger, Robert (1994) Sources of variation in ethnographic interview data: Food avoidances in the Ituri forest, Zaire. *Ethnology* 33(1):65–99.

Azuma, Hiroshi (1981) A note on cross-cultural study. *Quarterly Newsletter of the Laboratory of Comparative Human Cognition* 3(2):23–25.

Baas, Laura (2011) Ore mining in Bolivia. In G. Kristoffel Lieten (Ed.), *Hazardous Child Labour in Latin America*. pp. 105–123. Heidelberg: Springer.

Bachman, Jerald G., Safron, Deborah J., Sy, Susan Rogala, and Schulenberg, John E. (2003) Wishing to work: New perspectives on how adolescents' part-time work intensity is linked to educational disengagement, substance use, and other problem behaviours. *International Journal of Behavioral Development* 27(4):301–315.

Baer, Justin D., Cook, Andrea L., and Baldi, Stephane (2006) *The Literacy of America's College Students*. Washington, DC: American Institutes for Research.

Bai, Limin (2005) *Shaping the Ideal Child: Children and Their Primers in Late Imperial China*. Hong Kong: Chinese University Press.

Bailey, Drew H. and Geary, David C. (2009) Hominid brain evolution: Testing climatic, ecological, and social competition. *Human Nature* 20:67–79.

Bailey, Robert C. and Aunger, Robert (1989) Net hunters vs. archers: Variation in women's subsistence strategies in the Ituri Forest. *Human Ecology* 17:273–297.

Baillargeon, Renée and Carey, Susan (2012) Core cognition and beyond: The acquisition of physical and numerical knowledge. In Sabina Pauen (Ed.), *Early Childhood Development and Later Outcome*. pp. 33–65. Cambridge: Cambridge University Press.

Bakeman, Roger, Adamson, Lauren B., Konner, Melvin, and Barr, Ronald G. (1990) !Kung infancy: The social context of object exploration. *Child Development* 61(4):794–809.

Baker, Rachel and Panter-Brick, Catherine (2000) A comparative perspective on children's "careers" and abandonment in Nepal. In Catherine Panter-Brick and Malcolm T. Smith (Eds.), *Abandoned Children*. pp. 161–181. Cambridge: Cambridge University Press.

Baldwin, John D. and Baldwin, Janice I. (1972) The ecology and behavior of squirrel monkeys (*Saimiri*) in a natural forest in western Panama. *Folia Primatologica* 18(1):161–184.

  (1977) The role of learning phenomena in the ontogeny of exploration and play. In Suzanne Chevalier-Skolnikoff and Frank E. Poirier (Eds.), *Primate Bio-Social Development: Biological, Social, and Ecological Determinants*. pp. 343–406. New York, NY: Garland.

  (1978) Exploration and play in howler monkeys (*Aloutta palliata*). *Primates* 19(3):411–422.

Balicki, Asen (1967) Female infanticide on the Arctic coast. *Man* 2:615–625.

  (1970) *The Netsilik Eskimo*. Garden City, NY: Natural History Press.

Bamford, Sandra C. (2004) Embodiments of detachment: Engendering agency in the Highlands of Papua New Guinea. In Pascale Bonnemère (Ed.), *Women as Unseen Characters*. pp. 34–56. Philadelphia, PA: University of Pennsylvania Press.

Bandura, Albert (1977) *Social Learning Theory*. Englewood Cliffs, NJ: Prentice Hall.

Barber, Elizabeth W. (1994) *Women's Work: The First 20,000 Years. Women, Cloth and Society in Early Times*. New York, NY: W. W. Norton.

Barber, Nigel (1991) Play and regulation in mammals. *The Quarterly Review of Biology* 66(2):129–146.

  (2000) *Why Parents Matter: Parental Investment and Child Outcomes*. Westport, CT: Bergin and Garvey.

  (2002) Does parental investment increase wealth, or does wealth increase parental investment? *Cross-Cultural Research* 36(4):362–378.

Bard, Katherine A. (1995) Parenting in primates. In Marc H. Bornstein (Ed.), *Handbook of Parenting*. Vol. II: *Biology and Ecology of Parenting*. pp. 27–58. Mahwah, NJ: Erlbaum.

Bardo, Massimo, Petto, Andrew J., and Lee-Parritz, David E. (2001) Parental failure in captive cotton-top tamarins (*Saguinus oedipus*). *American Journal of Primatology* 54(2):159–169.

Bargh, John A. and Chartrand, Tanya L. (1999) The unbearable automaticity of being. *American Psychologist* 54:462–479.

Barley, Nigel (1983/2000) *The Innocent Anthropologist: Notes from a Mud Hut.* Long Grove, IL: Waveland Press.

Barlow, Kathleen (2001) Working mothers and the work of culture in a Papua New Guinea society. *Ethos* 29(1):78–107.

Barnett, Homer G. (1955) *The Coast Salish of British Columbia.* Eugene, OR: University of Oregon Press.

(1979) *Being a Palauan.* New York: Holt, Rinehart, and Winston.

Barnhart, Richard and Barnhart, Catherine (2002) Images of children in Song painting and poetry. In Ann Barrott Wicks (Ed.), *Children in Chinese Art.* pp. 21–56. Honolulu, HI: University of Hawai'i, Press.

Barrett, Autumn R. (2014) Childhood, colonialism, and nation-building: Virginia and New York. In Jennifer L. Thompson, Marta P. Alfonso-Durruty, and John J. Crandall (Eds.), *Tracing Childhood: Bioarchaeological Investigations of Early Lives in Antiquity.* pp. 159–182. Gainesville, FL: University Press of Florida.

Barrett, H. Clark (2005) Adaptations to predators and prey. In David M. Buss (Ed.), *Handbook of Evolutionary Psychology.* pp 200–223. New York, NY: Wiley.

Barrett, H. Clark and Broesch, James (2012) Prepared social learning about dangerous animals in children. *Evolution and Human Behavior* 33(5):499–508.

Barrett, Louise, Dunbar, Robin, and Lycett, John (2002) *Human Evolutionary Psychology.* Princeton, NJ: Princeton University Press.

Barry, Herbert L., III. (2007) Customs associated with premarital sexual freedom in 143 societies. *Cross-Cultural Research* 41:261–272.

Barry, Herbert L., III and Paxson, Leonora M. (1971) Infancy and early childhood: Cross-cultural codes 2. *Ethnology* 10(3):466–508.

Barth, Fredrik (1975) *Ritual and Knowledge among the Baktaman of New Guinea.* New Haven, CT: Yale University Press.

(1993) *Balinese Worlds.* Chicago, IL: University of Chicago Press.

Bascom, William (1969) *The Yoruba of Southwest Nigeria.* New York, NY: Holt, Rinehart, and Winston.

Basden, George T. (1966) *Niger Ibos.* London: Cass.

Basedow, Herbert (1925) *The Australian Aboriginal.* Adelaide: F. W. Preece and Sons.

Bass, Loreta E. (2004) *Child Labor in Sub-Saharan Africa.* Boulder, CO: Lynne Rienner.

Basso, Keith H. (1972) Ice and travel among the Fort Norman Slave: Folk taxonomies and cultural rules. *Language in Society* 1(1):31–49.

Bastian, Misty L. (2001) "The demon superstition": Abominable twins and mission culture in Onitsha history. *Ethnology* 40(1):13–27.

Batels, Lambert (1969) Birth customs and birth songs of the Macha Galla. *Ethnology* 8(4):406–422.

Baten, Jörg, a'Hearn, Brian and Crayen, Dorothee (2009) Quantifying quantitative literacy: Age heaping and the history of human capital. *Journal of Economic History* 69:783–808.

Bates, Brian and Turner, Allison N. (2003) Imagery and symbolism in the birth practices of traditional cultures. In Lauren Dundes (Ed.), *The Manner Born: Birth Rites in Cross-Cultural Perspective.* pp. 87–97. Lanham, MD: AltaMira Press.

Bateson, Gregory and Mead, Margaret (1942) *Balinese Character: A Photographic Analysis*. New York, NY: New York Academy of Sciences.

Bauerlein, Mark (2009) *The Dumbest Generation: How the Digital Age Stupefies Young Americans and Jeopardizes Our Future*. New York, NY: Penguin.

Baumeister, Roy F., Campbell, Jennifer D., Krueger, Joachim I., and Vohs, Kathleen D. (2005) Exploding the self-esteem myth. *Scientific American Mind* 16(4):50–57.

Baumrind, Diana (1971) Current patterns of parental authority. *Developmental Psychology Monographs* 4 (no. 1, part 2):1–103.

Baxter, Paul T. W. and Butt, Audrey (1953) *The Azande, and Related Peoples of the Anglo-Egyptian Sudan and Belgian Congo*. London: International African Institute.

Beach, Betty A. (2003) Rural children's play in the natural environment. In Donald E. Lytle (Ed.), *Play and Educational Theory and Practice*. pp. 183–194. Westport, CT: Praeger.

Beals, Diane E. (2001) Eating and reading: Links between family conversations with preschoolers and later language and literacy. In David K. Dickinson and Patton O. Tabors (Eds.), *Beginning Literacy with Language*. pp. 75–92. Baltimore, MD: Paul H. Brooks.

Beaumont, Lesley A. (1994) Constructing a methodology for the interpretation of childhood age in classical Athenian iconography. *Archaeological Review from Cambridge* 13(2):81–96.

Beazley, Harriot (2008) The geographies and identities of street girls in Indonesia. In Marta Gutman and Ning de Coninck-Smith (Eds.), *Designing Modern Childhoods: History, Space, and the Material Culture of Children*. pp. 233–249. New Brunswick, NJ: Rutgers University Press.

Beck, Frederick, A. G. (1975) *Album of Greek Education: The Greeks at School and at Play*. Sydney: Cheiron Press.

Becker, Marshall J. (2007) Childhood among the Etruscans: Mortuary programs at Tarquinia as indicators of the transition to adult status. In Ada Cohen and Jeremy B. Rutter (Eds.), *Constructions of Childhood in Ancient Greece and Italy* (Hesperia Supplement 410). pp. 281–292. Athens: American School of Classical Studies at Athens.

Beckerman, Stephan, Lizarralde, Roberto, Ballew, Carol, Schroeder, Sissel, Fingelton, Cristina, Garrison, Angela, and Smith, Helen (1998) The Bari partible paternity project: Preliminary results. *Current Anthropology*, 39(1):164–167.

Beckerman, Stephan and Valentine, Paul (2002) *Cultures of Multiple Fathers: The Theory and Practice of Partible Paternity in Lowland South America*. Gainesville, FL: University of Florida Press.

Belaunde, Luisa E. (2001) Menstruation, birth observances and the couple's love amongst the Airo-Pai of Amazonian Peru. In Soraya Tremayne (Ed.), *Managing Reproductive Life: Cross-Cultural Themes in Sexuality and Fertility*. pp. 127–139. Oxford: Berghahn Books.

Bellman, Berryl L. (1975) *Village of Curers and Assassins*. The Hague: Mouton.

Belo, Jane (1949) *Bali: Rangda and Barong*. New York: J. J. Augustin.

(1980) A study of customs pertaining to twins in Bali. In Jane Belo (Ed.), *Traditional Balinese Culture*. New York, NY: Columbia University Press.

Belsky, Jay, Steinberg, Lawrence, and Draper, Patricia (1991) Childhood experience, interpersonal development, and reproductive strategy: An evolutionary theory of socialization. *Child Development* 62(4):647–670.

Benedict, Ruth F. (1922) The vision in Plains culture. *American Anthropologist* 24(1):1– 23.

Bengston, Vern L., Biblarz, Timothy J., and Roberts, Robert E. L. (2002) *How Families Still Matter: A Longitudinal Study of Youth in Two Generations.* Cambridge: Cambridge University Press.

Benjamin, Gail R. (1997) *Japanese Lessons.* New York, NY: New York University Press.

Berdan, Frances F. and Anawalt, Patricia Rieff (1997) *The Essential Codex Mendoza.* Berkeley, CA: University of California Press.

Bereczkei, Tamas (2001) Maternal trade-off in treating high-risk children. *Evolution and Human Behavior* 22(2):197–212.

Bereczkei, Tamas and Csanaky, Andras (2001) Stressful family environment, mortality, and child socialisation: Life-history strategies among adolescents and adults from unfavourable social circumstances. *International Journal of Behavioral Development* 25(6):501–508.

Bereczkei, Tamas and Dunbar, Robin I. M. (1997) Female-biased reproductive strategies in a Hungarian Gypsy population. *Proceedings of the Royal Society of London*, Series B 264:17–22.

Bérenguier, Nadine (2011) *Conduct Books for Girls in Enlightenment France.* Farnham: Ashgate.

Berentzen, Sigurd (1984) *Children Constructing Their Social World: An Analysis of Gender Constrast in Children's Interaction in a Nursery School.* University of Bergen: Occasional Papers in Social Anthropology, No. 36.

Berk, Sarah F. (1985) *The Gender Factor: The Apportionment of Work in American Households.* New York, NY: Plenum Press.

Bernstein, Gaia and Triger, Zvi (2011) Over-parenting. *UC Davis Law Review*, 44:1221–1280.

Bernstein, Robin, Sterner, Kirsten N., and Wildman, Derek E. (2012) Adrenal androgen production in Catarrhine primates and the evolution of adrenarche. *American Journal of Physical Anthropology* 147:389–400.

Berón, Mónica A., Aranda, Claudia M., and Luna, Leandro H. (2012) Mortuary behaviour in subadults: Children as social actors in the hunter-gatherer societies of Argentine Pampas. *Childhood in the Past* 5:51–69.

Berrelleza, Juan A. R. and Balderas, Ximena C. (2006) The role of children in the ritual practices of the Great Temple of Tenochtitlan and the Great Temple of Tlatelolco. In Traci Adren and Scott R. Hutson (Eds.), *The Social Experience of Childhood in Ancient Mesoamerica.* pp. 233–248. Boulder, CO: University of Colorado Press.

Berrick, Jill Duerr (1995) *Faces of Poverty: Portraits of Women and Children on Welfare.* New York, NY: Oxford University Press.

Berrol, Selma (1992) Immigrant children at school, 1880–1940: A child's-eye view. In Elliot West and Paula Petrick (Eds.), *Small Worlds: Children and Adolescents in America, 1850–1950.* pp. 42–60. Lawrence, KS: University Press of Kansas.

Besom, Thomas (2009) *Of Summits and Sacrifice: An Ethnohistoric Study of Inka Religious Practices*. Austin, TX: University of Texas Press.

Best, Amy L. (2000) *Prom Night: Youth, Schools, and Popular Culture*. New York, NY: Routledge.

Best, Joel and Horiuchi, Gerald T. (1985) The razor blade in the apple: The social construction of urban legends. *Social Problems* 32(5):488–499.

Beverly, Elizabeth A. and Whittemore, Robert D. (1993) Mandinka children and the geography of well-being. *Ethos* 21(3):235–272.

Bey, Marguerite (2003) The Mexican child: From work with the family to paid employment. *Childhood* 10(3):287–299.

Biben, Maxine, Symmes, David, and Bernard, Deborah (1989) Vigilance during play in squirrel monkeys. *American Journal of Primatology* 17(1):41–49.

Biersack, Aletta (1998) Horticulture and hierarchy: The youthful beautification of the body in the Paiela and Porgera Valleys. In Gilbert H. Herdt and Stephen C. Leavitt (Eds.), *Adolescence in Pacific Island Societies*. pp. 71–91. Pittsburgh, PA: University of Pittsburgh Press.

Biesele, Megan (1993) *"Women Like Meat": The Folklore and Foraging Ideology of the Kalahari Ju/'hoan*. Bloomington, IN: Indiana University Press.

   (1997) An ideal of unassisted birth: Hunting, healing, and transformation among the Kalahari Ju/'hoansi. In Robbie E. Davis-Floyd and Carolyn F. Sargent (Eds.), *Childbirth and Authoritative Knowledge*. pp. 474–492. Berkeley, CA: University of California Press.

Binkley, David A. (2006) From grasshoppers to Babende: The socialization of Southern Kuba boys to masquerade. In Simon Ottenberg and David A. Binkley (Eds.), *Playful Performers: African Children's Masquerades*. pp. 105–115. New Brunswick, NJ: Transaction Publishers.

Binser, Martin J. (2004) "Sadder but fitter": Die evolutionäre Funktion von depressiven Symptomen nach Fehl-und Totgeburten. *Zeitschrift für Sozialpsychologie* 35(3):157–170.

Bird, Douglas W. and Bird, Rebecca B. (2002) Children on the reef: Slow learning or strategic foraging? *Human Nature* 13(2):269–297.

   (2005) Martu children's hunting strategies in the western desert, Australia. In Barry S. Hewlett and Michael E. Lamb (Eds.) *Hunter Gatherer Childhoods: Evolutionary, Developmental, and Cultural Perspectives*. pp. 129–146. New Brunswick, NJ: Aldine/Transaction Publishers.

Bird, Rebecca B. and Bird, Douglas W. (2002) Constraints of knowing or constraints of growing? Fishing and collection by the children of Mer. *Human Nature* 13(2):239–267.

Bird-David, Nurit (2005) Studying children in "hunter-gatherer" societies: Reflections from a Nayaka perspective. In Barry S. Hewlett and Michael E. Lamb (Eds.), *Hunter-Gatherer Childhoods: Evolutionary, Developmental, and Cultural Perspectives*. pp. 92–101. New Brunswick, NJ: Aldine/Transaction Publishers.

Bjorklund, David F. (2007) *Why Youth is Not Wasted on the Young*. Malden, MA: Wiley-Blackwell.

Black, Maureen M., Dubowitz, Howard, and Starr, Raymond H., Jr. (1999) African American fathers in low income, urban families: Development, behavior, and home environment of their three-year-old children. *Child Development* 70(4):967–978.

Blackburn, Roderic H. (1996) Fission, fusion, and foragers in East Africa: Micro-and macro-processes of diversity and integration among Okiek groups. In Susan Kent (Ed.), *Cultural Diversity among Twentieth-Century Foragers*. pp. 188–212. Cambridge: Cambridge University Press.

Blackwood, Evelyn (2001) Women's intimate friendships and other affairs: An ethnographic overview. In Caroline B. Brettell and Carolyn F. Sargent (Eds.), *Gender in Cross-Cultural Perspective*. pp. 237–247. Upper Saddle River, NJ: Prentice Hall.

Blakemore, Sarah-Jayne (2008) The social brain in adolescence. *Nature Reviews: Neuroscience* 9:267–277.

Blanchard, Ray and Bogaert, Anthony F. (1997) The relation of close birth intervals to the sex of the preceding child and the sexual orientation of the succeeding child. *Journal of Biosocial Science* 29(1):111–118.

Blanchy, Sophie (2007) Le tambavy des bébés à Madagascar: Du soin au ritual d'ancestralité. In Doris Bonnet and Laurence Pourchez (Eds.), *Du Soin au Rite dans L'Infance*. pp. 146–166. Paris: IRD.

Blau, Zena S. (1969) In defense of the Jewish mother. In Peter I. Rose (Ed.), *The Ghetto and Beyond*. pp. 57–68. New York, NY: Random House.

Bledsoe, Caroline H. (1980a) The manipulation of Kpelle social fatherhood. *Ethnology* 19(1):29–45.

(1980b) *Women and Marriage in Kpelle Society*. Stanford, CA: Stanford University Press.

(1992) The cultural transformation of Western education in Sierra Leone, *Africa: Journal of the International African Institute* 62(2):182–202.

(2001) The bodily costs of childrearing: Western science through a West African lens. In Helen B. Schwartzman (Ed.), *Children and Anthropology: Perspectives for the 21st Century*. pp. 57–81. Westport, CT: Bergin and Garvey.

Bledsoe, Caroline H. and Cohen, Barney (Eds.) (1993) *Social Dynamics of Adolescent Fertility in Sub-Saharan Africa*. Washington, DC: National Research Council.

Bledsoe, Caroline H. and Isiugo-Abanihe, Uche (1989) Strategies of child-fosterage among Mende grannies in Sierra Leone. In Ron J. Lesthaeghe (Ed.), *Reproduction and Social Organization in Sub-Saharan Africa*. pp. 443–474. Berkeley, CA: University of California Press.

Bledsoe, Caroline H. and Robey, Kenneth M. (1986) Arabic literacy and secrecy among the Mende of Sierra Leone. *Man* 21(2):202–226.

Blinn-Pike, Lynn, Kuschel, Diane, McDaniel, Annette, Mingus, Suzanne, and Mutti, Megan Poole (1998) The process of mentoring pregnant adolescents: An exploratory study. *Family Relations* 47(2):119–127.

Blitz, Jeffrey. (dir.) (2002) *Spellbound* (film). Los Angeles, CA: Columbia Tristar.

Bloch, Marianne N. (1989) Young boys' and girls' play at home and in the community: A cultural-ecological framework. In Marianne N. Bloch and Anthony D. Pellegrini (Eds.), *The Ecological Context of Children's Play*. pp. 120–154. Norwood, NJ: Ablex.

Bloch, Maurice E. F. (1988) *How We Think They Think: Anthropological Approach to Cognition, Memory, and Literacy.* Boulder, CO: Westview Press.

Bloch, Maurice E. F., Solomon, Gregg E. A., and Carey, Susan (2001) Zafimaniry: An understanding of what is passed on from parents to children: A cross-cultural investigation. *Journal of Cognition and Culture* 1(1):43–68.

Bloom, Paul (1999) The evolution of certain novel human capacities. In Michael C. Corballis and Stephen E. G. Lea (Eds.), *The Descent of the Mind.* pp 295–310. Oxford: Oxford University Press.

Bloom-Feshbach, Jonathan (1981) Historical perspectives on the father's role. In Michael E. Lamb (Ed.), *The Role of the Father in Child Development.* pp. 71–112. New York, NY: Wiley.

Blount, Benjamin J. (1972) Parental speech and language acquisition: Some Luo and Samoan examples. *Journal of Anthropological Linguistics* 14(4):119–130.

Blurton-Jones, Nicholas G. (1967) An ethological study of some aspects of social behavior of children in nursery school. In Desmond Morris (Ed.), *Primate Ethology.* pp. 347–367. London: Weidenfeld and Nicolson.

(1993) The lives of hunter-gatherer children: Effects of parental behavior and parental reproduction strategy. In Michael Pererira and Lynn Fairbanks (Eds.), *Juveniles: Comparative Socioecology.* pp. 405–426.Oxford: Oxford University Press.

(2005) Why childhood? In Barry S. Hewlett and Michael E. Lamb (Eds.), *Hunter-Gatherer Childhoods.* pp. 105–108. New Brunswick, NJ: Aldine/Transaction Publishers.

(2006) Contemporary hunter-gatherers and human life history evolution. In Kristen Hawkes and Richard R. Paine (Eds.), *The Evolution of Human Life History.* pp. 231–266. Santa Fe, NM: SAR Press.

Blurton-Jones, Nicholas G., Hawkes, Kristen, and O'Connell, James F. (1996) The global process and local ecology: How should we explain differences between the Hadza and the Kung? In Susan Kent (Ed.), *Cultural Diversity among Twentieth-Century Foragers.* pp. 159–187. Cambridge: Cambridge University Press.

(1997) Why do Hadza children forage? In Nancy L. Segal, Glenn E. Weisfeld, and Carol C. Weisfeld (Eds.), *Uniting Psychology and Biology: Integrative Perspectives on Human Development.* pp. 279–313. Washington, DC: American Psychological Association.

(2005) Older Hadza men and women as helpers. In Barry S. Hewlett and Michael E. Lamb (Eds.), *Hunter Gatherer Childhoods: Evolutionary, Developmental, and Cultural Perspectives.* pp. 214–236. New Brunswick, NJ: Aldine/Transaction Publishers.

Blurton-Jones, Nicholas G. and Konner, Melvin (1973) Sex differences in the behavior of Bushman and London two- to five-year-olds. In Richard P. Michael and John H. Crook (Eds.), *Comparative Ecology and Behavior of Primates.* pp. 689–750. New York, NY: Academic Press.

Blurton-Jones, Nicholas G. and Marlowe, Frank W. (2002) Selection for delayed maturity: Does it take 20 years to learn to hunt and gather? *Human Nature* 13(2):199–238.

Blurton-Jones, Nicholas G., Marlowe, Frank W., Hawkes, Kristen, and O'Connell, James F. (2000) Paternal investment and hunter-gatherer divorce rates. In Lee Cronk, Napoleon Chagnon, and William Irons (Eds.), *Adaptation and Human Behavior: An Anthropological Perspective*. pp. 69–90. New York, NY: Aldine De Gruyter.

Boas, Franz (1901) The Eskimo of Baffin Land and Hudson Bay. *Bulletin of the American Museum of Natural History* 15(1):1–370.

Bock, John (2002a) Learning, life history, and productivity: Children's lives in the Okavango Delta of Botswana. *Human Nature* 13(2):161–198.

(2002b) Evolutionary demography and intrahousehold time allocation: School attendance and child labor among the Okavango Delta peoples of Botswana. *American Journal of Human Biology* 14(2):206–221.

(2005) Farming, foraging, and children's play in the Okavango Delta, Botswana. In Anthony Pellegrini and Peter K. Smith (Eds.), *The Nature of Play: Great Apes and Humans*. pp. 254–281. New York, NY: Guilford Press.

(2010) An evolutionary perspective on learning in social, cultural, and ecological context. In David F. Lancy, Suzanne Gaskins, and John Bock (Eds.), *The Anthropology of Learning in Childhood*. pp. 11–34. Lanham, MD: AltaMira Press.

Bock, John and Johnson, Sara E. (2002) Male migration, remittances, and child outcome among the Okavango Delta peoples of Botswana. In Catherine S. Tamis-LaMonda and Natasha Cabrera (Eds.), *Handbook of Father Involvement: Multidisciplinary Perspectives*. pp. 308–335. Mahwah, NJ: Erlbaum.

(2004) Subsistence ecology and play among the Okavango Delta peoples of Botswana. *Human Nature* 15(1):63–82.

(2008) Grandmothers' productivity and the HIV/AIDS pandemic in Sub-Saharan Africa. *Journal of Cross-Cultural Gerontology* 25:131–145.

Bodenhorn, Barbara (1988) Whales, souls, children, and other things that are "good to share": Core metaphors in a contemporary whaling society. *Cambridge Anthropology* 13:1–19.

Boesch, Christophe (2005) Joint cooperative hunting among wild chimpanzees: Taking natural observations seriously. *Behavioral and Brain Sciences* 28:692–693.

Bogin, Barry (1994) Adolescence in evolutionary perspective. *Acta Paediatrica Scandinavia (Suppl.)* 406:29–35.

(1998) Evolutionary and biological aspects of childhood. In Catherine Panter-Brick (Ed.), *Biosocial Perspectives on Children*. pp. 10–44. Cambridge: Cambridge University Press.

(1999) *Patterns of Human Growth*, 2nd edn. Cambridge: Cambridge University Press.

(2009) Childhood, adolescence, and longevity: A multilevel model of the evolution of reserve capacity in human life history. *American Journal of Human Biology* 21:567–577.

(2013) Childhood, adolescence, and longevity: A chapter on human evolutionary life history. In Bonnie L. Hewlett (Ed.), *Adolescent Identity: Evolutionary, Cultural and Development Perspectives*. pp. 23–39. New York, NY: Routledge.

Bogin, Barry and Smith, Brian H. (1996) Evolution of the human life cycle. *American Journal of Human Biology* 8(6):703–716.

Bolin, Inge (2006) *Growing up in a Culture of Respect: Childrearing in Highland Peru*. Austin, TX: University of Texas Press.

Bonnemere, Pascale (2006) Variations on a theme: Fertility, sexuality and masculinity in Highland New Guinea. In Stanley J. Ulijaszek (Ed.), *Population, Reproduction, and Fertility in Melanesia*. pp. 201–238. Oxford: Berghahn Books.

Bonnet, Doris (2007) La toilette des nourissons au Burkina Faso: Une manipulation gestuelle et sociale du corps de l'enfant (Bathing Mossi babies: A social and cultural practice). In Doris Bonnet and Laurence Pourchez (Eds.), *Du Soin au Rite dans L'Infance*. pp. 113–28. Paris: IRD.

Boone, James and Kessler, Karen L. (1999) More status or more children? Social status, fertility reduction, and long-term fitness. *Evolution and Human Behavior* 20(2):257–277.

Booth, Marilyn (2002) Arab adolescents facing the future: Enduring ideals and pressure to change. In Bradford B. Brown, Reed W. Larson, and T. S. Saraswathi (Eds.), *The World's Youth: Adolescence in Eight Regions of the Globe*. pp. 207–242. Cambridge: Cambridge University Press.

Borgerhoff Mulder, Monique (1992) Reproductive decisions. In Eric A. Smith and Bruce Winterhalder (Eds.), *Evolutionary Ecology and Human Behavior*. pp. 339–374. New York, NY: Aldine.

Borofsky, Robert (1987) *Making History: Pukapukan and Anthropological Constructions of Knowledge*. Cambridge: Cambridge University Press.

Boserup, Esther (1970) *Women's Role in Economic Development*. London: George Allen and Unwin.

Boswell, John (1988) *The Kindness of Strangers*. New York: Pantheon Books.

Boulton, Michael J. and Smith, Peter K. (1992) The social nature of play fighting and play chasing: Mechanisms and strategies underlying cooperation and compromise. In Jerome H. Barkow, Leda Cosmides, and John Tooby (Eds.), *The Adapted Mind: Evolutionary Psychology and the Generation of Culture*. pp. 430–440. Oxford: Oxford University Press.

Boum, Aomar (2008) The political coherence of education incoherence: The consequences of education specialization in a Southern Moroccan community. *Anthropology and Education Quarterly* 39:205–223.

Bourdieu, Pierre (1973) Cultural reproduction and social reproduction. In Richard Brown (Ed.), *Knowledge, Education and Social Change*. pp. 49–76. London: Tavistock publications.

(1977) *Outline of a Theory of Practice*. Cambridge: Cambridge University Press.

Bourdillon, Michael (2000) Children at work on tea and coffee estates. In Michael Bourdillon, *Earning a Life: Working Children in Zimbabwe*. pp. 1–24. Harare, Zimbabwe: Weaver Press.

Bourdillon, Michael and Spittler, Gerd (2012) Introduction. In Gerd Spittler and Michael Bourdillon (Eds.), *African Children at Work: Working and Learning in Growing Up*. pp. 1–22. Berlin: LitVerlag.

Bourgois, Philippe (1998) Families and children in pain in the US inner city. In Nancy Scheper-Hughes and Carolyn F. Sargent (Eds.), *Small Wars: The Cultural Politics of Childhood*. pp. 331–351. Berkeley, CA: University of California Press.

424   References

Bove, Riley B., Valeggia, Claudia R., and Ellison, Peter T. (2002) Girl helpers and time allocation of nursing women among the Toba of Argentina. *Human Nature* 13(4):457–472.

Bowers, Nancy (1965) Permanent bachelorhood in the Upper Kaugel Valley of Highland New Guinea. *Oceania* 36:27–37.

Bowlby, John (1980) *Loss: Sadness and Depression*. New York: Basic Books.

Bowser, Brenda J. and Patton, John Q. (2008) Learning and transmission of pottery style: Women's life histories and communities of practice in the Ecuadorian Amazon. In Miriam T. Stark, Brenda J. Bowser, and Lee Horne (Eds.), *Breaking Down Boundaries: Anthropological Approaches to Cultural Transmission, Learning, and Material Culture*. pp. 105–129. Tucson, AZ: University of Arizona Press.

Boyd, Robert and Richerson, Peter J. (1985) *Culture and the Evolutionary Process*. Chicago, IL: University of Chicago Press.

   (1996) Why culture is common, but cultural evolution is rare. *Proceedings of the British Academy* 88:77–93.

   (2006) Culture and the evolution of the human social instincts. In Nick J. Einfield and Stephen C. Levinson (Eds.), *Roots of Human Socialization: Culture, Cognition and Interaction*. pp. 453–477. Oxford: Berg.

Boyd, Robert, Richerson, Peter J., and Henrich, Joseph (2011) The cultural niche: why social learning is essential for human adaptation. *PNAS* 108:10918–10925.

Boyden, Jo (2004) Anthropology under fire: Ethics, researchers and children in war. In Jo Boyden and Joanna de Berry (Eds.), *Children and Youth on the Front Line: Ethnography, Armed Conflict and Displacement*. pp. 237–258. Oxford: Berghahn Books.

Boyette, Adam H. (2013) Social learning during middle childhood among Aka foragers and Ngandu farmers of the Central African Republic. Unpublished PhD dissertation, Washington State University.

Bradley, Keith R. (1991) *Discovering the Roman Family: Studies in Roman Social History*. Oxford: Oxford University Press.

Braff, Lara (2009) Assisted reproduction and population politics: Creating "modern" families in Mexico City. *Anthropology News* 50(2):5–6.

Brase, Gary L. (2006) Cues of parental investment as a factor in attractiveness. *Evolution and Human Behavior* 27(2):145–157.

Brazelton, T. Barry (1977) Implications of infant development among the Mayan Indians of Mexico. In P. Herbert Leiderman, Steven R. Tulkin, and Anne Rosenfeld (Eds.), *Culture and Infancy: Variations in the Human Experience*. pp. 151–187. New York, NY: Academic Press.

Brenner, Suzanne (2001) Why women rule the roost: Rethinking Javanese ideologies of gender and self-control. In Caroline B. Brettell and Carolyn F. Sargent (Eds.), *Gender in Cross–Cultural Perspective*. pp. 135–156. Upper Saddle River, NJ: Prentice Hall.

Briggs, Jean L. (1970) *Never in Anger: Portrait of an Eskimo Family*. Cambridge, MA: Harvard University Press.

   (1990) Playwork as a tool in the socialization of an Inuit child. *Arctic Medical Research* 49:34–38.

Bril, Blandine (1986) The acquisition of an everyday technical motor skill: The pounding of cereals in Mali (Africa). In Harold Thomas, Anthony Whiting, and Michael G. Wade (Eds.), *Themes in Motor Development*. pp 315–326. Dordrecht: Martinus Nijhoff Publishers.

Bril, Blandine, Zack, Martine, and Nkounkou-Hombessa, Estelle (1989) Ethnotheories of development and education: A view from different cultures. *European Journal of Psychology of Education* 4:307–318.

Brison, Karen J. (1999) Hierarchy in the world of Fijian children. *Ethnology* 38(2):97– 119.

 (2009) Shifting conceptions of self and society in Fijian kindergarten. *Ethos* 37:314–333.

Broch, Harald B. (1990) *Growing up Agreeably: Bonerate Childhood Observed*. Honolulu, HI: University of Hawai'i Press.

Brooks, David (2011) Organization within disorder: The present and future of young people in the Ngaanyatjarra lands. In Ute Eickelkamp (Ed.), *Growing up in Central Australia: New Anthropological Studies of Aboriginal Childhood and Adolescence*. pp 183–212. Oxford: Berghahn Books.

Broude, Gwen J. (1975) Norms of premarital sexual behavior: A cross-cultural study. *Ethos* 3:381–401.

Broude, Gwen J. and Greene, Sarah J. (1976) Cross-cultural codes on twenty sexual attitudes and practices. *Ethnology* 15:409–429.

Brown, Ann L. (1990) Domain-specific principles affect learning and transfer in children. *Cognitive Science* 14:107–133.

Brown, Penelope (2011) The cultural organization of attention. In Alessandro Duranti, Elinor Ochs, and Bambi B. Schieffelin (Eds.) *The Handbook of Language Socialization*. Chichester: Wiley-Blackwell.

Brown, Shelby (1991) *Late Carthaginian Child Sacrifice and Sacrificial Monuments in their Mediterranean Context*. Sheffield: Sheffield Academic Press.

Browner, Carole H. (2001) The politics of reproduction in a Mexican village. In Caroline B. Brettell and Carolyn F. Sargent (Eds.), *Gender in Cross-Cultural Perspective*. pp. 460–470. Upper Saddle River, NJ: Prentice Hall.

Broyon, Marie A. (2004) L'éducation sanskrite à Bénares, enjeu d'une socié qui oscille entre traditions et transition. Paper presented at a seminar on Learning Processes and Everyday Cognition: The Role of Play and Games, April 16, Charmey.

Bruner, Jerome S. (1966) *Toward a Theory of Instruction*. Cambridge, MA: Harvard University Press

Bruner, Jerome S. and Sherwood, Virginia (1976) Peekaboo and the learning of rule structure. In Jerome S. Bruner, Allison Jolly, and Kathy Sylva (Eds.), *Play: Its Role in Development and Evolution*. pp. 277–286. New York, NY: Basic Books.

Bucher, Julia B. and d'Amorim, Maria A. (1993) Brazil. In Leonore Loeb Adler (Eds.), *International Handbook on Gender Roles*. pp. 16–27. Westport, CT: Greenwood Press.

Buckingham, David and Scanlon, Margaret (2003) *Education, Entertainment, and Learning in the Home*. Maidenhead: Open University Press.

Budwig, Nancy, Strage, Amy, and Bamberg, Michael (1986) The construction of joint activities with and age-mate: The transition from caregiver-child to peer play.

In Jenny Cook-Gumperz, William A. Corsaro, and Jürgen Streek (Eds.), *Children's Worlds and Children's Language*. pp. 83–108. Berlin: Mouton.

Bugos, Peter E., Jr. and McCarthy, Lorraine M. (1984) Ayoreo infanticide: A case study. In Glen Hausfater and Sarah Blaffer Hrdy (Eds.), *Infanticide: Comparative and Evolutionary Perspectives*. pp. 503–520. New York, NY: Aldine.

Burgess, Robert L. and Drias-Parrillo, Alicia A. (2005) An analysis of child maltreatment: From behavioral psychology to behavioral ecology. In Robert L. Burgess and Kevin MacDonald (Eds.), *Evolutionary Perspectives on Human Development*. pp. 305–330. Thousand Oaks, CA: Sage.

Burghardt, Gordon M. (2005) *The Genesis of Animal Play*. Cambridge, MA: MIT Press.

Burling, Robbins (1963) *Rengsanggri: Family and Kinship in a Garo Village*. Philadelphia, PA: University of Pennsylvania Press.

Burr, Rachael (2006) *Vietnam's Children in a Changing World*. New Brunswick, NJ: Rutgers University Press.

Burridge, Kenelm O. (1957) A Tangu game. *Man* 57:88–89.

Burrows, Edwin G. and Shapiro, Melford E. (1957) *An Atoll Culture*. Westport, CT: Greenwood Press.

Buss, David M. (1994) *The Evolution of Desire*. New York, NY: Basic Books.

Byrne, Richard W. (1995) *The Thinking Ape*. Oxford: Oxford University Press.
  (2006) Parsing behavior: A mundane origin for an extraordinary ability? In Nicholas J. Enfield and Stephen C. Levinson (Eds.), *Roots of Human Socialization: Culture, Cognition and Interaction*. pp. 478–505. Oxford: Berg.

Caine, Mead T. (1977) The economic activities of children in a village in Bangladesh. *Population and Development Review* 13:201–227.

Caldwell, John C. (1982) *"The Great Transition": Theory of Fertility Decline*. New York, NY: Academic Press.

Caldwell, John C. and Caldwell, Bruce K. (2005) Family size control by infanticide in the great agrarian societies of Asia. *Journal of Comparative Family Studies* 36:205–226.

Caldwell, John C., Caldwell, Pat, Caldwell, Bruce K., and Pieris, Indrani (1998) The construction of adolescence in a changing world: Implications for sexuality, reproduction, and marriage. *Studies in Family Planning* 29:137–153.

Callaghan, Tara, Moll, Henrike, Rakoczy, Hannes, Warneken, Felix, Liszkowski, Ulf, Behne, Tanya, and Tomasello, Michael (2011) Early social cognition in three cultural contexts. *Monographs of the Society for Research in Child Development* 76 (2):i–viii, 1–142.

Callimachi, Rukmini (2008) Islamic schools lure African boys into begging. *USA Today*, April 20. Available at http://usatoday30.usatoday.com/news/world/2008-04-20-4101720588_x.htm. Accessed February 1, 2014.
  (2013) Child soldier's tale illustrates Mali's dirty war. Associated Press, January 27. Available at www.boston.com/news/world/africa/2013/01/26/child-soldier-tale-illustrates-mali-dirty-war/cG7QOL44QVn6FQO6wCqY5K/story.html. Accessed October 14, 2013.

Calvert, Karin (1992) *Children in the House: The Material Culture of Early Childhood, 1600–1900*. Boston, MA: Northeastern University Press.

(2003) Patterns of childrearing in America. In Willem Koops and Michael Zucherman (Eds.), *Beyond the Century of the Child: Cultural History and Developmental Psychology*. pp. 62–81. Philadelphia, PA: University of Pennsylvania Press.

Cameron, Lisa, Erkal, Nisvan, Gangadharan, Lata, and Meng Xin (2013) Little emperors: Behavioral impacts of China's one-child policy. *Science*, January 10. Available at www.sciencemag.org/content/early/2013/01/09/science.1230221. Accessed January 13, 2013.

Campbell, John K. (1964) *Honour, Family, and Patronage: A Study of Institutions and Moral Values in a Greek Mountain Community*. Oxford: Clarendon Press.

Campos, Regina, Raffaelli, Marcela, Ude, Walter, Greco, Marilia, Ruff, Andrea, Rolf, Jon, Antunes, Carlos M., Halsey, Nea, and Greco, Dirceu (1994) Social networks and daily activities of street youth in Belo Horizonte, Brazil. *Child Development* 65:319–330.

Canaan, Joyce (1987) A comparative analysis of American suburban middle class, middle school, and high school teenage cliques. In George Spindler and Louise Spindler (Eds.), *Interpretive Ethnography of Education: At Home and Abroad*. pp. 385–406. Hillsdale, NJ: Erlbaum.

Cantrell, Eileen M. (1998) Woman the sexual, a question of when: A study of Gebusi adolescence. In Gilbert H. Herdt and Stephen C. Leavitt (Eds.), *Adolescence in Pacific Island Societies*. pp. 92–120. Pittsburgh, PA: University of Pittsburgh Press.

Caplan, Nathan S., Whitmore, John K., and Choy, Marcella H. (1991) *Children of the Boat People: A Study of Educational Success*. Ann Arbor, MI: University of Michigan Press.

Carey, Susan and Spelke, Elizabeth (1996) Science and core knowledge. *Philosophy of Science* 63:515–533.

Caro, Timothy M. and Hauser, Marc D. (1992) Is there teaching in nonhuman animals? *Quarterly Review of Biology* 67:151–171.

Carpenter, Edmund S. (1973) *Eskimo Realities*. New York: Holt, Rinehart, and Winston.

Carrasco, David (1999) *City of Sacrifice: The Aztec Empire and the Role of Violence in Civilization*. Boston, MA: Beacon Press.

Carrier, Achsah H. (1985) Infant care and family relations on Ponam Island, Manus Province, Papua New Guinea. In Leslie B. Marshall (Ed.), *Infant Care and Feeding in the South Pacific*. pp. 189–205. New York: Gordon and Breach.

Carrier, James G. (1981) Labour migration and labour export on Ponam Island. *Oceania* 51:237–255.

Case, Anne, Paxson, Christina, and Ableidinger, Joseph (2004) *Orphans in Africa: Parental Death, Poverty and School Enrollment*. Princeton, NJ: Princeton University Center for Health and Wellbeing Research Program in Development Studies.

Casimir, Michael J. (2010) *Growing Up in a Pastoral Society: Socialization among Pashtu Nomads*. Kölner Ethnologische Beiträge. Cologne: Druck & Bindung.

Cassidy, Claire (1980) Benign neglect and toddler malnutrition. In Lawrence Greene and Francis Johnston (Eds.), *Social and Biological Predictors of Nutritional*

Status, Physical Growth, and Neurological Development. pp. 109–139. New York, NY: Academic Press.

Castle, Sarah E. (1994) The (re)negotiation of illness diagnoses and responsibility for child death in rural Mali. *Medical Anthropology Quarterly* 8(3):314–335.

Castro, Laureano and Toro, Miguel A. (2004) The evolution of culture: From primate social learning to human culture. *Proceedings of the National Academy of Sciences* 101:10235–10240.

Caudill, William (1988) Tiny dramas: Vocal communication between mother and infant in Japanese and American families. In Gerald Handel (Ed.), *Childhood Socialization*. pp. 49–72. New York, NY: Aldine.

Cazden, Courtney B. (1988) *Classroom Discourse: The Language of Teaching and Learning*. Portsmouth, NH: Heinemann.

Cekaite, Asta (2010) Shepherding the child: Embodied directive sequences in parent–child interaction. *Text and Talk* 30–1:1–25.

Chagnon, Napoleon A. (1968/1992) *Yanomamö: The Fierce People*. Fort Worth, TX: Harcourt Brace Jovanovich.

   (1979) Is reproductive success equal in egalitarian societies? In Napoleon A. Chagnon and William Irons (Eds.), *Evolutionary Biology and Human Social Behavior: An Anthropological Perspective*. pp. 374–401. North Scituate, MA: Duxbury Press.

Chang, Heewon (1992) *Adolescent Life and Ethos: An Ethnography of a US High School*. Washington, DC: Falmer Press.

Chanthavong, Samlanchith (2002) *Chocolate and Slavery: Child Labor in Cote d'Ivoire*. TED Case Studies, 664. Available at www1.american.edu/ted/chocolate-slave.htm. Accessed July 27, 2013.

Chapin, Bambi L. (2011) "We have to give": Sinhala mothers' responses to children's expression of desire. *Ethos* 38: 354–368.

Chapman, Charlotte G. (1971) *Milocca: A Sicilian Village*. Cambridge, MA: Schenkman.

Chatty, Dawn (2006) Boarding schools for mobile peoples: The Harasiis in the Sultanate of Oman. In Caroline Dyer (Ed.), *The Education of Nomadic Peoples: Current Issues, Future Prospects*. pp. 212–230. Oxford: Berghahn Books.

Chavajay, Pablo (2006) How Mayan mothers with different amounts of schooling organize a problem-solving discussion with children. *International Journal of Behavioral Development* 30:371–382.

Chavajay, Pablo and Rogoff, Barbara (1999) Cultural variation in management of attention by children and their caregivers. *Developmental Psychology* 35:1079–1090.

Chee, Bernadine W. L. (2000) Eating snacks, biting pressure: Only children in Beijing. In Jun Jing (Ed.), *Feeding China's Little Emperors: Food, Children, and Social Change*. pp. 48–70. Stanford, CA: Stanford University Press.

Cheney, Kristen E. (2012) Seen but not heard: African orphanhood in the age of HIV/AIDS. In Marisa O. Ensor (Ed.), *African Childhoods: Education, Development, Peacebuilding and the Youngest Continent*. pp. 95–108. New York, NY: Palgrave Macmillan.

Chernela, Janet (2008) Translating ideologies: Tangible meaning and spatial politics in the northwest Amazon of Brazil. In Miriam T. Start, Brenda J. Bowser, and

Lee Horne (Eds.), *Cultural Transmission and Material Culture: Breaking Down Boundaries*. pp. 130–149. Tucson, AZ: University of Arizona Press.

Chevalier-Skolnikoff, Suzanne (1977) A Piagetian model for describing and comparing socialization in monkey, ape, and human infants. In Suzanne Chevalier-Skolnikoff and Frank E. Poirier (Eds.), *Primate Bio-Social Development: Biological, Social, and Ecological Determinants*. pp. 159–187. New York, NY: Garland.

Chick, Garry (2001) What is play for? Sexual selection and the evolution of play. In Stuart Reifel (Ed.), *Theory in Context and Out*. pp. 3–26. Westport, CT: Ablex.

Chipeniuk, Raymond (1995) Childhood foraging as a means of acquiring competent human cognition about biodiversity. *Environment and Behavior* 27:490–512.

Chirwa, Yotamu and Bourdillon, Michael (2000) Small-scale commercial farming: Working children in Nyangadzi Irrigation Scheme. In Michael Bourdillon (Ed.), *Earning a Life: Working Children in Zimbabwe*. pp. 127–145. Harare: Weaver Press.

Chirwa, Yotamu and Wakatama, Markim (2000) Working street children in Harare. In Michael Bourdillon (Ed.), *Earning a Life: Working Children in Zimbabwe*. pp. 45–58. Harare: Weaver Press.

Chisholm, James S. (1983/2009) *Navajo Infancy: An Ethological Study of Child Development*. New Brunswick, NJ: Aldine/Transaction Publishers.

   (1996) Learning respect for everything: Navaho images of development. In C. Philip Hwang, Michael E. Lamb, and Irving E. Sigel (Eds.), *Images of Childhood*. pp 167–183. Mahwah, NJ: Erlbaum.

Cho, Hae-Joang (1995) Children in the examination war in South Korea: A cultural analysis. In Sharon Stephens (Ed.), *Children and the Politics of Culture*. pp. 141–168. Princeton, NJ: Princeton University Press.

Chua, Amy (2011) *Battle Hymn of the Tiger Mom*. New York: Penguin.

Ciaccio, Nicholas V. and el Shakry, Omnia Sayed (1993) Egypt. In Leonore Loeb Adler (Ed.), *International Handbook on Gender Roles*. pp. 46–58. Westport, CT: Greenwood Press.

Clark, Cindy D. (2005) Tricks of festival: Children, enculturation, and American Halloween. *Ethos* 33:180–205.

Clark, Eric (2007) *The Real Toy Story: Inside the Ruthless Battle for America's Youngest Consumers*. New York, NY: Free Press.

Clark, Eve V. (2005) *First Language Acquisition*. Cambridge: Cambridge University Press.

Clark, Gracia (1994) *Onions Are My Husband: Survival and Accumulation by West African Market Women*. Chicago, IL: University of Chicago Press.

Clark, Sam, Colson, Elizabeth, Lee, J., and Scudder, Thayer (1995) Ten thousand Tonga: A longitudinal anthropological study from southern Zambia, 1956–1991. *Population Studies* 49:91–109.

Clark, Scott (1998) Learning at the public bathhouse. In John Singleton (Ed.), *Learning in Likely Places: Varieties of Apprenticeship in Japan*. pp. 239–252. Cambridge: Cambridge University Press.

Clarke, Alison J. (2008) Coming of age in suburbia: Gifting the consumer child. In Marta Gutman and Ning de Coninck-Smith (Eds.), *Designing Modern*

Childhoods: History, Space, and the Material Culture of Children. pp. 253–268.
    New Brunswick, NJ: Rutgers University Press.
Clement, Priscilla F. (1997) *Growing Pains: Children in the Industrial Age,*
    1850–1890. New York, NY: Twayne.
Clinton, Hillary R. (1996) *It Takes a Village.* New York: Simon and Schuster.
Clower, Robert W., George, Dalton, Harwitz, Mitchell, Walters, A. A., Armstrong,
    Robert P., Cole, Johnetta, Cole, Robert E., and Lamson, George (1966) *Growth*
    without Development: An Economic Survey of Liberia. Evanston, WY:
    Northwestern University Press.
Coe, Cati (2005) *Dilemmas of Culture in African Schools: Youth, Nationalism,*
    and the Transformation of Knowledge. Chicago, IL: University of
    Chicago Press.
Cole, Jennifer (2008) Fashioning distinction: Youth and consumerism in urban
    Madagascar. In Jennifer Cole and Deborah Durham (Eds.), *Figuring the Future:*
    Globalism and the Temporalities of Children and Youth. pp. 99–124. Santa Fe,
    NM: SAR Press.
Cole, Michael, Gay, John A., Glick, Joe, Sharp, Don W., Ciborowski, Tom,
    Frankel, Fred, Kellemu, John, and Lancy, David F. (1971) *The Cultural Context of*
    Learning and Thinking. New York, NY: Basic Books.
Coleman, Simon (1999) God's children: Physical and spiritual growth among
    evangelical Christians. In Susan J. Palmer and Charlotte E. Hardman (Eds.),
    Children in New Religions. pp. 71–87. New Brunswick, NJ: Rutgers
    University Press.
Coley, Rebekah Levine, Votruba-Drzal, Elizabeth, and Schindler, Holly S. (2009)
    Fathers' and mothers' parenting: Predicting and responding to adolescent sexual
    risk behaviors. *Child Development* 80:808–827.
Coll, Cynthia G. and Marks, Amy K. (2009) *Immigrant Stories: Ethnicity and*
    Academics in Middle Childhood. New York, NY: Oxford University Press.
Collings, Peter (2009) Birth order, age, and hunting success in the Canadian Arctic.
    Human Nature 29:354–374.
Colón, Angel R. with Colón, Patricia A. (2001) *A History of Children: A Socio-*
    Cultural Survey across Millennia. Westport, CT: Greenwood Press.
Conde-Agudelo, Agustin, Rosas-Bermudez, Anyeli, and Kafury-Goeta, Ana Cecilia
    (2006) Birth spacing and risk of adverse perinatal outcomes. *Journal of the*
    American Medical Association 295:1809–1823.
Condon, Richard G. (1987) *Inuit Youth: Growth and Change in the Canadian Arctic.*
    New Brunswick, NJ: Rutgers University Press.
Conklin, Beth A. (2001) Women's blood, warrior's blood and the conquest of
    vitality in Amazonia. In Thomas A. Gregor and Donald Tuzin (Eds.), *Gender in*
    Amazonia and Melanesia: An Exploration of the Comparative Method.
    pp. 141–172. Berkeley, CA: University of California Press.
Conklin, Beth A. and Morgan, Lynn M. (1996) Babies, bodies, and the production
    of personhood in North America and a native Amazonian society. *Ethos*
    24(4):657–694.
Consnoe, Robert (2011) *Fitting In, Standing Out: Navigating the Social*
    Challenges of High School to Get an Education. Cambridge: Cambridge
    University Press.

Conticini, Alessandro (2007) Children on the streets of Dhaka and their coping strategies. In James Staples (Ed.), *Livelihoods at the Margins: Surviving the City.* pp. 75–100. Walnut Creek, CA: Left Coast Press.

Cornwall, Andrea (2001) Looking for a child: Coping with infertility in Ado-Odo, south-western Nigeria. In Soraya Tremayne (Ed.), *Managing Reproductive Life: Cross-Cultural Themes in Sexuality and Fertility.* pp. 140–156. Oxford: Berghahn Books.

Correa-Chavez, Maricela and Rogoff, Barbara (2005) Cultural research has transformed our ideas of cognitive development. *International Society for the Study of Behavioral Development Newsletter* 47(1):7–10.

Corsaro, William A. (1996) Transitions in early childhood: The promise of comparative, longitudinal ethnography. In Richard Jessor, Anne Colby, and Richard A. Sweder (Eds.), *Ethnography and Human Development: Context and Meaning in Social Inquiry.* pp. 419–457. Chicago, IL: University of Chicago Press.

Cosminsky, Sheila (1985) Infant feeding practices in rural Kenya. In Valeria Hull and Mayling Simpson (Eds.), *Breastfeeding, Child Health and Birth Spacing: Cross-Cultural Perspectives.* pp. 35–54. London: Croom Helm.

  (1994) Childbirth and change: A Guatemalan study. In Carol P. MacCormack (Ed.), *Ethnography of Fertility and Birth.* pp. 195–219. Prospect Heights, IL: Waveland Press.

Coulter, Chris (2009) *Bush Wives and Girl Soldiers.* Ithaca, NY: Cornell University Press.

Counts, Dorothy A. (1985) Infant care and feeding in Kaliai, West New Britain, Papua New Guinea. In Leslie B. Marshall (Ed.), *Infant Care and Feeding in the South Pacific.* pp. 155–169. New York: Gordon and Breach.

Covarrubias, Miguel (1937) *Island of Bali.* New York: Alfred A. Knopf.

Cox, Caroline (2007) Boy soldiers: Lessons from the American Revolution. *Society for the History of Children and Youth Newsletter* 9:20–21.

Coy, Michael W. (1989) Being what we pretend to be: The usefulness of apprenticeship as a field method. In Michael W. Coy (Ed.), *Apprenticeship: From Theory to Method and Back Again.* pp. 115–135. Albany, NY: State University of New York Press.

Crago, Martha B. (1992) Communicative interaction and second language acquisition: An Inuit example. *TESOL Quarterly* 26:487–505.

Craig, Sienna R. (2009) Pregnancy and childbirth in Tibet: Knowledge, perspective, and practices. In Helaine Selin and Pamela K. Stone (Eds.), *Childhood across Cultures: Ideas and Practices of Pregnancy, Childbirth and the Postpartum.* pp. 145–160. Amherst, MA: Springer.

Crain, Caleb (2008) Twilight of the books. *The New Yorker* 83(41):134–39.

Crary, David (2012) Russia's move on adoptions discouraging: Eliminates American parents as retaliation. *The Washington Times*, December 23. Available at www.washingtontimes.com/news/2012/dec/23/russias-move-on-adoptions-discouraging. Accessed December 29, 2012.

Crawford, Sally (1999) *Childhood in Anglo-Saxon England.* Stroud: Sutton.

  (2009) The archaeology of play things: Theorizing a toy stage in the biography of objects. *Childhood in the Past* 2:56–71.

Creed, Gerald W. (1984) Sexual subordination: Institutionalized homosexuality and social control in Melanesia. *Ethnology* 23:157–176.

Crews, Douglas (2003) *Human Senescence: Evolutionary and Biocultural Perspectives*. Cambridge: Cambridge University Press.

Crittenden, Alyssa N., Conklin-Brittain, Nancy L., Zes, David A., Schoeninger, Margaret J., and Marlowe, Frank W. (2013) Juvenile foraging among the Hadza: Implications for human life history. *Evolution and Human Behavior* 34:299–304.

Crittenden, Alyssa N. and Marlowe, Frank W. (2008) Allomaternal care among the Hadza of Tanzania. *Human Nature* 19:249–262.

Crocker, William and Crocker, Jean (1994) *The Canela: Bonding through Kinship, Ritual and Sex*. New York, NY: Harcourt, Brace.

Crognier, Emile, Baali, A. and Hilali, Mohamed Kamal (2001) Do "helpers-at-the-nest" increase their parents' reproductive success? *American Journal of Human Biology* 13:365–373.

Cronk, Lee (1993) Parental favoritism toward daughters. *American Scientist* 81:272–280.

  (2000) Female-biased parental investment and growth performance among the Mukogodo. In Lee Cronk, Napoleon Chagnon, and William Irons (Eds.), *Adaptation and Human Behavior: An Anthropological Perspective*. pp. 203–221. New York, NY: Aldine.

Cronk, Lee, Gerkey, Drew, and Irons, William (2009) Interviews as experiments: Using audience effects to examine social relationships. *Field Methods* 21:331–346.

Cross, Gary (2004) *The Cute and the Cool: Wondrous Innocence and Modern American Children's Culture*. New York, NY: Oxford University Press.

Cross, Mary (1995) *Morocco: Sahara to the Sea*. New York, NY: Abbeville Press.

Crown, Patricia L. (2002) Learning and teaching in the Prehispanic American southwest. In Katheryn A. Kamp (Eds.), *Children in the Prehistoric Puebloan Southwest*. pp. 108–124. Salt Lake City, UT: University of Utah Press.

Culwick, Arthur T. (1935) *Ubena of the Rivers*. London: George Allen and Unwin.

Cunningham, Hugh (1995) *Children and Childhood in Western Society since 1500*. White Plains, NY: Longman.

d'Amato, John (1993) Resistance and compliance in minority classrooms. In Evelyn Jacob and Catbie Jordan (Eds.), *Minority Education: Anthropological Perspectives*. pp. 95–112. Norwood, NJ: Ablex.

d'Andrade, Roy G. (1984) Cultural meaning systems. In Richard A. Shweder and Robert A. LeVine (Eds.), *Culture Theory: Essays on Mind, Self, and Emotion*. pp. 88–119. Cambridge: Cambridge University Press.

Dahlberg, Gunilla (1992) The parent–child relationship and socialization in the context of modern childhood: The case of Sweden. In Jaipaul L. Roopnarine and D. Bruce Carter (Eds.), *Parent–Child Socialization in Diverse Cultures*. pp. 121–137. Norwood, NJ: Ablex.

Daly, Martin and Wilson, Margo (1984) A sociobiological analysis of human infanticide. In Glenn Hausfater and Sarah Blaffer Hrdy (Eds.), *Infanticide: Comparative and Evolutionary Perspectives*. pp. 487–502. New York, NY: Aldine.

Danielsson, Bengt (1952) *The Happy Island*. Translated by F. H. Lyon. London: George Allen and Unwin.

Dardess, John (1991) Childhood in premodern China. In Joseph M. Hawes and N. Ray Hiner (Eds.), *Children in Historical and Comparative Perspective*. pp. 71–94. Westport, CT: Greenwood Press.

Das Gupta, Monika (1987) Selective discrimination against female children in rural Punjab, India. *Population and Development Review* 13:77–100.

Dasen, Véronique (2010) Des nourrices grecques à Rome? *Paedagogica Historica* 46(6):699–713.

Davenport, Richard K. and Rogers, Charles M. (1970) Differential rearing of the chimpanzee. *The Chimpanzee* 3:337–360.

Davies, Matthew (2008) A childish culture? Shared understandings, agency and intervention: An anthropological study of street children in northwest Kenya. *Childhood* 15:309–330.

Davis, John (1992) The anthropology of suffering. *Journal of Refugee Studies*, 5(2):149–161.

Davis, Susan S. and Davis, Douglas A. (1989) *Adolescence in a Moroccan Town: Making Social Sense*. New Brunswick, NJ: Rutgers University Press.

Dawe, Bob (1997) Tiny arrowheads: Toys in the toolkit. *Plains Anthropology* 42(161):303–318.

Dawkins, Richard (1989) *The Selfish Gene*. New York, NY: Oxford University Press.

Day, Lynda R. (1998) Rites and reason: Precolonial education and its relevance to the current production and transmission of knowledge. In Marianne Bloch, Josephine A. Beoku–Betts, and B. Robert Tabachnick (Eds.), *Women and Education in Sub-Saharan Africa: Power, Opportunities, and Constraints*. pp. 49–72. Boulder, CO: Lynne Rienner.

de Berry, Joanna (2004) The sexual vulnerability of adolescent girls during civil war in Teso, Uganda. In Jo Boyden and Joanna de Berry (Eds.), *Children and Youth on the Front Line: Ethnography, Armed Conflict, and Displacement*. pp. 45–62. Oxford: Berghahn Books.

de Boeck, Filip (2005) The divine seed: Children, gift, and witchcraft in the Democratic Republic of Congo. In Alcinda Honwana and Filip de Boeck (Eds.), *Makers and Breakers: Children and Youth in Post-Colonial Africa*. pp. 188–214. Trenton, NJ: Africa World Press.

de Haan, Mariëtte (2001) Intersubjectivity in models of learning and teaching: Reflection from a study of teaching and learning in a Mexican Mazahua Community. In Seth Chaiklin (Ed.), *The Theory and Practice of Cultural-Historical Psychology*. pp. 174–199. Aarhus: Aarhus University Press.

de Laguna, Frederica (1965) Childhood among the Yakutat Tlingit. In Melford E. Spiro (Ed.), *Context and Meaning in Cultural Anthropology*. pp. 3–23. New York, NY: Free Press.

(1972) *Under Mount Saint Elias: The History and Culture of the Yakutat Tlingit*. Washington, DC: Smithsonian Institution Press.

de León, Lourdes (2000) The emergent participant: Interactive patterns in the socialization of Tzotzil (Mayan) infants. *Journal of Linguistic Anthropology* 8(2):131–161.

(2011) Language socialization and multiparty participation frameworks. In Alessandro Duranti, Elinor Ochs, and Bambi B. Schieffelin (Eds.), *The Handbook of Language Socialization*. pp. 81–111. Chichester: Wiley-Blackwell.

(2012) *Socializing attention: Directive sequences, participation, and affect in a Mayan family at work.* Unpublished MS, CIESAS. Mexico D.F., Mexico.

de Lucia, Kristin (2010) A child's house: Social memory, identity, and the construction of childhood in early postclassic Mexican households. *American Anthropologist* 112:607–24.

de Marrais, Katherine B., Nelson, Patricia A., and Baker, Jill H. (1992) Meaning in mud: Yup'ik Eskimo girls at play. *Anthropology and Education Quarterly* 23:120–145.

de Mause, Lloyd (1974) The evolution of childhood. In E. Lloyd de Mause (Ed.), *The History of Childhood*. pp. 1–73. New York, NY: Harper and Row.

de Oliveria, Marta K. (1995) The meaning of intellectual competence: Views from a Favela. In Jaan Valsiner (Ed.), *Child Development Within Culturally Structured Environments: Comparative-Cultural and Constructivist Perspectives.* pp. 245–270. Norwood, NJ: Ablex.

de Sahagun, Fray Bernardino (1829/1978) *General History of the Things of Spain*, 2nd edn. Arthur J. O. Anderson and Charles E. Dibble (Eds.). Santa Fe, NM: SAR Press.

de Suremain, Charles-Édouard (2000) Coffee beans and the seeds of labour: Child labour on Guatemalan plantations. In Bernard Schlemmer (Ed.), *The Exploited Child*. pp. 231–238. New York, NY: Zed Books.

(2007) Au fil de la faja: Enrouler et dérouler la vie en Bolivie. In Doris Bonnet and Laurence Pourchez (Eds.), *Du Soin au Rite dans L'Infance*. pp. 85–102. Paris: IRD.

de Suremain, Charles-Édouard, Lefevre, Pierre, Maire, Bernard, and Kolsteren Patrick (2001) Un buen cuerpo bien hecho: The perceptions of Bolivian mothers on health, growth and development. *The Oriental Anthropologist* 1(2):46–55.

de Vries, Marten W. (1987a) Alternatives to mother–infant attachment in the neonatal period. In Charles M. Super (Ed.), *The Role of Culture in Developmental Disorder*. pp. 109–130. New York, NY: Academic Press.

(1987b) Cry babies, culture, and catastrophe: Infant temperament among the Masai. In Nancy Scheper-Hughes (Ed.), *Child Survival: Anthropological Perspectives on the Treatment and Maltreatment of Children*. pp. 165–185. Dordrecht: Reidel.

de Waal, Frans (2001) *The Ape and the Sushi Master*. New York, NY: Basic Books.

Dean, Carolyn (2002) Sketches of childhood: Children in Colonial Andean art and society. In Tobias Hecht (Ed.), *Minor Omissions: Children in Latin American History and Society*. pp. 21–51. Madison, WI: University of Wisconsin Press.

Deka, Nalini (1993) India. In Leonore Loeb Adler (Ed.), *International Handbook on Gender Roles*. pp. 122–143. Westport, CT: Greenwood Press.

del Giudice, Marco and Belsky, Jay (2011) The development of life history strategies: Toward a multi-stage theory. In David M. Buss and Patricia H. Hawley (Eds.), *The Evolution of Personality and Individual Differences*. pp. 154–176. Oxford: Oxford University Press.

Delaney, Cassandra H. (1995) Rites of passage in adolescence. *Adolescence* 30:891–898.

Delgado-Gaitan, Concha (1994) Russian refugee families: Accommodating aspiration through education. *Anthropology and Education Quarterly* 25:137–155.

Demerath, Peter (1999) The cultural production of educational utility in Pere Village: Papua New Guinea. *Comparative Education Review* 43:162–192.

(2000) The social cost of acting "extra": Students' moral judgments of self, social relations, and academic success in Papua New Guinea. *American Journal of Education* 108:196–235.

Demerath, Peter, Lynch, Jill, and Davidson, Mario (2008) Dimensions of psychological capital in a U.S. suburb and high school: Identities for neoliberal times. *Anthropology and Education Quarterly* 39:270–292.

Demian, Melissa (2004) Transactions in right, transactions in children: A view of adoption from Papua New Guinea. In Fiona Bowie (Ed.), *Cross-Cultural Approaches to Adoption.* pp. 97–110. London: Routledge.

Demmert, William G., Jr. and Towner, John C. (2003) *A Review of the Research Literature on the Influence of Culturally Based Education on the Academic Performance of Native American Students.* Portland, OR: Northwest Regional Lab.

Demuth, Katherine (1986) Prompting routines in the language socialization of Basotho children. In Bambi B. Schiefflin and Elinor Ochs (Eds.), *Language Socialization across Cultures.* pp. 51–79. Cambridge: Cambridge University Press.

Deng, Francis M. (1972) *The Dinka of the Sudan.* Prospect Heights, IL: Waveland Press.

Denham, Aaron R. (2012) Shifting maternal responsibilities and the trajectory of blame in Northern Ghana. In Lauren Fordyce and Aminata Maraesa, (Eds.), *Risk Reproduction and Narratives of Experience.* pp. 173–190. Nashville, TN: Vanderbilt University Press.

Denham, Aaron R., Adongo, Philip B., Freydberg, Nicole, and Hodgson, Abraham (2010) Chasing spirits: Clarifying the spirit child phenomenon and infanticide in Northern Ghana. *Social Science and Medicine* 71:608-615.

Dentan, Robert K. (1978) Notes on childhood in a nonviolent context: The Semai case. In Ashley Montague (Ed.), *Learning Non-Aggression: The Experience of Non-Literate Societies.* pp. 94–143. Oxford: Oxford University Press.

Derby, C. Nana (2012) Are the barrels empty? Are the children any safer? Child domestic labor and servitude in Ghana. In Marisa O. Ensor (Ed.), *African Childhoods: Education, Development, Peacebuilding and the Youngest Continent.* pp. 19–32. New York, NY: Palgrave Macmillan.

Dettwyler, Katherine A. (1994) *Dancing Skeletons: Life and Death in West Africa.* Prospect Heights, IL: Waveland Press.

Devereux, George (1955) *A Story of Abortion in Primitive Societies.* New York, NY: Julian Press.

Devlieger, Patrick (1995) Why disabled? The cultural understanding of physical disability in an African Society. In Benedicte Ingstad and Susan Reynolds Whyte (Eds.), *Disability and Culture.* pp. 94–133. Berkeley, CA: University of California Press.

Deyhle, Donna (1986) Break dancing and breaking out: Anglos, Utes and Navajos in a border reservation high school. *Anthropology and Education Quarterly* 17: 111– 127.

(1991) Empowerment and cultural conflict: Navajo parents and the schooling of their children. *Qualitative Studies in Education* 4:277–297.

(1992) Constructing failure and maintaining cultural identity: Navajo and Ute school leavers. *Journal of American Indian Education* 31: 24–47.

Dickeman, Mildred (1975) Demographic consequences of infanticide in man. *Annual Review of Ecology and Systematics* 6:107–137.

(1979) Female infanticide, reproductive strategies, and social stratification: A preliminary model. In Napoleon A. Chagnon and William G. Irons (Eds.), *Evolutionary Biology and Human Social Behavior: An Anthropological Perspective*. pp. 321–367. North Scituate, MA: Duxbury Press.

Dickens, Charles (1836/1964) *The Pickwick Papers*. New York, NY: New American Library.

Dickson-Gómez, Julia (2003) Growing up in guerilla camps: The long-term impact of being a child soldier in El Salvador's civil war. *Ethos* 30:327–356.

Dilley, Roy M. (1989) Secrets and skills: Apprenticeship among Tukolor weavers. In Michael W. Coy (Ed.), *Apprenticeship: From Theory to Method and Back Again*. pp. 181–198. Albany, NY: State University of New York Press.

Dillon, Sam (1999) Smaller families to bring big change in Mexico. *New York Times*, June 8. Available at www.nytimes.com/1999/06/08/world/smaller-families-to-bring-big-change-in-mexico.html?pagewanted=all&src=pm. Accessed October 15, 2013.

Disma, Gérald, Sokolowski, Michel B. C., and Tonneau, François (2011) Children's competition in a natural setting: Evidence for the ideal free distribution. *Evolution and Human Behavior* 32:373–379.

Dolnick, Sam (2008) Birth is latest job to be outsourced in India. *ABCNews,com*, December 30. Available at www.today.com/id/22441355/ns/today-today_health/t/giving-birth-latest-job-outsourced-india/#.UlxY6SR4Mgo. Accessed October 14, 2013.

Donald, Merlin (1991) *Origins of the Modern Mind: Three Stages in the Evolution of Culture and Cognition*. Cambridge, MA: Harvard University Press.

Donohue, John J. (1994) *Warrior Dreams: The Martial Arts and the American Imagination*. Westport, CT: Bergin and Garvey.

Dorjahn, Vernon R. (1982) The initiation and training of Temne Poro members. In Simon Ottenberg (Ed.), *African Religious Groups and Beliefs*. pp. 35–62. Meerut: Archana.

dos Guimarães Sá, Isabel (2007) Up and out: Children in Portugal and the Empire (1500–1800). In Ondina E. Gonzáles and Bianca Premo (Eds.), *Raising an Empire: Children in Early Modern Iberia and Colonial Latin America*. pp. 17–40. Albuquerque, NM: University of New Mexico Press.

Draper, Patricia (1976) Social and economic constraints on child life among the !Kung. In Richard B. Lee and Irven DeVore (Eds.), *Kalahari Hunter-Gatherers: Studies of the !Kung San and their Neighbors*. pp. 199–217. Cambridge, MA: Harvard University Press.

(1978) The learning environment for aggression and anti-social behavior among the !Kung. In Ashley Montague (Ed.), *Learning Non-Aggression: The Experience of Non-Literate Societies*. pp. 31–53. Oxford: Oxford University Press.

Draper, Patricia and Cashdan, Elizabeth (1988) Technological change and child behavior among the !Kung. *Ethnology* 27:339–365.

Draper, Patricia and Harpending, Henry (1982) Father absence and reproductive strategy: An evolutionary perspective. *Journal of Anthropological Research* 38:255–273.

Droogers, André (1980) *The Dangerous Journey*. The Hague: Mouton.

Droz, Yvan (2006) Street children and the work ethic: New policy for an old moral, Nairobi (Kenya). *Childhood* 13:349–363.

Druckerman, Pamela (2012) *Bringing up Bébé*. New York, NY: Penguin.

Du Bois, Cora A. (1941) Attitudes toward food and hunger in Alor. In Leslie Spier, A. Irving Hallowell, and Stanley S. Newman (Eds.), *Language, Culture, and Personality*. Menasha, WI: Sapir Memorial Publication Fund.

  (1944) *The People of Alor: A Social-Psychological Study of an East Indian Island*. Minneapolis, MN: University of Minnesota Press.

Duffett, Ann and Johnson, Jean (2004) *All Work and No Play: Listening to What KIDS and PARENTS Really Want from Out-of-School Time*. Washington, DC: Public Agenda.

Dugatkin, Lee A. and Bekoff, Marc (2003) Play and the evolution of fairness: A game theory model. *Behavioural Processes* 60:209–214.

Dugstad, Sogrod A. (2010) Early child caught knapping: A novice Early Mesolithic flintknapper in south-west Norway. In *Proceedings from the 2nd International Conference of the Society for the Study of Childhood in the Past*. pp. 65–74. Stavanger: University of Stavanger.

Dunbar, Robin I. M. (1998) The social brain hypothesis. *Evolutionary Anthropology* 6:178–190.

Dunn, Patrick (1974) "That enemy is the baby": Childhood in imperial Russia. In Lloyd de Mause (Ed.), *The History of Childhood*. pp. 383–405. New York, NY: Harper and Row.

Dupire, Marguerite (1963) The position of women in pastoral society (the Fulani WoDaaBee, nomads of the Niger). In Denise Paulme (Ed.), *Women of Tropical Africa*. pp. 47–92. Berkeley, CA: University of California Press.

Durantini, Mary F. (1983) *The Child in Seventeenth-Century Dutch Painting*. Ann Arbor, MI: UMI Research Press.

Durham, Deborah (2008) Apathy and agency: The romance of agency and youth in Botswana. In Jennifer Cole and Deborah Durham (Eds.), *Figuring the Future: Globalism and the Temporalities of Children and Youth*. pp. 151–178. Santa Fe, NM: SAR Press.

Dybdahl, Ragnhild and Hundeide, Karsten (1998) Childhood in the Somali context: Mothers' and children's ideas about childhood and parenthood. *Psychology and Developing Societies* 10:131–145.

Dyer, Caroline and Choksi, Archana (2006) With God's grace and with education, we will find a way: Literacy, education, and the Rabaris of Kutch, India. In Caroline Dyer (Ed.), *The Education of Nomadic Peoples: Current Issues, Future Prospects*. pp. 159–174. Oxford: Berghahn Books.

Dyhouse, Carol (1978) Working-class mothers and infant mortality in England, 1895–1914. *Journal of Social History* 12:248–67.

Eberstadt, Mary (2004) *Home Alone America: The Hidden Toll of Daycare, Behavioral Drugs, and Other Parent Substitutes*. New York, NY: Penguin.

Eckholm, Erik (2009) Discipline of military redirects dropouts. *New York Times*, March 7. Available at www.nytimes.com/2009/03/08/us/08cadet.html?_r=0. Accessed April 4, 2013.

Edel, May M. (1957/1996) *The Chiga of Uganda*, 2nd edn. New Brunswick, NJ: Transaction Publishers.

Edgerton, Robert B. (1988) *Like Lions They Fought: The Zulu War and the Last Black Empire in South Africa*. New York, NY: Collier Macmillan.

(1992) *Sick Societies: Challenging the Myth of Primitive Harmony*. New York, NY: Free Press.

Edwards, Carolyn Pope (2005) Children's play in cross-cultural perspective: A new look at the Six Culture Study. In Felicia F. McMahon, Donald E. Lytle, and Brian Sutton Smith (Eds.), *Play: An Interdisciplinary Synthesis*. pp. 81–96. Lanham, MD: University Press of America.

Edwards, Carolyn Pope and Whiting, Beatrice B. (1980) Differential socialization of girls and boys in light of cross-cultural research. *New Directions for Child Development* 8:45–57.

Eggan, Dorothy (1956) Instruction and affect in Hopi cultural continuity. *Southwestern Journal of Anthropology* 12(4):347–370.

Eibl-Eibesfeldt, Irenäus (1983) Patterns of parent–child interaction in a cross-cultural perspective. In Alberto Oliverio (Ed.), *The Behavior of Human Infants*. pp. 177–217. New York, NY: Plenum Press.

(1989) *Human Ethology*. New York, NY: Aldine de Gruyter.

Eifermann, Rivka (1971) Social play in childhood. In Robert E. Herron and Brian Sutton-Smith (Eds.), *Child's Play*. pp. 270–297. New York, NY: Wiley.

Einarsdóttir, Jónína (2004) *Tired of Weeping: Mother Love, Child Death, and Poverty in Guinea-Bissau*. Madison, WI: University of Wisconsin Press.

(2008) The classification of newborn children: Consequences for survival. In Luke Clements and Janet Read (Eds.), *Disabled People and the Right to Life*. pp. 406–432. London: Routledge.

Eisenberg, Ann R. (1986) Teasing: Verbal play in two Mexicano homes. In Bambi B. Schieffelin and Elinor Ochs (Eds.), *Language Socialization across Cultures*. pp. 182–198. Cambridge: Cambridge University Press.

Eksner, H. Julia and Orellana, Marjorie F. (2012) Shifting in the zone: Latina/o child language brokers and the co-construction of knowledge. *Ethos* 40:196–220.

Elder, Glen (1969) Appearance and education in marriage mobility. *American Sociological Review* 34:519–533.

Ellis, Bruce J. (2013) Risky adolescent behavior: An evolutionary perspective. In Bonnie L. Hewlett (Ed.), *Adolescent Identity*. pp 40–72. New York, NY: Routledge.

Elmendorf, Mary L. (1976) *Nine Mayan Women: A Village Faces Change*. Cambridge, MA: Schenkman.

Elster, Arthur B. and Lamb, Michael E. (1986) Adolescent fathers: The under-studied side of adolescent pregnancy. In Jane B. Lancaster and Beatrix A.

Hamburg (Eds.), *School-Age Pregnancy and Parenthood: Biosocial Dimensions*. pp. 177–190. New York, NY: Aldine de Gruyter.

Elwin, Verrier (1947) *The Muria and their Ghotul*. Calcutta: Oxford University Press.

Ember, Carol R. (1973) Feminine task assignment and the social behavior of boys. *Ethos* 1:424–439.

(1983) The relative decline of women's contribution to agriculture with intensification. *American Anthropologist* 85:285–304.

Ember, Carol R. and Ember, Melvin (1994) War, socialization, and interpersonal violence: A cross-cultural study. *Journal of Conflict Resolution* 38:620–646.

(2005) Explaining corporal punishment of children: A cross-cultural study. *American Anthropologist* 107:609–619.

(2007) Effects of war and peace socialization: Comparing evolutionary models. Paper presented at the annual meeting of the Society for Cross-Cultural Research February 21–24, San Antonio, TX.

Emery, Patrizia B. (2010) De la nourrice à la dame de compagnie: Le cas de la trophos en Grèce antique. *Paedagogica Historica* 46:751–761.

Endicott, Karen L. (1992) Fathering in an egalitarian society. In Barry S. Hewlett (Ed.), *Father–Child Relations: Cultural and Biosocial Contexts*. pp. 291–295. New York, NY: Aldine.

Ensing, Anna (2011) Child labour in an urban setting: Markets and waste collection in Lima. In G. Kristoffel Lieten (Ed.), *Hazardous Child Labour in Latin America*. pp. 21–24. Heidelberg: Springer.

Erchak, Gerald M. (1977) *Full Respect: Kpelle Children in Adaptation*. New Haven, CT: Hraflex Books.

(1980) The acquisition of cultural rules by Kpelle children. *Ethos* 8:40–44.

(1992) *The Anthropology of Self and Behavior*. New Brunswick, NJ: Rutgers University Press.

Erkens, Jelmer W. and Lipo, Carl P. (2007) Cultural transmission theory and the archaeological record: Providing context to understanding variation and temporal changes in material culture. *Journal of Archaeological Research* 15:239–274.

Evans, Ruth M. C. (2004) Tanzanian childhoods: Street children's narratives of "home." *Journal of Contemporary African Studies* 22:69–92.

Evans-Pritchard, Edward E. (1932) Heredity and gestation, as the Azande see them. *Sociologus* 8:400–414.

(1956) *Nuer Religion*. Oxford: Clarendon Press.

Eveleth, Phyllis B. and Tanner, James M. (1990) *Worldwide Variation in Human Growth*. Cambridge: Cambridge University Press.

Everett, Daniel L. (2005) Cultural constraints on grammar and cognition in Pirahã: Another look at the design features of human language. *Current Anthropology* 46:621–646.

(2014) Concentric circles of attachment in Pirahã: A brief survey. In Hiltrud Otto and Heidi Keller (Eds.), *Different Faces of Attachment: Cultural Variations of a Universal Human Need*. pp. 169–186. Cambridge: Cambridge University Press.

Fagen, Robert (1981) *Animal Play Behavior*. New York, NY: Oxford University Press.

Fairbanks, Lynn A. (1990) Reciprocal benefits of allomothering for female vervet monkeys. *Animal Behaviour* 40:553–562.

(1995) Developmental timing of primate play. In Sue Taylor Parker, Jonas Langer, and Michael L. McKinney (Eds.), *Biology, Brains, and Behavior: The Evolution of Human Development*. pp. 131–158. Santa Fe, NM: SAR Press.

Fajans, Jane (1997) *They Make Themselves: Work and Play among the Baining of Papua New Guinea*. Chicago, IL: University of Chicago Press.

Falgout, Suzanne (1992) Hierarchy vs. democracy: Two management strategies for the management of knowledge in Pohnpei. *Anthropology and Education Quarterly* 23:30–43.

Faramarzi, Scheherazade (2005) Some in France ask: Where are the parents? Associated Press, November 12. Available at www.highbeam.com/doc/1P1-115146730.html. Accessed January 21, 2013.

Faron, Louis C. (1964) *Hawks of the Sun: Mapuche Morality and its Ritual Attributes*. Pittsburgh, PA: University of Pittsburgh Press.

Farrell, Allan P. (Trans., Ed.) (1970) *The Jesuit Ratio Studiorum of 1599*. Washington, DC: Conference of Major Superiors of Jesuits.

Farver, Jo Ann M. (1993) Cultural differences in scaffolding pretend play: A comparison of American and Mexican mother–child and sibling–child pairs. In Kevin MacDonald (Ed.), *Parent–Child Play: Descriptions and Implications*. pp. 349–366. Albany, NY: State University of New York Press.

Farver, Jo Ann M. and Howes, C. (1993) Cultural differences in American and Mexican mother–child pretend play. *Merrill-Palmer Quarterly* 39:344–358.

Fass, Paula (1997) *Kidnapped: Child Abduction in America*. New York, NY: Oxford University Press.

Fasulo, Alessandra, Loyd, Heather, and Padiglione, Vincenzo (2007) Children's socialization into cleaning practices: A cross-cultural perspective. *Discourse and Society* 18:11–33.

Faulkingham, Ralph H. (1970) Bases of legitimacy for social control in a Hausa village. Unpublished PhD dissertation, Michigan State University.

Fedigan, Linda M. and Zohar, Sandra (1997) Sex differences in mortality of Japanese macaques: Twenty-one years of data from Arashiyama West population. *American Journal of Physical Anthropology* 102:161–175.

Fehr, Ernst, Bernhard, Helen, and Rockenbach, Bettina (2008) Egalitarianism in young children. *Nature* 454:1079–1084.

Feifer, Gregory (2007) Russia's halt on adoptions spotlights conditions. *NPR Morning Edition*, April 25. Available at www.npr.org/templates/story/story.php?storyId=9810880. Accessed February 1, 2014.

Fermé, Mariane C. (2001) *The Underneath of Things: Violence, History, and the Everyday in Sierra Leone*. Berkeley, CA: University of California Press.

Fernald, Anne (1992) Human maternal vocalizations to infants as biologically relevant signals: An evolutionary perspective. In Jerome H. Barkow, Leda Cosmides, and John Tooby (Eds.), *The Adapted Mind: Evolutionary Psychology and the Generation of Culture*. pp. 391–428. New York, NY: Oxford University Press.

Fernea, Elizabeth (1991) Muslim Middle East. In Joseph M. Hawes and N. Ray Hiner (Eds.), *Children in Historical and Comparative Perspective*. pp. 447–470. Westport, CT: Greenwood Press.

Ferraro, Joanne M. (2008) *Nefarious Crimes, Contested Justice: Illicit Sex and Infanticide in the Republic of Venice, 1557–1789*. Baltimore, MD: Johns Hopkins University Press.

Field, Margaret J. (1970) *Search for Security: An Ethno-Psychiatric Study of Rural Ghana*. New York: W. W. Norton.

Field, Tiffany M., Shostak, A. Marjorie, Vietze, P., and Leiderman, Phillip H. (1981) *Culture and Early Interactions*. Hillsdale, NJ: Erlbaum.

Field, Tiffany M. and Widmayer, Susan M. (1981) Mother–infant interaction among lower SES black, Cuban, Puerto Rican and South American immigrants. In Tiffany M. Field, Anita M. Sostek, Peter Vietze, and P. Herbert Leiderman (Eds.), *Culture and Early Interactions*. pp. 41–62. Hillsdale, NJ: LEA.

Field, Tiffany M., Widmayer, Susan M., Adler, Sherilyn, and de Cubas, Mercedes (1992) Mother–infant interactions of Haitian immigrants and Black Americans living in Miami. In Jaipaul L. Roopnarine and D. Bruce Carter (Eds.), *Parent–Child Socialization in Diverse Cultures*. pp. 173–184. Norwood, NJ: Ablex.

Fiese, Barbara H., Foley, Kimberly P., and Spagnola, Mary (2006) Routine and ritual elements in family mealtimes: Contexts for child wellbeing and family identity. *New Directions for Child Development* 111:67–89.

Fine, Gary A. (1987) *With the Boys: Little League Baseball and Preadolescent Culture*. Chicago, IL: University of Chicago Press.

Finkel, Michael (2012) Tibet's golden "worm." *National Geographic* 222(2):114–129.

Finnan, Christine R. (1987) The influence of the ethnic community on the adjustment of Vietnamese refugees. In George Spindler and Louise Spindler (Eds.), *Interpretive Ethnography of Education: At Home and Abroad*. pp. 313–330. Hillsdale, NJ: Erlbaum.

Firestone, Shulamith (1971) *The Dialectic of Sex: The Case for Feminist Revolution*. London: Jonathan Cape.

Firth, Raymond (1970) Education in Tikopia. In John Middleton (Ed.), *From Child to Adult*. pp. 75–90. Garden City, NY: Natural History Press.

Fisher, Ann (1963) Reproduction in Truk. *Ethnology* 2:526–540.

Fisher, Edward P. (1992) The impact of play on development: A meta-analysis. *Play and Culture* 5:159–181.

Fitchen, Janet M. (1981) *Poverty in Rural America: A Case Study*. Boulder, CO: Westview Press.

Flinn, Juliana (1992) Transmitting traditional values in new schools: Elementary education of Pulap Atoll. *Anthropology and Education Quarterly* 23(1):44–58.

Flinn, Mark V. (1988) Parent–offspring interactions in a Caribbean village: Daughter guarding. In Laura Betzig, Monique Borgerhoff Mulder, and Paul Turke (Eds.), *Human Reproductive Behavior: A Darwinian Perspective*. pp. 189–200. Cambridge: Cambridge University Press.

  (1989) Household composition and female reproductive strategies. In Anne E. Rasa, Christian Vogel, and Eckart Voland (Eds.), *The Sociobiology of Sexual and Reproductive Strategies*. pp. 206–233. London: Chapman and Hall.

  (2005) Culture and developmental plasticity. In Robert L. Burgess and Kevin MacDonald (Eds.), *Evolutionary Perspectives on Human Development*, 2nd edn, pp. 73–98. Thousand Oaks, CA: Sage.

Flinn, Mark V. and England, Barry G. (1995) Childhood stress and family environment. *Current Anthropology* 36(5):854–866.

(2002) Childhood stress: Endocrine and immune responses to psychosocial events. In James M. Wilce (Ed.), *Social and Cultural Lives of Immune Systems*. pp. 107–147. London: Routledge.

Flinn, Mark V. and Ward, Carol V. (2005) Ontogeny and evolution of the social child. In Bruce J. Ellis and David F. Bjorklund (Eds.), *Origins of the Social Mind: Evolutionary Psychology and Child Development*. pp. 19–65. New York, NY: Guilford Press.

Fogel, Allen, Barratt, Marguerite Stevenson, and Messinger, Daniel (1992) A comparison of the parent–child relationship in Japan and the United States. In Jaipaul L. Roopnarine and D. Bruce Carter (Eds.), *Parent–Child Socialization in Diverse Cultures*. pp. 35–51. Norwood, NJ: Ablex.

Fonseca, Isabel (1995) *Bury Me Standing: The Gypsies and Their Journey*. New York, NY: Vintage Books.

Ford, Clellan S. (1964) *A Comparative Study of Human Reproduction*. New Haven, CT: Yale University Publications in Anthropology, Human Relations Area Files Press.

Fordham, Signithia (1999) "Dissin' the standard": Ebonics as guerilla warfare at Capital High. *Anthropology and Education Quarterly* 30:272–293.

Fordham, Signithia and Ogbu, John U. (1986) Black students' school success: Coping with the burden of "acting white." *The Urban Review* 18:176–206.

Formanek-Brunell, Miriam (1992) Sugar and spite: The politics of doll play in nineteenth-century America. In Elliott West and Paula Petrik (Eds.), *Small Worlds: Children and Adolescents in America, 1850–1950*. pp. 107–124. Lawrence, KS: University Press of Kansas.

Fortes, Meyer (1938/1970) Social and psychological aspects of education in Taleland. In John Middleton (Ed.), *From Child to Adult: Studies in the Anthropology of Education*. pp. 14–74. Garden City, NY: Natural History Press.

(1950) Kinship and marriage among the Ashanti. In A. R. Radcliffe-Brown and Daryll Forde (Eds.), *African Systems of Kinship and Marriage*. pp. 252–284. Oxford: Oxford University Press.

Fosburg, Steven (1982) Family day care: The role of surrogate mother. In Luis M. Laosa and Irving E. Sigel (Eds.), *Families as Learning Environments for Children*. pp. 223–260. New York, NY: Plenum Press.

Fouts, Hillary N. (2004a) Social contexts of weaning: The importance of cross-cultural studies. In Uwe P. Gielen and Jaipaul L. Roopnarine (Eds.), *Childhood and Adolescence: Cross-Cultural Perspectives and Applications*. pp. 133–148. Westport, CT: Praeger.

(2004b) Social and emotional contexts of weaning among Bofi farmers and foragers. *Ethnology* 43:65–81.

(2005) Families in Central Africa: A comparison of Bofi farmer and forager families. In Jaipaul L. Roopnarine and Uwe P. Gielen (Eds.), *Families in Global Perspective*. pp. 347–363. Boston, MA: Allyn and Bacon.

(2008) Father involvement with young children among the Aka and Bofi foragers. *Cross-Cultural Research* (42):290–312.

Fouts, Hillary N. and Brookshire, Robyn A. (2009) Who feeds children? A child's-eye-view of caregiver feeding patterns among the Aka Foragers in Congo. *Social Science & Medicine* 69:285–292.

Fouts, Hillary N., Hallam, Rena A., and Purandare, Swapna (2013) Gender segregation in early-childhood social play among the Bofi foragers and Bofi farmers in Central Africa. *American Journal of Play* 5:333–356.

Fouts, Hillary N., Hewlett, Barry S., and Lamb, Michael E. (2001) Weaning and the nature of early childhood interactions among Bofi foragers in Central Africa. *Human Nature* 12:27–46.

Fouts, Hillary N. and Lamb, Michael E. (2009) Cultural and developmental variation in toddlers' interactions with other children in two small-scale societies in Central Africa. *European Journal of Developmental Science* 4: 259–277.

Fox, Robin (1972) Alliance and constraint: Sexual selection in the evolution of human kinship systems. In Bernard Campbell, (Ed.) *Sexual Selection and the Descent of Man*. pp. 283–331. Chicago, IL: Aldine.

Franco, Patricia, Seret, Nicole, Van Hees, Jean-Noël, Scaillet, Sonia, Groswasser, José, and Kahn, André (2005) Influence of swaddling on sleep and arousal characteristics of healthy infants. *Pediatrics* 115:1307–1311.

Frankland, Stan (2007) No money, no life: Surviving on the streets of Kampala. In James Staples (Ed.), *Livelihoods at the Margins: Surviving the City*. pp. 31–51. Walnut Creek, CA: Left Coast Press.

Freely, John (1996) *Istanbul: The Imperial City*. London: Penguin.

Freeman, Derek (1970) *Report on the Iban (Sarawak)*. Atlantic Highlands, NJ: Humanities Press.

  (1983) *Margaret Mead and Samoa: The Making and Unmaking of an Anthropological Myth*. Cambridge, MA: Harvard University Press.

Freeman, Milton M. R. (1971) A social and ecologic analysis of systematic female infanticide among the Netsilik Eskimo. *American Anthropologist* 73:1011–1018.

Freie, Carrie (1999) Rules in children's games and play. In Stuart Reifel (Ed.), *Play Contexts Revisited*. pp. 83–100. Stamford, CT: Ablex.

French, Valerie (1991) Children in antiquity. In Joseph M. Hawes and N. Ray Hiner (Eds.), *Children in Historical and Comparative Perspective*. pp. 13–29. Westport, CT: Greenwood Press.

Fricke, Tom (1994) *Himalayan Households: Tamang Demography and Domestic Process*. New York, NY: Columbia University Press.

Friedl, Erika (1997) *Children of Deh Koh: Young Life in an Iranian Village*. Syracuse, NY: Syracuse University Press.

Friedl, Ernestine (1992) Moonrose watched through a sunny day. *Natural History* 101(8):34–44.

Froerer, Peggy (2012) Learning, livelihoods, and social mobility: Valuing girls' education in central India. *Anthropology and Education Quarterly* 43:344–357.

Frost, Joe L. (2010) *A History of Children's Play and Play Environments: Toward a Contemporary Child-Saving Movement*. New York, NY: Routledge.

Fry, Douglas P. (1987) Differences between playfighting and serious fights among Zapotec children. *Ethology and Sociobiology* 8:285–306.

(2005) Rough-and-tumble social play in humans. In Anthony D. Pellegrini and Peter K. Smith (Eds.), *The Nature of Play: Great Apes and Humans*. pp. 54–85. New York, NY: Guilford Press.

Fry, Richard (2013) A rising share of young adults live in their parents' home. *Pew Research Social and Demographic Trends*. Washington, DC: Pew Research Center. Available at www.pewsocialtrends.org/2013/08/01/a-rising-share-of-young-adults-live-in-their-parents-home/ Accessed September 14, 2013.

Fujimura, Clementine K. (2003) Adult stigmatization and the hidden power of homeless children in Russia. *Children, Youth, and Environments* (online journal) 14(1). Available at www.colorado.edu/journals/cye. Accessed September 14, 2013.

(2005) *Russia's Abandoned Children: An Intimate Understanding*. Westport, CT: Praeger.

Fung, Heidi (1999) Becoming a moral child: The socialization of shame among young Chinese children. *Ethos* 27:180–209.

Gallimore, Ronald, Howard, Alan, and Jordan, Cathie (1969) Independence training among Hawaiians: A cross-cultural study. In Henry Clay Lindgren (Ed.), *Contemporary Research in Social Psychology*. pp. 392–397. New York, NY: Wiley.

Gamlin, Jennie B. (2011) "My eyes are red from looking and looking": Mexican working children's perspectives of how tobacco labour affects their bodies. *Vulnerable Children and Youth Studies* 6(4):339–345.

Gardner, Robert and Heider, Karl G. (1969) *Gardens of War: Life and Death in the New Guinea Stone Age*. New York, NY: Random House.

Garrels, Anne (2008) Russian attitudes colder toward foreign adoptions. *NPR Morning Edition*, December 17. Available at www.npr.org/templates/story/story.php?storyId=98360183. Accessed January 14, 2013.

Gaskins, Suzanne (2006) Cultural perspectives on infant–caregiver interaction. In Nicholas J. Enfield and Steven C. Levinson (Eds.), *The Roots of Human Sociality: Culture, Cognition, and Human Interaction*. pp. 279–298. Oxford: Berg.

Gaskins, Suzanne and Göncü, Artin (1992) Cultural variation in play: A challenge to Piaget and Vygotsky. *Quarterly Newsletter of the Laboratory of Comparative Human Cognition* 14:31–41.

Gaskins, Suzanne, Haight, Wendy, and Lancy, David F. (2007) The cultural construction of play. In Artin Göncü and Suzanne Gaskins (Eds.), *Play and Development: Evolutionary, Sociocultural, and Functional Perspectives*. pp. 179–202. Mahwah, NJ: Erlbaum.

Gaskins, Suzanne and Miller, Peggy J. (2009) The cultural roles of emotions in pretend play. In Cindy D. Clark (Ed.), *Transactions at Play*. pp. 5–21. Lanham, MD: University Press of America.

Gaskins, Suzanne and Paradise, Ruth (2010). Learning through observation in daily life. In David F. Lancy, Suzanne Gaskins, and John Bock (Eds.), *The Anthropology of Learning in Childhood*. pp. 85–117. Lanham, MD: AltaMira Press.

Gauvain, Mary (2001) *The Social Context of Cognitive Development*. New York, NY: Guilford Press.

Gavitt, Phillip (1990) *Charity and Children in Renaissance Florence: The Ospedale degli Innocenti, 1410–1536.* Ann Arbor, MI: University of Michigan Press.

Gay, John (2014) *Africa: A Dream Denied.* Porter Ranch, CA: New World African Press.

Gay, John and Cole, Michael (1967) *The New Mathematics and an Old Culture: A Study of Learning among the Kpelle.* New York, NY: Holt, Rinehart, and Winston.

Geary, David C. (1998) *Male, Female: The Evolution of Human Sex Differences.* Washington, DC: American Psychological Association.

Geertz, Hildred (1961) *The Javanese Family: A Study of Kinship and Socialization.* New York, NY: Free Press.

Gegeo, David W. and Watson-Gegeo, Karen A. (1985) Kwara'ae mothers and infants: Changing family practices in health, work, and childrearing. In Leslie B. Marshall (Ed.), *Infant Care and Feeding in the South Pacific.* pp. 235–253. New York, NY: Gordon and Breach.

Geisler, Charles and Roshani, Niousha (2006) The role of young IDPs as child soldiers, *Columbia Journal Online*, July 17. Available at http://colombiajournal.org/category/armed-conflict/page/8. Accessed July 8, 2013.

Gelles, Richard J. (1986) School-age parents and child abuse. In Jane B. Lancaster and Beatrix A. Hamburg (Eds.), *School-Age Pregnancy and Parenthood: Biosocial Dimensions.* pp. 347–359. New York, NY: Aldine de Gruyter.

Gergely, György, Egyed, Katalin, and Király, Ildikó (2007) On pedagogy. *Developmental Science* 10:139–146.

Geronimus, Arline T. (1992) The weathering hypothesis and the health of African-American women and infants: Evidence and speculations. *Ethnicity and Disease* 2:207–221.

(1996) What teen mothers know. *Human Nature* 7:323–352.

Ghosh, Amitav (1992) *An Antique Land.* London: Granta Books.

Gibbons, Judith L. (2004) Adolescents in the developing world. In Uwe P. Gielen and Jaipaul L. Roopnarine (Eds.), *Childhood and Adolescence: Cross-Cultural Perspectives and Applications.* pp. 255–276. Westport, CT: Praeger.

Gibbs, Nancy (2005) Parents behaving badly. *Time Magazine* 165(8):40–49.

Gibson, Margaret A. (1987) Punjabi immigrants in an American high school. In George Spindler and Louise Spindler (Eds.), *Interpretive Ethnography of Education: At Home and Abroad.* pp. 281–310. Hillsdale, NJ: Erlbaum.

(1988) *Accommodation without Assimilation: Sikh Immigrants in an American High School.* Ithaca, NY: Cornell University Press.

Gibson, Mhairi A. and Mace, Ruth (2005) Helpful grandmothers in rural Ethiopia: A study of the effect of kin on child survival and growth. *Evolution and Human Behavior* 26:469–482.

Gielen, Uwe P. (1993) Traditional Tibetan societies. In Leonore Loeb Adler (Ed.), *International Handbook on Gender Roles.* pp. 413–437. Westport, CT: Greenwood Press.

Gielen, Uwe P. and Chumachenko, Oksana (2004) All the world's children: The impact of global demographic trends and economic disparities. In Uwe P. Gielen and Jaipaul L. Roopnarine (Eds.), *Childhood and Adolescence: Cross-Cultural Perspectives and Applications.* pp. 81–109. Westport, CT: Praeger.

Gies, Frances and Gies, Joseph (1987) *Marriage and the Family in the Middle Ages.* New York, NY: Harper and Row.

Gilliam, Laura (2008) Calm children, wild children: Exploring the relation between civilizing projects and children's school identities. Paper presented at the annual meeting of the American Anthropological Association, November, San Francisco, CA.

Gillis, John R. (2003) The birth of the virtual child: A Victorian progeny. In Willem Koops and Michael Zuckerman (Eds.), *Beyond the Century of the Child: Cultural History and Developmental Psychology.* pp. 82–95. Philadelphia, PA: University of Pennsylvania Press.

Gilmore, David D. (2001) The manhood puzzle. In Caroline B. Brettell and Carolyn F. Sargen (Eds.), *Gender in Cross-Cultural Perspective.* pp. 207–220. Upper Saddle River, NJ: Prentice Hall.

Giroux, Henry A. (1998) Stealing innocence: The politics of child beauty pageants. In Henry Jenkins (Eds.), *The Children's Culture Reader.* pp. 265–282. New York, NY: New York University Press.

Gladwin, Thomas (1970) *East is a Big Bird: Navigation and Logic on Puluwat Atoll.* Cambridge, MA: Harvard University Press.

Gladwin, Thomas and Sarason, Seymour B. (1953) *Truk: Man in Paradise.* New York, NY: Wenner-Gren Foundation.

Glassner, Barry (1999) *The Culture of Fear.* New York, NY: Basic Books.

Gleason, Judith and Ibubuya, Allison (1991) My year reached, we heard ourselves singing: Dawn songs of girls becoming women in Ogbogbo, Okirka, Rivers State, Nigeria. *Research in African Literature* 2:135–147.

Goddard, Victoria (1985) Child labour in Naples: The case of outwork. *Anthropology Today* 1(5):18–21.

Golden, Mark (1990) *Children and Childhood in Classical Athens.* Baltimore, MD: Johns Hopkins University Press.

(2003) Childhood in ancient Greece. In Jennifer Neils and John H. Oakley (Eds.), *Coming of Age in Ancient Greece.* pp. 13–29. New Haven, CT: Yale University Press.

Goldman, Laurence R. (1998) *Child's Play: Myth, Mimesis and Make-Believe.* Oxford: Berg.

Goldschmidt, Walter (1976) *Culture and Behavior of the Sebei.* Berkeley, CA: University of California Press.

(1986) *The Sebei: A Study in Adaptation.* New York, NY: Holt, Rinehart, and Winston.

Goldstein, Donna M. (1998) Nothing bad intended: Child discipline, punishment, and survival in Shantytown in Rio de Janeiro, Brazil. In Nancy Scheper-Hughes and Carolyn F. Sargent (Eds.), *Small Wars: The Cultural Politics of Childhood.* pp. 389–415. Berkeley, CA: University of California Press.

Goldstein, Jeffrey (1998) Why we watch. In Jeffery Goldstein (Ed.), *Why We Watch: The Attractions of Violent Entertainment.* pp. 212–226. New York, NY: Oxford University Press.

Goldstein, Joshua R. (2011) A secular trend toward earlier male sexual maturity: Evidence from shifting ages of male young adult mortality. *PLoS One* 6(8):14826.

Goldstein-Gidoni, Ofra (1999) Kimono and the construction of gendered and cultural identities. *Ethnology* 38:351–370.

Göncü, Artin, Mistry, Jayanthi, and Mosier, Christine (2000) Cultural variations in the play of toddlers. *International Journal of Behavioral Development* 24:321–329.

Goodale, Jane C. (1980) Gender, sexuality, and marriage: A Kaulong model of nature and culture. In Carol P. MacCormack (Ed.), *Nature, Culture and Gender*. pp. 119–143. Cambridge: Cambridge University Press.

Goodich, Michael E. (1989) *From Birth to Old Age: The Human Life Cycle in Medieval Thought, 1250–1350*. Lanham, MD: University Press of America.

Goodkind, Daniel (1996) On substituting sex preference strategies in East Asia: Does prenatal sex selection reduce postnatal discrimination? *Population and Development Review* 22:111–125.

Goodnow, Jacqueline J. (1976) The nature of intelligent behavior: Questions raised by cross-cultural studies. In Lauren B. Resnick (Ed.), *The Nature of Intelligence*. pp. 169–188. Hillsdale, NJ: Erlbaum.

　(1990) The socialization of cognition. In James W. Stigler, Richard A. Shweder, and Gilbert H. Herdt (Eds.), *Cultural Psychology*. pp. 259–286. Cambridge: Cambridge University Press.

　(1996) From household practices to parents' ideas about work and interpersonal relationships. In Sara Harkness and Charles M. Super (Eds.), *Parents' Cultural Belief Systems: Their Origins, Expressions, and Consequences*. pp. 313–344. New York, NY: Guilford Press.

Goodwin, Bryan (2012) Research says: New teachers face three common challenges. *Educational Leadership* 69(8):84–85.

Goodwin, Grenville and Goodwin, Janice T. (1942) *The Social Organization of the Western Apache*. Chicago, IL: University of Chicago Press.

Goodwin, Marjorie H. (1998) Games of stance: Conflict and footing in hopscotch. In Susan M. Hoyle and Carolyn T. Adger (Eds.), *Kids Talk: Strategic Language Use in Later Childhood*. pp. 23–46. New York, NY: Oxford University Press.

　(2006) *The Hidden Life of Girls: Games of Stance, Status, and Exclusion*. Oxford: Blackwell.

Goody, Esther N. (1982a) Daboya weavers: Relations of production, dependence and reciprocity. In Esther N. Goody (Ed.), *From Craft to Industry: The Ethnography of Proto-Industrial Cloth Production*. pp. 50–84. Cambridge: Cambridge University Press.

　(1982b) *Parenthood and Social Reproduction*. Cambridge: Cambridge University Press.

　(1992) From play to work: Adults and peers as scaffolders of adult role skills in northern Ghana. Paper presented at the 91st annual meeting of the American Anthropological Association, December, San Francisco, CA.

　(2006) Dynamics of the emergence of sociocultural institutional practices. In David R. Olson and Michael Cole (Eds.), *Technology, Literacy, and the Evolution of Society*. pp. 241–264. Mahwah, NJ: Erlbaum.

Goody, Jack (1977) *The Domestication of the Savage Mind*. Cambridge: Cambridge University Press.

Gopnik, Alison, Meltzoff, Andrew N., and Kuhl, Patricia K. (2000) *The Scientist in the Crib: What Early Learning Tells Us About the Mind*. New York, NY: Harper.

Gorer, Geoffrey (1967) *Himalayan Village: An Account of the Lepchas of Sikkim*. New York, NY: Basic Books.

Gorshkov, Boris B. (2009) *Russia's Factory Children: State, Society, and Law, 1800–1917*. Pittsburgh, PA: University of Pittsburgh Press.

Gosselain, Olivier P. (2008) Mother Bella was not a Bella: Inherited and transformed traditions in Southwestern Niger. In Miriam T. Start, Brenda J. Bowser, and Lee Horne (Eds.), *Cultural Transmission and Material Culture: Breaking Down Boundaries*. pp. 150–177. Tucson, AZ: University of Arizona Press.

Gosso, Yumi, Morais, Maria, and Otta, Emma (2007) Pretend play of Brazilian children: A window into different cultural worlds. *Journal of Cross-Cultural Psychology* 38:539–558.

Gosso, Yumi, Otta, Emma, De Lima Salum e Morais, Maria, Ribeiro, Fernando José Leite, and Raad Bussab, Vera Silvaia (2005.) Play in hunter-gatherer society. In Anthony D. Pellegrini and Peter K. Smith (Eds.), *The Nature of Play: Great Apes and Humans*. pp. 213–253. New York, NY: Guilford Press.

Goto, Stanford T. (1997) Nerds, normal people and homeboys: Accommodation and resistance among Chinese-American students. *Anthropology and Education Quarterly* 28:70–84.

Gottfredson, Linda S. (2004) Schools and the *g* factor. *The Wilson Quarterly* 28 (3):35–45.

Gottlieb, Alma (1992) *Under the Kapok Tree: Identity and Difference in Beng Thought*. Bloomington, IN: Indiana University Press.

(1995) Of cowries and crying: A Beng guide to managing colic. *Anthropology and Humanism* 20:20–28.

(2000) Luring your child into this life: A Beng path for infant care. In Judy DeLoache and Alma Gottlieb (Eds.), *A World of Babies: Imagined Childcare Guides for Seven Societies*. pp. 55–90. Cambridge: Cambridge University Press.

Gowlland, Geoffrey (2012) Learning craft skills in China: Apprenticeship and social capital in an artisan community of practice. *Anthropology and Education Quarterly* 43:358–371.

Graff, Harvey J. (2010) The literacy myth: Literacy, education and demography. *Vienna Yearbook of Population Research* 8:17–23.

Grammer, Karl, Kruck, Kirsten, Juette, Astrid, and Fink, Bernhard (2000) Non-verbal behavior as courtship signals: The role of control and choice in selecting partners. *Evolution and Human Behavior* 21:371–390.

Gray, Brenda M. (1994) Enga birth, maturation and survival: Physiological characteristics of the life cycle in the New Guinea Highlands. In Carol P. MacCormack (Ed.), *Ethnography of Fertility and Birth*. pp. 65–103. Prospect Heights, IL: Waveland Press.

Gray, Peter B. and Anderson, Kermyt G. (2010) *Fatherhood*. Cambridge, MA: Harvard University Press.

Gray, Peter O. (2009) Play as a foundation for hunter-gatherer social existence. *American Journal of Play* 1:476–522.

(2013) *Freedom to Learn*. New York, NY: Basic Books.

Green, Edward C., Jurg, Annemarie, and Djedje, Armando (1994) The snake in the stomach: Child diarrhea in Central Mozambique. *Medical Anthropology Quarterly* 8:4–24.

Green, Miranda A. (1999) Human sacrifice in Iron Age Europe. *Discovering Archeology* 1(2):56–80.

Greenfield, Patricia M. (1966) On culture and conservation. In Jerome S. Bruner, Rose R. Olver, and Patricia M. Greenfield (Eds.), *Studies in Cognitive Growth.* pp. 225–256. New York, NY. Wiley.

  (2004) *Weaving Generations Together: Evolving Creativity in the Maya of Chiapas.* Santa Fe, NM: SAR Press.

Greenfield, Patricia M., Brazelton, T. Barry, and Childs, Carla P. (1989) From birth to maturity in Zinacantan: Ontogenesis in cultural context. In Victoria Bricker and Gary Gosen (Eds.), *Ethnographic Encounters in Southern Mesoamerica: Celebratory Essays in Honor of Evon Z. Vogt.* pp. 177–216. Albany, NY: State University of New York Press.

Greenfield, Patricia M. and Cocking, Rodney R. (Eds.) (1994) *Cross-Cultural Roots of Minority Child Development.* Hillsdale, NJ: Erlbaum.

Greenfield, Patricia M. and Lave, Jean (1982) Cognitive aspects of informal education. In Dan A. Wagner and Harold W. Stevenson (Eds.), *Cultural Perspectives on Child Development.* pp.181–207. San Francisco, CA: W. H. Freeman.

Greenfield, Patricia M., Maynard, Ashley E., Boehm, Christopher, and Schmidtling, Emily Yut (1995) Cultural apprenticeship and cultural change. In Sue Taylor Parker, Jonas Langer, and Michael L. McKinney (Eds.), *Biology, Brains, and Behavior: The Evolution of Human Development.* pp. 237–277. Santa Fe, NM: SAR Press.

Greenfield, Patricia M., Yut, Emily, Chung, Mabel, Land, Deborah, Kreider, Holly, Pantoja, Maurice, and Horsley, Kris (1990) The program-length commercial: A study of the effects of television toy tie-ins on imaginative play. *Psychology and Marketing* 7(4):237–255.

Gregor, Thomas (1970) Exposure and seclusion: A study of institutionalized isolation among the Mehinacu Indians of Brazil. *Ethnology* 9:234–250.

  (1988) *Mehinacu: The Drama of Daily Life in a Brazilian Indian Village.* Chicago, IL: University of Chicago Press.

  (1990) Male dominance and sexual coercion. In James. W. Stigler, Richard A. Shweder, and Gilbert H. Herdt (Eds.), *Cultural Psychology.* pp. 477–495. Cambridge: Cambridge University Press.

Grendler, Paul R. (1989) *Schooling in Renaissance Italy.* Baltimore, MD: Johns Hopkins University Press.

Grier, Beverly C. (2006) *Invisible Hands: Child Labor and the State in Colonial Zimbabwe.* Portsmouth, NH: Heinemann.

Griffin, P. Bion, and Griffin, Marcus B. (1992) Fathers and childcare among the Cagayan Agta. In Barry S. Hewlett (Ed.), *Father–Child Relations: Cultural and Biosocial Contexts.* pp. 297–320. Hawthorne, NY: Aldine de Gruyter.

Grindal, Bruce T. (1972) *Growing up in Two Worlds: Education and Transition among the Sisala of Northern Ghana.* New York, NY: Holt, Rinehart, and Winston.

Grinnel, George B. (1923) *The Cheyenne Indians: Their History and Ways of Life,* 2 vols. New Haven, CT: Yale University Press.

Groos, Karl (1898/1976) *The Play of Animals*. Translated by E. L. Baldwin. New York, NY: Appleton.

Gross-Loh, Christine (2013) *Parenting without Borders*. New York, NY: Avery.

Grove, M. Annette (2009) "All the world's a stage": Parental ethnotheories and children's extracurricular activities. Unpublished MS thesis, Department of Family, Consumer and Human Development, Utah State University.

Grove, M. Annette and Lancy, David F. (in press) Cultural views of life phases. In James D. Wright (Ed.), *International Encyclopedia of Social and Behavioral Sciences*, 2nd edn. Oxford: Elsevier.

Guemple, D. Lee (1969) The Eskimo ritual sponsor: A problem in the fusion of semantic domains. *Ethnology* 8:468–483.

(1979) Inuit socialization: A study of children as social actors in an Eskimo community. In Ishwaran Karigoudar (Ed.), *Childhood and Adolescence in Canada*. pp. 39–71. Toronto: McGraw-Hill Ryerson.

Guillaumin, Emile (1983) *The Life of a Simple Man*. Translated by Margaret Crosland. Hanover, NH: University Press of New England.

Gurven, Michael, Kaplan, Hillard, and Gutierrez, Maguin (2006) How long does it take to become a proficient hunter? Implications for the evolution of extended development and long life span. *Journal of Human Evolution* 51:454–470.

Gurven, Michael and Walker, Robert (2006) Energetic demand of multiple dependents and the evolution of slow human growth. *Proceedings of the Royal Society* 273:835–841.

Gusinde, Martin (1937) *The Yahgan: The Life and Thought of the Water Nomads of Cape Horn*. Mödling bei Wien: Anthropos-Bibliothek.

Guss, David M. (1982) The enculturation of Makiritare women. *Ethnology* 21:259–269.

Guttmann, Allen (2010) The Progressive Era appropriation of children's play. *Journal of the History of Childhood and Youth* 3:147–151.

Guy, Donna J. (2002) The state, the family, and marginal children in Latin America. In Tobias Hecht (Ed.), *Minor Omissions*. pp. 139–164. Madison, WI: University of Wisconsin Press.

Haffter, Carl (1986) The changeling: History and psychodynamics of attitudes to handicapped children in European folklore. *Journal of the History of Behavioral Sciences* 4:55–61.

Hagen, Edward H. (1999) The functions of post-partum depression. *Evolution and Human Behavior* 20:325–359.

Hagstrum, Melissa B. (1999) The goal of domestic autonomy among the Highland Peruvian farmer-potters: Home economics of rural craft specialists. In Barry L. Isaac (Ed.), *Research in Economic Anthropology*. Vol. 20. pp. 265–298. Stamford, CT: JAI Press.

Haight, Wendy, Wang, Xiao-lei, Fung, Heidi Han-tih, Williams, Kimberley, and Mintz, Judith (1999) Universal, developmental, and variable aspects of young children's play: A cross-cultural comparison of pretending at home. *Child Development* 70(6):1477–1488.

Halioua, Bruno and Ziskind, Bernard (2005) *Medicine in the Days of the Pharaohs*. Cambridge, MA: Harvard University Press.

Hall, Granville S. (1904) *Adolescence: Its Psychology and its Relations to Physiology, Anthropology, Sociology, Sex, Crime, Religion, and Education.*New York, NY: Appleton.

Hames, Raymond (1992) Time allocation. In Eric A. Smith and Bruce Winterhalder (Eds.), *Evolutionary Ecology and Human Behavior.* pp. 203–235. Hawthorne, NY: Aldine de Gruyter.

Hames, Raymond and Draper, Patricia (2004) Women's work, childcare, and helpers-at-the-nest in a hunter-gatherer society. *Human Nature* 15:319–334.

Hampshire, Kate (2001) The impact of male migration on fertility decisions and outcomes in northern Burkina Faso. In Soraya Tremayne (Ed.), *Managing Reproductive Life: Cross-Cultural Themes in Sexuality and Fertility.* pp. 107–125. Oxford: Berghahn Books.

Han, Sallie (2009) Imagining babies through belly talk. *Anthropology News* 50(2):13.

Hanawalt, Barbara A. (1986) *The Ties that Bound.* Oxford: Oxford University Press.
  (2003) The child in the Middle Ages and the Renaissance. In Willem Koops and Michael Zuckerman (Eds.), *Beyond the Century of the Child: Cultural History and Developmental Psychology.* pp. 21–42. Philadelphia, PA: University of Pennsylvania Press.

Harden, Blaine and Hedgpeth, Dana (2005) Minnesota killer chafed at life on reservation: Teen faced cultural obstacles and troubled family history. *Washington Post*, March 24. Available at www.washingtonpost.com/wp-dyn/articles/A64315-2005Mar24.html. Accessed October 4, 2013.

Hardenberg, Roland (2006) Hut of the young girls: Transition from childhood to adolescence in a middle Indian tribal society. In Deepak K. Behera (Ed.), *Childhoods in South Asia.* pp. 65–81. Singapore: Pearson Education.

Hardman, Charlotte (1980) Can there be an anthropology of children? *Journal of the Anthropological Society of Oxford* 4:85–89.

Harkness, Sara and Super, Charles M. (1985) The cultural context of gender segregation in children's peer groups. *Child Development* 56:219–224.
  (1986) The cultural structuring of children's play in a rural African community. In Kendall Blanchard (Ed.), *The Many Faces of Play.* pp. 96–103. Champaign, IL: Human Kinetics.
  (1991) East Africa. In Joseph M. Hawes and N. Ray Hiner (Eds.), *Children in Historical and Comparative Perspective.* pp. 217–239. Westport, CT: Greenwood Press.
  (2006) Themes and variations: Parental ethnotheories in Western cultures. In Kenneth H. Rubin and Ock Boon Chung (Eds.), *Parenting Beliefs, Behaviors, and Parent–Child Relations: A Cross-Cultural Perspective.* pp. 61–79. New York, NY: Psychology Press.

Harkness, Sara, Super, Charles M., and Keefer, Constance H. (1992) Learning to be an American parent: How cultural models gain directive force. In Roy D'Andrade and Claudia Strauss (Eds.), *Human Motives and Cultural Models.* pp. 163–178. Cambridge: Cambridge University Press.

Harkness, Sara, Super, Charles M., Parmar, Parmindar, Hidalgo, Victoria, and Welles-Nystrom, Barbara (2006) The isolated nuclear family – how isolated? How nuclear? A study in seven Western cultures. Paper presented at the 35th annual meeting of the Society for Cross-Cultural Research, February 24, Savannah, GA.

Harris, Colette (2006) *Muslim Youth: Tensions and Transitions in Tajikistan.* Boulder, CO: Westview Press.

Harris, Judith R. (1998) *The Nurture Assumption: Why Children Turn Out the Way They Do.* New York, NY: Free Press.

(2006) *No Two Alike: Human Nature and Human Individuality.* New York, NY: W. W. Norton.

Harris, Marvin (1990) *Our Kind: Who We Are, Where We Came From, Where We Are Going.* New York, NY: Harper and Row.

Hart, Betty and Risley, Todd (1995) *Meaningful Differences in the Everyday Experience of Young American Children.* Baltimore, MD: Paul H. Brookes.

Hart, Don V. (1965) From pregnancy through birth in a Bisayan Filipino village. In Don V. Hart and Richard I. Coughlin (Eds.), *Southeast Asian Birth Customs.* Behavior Science Monographs. New Haven, CT: HRAF Press.

Harvey, Travis A. and Buckley, Lila (2009) Childbirth in China. In Helaine Selin and Pamela K. Stone (Eds.), *Childhood across Cultures: Ideas and Practices of Pregnancy, Childbirth and the Postpartum.* pp. 55–69. Amherst, MA: Springer.

Hassig, Ros (1945) *Aztec Warfare.* Norman, OK: University of Oklahoma Press.

Hatley, Nancy B. (1976) Cooperativism and enculturation among the Cuna Indians of San Blas. In Johannes Wilbert (Ed.), *Enculturation in Latin America.* pp. 67–94. Los Angeles, CA: UCLA Latin American Center Publications.

Hatt, Doyle G. (1974) Skullcaps and turbans: Domestic authority and public leadership among the Idaw Tanan of the Western High Atlas, Morocco. Unpublished PhD dissertation, University of California, Los Angeles.

Hauser-Schaublin, Brigitta (1995) Puberty rites, women's Naven, and initiation: Women's rituals of transition in Abelam and Iatmul culture. In Nancy C. Lutkehaus and Paul B. Roscoe (Eds.), *Gender Rituals: Female Initiation in Melanesia.* pp. 33–53. London: Routledge.

Hawkes, Kristen (1991) Showing off: Tests of another hypothesis about men's foraging goals. *Ethology and Sociobiology* 11:29–54.

Hawkes, Kristen, O'Connell, James F., and Blurton-Jones, Nicholas G. (1997) Hadza women's time allocation, offspring provisioning, and the evolutions of long postmenopausal life spans. *Current Anthropology* 38:551–577.

Hawkes, Kristen, O'Connell, James F., Blurton-Jones, Nicholas G., Alvarez, Helen, and Charnov, Eric L. (2000) The grandmother hypothesis and human evolution. In Lee Cronk, Napoleon Chagnon, and William Irons (Eds.), *Adaptation and Human Behavior: An Anthropological Perspective.* pp. 237–258. Hawthorne, NY: Aldine de Gruyter.

Hawks, John, Wang, Eric T., Cochran, Gregory M., Harpending, Henry C., and Moyzis, Robert K. (2007) Recent acceleration of human adaptive evolution. *Proceedings National Academy of Sciences* 104:20753–20758.

Hayden, Brian and Cannon, Aubrey (1984) Interaction inferences in archaeology and learning frameworks of the Maya. *Journal of Anthropological Archaeology* 3:325–367.

Heald, Suzette (1982) The making of men: The relevance of vernacular psychology to the interpretation of a Gisu ritual. *Africa* 52:15–36.

Heath, Shirley B. (1982) What no bedtime story means: Narrative skills at home and school. *Language in Society* 11:49–76.

(1983) *Ways with Words*. Cambridge: Cambridge University Press.

(1990) The children of Tracton's children. In James W. Stigler, Richard A. Shweder, and Gilbert H. Herdt (Eds.), *Cultural Psychology*. pp. 496–519. Cambridge: Cambridge University Press.

Hecht, Tobias (1998) *At Home in the Street*. Cambridge: Cambridge University Press.

Helander, Bernhard (1988) *The Slaughtered Camel: Coping with Fictitious Descent Among the Hubeer of Southern Somalia*. Uppsala: University of Uppsala, Department of Anthropology.

Hemmings, Annette B. (2004) *Coming of Age in US High Schools: Economic, Kinship, Religious, and Political Crosscurrents*. Mahwah, NJ: Erlbaum.

Henderson, Helen K. (1970) Ritual roles of women in Onitsha Ibo society. Unpublished PhD dissertation, University of Michigan.

Henderson, Patricia C. (2006) South African AIDS orphans: Examining assumptions around vulnerability from the perspective of rural children and youth. *Childhood* 13:303–327.

Hendry, Joy (1986) *Becoming Japanese: The World of the Pre-School Child*. Honolulu, HI: University of Hawai'i Press.

Henrich, Joseph (2004) Demography and cultural evolution: How adaptive cultural processes can produce maladaptive losses – the Tasmanian case. *American Antiquity* 69:197–214.

Henrich, Joseph, Heine, Stephen J., and Norenzayan, Ara (2010) The weirdest people in the world? *Behavioural and Brain Sciences* 33:61–81.

Henrich, Joseph, McElreath, Richard, Barr, Abigail, Ensminger, Jean, Barrett, Clark, Bolyanatz, Alexander, Cardenas, Juan Camilo, Gurven, Michael, Gwako, Edwins, Henrich, Natalie, Lesorogol, Carolyn, Marlowe, Frank, Tracer, David, and Ziker, John (2006) Costly punishment across human societies. *Science* 312:1767–1770.

Henry, Jules (1941/1964) *Jungle People: A Kaingáng Tribe of the Highlands of Brazil*. New York, NY: Random House.

Henry, Paula I., Morelli, Gilda A., and Tronick, Edward Z. (2005) Child caretakers among Efe foragers of the Itruri Forest. In Barry S. Hewlett and Michael E. Lamb (Eds.), *Hunter-Gatherer Childhoods: Evolutionary, Developmental, and Cultural Perspectives*. pp. 191–213. New Brunswick, NJ: Aldine/Transaction Publishers.

Herdt, Gilbert H. (1990) Sambia nosebleeding rites and male proximity to women. In James W. Stigler, Richard A. Shweder, and Gilbert H. Herdt (Eds.), *Cultural Psychology*. pp. 366–400. Cambridge: Cambridge University Press.

(2001) Rituals in manhood: Male initiation in Papua New Guinea. In Caroline B. Brettell and Carolyn F. Sargent (Eds.), *Gender in Cross-Cultural Perspective*. pp. 162–166. Upper Saddle River, NJ: Prentice Hall.

Hermes, Mary (2005) "Ma'iingan is just a misspelling of the word wolf": A case for teaching culture through language. *Anthropology and Education Quarterly* 36:43–56.

Hern, Warren M. (1992) Family planning, Amazon style. *Natural History* 101(12):30–37.

Hernandez, Theodore (1941) Children among the Drysdale River tribes. *Oceania* 12:122–133.

Herzfeld, Michael (1995) It takes one to know one: Collective resentment and mutual recognition among Greeks in local and global contexts. In Richard Fardon (Ed.), *Counterworks: Managing the Diversity of Knowledge*. pp. 124–142. London: Routledge.

Heth, C. Donald and Cornell, Edward H. (1985) A comparative description of representation and processing during search. In Henry M. Wellman (Ed.), *Children's Searching: The Development of Search Skill and Spatial Representation*. pp. 215–249. Hillsdale, NJ: Erlbaum.

Hewlett, Barry S. (1986) Intimate fathers: Paternal patterns of holding among Aka Pygmies. In Michael E. Lamb (Ed.), *Father's Role in Cross-Cultural Perspective*. pp. 34–61. Hillsdale, NJ: Erlbaum.

(1988) Sexual selection and paternal investment among Aka Pygmies. In Laura Betzing, Monique Borgerhoff Mulder, and Paul Turke (Eds.), *Human Reproductive Behavior: A Darwinian Perspective*. pp. 263–276. Cambridge: Cambridge University Press.

(1991a) Demography and childcare in preindustrial societies. *Journal of Anthropological Research* 47:1–37.

(1991b) *Intimate Fathers: The Nature and Context of Aka Pygmy Paternal-Infant Care*. Ann Arbor, MI: University of Michigan Press.

(1992) The parent-infant relationship and social-emotional development among Aka Pygmies. In Jaipaul L. Roopnarine and D. Bruce Carter (Eds.), *Parent–Child Socialization in Diverse Cultures*. pp. 223–243. Norwood, NJ: Ablex.

(1996) Cultural diversity among African Pygmies In Susan Kent (Ed.), *Cultural Diversity among Twentieth-Century Foragers*. pp. 215–244. Cambridge: Cambridge University Press.

(2001) The cultural nexus of father–infant bonding. In Caroline B. Brettell and Carolyn F. Sargent (Eds.), *Gender in Cross-Cultural Perspective*. pp. 45–56. Upper Saddle River, NJ: Prentice Hall.

Hewlett, Barry S. and Cavalli-Sforza, Luca L. (1986) Cultural transmission among Aka Pygmies. *American Anthropologist* 88:922–934.

Hewlett, Barry S., Fouts, Hillary N., Boyette, Adam H., and Hewlett, Bonnie L. (2011) Social learning among Congo Basin hunter-gatherers. *Philosophical Transactions of the Royal Society: Biology* 366:1168–1178.

Hewlett, Barry S., Lamb, Michael E., Leyendecker, Birgit, and Schölmerich, Axel (2000) Parental investment strategies among Aka foragers, Ngandu farmers, and Euro-American urban-industrialists. In Lee Cronk, Napoleon Chagnon, and William Irons (Eds.), *Adaptation and Human Behavior: An Anthropological Perspective*. pp. 155–178. New York, NY: Aldine de Gruyter.

Hewlett, Barry S., Lamb, Michael E., Shannon, Donald, Leyendecker, Birgit, and Schölmerich, Helge (1998) Culture and infancy among Central African foragers and farmers. *Developmental Psychology* 34:653–661.

Hewlett, Bonnie L. (2013) *Listen, Here is a Story*. New York: Oxford University Press.

Hewlett, Bonnie L. and Hewlett, Barry S. (2013) Hunter-gatherer adolescence. In Bonnie L. Hewlett (Ed.), *Adolescent Identity*. pp. 73–101. New York, NY: Routledge.

Heywood, Colin (1988) *Childhood in Nineteenth-Century France: Work, Health and Education Among the "Classes Populaires."* Cambridge: Cambridge University Press.

(2001) *A History of Childhood: Children and Childhood in the West from Medieval to Modern Times.* Cambridge: Polity.

Higgens, Kathleen (1985) Ritual and symbol in Baka life history. *Anthropology and Humanism Quarterly* 10(4):100–106.

Hilger, M. Inez (1951) *Chippewa Child Life and its Cultural Background.* Washington, DC: US Government Print Office.

(1957) *Araucanian Child Life and Cultural Background. Smithsonian Miscellaneous Collections*, vol. 133. Washington, DC: Smithsonian Institution.

Hill, Jacquette F. and Plath, David W. (1998) Moneyed knowledge: How women become commercial shellfish divers. In John Singleton (Ed.), *Learning in Likely Places: Varieties of Apprenticeship in Japan.* pp. 211–225. Cambridge: Cambridge University Press.

Hill, Kim and Hurtado, A. Magdalena (1996) *Ache Life History: The Ecology and Demography of a Foraging People.* New York, NY: Aldine de Gruyter.

Hill, Sarah E. and Reeve, H. Kern (2004) Mating games: The evolution of human mating transactions. *Behavioral Ecology* 15:748–756.

Hilson, Gavin (2010) Child labour in African artisanal mining communities: Experiences from Northern Ghana. *Development and Change* 41:445–473.

Hine, Thomas (1999) *The Rise and Fall of the American Teenager.* New York NY: HarperCollins.

Hirasawa, Ayako (2005) Infant care among the sedentarized Baka hunter-gatherers in Southeastern Cameroon. In Barry S. Hewlett and Michael E. Lamb (Eds.), *Hunter-Gatherer Childhoods: Evolutionary, Developmental, and Cultural Perspectives.* pp. 365–384. New Brunswick, NJ: Aldine/Transaction Publishers.

Hirschfeld, Lawrence E. (2002) Why don't anthropologists like children? *American Anthropologist* 104:611–627.

Ho, David Y. F. (1994) Cognitive socialization in Confucian heritage cultures. In Patricia M. Greenfield and Rodney R. Cocking (Eds.), *Cross-Cultural Roots of Minority Child Development.* pp. 285–313. Hillsdale, NJ: Erlbaum.

Hobart, Angela (1988) The shadow play and operetta as mediums of education in Bali. In Gustav Jahoda and Ioan M. Lewis (Eds.), *Acquiring Culture: Cross-Cultural Studies in Child Development.* pp. 113–144. London: Croom Helm.

Hobart, Angela, Ramseyer, Urs, and Leeman, Albert (1996) *The Peoples of Bali.* Oxford: Blackwell.

Hodges, Glenn (2003) Mongolian crossing. *National Geographic* 204(4):102–121.

Hoechner, Hannah (2012) Striving for knowledge and dignity: Young Qur'anic students in Kano, Nigeria. In Marisa O. Ensor (Ed.), *African Childhoods: Education, Development, Peacebuilding and the Youngest Continent.* pp. 157–170. New York, NY: Palgrave Macmillan.

Hofferth, Sandra, Brayfield, April, Deich, Sharon G., and Holcomb, Pamela (1991) *National Childcare Survey 1990.* Washington, DC: Urban Institute Press.

Hoffman, Diane M. (2012) Power struggles: The paradoxes of emotion and control among child-centered mothers in the privileged United States. *Ethos* 41:75–79.

Hoffman, Lois W. (1988) Cross-cultural differences in childrearing goals. In Robert A. LeVine, Patricia M. Miller, and Mary M. West (Eds.), *Parental Behavior in Diverse Societies, special issue of New Directions for Child Development* 40:99–122.

Hogbin, H. Ian (1946) A New Guinea childhood: From weaning till the eighth year in Wogeo *Oceania* 16:275–296.

   (1969) *A Guadalcanal Society: The Kaoka Speakers*. New York, NY: Holt, Rinehart, and Winston.

   (1970) *The Island of Menstruating Men*. Scranton, PA: Chandler.

Holbreich, Mark, Genuneit, Jon, Weber, Juliane, Braun-Fahrländer, Charlotte, Waser, Marco, and von Mutius, Erika (2012) Amish children living in northern Indiana have a very low prevalence of allergic sensitization. *The Journal of Allergy and Clinical Immunology* 129:1671–1673.

Holland, Dorothy C. and Eisenhart, Margaret A. (1990) *Educated in Romance: Women, Achievement and College Culture*. Chicago, IL: University of Chicago Press.

Hollos, Marida C. (1998) The status of women in southern Nigeria: Is education a help or a hindrance? In Marianne Bloch, Josephine A. Beoku–Betts, and B. Robert Tabachnick (Eds.), *Women and Education in Sub-Saharan Africa: Power, Opportunities, and Constraints*. pp. 247–276. Boulder, CO: Lynne Rienner.

   (2002) The cultural construction of childhood: Changing concepts among the Pare of Northern Tanzania. *Childhood* 9:167–189.

Hollos, Marida C. and Leis, Philip E. (1989) *Becoming Nigerian in Ijo Society*. New Brunswick, NJ: Rutgers University Press.

Holloway, Sarah L. and Valentine, Gill (2000) Children's geographies and the new social studies of childhood. In Sarah L. Holloway and Gill Valentine (Eds.), *Children's Geographies: Playing, Living, Learning*. pp. 1–26. London: Routledge.

Holmes, Hilary (1994) Pregnancy and birth as rites of passage for two groups of women in Britain. In Carol P. MacCormack (Ed.), *Ethnography of Fertility and Birth*. pp. 221–258. Prospect Heights, IL: Waveland Press.

Honigmann, Irman and Honigmann, John (1953) Child-rearing patterns among the Great Whale River Eskimo. *Anthropological Papers of the University of Alaska* 2(1):31–50.

Honwana, Alcinda (2005) The pain of agency: The agency of pain. In Alcinda Honwana and Filip de Boeck (Eds.), *Makers and Breakers: Children and Youth in Post-Colonial Africa*. pp. 31–52. Trenton, NJ: Africa World Press.

   (2006) *Child Soldiers in Africa*. Philadelphia, PA: University of Pennsylvania Press.

Hopcroft, Rosemary L. (2006) Sex, status, reproductive success in the contemporary United States. *Evolution and Human Behavior* 27:104–120.

Hopper, Lydia M., Marshall-Pescini, Sarah, and Whiten, Andrew (2012) Social learning and culture in child and chimpanzee. In Frans B. M. de Waal and Pier Francesco Ferrari (Eds.), *The Primate Mind: Built to Connect with Other Minds*. pp. 99–118. Cambridge, MA: Harvard University Press.

Hoppitt, William J. E., Brown, Gillian R., Kendal, Rachel, Rendell, L. Thornton, Alex, Webster, Mike M., and Laland, Kevin N. (2008) Lessons from animal teaching. *Trends in Ecology and Evolution* 23:486–493.

Horn, Cornelia B. and Martens, John W. (2009) *"Let the Little Children Come to Me":*
Childhood and Children in Early Christianity. Washington, DC: Catholic
University Press.

Horn, Wade F. (2003) Fatherhood, cohabitation, and marriage. In Douglas J. Besharov
(Ed.), *Family and Child Wellbeing after Welfare Reform.* pp. 129–144.
New Brunswick, NJ: Transaction Publishers.

Horr, David A. (1977) Orangutan maturation: Growing up in a female world. In
Suzanne Chevalier-Skolnikoff and Frank E. Poirier (Eds.), *Primate Bio-Social*
Development: Biological, Social, and Ecological Determinants. pp. 289–321.
New York, NY: Garland.

Horrell, Sara and Humphries, Jane (1995) "The exploitation of little children": Child
labour and the family economy in the Industrial Revolution. *Explorations in*
Economic History 32:485–516.

Hostetler, John A. (1964) Persistence and change patterns in Amish society. *Ethnology*
3:185–198.

Hostetler, John A. and Huntington, Gertrude E. (1971/1992) *Amish Children:*
Education in the Family, School, and the Community, 2nd edn. Orlando, FL:
Harcourt Brace Jovanovich.

Hotvedt, Mary E. (1990) Emerging and submerging adolescent sexuality: Culture and
sexual orientation. In John Bancroft and June M. Reinisch (Eds.), *Adolescence*
and Puberty. pp. 157–172. New York, NY: Oxford University Press.

Houby-Nielsen, Sanne (2000) Child burials in ancient Athens. In Joanna S. Derevenski
(Ed.), *Children and Material Culture.* pp. 151–166. London: Routledge.

Hough, Walter (1915) *The Hopi Indians.* Cedar Rapids, IA: Torch Press.

Houreld, Katherine (2007) Sexual harassment plagues Nigeria's schools. *Los Angeles*
Times, March 25. Available at http://articles.latimes.com/2007/mar/25/news/adfg-
lecherous25. Accessed July 11, 2013.

House, Bailey R., Henrich, Joseph, Brosnan, Sarah F., and Silk, Joan B. (2012)
The ontogeny of human prosociality: Behavioral experiments with children aged
3 to 8. *Evolution and Human Behavior* 33:291–308.

Howard, Alan (1970) *Learning to be Rotuman.* New York, NY: Teachers College
Press.

(1973) Education in 'Aina Pumehana: The Hawaiian-American student as hero.
In Solon T. Kimball, and Jacquette H. Burnett (Eds.), *Learning and Culture.*
pp. 115–129. Seattle, WA: University of Washington Press.

Howard, Kathryn M. (2012) Language socialization and hierarchy. In Alessandro
Duranti, Elinor Ochs, and Bambi B. Schieffelin (Eds.), *The Handbook of*
Language Socialization. pp. 341–364. Chickester: Wiley-Blackwell.

Howell, Nancy (1979) *Demography of the Dobe !Kung.* New York, NY: Academic
Press.

(2010) *Life Histories of the Dobe !Kung: Food, Fatness, and Well-Being Over the*
Life Span. Berkeley, CA: University of California Press.

Howell, Signe (1988) From child to human: Chewong concepts of self. In Gustav
Jahoda and Ioan M. Lewis (Eds.), *Acquiring Culture: Cross-Cultural Studies in*
Child Development. pp. 147–168. London: Croom Helm.

Howrigan, Gail, A. (1988) Fertility, infant feeding, and change in Yucatan. In Robert A.
LeVine, Patrice M. Miller, and Mary M. West (Eds.), *Parental Behavior in*

Diverse Societies, special issue of New Directions for Child Development 40:37–50.

Hrdy, Sarah B. (1976) Care and exploitation of nonhuman primate infants by conspecifics other than the mother. *Advances in the Study of Behavior* 6:101–158.

(1992) Fitness tradeoffs in the history and evolution of delegated mothering with special reference to wet-nursing, abandonment, and infanticide. *Ethology and Sociobiology* 13:409–442.

(1999) *Mother Nature: Maternal Instincts and How They Shape the Human Species.* New York, NY: Ballantine.

(2005a) On why it takes a village: Cooperative breeders, infant needs, and the future. In Robert L. Burgess and Kevin MacDonald (Eds.), *Evolutionary Perspectives on Human Development*, 2nd edn pp. 167–188. Thousand Oaks, CA: Sage.

(2005b) Comes the child before man: How cooperative breeding and prolonged postweaning dependence shaped human potential. In Barry S. Hewlett and Michael E. Lamb (Eds.), *Hunter-Gatherer Childhoods: Evolutionary, Developmental, and Cultural Perspectives.* pp. 65–91. New Brunswick, NJ: Aldine/Transaction Publishers.

(2006) Evolutionary context of human development: The cooperative breeding model. In C. Sue Carter, Lieselotte Ahnert, K. E. Grossmann, Sarah B. Hrdy, Michael E. Lamb, Stephen W. Porges, and Norbert Sachser (Eds.), *Attachment and Bonding: A New Synthesis.* pp 9–32. Cambridge, MA: MIT Press.

(2009) *Mothers and Others: The Evolutionary Origins of Mutual Understanding.* Cambridge, MA: Belknap Press.

(in press) Development and social selection in the emergence of "emotionally modern" humans. In Courtney L. Mehan and Alyssa Crittenden (Eds.), *Origins and Implications of the Evolution of Childhood.* Santa Fe, NM: SAR Press.

Hua, Cai (2001) *A Society without Fathers or Husbands: The Na of China.* Translated by Asti Hustvedt. Brooklyn, NY: Zone Books.

Huang, Julia. (2009). *Tribeswomen of Iran: Weaving Memories among Qashqa'i Nomads.* London: I. B. Tauris.

Huber, Brad R. and Breedlove, William L. (2007) Evolutionary theory, kinship, and childbirth in cross-cultural perspective. *Cross-Cultural Research* 41:196–219.

Hubert, Jane (1974) Belief and reality: Social factors in pregnancy and childbirth. In Martin P. M. Richards (Ed.), *The Integration of a Child into a Social World.* pp. 37–51. Cambridge: Cambridge University Press.

Hudson, Valerie M. and den Boer, Andrea M. (2005) *Bare Branches: The Security Implications of Asia's Surplus Male Population.* Cambridge, MA: MIT Press.

Hunn, Eugene S. (2002) Evidence for the precocious acquisition of plant knowledge by Zapotec children. In John R. Stepp, Felice S. Wyndham, and Rebecca K. Zarger (Eds.), *Ethnobiology and Biocultural Diversity: Proceedings of the Seventh International Congress of Ethnobiology.* pp. 604–613. Athens, GA: University of Georgia Press.

Husu, Lisa and Niemela, Pirkko (1993) Finland. In Leonore Adler (Ed.), *International Handbook on Gender Roles.* pp. 59–76. Westport, CT: Greenwood Press.

Ingold, Tim (2001) From the transmission of representations to the education of attention. In Harvey Whitehouse (Ed.), *The Debated Mind: Evolutionary Psychology versus Ethnography.* pp. 113–153. Oxford: Berg.

Inhelder, Bärbel and Piaget, Jean (1964) *The Early Growth of Logic in the Child.* Atlantic Highlands, NJ: Humanities Press.

Irons, William (2000) Why do the Yomut raise more sons than daughters? In Lee Cronk, Napoleon Chagnon, and William Irons (Eds.), *Adaptation and Human Behavior: An Anthropological Perspective.* pp. 223–236. New York, NY: Aldine.

Irvine, Judith T. (1978) Wolof "magical thinking": Culture and conservation revisited. *Journal of Cross-Cultural Psychology* 9:300–310.

Isaac, Barry L. and Conrad, Shelby R. (1982) Child fosterage among the Mende of Upper Bambara Chiefdom, Sierra Leone: Rural–urban and occupational comparisons. *Ethnology* 21:243–247.

Isaac, Barry L. and Feinberg, William E. (1982) Marital form and infant survival among the Mende of rural Upper Bambara Chiefdom, Sierra Leone. *Human Biology* 54:627–634.

Isaacson, Nicole (2002) Preterm babies in the "Mother Machine": Metaphoric reasoning and bureaucratic rituals that finish the "unfinished infant." In Karen A. Cerulo (Ed.), *Culture in Mind: Toward a Sociology of Culture and Cognition.* pp. 89–100. New York, NY: Routledge.

Istomin, Kirill V. and Dwyer, Mark J. (2009) Finding the way: A critical discussion of anthropological theories of human spatial orientation with reference to reindeer herders of northeastern Europe and western Siberia. *Current Anthropology* 50:29–49.

Iversen, Vegard and Raghavendra, P. S. (2005) Work and hardship, friendship and learning. Paper presented at a conference on Children and Youth in Emerging and Transforming Societies, June. Oslo.

Jacquemin, Melanie Y. (2004) Children's domestic work in Abidjan, Côte d'Ivoire: Petites bonnes have the floor. *Childhood* 11:383–397.
   (2006) Can the language of rights get hold of the complex realities of child domestic work? *Childhood* 13:389–406.

Jalil, Nasir and McGinn, Noel F. (1992) Pakistan. In R. Murray Thomas (Eds.), *Education's Role in National Development Plans: Ten Country Cases.* pp. 89–108. New York, NY: Praeger.

James, Wendy (1979) *"Kwanim Pa": The Making of the Uduk People.* Oxford: Clarendon Press.

James, William (1890/1981) *Principles of Psychology.* Cambridge, MA: Harvard University Press.

Jamin, Jacqueline R. (1994) Language and socialization of the child in African families living in France. In Patricia M. Greenfield and Rodney R. Cocking (Ed.), *Cross-Cultural Roots of Minority Child Development.* pp. 147–167. Hillsdale, NJ: Erlbaum.

Jankowiak, William (2011) The Han Chinese family: The realignment of parenting ideals, sentiments, and practices. In Shanshan Du and Yah-Chen Chen (Eds.), *Women and Gender in Contemporary Chinese Societies: Beyond Han Patriarchy.* pp. 109–132. Lanham, MD: Lexington Publishers.

Jankowiak, William, Joiner, Amber, and Khatib, Cynthia (2011) What observation studies can tell us about single child play patterns, gender, and changes in society. *Cross-Cultural Research* 45:155–177.

Janssen, Rosalind M. and Janssen, Jac J. (1990) *Growing Up in Ancient Egypt*. London: Rubicon Press.

Jay, Robert R. (1969) *Javanese Villagers: Social Relations in Rural Modjokuto*. Cambridge, MA: MIT Press.

Jelliffe, D. B., Woodburn, J., Bennett, F. J., and Jelliffe, E. F. B. (1962) The children of Hadza hunters. *Tropical Pediatrics* 60(2):907–913.

Jenkins, Carol L., Orr-Ewing, Alison K., and Heywood, Peter F. (1985) Cultural aspects of early childhood growth and nutrition among the Amele of Lowland Papua New Guinea. In Leslie B. Marshall (Ed.), *Infant Care and Feeding in the South Pacific*. pp. 29–50. New York, NY: Gordon and Breach.

Jenness, Diamond (1922) *The Life of the Copper Eskimos: Report of the Canadian Arctic Expedition, 1913–18. Vol. 12(A)*. Ottawa: King's Printer.

Jensen, Gordon D. and Suryani, Luh K. (1992) *The Balinese People: A Reinvestigation of Character*. Singapore: Oxford University Press.

Jensen de López, Kristine (2005) *Weddings, Funerals and Other Important Games: Zapotec (Southern Mexico) Children's Sociocultural Play as Cultural Bootstrapping*. Aalborg University VBN Working Paper.

Jocano, F. Landa (1969) *Growing Up in a Philippine Barrio*. New York, NY: Holt, Rinehart, and Winston.

Johannes, Robert E. (1981) *Words of the Lagoon: Fishing and Marine Lore in the Palau District of Micronesia*. Berkeley, CA: University of California Press.

Johnson, Kay A. (2004) *Wanting a Daughter, Needing a Son*. St. Paul, MN: Yeong and Yeong.

Johnson, Sara E. and Bock, John (2004) Trade-offs in skill acquisition and time allocation among juvenile Chacma baboons. *Human Nature* 15:45–62.

Jolivet, Muriel (1997) *Japan: The Childless Society? The Crisis of Motherhood*. London: Routledge.

Jones, Rhys (1977) The Tasmanian paradox. In R. V. S. Wright (Ed.), *Stone Tools as Cultural Markers: Change, Evolution and Complexity*. pp 189–204. Atlantic Highlands, NJ: Humanities Press.

Jordan, Brenda G. (1998) Education in the Kanō school in nineteenth-century Japan: Questions about the copybook method. In John Singleton (Ed.), *Learning in Likely Places: Varieties of Apprenticeship in Japan*. pp. 45–67. Cambridge: Cambridge University Press.

Josephson, Steven C. (2002) Fathering as reproductive investment. In Catherine S. Tamis-LeMonda and Natasha Cabrera (Eds.), *Handbook of Father Involvement: Multidisciplinary Perspectives*. pp. 359–382. Mahwah, NJ: Erlbaum.

Jourdan, Christine (1995) Masta Liu. In Vered Amit-Talai and Helena Wulff (Eds.), *Youth Cultures: A Cross-Cultural Perspective*. pp. 202–222. London: Routledge.

Junod, Henri A. (1927) *The Life of a South African Tribe*. London: Macmilllan.

Juul, Kristine (2008) Nomadic schools in Senegal: Manifestations of integration or ritual performance? In Marta Gutman and Ning de Coninck-Smith (Eds.), *Designing Modern Childhoods: History, Space, and the Material Culture of Children*. pp. 152–170. New Brunswick, NJ: Rutgers University Press.

Kagitçibasi, Çigdem and Ataca, Bilge (2005) Value of children and family change: A three-decade portrait from Turkey. *Applied Psychology* 54:317–337.

Kagitçibasi, Çigdem and Sunar, Diane (1992) Family and socialization in Turkey. In Jaipaul L. Roopnarine and D. Bruce Carter (Eds.), *Parent–Child Socialization in Diverse Cultures*. pp. 75–88. Norwood, NJ: Ablex.

Kahlenberg, Sonya M. and Wrangham, Richard W. (2010) Sex differences in chimpanzees' use of sticks as play objects resemble those of children. *Current Biology* 20:1067–1068.

Kahneman, Daniel, Krueger, Alan B., Schkade, David A., Schwarz, Norbert, and Stone, Arthur A. (2004) A survey method for characterizing daily life experience: The day reconstruction method. *Science* 306:1776–1780.

Kamat, Vinay R. (2008). Dying under the bird's shadow: Narrative representations of Degedege and child survival among the Zaramo of Tanzania. *Medical Anthropology Quarterly* 22:67–93.

Kamei, Nobutaka (2005) Play among Baka children in Cameroon. In Barry S. Hewlett and Michael E. Lamb (Eds.), *Hunter-Gatherer Childhoods: Evolutionary, Developmental, and Cultural Perspectives*. pp. 343–364. New Brunswick, NJ: Aldine/Transaction Publishers.

Kamp, Kathryn A. (2002) Working for a living. In Kathryn A. Kamp (Ed.), *Children in the Prehistoric Puebloan Southwest*. pp. 71–89. Salt Lake City, UT: University of Utah Press.

Kanazawa, Satoshi and Still, Mary C. (2000) Parental investment as a game of chicken. *Politics and the Life Sciences* 10(1):17–26.

Kantor, Harvey and Lowe, Robert (2004) Reflections on history and quality education. *Educational Researcher* 33(5):6–10.

Kaplan, Hillard S. (1994) Evolutionary and wealth flows theories of fertility: Empirical tests and new models. *Population and Development Review* 20:753–791.

Kaplan, Hillard S. and Bock, John A. (2001) Fertility theory: The embodied capital theory of life history evolution. In Jan M. Hoem (Ed.), *International Encyclopedia of the Social and Behavioral Sciences* 3.3(155):5561–5568. New York: Elsevier Science.

Kaplan, Hillard S. and Dove, Heather (1987) Infant development among the Ache of eastern Paraguay. *Developmental Psychology* 23:190–198.

Kaplan, Hillard S. and Hill, Kim (1992) The evolutionary ecology of food acquisition. In Eric A. Smith and Bruce Winterhalder (Eds.), *Evolutionary Ecology and Human Behavior*. pp. 167–201. New York, NY: Aldine.

Kaplan, Hillard, Hill, Kim, Lancaster, Jane B., and Hurtado, A. Magdalena (2000) A theory of human life history evolution: Brains, learning, and longevity. *Evolutionary Anthropology* 9:156–185.

Kaplan, Hillard S. and Lancaster, Jane B. (2000) The evolutionary economics and psychology of the demographic transition to low fertility. In Lee Cronk, Napoleon Chagnon, and William Irons (Eds.), *Adaptation and Human Behavior: An Anthropological Perspective*. pp. 283–322. New York, NY: Aldine.

Kaplan, Sam (2006) *The Pedagogical State: Education and the Politics of National Culture in Post-1980 Turkey*. Palo Alto, CA: Stanford University Press.

Kaplan, Steven (2007) Reconsidering apprenticeship: Afterthoughts. In Bert de Munck, Steven L. Kaplan, and Hugo Soly (Eds.), *On the Shop Floor: Historical Perspectives on Apprenticeship Learning*. pp. 203–218. Oxford: Berghahn Books.

Karsten, Lia (2003) Children's use of public space: The gendered world of the playground. *Childhood* 10:457–473.

Katz, Cindi (1986) Children and the environment: Work, play and learning in rural Sudan. *Children's Environment Quarterly* 3(4):43–51.

(2001) Vagabond capitalism and the necessity of social reproduction. *Antipode* 33:709–728.

(2004) *Growing up Global: Economic Restructuring and Children's Everyday Lives.* Minneapolis, MN: University of Minnesota Press.

(2005) The terrors of hypervigilance: Security and the compromised spaces of contemporary childhood. In Jens Qvortrup (Ed.), *Studies in Modern Childhood.* pp. 99–114. Houndmills: Palgrave Macmillan.

Katz, Jane R. (2001) Playing at home: The talk of pretend play. In David K. Dickinson and Patton O. Tabors (Eds.), *Beginning Literacy with Language.* pp. 53–73. Baltimore, MD: Paul H. Brooks.

Katz, Phyllis B. (2007) Educating Paula: A proposed curriculum for raising a 4th-century Christian infant. In Ada Cohen and Jeremy B. Rutter (Eds.), *Constructions of Childhood in Ancient Greece and Italy.* pp. 115–127. Princeton, NJ: American School of Classical Study at Athens.

Katz, Richard (1981) Education is transformation: Becoming a healer among the !Kung and the Fijians. *Harvard Education Review* 51:57–78.

Kay, Verla (2003) *Orphan Train.* New York: G. P. Putnam's Sons.

Kearins, Judith (1986) Visual spatial memory in Aboriginal and white Australian children. *Australian Journal of Psychology* 38:203–213.

Keeler, Ward (1983) Shame and stage fright in Java. *Ethos* 11:152–165.

Keller, Heidi (2007) *Cultures of Infancy.* Mahwah, NJ: Erlbaum.

Kellet, Mary (2009) Children and young people's voice. In Mary Kellet and Heather K. Montgomery (Eds), *Children and Young People's Worlds: Developing Frameworks for Integrated Practice.* pp. 237–252. Bristol: Policy Press.

Kenny, Mary L. (1999) No visible means of support: Child labor in urban northeast Brazil. *Human Organization* 58:375–386.

(2007) *Hidden Heads of Households: Child Labor in Urban Northeast Brazil.* Buffalo, NY: Broadview Press.

Kenyon, Dienje and Arnold, Charles D. (1985). Toys as indicators of socialization in Thule culture. In Marc Thompson, Maria Teresa Garcia, and François J. Kense (Eds.), *Status, Structure and Stratification: Current Archaeological Reconstructions.* pp. 347–353. Calgary, AL: Archaeological Association of the University of Calgary.

Kertzer, David (1993) *Sacrificed for Honor: Italian Infant Abandonment and the Politics of Reproductive Control.* Boston, MA: Beacon Press.

Keshavjee, Salmaan (2006) Bleeding babies in Badakhshan: Symbolism, materialism, and the political economy of traditional medicine in Post-Soviet Tajikistan. *Medical Anthropology Quarterly* 20:72–93.

Khair, Sumaiya (2011) *Child Labour Revisited: Gender, Culture, Economics and Human Rights.* Daka: University Press.

Khosravi, Shahram (2008) *Young and Defiant in Tehran.* Philadelphia, PA: University of Pennsylvania Press.

Kilbride, Janet E. (1975) Sitting and smiling behavior of Baganda infants: The influence of culturally constituted experience. *Journal of Cross-Cultural Psychology* 6:88–107.

Kilbride, Philip L. and Kilbride, Janet C. (1990) *Changing Family Life in East Africa: Women and Children at Risk.* University Park, PA: Penn State University Press.

Kilbride, Philip, Suda, Collette, and Njeru, Enos (2000) *Street Children in Kenya: Voices of Children in Search of a Childhood.* Westport, CT: Bergin.

Kim, Kyung-hak and Chun, Kyung-soo (1989) Cultural transmission and culture acquisition in a Korean village: The systems model in ethnographic terms. In Mary Anne Pitman, Rivka A. Eisikovits, and Marion Lundy Dobbert (Eds.), *Culture Acquisition: A Holistic Approach to Human Learning.* pp. 169–184. New York: Praeger.

Kim, Tae L. (1993) Korea. In Leonore Loeb Adler (Ed.), *International Handbook on Gender Roles.* pp. 187–198. Westport, CT: Greenwood Press.

Kim, Uichol and Choi, So-Hyang (1994) Individualism, collectivism, and child development: A Korean perspective. In Patricia M. Greenfield and Rodney R. Cocking (Eds.), *Cross-Cultural Roots of Minority Child Development.* pp. 227–259. Hillsdale, NJ: Erlbaum.

Kincheloe, Joe L. (2002) The complex politics of McDonald's and the new childhood: Colonizing kidworld. In Gaile S. Cannella and Joe L. Kincheloe (Eds.), *Kidworld: Childhood Studies, Global Perspectives, and Education.* pp. 75–121. New York: Peter Lang.

Kindermann, Thomas A. (1993) Natural peer groups as contexts for individual development: The case of children's development within natural peer contexts. *Developmental Psychology* 29:970–977.

King, Barbara J. (1994) *The Information Continuum: Evolution of Social Information Transfer in Monkeys, Apes and Hominids.* Santa Fe, NM: SAR Press.
    (1999) New directions in the study of primate learning. In Hilary O. Box and Kathleen R. Gibson (eds.), *Mammalian Social Learning: Comparative and Ecological Perspectives.* pp. 17–32. Cambridge: Cambridge University Press.
    (2005) How gorillas and chimpanzees can help our children. *Anthropology News* 46(3):9.

King, Phillip J. (2006) Who did it, who didn't and why: Circumcision. *Biblical Archaeology Review* 32(4):48–55.

King, Stacie M. (2006) The coming of age in ancient coastal Oaxaca. In Traci Adren and Scott R. Hutson (Eds.), *The Social Experience of Childhood in Ancient Mesoamerica.* pp. 169–200. Boulder, CO: University of Colorado Press.

Kingston, Jeff (2004) *Japan's Quiet Transformation: Social Change and Civil Society in the Twenty-Frst Century.* Abingdon: Routledge Curzon.

Kinney, Anne B. (1995) Dyed silk: Han notions of the moral development of children. In Anne B. Kinney (Ed.), *Chinese Views of Childhood.* pp. 17–56. Honolulu, HI: University of Hawai'i Press.

Kipling, Rudyard (1901/2003) *Kim.* New York, NY: Barnes and Noble.

Kipnis, Andrew (2001) The disturbing educational discipline of "peasants." *The China Journal* 46:1–24.

Klapisch-Zuber, Christiane (1985) *Women, Family, and Ritual in Renaissance Italy.* Translated by Lydia Cochrane. Chicago, IL: University of Chicago Press.

Klaus, Haagen, Centurion, Jorge, and Curo, Manuel (2010) Bioarchaeology of human sacrifice: Violence, identity and the evolution of ritual killing at Cerro Cerrillos, Peru. *Antiquity* 84:1102–1122.

Kleijueqgt, Marc (2009) Ancient Mediterranean world, childhood and adolescence. In Richard A. Shweder, Thomas R. Bidell, Anne C. Dailey, Suzanne D. Dixon, Peggy J. Miller, and John Modell (Eds.), *The Child: An Encyclopedic Companion.* pp 54–56. Chicago, IL: University of Chicago Press.

Kleppe, Else J. (2012) Gendered Sámi childhoods: Traditions in the Lule Sámi region 1100–1950. *Childhood in the Past* 5:70–95.

Kline, Michelle A., Robert Boyd, and Joseph Henrich (2013) Teaching and the life history of cultural transmission in Fijian villages. *Human Nature* 24:351–374.

Klinnert, Mary D., Campos, Joseph J., Sorce, James F., Emde, Robert N., and Svejda, Marylin (1983) Emotions as behavior regulators: Social referencing in infancy. In Robert Plutchik and Henry Kellerman (Eds.), *Emotion: Theory, Research, and Experience.* pp. 57–86. New York, NY: Academic Press.

Kloek, Els (2003) Early modern childhood in the Dutch context. In Willem Koops and Michael Zucherman (Eds.), *Beyond the Century of the Child: Cultural History and Developmental Psychology.* pp. 43–61. Philadelphia, PA: University of Pennsylvania Press.

Knott, Cheryl (2003) Code red. *National Geographic* 204(4):76–81.

Kogel, Amy, Bolton, Ralph, and Bolton, Charlene (1983) Time allocation in four societies. *Ethnology* 22:355–370.

Köhler, Iris (2012) Learning and children's work in a pottery-making environment in Northern Côte d'Ivoire. In Gerd Spittler and Michael Bourdillon (Eds.), *African Children at Work: Working and Learning in Growing Up.* pp. 113–141. Berlin: LitVerlag.

Kojima, Hideo (2003). The history of children and youth in Japan. In Willem Koops and Michael Zucherman (Eds.) *Beyond the Century of the Child: Cultural History and Developmental Psychology.* pp. 112–135. Philadelphia, PA: University of Pennsylvania Press.

Konner, Melvin J. (1975) Relations among infants and juveniles in comparative perspective. In Michael Lewis and Leonard A. Rosenblum (Eds.), *Friendship and Peer Relations.* pp. 99–129. New York, NY: Wiley.

(1976) Maternal care, infant behavior and development among the Kung. In Richard B. Lee and Irven DeVore (Eds.), *Studies of the !Kung San and Their Neighbors.* pp. 218–245. Cambridge, MA: Harvard University Press.

(2005) Hunter-gatherer infancy and childhood. In Barry S. Hewlett and Michael E. Lamb (Eds.), *Hunter-Gatherer Childhoods: Evolutionary, Developmental, and Cultural Perspectives.* pp. 19–64. New Brunswick, NJ: Aldine/Transaction Publishers.

(2010) *The Evolution of Childhood: Relationships, Emotion, Mind.* Cambridge, MA: Belknap Press.

(in press) Hunter-gatherer infancy and childhood in the context of human evolution. In Courtney L. Mehan and Alyssa Crittenden (Eds.), *Origins and Implications of the Evolution of Childhood.* Santa Fe, NM: SAR Press

Konner, Melvin J. and Worthman, Carol (1980) Nursing frequency, gonadal function and birth spacing among !Kung hunter-gatherers. *Science* 207:788–791.

Kopp, Claire B., Khoka, Ellen W., and Sigman, Marian (1977) A comparison of sensorimotor development among infants in India and the United States. *Journal of Cross-Cultural Psychology* 8(4):435–451.

Korbin, Jill E. (1987a) Child maltreatment in cross-cultural perspective: Vulnerable children and circumstances. In Richard J. Gelles and Jane B. Lancaster (Eds.), *Child Abuse and Neglect: Biosocial Dimensions*. pp. 31–56. New York, NY: Aldine de Gruyter.

(1987b) Child sexual abuse: Implications from the cross-cultural record. In Nancy Scheper-Hughes (Ed.), *Child Survival: Anthropological Perspectives on the Treatment and Maltreatment of Children*. pp. 247–265. Dordrecht: Reidel.

Kotlowitz, Alex (1991) *There are no Children Here*. New York, NY: Doubleday.

Kousholt, Dorte (2011) Researching family through the everyday lives of children across home and day care in Denmark. *Ethos*, 39:98–114.

Kovats-Bernat, J. Christopher (2006) *Sleeping Rough in Port-au-Prince*. Gainsville, FL: University of Florida Press.

(2013) "The bullet is certain": Armed children and gunplay on the streets of Haiti. In Bonnie L. Hewlett (Ed.), *Adolescent Identity*. pp 186–221. New York, NY: Routledge.

Kramer, Karen L. (2002) Variation in juvenile dependence: Helping behavior among Maya children. *Human Nature* 13:299–325.

(2005) *Maya Children: Helpers on the Farm*. Cambridge, MA: Harvard University Press.

Kramer, Karen L. and Greaves, Russell D. (2007) Changing patterns of infant mortality and maternal fertility among Pumé foragers and horticulturalists. *American Anthropologist* 109:713–726.

(2011) Juvenile subsistence effort, activity levels, and growth patterns. *Human Nature* 22:303–326.

Kramer, Samuel N. (1963) *The Sumerians: Their History, Culture and Character*. Chicago, IL: University of Chicago Press.

Kratz, Corinne A. (1990) Sexual solidarity and the secrets of sight and sound: Shifting gender relations and their ceremonial constitution. *American Ethnologist* 17:449–469.

Krause, Richard A. (1985) *The Clay Sleeps: An Ethnoarchaeological Study of Three African Potters*. Birmingham, AL: University of Alabama Press.

Kremer-Sadlik, Tamar, Izquierdo, Carolina, and Fatigante, Marilena (2010) Making meaning of everyday practices: Parents' attitudes toward children's extra-curricular activities in the United States and in Italy. *Anthropology of Education Quarterly* 4:35–54.

Kress, Howard (2005) The role of culture, economics, and education in reproductive decision making in Otavalo, Ecuador. Paper presented at the annual meeting of the American Anthropological Association, December, Washington, DC.

(2007) An evaluation of infant mortality and embodied capital models of fertility transition in Otavalo, Ecuador. Paper presented at the 36th annual meeting, of the Society for Cross-Cultural Research, and third general meeting of the Society for Scientific Anthropology, February 21–24, San Antonio, TX

Krige, Eileen J. (1965/2005) *The Social System of the Zulus*. Pietermaritzburg: Shuter and Shooter; New Haven, CT: HRAF.

Kruger, Ann Cale and Konner, Melvin (2010) Who responds to crying? Maternal care and allocare among the !Kung. *Human Nature* 21:309–329.

Kulick, Don (1992) *Language Shift and Cultural Reproduction: Socialization, Self, and Syncretism in a Papua New Guinea Village*. Cambridge: Cambridge University Press.

Kulick, Don and Stroud, Christopher (1993) Conceptions and uses of literacy in a Papua New Guinean village. In Brian Street (Ed.), *Cross-Cultural Approaches to Literacy*. pp. 30–61. Cambridge: Cambridge University Press.

Kuroda, Hideo (1998) A social historical view of the children of the Edo period. In Kumon Children's Research Institute (Ed.), *Children Represented in Ukiyo-e*. pp. 10–12. Osaka: Kumon Institute of Education.

Kusserow, Adrie S. (2004) *American Individualisms: Child Rearing and Social Class in Three Neighborhoods*. New York, NY: Palgrave Macmillan.

Kuznesof, Elizabeth A. (2007) Slavery and childhood in Brazil (1550–1888). In Ondina E. Gonzáles and Bianca Premo (Eds.), *Raising an Empire: Children in Early Modern Iberia and Colonial Latin America*. pp. 187–218. Albuquerque: NM: University of New Mexico Press.

Kyratzis, Amy (2004) Talk and interaction among children and the co-construction of peer groups and peer culture. *Annual Review of Anthropology* 33:625–649.

La Russo, Maria G. (1988) *A Portrait of Third Generation Italian-American Family Life: Interviews and Observations with Six Families*. Ann Arbor, MI: University Microfilms.

Laes, Christian (2011) *Children in the Roman Empire*. Cambridge: Cambridge University Press.

La Franiere, Sharon (2007) African crucible: Cast as witches, then cast out. *New York Times*, November 15. Available at www.nytimes.com/2007/11/15/world/africa/15witches.html?pagewanted=all. Accessed October 10, 2013.

La Freniere, Peter (2005) Human emotions as multipurpose adaptations: An evolutionary perspective on the development of fear. In Robert L. Burgess and Kevin MacDonald (Eds.). *Evolutionary Perspectives on Human Development*, 2nd edn pp. 189–205. Thousand Oaks, CA: Sage.

Lahai, John I. (2012) Youth agency and survival strategies in Sierra Leone's postwar informal economy. In Marisa O. Ensor (Ed.), *African Childhoods: Education, Development, Peacebuilding and the Youngest Continent*. pp. 47–59. New York: Palgrave Macmillan.

Lancaster, Jane B. (1984) Evolutionary perspectives on sex differences in the higher primates. In Alice Rossi (Ed.), *Gender and the Life Course*. pp. 3–28. New York, NY: Aldine.

(1986) Human adolescence and reproduction: Evolutionary perspectives. In Jane B. Lancaster and Beatrix A. Hamburg (Eds.), *School-Age Pregnancy and Parenthood: Biosocial Dimensions*. pp. 17–37. New York, NY: Aldine.

Lancaster, Jane B. and Kaplan, Hillard S. (2000) Parenting other men's children: Costs, benefits, and consequences. In Lee Cronk, Napoleon Chagnon, and William Irons (Eds.), *Adaptation and Human Behavior: An Anthropological Perspective*. pp. 179–201. New York, NY: Aldine.

Lancaster, Jane B. and Lancaster, Chet S. (1983) Parental investment: The hominid adaptation. In Douglas J. Ortner (Ed.), *How Humans Adapt*. pp. 33–65. Washington, DC: Smithsonian Institution Press.

Lancy, David F. (1975) The social organization of learning: Initiation rituals and public schools. *Human Organization* 34:371–380.

  (1979) Introduction. In David Lancy (Ed.), *The Community School, special issue of Papua New Guinea Journal of Education* 15(1):1–9.

  (1980a) Speech events in a West African court. *Communication and Cognition* 13 (4):397–412.

  (1980b) Becoming a blacksmith in Gbarngasuakwelle. *Anthropology and Education Quarterly* 11:266–274.

  (1980c) Play in species adaptation. In Bernard J. Siegel (Ed.), *Annual Review of Anthropology* 9:471–495.

  (1982) Some missed opportunities in theories of play. *The Behavioral and Brain Sciences* 5:165–166.

  (1983) *Cross-Cultural Studies in Cognition and Mathematics*. New York, NY: Academic Press.

  (1984) Play in anthropological perspective. In Peter K. Smith (Ed.), *Play in Animals and Humans*. pp. 295–304. Oxford: Blackwell.

  (1989) An information processing framework for the study of culture and thought. In Donald Topping, Doris Crowell, and Victor Kobayashi (Eds.), *Thinking Across Cultures*. pp. 13–26. Hillsdale, NJ: Erlbaum.

  (1994) The conditions that support emergent literacy. In David F. Lancy (Ed.), *Children's Emergent Literacy: From Research to Practice*. pp. 1–19. Westport, CT: Praeger.

  (1996) *Playing on the Mother Ground: Cultural Routines for Children's Development*. New York, NY: Guilford Press.

  (2001a) *Studying Children and Schools: Qualitative Research Traditions*. Prospect Heights, IL: Waveland Press.

  (2001b) Cultural constraints on children's play. *Play and Culture Studies* 4:3–62.

  (2007) Accounting for the presence/absence of mother–child play. *American Anthropologist* 109(2):273–284.

  (2008) *The Anthropology of Childhood: Cherubs, Chattel, Changelings*, 1st edn Cambridge: Cambridge University Press.

  (2010a) Learning "from nobody": The limited role of teaching in folk models of children's development. *Childhood in the Past* 3:79–106.

  (2010b) Children's learning in new settings. In David F. Lancy, Suzanne Gaskins, and John Bock (Eds.), *The Anthropology of Learning in Childhood*. pp. 443–463. Lanham, MD: AltaMira Press.

  (2010c) What price happiness? *Psychology Today*, Available at www. psychologytoday.com/blog/benign-neglect/201011/what-price-happiness. Accessed January 1, 2013.

  (2012a) "First you must master pain": The nature and purpose of apprenticeship. *Society for the Anthropology of Work Review* 33:113–126.

  (2012b) Unmasking children's agency. *Anthropology of Children* (2/October). Available at http://popups.ulg.ac.be/AnthropoChildren/document.php?id=1253.

(2012c) The chore curriculum. In Gerd Spittler and Michael Bourdillion (Eds.), *African Children at Work: Working and Learning in Growing Up.* pp. 23–57. Berlin: LitVerlag.

(2014) "Babies aren't persons": A survey of delayed personhood. In Hiltrud Otto and Heidi Keller (Eds.), *Different Faces of Attachment: Cultural Variations of a Universal Human Need.* pp. 66–112. Cambridge: Cambridge University Press.

Lancy, David F. and Grove, M. Annette (2010) The role of adults in chidren's learning. In David F. Lancy, Suzanne Gaskins, and John Bock (Eds.), *The Anthropology of Learning in Childhood.* pp. 145–179. Lanham, MD: AltaMira Press.

(2011a) "Getting noticed": Middle childhood in cross-cultural perspective. *Human Nature* 22:281–302.

(2011b) Marbles and Machiavelli: The role of game play in children's social development. *American Journal of Play* 3:489–499.

Lancy, David F. and Madsen, Millard C. (1981) Cultural patterns and the social behavior of children: Two studies from Papua New Guinea. *Ethos* 9:201–216.

Lancy, David F. and Strathern, Andrew J. (1981) Making-twos: Pairing as an alternative to the taxonomic mode of representation. *American Anthropologist* 81:773–795.

Landsman, Gail Heidi (2009) *Reconstructing Motherhood and Disability in the Age of "Perfect" Babies.* New York, NY: Routledge.

Landy, David (1959) *Tropical Childhood: Cultural Transmission and Learning in a Puerto Rican Village.* New York: Harper Torchbooks.

Lange, Garret and Rodman, Hyman (1992) Family relationships and patterns of child-rearing in the Caribbean. In Jaipaul L. Roopnarine and D. Bruce Carter (Eds.), *Parent–Child Socialization in Diverse Cultures.* pp. 185–198. Norwood, NJ: Ablex.

Langness, Louis L. (1981) Child abuse and cultural values: The case of New Guinea. In Jill E. Korbin (Ed.), *Child Abuse and Neglect: Cross-Cultural Perspectives.* pp. 13–34. Berkeley, CA: University of California Press.

Lansing, J. Stephen (1994) *The Balinese.* Fort Worth, TX: Harcourt Brace.

Lareau, Annette (1989) *Home Advantage: Social Class and Parental Intervention in Elementary Education.* New York: Falmer.

(2003) *Unequal Childhoods: Class, Race, and Family Life.* Berkley, CA: University of California Press.

Larson, Reed W., Branscomb, Kathryn R., and Wiley, Angela R. (2006) Forms and functions of family mealtimes: Multidisciplinary perspectives. *New Directions for Child and Adolescent Development* 111:1–15.

Larson, Reed W. and Suman, Verma (1999) How children and adolescents spend time across the world: Work, play, and development opportunities. *Psychological Bulletin* 125:701–736.

Lasker, Gabriel (1969) Human biological adaptability: The ecological approach in physical anthropology. *Science* 166: 1480–1486.

Lassonde, Stephen (2005) *Learning to Forget: Schooling and Family Life in New Haven's Working Class, 1870–1940.* New Haven, CT: Yale University Press.

Lattimore, Owen (1941) *Mongol Journeys.* London: Jonathan Cape.

Lave, Jean (1982) A comparative approach to educational forms and learning processes. *Anthropology and Education Quarterly* 132:181–187.

Lave, Jean and Wenger, Etienne (1991) *Situated Learning: Legitimate Peripheral Participation*. Cambridge: Cambridge University Press.

Lawson, David W. and Mace, Ruth (2009) Trade-offs in modern parenting: A longitudinal study of sibling competition for parental care. *Human Behavior* 30:170–183.

   (2010) Optimizing modern family size. *Human Nature* 21:39–61.

Lawton, Carol (2007) Children in classical Attic votive reliefs. In Ada Cohen, and Jeremy B. Rutter (Eds.), *Constructions of Childhood in Ancient Greece and Italy*. pp. 41–60. Princeton, NJ: American School of Classical Study at Athens.

Le Mort, Francis (2008) Infant burials in pre-pottery Neolithic Cyprus: Evidence from Khiroitia. In Krum Bacvarov (Ed.), *Babies Reborn: Infant/Child Burials in Pre- and Protohistory*. pp. 23–32. BAR International Series 1832. Oxford: Archaeopress.

Leavitt, Stephen C. (1989) Cargo, Christ, and nostalgia for the dead: Themes of intimacy and abandonment in Bumbita Arapesh social experience. Unpublished PhD. dissertation, University of California, San Diego.

   (1998) The *bikhet* mystique: Masculine identity and patterns of rebellion among Bumbita adolescent males. In Gilbert H. Herdt and Stephen Leavitt (Eds.), *Adolescence in Pacific Island Societies*. pp. 173–194. Pittsburgh, PA: University of Pittsburgh Press.

Lebegyiv, Judit (2009) Phases of childhood in early Mycenaean Greece. *Childhood in the Past* 2:15–32.

Lebra, Takie S. (1994) Mother and child in Japanese socialization: A Japan–US comparison. In Patricia M. Greenfield and Rodney R. Cocking (Eds.), *Cross-Cultural Roots of Minority Child Development*. pp. 259–274. Hillsdale, NJ: Erlbaum.

Lee, K. Alexandra (1994) Attitudes and prejudices towards infanticide: Carthage, Rome and today. *Archaeological Review from Cambridge* 13:65–79.

Lee, Kwan C. (1998) *Gender and the South China Miracle: Two Worlds of Factory Women*. Berkeley, CA: University of California Press.

Lee, Phyllis C. (1996) The meanings of weaning: Growth, lactation, and life history. *Evolutionary Anthropology* 5:87–96.

Lee, Richard B. (1979) *The !Kung San: Men, Women and Work in a Foraging Society*. Cambridge: Cambridge University Press.

Lee, Sang-hyop and Mason, Andrew (2005) Mother's education, learning-by-doing, and child health care in rural India. *Comparative Education Review* 49:534–551.

Leff, Jonah (2009) Pastoralists at war: Violence and security in the Kenya–Sudan–Uganda border region. *International Journal of Conflict and Violence* 3 (2):188–203.

Leighton, Dorothea and Kluckhohn, Clyde C. (1948) *Children of the People*. Cambridge, MA: Harvard University Press.

Leinaweaver, Jessaca B. (2008a) Improving oneself: Young people getting ahead in the Peruvian Andes. In *Youth, Culture, and Politics in Latin America*, Special Issue of *Latin American Perspectives* 35(4):60–78.

   (2008b) *The Circulation of Children: Kinship, Adoption, and Morality in Andean Peru*. Durham, NC: Duke University Press.

Leinhardt, Gaea and Knutson, Karen (2004) *Listening in on Museum Conversations*. Lanham, MD: AltaMira Press.

Leis, Phillip E. (1982) The not-so-supernatural power of Ijaw children. In Simon Ottenberg (Ed.), *African Religious Groups and Beliefs*. pp. 151–169. Meerut: Folklore Institute.

Leonetti, Donna L., Nath, Dilip C., Heman, Natabar S., and Neill, Dawn B. (2005) Kinship organization and the impact of grandmothers on reproductive success among the matrilineal Khasis and patrilineal Bengali of Northeast India. In Eckart Voland, Athanasios Chasiotis, and Wulf Schiefendhövel (Eds.), *Grandmotherhood: The Evolutionary Significance of the Second Half of the Female Life*. pp 194–214. New Brunswick, NJ: Rutgers University Press.

Lepowsky, Maria A. (1985) Food taboos, malaria and dietary change: Infant feeding and cultural adaptation on a Papua New Guinea Island. In Leslie B. Marshall (Ed.), *Infant Care and Feeding in the South Pacific*. pp. 51–81. New York, NY: Gordon and Breach.

(1987) Food taboos and child survival: A case study from the Coral Sea. In Nancy Scheper-Hughes (Ed.), *Child Survival: Anthropological Perspectives on the Treatment and Maltreatment of Children*. pp. 71–92. Dordrecht: Reidel.

(1993) *Fruit of the Motherland: Gender in an Egalitarian Society*. New York: Columbia University Press.

(1998) Coming of age on Vanatinai: Gender, sexuality, and power. In Gilbert H. Herdt and Stephen C. Leavitt (Eds.), *Adolescence in Pacific Island Societies*. pp. 123–147. Pittsburgh, PA: University of Pittsburgh Press.

Lerer, Leonard B. (1998) Who is the rogue? Hunger, death, and circumstance in John Mampe Square. In Nancy Scheper-Hughes and Carolyn F. Sargent (Eds.), *Small Wars: The Cultural Politics of Childhood*. pp. 228–250. Berkeley, CA: University of California Press.

Lerner, Daniel (1958) *The Passing of Traditional Society*. New York, NY: Macmillan.

Lessa, William A. (1966) *Ulithi: A Micronesian Design for Living*. New York, NY: Holt, Rinehart, and Winston.

Levey, Hilary (2009) Pageant princesses and Math whizzes: Understanding children's activities as a form of children's work. *Childhood* 16:195–212.

Lévi-Strauss, Claude (1966) *The Savage Mind*. Chicago, IL: University of Chicago Press.

Levin, Paula (1992) The impact of preschool teaching and learning in Hawaiian families. *Anthropology and Education Quarterly* 23(1):59–72.

Levine, Donald N. (1965) *Wax and Gold: Tradition and Innovation in Ethiopian Culture*. Chicago, IL: University of Chicago Press.

LeVine, Robert A. (1966) Sex roles and economic change in Africa. *Ethnology* 5:186–193.

(1973) Patterns of personality in Africa. *Ethos* 1:123–152.

(1974) Children's kinship concepts: Cognitive development and early experience among the Hausa. *Ethnology* 13:25–44.

(1988) Human parental care: Universal goals, cultural strategies, individual behavior. *New Directions for Child Development* 40:3–11.

(2004) Challenging expert knowledge: Findings from an African study of infant care and development. In Uwe P. Gielen and Jaipaul L. Roopnarine (Eds.), *Childhood and Adolescence: Cross-Cultural Perspectives and Applications*. pp. 149–165. Westport, CT: Praeger.

(2007) Ethnographic studies of childhood: A historical overview. *American Anthropologist* 109:247–260.

(2011) Traditions in transition: Adolescents remaking culture. *Ethos* 39:426–431.

(2014) Attachment theory as cultural ideology. In Hiltrud Otto and Heidi Keller (Eds.), *Different Faces of Attachment: Cultural Variations of a Universal Human Need*. pp. 50–65. Cambridge: Cambridge University Press.

LeVine, Robert A. and LeVine, Sarah E. (1988) Parental strategies among the Gusii of Kenya. In Robert A. LeVine, Patricia M. Miller, and Mary Maxwell West (Eds.), *Parental Behavior in Diverse Societies, special issue of New Directions for Child Development* 40:27–36.

LeVine, Robert A., LeVine, Sarah, Dixon, Suzanne, Richman, Amy, Leiderman, P. Herbert, Keefer, Constance H., and Brazelton, T. Berry (1994) *Child Care and Culture: Lessons from Africa*. Cambridge: Cambridge University Press.

LeVine, Robert A., LeVine, Sarah E., Rowe, Meredith L., and Anzola-Schnell, Beatrice (2004) Maternal literacy and health behavior: A Nepalese case study. *Social Science and Medicine* 58:863–877.

LeVine, Robert A., LeVine Sarah, Schnell-Anzola, Beatrice, Rowe, Meredith L., and Dexter, Emily (2012) *Literacy and Mothering: How Women's Schooling Changes the Lives of the World's Children*. New York, NY: Oxford University Press.

LeVine, Robert A. and White, Merrie I. (1986) *Human Conditions*. New York, NY: Routledge and Kegan Paul.

LeVine, Sarah E. (2006) Getting in, dropping out, and staying on: Determinants of girls' school attendance in the Kathmandu Valley in Nepal. *Anthropology and Education Quarterly* 37:21–41.

LeVine, Sarah and LeVine, Robert A. (1981) Child abuse and neglect in sub-Saharan Africa. In Jill E. Korbin (Ed.), *Child Abuse and Neglect*. pp. 35–55. Berkeley, CA: University of California Press.

Levine, Susan (2013) *Children of a Bitter Harvest*. Cape Town: Bested.

Levy, Robert I. (1973) *The Tahitians*. Chicago, IL: University of Chicago Press.

(1996) Essential contrasts: Differences in parental ideas about learners and teaching in Tahiti and Nepal. In Sara Harkness and Charles M. Super (Eds.), *Parents' Cultural Belief Systems: Their Origins, Expressions, and Consequences*. pp. 123–142. New York, NY: Guilford Press.

Lew, Jamie (2004) The "other" story of model minorities: Korean American high school dropouts in an urban context. *Anthropology and Education Quarterly* 35:303–323.

Lewin, Tamar (2009) College dropouts cite low money and high stress. *New York Times*, December 9. Available at www.nytimes.com/2009/12/10/education/10graduate.html?_r=0. Accessed October 4, 2013.

Lewis, Amanda E. and Forman, Tyrone A. (2002) Contestation or collaboration? A comparative study of home–school relations. *Anthropology and Education Quarterly* 33:60–89.

Lewis, Jerome (2008) Ekila: Blood bodies, egalitarian societies. *Journal of the Royal Anthropological Institute* 14:297–315.

Lewis, Kerrie P. and Barton, Robert A. (2004) Playing for keeps: Evolutionary relationships between social play and the cerebellum in nonhuman primates. *Human Nature* 15:5–21.

Lewis, Mary E. (2007) *The Bioarchaeology of Children: Perspectives from Biological and Forensic Anthropology.* Cambridge: Cambridge University Press.

Lewis, Oscar (1961) *The Children of the Sanchez.* New York, NY: Random House.

Li, Jin (2003) US and Chinese cultural beliefs about learning. *Journal of Educational Psychology* 95:258–267.

   (2012) *Cultural Foundations of Learning: East and West.* Cambridge: Cambridge University Press.

Li, Jin, Wang, Lianquin, and Fischer, Kurt W. (2004) The organization of Chinese shame concepts. *Cognition and Emotion* 18:767–797.

Liamputtong, Prancee (2009) Nyob Nruab Hlis: Thirty days' confinement in Hmong culture. In Helaine Selin and Pamela K. Stone (Eds.) *Childhood across Cultures: Ideas and Practices of Pregnancy, Childbirth and the Postpartum.* pp. 161–173. Amherst, MA: Springer.

Liapis, Vayos (2004) Choes, Anthesteria, and the dead: A re-appraisal. Paper presented at the American Philological Association annual meeting, January, San Francisco, CA.

Liden, Hilde (2003) Common neighbourhoods, diversified lives: Growing up in urban Norway. In Karen Fog Olwig and Eva Gullov (Eds.), *Children's Places: Cross-Cultural Perspectives.* pp. 119–137. New York, NY: Routledge.

Liefsen, Esben (2004) Person, relation, and value: The economy of circulating Ecuadorian children in international adoption. In Fiona Bowie (Ed.), *Cross-Cultural Approaches to Adoption.* pp. 182–196. London: Routledge.

Lindenbaum, Shirley (1973) Sorcerers, ghosts, and polluting women: An analysis of religious beliefs and population control. *Ethnology* 2:241–253.

Lindstrom, Lamont (1990) *Knowledge and Power in a South Pacific Society.* Washington, DC: Smithsonian Institution Press.

Lipka, Jerry, Hogan, Maureen P., Webster, Joan Parker, Yanez, Evelyn, Adams, Barbara, Clark, Stacy, and Lacy, Doreen (2005) Math in a cultural context: Two case studies of a successfully culturally based math project. *Anthropology Education Quarterly* 26:367–385.

Little, Christopher A. J. L. (2008) Becoming an Asabano: The socialization of Asabano children, Duranmin, West Sepik Province, Papua New Guinea. Unpublished Master's thesis, Trent University, Peterborough, Ontario.

   (2011) How Asabano children learn; or, formal schooling amongst informal learners. *Oceania* 81:146–166.

Little, Kenneth (1970) The social cycle and initiation among the Mende. In John Middleton (Ed.), *From Child to Adult.* pp. 207–225. Garden City, NY: Natural History Press.

Lloyd, Peter (1953) Craft organization in Yoruba towns. *Africa* 23:30–44.

Locke, John J. (1693/1994) *Some Thoughts on Education.* Ed. Frances W. Garforth. Woodbury, NY: Barron's Education Series.

Lonsdorf, Elizabeth (2005) Sex differences in the development of termite-fishing skills in the wild chimpanzees, *Pan troglodytes schweinfurthii,* of Gombe National Park, Tanzania. *Animal Behavior* 70:673–683.

Lord, Jack (2011) Child labor in the Gold Coast: The economics of work, education, and the family in late-colonial African households, c.1940–57. *Journal of the History of Childhood and Youth* 4.(1):86–115.

Lorenz, John M., Paneth, Nigel, Jetton, James R., Ouden, Lyaden, and Tyson, Jon E. (2001) Comparison of management strategies for extreme prematurity in New Jersey and the Netherlands: Outcomes and resource expenditure. *Pediatrics* 108:1269–1274.

Loudon, John. B. (1970) Teasing and socialization on Tristan da Cunha. In Phillip Maye (Ed.), *Socialization: The Approach from Social Anthropology*. pp. 293–332. London: Tavistock Publications.

Loveless, Tom (2010). *The 2009 Brown Center Report on American Education. Vol. 11: How Well Are American Students Learning?* Washington, DC: Brookings Institution.

Low, Bobbi S. (1989) Cross-cultural patterns in the training of children: An evolutionary perspective. *Journal of Comparative Psychology* 103:311–319.

(2000) Sex, wealth, and fertility: old rules, new environments. In Lee Cronk, Napoleon Chagnon, and William Irons (Eds.), *Adaptation and Human Behavior: An Anthropological Perspective*. pp. 323–344. New York, NY: Aldine de Gruyter.

(2005) Families: An evolutionary anthropological perspective. In Jaipaul L. Roopnarine and Uwe P. Gielen (Eds.), *Families in Global Perspective*. pp. 14–32. Boston, MA: Allyn and Bacon.

Low, Bobbi S., Hazel, Ashley, Parker, Nicholas, and Welch, Kathleen B. (2008) Influences on women's reproductive lives: Unexpected ecological underpinnings. *Cross-Cultural Research* 42:201–219.

Lowe, Edward D. and Johnson, Allen (2007) Tales of danger: Parental protection and child development in stories from Chuuk. *Ethnology* 46:151–168.

Lozoff, Betsy and Brittenham, Gary (1979) Infant care: Cache or carry. *Journal of Pediatrics* 95(3):478–483.

Lupher, Mark (1995) Revolutionary little red devils: The social psychology of rebel youth, 1966–1967. In Anne B. Kinney (Ed.), *Chinese Views of Childhood*. pp. 321–343. Honolulu, HI: University of Hawai'i Press.

Luria, Alexander R. (1976) *Cognitive Development: Its Cultural and Social Foundations*. Cambridge, MA: Harvard University Press.

Luthar, Suniya S. and Shoum, Karen A. (2006) Extracurricular involvement among affluent youth: A scapegoat for "ubiquitous achievement pressures"? *Developmental Psychology* 42:583–597.

Lutz, Catherine A. (1983) Parental goals, ethnopsychology, and the development of emotional meaning. *Ethos* 11:246–262.

(1988) *Unnatural Emotions: Everyday Sentiments on a Micronesian Atoll and their Challenge to Western Theory*. Chicago, IL: University of Chicago Press.

Lutz, Catherine and LeVine, Robert A. (1983) Culture and intelligence in infancy: An ethnographic view. In Michael Lewis (Ed.), *Origins of Intelligence*, 2nd edn pp. 327–345. New York, NY: Plenum Press.

Lynch, Caitrin (2007) *Juki Girls, Good Girls: Gender and Cultural Politics in Sri Lanka's Global Garment Industry*. Ithaca, NY: Cornell University Press.

Lynd, Robert S. and Lynd, Helen M. (1929) *Middletown: A Study in American Culture*. New York, NY: Harcourt, Brace.

Lyon, Karen (2009) Educating Ben: Johnson's school days. *Folger Magazine, Fall* 22–25.

Mabilia, Mara (2000) The cultural context of childhood diarrhoea among Gogo infants. *Anthropology and Medicine* 7:191–208.

(2005) *Breast Feeding and Sexuality: Beliefs and Taboos among the Gogo Mothers in Tanzania.* Oxford: Berghahn Books.

MacCormack, Carol P. (1994) Health, fertility and birth in Moyamba District, Sierra Leone. In Carol P. MacCormack (Ed.), *Ethnography of Fertility and Birth.* pp. 105–129. Prospect Heights, IL: Waveland Press.

MacDonald, Katherine (2007) Cross-cultural comparison of learning in human hunting: Implication for life history evolution. *Human Nature* 18:386–402.

MacDonald, Kevin and Hershberger, Scott L. (2005) Theoretical issues in the study of evolution and development. In Robert L. Burgess and Kevin MacDonald (Eds.), *Evolutionary Perspectives on Human Development*, 2nd ed,. pp. 21–72. Thousand Oaks, CA: Sage.

Macedo, Silva Loped da Silva (2009) Indigenous school policies and politics: The sociopolitical relationship of Wayãpi Amerindians to Brazilian and French Guyana schooling. *Anthropology and Education Quarterly* 40:170–186.

MacElroy, Mary H. (1917) *Work and Play in Colonial Days.* New York, NY: The MacMillan.

MacGinnis, John (2011) Aspects of child labour and the status of children in Mesopotamia in the first millennium BC. Paper presented at the fourth annual conference of the Society for the Study of Childhood in the Past, October, Cambridge.

Machado Neto, Zahidé (1982). Children and adolescents in Brazil: Work, poverty, starvation. *Development and Change* 13:527–536.

MacKenzie, Maureen A. (1991) *Androgynous Objects: String Bags and Gender in Central New Guinea.* Reading: Harwood.

Maclean, Una (1994) Folk medicine and fertility: Aspects of Yoruba medical practice affecting women. In Carol P. MacCormack (Ed.), *Ethnography of Fertility and Birth.* pp. 151–169. Prospect Heights, IL: Waveland Press.

MacNall, Miles, Dunnigan, Timothy, and Mortimer, Jeylan T. (1994) The educational achievement of the St. Paul Hmong. *Anthropology and Education Quarterly* 25:44–65.

MacNeilage, Peter F. and Davis, Barbara L. (2005) The evolution of language. In David M. Buss (Ed.), *Handbook of Evolutionary Psychology.* pp 698–723. New York, NY: Wiley.

Madsen, Millard C. (1971) Developmental and cross-cultural differences in the cooperation and competitive behavior of young children. *Journal of Cross-Cultural Psychology* 2:365–371.

Maestripieri, Dario (2007) *Macachiavellian Intelligence: How Rhesus Macaques and Humans Have Conquered the World.* Chicago, IL: University of Chicago Press.

Maestripieri, Dario and Pelka, Suzanne (2001) Sex differences in interest in infants across the lifespan: A biological adaptation for parenting? *Human Nature* 13:327–344.

Magvanjav, Oyunbileg, Undurraga, Eduardo A., Eisenberg, Dan T. Zeng, Wu, Dorjgochoo, Tsogzolmaa, Leonard, William R., and Godoy, Ricardo A. (2012)

Sibling composition and children's anthropometric indicators of nutritional status: Evidence from native Amazonians in Bolivia. Waltham, MA: Brandeis University Tsimane' Amazonian Panel Study Working Paper 73, April 13. Available at: http://heller.brandeis.edu/academic/sid/tsimane.

Maiden, Annet H. and Farwell, Edie (1997) *The Tibetan Art of Parenting*. Boston, MA: Wisdom Publications.

Makey, Wade C. (1983) A preliminary test for the validation of the adult male–child bond as a species-characteristic trait. *American Anthropologist* 85:391–402.

Malinowski, Bronislaw (1927/2012) *The Father in Primitive Psychology*. Hackensack, NJ: Morrison Press.

  (1929) *The Sexual Life of Savages: An Ethnographic Account of Courtship, Marriage, and Family Life Among the Natives of the Trobriand Islands, British New Guinea*. London: Routledge, Kegan, Paul.

Manderson, Lenore (2003) Roasting, smoking, and dieting in response to birth: Malay confinement in cross-cultural perspective. In Lauren Dundes (Ed.), *The Manner Born: Birth Rites in Cross-Cultural Perspective*. pp. 137–159. Lanham, MD: AltaMira Press.

Mann, Gillian (2004) Separated children: Care and support in context. In Jo Boyden and Joanna de Berry (Eds.), *Children and Youth on the Front Line: Ethnography, Armed Conflict and Displacement*. pp. 3–22. Oxford: Berghahn Books.

Mann, Janet (2002) Nurturance or negligence: Maternal psychology and behavioral preference among preterm twins. In James Tooby, Leeda Cosmides, and Jerome Barkow (Eds.), *The Adapted Mind: Evolutionary Psychology and the Generation of Culture*. pp. 367–390. Oxford: Oxford University Press.

Mann, Rann S. (1979) *The Bay Islander*. Calcutta: Institute of Social Research and Applied Anthropology.

Mannon, Susan E. and Eagan Kemp (2010) Pampered sons, (wo)manly men, or do nothing machos? Costa Rican men coming of age under neo-liberalism. *Bulletin of Latin American Research* 29:477–491.

Mapedzahama, Virginia and Bourdillon, Michael (2000) Street workers in a Harare suburb. In Michael Bourdillon (Ed.), *Earning a Life: Working Children in Zimbabwe*. pp. 25–44. Harare: Weaver Press.

Marano, Hara E. (2008) *A Nation of Wimps*. New York, NY: Broadway Books.

Marchand, Trevor H. J. (2001) *Minaret Building and Apprenticeship in Yemen*. Richmond: Curzon Press.

Maretzki, Thomas W. and Maretzki, Hatsumi (1963) Taira: An Okinawan village. In Beatrice B. Whiting, (Ed.), *Six Cultures: Studies of Child Rearing*. pp. 363–539. New York, NY: Wiley.

Marks, Jonathan (2003) *What It Means to be 98% Chimpanzee: Apes, People and their Genes*. Berkeley, CA: University of California Press.

Markstrom, Carol A. (2008) *Empowerment of North American Indian Girls: Ritual Expressions at Puberty*. Lincoln, NE: University of Nebraska Press.

Marlowe, Frank W. (1999) Showoffs or providers? The parenting effort of Hadza men. *Evolution and Human Behavior* 20:391–404.

(2004) Mate preferences among Hadza hunter-gatherers. *Human Nature* 15(4):365–376.

(2005) Who tends Hadza children? In Barry S. Hewlett and Michael E. Lamb (Eds.), *Hunter Gatherer Childhoods: Evolutionary, Developmental, and Cultural Perspectives.* pp. 177–190. New Brunswick, NJ: Aldine Transaction.

(2007) Hunting and gathering: The human sexual division of foraging labor. *Cross-Cultural Research* 41(2):170–195.

(2010) *The Hadza: Hunter-Gatherers of Tanzania.* Berkeley, CA: University of California Press.

Maron, Dina F. (2013) Flame retardants linked to lower IQs, hyperactivity in children. *Scientific American*, May 6. Available at www.scientificamerican.com/article.cfm?id=flame-retardants-linked-lower-iq-hyperactivitiy-children. Accessed August 8, 2013.

Márquez, Patricia C. (1999) *The Street Is My Home: Youth and Violence in Caracas.* Palo Alto, CA: Stanford University Press.

Marshall, John (1972) *Playing with Scorpions* (film). Watertown, MA: Documentary Educational Resources.

Martin, Diana (2001) The meaning of children in Hong Kong. In Soraya Tremayne (Ed.), *Managing Reproductive Life: Cross-Cultural Themes in Sexuality and Fertility.* pp. 157–171. Oxford: Berghahn Books.

Martin, Jeannett (2012) Child fosterage, children's work and the spread of schooling in Northern Benin. In Gerd Spittler and Michael Bourdillion (Eds.), *African Children at Work: Working and Learning in Growing Up.* pp. 195–226. Berlin: LitVerlag.

Martin, Kay and Voorhies, Barbara (1975) *Female of the Species.* New York, NY: Columbia University Press.

Martini, Mary (1994) Peer interactions in Polynesia: A view from the Marquesas. In Jaipaul L. Roopnarine, James E. Jonson, and Frank H. Hooper (Eds.), *Children's Play in Diverse Cultures.* pp. 73–103. Albany, NY: State University of New York Press.

(1995) Features of home environments associated with children's school success. *Early Child Development and Care* 111:49–68.

(1996) "What's new?" at the dinner table: Family dynamics during mealtimes in two cultural groups in Hawaii. *Early Development and Parenting* 5:23–34.

(2005) Family development in two island cultures in the changing Pacific. In Jaipaul L. Roopnarine and Uwe P. Gielen (Eds.), *Families in Global Perspective.* pp. 120–147. Boston, MA: Allyn and Bacon.

Martini, Mary and Kirkpatrick, John (1981) Early interaction in the Marquesas Islands. In Tiffany M. Field, Anita M. Sostek, Peter Vietze, and P. Herbert Leiderman (Eds.), *Culture and Early Interactions.* Hillsdale, NJ: Lawrence Erlbaum.

(1992) Parenting in Polynesia: A view from the Marquesas. In Jaipaul L. Roopnarine and D. Bruce Carter (Eds.), *Parent–Child Socialization in Diverse Cultures. Vol. V: Annual Advances in Applied Developmental Psychology.* pp. 199–222. Norwood, NJ: Ablex.

Maschio, Thomas (1995) Mythic images and objects of myth in Rauto female puberty ritual. In Nancy C. Lutkehaus and Paul B. Roscoe (Eds.), *Gender Rituals: Female Initiation in Melanesia*. pp. 131–161. London: Routledge.

Matchar, Emily (2013) How parenting became a DIY project. *Atlantic Monthly*, February 4. Available at www.theatlantic.com/sexes/archive/2013/02/how-parenting-became-a-diy-project/272792. Accessed February 6, 2013.

Mathews, Holly F. (1992) The directive force of morality tales in a Mexican community. In Roy D'Andrade and Claudia Strauss (Eds.), *Human Motives and Cultural Models*. pp. 127–162. Cambridge: Cambridge University Press.

Matias, Aisha S. (1996) Female circumcision in Africa. *Africa Update* (online) 3(2). Available at http://web.ccsu.edu/afstudy/upd3-2.html#Z3. Accessed October 4, 2013.

Matsuzawa, Tetsuro, Biro, Dora, Humle, Tatyana, Inoue-Nakamura, Noriko, Tonooka, Rikako, and Yamakoshi, Gen (2001) Emergence of culture in wild chimpanzees: Education by master apprenticeship. In Tetsuro Matsuzawa (Ed.), *Primate Origins of Human Cognition and Behavior*. pp. 557–74. Heidelberg: Springer.

Matthiasson, John S. (1979) But teacher, why can't I be a hunter: Inuit adolescence as a double-blind situation. In Ishwaran Karigoudar (Ed.), *Childhood and Adolescence in Canada*. pp. 72–82. Toronto: McGraw-Hill Ryerson.

Mattison, Siobhán M. and Neill, Dawn B. (2013) The effects of residential ecology on patterns of child work and mother's reproductive success among Indo-Fijians. *Evolution and Human Behavior* 34:207–215.

Mauss, Marcel (1967) *The Gift: Forms and Functions of Exchanges in Archaic Societies*. New York, NY: W.W. Norton.

Mawson, Andrew (2004) Children, impunity and justice: Some dilemmas from northern Uganda. In Jo Boyden and Joanna de Berry (Eds.), *Children and Youth on the Front Line: Ethnography, Armed Conflict and Displacement*. pp. 130–141. Oxford: Berghahn Books.

Maxwell, Kevin B. (1983) *Bemba Myth and Ritual: The Impact of Literacy on an Oral Culture*. New York, NY: Peter Lang.

Mayer, Philip and Mayer, Iona (1970) Socialization by peers: The youth organization of the Red Xhosa. In Philip Mayer (Ed.), *Socialization: The Approach from Social Anthropology*. pp. 159–189. London: Tavistock Publications.

Maynard, Ashley E. (2002) Cultural teaching: The development of teaching skills in Maya sibling interactions. *Child Development* 7:969–982.
    (2004a) Sibling interactions. In Uwe P. Gielen and Jaipaul L. Roopnarine (Eds.), *Childhood and Adolescence: Cross-Cultural Perspectives and Applications*. pp. 229–252. Westport, CT: Praeger.
    (2004b) Cultures of teaching in childhood: Formal schooling and Maya sibling teaching at home. *Cognitive Development* 19:517–535.

Maynard, Ashley E., Greenfield, Patricia M., and Childs, Carla P. (1999) Culture, history, biology and body: Native and non-native acquisition of technological skill. *Ethos* 27:379–402.

Maynard, Ashley E. and Tovote, Katherine E. (2010) Learning from other children. In David F. Lancy, Suzanne Gaskins, and John Bock (Eds.), *The Anthropology of Learning in Childhood*. pp. 181–205. Lanham, MD: AltaMira Press.

Mays, Sam (2000) The archaeology and history of infanticide, and its occurrence in earlier British populations. In Joanna S. Derevenski (Ed.), *Children and Material Culture*. pp. 180–190. London: Routledge.

McCabe, Donald L. Butterfield, Kenneth D., and Treviño, Linda K. (2012) *Cheating in College: Why Students Do It and What Educators Can Do about It*. Baltimore, MD: Johns Hopkins University Press.

McCafferty, Geoffery G. and McCafferty, Sharisse D. (2006) Boys and girls interrupted: Mortuary evidence of children from postclassical Cholula, Puebla. In Traci Adren and Scott R. Hutson (Eds.), *The Social Experience of Childhood in Ancient Mesoamerica*. pp. 25–82. Boulder, CO: University of Colorado Press.

McCorkle, Thomas (1965) Fajardo's people: Cultural adjustment in Venezuela; and the little community in Latin American and North American contexts. In *Latin American Studies. Vol. 1*. Los Angeles: UCLA Latin American Center.

McCosker, Sandra (1976) San Blas Cuna Indian lullabies: A means of informal learning. In Johannes Wilbert (Ed.), *Enculturation in Latin America*. pp. 29–66. Los Angeles, CA: UCLA Latin American Center Publications.

McDonald, Mark (2012) Buy, sell, adopt: Child trafficking in China. *International Herald Tribune*, December 26. Available at http://rendezvous.blogs. nytimes.com/2012/12/26/buy-sell-adopt-child-trafficking-in-china. Accessed February 1, 2014.

McElreath, Richard (2004) Social learning and the maintenance of cultural variation: An evolutionary model and data from East Africa. *American Anthropologist* 106:308–321.

McGaugh, James L. (2006) Make mild moments memorable: Add a little arousal. *Trends in Cognitive Sciences* 10:345–347.

McGilvray, Dennis B. (1994) Sexual power and fertility in Sri Lanka: Batticaloa Tamils and Moors. In Carol P. MacCormack (Ed.), *Ethnography of Fertility and Birth*. pp. 15–63. Prospect Heights, IL: Waveland Press.

McGirk, Jan (2012) Tomb of sixth-century Maya king discovered. *National Geographic Online Magazine*, May 30. Available at http://news. nationalgeographic.com/news/2001/05/0530_mayafind.html. Accessed February 1, 2014.

McGrew, William C. (1977) Socialization and object manipulation of wild chimpanzees. In Suzanne Chevalier-Skolnikoff and Frank E. Poirier (Eds.), *Primate Bio-Social Development: Biological, Social, and Ecological Determinants*. pp. 261–288. New York: Garland.

McIvor, Chris (2000) Child labour in informal mines in Zimbabwe. In Michael Bourdillon (Ed.), *Earning a Life: Working Children in Zimbabwe*. pp. 173–185. Harare: Weaver Press.

McNaughton, Peter R. (1988) *The Mande Blacksmiths*. Bloomington, IN: Indiana University Press.

McNaughton, Stuart (1996) Ways of parenting and cultural identity. *Culture and Psychology* 2:173–201.

McPhee, Colin (1955) Children and music in Bali. In Margaret Mead and Martha Wolfenstein (Eds.), *Childhood in Contemporary Cultures*. pp. 70–98. Chicago, IL: University of Chicago Press.

Mead, Margaret (1928/1961) *Coming of Age in Samoa*. New York, NY: New American Library.

(1932) An investigation of the thought of primitive children with special reference to animism. *Journal of the Royal Anthropological Institute* 62:173–190.

(1954) The swaddling hypothesis: Its reception. *American Anthropologist* 56:395–409.

(1955) Children and ritual in Bali. In Margaret Mead and Martha Wolfenstein (Eds.), *Childhood in Contemporary Cultures*. pp. 40–51. Chicago, IL: University of Chicago Press.

(1964) *Continuities in Cultural Evolution*. New Haven, CT: Yale University Press.

Medaets, Chantal V. (2011) "Tu garante?" Reflections on the transmission practices and learning in the Lower Tapajós, Brazilian Amazon. Paper presented at the 34th Annual Meeting of ANPEd (Brazilian Educational Research and Post-Graduate Association), October.

(2013) "*Tu garante?*" Local ideas on childhood, cultural transmission and learning practices along the Tapajós river. Paper presented at the joint SPA/AYCIG meeting, February, San Diego, CA.

Mederer, Helen J. (1993) Division of labor in two-earner homes: Task accomplishment versus household management as critical variables in perceptions about family work. *Journal of Marriage and the Family* 55: 133–145.

Meehan, Courtney L. (2005) The effects of residential locality on parental and alloparental investment among the Aka foragers of the Central African Republic. *Human Nature* 16:58–80.

(2009) Maternal time allocation in two cooperative childrearing societies. *Human Nature* 20:375–393.

Meinert, Lotte (2003) Sweet and bitter places: The politics of schoolchildren's orientation in rural Uganda. In Karen Fog Olwig and Eva Gullov (Eds.), *Children's Places: Cross-Cultural Perspectives*. pp. 179–196. New York, NY: Routledge.

Mejia-Arauz, Rebecca, Rogoff, Barbara, and Paradise, Ruth (2005) Cultural variation in children's observation during a demonstration. *International Journal of Behavioral Development* 29:282–291.

Meltzoff, Andrew N. and Williamson, Rebecca A. (2009) Imitation. In Richard A. Shweder, Thomas R. Bidell, Anne C. Dailey, and Suzanne D. Dixon (Eds.), *The Child: An Encyclopedic Companion*. pp. 480–481. Chicago, IL: University of Chicago Press.

Menon, Shanti (2001) Male authority and female autonomy: A study of the matrilineal Nayars of Kerala, south India. In Caroline B. Brettell and Carolyn F. Sargent (Eds.), *Gender in Cross-Cultural Perspective*. pp. 352–361. Upper Saddle River, NJ: Prentice Hall.

Meskell, Lynn (1994) Dying young: The experience of death at Deir el Medina. *Archaeological Review from Cambridge* 13:35–45.

Messing, Simon D. (1985) *Highland Plateau Amhara of Ethiopia*. New Haven, CT: Human Relations Area Files.

Michaels, Sarah and Cazden, Courtney B. (1986) Teacher/child collaboration as oral preparation for literacy. In Bambi B. Schiefflin and Perry Gilmore (Eds.), *The Acquisition of Literacy: Ethnographic Perspectives*. pp. 132–154. Norwood, NJ: Ablex.

Michalchik, Vera S. (1997) The display of cultural knowledge in cultural transmission: Models of participation from the Pacific Island of Kosrae. In George D. Spindler (Ed.), *Education and Cultural Process: Anthropological Approaches*. pp. 393–426. Prospect Heights, IL: Waveland Press.

Michaud, Francine (2007) From apprentice to wage-earner: Child labour before and after the Black Death. In Joel T. Rosenthal (Ed.), *Essays on Medieval Childhood: Responses to Recent Debate*. pp. 73–90. Donington: Shaun Tyas.

Mickelson, Roslyn A. (2000) Globalization, childhood poverty and education in the Americas. In Roslyn A. Mickelson (Ed.), *Children on the Streets of the Americas: Globalization, Homeless-ness and Education in the United States, Brazil and Cuba*. pp. 11–42. New York, NY: Routledge.

Millard, Ann V. and Graham, Margaret A. (1985) Breastfeeding in two Mexican villages: Social and demographic perspectives. In Valerie Hull and Mayling Simpson (Eds.), *Breastfeeding, Child Health and Birth Spacing: Cross-Cultural Perspectives*. pp. 55–74. London: Croom Helm.

Miller, Barbara D. (1987) Female infanticide and child neglect in rural north India. In Nancy Scheper-Hughes (Ed.), *Child Survival: Anthropological Perspectives on the Treatment and Maltreatment of Children*. pp. 95–112. Dordrecht: Reidel.

(1995) Precepts and practices: Researching identity formation among Indian Hindu adolescents in the United States. In Jacqueline J. Goodnow, Peggy J. Miller, and Frank Kessel (Eds.), *Cultural Practices as Contexts for Development*. pp. 71–90. San Francisco, CA: Jossey-Bass.

Miller, Peggy J., Sandel, Todd L., Liang, Chung-Hui, and Fung, Heidi (2001) Narrating transgressions in U.S. and Taiwan. *Ethos* 29:159–186.

Milner, Murray Jr. (2006) *Freaks, Geeks, and Cool Kids: American Teenagers, Schools, and the Culture of Consumption*. New York, NY: Routledge.

Minehan, Thomas (1934) *Boy and Girl Tramps of America*. New York, NY: Farrar and Rinehart.

Mintz, Steven (2004) *Huck's Raft: A History of American Childhood*. Cambridge, MA: Belknap Press.

Mitchell, George (1981) *Human Sex Differences: A Primatologists' Perspective*. New York, NY: Van Nostrand Reinhold.

Mitchell, Robbyn (2008) One-year-old, one lavish birthday bash. *Tampa Bay Times*, February 24, B1. Available at www.sptimes.com/2008/02/24/Hillsborough/One_year_old_one_lav.shtml. Accessed February 1, 2014.

Mithen, Steven (1998) The supernatural beings of prehistory and the external storage of religious ideas. In Colin Renfrew and Chris Scarre (Eds.), *Cognition and Material Culture: The Archaeology of Symbolic Storage*. pp. 97–106. Oxford: Oxbow Books.

(1999) Imitation and cultural change: A view from the Stone Age, with specific reference to the manufacture of handaxes. In Hilary O. Box and Kathleen R. Gibson (Eds.), *Mammalian Social Learning: Comparative and Ecological Perspectives*. pp: 389–399. Cambridge: Cambridge University Press.

Mitterauer, Michael (1992) *A History of Youth*. Oxford: Blackwell.

Mitterauer, Michael and Sieder, Reinhard (1997) *The European Family: Patriarchy to Partnership from the Middle Ages to the Present*. Chicago, IL: University of Chicago Press.

Modiano, Nancy (1973) *Indian Education in the Chiapas Highlands*. New York, NY: Holt, Rinehart, and Winston.

Mohammad, Patel H. (1997) Child rearing and socialization among the Savaras. *Man and Life* 23:173–182.

Monberg, Torben (1970) Determinants of choice in adoption and fosterage on Bellona Island. *Ethnology* 9:99–136.

Montague, Susan P. (1985) Infant feeding and health care in Kaduwaga Village, the Trobriand Islands. In Leslie B. Marshall (Ed.), *Infant Care and Feeding in the South Pacific*. pp. 83–96. New York, NY: Gordon and Breach.

Montandon, Cleopatre (2001) The negotiation of influence: Children's experience of parental educational practices in Geneva. In Leena Alanen and Berry Mayall (Eds.), *Conceptualizing Child–Adult Relations*. pp. 54–69. New York, NY: Routledge.

Montgomery, Heather (2001a) Motherhood, fertility and ambivalence among young prostitutes in Thailand. In Soraya Tremayne (Ed.), *Managing Reproductive Life: Cross-Cultural Themes in Sexuality and Fertility*. pp. 71–84. Oxford: Berghahn Books.

(2001b) *Modern Babylon: Prostituting Children in Thailand*. Oxford: Berghahn Books.

(2008) *An Introduction to Childhood: Anthropological Perspectives on Children's Lives*. Oxford: Blackwell.

Moore, Leslie C. (2006) Learning by heart in Qur'anic and public schools in northern Cameroon. *Social Analysis: The International Journal of Cultural and Social Practice* 50:109–126.

Morelli, Camilla (2011) Learning to sit still: The physical implications of schooling for Matses children in the Peruvian Amazon. Paper presented at the workshop on Schooling in Anthropology: Learning the "Modern Way," December 5, Brunel University.

(2012) Teaching in the rainforest: Exploring Matses children's affective engagement and multisensory experiences in the classroom environment. *Teaching Anthropology* 2(2):53–65.

Morelli, Gilda A., Rogoff, Barbara, and Angelillo, Cathy (2003) Cultural variation in young children's access to work or involvement in specialized child-focused activities. *International Journal of Behavioral Development* 27:264–274.

Morelli, Gilda A. and Tronick, Edward Z. (1991) Parenting and child development in the Efe foragers and Lese farmers of Zaire. In Mark H. Bornstein (Ed.), *Cultural Approaches to Parenting*. pp. 91–113. Hillsdale, NJ: Erlbaum.

Morgan, Lynn M. (1998) Ambiguities lost: Fashioning the fetus into a child in Ecuador and the United States. In Nancy Scheper-Hughes and Carolyn F. Sargent (Eds.),

Small Wars: The Cultural Politics of Childhood. pp. 58–74. Berkeley, CA: University of California Press.

Moritz, Mark (2008) A critical examination of honor cultures and herding societies in Africa. *African Studies Review* 51:99–117.

Mortimer, Jeylan T. and Krüger, Helga (2000) Pathways from school to work in Germany and the United States. In Maureen T. Hallinan (Ed.), *Handbook of the Sociology of Education.* pp. 475–497. New York: Plenum Press.

Morton, Helen (1996) *Becoming Tongan: An Ethnography of Childhood.* Honolulu, HI: University of Hawai'i Press.

Moses, Sharon (2008) Çatalhöyük's foundation burials: Ritual sacrifice or convenient deaths? In Krum Bacvarov (Ed.), *Babies Reborn: Infant/Child Burials in Pre- and Protohistory.* BAR International Series 1832. pp. 45–52. Oxford: Archaeopress.

Mueller, Claudia M. and Dweck, Carol S. (1998) Praise for intelligence can undermine children's motivation and performance. *Journal of Personality and Social Psychology* 75:33–52.

Mull, Dorothy S. and Mull, J. Dennis (1987) Infanticide among the Tarahumara of the Mexican Sierra Madre. In Nancy Scheper-Hughes (Ed.), *Child Survival: Anthropological Perspectives on the Treatment and Maltreatment of Children.* pp. 113–132. Dordrecht: Reidel.

Mungai, Anne M. (2002) *Rethinking Childhood: Growing up and Schooling for Females in Rural Kenya.* New York, NY: Peter Lang.

Munroe, Robert L. (2005) Fatherhood and effects on children in four cultures. Paper presented at the 34th annual meeting of the Society for Cross-Cultural Research February 25, Santa Fe, NM.

Munroe, Robert L. and Munroe, Ruth H. (1992) Fathers in children's environments: A four culture study. In Barry S. Hewlett (Ed.), *Father–Child Relations: Cultural and Biosocial Contexts.* pp. 213–229. New York, NY: Aldine de Gruyter.

Munroe, Ruth H., Munroe, Robert L., and Shimmin, Harold S. (1984) Children's work in four cultures: Determinants and consequences. *American Anthropologist* 86:369–379.

Muraskas, Jonathan and Parsi, Kayhan (2008) The cost of saving the tiniest lives: NICUS versus prevention. *Virtual Mentor* 10:655–658.

Murdock, George P. (1967) *Ethnographic Atlas.* Pittsburgh, PA: University of Pittsburgh Press.

Murphy, Elizabeth (2007) Images of childhood in mothers' accounts of contemporary childrearing. *Childhood* 14:105–127.

Murphy, William P. (1980) Secret knowledge as property and power in Kpelle society: Elders versus youth. *Africa* 50:193–207.

Musharbash, Yasmine (2011) Warungka: Becoming and unbecoming a Warlpiri person. In Ute Eickelkamp (Ed.), *Growing up in Central Australia: New Anthropological Studies of Aboriginal Childhood and Adolescence.* pp. 63–81. Oxford: Berghahn Books.

Musil, Alois (1928) *The Manners and Customs of the Rwala Bedouin.* New York, NY: American Geographical Society.

Mygland, Sigrid Samset (2008) Beyond fragments and shards: Children in medieval Bergen. In *Proceedings from the 2nd International Conference of the Society for the Study of Childhood in the Past, Stavanger.* pp. 83–93. Stavanger: University of Stavanger.

Nag, Moni, White, Benjamin N. F., and Peet, R. Creighton (1978) An anthropological approach to the study of the economic value of children in Java and Nepal. *Current Anthropology* 19:293–306.

Naito, Takashi and Gielen, Uwe P. (2005) The changing Japanese family: A psychological portrait. In Jaipaul L. Roopnarine and Uwe P. Gielen (Eds.), *Families in Global Perspective.* pp. 63–84. Boston, MA: Allyn and Bacon.

Naji, Myriem (2012) Learning to weave the threads of honor: Understanding the value of female schooling in southern Morocco. *Anthropology and Education Quarterly* 43:372–384.

Nakazawa, Jun and Shwalb, David W. (2012) Fathering in Japan: Entering an era of involvement. In David W. Shwalb, Barbara J. Shwalb, and, Michael E. Lamb (Eds.), *Fathers in Cultural Context.* pp. 42–67. New York, NY: Routledge.

Naraindas, Harish (2009) A sacramental theory of childbirth in India. In Helaine Selin and Pamela K. Stone (Eds.), *Childhood across Cultures: Ideas and Practices of Pregnancy, Childbirth and the Postpartum.* pp. 95–106. Amherst, MA: Springer.

Nasaw, David (1992) Children and commercial culture. In Elliott West and Paula Petrik (Eds.), *Small Worlds: Children and Adolescents in America, 1850–1950.* pp. 14–25. Lawrence, KS: University Press of Kansas.

Nash, Manning (1958) *Machine Age Maya.* Glencoe, IL: Free Press.

Nath, Y. V. Surendra (1960) *Bhils of Ratanmal: An Analysis of the Social Structure of a Western Indian Community.* M.S. University Sociological Monograph Series I. Baroda: Maharaja Sayajirao University of Baroda.

Ndege, George O. (2007) *Culture and Customs of Mozambique.* Westport, CT: Greenwood Press.

Neel, James V. (1970) Lessons from a "primitive" people. *Science* 170:815–822.

Neill, Sean R. (1983) Children's social relationships and education: An evolutionary effect? *Social Biology and Human Affairs* 47:48–55.

Neils, Jennifer and Oakley, John H. (2003) *Coming of Age in Ancient Greece* (DVD). Cincinnati, OH: Institute of Mediterranean Studies.

Nerlove, Sarah B. (1974) Women's workload and infant feeding practices: A relationship with demographic implications. *Ethnology* 13:207–214.

Nerlove, Sarah B., Roberts, John M., Klein, Robert E., Yarbrough, Charles, and Habicht, Jean-Pierre (1974) Natural indicators of cognitive development: An observational study of rural Guatemalan children. *Ethos* 2:265–295.

Neuwelt-Truntzer, Sandra (1981) Ecological influences on the physical, behavioral, and cognitive development of Pygmy children. Unpublished PhD dissertation, University of Chicago.

New, Rebecca S. (1994) Child's play – *una cosa naturale*: An Italian perspective. In Jaipaul L. Roopnarine, James E. Johnson, and Frank H. Hooper (Eds.), *Children's Play in Diverse Cultures.* pp. 123–147. Albany, NY: State University of New York Press.

Nichter, Mimi and Nichter, Mark (1987) A tale of Simeon: Reflections on raising a child while constructing fieldwork in rural South India. In Joan Cassell (Ed.), *Children in the Field: Anthropological Experiences.* pp. 65–89. Philadelphia, PA: Temple University Press.

Nicolaisen, Ida (1988) Concepts and learning among the Punan Bah of Sarawak. In Gustav Jahoda and Ioan Lewis (Eds.), *Acquiring Culture: Cross-Cultural Studies in Child Development.* pp. 193–221. London: Croom Helm.

Nicolas, David (1991) Children in medieval Europe. In Joseph M. Hawes and N. Ray Hiner (Eds.), *Children in Historical and Comparative Perspective.* pp. 31–52. Westport, CT: Greenwood Press.

Nicolson, Nancy A. (1977) A comparison of early behavioral development in wild and captive chimpanzees. In Suzanne Chevalier-Skolnikoff and Frank E. Poirier (Eds.), *Primate Bio-Social Development: Biological, Social, and Ecological Determinants.* pp. 529–600. New York, NY: Garland.

Nielson, John (2006) Video games favored over national parks, National Public Radio, July 19. Available at www.npr.org/templates/story/story.php?storyId=5567214. Accessed October 5, 2013.

Nieuwenhuys, Olga (1994) *Children's Lifeworlds: Gender, Welfare, and Labour in the Developing World.* London: Routledge.

(1996) The paradox of child labor and anthropology. *Annual Review of Anthropology* 25:237–251.

(2003) Growing up between places of work and non-places of childhood: The uneasy relationship. In Karen Fog Olwig and Eva Gullov (Eds.), *Children's Places: Cross-Cultural Perspectives.* pp. 99–118. London: Routledge.

(2005) The wealth of children: Reconsidering the child labor debate. In Jens Qvortrup (Ed.), *Studies in Modern Childhood.* pp. 167–183. Houndsmills: Palgrave Macmillian.

Nimmo, H. Arlo (1970) Bajau sex and reproduction. *Ethnology* 9:251–262.

Noonan, John T. (1970) An almost absolute value in history. In John T. Noonan (Ed.), *The Morality of Abortion: Legal and Historical Perspectives.* pp. 1–59. Cambridge, MA: Harvard University Press.

Norenzayan, Ara and Atran, Scott (2004) Cognitive and emotional processes in the cultural transmission of natural and nonnatural beliefs. In Mark Schaller and Christian S. Crandall (Eds.), *The Psychological Foundations of Culture.* pp. 149–169. Mahwah, NJ: Erlbaum.

Notermans, Catrien (2004) Sharing home, food, and bed: Paths of grandmotherhood in East Cameroon. *Africa* 74:6–27.

Nsamenang, Bame A. (2002) Adolescence in sub-Saharan Africa: An image constructed from Africa's triple inheritance. In Bradford B. Brown, Reed W. Larson, and T. S. Saraswathi (Eds.), *The World's Youth: Adolescence in Eight Regions of the Globe.* pp. 61–105. Cambridge: Cambridge University Press.

Nunes, Angela (2005) Childhood dynamics in a changing culture: Examples from the Xavante people of central Brazil. In Jacqueline Knörr (Ed.), *Childhood and Migration: From Experience to Agency.* pp. 207–226. Bielefeld: Transcript.

Nutter-El Ouardani, Christine (2013) *Discipline and development: Negotiating childhood and authority in rural Morocco.* Unpublished PhD dissertation, University of Chicago.

Nwokah, Evangeline E. and Ikekonwu, Clara (1998) A sociocultural comparison of Nigerian and American children's games. In Margaret C. Duncan, Garry Chick, and Alan Aycock (Eds.), *Diversions and Divergences in Fields of Play.* pp. 59–76. Westport, CT: Ablex.

Oakley, John H. (2003) Antiquities exhibit explores childhood in ancient Greece. *National Geographic News*, September 12. Available at http://news. nationalgeographic.com/news/2003/09/0912_030912_ancientgreece.html. Accessed February 3, 2014.

Obendick, Helena (2013) When siblings determine your "fate." In Erdmute Alber, Cati Coe, and Tatjana Thelen (Eds.). *The Anthropology of Sibling Relations.* pp. 97–121. London: Palgrave Macmillan.

Obidi, S. S. (1995) Skill acquisition through indigenous apprenticeship: A case study of the Yoruba blacksmith in Nigeria. *Comparative Education* 313:369–383.

Ochs, Elinor (1986) Introduction. In Bambi B. Schieffelin and Elinor Ochs (Eds.), *Language Socialization across Cultures.* pp. 1–13. Cambridge: Cambridge University Press.

(1988) *Culture and Language Development: Language Socialization and Language Acquisition in a Samoan Village.* Cambridge: Cambridge University Press.

Ochs, Elinor and Izquierdo, Carolina (2009) Responsibility in childhood: Three developmental trajectories. *Ethos* 37:391–413.

Ochs, Elinor and Schieffelin, Bambi B. (1984) Language acquisition and socialization: Three developmental stories and their implications. In Richard A. Shweder and Robert A. LeVine (Eds.), *Culture Theory: Essays on Mind, Self and Society.* pp. 276–320. Cambridge: Cambridge University Press.

Ochs, Elinor, Taylor, Carolyn, Rudolph, Dina, and Smith, Ruth (1992) Storytelling as a theory-building activity. *Discourse Processes* 15:37–72.

Odden, Harold and Rochat, Phillipe (2004) Observational learning and enculturation. *Educational and Child Psychology* 21:39–50.

Ofosu-Kusi, Yaw and Mizen, Phil (2012) No longer willing to be dependent: Young people moving beyond learning. In Gerd Spittler and Michael Bourdillon (Eds.), *African Children at Work: Working and Learning in Growing Up.* pp. 279–302. Berlin: LitVerlag.

Ogbu, John U. (1987) Variability in minority school performance: A problem in search of an explanation. *Anthropology and Education Quarterly* 18(4):312–334.

(2003) *Black American Students in an Affluent Suburb: A Study of Academic Disengagement.* Mahwah, NJ: Erlbaum.

Ohmagari, Kayo and Berkes, Fikret (1997) Transmission of indigenous knowledge and bush skills among the Western James Bay Cree women of subarctic Canada. *Human Ecology* 23:197–222.

Okamoto-Barth, Sanae, Moore, Chris, Barth, Jochen, Subiaul, Francys, and Povinelli, Daniel J. (2011) Carryover effect of joint attention to repeated events in chimpanzees and young children. *Developmental Science* 14:440–452.

Oleke, Christopher, Blystad, Astrid, Moland, Karen Marie, Rekdal, Ole Bjorn, and Heggenhougen, Kristian (2005) The varying vulnerability of African orphans: The case of the Langi, northern Uganda. *Childhood* 13:267–284.

Oloko, Beatrice A. (1994) Children's street work in urban Nigeria: Dilemma of modernizing tradition. In Patricia M. Greenfield and Rodney R. Cocking (Eds.), *Cross-Cultural Roots of Minority Child Development.* pp. 197–224. Hillsdale, NJ: Erlbaum.

Olson, David R. (2003) *Psychological Theory and Educational Reform: How School Remakes Mind and Society*. Cambridge: Cambridge University Press.

Olusanya, P. O. (1989) Human reproduction in Africa: Fact, myth and the martyr syndrome. *Research for Development* 6:69–97.

Opie, Iona and Opie, Peter (1969) *Children's Games in Street and Playground*. Oxford: Clarendon Press.

(1997) *Children's Games with Things*. Oxford: Oxford University Press.

Orellana, Marjorie F. (2001) The work kids do: Mexican and Central American immigrant children's contributions to households and schools in California. *Harvard Educational Review* 71:366–389.

(2009) *Translating Childhoods: Immigrant Youth, Language, and Culture*. New Brunswick, NJ: Rutgers University Press.

Orme, Nicholas (2003) *Medieval Children*. London: Yale University Press.

(2006) *Medieval Schools: From Roman Britain to Renaissance England*. London: Yale University Press.

Orrelle, Estelel (2008) Infant jar burials: A ritual associated with early agriculture? In Krum Bacvarov (Ed.), *Babies Reborn: Infant/Child Burials in Pre- and Protohistory*. pp. 71–78. BAR International Series 1832. Oxford: Archaeopress.

Ottenberg, Simon (1968) *Double Descent in an African Society: The Afikpo Village-Group*. Seattle, WA: University of Washington Press.

(1989) *Boyhood Rituals in an African Society: An Interpretation*. Seattle, WA: University of Washington Press.

(2006) Emulation in boy's masquerades: The Afikpo case. In Simon Ottenberg and David A. Binkley (Eds.), *Playful Performers: African Children's Masquerades*. pp. 117–127. New Brunswick, NJ: Transaction Publishers.

Otto, Hiltrud (2014) Don't show your emotions! Emotion regulation and attachment in the Cameroonian Nso. In Hiltrud Otto and Heidi Keller (Eds.), *Different Faces of Attachment: Cultural Variations of a Universal Human Need*. pp. 215–229. Cambridge: Cambridge University Press.

Otto, Hiltrud and Keller, Heidi (in press) A good child is a calm child: Mothers' social status, maternal conceptions of proper demeanor, and stranger anxiety in one-year-old Cameroonian Nso children. *Psychological Topics*.

Overing, Joanna (1988) Personal autonomy and the domestication of the self in Piaroa society. In Gustav Jahod and Ioan M. Lewis (Ed.), *Acquiring Culture: Cross-Cultural Studies in Child Development*. pp. 169–192. London: Croom Helm.

Oxenham, Marc, Matsumura, Hirofumi, Domett, Kate, Nguyen, Kim Thuy, Nguyen, Kim Dung, Nguyen, Lan Cuong, Huffer, Damien, and Muller, Sarah (2008) Childhood in late Neolithic Vietnam: Bio-mortuary insights into an ambiguous life stage. In Krum Bacvarov (Ed.), *Babies Reborn: Infant/Child Burials in Pre- and Protohistory*. pp. 123–126. BAR International Series 1832. Oxford: Archaeopress.

Packer, Boyd K. (1993) For time and all eternity. *Ensign*, January:21–25.

Pagel, Mark (2012) *Wired for Culture: Origins of the Human Social Mind*. New York, NY: W. W. Norton.

Palley, Thomas I. (2002) The child labor problem and the need for international labor standards. *Journal of Economic Issues* 36(3):1–15.

Paltrow, Lynn and Flavin, Jeanne (2013) Arrests of and forced interventions on pregnant women in the United States, 1973–2005: Implications for women's legal status and public health. *Journal of Health Politics, Policy, and Law* 38:299–343.

Pandya, Vishvajit (2005) Deforesting among Adamanese children. In Barry S. Hewlett and Michael E. Lamb (Eds.), *Hunter-Gatherer Childhoods: Evolutionary, Developmental, and Cultural Perspectives.* pp. 385–406. New Brunswick, NJ: Aldine/Transaction Publishers.

Panter-Brick, Catherine (1989) Motherhood and subsistence work: The Tamang of rural Nepal. *Human Ecology* 17:205–228.

Paradise, Ruth (1996) Passivity or tacit collaboration: Mazahua interaction in cultural context. *Learning and Instruction* 6:379–389.

Paradise, Ruth and de Haan, Mariëtte (2009) Responsibility and reciprocity: Social organization of Mazahua learning practices. *Anthropology and Education Quarterly* 40:187–204.

Paradise, Ruth and Rogoff, Barbara (2009) Side by side: Learning by observing and pitching in. *Ethos* 37:102–138.

Parin, Paul (1963) *The Whites Think Too Much: Psychoanalytic Investigations among the Dogon in West Africa.* Zurich: Atlantis.

Park, Robert W. (2006) Growing up north: Exploring the archaeology of childhood in the Thule and Dorset cultures of Arctic Canada. *Archeological Papers of the American Anthropological Association* 15:53–64.

Park, Young-Shin and Kim, Uichol (2006) Family, parent–child relationship, and academic achievement in Korea: Indigenous, cultural, and psychological analysis. In Uichol Kim, Kuo-Shu Yang, and Kwang-Kuo Hwang (Eds.), *Indigenous and Cultural Psychology: Understanding People in Context.* pp. 421–443. New York, NY: Springer.

Parker, Sue T. (1984) Playing for keeps: An evolutionary perspective on human games. In Peter K. Smith (Ed.), *Play in Animals and Humans.* pp. 271–294. Oxford: Blackwell.

Parmar, Parminder, Harkness, Sara and Super, Charles M. (2008) Teacher or playmate? Asian immigrant and Euro-American parents' participation in their young children's daily activities. *Social Behavior and Personality* 36:163–176.

Patterson, Cynthia (1985) "Not worth rearing": The causes of infant exposure in ancient Greece. *Transactions of the American Philological Association* 115:103–123.

Paugh, Amy (2012) Local theories of child rearing. In Alessandro Duranti, Elinor Ochs, and Bambi B. Schieffelin (Eds.), *The Handbook of Language Socialization.* pp. 150–168. Chichester: Wiley-Blackwell.

Paul, Pamela (2008) *Parenting Inc.: How We are Sold on $800 Strollers, Fetal Education, Baby Sign Language, Sleep Coaches, Toddler Couture, and Diaper Wipe Warmers – and What It Means to Our Children.* New York, NY: Henry Holt.

Pauli, Julia (2005) "We didn't grow up together!" Relatedness among the Damara/ Nama of Fransfontein, Namibia. Paper presented at the conference on Familie und Verwandtschaft, July, Bayreuth.

Paulme, Denise (1940) *Social Organization of the Dogon.* Paris: Editions Domat-Montchrestien.

Pearsall, Marion (1950) *Klamath Childhood and Education.* Berkeley, CA: University of California Press.

Peil, Margaret (1970) The apprenticeship system in Accra. *Africa* 40:137–150.

Peisner, Ellen S. (1989) To spare or not to spare the rod: A cultural-historical view of child discipline. In Jaan Valsiner (Ed.), *Child Development in Cultural Context.* pp. 111–141. Lewiston, NY: Hogrefe and Huber.

Peissel, Michel (1992) *Mustang: A Lost Tibetan Kingdom.* Delhi: South Asia Books.

Pelissier, Catherine (1991) The anthropology of teaching and learning. *Annual Review of Anthropology* 20:75–95.

Pellegrini, Anthony D. (2004) Sexual segregation in childhood: A review of evidence for two hypotheses. *Animal Behaviour* 68(3):435–443.

Penn, Helen (2001) Culture and childhood in pastoralist communities: The example of Outer Mongolia. In Leena Alanen and Berry Mayall (Eds.), *Conceptualizing Child–Adult Relations.* pp. 86–98. Abingdon: Routledge.

Pennington, Renee and Harpending, Henry (1993) *The Structure of an African Pastoralist Community: Demography, History, and Ecology of the Ngamiland Herero.* Oxford: Oxford University Press.

Peters, John F. (1998) *Life among the Yanomami: The Story of Change among the Xilixana on the Mucajai River in Brazil.* Orchard Park, NY: Broadview Press.

Peterson, Jean T. (1978) *The Ecology of Social Boundaries: Agta Foragers of the Philippines.* Urbana, IL: University of Illinois Press.

Philbrick, Nathaniel (2000) *In the Heart of the Sea.* London: HarperCollins.

Phillips, Susan U. (1983) *Invisible Culture: Communication in Classroom and Community on the Warm Springs Indian Reservation.* White Plains, NY: Longman.

Piaget, Jean (1929) *The Child's Conception of the World.* New York, NY: Harcourt. (1932/1965) *The Moral Judgment of the Child.* Translated by Marjorie Gabain. New York, NY: Free Press.

Pickering, Apryle J. (2005) Individual agency in the context of powerful cultural forces: Fertility strategies in contemporary Nepal. Paper presented at the annual meeting of the American Anthropological Association, December, Washington, DC.

Piel, L. Halliday (2012) Food rationing and children's self-reliance in Japan, 1942–1952. *Journal of the History of Childhood and Youth* 5:393–418.

Pigeot, Nicole (1990) Technical and social actors: Flintknapping specialists at Magdalenian Etiolles. *Archaeological Review from Cambridge* 9:126–141.

Pitman, Mary A., Eisikovits, Rivka A., and Dobbert, Marion L. (1989) Introduction. In Mary A. Pitman, Rivka A. Eisikovits, and Marion L. Dobbert (Eds.), *Culture Acquisition: A Holistic Approach to Human Learning.* pp. 1–20, New York, NY: Praeger.

Platt, Brian (2005) Japanese childhood, modern childhood: The nation-state, the school, and 19th-century globalization. *Journal of Social History* 38:965–985.

Platt, Katherine (1988) Cognitive development and sex roles of the Kerkennah Islands of Tunisia. In Gustav Jahoda and Ioan M. Lewis (Eds.), *Acquiring Culture: Cross-Cultural Studies in Child Development.* pp. 271–287. London: Croom Helm.

Pleck, Joseph (1987) American fathering in historical perspective. In Michael S. Kimmel (Ed.), *Changing Men: New Directions in Research on Men and Masculinity.* pp. 83–97. Beverly Hills, CA: Sage.

Plooij, Frans (1979) How wild chimpanzee babies trigger the onset of mother–infant play and what the mother makes of it. In Margaret Bullowa (Ed.), *Before Speech:*

The Beginning of Interpersonal Communication. pp. 223–243. Cambridge: Cambridge University Press.

Polak, Barbara (1998) Wie Bamana kinder feldarbeit lernen. In Heike Schmidt and Albert Wirz (Eds.), *Afrika und das Andere: Alterität und Innovation.* pp. 103–114. Münster: LitVerlag.

(2003) Little peasants: On the importance of reliability in child labour. In Hélène d'Almeida-Topor, Monique Lakroum, and Gerd Spittler (Eds.), *Le travail en Afrique noire: Représentations et pratiques à l'époque contemporaine.* pp. 125–136. Paris: Karthala.

(2011) Die Könige der Feldarbeit. Unpublished PhD dissertation, Kulturwissenschaftlichen Fakultät der Universität Bayreuth.

(2012) Peasants in the making: Bamana children at work. In Gerd Spittler and Michael Bourdillon (Eds.), *African Children at Work: Working and Learning in Growing Up.* pp. 87–112. Berlin: LitVerlag.

Polaski, Sandra (2011) *US Department of Labor's 2010 Findings on the Worst Forms of Child Labor.* Washington, DC: US Government Printing Office.

Politis, Gustavo G. (2007) *Nukak: Ethnoarchaeology of an Amazonian People.* Translated by Benjamin Alberti. Walnut Creek, CA: University College London Institute of Archaeology Publications.

Pollock, Linda A. (1983) *Forgotten Children: Parent–Child Relations from 1500 to 1900.* Cambridge: Cambridge University Press.

Poluha, Eva (2004) *The Power of Continuity: Ethiopia through the Eyes of its Children.* Stockholm: Nordiska Afrikainstitutet.

Pomerantz, Eva M. and Moorman, Elizabeth A. (2007) The how, whom, and why of parental involvement in children's academic lives: More is not always better. *Review of Educational Research* 77:373–410.

Pomponio, Alice (1981) School, fish and timber: Economic development and culture change on Mandok Island, Siassi Sub District, Morobe Province. Seminar presented to the Papua New Guinea Institute of Applied Social and Economic Research, March, Port Moresby, Papua New Guinea.

(1992) *Seagulls Don't Fly into the Bush.* Belmont, CA: Wadsworth.

Pomponio, Alice and Lancy, David F. (1986) A pen or a bush knife: School, work and personal investment in Papua New Guinea. *Anthropology and Education Quarterly* 17:40–61.

Pontecorvo, Clotilde, Fasulo, Allesandra, and Sterponi, Laura (2001) Mutual apprentices: The making of parenthood and childhood in family dinner conversations. *Human Development* 44:340–361.

Portes, Pedro, Dunham, Richard M., King, F. J., and Kidwell, Jeannie S. (1988) Early age intervention and parent–child interaction: Their relation to student achievement. *Journal of Research and Development in Education* 21(4):78–86.

Portisch, Anna O. (2010) The craft of skillful learning: Kazakh women's everyday craft practices in western Mongolia. *Journal of the Royal Anthropological Institute,* Supplement: 62–79.

Potts, Malcolm and Short, Roger (1999) *Ever since Adam and Eve: The Evolution of Human Sexuality.* Cambridge: Cambridge University Press.

Poveda, David, Morgade, Marta, and González-Patiño, Javier (2012) *Children at Home in Madrid*. Cuadernos de Investigación Etnográfica sobre Infancia, Adolescencia y Educación del IMA/FMEE 4.

Povinelli, Daniel J., Prince, Christopher, G., and Preuss, Todd M. (2005) Parent–offspring conflict and the development of social understanding. In Peter Carruthers, Stephen Laurence, and Stephen Stitch (Eds.), *The Innate Mind*. pp. 239–253. Oxford: Oxford University Press.

Power, Thomas G. (2000) *Play and Exploration in Children and Animals*. Mahwah, NJ: Erlbaum.

Power, Thomas G. and Parke, Ross, D. (1982) Play as a context for early learning: Lab and home analyses. In Luis M. Laosa and Irving E. Sigel (Eds.), *Families as Learning Environments for Children*. pp. 147–178. New York, NY: Plenum Press.

Prosser, G. V., Hutt, Corinne, Hutt, Stephen J., Mahindadasa, K. J., and Goonetilleke, M. D. J. (1986) Children's play in Sri Lanka: A cross-cultural study. *The British Psychological Society* 4: 179–186.

Prothro, Edwin Terry (1961) *Child Rearing in the Lebanon*. Cambridge, MA: Harvard University Press.

Pugh, Allison J. (2009) *Longing and Belonging: Parents, Children, and Consumer Culture*. Berkeley, CA: University of California Press.

Punch, Samantha (2001) Negotiating autonomy: Childhoods in rural Bolivia. In Leena Alanen and Berry Mayall (Eds.), *Conceptualizing Child–Adult Relations*. pp. 23–36. Abingdon: Routledge.

Puri, Rajindra K. (2005) *Deadly Dances in the Bornean Rainforest: Hunting Knowledge of the Punan Benalui*. Leiden: KITLV Press.

  (2013) Transmitting Penan basketry knowledge and practice. In Roy Ellen, Stephen J. Lycett, and Sarah E. Johns (Eds.), *Understanding Cultural Transmission: A Critical Anthropological Synthesis*. pp. 266–299. Oxford: Berghahn Books.

Pye, Clifton (1991) The acquisition of K'iché (Maya). In Dan I. Slobin (Ed.), *The Cross-Linguistic Study of Language Acquisition*. pp. 221–308. Hillsdale, NJ: Erlbaum.

Queller, David C. (1997) Why do females care more than males? *Biological Sciences* 264:1555–1557.

Quinlan, Marsha B. and Hansen, Jenna R. (2013) Introduction of television and Dominican youth. In Bonnie L. Hewlett (Ed.), *Adolescent Identity*. pp. 245–276. New York, NY: Routledge.

Quinn, Naomi (1978) Do Mfantse fish sellers estimate probability in their heads? *American Ethnologist* 5:206–226.

  (2005) Universals of child rearing. *Anthropological Theory* 5:477–516.

Qvortrup, Jens (2005) Varieties of childhood. In Jens Qvortrup (Ed.), *Studies in Modern Childhood: Society, Agency, Culture*. pp. 1–20. New York, NY: Palgrave.

Rabain, Jean (1979) *L'enfant du lignage: Du sevrage à la classe d'age*. Paris: Payot.

Rae-Espinoza, Heather (2006) Methodological techniques in the psychological evaluation of the children left behind. Paper presented at the 35th annual meeting of the Society for Cross-Cultural Research, February 23, Savannah, GA.

Raffaele, Paul (2003) *The Last Tribes on Earth: Journeys among the World's Most Threatened Cultures*. Sydney: Pan Macmillan.

(2005) Born into bondage. *Smithsonian Magazine* 36(6):64–73.

(2006) Sleeping with cannibals. *Smithsonian Magazine* 37(8):10–11.

Rahman, Anika and Toubia, Nahid (2000) Background and history. In Anika Rahman and Nahid Toubia (Eds.), *Female Genital Mutilation: A Guide to Laws and Policies Worldwide*. pp. 3–14. London: Zed Books.

Raitt, Margaret and Lancy, David F. (1988) Rhinestone cowgirl: The education of a rodeo queen. *Play and Culture* 1(4):267–281.

Rakoczy, Hannes, Tomasello, Michael, and Striano, Tricia (2005) On tools and toys: How children learn to act on and pretend with "virgin objects." *Developmental Science* 8:57–73.

Rampal, Anita (2003) The meaning of numbers: Understanding street and folk mathematics. In Brij Kothari, P. G. Vijaya, Sherry Chand, and Michael Norton (Eds.), *Reading Beyond the Alphabet: Innovations in Lifelong Literacy*. pp. 241–258. New Delhi: Sage.

Rao, Aparna (1998) *Autonomy: Life Cycle, Gender, and Status among Himalayan Pastoralists*. Oxford: Berghahn Books.

(2006) The acquisition of manners, morals and knowledge: Growing into and out of Bakkarwal society. In Caroline Dyer (Ed.), *The Education of Nomadic Peoples: Current Issues, Future Prospects*. pp. 53–76. Oxford: Berghahn Books.

Rao, Vijay (1993) The rising price of husbands: A hedonic analysis of dowry increases in rural India. *Journal of Political Economy* 101:666–677.

(1997) Wife-beating in rural south India: A qualitative and econometric analysis. *Journal of Sociology, Science and Medicine* 44:1169–1180.

Raphael, Dana L. (1966) The lactation–suckling process within a matrix of supportive behavior. Unpublished PhD dissertation Columbia University.

Raphael, Dana L. and Davis, Flora (1985) *Only Mothers Know: Patterns of Infant Feeding in Traditional Cultures*. Westport, CT: Greenwood Press.

Rappaport, Roy A. (1967) *Pigs for the Ancestors: Ritual in the Ecology of a New Guinea People*. New Haven, CT: Yale University Press.

Rattray, Robert S. (1927) *Religion and Art in Ashanti*. Oxford: Clarendon Press.

Raum, Otto F. (1940) *Chaga Childhood*. Oxford: Oxford University Press.

Ravololomanga, Bodo and Schlemmer, Bernard (2000) "Unexploited" labour: Social transition in Madagascar. In Bernard Schlemmer (Ed.), *The Exploited Child*. pp. 300–313. New York, NY: Zed Books.

Rawson, Beryl (1991) Adult–child relationships in Roman society. In Beryl Rawson (Ed.), *Marriage, Divorce, and Children in Ancient Rome*. pp. 7–30. Canberra: Clarendon Press.

(2003) *Children and Childhood in Roman Italy*. Oxford: Oxford University Press.

Razy, Élodie (2007) *Naître et devenir: Anthropologie de la petite enfance en pays Soninké, Mali*. (Birth and Becoming: The Anthropology of Infancy in Soninké, Mali.) Nanterre: Société D'ethnologie.

Read, Dwight W. (2001) Formal analysis of kinship terminologies and its relationship to what constitutes kinship. *Mathematical Anthropology and Cultural Theory* 1:239–267.

Read, Margaret (1960) *Children of their Fathers: Growing up among the Ngoni of Malawi*. New Haven, CT: Yale University Press.

Reay, Marie (1959) *The Kuma: Freedom and Conformity in the New Guinea Highlands*. Melbourne: Melbourne University Press.

Redfield, Robert (1943/1970) Culture and education in the midwestern highlands of Guatemala. In John Middleton (Ed.), *From Child to Adult: Studies in the Anthropology of Education*. pp. 287–300. Garden City, NY: Natural History Press.

Reichard, Gladys (1934) *Spider Woman: A Story of Navaho Weavers and Chanters*. New York, NY: Macmillan.

Reichel-Dolmatoff, Gerardo (1976) Training for the priesthood among the Kogi of Columbia. In Johannes Wilbert (Ed.), *Enculturation in Latin America*. pp. 265–288. Los Angeles, CA: UCLA Latin American Center Publications.

Remorini, Carolina (2011) Becoming a person from the Mbya Guarani perspective. Unpublished MS thesis, National University of La Plata, Argentina.

    (2012) Childrearing and the shaping of children's emotional experiences and expressions in two Argentinian communities. *Global Studies of Childhood* 2:144–157.

Renfrew, Colin (1998) Mind and matter: Cognitive archaeology and external storage. In Colin Renfrew and Chris Scarre (Eds.), *Cognition and Material Culture: The Archaeology of Symbolic Storage*. pp. 1–6. Oxford: Oxbow Books.

Renne, Elisha P. (2005) Childhood memories and contemporary parenting in Ekiti, Nigeria. *Africa* 75(1):63–82.

Reynolds, Pamela (1991) *Dance Civet Cat: Child Labour in the Zambezi Valley*. Athens, OH: Ohio University Press.

Reynolds, Pamela, Nieuwenhuys, Olga, and Hanson, Karl (2006) Refractions of children's rights in development practice: A view from anthropology. Introduction. *Childhood* 13(3):291–302.

Reynolds, Suzanne (1996) *Medieval Reading: Grammar, Rhetoric and the Classical Text*. Cambridge: Cambridge University Press.

Rheingold, Harriet (1982) Little children's participation in the work of adults: A nascent prosocial behavior. *Child Development* 53:114–125.

Richards, Audrey I. (1956) *Chisungu*. London: Faber and Faber.

Richerson, Peter J. and Boyd, Robert (1992) Cultural inheritance and evolutionary ecology. In Eric A. Smith and Bruce Winterhalder (Eds.), *Evolutionary Ecology and Human Behavior*. pp. 61–92. New York, NY: Aldine de Gruyter.

Riches, David (1974) The Netsilik Eskimo: A special case of selective female infanticide. *Ethnology* 13:351–361.

Richman, Amy L., Miller, Patrice M., and Johnson Solomon, Margaret (1988) The socialization of infants in suburban Boston. In Robert A. LeVine, Peggy M. Miller, and Mary Maxwell West (Eds.), *Parental Behavior in Diverse Societies, special issue of New Directions for Child Development* 40:65–74.

Richtner, Linda and Kruglanski, Arie W. (2004) Motivated closed mindedness and the emergence of culture. In Mark Schaller and Christian S. Crandall (Eds.), *The Psychological Foundations of Culture*. pp. 101–121. Mahwah, NJ: Erlbaum.

Riesman, Paul (1992) *First Find Your Child a Good Mother*. New Brunswick, NJ: Rutgers University Press.

Riis, Jacob (1890/1996) *How the Other Half Lives*. New York, NY: Penguin.

Rindstedt, Camilla and Aronsson, Karin (2003) ¿Quieres bañar? Sibling caretaking, play and perspective-taking in an Andean community. Paper presented at the 33rd annual meeting of the Jean Piaget Society, June 5, Chicago, IL.

Ritchie, Jane and Ritchie, James (1979) *Growing up in Polynesia*. Sydney: George Allen and Unwin.

Ritter, Philip (1981) Adoption on Kosrae Island: Solidarity and sterility. *Ethnology* 20:45–61.

Rival, Laura M. (1998) Androgynous parents and guest children: The Huaorani couvade. *The Journal of the Royal Anthropological Institute* 4:619–642.

(2000) Formal schooling and the production of modern citizens in the Ecuadorian Amazon. In Bradley A. U. Levinson (Ed.), *Schooling the Symbolic Animal: Social and Cultural Dimensions of Education*. pp. 108–122. Lanham, MD: Rowman and Littlefield.

(2002) *Trekking through History: The Hauorani of Amazonian Ecuador*. New York, NY: Columbia University Press.

Robbins, Alexandra (2006) *The Overachievers: The Secret Lives of Driven Kids*. New York, NY: Hyperion.

Robbins, Joel (2004) *Becoming Sinners: Christianity and Moral Torment in a Papua New Guinean Society*. Berkeley, CA: University of California Press.

Roberts, John M. (1964) The self-management of cultures. In Ward H. Goodenough (Ed.), *Explorations in Cultural Anthropology*. pp. 433–454. New York, NY: McGraw-Hill.

Roberts, John M., Arth, Malcom J., and Bush, Robert R. (1959) Games in culture. *American Anthropologist* 61:597–605.

Roberts, John M. and Sutton-Smith, Brian (1962) Child training and game involvement. *Ethnology* 2:166–185.

Robinson, Julie A. (1988) What we've got here is a failure to communicate: The culture context of meaning. In Jaan Valsiner (Ed.), *Child Development within Culturally Structured Environments. Vol. II*. pp. 137–198. Norwood, NJ: Ablex.

Robson, Arthur J. and Kaplan, Hillard S. (2003) The evolution of human life expectancy and intelligence in hunter-gatherer economies. *American Economic Review* 93:150–169.

Rochat, Philippe (2005) Humans evolved to become *Homo negotiatus* . . . the rest followed. *Behavioral and Brain Sciences* 28: 714–715.

(2009) *Others in Mind: Social Origins of Self-Consciousness*. Cambridge: Cambridge University Press.

Rogers, Alan R. (1989) Does biology constrain culture? *American Anthropologist* 90(4):819–831.

Rogoff, Barbara (1981a) Adults and peers as agents of socialization: A Highland Guatemalan profile. *Ethos* 9:18–36.

(1981b) Schooling and the development of cognitive skills. In Harry Triandis and Alistair Heron (Eds.), *The Handbook of Cross-Cultural Psychology*. pp. 233–294. Boston: Allyn and Bacon.

(1990) *Apprenticeship in Thinking: Cognitive Development in Social Context*. New York, NY: Oxford University Press.

(2003) *The Cultural Nature of Human Development*. New York, NY: Oxford University Press.

Rogoff, Barbara, Mistry, Jayanthi, Göncü, Artin, and Mosier, Christine (1991)
Cultural variation in the role relations of toddlers and their families. In Mark H.
Bornstein (Ed.), *Cultural Approaches to Parenting*. pp. 173–183. Hillsdale, NJ:
Erlbaum.

(1993) Guided participation in cultural activity by toddlers and caregivers.
Monographs of the Society for Research in Child Development 58(8/236):v,
vi, 1–183.

Rogoff, Barbara, Sellers, Martha J., Pirotta, Sergio, Fox, Nathan, and White,
Sheldon H. (1975) Age of assignment of roles and responsibilities to children.
Human Development 18:353–369.

Rohlen, Thomas P. (1996) Building character. In Thomas P. Rohlen and Gerald K.
LeTendre (Eds.), *Teaching and Learning in Japan*. pp. 50–74. Cambridge:
Cambridge University Press.

Rohner, Ronald P. and Chaki-Sircar, Manjusri (1988) *Women and Children in a
Bengali Village*. Hanover, NH: University Press of New England.

Rojo, Roxane H. R. (2001) Family interaction as a source of being in society:
Language-games and everyday family discourse genres in language construction.
In Seth Chaiklin (Ed.), *The Theory and Practice of Cultural-Historical
Psychology*. pp. 56–83. Aarhus: Aarhus University Press.

Rollings-Magnusson, Sandra (2009) *Heavy Burdens on Small Shoulders: The Labour
of Pioneer Children on the Canadian Prairies*. Edmonton, AL: University of
Alberta Press.

Roopnarine, Jaipaul L., Bynoe, Pauline F., and Singh, Ronald (2004) Factors tied to the
schooling of children of English-speaking Caribbean immigrants in the United
States. In Uwe P. Gielen and Jaipaul L. Roopnarine (Eds.), *Childhood and
Adolescence: Cross-Cultural Perspectives and Applications*. pp. 319–349.
Westport, CT: Praeger.

Roopnarine, Jaipaul L., Fouts, Hilary N., Lamb, Michael E., and Lewis, Tracey (2005)
Mothers' and fathers' behaviors towards their 3–4-month-old infants in low-,
middle- and upper-socioeconomic African American families. Paper presented at
the 34th annual meeting of the Society for Cross-Cultural Research, February,
Santa Fe, NM.

Roopnarine, Jaipaul L. and Hossain, Ziarat (1992) Parent–child interaction patterns in
urban Indian families in New Delhi: Are they changing? In Jaipaul L. Roopnarine
and D. Bruce Carter (Eds.), *Parent–Child Socialization in Diverse Cultures*.
pp. 1–16. Norwood, NJ: Ablex.

Roopnarine, Jaipaul L., Hossain, Ziarat, Gill, Preeti, and Brophy, Holly (1994) Play
in the east Indian context. In Jaipaul L. Roopnarine, James E. Johnson, and
Frank H. Hooper (Eds.), *Children's Play in Diverse Cultures*. pp. 9–30. Albany,
NY: State University of New York Press.

Roopnarine, Jaipaul L., Krishnakumar, Ambika, Metindogan, Aysegul, and Evans,
Melanie (2006) Links between parenting styles, parent–child interaction,
parent–school interaction, and early academic skills and social behaviors in young
children of English-speaking Caribbean immigrants. *Early Childhood Research
Quarterly* 21:238–252.

Roscoe, John (1924) *The Bagesu and Other Tribes of the Uganda Protectorate*.
Cambridge: Cambridge University Press.

Roscoe, Paul B. (1995) In the shadow of the Tambaran: Female initiation among the Ndu of the Sepik Basin. In Nancy C. Lutkehaus and Paul B. Roscoe (Eds.), *Gender Rituals: Female Initiation in Melanesia.* pp. 55–82. London: Routledge.

Roscoe, Paul B. and Telban, Borut (2004) The people of the lower Arafundi: Tropical foragers of the New Guinea rainforest. *Ethnology* 43:93–115.

Rose, Harold M. and McClain, Paula D. (1990) *Race, Place, and Risk: Black Homicide in Urban America.* Albany, NY: State University of New York Press.

Rosen, David M. (2005) *Armies of the Young: Child Soldiers in War and Terrorism.* New Brunswick, NJ: Rutgers University Press.

Ross, Norbert O. (2002) Lacandon Maya intergenerational change and the erosion of folk biological knowledge. In John R. Stepp, Felice S. Wyndham, and Rebecca K. Zarger (Eds.), *Ethnobiology and Biocultural Diversity: Proceedings of the Seventh International Congress of Ethnobiology.* pp. 585–592. Athens, GA: University of Georgia Press.

   (2004) *Culture and Cognition: Implications for Theory and Method.* Thousand Oaks, CA: Sage.

Roth, Ann M. (2002) The meaning of menial labor: "Servant statues" in Old Kingdom serdabs. *Journal of the American Research Center in Egypt* 39:103–121.

Rousseau, Cecile, Said, Taher M., Gagné, Marie-Josée, and Bibeau, Gilles (1998) Resilience in unaccompanied minors from the north of Somalia. *Psychoanalytic Review* 85:615–637.

Roux, Valentine, Bril, Blandine, and Dietrich, Gilles (1995) Skills and learning difficulties involved in stone knapping: The case of stone-bead knapping in Khambhat, India. *World Archaeology* 27:63–87.

Rowell, Thelma E. (1975) Growing up in a monkey group. *Ethos* 3:113–128.

Rowley-Conwy (2001) Time, change, and the archaeology of hunter-gatherers: How original is the "original affluent society"? In Catherine Panter-Brick, Robert H. Layton, and Peter Rowley-Conwy (Eds.), *Hunter-Gatherers: An Interdisciplinary Perspective.* pp. 39–72. Cambridge: Cambridge University Press.

Rubenson, Birgitta, Hanh, Le Thi, Höjer, Bengt, and Johansson, Eva (2005) Young sex-workers in Ho Chi Minh City telling their life stories. *Childhood* 12:391–401.

Ruddle, Kenneth and Chesterfield, Ray (1977) *Education for Traditional Food Procurement in the Orinoco Delta.* Berkeley, CA: University of California Press.

Ruiz, Luisa F. M. (2011a) Stone quarries in Guatemala. In G. Kristoffel Lieten (Ed.), *Hazardous Child Labour in Latin America.* pp. 81–103. Heidelberg: Springer.

   (2011b) Coffee in Guatemala. In G. Kristoffel Lieten (Ed.), *Hazardous Child Labour in Latin America.* pp. 165–189. Heidelberg: Springer.

Rurevo, Rumbidazi and Bourdillion, Michael (2003) *Girls on the Street.* Harare: Weaver Press.

Saad, Ahmed Youssof (2006) Subsistence education: Schooling in a context of urban poverty. In Linda Herrara and Carolos Alberto Torres (Eds.), *Cultures of Arab Schooling: Critical Ethnographies from Egypt.* pp. 83–107. Albany, NY: State University of New York Press.

Sachs, Dana and Le, Quang Vu (2005) Vietnam unearths its royal past. *National Geographic* 207(6):3.

Saffran, Jenny R., Aslin, Richard N., and Newport, Elissa L. (1996) Statistical learning by 8-month-old infants. *Science* 274:1926–1928.

Saggs, H. W. F. (1987) *Everyday Life in Babylonia and Assyria*. New York, NY: Hippocrene Books.

Salmon, Catherine (2005) Parental investment and parent–offspring conflict. In David M. Buss (Ed.), *Handbook of Evolutionary Psychology*. pp. 506–527. New York, NY: Wiley.

Sánchez, Martha A. R. (2007) "Helping at home": The concept of childhood and work among the Nahuas of Tlaxcala, Mexico. In Betrice Hungerland, Manfred Leibel, Brian Milne, and Anne Wihstutz (Eds.), *Working to Be Someone: Child-Focused Research and Practice with Working Children*. pp. 87–95. London: Jessica Kingsley.

Sanghavi, Darshak M. (2006) Wanting babies like themselves, some parents choose genetic defects. *New York Times*, December 5, Available at www.nytimes.com/2006/12/05/health/05essa.html?_r=0. Accessed October 14, 2013.

Santa Maria, Madelene (2002) Youth in Southeast Asia: Living within the continuity of tradition and the turbulence of change. In Bradford B. Brown, Reed W. Larson, and T. S. Saraswathi (Eds.), *The World's Youth: Adolescence in Eight Regions of the Globe*. pp. 171–206. Cambridge: Cambridge University Press.

Sargent, Carolyn F. (1988) Born to die: Witchcraft and infanticide in Bariba culture. *Ethnology* 27:79–95.

Sargent, Carolyn F. and Harris, Michael (1998) Bad boys and good girls: The implications of gender ideology for child health in Jamaica. In Nancy Scheper-Hughes and Carolyn F. Sargent (Eds.), *Small Wars: The Cultural Politics of Childhood*. pp. 202–227. Berkeley, CA: University of California Press.

Sargent, Laurie W. (2003) *The Power of Parent–Child Play*. Wheaton, IL: Tynedale House.

Sastre, Béatriz S. Céspedes and Meyer, María-Isabel Zarama V. (2000) Living and working conditions: Child labour in the coal mines of Colombia. In Bernard Schlemmer (Ed.), *The Exploited Child*. pp. 83–92. New York, NY: Zed Books.

Savage, Anne, Ziegler, Toni E., and Snowdon, Charles T. (1988) Sociosexual development, pair bond formation, and mechanisms of fertility suppression in female cotton-top tamarins (*Saguinus oedipus oedipus*). *American Journal of Primatology* 14:345–359.

Savishinsky, Joel S. (1982) Vicarious emotions and cultural restraint. *Journal of Psychoanalytic Anthropology* 5:115–135.

Sax, Leonard (2005) *Why Gender Matters: What Parents and Teachers Need to Know about the Emerging Science of Sex Differences*. New York, NY: Doubleday.

Saxe, Geoffrey (1990) *Culture and Cognitive Development: Studies in Mathematical Understanding*. Mahwah, NJ: Erlbaum.

Scarr, Sandra (1997) Why child care has little impact on most children's development. *Current Directions in Psychological Science* 6:143–148.

Schade-Poulsen, Marc (1995) The power of love: Raï music and youth in Algeria. In Vered Amit-Talai and Helena Wulff (Eds.), *Youth Cultures: A Cross-Cultural Perspective*. pp. 81–113. London: Routledge.

Schaller, George B. (1976) *The Serengeti Lion: A Study of Predator–Prey Relations*. Chicago, IL: University of Chicago Press.

Schapera, Isaac (1930) *The Khoisan People of South Africa*. London: Routledge and Kegan Paul.

Scheer, Jessica and Groce, Nora (1988) Impairment as a human constant: Cross-cultural and historical perspectives on variation. *Journal of Social Issues* 44:23–37.

Scheper-Hughes, Nancy (1987a) "Basic strangeness": Maternal estrangement and infant death – A critique of bonding theory. In Charles M. Super (Ed.), *The Role of Culture in Developmental Disorder.* pp. 131–151. New York, NY: Academic Press.

(1987b) Cultures, scarcity, and maternal thinking: Mother love and child death in northeast Brazil. In Nancy Scheper-Hughes (Ed.), *Child Survival: Anthropological Perspectives on the Treatment and Maltreatment of Children.* pp. 187–208. Dordrecht: Reidel.

(2014) Family life as bricolage: Reflections on intimacy and attachment in "death without weeping". In Hiltrud Otto and Heidi Keller (Eds.), *Different Faces of Attachment: Cultural Variations of a Universal Human Need.* pp. 230–262. Cambridge: Cambridge University Press.

Scheper-Hughes, Nancy and Hoffman, Daniel (1998) Brazilian apartheid: Street kids and the struggle for urban space. In Nancy Scheper-Hughes and Carolyn F. Sargent (Eds.), *Small Wars: The Cultural Politics of Childhood.* pp. 352–388. Berkeley, CA: University of California Press.

Schiefenhovel, Wulf (1989) Reproduction and sex-ratio manipulation through preferential female infanticide among the Eipo, in the highlands of western New Guinea. In Anne E. Rasa, Christian Vogel, and Eckart Voland (Eds.), *The Sociobiology of Sexual and Reproductive Strategies.* pp. 170–193. New York: Chapman and Hall.

Schieffelin, Bambi B. (1986) Teasing and shaming in Kaluli children's interactions. In Bambi B. Schiefflin and Elinor Ochs (Eds.), *Language Socialization across Cultures.* pp. 165–181. Cambridge: Cambridge University Press.

(1990) *The Give and Take of Everyday Life: Language Socialization of Kaluli Children.* Cambridge: Cambridge University Press.

Schildkrout, Enid (1990) Children's roles: The young traders of northern Nigeria. In James P. Spradley and Davie W. McCurdy (Eds.), *Conformity amd Conflict.* pp. 221–228. Glenview, IL: Scott Foresman.

Schlegel, Alice (1973) The adolescent socialization of the Hopi girl. *Ethnology* 12(4):449–462.

(1991) Status, property, and the value on virginity. *American Ethnologist* 18(4).719–734.

(2000a) Strangers or friends? The need of adults in the life of adolescents. *Paideuma* 46:137–148.

(2000b) The global spread of adolescence in times of social change. In Lisa J. Crockett and Rainer K. Silbereisen (Eds.), *Negotiating Adolescence in Times of Social Change.* pp. 71–88. Cambridge: Cambridge University Press.

(2013) Perspectives on adolescent identity. In Bonnie L. Hewlett (Ed.), *Adolescent Identity.* pp. 301–318. New York, NY: Routledge.

Schlegel, Alice and Barry, Herbert L., III. (1980) The evolutionary significance of adolescent initiation ceremonies. *American Ethnologist* 7(4):696–715.

(1991) *Adolescence: An Anthropological Inquiry.* New York, NY: Free Press.

Schlemmer, Bernard (2007) Working children in Fez, Morocco: Relationship between knowledge and strategies for social and professional integration. In Beatrice Hungerland, Manfred Leibel, Brian Milne, and Anne Wihstutz (Eds.), *Working to Be Someone: Child-Focused Research and Practice with Working Children.* pp. 109–115. London: Jessica Kingsley.

Schönpflug, Ute (2009) Epilogue: Toward a model of cultural transmission. In Ute Schönpflug (Ed.),*Cultural Transmission: Psychological, Developmental, Social, and Methodological Aspects.* pp. 460–478. Cambridge University Press.

Schorsch, Anita (1979) *Images of Childhood: An Illustrated Social History.* New York, NY: Mayflower Books.

Schultz, T. Paul (1994) *Human Capital Investment in Woman and Men.* San Francisco, CA: ICS Press.

Schütze, Yvonne, Kreppner, Kurt, and Paulsen, Sibylle (1986) The social construction of the sibling relationship. In Jenny Cook-Gumperz, William A. Corsaro, and Jürgen Streek (Eds.), *Children's Worlds and Children's Language.* pp. 128–145. Berlin: Mouton.

Schwartz, Jeffrey H., Houghton, Frank, Macchiarelli, Roberto, and Bondioli, Luca (2010) Skeletal remains from Punic Carthage do not support systematic sacrifice of infants. *PLos ONE* (online), February 10. Available at www.plosone.org/article/info:doi/10.1371/journal.pone.0009177.

Schwartzman, Helen (1978) *Transformations: The Anthropology of Children's Play.* New York, NY: Plenum Press.

   (2001) Children and anthropology: A century of studies. In Helen B. Schwartzman (Ed.), *Children and Anthropology: Perspectives for the 21st Century.* pp. 15–37. Westport, CT: Bergin and Garvey.

Scott, Eleanor (1999) *The Archaeology of Infancy and Infant Death.* Oxford: Archaeopress.

Scrimshaw, Susan C. M. (1978) Infant mortality and behavior in the regulation of family size. *Population and Development Review* 4:383–403.

   (1984) Infanticide in human populations: Societal and individual concerns. In Gerald Hausfater and Sarah Blaffer Hrdy (Eds.), *Infanticide: Comparative and Evolutionary Perspectives.* pp. 439–462. New York, NY: Aldine.

Sear, Rebecca and Mace, Ruth (2008) Who keeps children alive? A review of the effects of kin on child survival. *Evolution and Human Behavior* 29:1–18.

Sear, Rebecca, Mace, Ruth, and McGregor, Ian A. (2003) The effects of kin on female fertility in rural Gambia. *Evolution and Human Behavior* 24:25–42.

Seiter, Ellen (1998) Children's desires/mothers' dilemmas: The social contexts of consumption. In Henry Jenkins (Ed.), *The Children's Culture Reader.* pp. 297–317. New York, NY: New York University Press.

Sellen, Daniel W. (1995) *The socioecology of young child growth among the Datoga pastoralists of northern Kenya.* PhD dissertation, Department of Anthropology, University of California, Davis.

   (1998a) Infant and young child feeding practices among African pastoralists: The Datoga of Tanzania. *Journal of Biosocial Science* 3:481–499.

   (1998b) Polygyny and child growth in a traditional pastoral society: The case of the Datoga of Tanzania. *Human Nature* 10:329–371.

(2001) Weaning, complementary feeding, and maternal decision making in a rural East African pastoral population. *Journal of Human Lactation* 17:233–244.

Sellen, Daniel W. and Mace, Ruth (1997) Fertility and mode of subsistence: A phylogenetic analysis. *Current Anthropology* 38:878–889.

Senior, Louise M. (1994) Babes in the 'hood: Concepts of personhood and the spatial segregation of infants from adults in archaeological burial practices. Paper presented at the 59th annual meeting of the Society for American Archaeology, April 22, Anaheim, CA.

Serpell, Robert (1993) *The Significance of Schooling: Life Journeys in an African Society.* Cambridge: Cambridge University Press.

Seymour, Susan C. (2001) Child care in India: An examination of the "household size/infant indulgence" hypothesis. *Cross-Cultural Research* 35:3–22.

Shack, Dorothy N. (1969) Nutritional processes and personality development among the Gurage of Ethopia. *Ethnology* 8:293–300.

Shahar, Shulaminth (1990) *Childhood in the Middle Ages.* London: Routledge.

Shahbazi, Mohammed (2001) The Qashqa'i nomads of Iran: Formal education. *Nomadic Peoples* 5:37–64.

Shaner, Andrew, Miller, Geoffery, and Mintz, Jim (2008) Autism as the low-fitness extreme of a parentally selected fitness indicator. *Human Nature* 19:389–413.

Shapiro, H. A. (2003) Fathers and sons, men and boys. In Jennifer Neils and John H. Oakley (Eds.), *Coming of Age in Ancient Greece.* pp. 85–112. New Haven, CT: Yale University Press.

Sharer, Robert J. (1994) *The Ancient Maya,* 5th edn. Palo Alto, CA: Stanford University Press.

Sharp, Lesley A. (2002) *The Sacrificed Generation: Youth, History, and the Colonized Mind.* Berkeley, CA: University of California Press.

Shein, Max (1992) *The Precolumbian Child.* Culver City, CA: Labyrinthos.

Shelton, Jo-Ann (1998) *As the Romans Did: A Sourcebook in Roman Social History.* Oxford: Oxford University Press.

Shennan, Stephen J. and Steele, James (1999) Cultural learning in hominids: A behavioral ecological approach. In Hilary O. Box and Kathleen R. Gibson (Eds.), *Mammalian Social Learning: Comparative and Ecological Perspectives.* pp. 367–388. Cambridge: Cambridge University Press.

Shon, Mee-Ryong (2002) Korean early childhood education: Colonization and resistance. In Gaile S. Cannella and Joe L. Kincheloe (Eds.), *Kidworld: Childhood Studies, Global Perspectives, and Education.* pp. 137–160. New York, NY: Peter Lang.

Shore, Brad (1996) *Culture in Mind: Cognition, Culture, and the Problem of Meaning.* Oxford: Oxford University Press.

Shorto, Russell (2008) No babies. *New York Times Magazine,* June 29. Available at www.nytimes.com/2008/06/29/magazine/29Birth-t.html?pagewanted=all&_r=0. Accessed January 14, 2013.

Shostak, Marjorie (1976) A !Kung woman's memories of childhood. In Richard B. Lee and Irvin DeVore (Eds.), *Kalahari Hunter-Gatherers.* pp. 246–278. Cambridge, MA: Harvard University Press.

(1981) *Nisa: The Life and Words of a !Kung Woman.* New York, NY: Vintage Books.

Shutt, Eagle J., Miller, Mitchell J., Schreck, Christopher J., and Brown, Nancy K. (2004) Reconsidering the leading myths of stranger child abduction. *Criminal Justice Studies* 17:127–134.

Shwalb, David W., Shwalb, Barbara J., and Shoji, Junichi (1996) Japanese mothers' ideas about infants and temperament. In Sara Harkness and Charles M. Super (Eds.), *Parents' Cultural Belief Systems: Their Origins, Expressions, and Consequences.* pp. 169–191. New York, NY: Guilford Press.

Shweder, Richard A. (1984) Preview: A colloquy of culture theorists. In Richard A. Shweder and Robert L. LeVine (Eds.), *Culture Theory: Essays on Mind, Self and Emotion.* pp. 1–26. Cambridge: Cambridge University Press.

Sigman, Marian, Neumann, Charlotte, Carter, Eric, Cattle, Dorothy J., D'Souza, Susan, and Bwibo, Nimrod (1988) Home interactions and the development of Embu toddlers in Kenya. *Child Development* 59:1251–1261.

Silk, Joan B. (1980) Adoption and kinship in Oceania. *American Anthropologist* 82:799–820.

(1987) Adoption among the Inuit. *Ethos* 15:320–330.

(2002) Kin selection in primate groups. *International Journal of Primatology* 23:849–875.

Silk, Joan B., Alberts, Susan C., and Altmann, Jeanne (2003) Social bonds of female baboons enhance infant survival. *Science* 302:1231–1235.

Sillar, Bill (1994) Playing with God: Cultural perceptions of children, play, and miniatures in the Andes. *Archaeological Review from Cambridge* 13:47–63.

Silva, Katie G., Correa-Chavéz, Maricela, and Rogoff, Barbara (2011) Mexican-heritage children's attention and learning from interactions directed at others. *Child Development* 81:898–912.

Silvers, Jonathan (1996) Child labor in Pakistan. *Atlantic Monthly*, February:79–85.

Simmons, Leo W. (Ed.) (1942) *Sun Chief: The Autobiography of a Hopi Indian.* New Haven, CT: Yale University Press.

Simon, Herbert A. (1956) Rational choice and the structure of the environment. *Psychological Review* 63(1):129–138.

Singleton, John (1989) Japanese folkcraft pottery apprenticeship: Cultural patterns of an educational institution. In Michael W. Coy (Ed.), *Apprenticeship: From Theory to Method and Back Again.* pp. 13–30. Albany, NY: State University of New York Press.

Siskind, Amy (1999) In whose interest? Separating children from mothers in the Sullivan Institute/Fourth Wall community. In Susan J. Palmer and Charlotte E. Hardman (Eds.), *Children in New Religions.* pp. 51–68. New Brunswick, NJ: Rutgers. University Press.

Sjögren-de Beauchaine, Annick (1998) *The Bourgeoisie in the Dining Room: Meal Ritual and Cultural Process in Parisian Families of Today.* Stockholm: Institutet for Folkslivsforskining.

Skenazy, Lenore (2009) *Free-Range Kids: Giving Our Children the Freedom We Had Without Going Nuts with Worry.* Danvers, MA: Jossey-Bass.

Skoufias, Emmanuel (1994) Market wages, family composition and the time allocation of children in agricultural households. *The Journal of Developmental Studies* 30:335–360.

Small, Meredith F. (1998) *Our Babies, Ourselves: How Biology and Culture Shape the Way We Parent*. New York, NY: Anchor Books.

Smith, Benjamin (2010) Of marbles and (little) men: Bad luck and masculine identification in Aymara boyhood. *Journal of Linguistic Anthropology* 20:225–239.

Smith, Patricia E. (2006) Children and ceramic innovation: A study in the archaeology of children. *Archeological Papers of the American Anthropological Association* 15:65–76.

Smith, Peter K. (2010) *Children and Play*. Chichester: Wiley-Blackwell.

Smith-Hefner, Nancy J. (1993) Education, gender, and generational conflict among Khmer refugees. *Anthropology and Education Quarterly* 24:135–158.

Snow, Catherine E. and Beals, Dianne E. (2006) Mealtime talk that supports literacy development. *New Directions for Child and Adolescent Development* 111:51–66.

Snow, Catherine E. and Uccelli, Paolo (2009) The challenge of academic language. In David R. Olson and Nancy Torrance (Eds.), *The Cambridge Handbook of Literacy*. pp. 112–133. Cambridge: Cambridge University Press.

Snow, Pamela and Powell, Martine B. (2008) Oral language competence, social skills, and high-risk boys: What are juvenile offenders trying to tell us? *Children and Society* 22(1):16–28.

Sober, Elliott and Wilson, David S. (1998) *Unto Others: The Evolution and Psychology of Unselfish Behavior*. Cambridge, MA: Harvard University Press.

Sobolik, Kristin D. (2002) Children's health in the prehistoric southwest. In Kathryn A. Kamp (Ed.), *Children in the Prehistoric Puebloan Southwest*. pp. 125–151. Salt Lake City, UT: University of Utah Press.

Sofue, Takao (1965) Childhood ceremonies in Japan: Regional and local variations. *Ethnology* 4:148–164.

Sokolove, Michael (2004) Constructing a teen phenom. *New York Times Magazine*, November 28:80–85.

Solomon, Olga (2012) Rethinking baby talk. In Alessandro Duranti, Elinor Ochs, and Bambi B. Schieffelin (Eds.), *The Handbook of Language Socialization*. pp. 121–149. Chichester: Wiley-Blackwell.

Sommerville, John C. (1982) *The Rise and Fall of Childhood*. Sage Library of Social Research, vol. 140. Beverly Hills, CA: Sage.

Sorenson, E. Richard (1976) *The Edge of the Forest: Land, Childhood and Change in a New Guinea Protoagricultural Society*. Washington, DC: Smithsonian Institution Press.

Sosis, Richard, Kress, Howard C., and Boster, James S. (2007) Scars for war: Evaluating alternative signaling explanations for cross-cultural variance in ritual costs. *Evolution and Human Behavior* 28:234–247.

Spelke, Elizabeth S. (1990) Principles of object perception. *Cognitive Science* 14:29–56.

Spelke, Elizabeth S. and Kinzler, Katherine D. (2007) Core knowledge. *Developmental Science* 10:89–96.

Spencer, Paul (1970) The function of ritual in the socialization of the Samburu Moran. In Philip Mayer (Ed.), *Socialization: The Approach from Social Anthropology*. pp. 127–157. London: Tavistock Publications.

Spielmann, Katherine A. (1989) Dietary restrictions on hunter-gatherer women and the implications for fertility and infant mortality. *Human Ecology* 17:321–45.

Spilsbury, James C. and Korbin, Jill E. (2004) Negotiating the dance: Social capital from the perspective of neighborhood children and adults. In Peter B. Pufall and Richard P. Unsworth (Eds.), *Rethinking Childhood*. pp. 191–206. New Brunswick, NJ: Rutgers University Press.

Spiro, Melford E. (1958) *Children of the Kibbutz*. Cambridge, MA: Harvard University Press.

Spittler, Gerd (1998) *Hirtenarbeit*. Cologne: Rüdiger Köppe.

(2012) Children's work in a family economy: A case study and theoretical discussion. In Gerd Spittler and Michael Bourdillon (Eds.), *African Children at Work: Working and Learning in Growing Up*. pp. 57–85. Berlin: LitVerlag.

Sprott, Julie W. (2002) *Raising Young Children in an Alaskan Iñupiaq Village: The Family, Cultural and Village Environment of Rearing*. Westport, CT: Bergin and Garvey.

Stafford, Charles (1995) *The Roads of Chinese Childhood*. Cambridge: Cambridge University Press.

Stafford, Dinaz and Nair, Mira (2003) *Still the Children are Here*. Mumbai: Mirabai Films.

Stager, Lawrence E. and Greene, Joseph A. (2000) Were living children sacrificed to the gods? *Archeology Odyssey* 3(6):29–31.

Stager, Lawrence E. and Wolff, Samuel R. (1984) Child sacrifice at Carthage: Religious rite or population control? *Biblical Archaeology Review* 10(1):31–51.

Stambach, Amy (1998a) "Too much studying makes me crazy": School-related illnesses on Mount Kilimanjaro. *Comparative Education Review* 42:497–512.

(1998b) "Education is my husband": Marriage, gender, and reproduction in northern Tanzania. In Marianne Bloch, Josephine A. Beoku-Betts, and B. Robert Tabachnick (Eds.), *Women and Education in Sub-Saharan Africa: Power, Opportunities, and Constraints*. pp. 185–200. Boulder, CO: Lynne Rienner.

Stasch, Rupert (2009) *Society of Others: Kinship and Mourning in a West Papuan Place*. Berkeley, CA: University of California Press.

Stearman, Allyn M. (1989) *Yuqui: Forest Nomads in a Changing World*. New York, NY: Holt, Rinehart, and Winston.

Stearns, Peter N. (2010) Defining happy childhoods: Assessing a recent change. *Journal of the History of Childhood and Youth* 3:165–186.

Steels, Luc (2006) Experiments on the emergence of human communication. *Trends in Cognitive Sciences* 10:347–349.

Steiner, Leslie M. (2007) *Mommy Wars: Stay-at-Home and Career Moms Face Off on Their Choices, Their Lives, Their Families*. New York, NY: Random House.

Stella, Alessandro (2000) Introduction: A history of exploited children in Europe. In Bernard Schlemmer (Ed.), *The Exploited Child*. pp. 21–38. New York, NY: Zed Books.

Stephens, Sharon (1995) Introduction: Children and the politics of culture in "late capitalism." In Sharon Stephens (Ed.), *Children and the Politics of Culture*. pp. 3–48. Princeton, NJ: Princeton University Press.

Stephenson, Svetlana (2001) Street children in Moscow: Using and creating social capital. *Sociological Review* 49:530–47.

Sternglanz, Sarah Hall, Gran, James L., and Murakami, Melvin (1977) Adult preferences for infantile facial features: An ethnological approach. *Animal Behavior* 25:108–115.

Sternheimer, Karen (2003) *It's Not the Media: The Truth about Pop Culture's Influence on Children.* Boulder, CO: Westview Press.

Sterponi, Laura (2003) Account episodes in family discourse: The making of morality in everyday interaction. *Discourse Studies* 5:79–100.

Sterponi, Laura and Santagata, Rossella (2000) Mistakes in the classroom and at the dinner table: A comparison between socialization practices in Italy and the United States. *Crossroads of Language, Interaction and Culture* 3:57–72.

Stevens, Phillips, Jr. (1996) Traditional sport in Africa: Wrestling among the Bachama of Nigeria. In Tsuneo Sogawa (Ed.), *Traditional Sport in the Twenty-First Century.* pp. 83–114. Tokyo: Taishukun-Shoten.

Stevenson, Harold, W., Chen, Chuansheng, and Lee, Shinying (1992) Chinese families. In Jaipaul L. Roopnarine and D. Bruce Carter (Eds.), *Parent–Child Socialization in Diverse Cultures.* pp. 17–33. Norwood, NJ: Ablex.

Stevenson, Harold W. and Zusho, Akane (2002) Adolescence in China and Japan: Adapting to a changing environment. In Bradford B. Brown, Reed W. Larson, and T. S. Saraswathi (Eds.), *The World's Youth: Adolescence in Eight Regions of the Globe.* pp. 141–170. Cambridge: Cambridge University Press.

Stieglitz, Jonathan, Gurven, Michael, Kaplan, Hillard and Hooper, Paul L. (2013) Household task delegation among high-fertility forager-horticulturalists of Lowland Bolivia. *Current Anthropology* 54:1–10.

Stipek, Deborah (1995) The development of pride and shame in toddlers. In June P. Tangney and Kurt W. Fischer (Eds.), *Self-Conscious Emotions: The Psychology of Shame, Guilt, Embarrassment, and Pride.* pp. 237–254. New York, NY: Guilford Press.

Stoffle, Richard W. (1977) Industrial impact on family formation in Barbados, West Indies. *Ethnology* 16:253–267.

Stoller, Paul (1989) *Fusion of the Worlds: An Ethnography of Possession among the Songhay of Niger.* Chicago, IL: University of Chicago Press.

Stout, Dietrich (2002) Skill and cognition in stone tool production: An ethnographic case study from Irian Jaya. *Current Anthropology* 43:693–715.

Strassmann, Beverly I. (1993) Menstrual hut visits by Dogon women: A hormonal test distinguishes deceit from honest signaling. *Behavioral Ecology* 7:304–315.

(1997) Polygyny as a risk factor for child mortality among the Dogon. *Current Anthropology* 38:688–695.

(2011) Cooperation and competition in a cliff-dwelling people. *Proceedings of the National Academy of Sciences* 108:10894–10901.

Strathern, Andrew (1970) Male initiation in New Guinea Highlands societies. *Ethnology* 9:373–379.

Strathern, Marilyn (1980) No nature, no culture: The Hagen case. In Carol MacCormack and Marilyn Strathern (Eds.), *Nature, Culture, and Gender.* pp. 174–222. Cambridge: Cambridge University Press.

(1988) Social relations and the idea of externality. In Colin Renfrew and Chris Scarre (Eds.), *Cognition and Material Culture: The Archaeology of Symbolic Storage.* pp. 135–147. Oxford: Oxbow Books.

Strauss, Claudia (1992) Models and motives. In Roy d'Andrade and Claudia Strauss (Eds.), *Human Motives and Cultural Models.* pp. 1–20. Cambridge: Cambridge University Press.

Strehl, Talinay (2011) The risks of becoming a street child: Working children on the streets of Lima and Cusco. In G. Kristoffel Lieten (Ed.), *Hazardous Child Labour in Latin America.* pp. 43–65. Heiderberg: Springer.

Strier, Karen B. (2003) *Primate Behavioral Ecology,* 2nd edn. Boston, MA: Allyn & Bacon.

Strom, Robert D., Strom, Paris S., Strom, Shirley K., Shen, Yuh-Ling, and Beckert, Troy E. (2004) Black, Hispanic, and white American mothers of adolescents: Construction of a national standard. *Adolescence* 39:669–685.

Strouhal, Eugen (1990) Life of ancient Egyptian children according to archaeological sources. In Gaston P. Beunen (Ed.), *Children and Exercise.* pp. 184–196. Stuttgart: Enke.

(1992) *Life of the Ancient Egyptians.* Norman, OK: University of Oklahoma Press.

Suarez-Orozco, Marcelo M. (1989) *Central American Refugees and US High Schools: A Psycho-social Study of Motivation and Achievement.* Palo Alto, CA: Stanford University Press.

Sugiyama, Lawrence S. and Chacon, Richard (2005) Juvenile responses to household ecology among the Yora of Peruvian Amazonia. In Barry S. Hewlett and Michael E. Lamb (Eds.), *Hunter-Gatherer Childhoods: Evolutionary, Developmental, and Cultural Perspectives.* pp. 237–261. New Brunswick, NJ: Aldine/Transaction Publishers.

Sugiyama, Yukimaru (1967) Social organization of Hanuman langurs. In Steven A. Altmann (Ed.), *Social Communication among Primates.* pp. 221–253. Chicago, IL: University of Chicago Press.

Sung, Jihyun and Hsu, Hui-Chin (2009) Korean mothers' attention regulation and referential speech: Associations with language and play in one-year-olds. *International Journal of Behavioral Development* 33(5):430–439.

Sunley, Robert (1955) Early nineteenth-century American literature on child rearing. In Margaret Mead and Martha Wolfenstein (Eds.), *Childhood in Contemporary Cultures.* pp. 150–167. Chicago, IL: University of Chicago Press.

Super, Charles M. (1976) Environmental effects on motor development: The case of "African infant precocity." *Developmental Medicine and Child Neurology* 18:561–567.

Sussman, George (1982) *Selling Mother's Milk: The Wet-Nursing Business in France, 1715–1914.* Urbana, IL: University of Illinois Press.

Sussman, Robert W. (1977) Socialization, social structure, and ecology of the two sympatric species of Lemur. In Suzanne Chevalier-Skolnikoff and Frank E. Poirier (Eds.), *Primate Bio-Social Development: Biological, Social, and Ecological Determinants.* pp. 515–528. New York, NY: Garland.

Sutton-Smith, Brian (1977) Commentary. *Current Anthropology* 18:184–185.

(1986) *Toys as Culture.* New York, NY: Gardner Press.

Sutton-Smith, Brian and Rosenborg, Barak G. (1961) Sixty years of historical change in the game preferences of American children. *Journal of American Folklore* 74:17–46.

Swadener, Beth B., Kabiru, Margaret, and Njenga, Anne (2000) *Does the Village Still Raise the Child? A Collaborative Study of Changing Child-Rearing and Early Education in Kenya.* Albany, NY: State University of New York Press.

Swanton, John R. (1928) Social organization and the social usages of the Creek confederacy. In *United States Bureau of American Ethnology Forty-Second Annual Report.* pp. 23–472. Washington, DC: US Government Printing Office.

Takada, Akira (2005) Mother–infant interactions among the !Xun: Analysis of gymnastic and breastfeeding behaviors. In Barry S. Hewlett and Michael E. Lamb (Eds.), *Hunter-Gatherer Childhoods: Evolutionary, Developmental, and Cultural Perspectives.* pp. 289–308. New Brunswick, NJ: Aldine/Transaction Publishers.

(2010) Changes in developmental trends of caregiver–child interactions among the San: Evidence from the !Xun of northern Namibia. *African Study Monographs* 40:155–177.

(2012) Preverbal infant–caregiver interaction. In Alessandro Duranti, Elinor Ochs, and Bambi B. Schieffelin (Eds.), *The Handbook of Language Socialization.* pp. 56–80. Chichester: Wiley-Blackwell.

Takeuchi, Kiyoshi (2013) Food restriction and social identity of Aka forager adolescents in the Republic of Congo. In Bonnie L. Hewlett (Ed.), *Adolescent Identity: Evolutionary, Cultural and Developmental Perspectives.* pp. 165–185. New York: Routledge.

Talle, Aud (2004) Adoption practices among the pastoral Maasai of East Africa. In Fiona Bowie (Ed.), *Cross-Cultural Approaches to Adoption.* pp. 64–78. London: Routledge.

Tanon, Fabienne (1994) *A Cultural View on Planning: The Case of Weaving in Ivory Coast.* Tillburg: Tilburg University Press.

Taracena, Elvira and Tavera, Maria-Luisa (2000) Stigmatization versus identity: Child street-workers in Mexico. In Bernard Schlemmer (Ed.), *The Exploited Child.* pp. 93–105. New York, NY: Zed Books.

Tatar, Maria (1992) *Off with Their Heads: Fairytales and the Culture of Childhood.* Princeton, NY: Princeton University Press.

Tayanin, Damrong and Lindell, Kristina (1991) *Hunting and Fishing in a Kammu Village.* Studies in Asian Topics 14. Copenhagen: Curzon Press.

Taylor, Lisa Rende (2002) Dangerous trade-offs: The behavioral ecology of child labor and prostitution in Thailand. Paper presented at the symposium on New Research in Human Behavior Ecology, American Anthropological Association, November New Orleans, LA.

Tehrani, Jamshid J. and Collard, Mark (2009) On the relationship between interindividual cultural transmission and population-level cultural diversity: A case study of weaving in Iranian tribal populations. *Evolution and Human Behavior* 30:286–300.

Templeton, Sarah-Kate (2007) Deaf demand right to designer deaf children. *The Times,* December 23. Available at www.geneticsandsociety.org/article.php?id=3860. Accessed February 1, 2014.

Thiessen, Erik D., Hill, Emily A., and Saffran, Jenny R. (2005) Infant-directed speech facilitates word segmentation. *Infancy* 7(1):53–71.

Thompson, Jennifer L., and Nelson, Andrew J. (2011) Middle childhood and modern human origins. *Human Nature* 22:249–280.

Thompson, Laura (1940) *Fijian Frontier*. San Francisco, CA: American Council, Institute of Pacific Relations.

Thorne, Barrie (1993) *Gender Play: Girls and Boys in School*. New Brunswick, NJ: Rutgers University Press.

Thornton, Alex and McAuliffe, Katherine (2006) Teaching in wild meerkats. *Science* 313:227–229.

Thornton, Alex and Raihani, Nichola J. (2008) The evolution of teaching. *Animal Behaviour* 75:1823–1836.

Thorsen, Dorte (2009) From shackles to links in the chain: Theorizing adolescent boys' relocation in Burkina Faso. *Forum for Development Studies* 36:301–327.

Tietjen, Anne M. (1985) Infant care and feeding practices and the beginnings of socialization among the Maisin of Papua New Guinea. In Leslie B. Marshall (Ed.), *Infant Care and Feeding in the South Pacific*. pp. 121–135. New York, NY: Gordon and Breach.

Timaeus, Ian and Graham, Wendy (1989) Labour circulation, marriage and fertility in southern Africa. In Ronald J. Lesthaeghe (Ed.), *Reproduction and Social Organization in Sub-Saharan Africa*. pp. 364–400. Berkeley, CA: University of California Press.

Tingey, Holly, Kiger, Gary, and Riley, Pamela J. (1996) Juggling multiple roles: Perceptions of working mothers. *Social Science Journal* 33:183–191.

Tjitayi, Katrina and Lewis, Sandra (2011) Envisioning lives at Ernabella. In Ute Eickelkamp (Ed.), *Growing up in Central Australia: New Anthropological Studies of Aboriginal Childhood and Adolescence*. pp. 49–62. Oxford: Berghahn Books.

Tomasello, Michael, Carpenter, Malinda, Call, Josep, Behne, Tanya and Moll, Henrike (2005) Understanding and sharing intentions: The origins of cultural cognition. *Behavioral and Brain Sciences* 28:675–735.

Tonkinson, Myrna (2011) Change and challenge for some Western Desert young people today. In Ute Eickelkamp (Ed.), *Growing up in Central Australia: New Anthropological Studies of Aboriginal Childhood and Adolescence*. pp. 213–238. Oxford: Berghahn Books.

Tooby, John and Cosmides, Leda (1992) The psychological foundations of culture. In John Tooby, Leda Cosmides, and Jerome Barkow (Eds.), *The Adapted Mind: Evolutionary Psychology and the Generation of Culture*. pp. 19–136. Oxford: Oxford University Press.

Toren, Christina (1988) Children's perceptions of gender and hierarchy in Fiji. In Gustav Jahoda and Ioan M. Lewis (Eds.), *Acquiring Culture: Cross-Cultural Studies in Child Development*. pp. 225–270. London: Croom Helm.

(1990) *Making Sense of Hierarchy: Cognition as Social Process in Fiji*. Houndsmills: Palgrave Macmillan.

(1993) Making history: The significance of childhood cognition for a comparative anthropology of mind. *Man* 28(3):461–478.

(2001) The child mind. In Harvey Whitehouse (Ed.), *The Debated Mind: Evolutionary Psychology versus Ethnography*. pp. 155–179. Oxford: Berg.

Toshisada, Nishida (2003) Individuality and flexibility of cultural behavior patterns in chimpanzees. In Frans B. M. de Waal and Peter L. Tyack (Eds.), *Animal Social*

Complexity: Intelligence, Culture, and Individualized Societies. pp. 392–413. Cambridge, MA: Harvard University Press.

Trevarthen, Colwyn (1983) Interpersonal abilities of infants as generators for transmission of language and culture. In Alberto Oliverio (Ed.), *The Behavior of Human Infants.* pp. 145–176. New York: Plenum Press.

(1988) Universal co-operative motives: How infants begin to know the language and culture of their parents. In Gustav Jahoda and Ioan M. Lewis (Eds.), *Acquiring Culture: Cross-Cultural Studies in Child Development.* pp. 37–90. London: Croom Helm.

(2005) "Stepping away from the mirror". Pride and shame in adventures of companionship: Reflections on the emotional needs of infant intersubjectivity. In C. Sue Carter, Liselotte Ahnert, K. E. Grossmann, Sarah B. Hrdy, Michael E. Lamb, Steven W. Porges, and Neil Sachser (Eds.), *Attachment and Bonding: A New Synthesis.* pp. 55–84. Cambridge, MA: MIT Press.

Trevathan, Wenda and McKenna, James J. (1994) Birth and infancy in evolutionary perspective: Insights for modern life. *Children's Environments* 11(2):1–17.

Trivers, Robert, L. (1972) Parental investment and sexual selection. In Bernard Campbell (Ed.), *Sexual Selection and the Descent of Man.* pp. 136–179. Chicago, IL: Aldine.

(1974) Parent–offspring conflict. *American Zoologist* 14:249–264.

Tronick, Edward Z., Morelli, Gilda A., and Winn, Steven (1987) Multiple caretaking of Efe (Pygmy) infants. *American Anthropologist* 89:96–106.

Tronick, Edward Z., Thomas, R. Brook, and Daltabuit, Magali (1994) The Quechua manta pouch: A caretaking practice for buffering the Peruvian infant against the multiple stressors of high altitude. *Child Development* 65:1005–1013.

Tucker, Bram and Young, Alyson G. (2005) Growing up Mikea: Children's time allocation and tuber foraging in southwestern Madagascar. In Barry S. Hewlett and Michael E. Lamb (Eds.), *Hunter-Gatherer Childhoods: Evolutionary, Developmental, and Cultural Perspectives.* pp. 147–171. New Brunswick, NJ: Aldine/Transaction Publishers.

Tudge, Jonathan (2008) *The Everyday Lives of Young Children: Culture, Class, and Child Rearing in Diverse Societies.* Cambridge: Cambridge University Press.

Turke, Paul W. (1988) Helpers at the nest: Childcare networks on Ifaluk. In Laura Betzig, Monique Borgerhoff Mulder, and Paul Turke (Eds.), *Human Reproductive Behavior.* pp. 173–188. Cambridge: Cambridge University Press.

(1989) Evolution and the demand for children. *Population and Development Review* 15:61–90.

Turnbull, Colin M. (1965) *The Mbuti Pygmies: An Ethnographic Survey.* New York, NY: American Museum of Natural History.

(1978) The politics of non-aggression. In Ashley Montague (Ed.), *Learning Non-Aggression: The Experience of Non-Literate Societies.* pp. 161–221. Oxford: Oxford University Press.

(1992) *The Mountain People.* New York, NY: Simon and Schuster.

Turner, Diane M. (1987) What happened when my daughter became a Fijian. In Barbara Butler and Diane Michalski Turner (Eds.), *Children and Anthropological Research.* pp. 92–114. New York, NY: Plenum Press.

Tuzin, Donald (1980) *The Voice of the Tambaran: Truth and Illusion in Ilahita Arapesh Religion*. Berkeley, CA: University of California Press.

Twohey, Megan (2013) Americans use the internet to abandon children adopted overseas. *Reuters Online*, September 9. Available at www.reuters.com/investigates/adoption/#article/part1. Accessed September 9, 2013.

Tyson, Karolyn (2002) Weighing in: Elementary-age students and the debate on attitudes toward school among Black students. *Social Forces* 80:1157–1189.

Ullrich, Helen E. (1995) A co-constructivist perspective of life-course changes among Havik Brahmins in a South India village. In Jaan Valsiner (Ed.), *Child Development within Culturally Structured Environments: Comparative-Cultural and Constructivist Perspectives*. pp. 14–187. Norwood, NJ: Ablex.

Ulturgasheva, Olga (2012) *Narrating the Future in Siberia*. Oxford: Berghahn Books.

UNICEF (2004) *Progress for Children: A Child Survival Report Card. Vol. I*. New York, NY: United Nations.

(2007) *Progress for Children: A World Fit For Children Statistical Review, Vol. 6*. New York, NY: United Nations.

Unnithan-Kumar, Maya (2001) Emotion, agency and access to healthcare: Women's experiences of reproduction in Jaipur. In Soraya Tremayne (Ed.), *Managing Reproductive Life: Cross-Cultural Themes in Sexuality and Fertility*. pp. 27–51. Oxford: Berghahn Books.

Uno, Kathleen S. (1991) Japan. In Joseph M. Hawes and N. Ray Hiner (Eds.), *Children in Historical and Comparative Perspective*. pp. 389–419. Westport, CT: Greenwood Press.

Uribe, F. Medardo, Uribe, Tapia, LeVine, Robert A., and LeVine, Sarah E. (1994) Maternal behavior in a Mexican community: The changing environments of children. In Patricia M. Greenfield and Rodney R. Cocking (Eds.), *Cross-Cultural Roots of Minority Child Development*. pp. 41–54. Hillsdale, NJ: Erlbaum.

Utas, Mats (2005) Agency of victims: Young women in the Liberian civil war. In Alcinda Honwana and Filip de Boeck (Eds.), *Makers and Breakers: Children and Youth in Post-Colonial Africa*. pp. 53–80. Trenton, NJ: Africa World Press.

Uttal, Lynet (2010) Liminal cultural work in family childcare: Latino immigrant family childcare providers and bicultural childrearing in the United States, 2002–2004. *Paedagogica Historica* 46:729–740.

Valdez, Marianna F., Dowrick, Peter W., and Maynard, Ashley E. (2007) Cultural misperceptions and goals for Samoan children's education in Hawai'i: Voices from school, home, and community. *The Urban Review* 39:67–92.

Valsiner, Jaan (2000). *Culture and Human Development*. Thousand Oaks, CA: Sage.

van Biema, David and Kamlani, Ratu (1994) Parents who kill. *Time Magazine* 144(20):50–51.

van den Berge, Martin P. (2011a) Child miners in Cajamarca, Peru. In G. Kristoffel Lieten (Ed.), *Hazardous Child Labour in Latin America*. pp. 67–79. Heidelberg: Springer.

(2011b) Children in traditional and commercial agriculture. In G. Kristoffel Lieten (Ed.), *Hazardous Child Labour in Latin America*. pp. 145–163. Heidelberg: Springer.

van Gennep, Arnold (1908/1960) *The Rites of Passage*. Chicago, IL: University of Chicago Press.

van Lawick-Goodall, Jane (1973) Behavior of chimpanzees in their natural habitat. *American Journal of Psychiatry* 130:1–12.

  (1976a) Chimpanzee locomotor play. In Jerome S. Bruner, Alison Jolly, and Kathy Sylva (Eds.), *Play: Its Role in Development and Evolution*. pp. 156–160. New York, NY: Basic Books.

  (1976b) Mother chimpanzees' play with their infants. In Jerome S. Bruner, Alison Jolly, and Kathy Sylva (Eds.), *Play: Its Role in Development and Evolution*. pp. 262–267. New York, NY: Basic Books.

van Stone, James W. (1965) *The Changing Culture of the Snowdrift Chipewyan*. Ottawa, ON: National Museum of Canada.

Vandermaas-Peeler, Maureen, Nelson, Jackie, von der Heide, Melissa, and Kelly, Erica (2009) Parental guidance with four-year-olds in literacy and play activities at home. In David Kuschner (Ed.), *From Children to Red Hatters*. pp. 93–112. Lanham, MD: University Press of America.

Verma, Suman and Saraswathi, T. S. (2002) Adolescence in India: Street urchins or Silicon Valley millionaires? In Bradford B. Brown, Reed W. Larson, and T. S. Saraswathi (Eds.), *The World's Youth: Adolescence in Eight Regions of the Globe*. pp. 105–140. Cambridge: Cambridge University Press.

Verma, Suman and Sharma, Deepali (2007) Cultural dynamics of family relations among Indian adolescents in varied contexts. In Kenneth H. Rubin and Ock Boon Chung (Eds.), *Parenting Beliefs, Behavior and Parent–Child Relationships: A Cross-Cultural Perspective*. pp. 185–205. New York, NY: Psychology Press.

Vermeulen, Eric (2004) Dealing with doubt: Making decisions in a neonatal ward in the Netherlands. *Social Science & Medicine* (59):2071–2085.

Vermonden, Daniel (2009) Reproduction and development of expertise within communities of practice: A case study of fishing activities in South Buton. In Serena Heckler (Ed.), *Landscape, Process, and Power: Re-Evaluating Traditional Environmental Knowledge*. Studies in Environmental Anthropology and Ethnobiology. pp. 205–229. Oxford: Berghahn Books.

Viccars, John D. (1949) Witchcraft in Bolobo, Belgian Congo. *Africa* 19:220–229.

Vigh, Henrik E. (2006) Social death and violent life chances. In Catrine Christiansen, Mats Utas, and Henrik E. Vigh (Eds.), *Navigating Youth, Generating Adulthood: Social Becoming in an African Context*. pp. 31–60. Uppsala: Nordiska Afrikainstitutet

Vigil, James D. (1988) Group processes and street identity: Adolescent Chicano gang members. *Ethos* 16:421–445.

  (2003) Urban violence and street gangs. *Annual Review of Anthropology* 32:225–242.

Visalberghi, Elisabetta and Fragasky, Dorothy M. (1990) Do monkeys ape? In Sue Taylor Parker and Katherine R. Gibson (Eds.), *Language and Intelligence in Monkeys and Apes*. pp. 247–273. Cambridge: Cambridge University Press.

Visano, Livy A. (1990) The socialization of street children: The development and transformation of identities. *Sociological Studies of Child Development* 3:139–161.

Vizedom, Monika and Zais, James P. (1976) *Rites and Relationships: Rites of Passage and Contemporary Anthropology*. Beverly Hills, CA: Sage.

Voget, Fred W. (1975) *A History of Ethnology*. New York, NY: Holt, Rinehart, and Winston.

Volk, Anthony A. and Atkinson, Jeremy A. (2013) Infant and child death in the human environment and evolutionary adaptation. *Evolution and Human Behavior* 34:182–192.

Volk, Anthony and Quinsey, Vernon L. (2002) The influence of infant facial cues on adoption preferences. *Human Nature* 13:437–455.

Wagley, Charles (1977) *Welcome of Tears: The Tapirapé Indians of Central Brazil*. Oxford: Oxford University Press.

Wagner, Claire M., Lyimo, Emmanuely D., and Lwendo, Steven (2012) Matches but no fire: Street children in Dar es Salaam, Tanzania. In Marisa O. Ensor (Ed.), *African Childhoods: Education, Development, Peacebuilding and the Youngest Continent*. pp. 33–46. New York, NY: Palgrave Macmillan.

Waldfogel, Jane (2006) *What Children Need*. Cambridge, MA: Harvard University Press.

Wallaert, Hélène (2008) The way of the potter's mother: Apprenticeship strategies among Dii potters from Cameroon, West Africa. In Miriam T. Start, Brenda J. Bowser, and Lee Horne (Eds.), *Cultural Transmission and Material Culture: Breaking Down Boundaries*. pp. 178–198. Tucson, AZ: University of Arizona Press.

Wallaert-Pêtre, Hélène (2001) Learning how to make the right pots: Apprenticeship strategies and material culture, a case study in handmade pottery from Cameroon. *Journal of Anthropological Research* 57:471–493.

Walsh, Daniel J. (2004) Frog boy and the American monkey: The body in Japanese early schooling. In Liora Bresler (Ed.), *Knowing Bodies, Moving Minds*. pp. 97–109. Dordrecht: Kluwer Academic.

Walter, Jeffrey R. (1987) Transition to adulthood. In Barbara B. Smuts, Dorothy L. Cheney, Robert M. Seyfarth, Richard W. Wrangham, and Thomas T. Struhsaker (Eds.), *Primate Societies*. pp. 358–369. Chicago, IL: University of Chicago Press.

Waltner, Ann (1995) Infanticide and dowry in Ming and early Qing China. In Anne B. Kinney (Ed.), *Chinese Views of Childhood*. pp. 193–217. Honolulu, HI: University of Hawai'i Press.

Wang, Feng, Tsai, Yaching, and Wang, William, S.-Y. (2009) Chinese literacy. In David R. Olson and Nancy Torrance (Eds.), *The Cambridge Handbook of Literacy*. pp. 386–417. Cambridge: Cambridge University Press.

Ward, Barbara E. (1970) Temper tantrums in Kau Sai: Some speculations upon their effects. In Philip Mayer (Ed.), *Socialization: The Approach from Social Anthropology*. pp. 107–125. London: Tavistock Publications.

Ward, Carol J. (2005) *Native Americans in the School System: Family, Community, and Academic Achievement*. Lanham, MD: AltaMira Press.

Ward, Martha C. (1971) *Them Children: A Study in Language Learning*. New York: Holt, Rinehart, and Winston.

Warneken, Felix and Tomasello, Michael (2006) Altruistic helping in human infants and young chimpanzees. *Science* 311:1301–1303.

Warren, Andrea (2001) *We Rode the Orphan Trains*. Boston, MA: Houghton Mifflin.

Watson, James L. (1976) Chattel slavery in Chinese peasant society: A comparative analysis. *Ethnology* 15:361–375.

Watson-Franke, Maria-Barbara (1976) To learn for tomorrow: Enculturation of girls and its social importance among the Guajiro of Venezuela. In Johannes Wilbert (Ed.), *Enculturation in Latin America*. pp. 191–211. Los Angeles, CA: UCLA Latin American Center Publications.

Watson-Gegeo, Karen A. and Gegeo, David W. (1989) The role of sibling interaction in child socialization. In Patricia G. Zukow (Ed.), *Sibling Interaction across Cultures*. pp. 54–76. New York, NY: Springer.

(1992) Schooling, knowledge, and power: Social transformation in the Solomon Islands. *Anthropology and Education Quarterly* 23:10–29.

(2001) "That's what children do": Perspectives on work and play in Kwara'ae. Paper presented at the annual meeting of the Association for the Study of Play, February, San Diego, CA.

Wax, Murray L. (2002) The school classroom as frontier. *Anthropology and Education Quarterly* 33(1):118–130.

Wee, Vivienne (1992) Children, population policy, and the state in Singapore. In Sharon Stephens (Ed.),*Children and the Politics of Culture*. pp. 184–217. Princeton, NJ: Princeton University Press.

Weisfeld, Glenn E. (1999) *Evolutionary Principles of Human Adolescence*. New York, NY: Basic Books.

Weisfeld, Glenn E. and Linkey, Harold E. (1985) Dominance displays as indicators of a social success motive. In Steve L. Ellyson and John F. Dovidio (Eds.), *Power, Dominance, and Nonverbal Behavior*. pp. 109–128. New York, NY: Springer.

Weisner, Thomas S. (1989) Cultural and universal aspects of social support for children: Evidence from the Abaluyia of Kenya. In Deborah Belle (Ed.), *Children's Social Networks and Social Supports*. pp. 70–90. New York, NY: Wiley.

(1996) Why ethnography should be the most important method in the study of human development. In Richard Jessor, Anne Colby, and Richard W. Shweder (Eds.), *Ethnography and Human Development: Context and Meaning in Social Inquiry*. pp. 305–324. Chicago, IL: University of Chicago Press.

Weisner, Thomas S. and Gallimore, Ronald (1977) My brother's keeper: Child and sibling caretaking. *Current Anthropology* 18:169–190.

Welles-Nyström, Barbara (1988) Parenthood and infancy in Sweden. *New Direction for Child Development* 40:75–96.

(1996) Scenes from a marriage: Equality ideology in Swedish family policy, maternal ethnotheories, and practice. In Sara Harkness and Charles M. Super (Eds.), *Parents' Cultural Belief Systems: Their Origins, Expressions, and Consequences*. pp. 192–214. New York, NY: Guilford Press.

Wellman, Henry M., Cross, David, and Watson, Julanne (2001) Meta-analysis of theory-of-mind development: The truth about false belief. *Child Development* 72:655–684.

Wenger, Martha (1989) Work, play and social relationships among children in a Giriama community. In Deborah Belle (Ed.), *Children's Social Networks and Social Supports*. pp. 91–115. New York, NY: Wiley.

512   References

West, Elliott (1992) Children on the plains frontier. In Elliott West and Paula
    Petrik (Eds.), *Small Worlds: Children and Adolescents in America, 1850–1950*.
    pp. 26–41. Lawrence, KS: University Press of Kansas.
West, Mary Maxwell (1988) Parental values and behavior in the outer Fiji islands. In
    Robert LeVine, Patrice M. Miller, and Mary Maxwell West (Eds.), *Parental
    Behaviour in Diverse Societies, special issue of New Directions for Child
    Development* 40:13–26.
West, Mary Maxwell and Konner, Melvin J. (1981) The role of the father:
    An anthropological perspective. In Michael E. Lamb (Ed.), *The Role of the Father
    in Child Development*. pp. 155–218. New York, NY: Wiley.
West-Eberhard, Mary Jane (2003) *Developmental Plasticity and Evolution*. Oxford:
    Oxford University Press.
White, Ben (2012) Changing childhoods: Javanese village children in three generations.
    Journal of Agrarian Change 12:81–97.
White, Merry I. (2002) *Perfectly Japanese: Making Families in an Era of Upheaval*.
    Berkeley, CA: University of California Press.
White, Robert W. (1959) Motivation reconsidered: The concept of competence.
    Psychological Review 66:297–333.
Whitehead, Ann, Hashim, Imam, and Iversen, Vegard (2005) *Child Migration, Child
    Agency and Intergenerational Relations in Africa and South Asia*. Working
    Paper 24. Development Research Centre on Migration, Globalisation and
    Poverty, University of Sussex.
Whiten, Andrew, Goodall, Jane, McGrew, William C., Nishida, T., Reynolds,
    Vernon, Sugiyama, Yakimaru, Tutin, Caroline E. G., Wrangham, Richard W.,
    and Boesch, Christophe (1999) Culture in chimpanzees. *Nature*
    399:682–685.
Whiting, Beatrice B. and Edwards, Carolyn Pope (1988a) *Children of Different Worlds:
    The Formation of Social Behavior*. Cambridge, MA: Harvard University Press.
    (1988b) A cross-cultural analysis of sex differences in the behavior of children
    aged 3 through 11. In Gerald Handel (Ed.), *Childhood Socialization*. pp. 281–297.
    New York, NY: Aldine.
Whiting, Beatrice B. and Whiting, John W. M. (1975) *Children of Six Cultures*.
    Cambridge, MA: Harvard University Press.
Whiting, John W. M. (1941) *Becoming a Kwoma*. New Haven, CT: Yale University
    Press.
    (1977) Infanticide. Paper presented to the Society for Research in Cross-Cultural
    Research, February, Ann Arbor, MI.
Whiting, John W. M., Burbank, Victoria, K., and Ratner, Mitchell S. (1986)
    The duration of maidenhood across cultures. In Jane B. Lancaster and Beatrix A.
    Hamburg (Eds.), *School-Age Pregnancy and Parenthood: Biosocial Dimensions*.
    pp. 273–302. New York, NY: Aldine de Gruyter.
Whittemore, Robert D. (1989) Child caregiving and socialization to the Mandinka way:
    Toward an ethnography of childhood. Unpublished PhD dissertation, UCLA,
    Los Angeles, CA.
Whittemore, Robert D. and Beverly, Elizabeth (1989) Trust in the Mandika way:
    The cultural context of sibling care. In Patricia Zukow (Ed.), *Sibling Interaction
    across Cultures*. pp. 26–53. New York, NY: Springer.

Whittlesey, Stephanie M. (2002) The cradle of death: Mortuary practices, bioarchaeology, and the children of Grasshopper Pueblo. In Kathryn A. Kamp (Ed.), *Children in the Prehistoric Puebloan Southwest*. pp. 152–168. Salt Lake City, UT: University of Utah Press.

Wicks, Ann Barrott and Avril, Ellen B. (2002) Introduction: Children in Chinese art. In Ann Barrott Wicks (Ed.), *Children in Chinese Art*. pp. 1–30. Honolulu, HI: University of Hawai'i Press.

Wiedemann, Thomas (1989) *Adults and Children in the Roman Empire*. New Haven, CT: Yale University Press.

Wieschhoff, Heinz (1937) Names and naming customs among the Mashona in southern Rhodesia. *American Anthropologist* 39:497–503.

Wihstutz, Anne (2007) The significance of care and domestic work to children: A German portrayal. In Beatrice Hungerland, Manfred Leibel, Brian Milne, and Anne Wihstutz (Eds.), *Working to Be Someone: Child-Focused Research and Practice with Working Children*. pp. 77–86. London: Jessica Kingsley.

Wilbert, Johannes (1976) To become a maker of canoes: An essay in Warao enculturation. In Johannes Wilbert (Ed.), *Enculturation in Latin America*. pp. 303–358. Los Angeles, CA: UCLA Latin American Center Publications.

Wilder, William (1970) Socialization and social structure in a Malay village. In Philip Mayer (Ed.), *Socialization: The Approach from Social Anthropology*. pp. 215–268. London: Tavistock Publications.

Wileman, Julie (2005) *Hide and Seek: The Archaeology of Childhood*. Stroud: Tempus.

Wiley, Andrea S. (2004) *An Ecology of High-Altitude Infancy*. Cambridge: Cambridge University Press.

Wilkie, David S. and Morelli, Gilda A. (1991) Coming of age in the Ituri. *Natural History* 100(10):54–62.

Wilkins, Sally (2002) *Sports and Games of Medieval Cultures*. Westport, CT: Greenwood Press.

Willerslev, Rane (2007) *Soul Hunters: Hunting, Animism, and Personhood among the Siberian Yukaghirs*. Berkeley, CA: University of California Press.

Williams, Francis E. (1936) *Papuans of the Trans-Fly*. Oxford: Clarendon Press.

Williams, Judith R. (1968) *The Youth of Haouch El Harimi, a Lebanese Village*. Cambridge, MA: Harvard University Press.

Williams, Thomas R. (1969) *A Borneo Childhood: Enculturation in Dusun Society*. New York, NY: Holt, Rinehart, and Winston.

(1983) *Socialization*. Englewood Cliffs, NJ: Prentice Hall.

Willis, Paul E. (1977) *Learning to Labour: How Working Class Kids Get Working Class Jobs*. Westmead: Saxon House.

Wilson, Margo and Daly, Martin (2002) The man who mistook his wife for a chattel. In James Tooby, Leeda Cosmides, and Jerome Barkow (Eds.), *The Adapted Mind: Evolutionary Psychology and the Generation of Culture*. pp. 289–322. New York, NY: Oxford University Press.

Wiltz, Nancy W. and Fein, Greta G. (1996) Evolution of a narrative curriculum: The contributions of Vivian Gussin Paley. *Young Children* 51:61–69.

Wingard, Leah (2007) Constructing time and prioritizing activities in parent–child interaction. *Discourse and Society* 18:75–91.

Winking, Jeffrey, Gurven, Michael, and Kaplan, Hillard (2010) Father death and adult success among the Tsimané: Implications for marriage and divorce. *Evolution and Human Behavior* 32:79–89.

Winzeler, Robert L. (2004) *The Architecture of Life and Death in Borneo*. Honolulu, HI: University of Hawai'i Press.

Wober, Mallory M. (1972) Culture and the concept of intelligence: A case in Uganda. *Journal of Cross-Cultural Psychology* 3: 327–328.

Wolf, Margery (1972) *Woman and the Family in Rural Taiwan*. Palo Alto, CA: Stanford University Press.

Wolfenstein, Martha (1955) Fun morality: An analysis of recent American child-training literature. In Margaret Mead and Martha Wolfenstein (Eds.), *Childhood in Contemporary Cultures*. pp. 168–178. Chicago, IL: University of Chicago Press.

Wolseth, Jon (2009) "Good times and bad blood": Violence, solidarity, and social organization on Dominican streets. In Dennis Rodgers and Gareth Jones (Eds.), *Youth Violence in Latin America: Gangs and Juvenile Justice in Perspective*. pp. 63–82. New York, NY: Palgrave.

   (2010) Learning on the streets: Peer socialization in adverse environments. In David F. Lancy, Suzanne Gaskins, and John Bock (Eds.), *The Anthropology of Learning in Childhood*. pp. 421–442. Lanham, MD: AltaMira Press.

Woolf, Alex (1997) At home in the long Iron Age: A dialogue between households and individuals in cultural reproduction. In Jenny Moore and Eleanor Scott (Eds.), *Invisible People and Processes*. pp. 68–78. London: Leicester University Press.

Worthman, Carol M. (2010) Survival and health. In Marc H. Bornstein (Ed.), *Handbook of Cultural Developmental Science*. pp. 39–59. New York, NY: Psychology Press.

Wu, Pei Yi (1995) Childhood remembered: Parents and children in China, 800 to 1700. In Anne B. Kinney (Ed.), *Chinese Views of Childhood*. pp. 129–156. Honolulu, HI: University of Hawai'i Press.

Wu, Peixia, Robinson, Clyde C., Yang, Chongming, Hart, Craig H., Olsen, Susanne F., Porter, Christin L., Jin, Shenghua, Wo, Jianzhong, and Wu, Xinzi (2002) Similarities and differences in mothers' parenting of preschoolers in China and the United States. *International Journal of Behavioural Development* 26:481–491.

Wylie, Laurence (1957) *Village in the Vaucluse*. New York, NY: Harper and Row.

Wyndham, Felice S. (2010) Environments of learning: Rarámuri children's plant knowledge and experience of schooling, family, and landscapes in the Sierra Tarahumara, Mexico. *Human Ecology* 38:87–99.

Yamakoshi, Gen (2001) Ecology of tool use in wild chimpanzees: Toward reconstruction of early hominid evolution. In Tetsuro Matsuzawa (Ed.), *Primate Origins of Human Cognition and Behavior*. pp. 537–556. Heidelberg: Springer.

Yanagisawa, Satoko (2009) Childbirth in Japan. In Helaine Selin and Pamela K. Stone (Eds.), *Childhood across Cultures: Ideas and Practices of Pregnancy, Childbirth and the Postpartum*. pp. 85–94. Amherst, MA: Springer.

Yimou, Zhang (1991) *Raise the Red Lantern* (film). New York: Miramax Films.

Yoshida, Kenji (2006) Kalumbu and Chisudzo: Boys' and girls' masquerades among the Chewa. In Simon Ottenberg and David A. Binkley (Eds.), *Playful Performers:*

African Children's Masquerades. pp. 221–236. New Brunswick, NJ: Transaction Publishers.

Young, Emma C. (2010) Growing up Koori, growing up kids: Aboriginal families in Griffith, New South Wales. Unpublished PhD dissertation, Department of Anthropology, University of Sydney.

Zarger, Rebecca K. (2002) Acquisition and transmission of subsistence knowledge by Q'equchi' Maya in Belize. In John R. Stepp, Felice S. Wyndham, and Rebecca K. Zarger (Eds.), *Ethnobiology and Biocultural Diversity*. pp. 593–603. Athens, GA: University of Georgia Press.

Zeiher, Helga (2001) Dependent, independent, and interdependent relations: Children as members of the family household in West Berlin. In Leena Alanen and Berry Mayall (Eds.), *Conceptualizing Child–Adult Relations*. pp. 37–53. London: Routledge.

Zeitlin, Marian (1996) My child is my crown: Yoruba parental theories and practices in early childhood. In Sara Harkness and Charles M. Super (Eds.), *Parents' Cultural Belief Systems: Their Origins, Expressions, and Consequences*. pp. 407–427. New York, NY: Guilford Press.

Zelazo, Phillip R., Zelazo, Nancy A., and Kolb, Sarah (1972) "Walking" in the newborn. *Science* 176:314–315.

Zelizer, Viviana A. (1985) *Pricing the Priceless Child: The Changing Social Value of Children*. New York, NY: Basic Books.

Zeller, Anthony C. (1987) A role for children in hominid evolution. *Man* 22:528–557.

Zempleni-Rabain, Jacqueline (1973) Food and strategy involved in learning fraternal exchange among Wolof children. In P. Alexandre (Ed.), *French Perspectives in African Studies*. pp. 220–233. London: Oxford University Press for the International African Institute.

Zheng, Yuan (1994) Local government schools in Sung China: A reassessment. *History of Education Quarterly* 34:193–213.

Ziegler, Toni E., Savage, Anne, Scheffler, Guenther, and Snowdon, Charles T. (1987) The endocrinology of puberty and reproductive functioning in female cotton-top tamarins (*Saguinus oedipus*). *Biology of Reproduction* 37:618–627.

Zimmerman, Jonathan (2002) *Whose America? Culture Wars in the Public Schools*. Cambridge, MA: Harvard University Press.

Zito, Julie Mango, Safer, Daniel J., dos Reis, Susan, Gardner, James F., Magder, Laurence, Soeken, Karen, Boles, Myde, Lynch, Frances, and Riddle, Mark A. (2003) Psychotropic practice patterns in youth. *Archives of Pediatrics and Adolescent Medicine* 157:17–25.

Zuckerman, Michael (1984) Sensation-seeking: A comparative approach to a human trait. *Behavioral and Brain Sciences* 7:413–471.

Zukow, Patricia G. (1989) Siblings as effective socializing agents: Evidence from Central Mexico. In Patricia Zukow (Ed.), *Sibling Interaction across Cultures*. pp. 79–105. New York, NY: Springer.

Author index

516

Topic index

Society index

SOCIETIES, HISTORICAL